SWITZERLAND

CONTENTS

▶ **Introduction** 1
  Planning Your Trip 2
  Before You Go 4
  Travel Smart 9

▶ **Switzerland** 12

▶ **Zürich** 21

▶ **Luzern & Central**
  Switzerland 57

▶ **Bern & Murten** 100

▶ **Berner Oberland** 146
  Interlaken 154
  Lauterbrunnen 171
  Gimmelwald 179
  Mürren 188
  Activities in the
    Berner Oberland 198
  More Berner Oberland
    Towns 222

▶ **Zermatt & the Matterhorn** . 226

▶ **Appenzell** 253
  Appenzell Town 255
  Ebenalp 266
  Liechtenstein 269

▶ **Lake Geneva &**
  French Switzerland 271
  Lausanne 273
  Château de Chillon 295
  Montreux 300
  French Swiss Countryside . . 303
  Gruyères 303
  Near Gruyères 307

▶ **Lugano** 315

▶ **Upper Engadine** 334
  Pontresina 339
  Samedan 349
  St. Moritz 353

▶ **Scenic Rail Journeys** 360
  Golden Pass 364
  Gotthard Panorama Express . 369
  Bernina Express 373
  Glacier Express 383
  Chur 389

▶ **Switzerland in Winter** 391

▶ **Switzerland:**
  Past & Present 397

▶ **Practicalities** 409
  Tourist Information 409
  Travel Tips 410
  Money 412
  Sightseeing 418
  Sleeping 419
  Eating 429
  Staying Connected 436
  Transportation 441
  Resources from Rick Steves . 454

▶ **Appendix** 457
  Holidays & Festivals 457
  Books & Films 459
  Conversions & Climate 462
  Packing Checklist 465
  Survival Phrases 467

▶ **Index** 473

▶ **Map Index** 487

LEGEND

▭A-12▭	Freeway/Autobahn
─────	Major Road
─────	Major Rail Line
··········	Mountain Lift
··········	Boat Route
✈	Airport
■	Ruin, Museum, Other Point of Interest
▲	Mountain Peak
♜	Castle, Monument, Palace

SCENIC RAIL JOURNEYS

─────	Golden Pass
─────	Gotthard Panorama Express
─────	Bernina Express
─────	Glacier Express

0 km   50 km

0 miles   25 miles

Cable car to the Schilthorn,
Thrill Walk fun at Birg Station,
on top of the Schilthorn,
Bern—the charming capital

*Alpabfahrt in Appenzell—
when the cows come home from
high pasture, cliffside dining at
Ebenalp, the Bernina Express,
relaxing at Lake Lugano*

Rick Steves®

SWITZERLAND

Welcome to Rick Steves' Europe

Travel is intensified living—maximum thrills per minute and one of the last great sources of legal adventure. Travel is freedom. It's recess, and we need it.

I discovered a passion for European travel as a teen and have been sharing it ever since—through my tours, public television and radio shows, and travel guidebooks. Over the years, I've taught thousands of travelers how to best enjoy Europe's blockbuster sights—and experience "Back Door" discoveries that most tourists miss.

This book on Switzerland offers you a balanced mix of cities and villages, mountaintop hikes and lake cruises, thought-provoking museums and sky-high gondola rides. And it's selective—rather than listing dozens of mountain getaways, I recommend only the best ones. My self-guided museum tours and city walks give insight into Switzerland's vibrant history and today's living, breathing culture.

I advocate traveling simply and smartly. Take advantage of my money- and time-saving tips on sightseeing, transportation, and more. Try local, characteristic alternatives to expensive hotels and restaurants. In many ways, spending more money only builds a thicker wall between you and what you traveled so far to see.

We visit Switzerland to experience it—to become temporary locals. Thoughtful travel engages us with the world, as we learn to appreciate other cultures and new ways to measure quality of life.

Judging from the positive feedback I receive from readers, this book will help you enjoy a fun, affordable, and rewarding vacation—whether it's your first trip or your tenth.

Gute Reise! Happy travels!

Rick Steves

INTRODUCTION

Little, mountainous, efficient Switzerland is one of Europe's most appealing destinations. Wedged neatly between Germany, Austria, France, and Italy, Switzerland melds the best of all worlds—and adds a healthy dose of chocolate, cowbells, and cable cars. Fiercely independent and decidedly high-tech, the Swiss stubbornly hold on to their quaint traditions, too. Join cheesemakers in a high valley, try to call the shepherds on an alphorn, and hike through some of the world's most stunning mountain scenery.

This book breaks Switzerland into its top big-city, small-town, and rural attractions. It gives you all the information and suggestions

tions necessary to wring the maximum value out of your limited time and money. If you plan three weeks or less in Switzerland, this lean and mean little book has all the information you need...unless you're a skier. (This is a fair-weather book—it focuses on the highlights of summertime fun—but for basic info for a winter visit, see the Switzerland in Winter chapter.)

Experiencing Europe's culture, people, and natural wonders economically and hassle-free has been my goal throughout my life of traveling, tour guiding, and writing. With this guidebook, I pass on to you the lessons I've learned.

This book covers the predictable biggies while mixing in a healthy dose of Back Door intimacy. Along with Luzern, the Matterhorn, and the Glacier Express, you'll experience windswept Roman ruins and ramble through traffic-free alpine towns. I've been selective, including only the top destinations. For example, the country is dotted with alpine villages—but Gimmelwald is a cut above.

The best is, of course, only my opinion. But after spending much of my life exploring and researching Europe, I've developed a sixth sense for what travelers enjoy. Just thinking about the places featured in this book makes me want to yodel.

Planning Your Trip

This section will help you get started planning your trip—with advice on trip costs, when to go, and what you should know before you take off.

TRIP COSTS

Five components make up your trip costs: airfare, surface transportation, room and board, sightseeing and entertainment, and shopping and miscellany.

Airfare to Europe: A basic round-trip flight from the US to Zürich can cost, on average, about $1,000-2,000 total, depending on where you fly from and when (cheaper in winter). If Switzerland is part of a longer trip, consider saving time and money in Europe by flying into one city and out of another; for instance, into Zürich and out of Paris. Overall, Kayak.com is the best place to start searching for flights on a combination of mainstream and budget carriers.

Transportation in Europe: For a two-week whirlwind trip of most of my recommended destinations by public transportation, allow $750 per person. This covers a second-class, 15-day consecutive Swiss Travel Pass, plus high-mountain trains and lifts, and reservation fees for scenic trains. You can purchase a Swiss Travel Pass before you leave home or wait until you arrive in Switzerland—they're also sold at local train stations.

If you plan to rent a car, allow at least $250 per week, not including tolls, gas, and supplemental insurance; figure on an additional $250 for mountain lifts sans car. If you need the car for three weeks or more, leasing can save you money on insurance and taxes.

A short flight can be cheaper than the train (check Skyscanner. com for intra-European flights).

Room and Board: You can manage comfortably in Switzerland on $190 a day per person for room and board (more in big cities). This allows $30 for lunch, $45 for dinner, $5 for chocolate, and $110 for lodging (based on two people splitting the cost of a

Top Destinations in Switzerland

Scenic Rail Journeys:
❶ Golden Pass
❷ Gotthard Panorama Express
❸ Bernina Express
❹ Glacier Express

$220 double room that includes breakfast). Students and tightwads can enjoy Switzerland for as little as $75 a day ($45 for a hostel bed, $30 for supermarket meals and snacks).

Sightseeing and Entertainment: Figure about $10-15 per sight, and about $90 for each major alpine lift. Though hiking is free, lifts to some of the best high-altitude trails aren't. An overall average of $55 a day works for most. Don't skimp here. After all, this category is the driving force behind your trip—you came to sightsee, enjoy, and experience Switzerland.

Shopping and Miscellany: Figure $5 per coffee, beer, and ice-cream cone. Shopping can vary in cost from nearly nothing to a small fortune. Good budget travelers find that this category has little to do with assembling a trip full of lifelong memories.

SIGHTSEEING PRIORITIES
So much to see, so little time. How to choose? Depending on the length of your trip, and taking geographic proximity into account, here are my recommended priorities:

   3 days: Berner Oberland
   5 days, add: Luzern and Central Switzerland
   7 days, add: Bern and Lake Geneva area, connecting them with Golden Pass scenic rail journey
   10 days, add: Zermatt and Appenzell, linking them with the Glacier Express train
   14 days, add: Lugano and Upper Engadine, connecting with

Bernina Express and Gotthard Panorama Express train rides

16 days, add: Zürich and Murten

21 days, add: More day trips (French Swiss countryside), more hikes, and time to slow down

This includes nearly everything on the map and itinerary in the "Switzerland's Best Two-Week Trip by Train" sidebar (later in this chapter), plus modifications for a longer or shorter trip. If you don't have time to see it all, prioritize according to your interests. This chapter's "Switzerland at a Glance" sidebar can help you decide where to go.

WHEN TO GO

The summer "tourist season" runs roughly from May through September, though in mountainous areas, it doesn't start until sometime in June. High summer (July-Aug) has its advantages: the best weather, snow-free alpine trails, very long days (light until after 21:00), and the busiest schedule of tourist fun. In late May and early October, travelers enjoy fewer crowds, mild weather, and the ability to grab a room almost whenever and wherever they like.

During the *Zwischenzeit* ("between time"—that is, between summer and ski seasons, roughly April, early May, late Oct, and Nov), the cities are pleasantly uncrowded, but mountain resort towns such as Zermatt and Mürren are completely dead (most hotels and restaurants are closed, and the weather is iffy).

During ski season (Dec-March), mountain resorts are crowded and expensive, while cities are quieter (some accommodations and sights are either closed or run on a limited schedule). The weather can be cold and dreary, and nighttime will draw the shades on your sightseeing before dinner. But Christmastime traditions (such as colorful markets and special holiday foods) can warm up your trip at this chilly time of year.

Pack warm clothing for the Alps, no matter when you go—the weather can change suddenly.

Before You Go

You'll have a smoother trip if you tackle a few things ahead of time. For more information on these topics, see the Practicalities chapter (and RickSteves.com, for helpful travel tips and talks).

Make sure your travel documents are valid. If your passport is due to expire within six months of your ticketed date of return, you need to renew it. Allow up to six weeks to renew or get a passport (www.travel.state.gov). Beginning in 2021, you may also need to register with the European Travel Information and Authorization System (ETIAS).

Switzerland at a Glance

▲▲**Zürich** Bustling cosmopolitan city—Switzerland's largest by far—with upscale shops and a charming riverside old-town quarter full of pointy church spires and pealing bells.

▲▲**Luzern and Central Switzerland** Touristy yet worthwhile town of historic wooden bridges, picturesque streets, and vintage steamships that ply lovely Lake Luzern, ringed by mountains with stunning vistas accessible by high-altitude lifts.

▲▲▲**Bern** Cozy capital of Switzerland tucked in a sharp river bend, with arcaded shopping promenades, medieval clock towers, and museums devoted to Albert Einstein and artist Paul Klee.

▲▲**Murten** Quaint, small, walled town sitting right next to the German/French linguistic fault line, with nearby Roman ruins and museum in Avenches.

▲▲▲**Berner Oberland** Mountainous region, highlighted by the Jungfrau and Schilthorn peaks, popular for its alpine towns (such as rustic Gimmelwald) and scenic hikes, lifts, and train rides. Touristy Interlaken is the gateway.

▲▲**Zermatt and the Matterhorn** Glitzy ski resort that sports some traditional old-fashioned touches, in a valley at the foot of the famous Matterhorn.

▲▲**Appenzell** The most traditional Swiss region, known for pastoral scenery, small towns, cows, folk museums, and, just a cable-car ride away, a rustic cliffside retreat at Ebenalp.

▲▲**Lake Geneva and French Switzerland** Small-but-sophisticated lakeside city of Lausanne, Switzerland's best castle experience at Château de Chillon, the cute cheesemaking center of Gruyères, and pleasant scenery in the surrounding countryside.

▲**Lugano** Leading city of Italian-speaking Switzerland, with a tidy—if dull—urban core, scenic boat trips on Lake Lugano, and mountain lifts to lakeside peaks.

▲**Upper Engadine** Romansh-speaking mountain resort region anchored by three towns: touristy Pontresina, humble Samedan, and swanky St. Moritz.

▲▲**Scenic Rail Journeys** Four famous train rides, each offering panoramic views and crisscrossing the country.

Switzerland's Best Two-Week Trip by Train

Day	Plan	Sleep in
1	Arrive Zürich Airport, head to Appenzell	Appenzell or Ebenalp
2	All day for Appenzell and Ebenalp	Appenzell or Ebenalp
3	Leave early for Luzern	Luzern
4	Luzern	Luzern
5	Boat, then train to Lugano along Gotthard Panorama Express route	Lugano
6	Bernina Express to Upper Engadine Valley	Pontresina
7	Upper Engadine (Pontresina, St. Moritz, and Samedan)	Pontresina
8	Take Glacier Express; if weather's good, head for Zermatt; if weather's bad, consider going straight to Lausanne (see below)	Zermatt
9	Zermatt and hikes, Matterhorn-view lifts	Zermatt
10	If weather's good, spend more time in Zermatt and go late to Lausanne; if weather's bad, leave early for Lausanne	Lausanne
11	Take the Golden Pass to the Berner Oberland. If weather's good, go early; if weather's bad, linger in Lausanne/Lake Geneva area and leave late	Gimmelwald or Mürren
12	All day for lifts and hikes in the Berner Oberland	Gimmelwald or Mürren
13	More time in the Berner Oberland	Gimmelwald or Mürren
14	Early to Bern, then on to Zürich	Zürich
15	More time in Zürich, or fly home	

Notes

Zermatt isn't worth the trip in bad weather. If your reservations are flexible, consider skipping that leg and going straight to Lausanne (take the Glacier Express only to Brig, then change for Lausanne).

To connect Luzern and Lugano, follow the Gotthard Panorama Express route, but don't spend extra for the official tourist package-trip.

If you have extra time in Switzerland, I'd suggest spending it in (listed in order of priority): Murten and Bern, Zürich, Lausanne and the Lake Geneva area, Lugano (relaxing) or the Luzern area (day trips). For a short trip of a week or so, I'd just focus on the Berner Oberland, Luzern, and Bern.

Rail Pass: The best rail pass for this itinerary is a Swiss Travel

Pass for 15 consecutive days ($525 second class, $825 first class, prices are per adult age 28 or older, confirm latest prices at www. ricksteves.com/rail; figure an additional $100 total in reservation fees for all four scenic rail journeys). This pass doesn't cover most higher mountain lifts, but it usually earns you a 50 percent discount.

By Car: Although this itinerary is designed for public transportation, it can be done by car with a few modifications. Obviously, you won't take the scenic rail trips. Instead, drive from Appenzell straight to the Upper Engadine, then continue through Tirano and on to Lugano (via Lake Como in Italy). From Lugano, drive to Zermatt (crossing again through Italy) and resume the above itinerary, visiting Luzern at the end before returning to Zürich. The French Swiss countryside and the area around Murten merit more time if you have a car.

Beyond Switzerland: Switzerland, right in the middle of Western Europe, splices neatly into a multicountry trip by car or train. For instance, the Appenzell region is a likely gateway to Germany's Bavaria or Austria's Tirol. Italy's Lake Como is a stone's throw from Lugano (in fact, the Bernina Express bus drives right alongside it)—and Milan is not much farther. If you're in Lausanne, you're literally looking at France (across Lake Geneva), and a handy train ride whisks you to Lyon or Chamonix. And big Swiss cities are efficiently connected by fast trains to destinations in all of these countries and beyond.

Budget Tips

Switzerland is pricey, but there are ways to stretch your dollars. For example, you can cut down on restaurant costs by having scenic picnics or seeking out self-service cafeterias (often attached to department or grocery stores), which offer good food at a fraction of the cost of dining out.

Many expensive alpine lifts offer discounted "early bird" tickets for the first (and sometimes last) trip of the day. Train trips get cheaper when you choose the right rail pass (for help, see page 443); the Swiss Travel Pass is a swinging deal for most travelers, covering more than just trains.

Save on Sightseeing with the Swiss Travel Pass

The Swiss Travel Pass offers consecutive-day or flexipass coverage of Switzerland's trains, boats, and buses, a 50 percent discount off most lifts, including the cable car to the Schilthorn from Mürren (about $525 for 15-day consecutive pass in second class). It also doubles as a Swiss Museum Pass (which otherwise costs about $170), covering admission to 500 museums or so on the days your pass is valid (the standard Swiss Museum Pass is good for a year). To get the most out of a flexipass, use it to visit a museum, ride a lake boat, or take a lift either on the same day you arrive at that destination or on the day you depart.

Arrange your transportation. Book your international flights. Figure out your transportation options within Switzerland. It's worth thinking about buying train tickets online in advance (and reserving popular **scenic trains** during summer—see the Scenic Rail Journeys chapter), getting a rail pass, renting a car, or booking cheap European flights. (You can wing it once you're there, but it may cost more.)

Book rooms well in advance, especially if your trip falls during peak season (see "When to Go," earlier) or any major holidays or festivals (see the appendix).

Consider travel insurance. Compare the cost of the insurance to the cost of your potential loss. Check whether your existing insurance (health, homeowners, or renters) covers you and your possessions overseas.

Call your bank. Alert your bank that you'll be using your debit and credit cards in Europe. Ask about transaction fees, and get the PIN number for your credit card. You don't need to bring Swiss francs for your trip; you can withdraw them from cash machines in Europe.

Use your smartphone smartly. Sign up for an international service plan to reduce your costs, or rely on Wi-Fi in Europe instead. Download any apps you'll want on the road, such as maps,

The following sights, described in this book, are covered by the Swiss Travel Pass and the Swiss Museum Pass (for a full list, see www.museumspass.ch):

Zürich: Swiss National Museum and Rietberg Museum

Luzern: Rosengart Collection, Depot History Museum, Bourbaki Panorama, Glacier Garden, Richard Wagner Museum, Museum of Art Luzern, and Museum of Natural History, plus Fortress Fürigen Museum nearby in Stansstad (Swiss Transport Museum is 50 percent off with the pass)

Bern: Museum of Fine Arts and Paul Klee Center

Near Murten: Roman Museum in Avenches

Interlaken: Museum of Tourism (Swiss Travel Pass only)

Near Interlaken: Ballenberg Open-Air Folk Museum in Brienz

Zermatt: Matterhorn Museum

Appenzell Region: Appenzell Museum and Appenzell's two modern art museums, and folk museums in Stein and Urnäsch

Lausanne: Collection de l'Art Brut, Olympic Museum, and City History Museum

Lake Geneva Region: Château de Chillon

French Swiss Countryside: Gruyères Castle, H. R. Giger Museum, and Tibet Museum

translators, transit schedules, and Rick Steves Audio Europe (see page 11).

Rip up this book! Turn chapters into mini guidebooks: Break the book's spine and use a utility knife to slice apart chapters, keeping gummy edges intact. Reinforce the chapter spines with clear, wide tape; use a heavy-duty stapler; or make or buy a cheap cover (see Travel Store at www.ricksteves.com), swapping out chapters as you travel.

Pack light. You'll walk with your luggage more than you think. I travel for weeks with a single carry-on bag and a daypack. Use the packing checklist in the appendix as a guide.

Travel Smart

If you have a positive attitude, equip yourself with good information (this book), and expect to travel smart, you will.

Read—and reread—this book. To have an "A" trip, be an "A" student. Note opening hours of sights, closed days, crowd-beating tips, and whether reservations are required or advisable. Check the latest at www.ricksteves.com/update.

Be your own tour guide. As you travel, get up-to-date info on sights, reserve tickets and tours, reconfirm hotels and travel arrangements, and check transit connections. Visit local tourist information offices (TIs). Upon arrival in a new town, lay the groundwork for a smooth departure; confirm the train, bus, or road you'll take when you leave.

Outsmart thieves. Pickpockets abound in crowded places where tourists congregate. Treat commotions as smokescreens for theft. Keep your cash, credit cards, and passport secure in a money belt tucked under your clothes; carry only a day's spending money in your front pocket. Don't set valuable items down on counters or café tabletops, where they can be quickly stolen or easily forgotten.

Minimize potential loss. Keep expensive gear to a minimum. Bring photocopies or take photos of important documents (passport and cards) to aid in replacement if they're lost or stolen. Back up photos and files frequently.

Guard your time and energy. To avoid long lines, follow my crowd-beating tips, such as making advance reservations, or sightseeing early or late. Buy a "Good Morning Ticket" for the Jungfraujoch in the Berner Oberland, and you'll beat the hordes and get a discount.

Be flexible. Even if you have a well-planned itinerary, expect changes, strikes, closures, sore feet, bad weather, and so on. Your Plan B could turn out to be even better. For example, you might plan on three days split between the city of Bern and the mountainous Berner Oberland region. If it's raining as you approach the area, head for Bern. If it's sunny, make a beeline for the mountains, then hit Bern on your way out of the area. To help decide, tune in to websites and TV stations that show the weather in various parts of the country. Many high-altitude observation decks have webcams that show you what you'll see when you get up top (for example, www.swisspanorama.com for the Berner Oberland, www.zermatt.ch for Zermatt).

Attempt the language. Many Swiss—especially in the tourist trade and in cities—speak English, but if you learn some Italian, German, or French, even just a few phrases, you'll get more smiles and make more friends. Practice the survival phrases near the end of this book, and even better, bring a phrase book.

Connect with the culture. Interacting with locals carbonates your experience. Enjoy the friendliness of the Swiss people.

Rick's Free Video Clips and Audio Tours

Travel smarter with these free, fun resources:

Rick Steves Classroom Europe, a powerful tool for teachers, is also useful for travelers. This video library contains over 400 short clips excerpted from my public television series. Enjoy these videos as you sort through options for your trip and to better understand what you'll see in Europe. Check it out

at Classroom.RickSteves.com (just enter a topic in the search bar to find everything I've filmed on a subject).

The **Rick Steves Audio Europe** app makes it easy to download audio content to enhance your trip. Use the app to listen to audio tours of Europe's top sights, plus interviews from my public radio show with experts from Europe and around the globe. Find it in your app store or at RickSteves.com/AudioEurope.

Ask questions; most locals are happy to point you in their idea of the right direction. Set up your own quest for the richest hot chocolate, cheeriest window box, biggest cowbell, or most densely packed stack of firewood. When an opportunity pops up, make it a habit to say "yes."

Switzerland...here you come!

SWITZERLAND

Switzerland is one of Europe's richest, best organized, most expensive countries. Like the Boy Scouts, the Swiss count cleanliness, neatness, punctuality, tolerance, independence, thrift, and hard work as virtues...and they love pocketknives. The country is an enjoyable mix of bucolic peace and daring adventure. Around every alpine turn, you feel you could get a glimpse of Heidi milking a cow or James Bond schussing past on skis.

Nearly half of Switzerland—Europe's most mountainous country—consists of uninhabitable rocks and rugged Alps. It seems that any flat land (and quite a bit of hilly land) is cultivated into tidy little farms. While landlocked, Switzerland has more than its share of clear rivers and big, beautiful lakes with a striking mountain backdrop (such as Lake Geneva, Lake Murten, Lake Luzern, and Lake Lugano—all covered in this book).

Despite the country's small size, Switzerland is unusually diverse. Its wild geography has kept people apart historically, helping its many regions maintain their distinct cultural differences. Switzerland has four official languages: German, French, Italian, and Romansh.

The abbreviation for Swiss Federal Railways—in German, French, and Italian

And yet, regardless of which language is spoken, the entire country is unmistakably Swiss. Everyday things like the grocery

Switzerland: Western Europe's Linguistic Crossroads

You'd be forgiven for thinking of Switzerland as a "German" country. The heart of Switzerland, with about three-fifths of

German | Italian
French | Romansh

the population and most of the famous cities and sights, is linguistically (as well as culturally) Germanic. But even here, Germans and Austrians don't feel quite at home. As if keeping alive an archaic code for insiders, the Swiss speak to each other in the lilting, fun-to-listen-to Swiss German, a.k.a. *Schwyzertütsch,* then switch seamlessly to standard German (or English) when interacting with outsiders.

Surrounding the German-speaking core is a more colorful Romance language-speaking fringe—French (to the west), Italian (to the south), and Romansh (tucked in the southeastern mountains). Switzerland's biggest canton, officially trilingual, is its linguistic melting pot: the southeastern region called Graubünden (in German), Grigioni (in Italian), and Grischun (in Romansh).

Subtle differences in cuisine, climate, and landscape seem to match the linguistic boundaries. German-speaking Switzerland enjoys a vigorous efficiency reminiscent of Germany's. The pace in genteel French-speaking Switzerland is a bit mellower, and the cuisine and lifestyle are more refined, resembling France's. And the relatively balmy Italian-speaking canton of Ticino comes with a touch of chaos and lust for life that's not far removed from Italy proper (which surrounds it on three sides). You can spend a week in Switzerland and feel almost as if you've traveled from Paris to Munich to Rome... without ever crossing a border.

store, train station, or familiar products have the same signage and logos, but in different languages. And everywhere you go, you'll notice a dedication to order and organization that distinguishes Swiss culture. It's refreshing to visit a predictable place where, once you've got the gist of things in one city, you generally know what to expect in the next.

That sort of orderliness doesn't happen by itself. The Swiss jealously guard their way of life. If you accidentally drop a scrap of paper on the ground, someone might cross the street to be sure you pick it up. As if belonging to an exclusive club that's careful about admitting new members, the Swiss strike some visitors as a

Switzerland Almanac

Official Name: The Confoederatio Helvetica, or Switzerland, has a different name in each of its four official languages: *Schweizerische Eidgenossenschaft* (German), *Confédération Suisse* (French), *Confederazione Svizzera* (Italian), and *Confederaziun Svizra* (Romansh). Locals shorten those to "die Schweiz," "la Suisse," "la Svizzera," and "la Svizra."

Population: Switzerland has 8.2 million people (similar to the population of Virginia); 63 percent speak German as their main language, 23 percent speak French, 8 percent speak Italian, and about 1 percent speak Romansh. About 22 percent of Swiss residents are not Swiss citizens; these range from EU businesspeople to immigrant workers. The populace is 37 percent Catholic, 25 percent Protestant, 6 percent other Christian, 5 percent Muslim, and the rest are other or unspecified.

Latitude and Longitude: 47°N and 8°E, similar latitude to Quebec, Canada.

Area: 16,000 square miles; twice the size of New Jersey, or half the size of South Carolina.

Geography: Switzerland sits at the crossroads between northern and southern Europe. The Alps are Europe's high point and continental divide, from which the major rivers flow—Rhine, Rhône, Danube, and Po. Switzerland's highest point is the 15,200-foot Monte Rosa (specifically, the summit called Dufourspitze), along the Italian border. Though Switzerland is mostly mountainous, the center of the country consists of rolling hills and large lakes.

Biggest Cities: One in seven Swiss lives in or near Zürich (pop. 430,000 in the city; 1.2 million in the metropolitan area). Geneva has 192,000 people, and Basel has 167,000. The capital is Bern (pop. 129,000).

Economy: Like a fine watch, Switzerland's economy just keeps on ticking. The gross domestic product is $523 billion. Its per-capita GDP of $62,100 is among Europe's highest (about equal to the

bit standoffish—polite but not gregarious, welcoming but perhaps a bit suspicious. If you find the Swiss to be a little buttoned-down, remember that the payoff is a beautiful country where the trains run on time, the streets are clean, and every flower petal is perfectly in place.

While it's one of Europe's most progressive "big-government" countries—with high taxation, ample social services, and liberal drug policies—Switzerland also has a conservative streak. Traditional mindsets persist in the remote mountain hamlets—for example, women weren't guaranteed the right to vote in federal elections until 1971 (and were still barred from local elections in one region until 1990).

SWITZERLAND

US). The franc is strong, workers are highly skilled, and unemployment is less than half the European Union average. Blessed with hydropower and using nuclear technology, Switzerland generates 99 percent of its electricity with virtually no oil.

Currency: 1 Swiss franc (CHF) = 100 rappen/centimes = about $1.

Government: Founded in 1291 as a confederation of cantons, the country is still a model of federalism, balancing the needs of its different linguistic/ethnic groups. No single political party (or two or even three parties) dominates. The president, chosen by the legislature, serves for just one calendar year. The two-house Federal Assembly consists of the 46-seat Council of States and the 200-seat National Council, elected for four-year terms.

Flag: Switzerland's white cross on a distinctively square red background may have been the inspiration for the red-on-white symbol of the International Red Cross. It's one of only two recognized flags that are perfect squares (the other being the flag of Vatican City).

The Average Swiss: He or she has 1.5 children and will live to be 82. A typical Swiss man serves at least 260 days of compulsory service in the military. The average woman earns almost 20 percent less than her similar male counterparts, and often doesn't return to the workforce after having children. He or she travels about 1,400 miles a year on a train, the equivalent of crossing the country six times. Every month, the average Swiss drinks almost a quart of alcohol and eats more than a pound and a half of chocolate.

Historically, Switzerland is one of Europe's oldest democracies. Born when three states (cantons) united in 1291, over time the Swiss Confederation grew to the 26 cantons of today. The "CH" decal on cars doesn't stand for chocolate...but for "Confoederatio Helvetica," the country's official title (using the Latin name avoids linguistic controversy). The country is named for the Celtic Helvetii tribe that lived here back in Roman times. (Stamp collectors know to identify a Swiss stamp by looking for the word *Helvetia*.) The confederation's government is decentralized, and cantonal loyalty is very strong.

Similar to US states, each canton is semi-independent. Just as we debate "states' rights," the Swiss wrangle with just how much autonomy to allow cantons. Considering that each comes with not only its own political concerns, but also its own dialect and cultural heritage, cantonal independence is particularly important and delicate.

With the exception of the Protestant Reformation and an almost bloodless civil war in 1847, Swiss history has been pretty quiet...and that's just how the Swiss like it. They're happy to be high and dry in the mountains, watching from above the fray as the tides of history swirl around them (for an overview, see the Switzerland: Past & Present chapter).

Stubbornly independent, or maybe just smart, Switzerland loves its neutrality and stayed out of both world wars. But it's far from lax when it comes to national defense—on the contrary, the Swiss are legendary for their military readiness. A vast reserve army and a countryside embedded with hidden fortresses have earned Switzerland its unique ability to preserve its right to self-determination well into the 21st century, even though it's surrounded by bigger, stronger nations. Through the tumult of the 20th century, no foreign invaders dared to try cracking this nut.

Even so, for more than a century and a half, a different kind of invasion—of tourists—has descended on Switzerland each summer (for hiking season, all summer long but busiest July-Aug) and each winter (for ski season, roughly Christmas through Easter). You'll share the trails and lifts with a deluge of international visitors—from Europe, the US, and the rest of the world. Partly because several Bollywood movies have used the Swiss Alps as a stand-in for Kashmir, Switzerland is popular with tourists from India. And Middle Eastern visitors flock here to escape the heat. Locals report a spike in Middle Eastern tourists in the weeks leading up to the sacred, month-long observance of Ramadan...when their numbers drop to virtually zero, as Muslims go back home to spend time with their families.

Though not a European Union member—in part because its agricultural lobby doesn't want competition from more efficiently produced EU products—Switzerland still conforms to EU standards to be able to conduct business easily. Major Swiss moneymakers include banking, insurance, watches (from top-of-the-line pieces to inexpensive Swatches), chemicals and pharmaceuticals, chocolate (Nestlé is the biggest producer), tourism, and precision instruments. Swiss-made equipment helps produce everything from clothing to ballpoint-pen tips to parts for the Mars Exploration Rover. Swiss ingenuity is nowhere more apparent than in the famous Swiss Army knives, which come in sizes big and small, with as many—or as few—tools as any armchair MacGyver might need.

Perhaps owing to its financial strength, Switzerland is one of

Europe's most expensive countries. A night on the town can be a major splurge. Locals call sitting on the pavement around a bottle of wine "going out." Double rooms with bath for less than $175 are rare. Even dormitory beds are expensive. If your budget is tight, be sure to chase down hostels (many have private rooms for couples and families), and keep your eyes peeled for *Matratzenlagers* ("mattress dorms"). Hiking is free, though most major alpine lifts cost at least $50.

Switzerland has more than its share of cosmopolitan cities. My favorites—Zürich, Luzern, Bern, Lausanne, and Lugano—

are covered in this book. Each one offers an enticing, I-could-live-here glimpse of the appealing and uniquely Swiss urban quality of life: efficient trams and buses gliding around town, manicured pedestrian zones teeming with locals enjoying their cities, crystal-clear rivers and lakes made accessible by scenic cruise boats, eclectic restaurants offering a tasty range of both Swiss and international cuisine, and low-key but generally compelling museums. While Switzerland lacks a world-class metropolis on par with Paris or Rome, all of these cities are engaging—especially if bad weather keeps you from heading for the hills.

But let's face it: Travelers don't flock to Switzerland for its cities. Spend most of your time getting high in the Alps. You can

climb onto a train in one of Switzerland's most bustling stations and, within an hour or two, step off into an idyllic time-warp world where traditional culture still thrives. Alpine villages (such as Gimmelwald) and towns (such as Appenzell) give you a taste of rural Switzerland, and are the perfect base for pastoral countryside hikes or riding lifts to dramatic cut-glass alpine panoramas.

If you're in the countryside on a Sunday, you'll most likely enjoy traditional music, clothing, and culture. At the end of a day of hiking, you can retreat to a village enclave preserving a colorful, rustic, rural way of life. Because the Swiss have chosen (at great cost) to protect their agricultural sector against competition from imports, the government subsidizes families who raise cows and make cheese the old-fashioned way. In the spring and again in the fall, you might be lucky

Understanding the Alps

Switzerland's snowy, rugged mountains are its claim to fame—and most likely a main reason for your visit. Fortunately, you don't have to be a mountain climber to see the Alps up close, as the Swiss transportation system is as remarkable as its mountains. Its cog railways, gondolas, and cable cars whisk you up into the type of scenery that's only accessible in some countries by ropes, pitons, and crampons.

The Alps were formed by the collision of two continents. About 100 million years ago, the African plate began pushing north against the stable plates of Europe and Asia. In the process, the sediments of the ancient Tethys Ocean (which once occupied the general real estate of the modern Mediterranean) became smooshed between the landmasses. Shoving all this material together made the rocks and sediments fold, shatter, and pile on top of each other; over millennia this growing jumble built itself up into today's Alps. Up in the mountains, look for folds and faults in the rocks that hint at this immense compression, which is still happening today: The Alps continue to rise by at least a millimeter each year (while erosion wears them down at about the same rate).

The current shape of the mountains and valleys is the handiwork of at least five ice ages over the last two million years. Glaciers flowed down the mountain valleys, scooped out Switzerland's beautiful alpine lakes, and carried rocks far away from where they had formed. The Alps were the first mountains extensively studied by geologists, and many of the geological terms that describe mountains originated here. Once you learn how to recognize a few of the landforms shaped by glaciers, you can easily spot these features when you visit other alpine areas. Study glacier exhibits to train your eye to recognize what you're seeing.

Glaciers are big and blunt, so they make simple, large-scale marks on the landscape. If a valley is U-shaped (with steep sides and a rounded base), it likely was scoured out by a glacier. Switzerland's Lauterbrunnen Valley and California's Yosemite Valley are classic examples.

A **cirque** (French for "circus") is the amphitheater-like depression carved out at the upper part of a valley by a glacier. If two adjacent cirques erode close to each other, a sharp steep-sided ridge forms, called an **arête** (French for "fishbone"). Cirques and arêtes are common in mountains with glaciers. More rarely, when three or more cirques erode toward one another, a pyramidal peak is created, called a **horn.** The Matterhorn is the world's most famous example. Glaciers flowed down all sides of this mountain, scooping material away and creating the distinctive sharp peak.

A common feature left behind by retreating glaciers is a **moraine,** a pile of dirt and rocks carried along on the glacier as it advanced, then dumped as the glacier melted. The Lindenhof in Zürich, a hilltop square once crowned with forts to defend the town, perches on a moraine.

Alpine glaciers can only originate above the snowline, so if you see any of these landforms (U-shaped valleys, cirques, horns, or moraines) in lower elevations, you know that the climate there used to be colder. The warming climate has profoundly affected the glaciers of Switzerland, which have lost at least a third of their volume since the 1950s. Some studies project that at that rate most glaciers in Switzerland could virtually disappear by the end of the century, affecting water storage and hydroelectric power generation.

In higher elevations, mountainsides have become less stable due to the melting of permafrost. A heat wave in 2003 caused several rockfalls on the Matterhorn, resulting in trail closures and the evacuation of dozens of climbers trapped on the summit. The ski resort of Pontresina built a dam in 2002 to protect the town from a potential landslide from its nearby mountain.

Another consequence of the warming climate is that winter weather no longer reliably produces snow at altitudes that it did in the past—which is bad news for Switzerland's huge ski industry. Seeing a future of ever-warmer winters, the Swiss are putting their ingenuity to the test. This goes beyond snow machines: Many resorts are investing hugely in new spas, convention centers, and other attractions that don't require snow.

With their acute awareness of their alpine climate's fragility, the Swiss are especially keen to explore green technology—even high up in the Alps. Now when they build mountain refuges, the favored design isn't necessarily a rustic stone-hut chalet, but a high-tech building that depends on solar power. Switzerland's technological innovation can help keep its mountains white and its valleys green.

enough to see a parade of cows on their way up to or back down from the high-mountain pastures.

The cows have also had a big impact on Swiss cuisine—especially cheese. Two of the most revered Swiss cheeses are the smooth Gruyère (from the town of Gruyères) and the stinky Appenzeller (from the region of Appenzell). In these areas, you can watch the cheese being made just as it has been for centuries...or at modern facilities using technology to carry out the same age-old processes (including robots that tenderly rub and flip each aging wheel of

cheese). Cheese shops (*Käserei* in German) sell a fragrant festival of mold, perfect for picnicking or for making two famous Swiss culinary specialties: fondue (a pot of cheese melted into wine) or raclette (cheese melted over potatoes and other vegetables). But after a few days of cheese plates for breakfast, cheese sandwiches for lunch, and cheese specialties for dinner, even the biggest cheese lovers might find they need a dairy detox.

Switzerland's public transportation system is tops, whether you want to go across the country or straight up into the mountains. The country is crisscrossed with fine autobahns and arguably Europe's most efficient rail system. Boats ply the tranquil waters of the country's many lakes, and PostBuses (operated by the post office) pick you up in the rare situations that trains let you down. You can even go *through* the mountains, thanks to long tunnels (but you'll miss the views). Try the variety of fun cogwheel trains, funiculars, and cable cars that deliver you—no matter the season—from sunny valleys up to dizzying heights and snowy vistas.

Switzerland's best attraction might just be hiding between the cities and the villages: In this land of dramatic mountains and picture-perfect farms, perhaps more than anywhere else in Europe, the journey is the destination. The Swiss Railway markets several scenic journeys that run along the country's prettiest routes, many with special panoramic trains designed to maximize views (for details, see the Scenic Rail Journeys chapter). But don't let the tourist hype give you tunnel vision. A sunny day spent on a train just about anywhere in Switzerland can rank as a memorable trip-capper.

From its famous efficiency, to its unique mingling of the modern and the traditional, to its flat-out spectacular scenery, Switzerland delights the Swiss...and their visitors.

ZÜRICH

Zürich is one of those cities that tourists tend to skip right through. Since it's a transportation hub, people fly in or change trains here, but don't give stopping a serious thought. The local graffiti jokes: *Zürich = zu reich, zu ruhig* ("too rich, too quiet"). But even though you won't find a hint of Swiss Miss in Switzerland's leading city, Zürich is rewarding and worth getting to know.

In prehistoric times, people lived on pilings near the shores of Lake Zürich. Later, the Romans founded a city here as a customs post. Roman Turicum eventually became Zürich. It gained city status in the 10th century, flourished thanks to the hard work of its many powerful guilds, and was a center of the Swiss Reformation. By the 19th century it was a leading European financial and economic center. Today, thanks largely to Switzerland's long-term economic and political stability, Zürich is a major hub of international banking. Assuming you've got the money to enjoy it, Zürich is by many measures the world's most livable city.

For the traveler, Zürich is a city of contrasts. It's urban and gritty, but also quiet and quaint. Fragrant fondue restaurants sit next door to cheap Thai takeout joints and designer boutiques that put Milan to shame. One-third of its residents come from countries other than Switzerland (169 nationalities, at last count), and one-third of its territory is nature ("if you count the river and lake," locals explain).

While not the capital, Zürich is far and away Switzerland's biggest city—a hub for both business and transportation (with the country's dominant train station and airport). Perhaps Zürich's hard-to-pin-down character is rooted in its role as home to Switzerland's Reformation: The city retains a no-fuss, no-muss, nose-to-the-grindstone Protestant work ethic that leaves little time for colorful flourishes. Locals pride themselves on being private, discreet, and no-drama.

Zürich is the only place in Switzerland where I've seen men in ties running in the streets. And it's the only place I've seen a shop clerk dispose of a cigarette by slipping it into the finger hole of a manhole cover, rather than just tossing it on the ground.

PLANNING YOUR TIME

While Luzern and Bern provide more charming and compact urban experiences, Zürich is worth a look. With two weeks in Switzerland, I'd spend a day here. Begin by visiting the impressive Swiss National Museum (a.k.a. Landesmuseum), then wander along the river, using my self-guided walk, and take a river/lake cruise. With less time, do only the walk. With more time, check out the excellent art museum, visit the up-and-coming Zürich West area, or head to the countryside (zoo or Uetliberg viewpoint). While there are more charming places to overnight, you won't regret sleeping in Zürich—the city offers plenty to keep visitors engaged.

Orientation to Zürich

Zürich—with about 430,000 people (1.4 million in greater Zürich)—is draped around the northern tip of the long, skinny Lake Zürich (Zürichsee). The grand Bahnhofstrasse cuts through the city's glitzy shopping center, connecting the train station with the lakefront (a 15-minute walk). Across the Limmat River is the Niederdorf neighborhood—a vibrant, cobbled, Old World zone of colorful little shops, cafés, and restaurants. West of the train station is the emerging Zürich West dining and nightlife zone.

TOURIST INFORMATION

The helpful TI is off the great hall of the train station, near the giant blue angel hanging from the ceiling (Mon-Sat 8:00-20:30, Sun 8:30-18:30; Nov-April Mon-Sat 8:30-19:00, Sun 9:00-18:00; tel. 044-215-4000, www.zuerich.com).

For a whirlwind visit, consider the TI's **Zürich Card**, which covers public transit (including trips to the airport and up to the Uetliberg viewpoint); river boats and the short lake cruise; admission to most of the city's museums, and discounts on others; half off the TI's city walking tour; and freebies in many restaurants (27 CHF/24 hours, 53 CHF/72 hours, sold at TI). The one-day card pays for itself if you do the walking tour and one museum.

ARRIVAL IN ZÜRICH

By Train: The slick train station is at the north end of downtown. Many platforms are underground; to orient yourself, follow signs for tracks 3-17, which dead-end at the great hall of the station.

In the hall (with your back to the tracks), the ticket office is to your left (daily 6:00-21:00), with the TI just beyond it. Exiting through the front doors—straight ahead—brings you to the river (cross it to reach most recommended hotels). Lockers are down one flight below the big blue angel, and a pricey WC (with showers) is down two flights. A long-hours Migros supermarket is in the maze-like shopping mall one level down. The right-hand doors of the hall lead to tram stops and Bahnhofstrasse, while the left-hand doors lead toward the Swiss National Museum.

By Plane: If arriving at Zürich Airport, see the end of the chapter.

GETTING AROUND ZÜRICH

Much of Zürich is walkable, but it's big enough that trams, buses, and boats can make things easier. Handy trams #4 and #11 run north and south along Limmatquai and Bahnhofstrasse, respectively. The riverboats and short lake cruise are part of the system, but longer lake cruises are not.

The Swiss Travel Pass, Eurail Global Pass, and **Zürich Card** cover all city transit. Otherwise, individual tickets cost 2.70 CHF for a "short stretch" ticket of a few stops *(Kurtzstrecke)*, or 4.40 CHF for one hour *(Einzelbillett)*. A 24-hour pass *(Tageskarte)* for 8.80 CHF is a good investment for a full day in Zürich (13.60 CHF for three-zone version that includes airport and other outlying sights). For transit information, visit www.zvv.ch or call 0848-988-988.

HELPFUL HINTS

Medical Help: The **Permanence** drop-in clinic on the main floor of the train station offers on-the-spot medical aid (daily 7:00-22:00, Bahnhofplatz 15, tel. 044-215-4444, www.permanence.ch). The **Bahnhof Apotheke** is a convenient pharmacy next door (daily 7:00-24:00). A dentist is on the lower level.

Laundry: A short ride from downtown, **Expresswäscherei Self-service** is next to the Kinkelstrasse tram stop for trams #9 and #10 (daily 7:00-22:00, Winterthurstrasse 62, mobile 079-346-4032 or 076-305-1111).

Parking: The **Central** parking garage, on Seilergraben, is close to downtown (34 CHF/day, tel. 044-229-5050, www.pls-zh.ch).

Shopping on Sunday: Though most stores are closed on Sunday, the vast mall under the train station is wide open.

Tours in Zürich

Walking Tours

The TI's two-hour **guided walk** is similar to the self-guided walk in this chapter (25 CHF, half-price with Zürich Card; leaves from TI daily at 15:00, Sat-Sun also at 11:00; Nov-March runs Wed and Sun at 11:00, Sat at 11:00 and 15:00). Unfortunately, this tour is usually given in both German and English (sometimes heavily favoring German—depending on who signs up).

Local Guide: Energetic **Nicole Berger** is an informative guide who enjoys sharing her city (280 CHF/2 hours, book through the TI and request Nicole, info@zuerich.com).

Bus Tours

If you'd rather ride than walk, consider a bus tour. Two companies offer a similar 2-hour tour for 34 CHF and leave from the bus lot behind the train station. **Best of Switzerland Tours** runs a "Best of Zürich City Tour," which includes a live guide who switches between German and English, and a short journey on a cogwheel train (daily at 10:00, 13:00, and 15:30; Nov-March daily at 13:00; tel. 044-710-5050, www.switzerland-tours.ch). **Gray Line** offers a "Zürich Experience City Tour," which has larger groups and re-corded headphone commentary (daily at 9:45, 12:00, and 14:00 year-round; tel. 044-383-7878, www.meiertours.ch).

Zürich Walk

If you're blitzing Zürich from the train station, this self-guided walk is a great way to connect the city center's main sights. It criss-crosses the river en route to the boat dock for a lazy lake-cruise finale (or a quick tram ride back to the station). Allow about 1.5 hours—add 30 minutes to enter the two major churches (Gross-münster and Fraumünster).

❶ Train Station

Step inside the main concourse of this major European hub. It handles 2,000 trains a day, including InterCity expresses to many major capitals. To keep up with Europe's ever-faster transporta-tion expectations, the station's tracks have been tunneled deep underground so trains can zip through the city rather than being hampered by an old-fashioned facility where tracks dead-end at

Zürich

Zürich Walk

1 Train Station
2 Bahnhofplatz
3 Bahnhofstrasse to Pestalozzi Park
4 Police Department
5 Schipfe
6 Lindenhof
7 St. Peter's Church
8 Weinplatz & Roman Bath
9 Rathausbrücke
10 Niederdorf
11 Grossmünster
12 River View
13 Fraumünster
14 Münsterhof
15 Paradeplatz
16 Lake Zürich

the station. Built in 1870, its vast main hall was once lined with six tracks. Today, this hall is a community-events venue busy with concerts, exhibitions, and even "beach" volleyball—and a farmers market (Wed 10:00-20:00). The station sits above a modern, underground shopping mall (Mon-Fri until 21:00, Sat-Sun until 20:00).

Above you hangs the *zäftig* blue angel, Zürich's **"Guardian Angel,"** protecting all travelers. The angel (sculpted by French-American artist Niki de St. Phalle) was placed here in 1997 to celebrate the 150th anniversary of the Swiss rail system.

If the angel hopped down, walked toward the tracks, turned right, and crossed the street, she'd arrive at the **Swiss National Museum** (Schweizerisches Nationalmuseum). It's the best museum in town, offering an essential introduction to Swiss history. Consider touring this museum before starting the walk (see listing, later).

• *Exit the station hall to the angel's left, following a passage leading to Bahnhofplatz (also well-signed).*

❷ Bahnhofplatz

Mile-long Bahnhofstrasse, stretching from the train station to the lake, is lined with all the big-name shops. Cross the street (watch for silent trams), but before heading down the street, pause on Bahnhofplatz and look back at the station.

The station facade is a huge triumphal **arch,** built in 1871 to symbolize the rise of industry. In the Industrial Age, Zürich

emerged as Switzerland's leading city. Sitting atop the arch and presiding over all this triumph is Helvetia, the personification of Switzerland (she sits beneath a Swiss flag). The Helvetii were the Celtic tribe that the Romans defeated in 58 BC to gain control of what is now Switzerland. Helvetia was adopted as a symbol of the Swiss confederation in 1848 (a Swiss version of France's Marianne), when the diverse cantons that banded together to create Switzerland needed some symbol of unity to transcend all their linguistic and regional differences. The same word was put to use in the Latin name for the new federal state *(Confoederatio Helvetica).* Today, this neutral name is used when there's a need to avoid favoring any of the country's four languages—thus the "CH" on Swiss license plates, in web addresses, and in the abbreviation for the country's currency (CHF).

Helvetia is flanked by allegories of river travel (the goddess sitting on the boat) and rail travel (another goddess sitting on a locomotive), reminding us that Zürich has long been a transportation hub. Zürich's river, the Limmat, starts from the lake and eventually flows into the Rhine (reaching the Atlantic at Rotterdam).

The statue in the foreground honors **Alfred Escher,** the Zürich-born politician who, in the mid-19th century, spearheaded the creation of the infrastructure—railways, universities, and banks—that allowed Switzerland to function efficiently within its mountains and connected this country with the rest of Europe. It was his idea, for example, to link the flat, urban north of Switzerland to Italy with the nearly 10-mile Gotthard Tunnel (completed in 1882). He was also instrumental in founding Credit Suisse bank and Swiss Life insurance company. Without Escher, it's quite possible Switzerland would never have become such an economic powerhouse. Infrastructure!

• *Start strolling down Bahnhofstrasse.*

❸ Bahnhofstrasse to Pestalozzi Park

Bahnhofstrasse was built in the 1860s, when the newfangled train station needed a suitable approach road. Long before there was a train station, this would have been the moat lining the town's 13th-century fortifications. Today, you can stroll the entire boulevard from here to the lakefront, lined with department stores, elegant shops, and banks. Locals say that prices go up and shops get fancier as you get closer to the lake. This city is all about the service industry: banking, insurance, conferences, and education (it's home to several important universities).

Among the Swiss, Zürichers have a reputation for being hardworking, impatient, and a bit snobby. Notice how the traffic lights flip from green to yellow to red at an unforgiving pace—nobody has time to waste.

Near the end of the first block are three chocolate shops: Lindt and Bachmann on the right, and Läderach on the left.

• *In two blocks (on the right), you'll see a park.*

The only park along this pedestrian- and tram-only boulevard is dedicated to a famous Swiss educational reformer, **Johann Hein-**

rich Pestalozzi (1746-1827). He promoted the then-radical no-tions that good education should focus on the whole child (not just on specific skills) and should be available to everyone (not only the sons of rich families). He's standing in front of the Globus build-ing, which used to be a school. Parks like this are rare in central Zürich because of sky-high property values—Swiss real estate is among the most expensive in the world.

In the park's far corner gurgles a green, Parisian-style **foun-tain.** More than 1,200 fun and fresh fountains are sprinkled around town, spouting water that's as good as bottled mineral water (the city regularly checks its quality). This is a blessing in a town where restaurants charge for a glass of tap water. Tourist brochures brag that Zürich is Europe's most "fountainous" city.

• *From the green fountain, turn left across the street and head two blocks down Werdmühlestrasse. Then follow white* Stadtpolizei *signs up and around to the river side of the grand building facing the water. This is the...*

❹ Police Department (Stadtpolizei)

Enter the big police building at Bahnhofquai 3 for a peek at a fine example of Swiss Art Nouveau, called *Jugendstil* in German (free, open daily 9:00-11:00 & 14:00-16:00). The Swiss artist Augusto Giacometti (1877-1947) painted the arched vaults of the build-ing's entry hall in the 1920s. Awash in vibrant orange and red, with flowery motifs, the "Hall of Flowers" reflects the re-lief and joy the artist felt when World War I ended. (Augusto's nephew, Alberto, is the more

famous Giacometti, well known for his tall, skinny statues.) This building dates from the early 20th century, when higgledy-piggle-dy outlying villages were being absorbed into the growing city of Zürich; this was the site of a huge cloister that was later used as a prison and an orphanage.

• *From the door of the police building, head to the right, upstream along the river. (Notice the towering old observatory off to your right.) Ahead of you, the inviting* **Schweizer Heimatwerk** *shop shows off Swiss folk crafts. It originated long ago as a place for farmers and mountain folk to showcase and retail the handiwork that the boredom of their long winters inspired.*

From there, go down the stairs and continue walking upstream. You'll pass curious and arty little shops and come to a delightful riverside

Switzerland's Clear-Headed Drug Policy

Like many of its neighbors, Switzerland has a progressive drug policy that aims to reduce the overall harm to its society, rather than focus on punishing users. Even by European standards, the country's approaches to soft and hard drugs are unusually pragmatic.

Switzerland's policy has swung harder and softer in recent years. When polls showed that more than 30 percent of Swiss people had used marijuana, the parliament decided to decriminalize the drug, rather than criminalize a third of its population. But the laws, which vary between cantons, remain a bit ambiguous: The Swiss can possess and use pot, but they can't sell it. Each spring, there's a push for stricter control. Word gets out that Switzerland is no haven for pot, and then things ease up. Now medical marijuana shops can legally sell very weak strains of marijuana that contain less than 1 percent THC. Smoking this gets you relaxed but not high.

Unlike marijuana, hard drugs remain illegal. Still, Swiss laws treat addicts as people needing medical help, rather than as criminals. Zürich was ground zero for junkies in the 1980s and early 1990s. Beginning in 1987, heroin use was tolerated in the park called Platzspitz, along the river just behind the Swiss National Museum. Dubbed "Needle Park," the space became a magnet for thousands of users, a hotbed of crime, and one big public health hazard. In a confrontation that looms large in local history, local police reclaimed Platzspitz in 1992.

That year, Zürich pivoted to a harm-reduction, addiction-maintenance model by providing the heroin replacement drug methadone (or actual heroin) to addicts who couldn't get clean. The city funds needle exchanges and counselor-staffed safe houses where addicts unable to recover can proceed, without endangering themselves or others. If you know where to look, you can see evidence of this policy. For instance, across the river from the station, on the far side of the Walchebrücke bridge, there's a big, nondescript vending machine bolted to the railing selling safe, government-subsidized syringes.

The policy shift worked. Nationally, the opioid-related death rate has dropped by two-thirds, and heroin use among young people has dwindled to historic lows. Crime also decreased, and you see very few street addicts in Zürich. A similar approach was quickly embraced nationwide, later confirmed by 70 percent of Swiss voters in a national referendum in 2008. As the US grapples with its own opioid crisis, perhaps we can take inspiration from the pragmatic, compassionate, and highly successful Swiss approach.

square. (High above you on the right is a viewpoint on a bluff. That's Lindenhof, where we're heading.)

❺ Schipfe

Back when the city's trade depended on river traffic, this small street was Zürich's harbor. Today it retains its old river-merchant ambience. This area has several businesses that are subsidized by the city government to support down-on-their-luck locals and worthy causes. On the left at #24, the **Marktlücke** shop aids single mothers; they sell interesting gifts, including items made from recycled materials. At the far end of the little square is a fun waterfront eatery—the recommended **Restaurant Schipfe 16**—that operates as a charity, employing people who are trying to get back on their feet.

Continue past the restaurant, admiring the antiques in the windows of the Voch shop (which painstakingly restores classic pieces). Bear left at the fork, and soon you'll reach an arcade that runs along the river. Head through it, passing an interesting strip of little artisan workshops and boutiques (also subsidized by the local government, to enliven this central area with traditional crafts).

• *Emerging at the far end of the arcade, near a fine fountain, turn right (away from the river) and head up the stairs. Bear right at the fork (with the Old Crow sign), then left at Wohllebgasse. Climbing up from the river, watch on the right for Pfalzgasse, which leads steeply to a park with fine views.*

❻ Lindenhof

Important forts and strategic buildings stood on this bluff from Roman times through the ninth-century Carolingian era. The statue commemorates the local women who cleverly defended the town in 1292. Their men were engaged in another battle when the Habsburgs encircled the city. The women put on armor and made like a big, rowdy army, tricking the Habsburgs into thinking the whole city was prepared to attack.

In the early 13th century, Zürich became a free city of the Holy Roman Empire, meaning it was relatively autonomous and self-ruling. The townspeople destroyed the fort here and established a law forbidding any new construction. The citizens realized that whoever lived on this hill would control the city—and they didn't want any more such rulers. Today, this is a people's square, where locals relax under linden trees (for which the square is named) and enjoy the commanding city view.

Look out and survey the city. **Zürich University** (behind the skinny green spire) is the largest in Switzerland, with 25,000 students (and was the first German-speaking university to allow women students, in 1847). Left of that is Zürich's renowned **technical college,** the ETH (Eidgenössische Technische Hochschule—the Federal Institute of Technology), with 15,000 students. The ETH has graduated more than 20 Nobel Prize winners, including Albert Einstein and Wilhelm Röntgen (who discovered X-rays). The ETH terrace offers a great city viewpoint (which you can visit later by riding the little Polybahn funicular). Below these storied institutions, lining the opposite side of the river, the **Niederdorf** is a lively district of restaurants, cafés, and bars. We'll walk through there soon. On a clear day, you can see the Alps beyond the twin domes of the Grossmünster.

• *Descend the stairs at the back corner of the park, just beyond where you entered (near the giant chessboard), to a little square with a fountain. The fountain's armpit points you down Glockengasse. Heading that way, you'll reach a big golden bell (at the Haus zur Glocke); take the narrow lane around its left side (Robert-Walser-Gasse). You'll pass a characteristic eatery, Restaurant Kaiser's Reblaube, made famous by visits from Goethe in 1779. He'd meet here for long, wine-fueled discussions with the minister of...*

❼ St. Peter's Church (St. Peterskirche)

Founded in the seventh century, this church—Zürich's oldest—has one of Europe's largest clock faces (28 feet in diameter). The town watchman used to live above the clock. If he spotted a fire, he would ring the alarm and hang a flag out of the window facing the blaze. This system seems to have worked—Zürich never suffered a devastating fire.

• *Continue past the church on Schlüsselgasse and take the first left, down the narrow Thermengasse (Bath Lane). Here we meet a bit of Roman Zürich. Glass cases in the wall contain artifacts, and under your feet are the excavations of a **Roman bath**, discovered by accident in 1984. You're standing over studs that elevated the floor, which was heated from below.*

The lane empties out on...

❽ Weinplatz

This pleasant spot was a wine market in centuries past (look for the happy grape picker on the fine little fountain). Zürich never had a centralized market hall, and this is just the first of many such market-themed squares that ran through town; I'll mention several of them in the next few blocks. (Notice the dock here for the riverboat-bus—described later, under "Sights in Zürich".)

• Now cross the wide...

❾ Rathausbrücke

Built on the site of the town's first bridge, this is, quite possibly, the ugliest bridge in Switzerland. You'll pass the c. 1880 carousel and see a fancy Neoclassical police station (on the left).

Near the far end of the bridge, the big building on the right is the 17th-century, Renaissance-style **Town Hall**. Below the second-story windows, find the fruits and vegetables carved into the stonework—a subtle reminder that this bridge was once the Gemüsebrücke, where produce (Gemüse) was sold. The bridge still hosts a farmers market on Saturdays in summer (and locals still call it by that old nickname). Above the ground-floor windows, you'll see busts of Greek, Roman, and Swiss heroes, including (at the far end just before the street) William Tell and his crossbow. Before crossing the tram tracks, look back, along the street-facing side of Town Hall. Instead of veggies, this side is decorated with fish—indicating the historic location of a fish market.

• At the end of the bridge, cross the street and walk a block straight uphill along Marktgasse. Pause where the street hits a T-intersection. You're standing in the heart of the bustling neighborhood called...

❿ Niederdorf

"Niederdorf" means "nether town"—across the river from the historic core of Zürich. Today Niederdorf is a district of colorful streets, fun shopping, restaurants, and nightlife. This is a great spot for dinner (scope out menus as we explore, and see my dining suggestions later, under "Eating in Zürich").

Let's take a little loop through Niederdorf to see some facets of this neighborhood that many visitors miss. Turn left to continue along narrow Marktgasse, which was the leading commercial street before the old city wall was torn down to create Bahnhofstrasse. After two short blocks, turn right up **Rindermarkt**—literally "Beef Market" (yet another street named for its onetime commerce). Follow this broad street one long block, past high-end shops, art boutiques, furniture shops, and some tempting restaurants. This atmospheric street is still lit with gas lamps.

Just after the Travel Book Shop (on your right), turn left on Froschaugasse. Then, just a few doors down, squeeze through the green doors on the right (just before #8), entering **Synagogengasse** (Lane of the Synagogues). Follow this narrow passage, which is where the city's Jews once lived, mixed in among their non-Jewish neighbors, until the pogrom of 1249. The alley bends right, passing the garden of the recommended Wirtschaft Neumarkt restaurant, before popping out at Neumarkt, where historically household goods were sold.

Head directly across wide Neumarkt—passing inviting café tables huddled around a fountain—and find the door at #4, with the stone plaque that says *Zvm Vntern Rech*. Enter the **City Archive** (free, closed Sun) and head straight back to a big room with a wonderfully detailed city model of Zürich around the year 1800 (based on the two maps you see hanging on the wall). Notice the moat—which is now Bahnhofstrasse—and the outer, star-shaped fortifications that beefed up the city in the 17th century. (You can still see echoes of this in a city map.)

Exiting the Archive, immediately turn left to head up the narrow lane called Spiegelgasse—watching on the left for a cute little interior garden (at #22). Locals brag about how green their city is; there are many such private, hidden gardens even in the dense medieval center.

Find #16, on the left. Now a clothing store, this was once a butcher. Notice the cleaver motif in the ornate window frames, and peek inside to see how old meat hooks still hang from a meat-themed ceiling fresco.

Next door, at #14, a plaque identifies where **Vladimir Lenin** lived in exile from February 1916 until April 1917. When he left here, he traveled north to Helsinki, boarded a train, and was greeted as a conquering hero upon arriving in St. Petersburg, where he took leadership of the revolution that would topple the monarchy and introduce communism to Russia.

Cresting the hill and passing a fountain, continue straight downhill along Spiegelgasse. On the right is the **Cabaret Voltaire,** where a different type of revolution was taking place. In 1916, the "anti-art" Dada movement was started here by a group of rebellious young artists and writers. Although the Dada movement picked up steam, the cabaret itself lasted only until 1917...complaints about excessive nightly noise forced its closure.

You've made a loop, and you're back near where we started our tour of Niederdorf. Turn left on Münstergasse. A couple of doors down on the right at #19, pop into **Schwarzenbach,** a delightful specialty grocery store that's been operating here for more than 100 years. They still sell things the old-fashioned way (in loose bags, by weight). Inhale. Pick up 100 grams of dried bananas from Togo or whatever appeals (closed Sun). They also roast coffee beans next door on Tuesday and Thursday mornings, making this whole street smell like coffee.

Across the street is Zürich's popular **Conditorei Schober,** a venerable chocolate shop that feels like a time warp, with a fine perch from which to enjoy a cup of coffee or hot chocolate. Across the lane to the left is a Swiss schnapps shop.

• *Farther along, Münstergasse runs into the...*

⓫ Grossmünster

Literally the "big cathedral," this is where Huldrych Zwingli—whose angry religious fervor made Martin Luther seem mellow—sparked the Reformation in German-speaking Switzerland. The domes of its towers (early examples of Neo-Gothic) are symbols of Zürich. They were rebuilt following a 1781 fire, and after much civic discussion, were left a plain stone color.

Cost and Hours: Church—free, Mon-Sat 10:00-18:00, Sun from 12:30, off-season until 17:00; tower climb—5 CHF, closes 1 hour earlier than church; cloister—free, Mon-Fri 10:00-17:00, closed Sat-Sun; pick up English story of the Swiss Reformation, www.grossmuenster.ch.

Visiting the Church: Step inside and sit down. Let the strength and purity of the 12th-century Romanesque architecture have its way with you. The simple round arches seem strong, and the pulpit—surrounded by none of the old Catholic ornamentation—gave you almost no alternative other than to be riveted by Zwingli's fiery sermons. Zwingli's reforms led to a clean sweep of Catholic decor in 1519.

Behind the altar in the apse are three **choir windows** by Augusto Giacometti (c. 1933). Mary and the Baby Jesus (at her feet) meet two of the three kings bearing their gifts, while angels hover above with offerings of flowers. You can walk to just below the windows for a closer look. While there, check out the 1531 Zürich Bible. (Like Luther, Zwingli was a fan of having the Bible available in the people's language—which is what got them in hot water with the Church.)

In the dank **crypt** (stairs below altar), you'll see an original 15th-century statue of Charlemagne (a copy now fills its niche on the river side of the church exterior).

For a sweeping city view, climb the 187 steps to the top of the **Karlsturm,** one of the church's twin towers.

Leaving the church, go right and into the corner, where a door leads to a fine Romanesque **cloister** ringed with fanciful 12th-century carvings. Upon entering, take 10 steps to the left and meet the sculptor (self-portrait on the highest arch).

Before moving on, circle around to the river side of the church. Up eight steps, find the **bronze door** depicting scenes from the life of Zwingli.

• *Head down to the bridge and walk halfway across the river. Pause in the middle of the bridge for a...*

⓬ River View

This spot—flanked by Zürich's two most important churches—is one of the most scenic places in town.

Look back toward the Grossmünster. The building sticking out into the river on your right is the **Wasserkirche** (Water Church). According to the city's foundational legend, two early Christians (Felix and Regula) were beheaded by Roman authorities on this spot in the third century. Miraculously, they picked up their heads, walked 40 paces up the hill, and lay back down again on the site of today's Grossmünster. (Later, they were joined by a third headless body—so you'll see the "three headless bodies" motif around the city.) Flash forward 600 years: It's said that Charlemagne was out hunting when he discovered the bodies, and decided that this would be the optimal site of the city's main church. The only statue that adorns the church—high up on the side of the steeple facing this bridge—shows Charlemagne, with his golden crown.

Looking left along the river, you see stately old houses. Many of these are **guildhouses** *(Zunfthaus)*. Merchant towns like Zürich were dominated by guilds—groups of like-minded, wealthy burghers, often of the same profession, who combined to have serious clout. In fact, guilds dominated the city's civic life; the city is sometimes called *Bürgertum* (town of burghers) or *Zunftstadt* (guild city). As we stand between two giant churches, notice that both are called Münster—not "cathedral." Zürich didn't want a cathedral—or the bishop who'd come along with it and constantly boss around the burghers.

Guilds have loomed so large in the story of Zürich, in fact, that they still survive today, as modern-day social institutions (similar to a Rotary or Elks club). There are about a dozen historical guilds, and about a dozen modern ones—but none of them admit women. Each *Zunft* (guild) meets in its own *Zunfthaus*, which have both meeting rooms and restaurants or reception halls that are open to the public. You can see three guildhouses along the water: Below and to the left of the Grossmünster (with the red turret) is the Zunfthaus zur Zimmerleuten (for carpenters); next door is the Haus zum Rüden ("House of the Hound," for an association of noblemen); and across the river is the big, pink fishermen's guild (now the swanky Hotel Storchen).

• *Continue the rest of the way over the river to the tall-steepled church with "1732" on the tower.*

⓭ Fraumünster

This ▲▲ church was founded along with a convent in 853, when Zürich was little more than a village. The current building, which sits on the same footprint as its predecessor, dates from 1250. With the Reformation of Zwingli, the church was taken by the Zürich

Switzerland's Zwingli Reformation

Today's Evangelical Reformed Church of Switzerland was founded by Huldrych Zwingli (1484-1531), who preached in Zürich from 1519 through 1531. A follower of the humanist philosopher Erasmus of Rotterdam, Zwingli believed that the Holy Scriptures should be preached freely—in the people's language, rather than in Latin. In 1522, most of German-speaking Switzerland embraced Zwingli's ideas...and that required leaving the Roman Catholic Church.

In 1517, when Zwingli was 33, German church reformer Martin Luther posted his revolutionary *95 Theses* (which questioned the practice of selling forgiveness, salvation, church offices, and so on). Within two years, sellers of indulgences were refused entry to Zürich. As the Reformation swept Switzerland, things heated up. In 1523, rioters were storming churches, and authorities called for an orderly removal of all images in Zürich houses of worship (except stained-glass windows, which were destroyed).

The new, reformed Swiss church let priests marry. (Zwingli, like Luther, promptly took advantage of this freedom.) Fancy Masses were replaced by simple services. At Zürich's main church, the Grossmünster, preachers studied Latin, Greek, and Hebrew in order to translate the Bible into the people's German. In 1531, the Zwingli Bible, a complete translation into Swiss German, was published. It's still used today (like the King James Bible is in English); you can see one in the Swiss National Museum here in Zürich.

Zwingli gave the Swiss church an unusual austerity: no altar, no pictures, and for a while, not even any music. Church services focused on preaching. Holy Communion was celebrated only on holidays. This puritanical simplicity permeated Swiss society in general. Zwingli was no fan of the "separation of church and

town council in 1524 and—you know the drill—gutted to fit Zwingli's taste. Today, the Fraumünster's claim to fame is a collection of 30-foot-tall stained-glass windows by Marc Chagall (1887-1985), the Russian-born French artist. The included audioguide also explains the rest of the church—including the historic crypt with fine and well-described artifacts (stairs from near the altar).

Cost and Hours: 5 CHF, includes excellent audioguide or a brochure; Mon-Sat 10:00-18:00, Sun from 12:00, Nov-March until 17:00; occasional evening concerts, www.fraumuenster.ch.

Background: In 1967, Zürich's art museum hosted a Chagall retrospective. It so impressed the Frau-state." Pushing for a theocracy, he established an ironclad city law: The government's duty was to oversee public worship, and only preaching that was true to the Bible was to be tolerated.

But Zwingli's reforms were by no means universally supported. The Reformation was a messy process. The Protestant movement split over the proper role of baptism. Luther and Zwingli split over the Eucharist (is Christ's body literally *in* the bread, or there only in a spiritual sense?). And, as old-school Catholics predicted, putting the Bible into the hands of regular people brought chaos—enabling every Tom, Dick, and Hans to "carve his own path to hell." Switzerland became embroiled in a religious civil war, as Protestant cantons fought Catholic ones. In 1531, while fighting as a "citizen soldier," Zwingli was killed in battle. His friend and partner Heinrich Bullinger succeeded him as the leader of German-speaking Swiss Protestantism.

Bullinger collaborated with John Calvin as Swiss Protestantism matured. The Protestant focus on preaching promoted the translation and interpretation of the Bible. Everyone was reading the Bible directly, which promoted literacy. The Reformation provided a basis for the autonomous community spirit, strong work ethic, and high literacy of a prosperous Switzerland for the future. The Swiss church became a place where equals would meet and worship God. As in other Protestant countries, Zwingli's heritage included transferring the notion of social charity from a church phenomenon to the responsibility of any self-respecting modern state. The foundations of Swiss democracy and its present social policies are rooted in Zwingli's teaching. And these Swiss reformers planted the seeds of what became the Presbyterian Church in the United States.

münster's pastor that he offered the world-famous artist a commission. To his surprise, the 80-year-old Chagall accepted. He designed the windows to stand in the church's spacious choir zone behind the altar—a space where he intuitively felt his unique mix of religious themes could flourish.

For the next three years, Chagall threw his heart and soul into the project, making the sketches at his home on the French Riviera, then working in close collaboration with a glassmaking factory in Reims, France. After the colored panes were made, he outlined the figures in black, which were then baked into the glass. Chagall spent weeks in Zürich overseeing the installation, completed in 1970.

Chagall's inimitable painting style—deep colors, simple figures, and shard-like Cubism—is perfectly suited to the medium of stained glass. Blending Jewish and Christian traditions, he created a work that can make people of many faiths comfortable.

Visiting the Church: Grab a seat in the front of the church with the five Chagall windows towering above you and enjoy the entire audioguide description (or follow this explanation).

The five windows depict Bible scenes, culminating in the central image of the crucified Christ. From left to right, they are:

The Prophets (red): The prophet Elisha (bottom) looks up to watch a horse-drawn chariot carry his mentor Elijah off to heaven. Farther up, Jeremiah (blue in color and mood) puts his hand to his head and ponders the destruction of wicked Jerusalem. Up in heaven (top), a multicolored, multifaceted God spins out his creation, sending fiery beams down to inspire his prophets on earth. This window is artificially lit, as it's built into an interior wall.

Jacob (blue—Chagall's favorite color): Jacob (bottom, riding a skateboard amid the deep blue) dreams of a ladder that snakes up to heaven, with red-tinged angels ascending and descending, symbolizing the connection between God above and Jacob's descendants (the Children of Israel) below.

Christ (green): The middle, and biggest, window depicts the central figure in God's plan of salvation—Jesus Christ, who, as the Messiah, fulfills the promises of the Old Testament prophets. Mother Mary suckles Baby Jesus (bottom) amid the leafy family tree of Jesus' Old Testament roots. The central area is an indistinct jumble of events from Christ's life, leading up to his Crucifixion. The life-size ascendant Christ is crucified in a traditional medieval pose, but he's surrounded by a circle that seems to be bearing him, resurrected, to heaven. Chagall signed and dated the work (1970).

Zion (yellow): King David (bottom right) strums his harp and sings a psalm, while behind him stands his mistress Bathsheba, who gave birth to Solomon, the builder of Jerusalem's temple. At the end of history, an angel (top) blows a ram's horn, announcing the establishment of a glorious New Jerusalem, which descends (center), featuring rust-colored, yellow, and green walls, domes, and towers.

The Law (blue): At the very top, Moses—with horns of light and the Ten Commandments—looks sternly down on law-breaking warriors on horseback wreaking havoc. At the bottom, an angel (in red) embraces the prophet Isaiah (very bottom) and inspires him to foretell the coming of the Messiah (in red, above the angel).

Everyone comes away with a different interpretation of this complex work, which combines images from throughout the Bible. Some feel that the tall, skinny windows seem to emphasize the vertical connection between heaven above and earth below, both bathed in the same colored light. Some think Chagall used colors symbolically: Blue and green represent the earth; red and yellow, heavenly radiance. But all recognize that the jumble of images—evoking the complexity of God's universe—reaches its Point

Omega in the central window, celebrating the idea of salvation through Christ's Crucifixion.

• *Head into the square alongside the church. This is the...*

⑭ Münsterhof

This original courtyard of a fortified convent was made into a traffic-free public space in 2016. Each spring, on the Monday after the equinox, people gather here to celebrate Sächsilüüte—the end of winter. In the middle of the square stands a six-story-tall pyre topped with a giant snowman figure (called the Böögg). The pyre is lit with great ceremony and burns its way up to the snowman, whose head is loaded with fireworks. The bigger the explosion, the better the spring will be.

This square is also home to more of Zürich's surviving **guilds**. At the bottom (river end) of the square is the elegant Zunfthaus zur Meisen, historically the guild for innkeepers, painters, and saddle makers. Near the top of the square, behind the fountain, is the Zunfthaus zur Waag—once the wool and linen weavers' guild.

Before moving on, consider a little detour to see some hidden illustrations of Zürich's legendary past: Circle around to face the "front door" of the Fraumünster, then duck through the gate on its right side, into the **Kreuzgang Fraumünster** (free, closed Sun). This passage, once a nunnery, is now part of the city administration building. The inside is painted with vivid, dreamy depictions of important local legends. In one, a magical, glowing deer shows two nuns the place where they should build what is today the Fraumünster. In the other, you can see those early Christian martyrs who, after being beheaded by Romans, picked up their heads and carried them to what's now the Grossmünster (in this version, they are guided by angels carrying doves).

• *Back out on Münsterhof, follow the small lane on the left side of Zunfthaus zur Waag, passing (or walking through) the recommended Zeughauskeller restaurant (500 years ago the city armory, it has a weapons theme for its decoration today—including what they call an "authentic replica" of William Tell's crossbow). As you round the corner, you'll hit busy...*

⑮ Paradeplatz

Survey the scene, a triumph of urban planning and people-friendly vision: The train station is a 10-minute walk to your right up Bahnhofstrasse, and the lake is a few minutes to your left, down the classiest stretch of Bahnhofstrasse. On the left is **$$$ Sprüngli**, Zürich's top café for the past century. Its "Luxemburgerli" *macarons*—little cream-filled, one-inch *macaron*-meringue treats —are a local favorite (you can buy just a couple; if you buy 100 grams, you'll get a selection of 12, see photo next page). Sprüngli also sells elegant sandwich lunches, either in its café (upstairs/outside) or to go (perfect for a lakeside snack; open Mon-Sat until 18:30, Sun until 17:30).

Across the square is Credit Suisse, with a luxurious ground floor full of fancy shops. If you like, detour a block back up Bahnhofstrasse to #31 and visit the fine little **Beyer Clock and Watch Museum,** in the basement of the elegant Beyer watch shop (10 CHF, Zürich Card valid but not Swiss Travel Pass, Mon-Fri 14:00-18:00, closed Sat-Sun).

• *From here, you've seen the heart of Zürich; if time is short, simply hop a tram back to the station.*

But if time allows and you'd like a peek at the city's lake—and the chance to go on a lake cruise—you can head several minutes farther down Bahnhofstrasse. From where you entered the square, turn left and follow Bahnhofstrasse past a few more elegant shops and mighty banks to the boats and riverside terrace at Bürkliplatz. We'll finish this walk at...

❻ Lake Zürich (Zürichsee)

Lake Zürich is 17 miles long, 2.5 miles wide, and—because it's relatively shallow—warm enough for swimming in the summer. From here, you can enjoy the lakeside promenade (a fine strolling path stretching 3 miles in either direction; left is sunnier and more interesting) or a short cruise. To go back to the

station, catch tram #11 (from the inland side, across the street) or the Limmat riverboat. Both cruise and riverboat options are described next.

Sights in Zürich

▲▲Swiss National Museum
(Schweizerisches Nationalmuseum)

By the late 19th century, it was clear that the world was changing, and the Swiss wanted to protect their unique heritage. A national competition was held, Zürich won, and it created the country's national museum. Located in a Neo-Gothic castle, this massive and interesting museum (still often called by its original name,

Landesmuseum) provides a solid background on Swiss history and identity. If Zürich is your first stop in Switzerland, visiting here for a primer on all things Swiss can help put the rest of your trip in context. Even if you're not staying the night in Zürich, the museum (just across the street from the train station) can be a worthwhile rainy-day excursion from other cities (especially if you have a train pass) or a quick stop while passing through.

Cost and Hours: 10 CHF, covered by Swiss Travel Pass and Zürich Card; Tue-Sun 10:00-17:00, Thu until 19:00, closed Mon; audioguide-5 CHF (or download the free app), English tours Tue and Fri at 11:00, mandatory bag check, Museumstrasse 2, quality café, tel. 044-218-6511, www.landesmuseum.ch.

Visiting the Museum: The museum is well-designed and well-described in English. Be prepared to walk up and down stairs, and down long hallways, to traverse the sprawling, mazelike layout; review the floor plan before you get going. I've described the permanent exhibits below, but there are good temporary exhibits, too. With limited time, prioritize the History of Switzerland exhibit.

History of Switzerland: The main exhibit tells the story of this unique land, using ample artifacts to illustrate each theme. (To get here, track signs to the left of the ticket desk, through a labyrinth of stairs and hallways.) The story begins in the **14th century,** as the cantons that would eventually become Switzerland started to unify. This is the time of William Tell and the Rütli Oath, in which the three founding cantons threw off the shackles of the aristocracy to assert self-rule. The bristling column of pikes and halberds symbolizes this militaristic age.

The exhibit proceeds through the **16th century,** when the Reformation split Switzerland—spiritually and ideologically—right down the middle. See Zwingli's Bible translation into German (from 1531, designed to put the Word of God into the hands of the people), and study the giant triptych painting of saints with old Zürich as a backdrop—completed in 1502, then removed by iconoclasts in 1524.

Meanwhile, Switzerland became famous for exporting its men as mercenaries in foreign wars (a tradition that continues with today's Swiss Guard at the Vatican). Find the tapestry of Swiss officials renewing their alliance with Louis XIV (inside Notre-Dame) to provide mercenaries. Compare the simply dressed, unpretentious Swiss on the left with the lavish court of the Sun King on the right. Cities also flourished during this age; see the huge cabinet from 1657, displaying the many guilds of Zürich (which survive today).

The **18th century** brought the Enlightenment, including the scientific study of the Alps, the development of alpine infrastructure, and a Romantic appreciation of the beauty of nature, as preached by French-Swiss philosopher Jean-Jacques Rousseau, who presented an idealized image of Switzerland.

In the **19th century,** the federal state of Switzerland was born (1848) with Bern as its seat of government (see model of the parliament). The 1829 painting of 135 Swiss founding fathers includes politicians, scholars, scientists, and Reformers (all identified by the touchscreen). Nationhood came with a single currency (see some of the 800 different coins, issued by 79 authorities, that were phased out in 1850). It also came with neutrality, which both defines Swiss identity and remains one of this country's most controversial features.

This age also saw the rise of tourism, including the first cogwheel train to Rigi (1871—it still runs today) and the Gotthard Tunnel connecting Swiss cities to Italy (1882). See the vintage travel posters and the official rail map from that era. But the mid-1800s were also difficult times for the poor, with many emigrating to find a better life in the New World. The painting *Pain of Parting* shows grief-stricken parents collapsing on the train platform after saying goodbye to their adult children forever.

The **20th century** was a tough time to be neutral, but Switzerland doubled down on not taking sides. See the machine gun and cannon that defended the Gotthard Pass from potential invasion (had it happened, Swiss leadership planned to abandon its cities and hole up in the rugged alpine interior, creating a fortified "Swiss National Redoubt"). To preserve its neutrality, Switzerland turned each of its citizens into a soldier, with standard-issue gear to protect against "NBC" (nuclear, biological, and chemical weapons). Meanwhile, to differentiate themselves from the Nazis ideologically, the Swiss created the Pro Helvetia movement (for "spiritual national defense"). At the Landi national exhibition on Lake Zürich in 1939, 10 million Swiss celebrated their folk culture and dialects; look for the flags from that event.

Switzerland did take in refugees, though critics say hardly enough: 26,000 in World War I, and 51,000—including 21,000 Jews—in World War II. The exhibit examines this issue with candor; contrast the postcard of Lady Switzerland comforting war refugees with illustrations of desperate refugees waiting at the border. The bullet-holed sign from the Swiss embassy in Budapest recalls how the Swiss diplomat Carl Lutz heroically saved some 62,000 Jews there—while others, including Switzerland's ambassador to Germany, ignored the crisis (find the tattered Swiss flag from the Berlin embassy).

The **postwar era** kicked off with an economic boom, but it also saw Switzerland grapple with social challenges, including workers' rights; the global student movement of 1968; and—in 1971—the vote that finally guaranteed Swiss women the right to vote, which passed by a two-thirds majority. The exhibit ends with a look at the rise of consumer culture and 21st-century challenges, including climate change, migration, and sovereignty in the age of the EU.

While that's the core of the museum, there are other permanent exhibits worth visiting:

Simply Zürich: This exhibit (upstairs) displays objects that symbolize Switzerland's largest city (each one explained by touch-screens), and giant sculpture by the local art collective Mickry 3.

Ideas of Switzerland: This small but thought-provoking exhibit explores what it means to be Swiss (enter from the opposite side of the building, past the ticket desk and near the café). Virtual "books" introduce you to four prominent Swiss figures: theologian John Calvin, historian Petermann Etterlin, philosopher Jean-Jacques Rousseau, and humanitarian Henry Dunant, who cofounded the Red Cross. A giant granite 3-D map of the Swiss Alps offers an enhanced-reality view of the country; aim the binoculars at the map on the wall to see Switzerland over time.

Archaeology in Switzerland: Find this exhibit by heading upstairs, then back down again. Here you'll see items found in prehistoric graves, a stela (carved pillar) showing a man from about 3000-2500 BC, an exquisite golden dish made as a gift for the gods (from around 1100 BC), and tools made from stone, bronze, and iron. Meet the Celts (Helvetii—see their large golden rings from around 390 BC, thought to help protect travelers), who were Romanized beginning around the second century BC. Most of the objects are in large cases on the wall; move the giant sliding screen into position over each item to learn more.

Before leaving, check out the **shop** (near the ticket desk), which has one of the city's best selections of quality Swiss souvenirs that go beyond the clichés (and, also, some clichés).

▲Kunsthaus Zürich

It's worth the tram/bus ride (or 10-minute stroll up from the heart of Niederdorf) to see Switzerland's top collection of fine art. The museum features a combination of quality works by European masters, mixed in with fine examples by Swiss artists (whom I've highlighted here). For art lovers, it's worth ▲▲. The curator embraces change, so the collection gets shuffled around frequently—and there are often high-quality special exhibitions, too. Pick up a map as you enter and go with the flow.

Cost and Hours: 16 CHF, more for special exhibits, includes audioguide, free on Wed, not covered by Swiss Travel Pass; Tue-Sun 10:00-18:00, Wed-Thu until 20:00, closed Mon; mandatory bag check, café; at Heimplatz 1—take tram #3, #5, #8, or #9, or bus #31 to Kunsthaus stop; tel. 044-253-8484, www.kunsthaus.ch.

Visiting the Museum: The collection runs the gamut, from

Old Masters (Guardi, Tiepolo, Rembrandt, Brueghel, Hals) to present-day greats.

In the 18th- and 19th-century section, look for works by three Swiss painters. **Johann Heinrich Füssli**—a.k.a. Henry Fuseli (1741-1825)—was born in Zürich but spent most of his career in London. Füssli's works exhibit a marked *chiaroscuro* technique (with a strong contrast between light and dark); the supernatural was a favorite theme of his. **Arnold Böcklin** (1827-1901), from Basel, was a Symbolist who painted fantastical landscapes and evocative creatures. *The War* (1896) began as four horsemen of the apocalypse—but then Böcklin went in a different direction, winding up with three grotesque horseback figures. **Ferdinand Hodler** (1853-1918) was also quite mystical, working with bright, cheery colors, symbolic figures, and shimmering landscapes. *The Day* (1904-1906) depicts five young women in a semicircle, who embody the way that light changes over the course of a day.

The excellent 20th-century collection includes works by Picasso, Kokoschka, Ernst, Beckmann, Corinth, Magritte, Miró, Degas, Renoir, Monet, and Chagall (whose stained-glass windows adorn the Fraumünster). The museum owns the best collection of **Edvard Munch** works outside of Norway; these typically share a room with works by **Giovanni Segantini** (1858-1899). While Italian-born and trained in Milan, Segantini later moved to the Graubünden and Engadine regions of Switzerland, where he did his best work. His gorgeous, grand-scale *Alpine Pasture* (1893-1894) shows off Segantini's mastery of his late-Impressionist style, where collages of dots and streaks form a vivid, beautiful scene of pastoral Swiss countryside.

There's usually a large exhibition of hauntingly stretched-out sculptures by **Alberto Giacometti** (1901-1966)—one of Switzerland's best-known artists beyond his homeland. Giacometti built on the foundation of Rodin but took things in a Surrealist direction, abstracting and elongating human figures until they were barely recognizable. Over time, Giacometti's style evolved—going through phases with sculptures just a few inches tall to figures several feet tall. Elsewhere, you'll also see paintings by Alberto's father, **Giovanni Giacometti** (1868-1933). Giovanni was the cousin of Augusto Giacometti, whose work we've already seen on the town walk, in the entrance hall of the police station and in the *Grossmünster*. And, of course, you'll see a few works by the great Swiss painter **Paul Klee** (1879-1940), with his exuberant, colorful, abstract, almost childlike compositions. The collection carries through to the present day, with pieces by Warhol, Lichtenstein, Rothko, Merz, Twombly, Beuys, Bacon, and Baselitz.

Cruises on Limmat River and Lake Zürich

A boat ride down the Limmat River or on Lake Zürich can be a nice, lazy contrast to your busy, urban visit. Small riverboat-buses take commuters and joy-riding visitors up and down the river and to points nearby on the lake. Big, romantic ships take tourists on longer rides around Lake Zürich. All boats are run by ZSG and do not include commentary (tel. 044-487-1333, www.zsg.ch). The first two options are fully covered by the Swiss Travel Pass, **Zürich Card,** or 24-hour transit pass (also covered by the Global Pass, but uses a flexi day—so do it the day you arrive or depart).

Riverboat-Buses: These low-to-the-water boats (designed to squeeze under the bridges) start where the Swiss National Museum and the Platzspitz Park meet on the banks of the Limmat River. These boats do a 50-minute loop, making several stops along the river en route to Bürkliplatz (pier #6, where lake cruises begin), and then do a quick circle around the lake before returning to their starting point. You can either do the full trip, or hop on and off as you like. They can be handy for connecting the museum and the lake (4.40 CHF/ride—up to the entire loop, runs daily 2/hour about 10:00-21:00, more frequent in summer, no boats in winter).

Big Lake-Only Excursion Boats: These start at Bürkliplatz and go farther down the lake. The basic 1.5-hour "short round trip" goes as far as Erlenbach (8.80 CHF; April-Oct daily 2/hour 9:10-19:40, fewer off-season, buy tickets near pier #3, boats depart from pier #1-#6). They also offer longer trips and jazz and dinner cruises (but these are not covered by the Zürich Card or transit passes). With plenty of time, you could even ride the boat all the way to Rapperswil (at the far end of Lake Zürich), enjoy that town for lunch, and then catch the train back to Zürich.

Zürich West (Züri Wescht)

This trendy, up-and-coming former industrial zone is just a few minutes' tram ride behind the train station. Though not as funky or interesting as similar zones in other European cities, it's worth a wander if you're curious to see a contemporary side of this otherwise staid city. Note that many shops here are closed Sundays.

From the train station area, ride tram #4, #13, or #17 to Dammweg, where you can visit **Markthalle Viadukt,** with bakeries, cheesemongers, greengrocers, microbrew and wine vendors, and a variety of eateries, including sushi, fresh pasta, and the good **$$$ Restaurant Markthalle,** with international plats du jour (check out the selection of vendors at www.im-viadukt.ch). Exit the market hall at the far end, and follow the **viaduct** toward the smokestack—checking out the many numbered shops tucked under the 36 arches (clothing, housewares, home decor, and more).

At the viaduct's end, turn right and head toward the city's

only skyscraper. Your next stop is the big tower of stacked shipping containers—the flagship store for **Freitag,** which started in Zürich manufacturing bags from recycled materials. Just beyond is **Frau Gerolds Garten,** with shops up front and a beer garden in back—all with a funky mismatched-furniture-under-twinkle-lights vibe.

You could retrace your steps, or turn right and walk under the overpass to head back along the tram tracks. Along with interesting eateries and modern condo and office developments, you'll find the Schiffbau theater, filling a former shipbuilding factory (as its name means). Heading back toward the river, you'll wind up at the Escher-Wyss-Platz tram stop—one stop from where you got off. From here, ride the tram back to the station.

Museum Rietberg

Filling historic villas set in a beautiful park, this museum houses art from Asia, Africa, the Americas, and the South Pacific.

Cost and Hours: 14 CHF, covered by Swiss Travel Pass and Zürich Card; Tue-Sun 10:00-17:00, Wed until 20:00, closed Mon; audioguide-5 CHF, tram #7 from station (direction: Wollishofen) to Museum Rietberg stop, Gablerstrasse 15, tel. 044-415-3131, www.rietberg.ch.

Zürich Zoo

With 360 species, an impressive Madagascar rainforest hall, and a huge indoor exhibit, the city's zoo is a fun place to see locals at play.

Cost and Hours: 26 CHF; daily 9:00-18:00, Nov-Feb until 17:00; tram #6 from Bahnhofstrasse in front of the station (direction: Zoo), ride to last stop, Zürichbergstrasse 221, tel. 044-254-2500, www.zoo.ch.

Nearby: James Joyce fans can find the grave of the Irish author (adorned with a life-size statue) in the parklike Friedhof Fluntern cemetery, next to the zoo.

Uetliberg

For an interesting 1.5-hour excursion high above the city and lake, take the small red/orange S10 excursion train that climbs from the main train station to this little mountain peak (17.60 CHF four-zone *Tageskarte* covers your round-trip and gives you 24 hours of free transport around town, also covered by Zürich Card; 2-3/hour, runs 6:30-24:00, 25 minutes, www.zvv.ch). From the Uetliberg station, it's a moderately steep, 10-minute climb up a paved pedestrian road to a hotel and a tall observation tower overlooking the city. The view is particularly striking at sunset.

Sleeping in Zürich

High season in Zürich is May, June, September, and October. In this business-oriented city, rooms tend to be cheaper on weekends and pricier during festivals and conventions (September can be particularly busy). If you're on a tight budget, some hotels let you save a little on the rate by skipping breakfast—ask.

I rank accommodations from **$** budget to **$$$$** splurge. For the best deal, contact hotels directly by phone or email. When you book direct, the owner avoids a commission and may be able to offer a discount. Book well in advance for peak season or if your trip coincides with a major holiday or festival (see the appendix). For more details on reservations, short-term rentals, and more, see the "Sleeping" section in the Practicalities chapter.

Most of my listings are across the river from the train station (about a 10- to 15-minute walk)—ideal for those passing through or leaving on an early-morning train or plane. To avoid nighttime noise, ask for a room on a high floor.

ACROSS FROM THE TRAIN STATION

With this efficient neighborhood as your home base, you're a quick stroll away from the train station, Swiss National Museum, riverboat-bus dock, a huge underground mall of services and shops (under the station), and the Niederdorf restaurant and nightlife zone. From the station, exit through the front doors of the great hall and cross the river.

$$$ Leoneck Swiss Hotel, sharp and well-run, offers 82 comfortable rooms with small bathrooms and a tasteful touch of modernized Swiss kitsch. Consider booking one of the 14 "alpine rooms" for a bit more space. The large lobby and its restaurant/bar are a nice place to relax (family rooms, some rooms with balconies, air-con, elevator, limited pay garage parking, Leonhardstrasse 1, tel. 044-254-2222, www.leoneck.ch, info@leoneck.ch). From the Walchebrücke bridge, it's a 12-minute uphill walk (faster if you take the many stairs). To save some walking, ride tram #6 or #10 from the station (direction: Flughafen Zürich) two stops to Haldenegg. You can also take tram #10 directly to or from the airport (30 minutes).

$$ Hotel Bristol, well-run by Martin Hämmerli and his staff, has 56 rooms that are handy to the train station. It's a bit dated, but comfortable. Martin loves our readers and gives a 12 percent discount when you book directly by email (RS%, family rooms, air-con, elevator, pay laundry, Stampfenbachstrasse 34, tel. 044-258-4444, www.hotelbristol.ch, info@hotelbristol.ch).

$$ Hotel Arlette is stuck in a time warp, with 28 comfortable, no-frills rooms. The central location and affordable rates help make up for the often gruff reception staff (air-con, elevator, Stampfenbachstrasse 26, tel. 044-252-0032, www.hotelarlette.ch, hotel@hotelarlette.ch, Schlotter family).

NIEDERDORF DISTRICT

The atmospheric, cobblestoned old town of Zürich is just a few minutes farther from the station than the previous listings. During the day, it's busy with shoppers and workers on lunch breaks; at night, restaurants and clubs keep the pedestrian streets vibrant (and, in some places, noisy). From the train station, cross the Bahnhofbrücke bridge (to your right as you leave the main hall), go through the square called Central, and head to the right along Niederdorfstrasse.

$$$$ Marktgasse Hotel impresses well-heeled urbanites. Located at the quiet end of Niederdorf, its 39 rooms feel sophisticated, with hip, minimalist decor. The first-floor lounge/reception area, with free coffee and big windows, is a tempting place to hang out (breakfast extra, air-con, elevator, Marktgasse 17, tel. 044-266-1010, www.marktgassehotel.ch, info@marktgassehotel.ch).

$$$ Hotel Adler, nestled in the heart of the Niederdorf, is the place to stay if you don't want to risk forgetting that you're in Switzerland. It has a popular Swiss restaurant on the ground floor, a cow peeking out over the balcony, and 52 pleasantly cheesy rooms with woody, half-timbered accents (air-con, elevator, Rosengasse 10—at Hirschenplatz, tel. 044-266-9696, www.hotel-adler.ch, info@hotel-adler.ch).

$$$ Hotel Alexander is a 41-room business-class hotel in a busy central location offering a decent value (especially if you book well in advance). It's right at the edge of a somewhat seedier side of Niederdorf, but it feels solid, well-designed, and well-run, and the serious windows help keep out street noise (RS%, family rooms, air-con, elevator, Niederdorfstrasse 40, tel. 044-251-8203, www.hotel-alexander.ch, info@hotel-alexander.ch). They also run the **$ Alexander Guest House** a block away at Zähringerstrasse 16, housing 20 twin-bedded rooms with modern bathrooms and cheaper prices (breakfast extra, check in at Hotel Alexander, www.alexander-guesthouse.ch).

$$$ Hotel du Théâtre occupies a renovated little trapezoid-shaped theater around the corner from Central square, beneath the Polybahn funicular. The 50 thespian-themed rooms are dark but comfortable, with triple-paned windows that keep out most of the street noise (a few rooms have air-con, elevator, Seilergraben 69, tel. 044-267-2670, www.byfassbind.com, dt@byf.ch).

$$ Hotel Marta, on a side street near Central square, is run by a nonprofit foundation that assists women with disabilities in finding employment. The 39 sparse yet modern rooms vary in size

Zürich Hotels & Restaurants

ZÜRICH

and quietness (street-facing rooms can be noisy). The hotel's website describes them with unusual honesty and lets you choose (fans, elevator, Zähringerstrasse 36, tel. 044-269-9595, www.hotelmarta.ch, info@hotelmarta.ch).

¢ **City Backpacker Hotel Biber,** buried in the middle of the Niederdorf action three floors above a restaurant, offers the cheapest backpacker beds in the old center, with a cool, rough-at-the-edges ambience aimed at young travelers who don't mind climbing lots of narrow stairs. Families will feel more comfortable at the official hostel (private rooms, no breakfast, rooftop terrace, street noise at night, no curfew, reception open daily 8:00-12:00 & 15:00-22:00, 8-minute walk from station at Niederdorfstrasse 5, tel. 044-251-9015, www.city-backpacker.ch, sleep@city-backpacker.ch).

ZÜRICH

FARTHER FROM THE CENTER

You can sleep a little more cheaply if you're willing to compromise a bit on rooms and location. The first two listings are located in an area known for its bar scene; they're still just a short walk from the station.

$ **Dakini's B&B,** run by well-traveled Susanne Seiler, rents eight creatively decorated rooms on three floors above an Italian restaurant in a lively urban neighborhood. Each floor has a shared bathroom and a kitchen (no elevator, Brauerstrasse 87, mobile 078-661-8374, www.dakini.ch, sleep@dakini.ch). From the station, walk 15 minutes or take bus #31 (direction: Schlieren or Farbhof) to the Bäckeranlage stop, cross the street on the yellow crossing behind the bus stop, continue onto Brauerstrasse, and look for the restaurant in the wine-red house. The Dakini's entrance is on the side.

$ **EasyHotel** is a decent value in this pricey town, with 33 small, modern rooms located away from all the sights, a 10-minute walk from the station. There are several catches: It has four floors but no elevator (except for a luggage dumbwaiter); no common space aside from the basement computer room; most bathrooms are teeny, modular installations with opaque glass; and rooms are cleaned after four nights (no breakfast, Zwinglistrasse 14, tel. 043-322-0551, www.easyhotel.com). From the station: walk or take bus #31 (direction: Schlieren Zentrum) to Kanonengasse stop, walk a block down Kanonengasse with back to train station, then right on Zwinglistrasse to #14.

¢ **Zürich Youth Hostel** is big, modern, and well-equipped with lots of services in a pleasant neighborhood near the lake that's easy to reach from the station. Its rooms with private bath compete favorably with hotels (fair-trade breakfast, lunch or dinner extra, packed lunch, elevator, no curfew, pay parking, Mutschellenstrasse 114, tel. 043-399-7800, www.youthhostel.ch/zuerich, zuerich@

youthhostel.ch). From the station, take tram #7 (direction: Wollishofen) to Morgental, then walk back 5 minutes along Mutschellenstrasse.

Eating in Zürich

While famously expensive and formal, Zürich has a good variety
of places to eat memorably. My recommendations include romantic
Swiss places (both traditional and modern), cheesy raclette bars,
beer gardens, and quality vegetarian choices. If you're up for a
splurge, many of Zürich's venerable guildhouses are now convivial
traditional restaurants. At finer places, reservations are wise.

Zürich's most typical dish is *Kalbsgeschnetzeltes (or Zürcher
Geschnetzeltes)*—diced veal with mushrooms in cream sauce, often
served with *Rösti. Zürcher Eintopf* is a stew of pork, vegetables, and
white wine that's satisfying in the winter. You'll also see quite a few
traditional country Swiss restaurants featuring raclette and fondue.
These are designed entirely for tourists; when the Swiss want these
foods, they have them at home. Also, much as the Swiss love their
cheese, they're almost comically sensitive about it stinking up their
clothing (they don't like the smell unless they're actually eating it).
It seems that restaurants either do cheese or don't do cheese.

I rank eateries from **$** budget to **$$$$** splurge. For more
advice on eating in Switzerland, including ordering, tipping,
and Swiss cuisine and beverages, see the "Eating" section of the
Practicalities chapter.

NIEDERDORF DISTRICT

Niederdorf is Zürich's dining district, and the traffic-free Nieder-
dorfstrasse is its restaurant row. The countless eateries lining this
main drag don't offer the best values, though the people-watching
is hard to beat. Just a block or two away, you'll feel like you're far
from the tourist crush and rubbing elbows with a smarter clientele.

$$$ Wirtschaft Neumarkt, tucked away in the old town, is
packed with in-the-know locals eating well under chestnut trees in
their big "summer night dream garden." The creative, international
menu uses healthy, organic ingredients. The interior is modern
Swiss, with a classic wood-paneled upstairs, and the garden creates
a wonderful backyard feel. Alex enjoys greeting guests and being
sure they get the most out of his menu (lunch specials, always a
vegetarian plate, Mon-Sat 11:30-14:00 & 18:00-24:00, closed Sun,
extensive wine list and good beer on tap, Neumarkt 5, tel. 044-252-
7939, www.wirtschaft-neumarkt.ch).

$$ Café Zähringer is an artsy, bohemian co-op with a pas-
sion for serving reasonably priced, healthy food. Linger in the stay-
awhile interior, or enjoy the leafy seating with the older hippies out

on the square (daily special served all day, always good veggie and vegan plates, breakfasts, organic produce, salads, also meat dishes and wok dishes, good coffee, kitchen open daily 11:30-15:00 & 17:30-23:00, facing the tall steeple at Zähringerplatz 11, tel. 044-252-0500, www.zaehringer.ch).

$$$ Bauernschänke (Farmer's Tavern), facing Rindermarkt, is a favorite of upscale local foodies. While the setting is traditional, with inviting wooden tables and paneling, the menu has a modern sensibility. Chef Nenad Mlinarevic—who won "Swiss Chef of the Year" in 2016 and owns two Michelin stars at another location—combines fresh-from-the-market ingredients, classic Swiss inspiration, and creative and precise preparation. Reservations are wise (Mon-Fri 11:30-14:30 & 18:00-24:00, Sat 18:00-24:00, closed Sun, Rindermarkt 24, tel. 044-262-4130, www.bauernschaenke.ch).

$$$ Restaurant Mère Catherine is a little oasis of Provençal elegance tucked away in the old town, popular for its south-of-France menu and good wines by the glass. Both the interior and its tiny courtyard are delightful and cozy (daily 11:30-22:15, Nägelihof 3, tel. 044-250-5940).

Cheesy Swiss Clichés, Old and New: While having traditional Swiss food in Zürich is like having Southern comfort food in New York City, there are plenty of touristy options to choose from. These two are a good value for getting your melted cheese fix. **$$ Raclette Stube** is the traditional choice, and the place to go if you want your clothes to smell like good Swiss cheese for days to come. In a bright, modern mountain chalet interior they do only the cheese specialties: raclette and fondue (nightly from 18:00, Zähringerstrasse 16, tel. 044-251-4130). **$$ Raclette Factory,** the IHOP of melted Swiss cheese, serves your choice on a variety of potatoes with the traditional onion and pickle. You can even do a raclette tasting, combining a selection of different types. Their big, open windows ventilate the place, making it less cheesy inside. It's a fun perch, overlooking the action in the heart of the Niederdorf district (daily 11:00-22:00, Rindermarkt 1, tel. 044-261-0410).

Ice Cream: Tucked behind the Grossmünster, **Hasta** is a quality shop with lots of creative flavors (daily 12:30-18:30, Zwingliplatz 3).

Popular Sausage Stand: Locally beloved since 1963, **$ Sternen Grill,** about a five-minute walk south of the Grossmünster (at the Bellevue transit hub, by the lake) is Zürich's favorite place to grab a cheap, good-quality sausage. They have a few indoor tables and lots of outdoor ones, or you can get your sausage to go and eat along the water. Locals from every walk of life—from scruffy artists to well-dressed theatergoers to formal businesspeople—line up here (daily 10:30-23:45, Theaterstrasse 22, tel. 043-268-2080).

ON OR JUST OFF BAHNHOFSTRASSE

$$$ Zeughauskeller is a massively popular tourist trap filling an atmospheric 500-year-old armory with medieval battle gear (including a "William Tell crossbow") and the lively energy of happy eaters enjoying typical German-Swiss cuisine. Their fun, accessible menu—designed to stuff out-of-towners—offers big (splittable) portions, traditional dishes (their *Kalbsgeschnetzeltes is the house special*), and lots of soft meats. While it has a few outdoor tables, the interior has all the character and stays cool even when it's hot. On busy evenings, there are lines out the door; you may find yourself sharing a table (weekday lunch specials for 23 CHF, daily 11:30-23:00, plenty of beer and wine, kid-friendly, near Paradeplatz at Bahnhofstrasse 28, tel. 044-220-1515, www.zeughauskeller.ch).

$$$ Restaurant zum Kropf serves traditional Zürich cuisine in a grand and dressy beer hall with a sophisticated yet cozy atmosphere (26-CHF weekday lunch specials, Mon-Sat 11:30-23:00, closed summer weekends and first half of Aug, tel. 044-221-1805, next to Zeughauskeller at In Gassen 16).

$$$$ Restaurant Zunfthaus zur Waag is your chance to dine inside one of Zürich's historic guildhouses (from 1315), overlooking Münsterhof and the Fraumünster. It's dressy and expensive—a memorable place to enjoy a special occasion (70-CHF fixed-price dinners, Mon-Sat 11:30-14:00 & 18:00-22:00, closed Sun, Münsterhof 8, tel. 044-216-9966, www.zunfthaus-zur-waag.ch).

$$ Hiltl Vegetarian Restaurant is a popular treat for vegetarians. In 1898, Ambrosius Hiltl was fighting rheumatoid arthritis. His doctor said, "No more meat," so Ambrosius established what may have been Europe's first vegetarian restaurant. Over a century later, it's still in the family and a Zürich institution (claiming to be the oldest vegetarian restaurant in the world). The vast and appetizing buffet is what people come for. Choose your seating section from three zones: regular self-service (plain tables); self-service in the bar area (your food will be weighed at a 10 percent discount); and fancier dining with table service. Food is sold by weight and can add up quickly—generally 25-30 CHF per plate. For self-service, find the cashier to get weighed and pay. For table service, weigh your food and present your ticket to waitstaff. Tap water is free. The à la carte menu comes with delightful salads, curries, and fancy fruit juices. Hiltl's food is legendary for its freshness and lack of preservatives (buffet open daily 6:00-23:00, 2 blocks off Bahnhofstrasse where it kinks, Sihlstrasse 30, tel. 044-227-7000, www.hiltl.ch).

$$ Hiltl Dachterrasse, closer to Bahnhofstrasse and a bit hipper, is on the third floor of an upscale women's clothing store. The glassy, convivial space, which feels like a chirpy birdhouse, is jammed with locals taking a break from shopping to meet up with

ZURICH

friends. It's self-service—line up at the counter and pay by weight (Mon-Sat 9:00-23:00, Sun 10:00-22:00, inside the PKZ store at Bahnhofstrasse 88, ride elevator to third floor).

Supermarkets near the Train Station: A convenient, mid-sized, long-hours **Migros** supermarket is in the underground mall at the train station, near the Landesmuseum (Swiss National Museum) entrance/exit. Around the corner (also under the station) is the **Migros Takeaway,** which sells big portions of daily main dishes, packaged to go for about 10 CHF (both open daily until 22:00). A much larger **Co-op** supermarket is kitty-corner from the station by the Bahnhofbrücke bridge (Mon-Sat until 22:00, closed Sun).

ALONG THE WEST BANK OF THE RIVER

$$ Restaurant Bauschänzli is a leisurely beer garden with a huge buffet line, lots of picnic-table seating, and a fine riverside setting. A block inland from the boat docks at Bürkliplatz, it fills a small island on the river. Its fun-loving and popular self-serve restaurant offers a great beer-garden experience—like a Munich *Biergarten* without the kraut—and it's reasonably priced. Help yourself to the salad bar and the beer and wine from big casks (grab the glass or carafe of your choice). A little vocabulary is helpful: *Bürl* is a roll; *Beilage* is a side dish; *Penache* is a Radler (beer with lemonade). It's open from mid-April through mid-September in good weather only (daily 11:00-23:00, Stadthausquai 2, tel. 044-212-4919, www. bauschaenzli.ch). Live music (daily 15:00-17:00 & 19:00-22:30) has people up and dancing, giving the place a polka-party feel. For a little peace, grab a table at the quieter tip of the island. The small restaurant section, off to the side, is more expensive. (While it tries to be elegant, the sloppy and noisy beer-garden fun splashes over the little fence.)

$$ Restaurant Schipfe 16, gorgeously and peacefully situated on the river with an old-town view, is part of a city-run organization providing work for hard-to-employ people. It was originally a soup kitchen, but the location was just too charming to stay that way, so it was turned into a restaurant open to everyone. Don't expect polished service; instead, feel good that you're contributing to a worthy cause and enjoying healthy and decent food at a great price. The menu is small—always with a fish, meat, and veggie dish—with lighter dishes available after 14:00. The best seats are right along the river (two-course daily specials, Mon-Sat 10:00-22:00, closed Sun, Schipfe 16, tel. 044-211-2122, www.stadt-zuerich.ch/schipfe, reservations smart).

Zürich Connections

BY TRAIN

From Zürich by Train to: Luzern (2/hour direct, 1 hour, more with transfers), **Interlaken** (2/hour, 2 hours, transfer in Bern and sometimes Spiez), **Bern** (4/hour direct, 1-1.5 hours, more with transfers), **Murten** (2/hour, 2 hours, 1-2 transfers), **Appenzell** (2-3/hour, 2 hours, change in Gossau), **Lausanne** (2/hour direct, 2 hours, more with change), **Zermatt** (1-2/hour, 3.5 hours, change in Visp), **Chur** (2-3/hour direct, 1.5-2.5 hours, more with changes), **Lugano** (1-3/hour, 2.5 hours), **Berlin** (1-2/hour, 9 hours, 1-2 transfers; one direct overnight option, 12 hours), **Munich** (3/day direct, 5 hours; or go by bus from Sihlqual bus terminal, 3/day, 4 hours, reserve through train system), **Frankfurt** (hourly, 4 hours, more with change in Basel), **Vienna** (5/day direct, 8.5 hours; 1 night train, 11 hours), **Paris** (5/day direct, 4 hours, more with transfers). Train info: www.sbb.ch.

BY PLANE

User-friendly **Zürich Airport** (code: ZRH, www.zürich-airport.com) has three levels and is an eye-opening introduction to Swiss efficiency. On the lower level you'll find a train station (with ticket desk). The main level has a top-end food court, Migros and Co-op supermarkets, fancy souvenir shops, a post office, mobile-phone shops, banks, ATMs, and lockers. The upper level has departures, TI, lockers, rental car desks, and an observation deck. Check-in areas (numbered 1 through 3) are scattered around the complex; use the screens to identify your zone, then follow signs.

Getting Between the Airport and Downtown: From the station underneath the airport, trains whisk you to **downtown Zürich** in about 10 minutes (6.80 CHF for three-zone single ticket, 13.60 CHF for three-zone 24-hour pass, leaves every 10 minutes 5:00-24:00). You can also ride tram #10 into town (takes much longer—35 minutes; same price as the train). Your ticket into Zürich is also good for

one hour on all city public transportation. Either option is much cheaper than the 60-CHF taxi ride.

Sleeping at the Airport: Since most of my recommended accommodations are near the station, and the train connection to the airport is so fast and frequent, there's little reason to sleep at the airport. But if you really want to stay close to the airport, choose a hotel within a few miles that has a free shuttle service, such as the **Ibis Zürich Messe Airport** or the **Mövenpick Hotel** in Glattbrugg.

Zürich Airport Connections: From the airport you can take the train to **Luzern** (hourly, 1 hour, more with change at Zürich main station), **Interlaken** (2/hour, 2.5 hours, change in Bern and sometimes Spiez), **Bern** (2/hour, 75 minutes), **Murten** (hourly, 2 hours, change in Bern or Neuchâtel), **Appenzell** (2/hour, 2 hours, change in Gossau), **Lausanne** (2/hour, 2.5 hours), **Zermatt** (hourly, 3.5 hours, change in Visp), **Chur** (2/hour, 2 hours, change at Zürich main station), **Lugano** (2/hour, 2.5 hours, change at Zürich main station and sometimes Arth-Goldau), **Munich** (4/day direct, 4 hours, more with transfers).

ZÜRICH

LUZERN & CENTRAL SWITZERLAND

Luzern has long been Switzerland's tourism capital. Situated on the edge of its namesake lake, with a striking alpine panorama as a backdrop, Luzern was a regular stop on the Grand Tour route of Europe during the Romantic era, entertaining visitors such as Mark Twain, Goethe, and Queen Victoria. And with a charming old town, a pair of picture-perfect wooden bridges, a gaggle of fine museums, and a famous weeping lion, there's enough in Luzern to earn it a place on any Swiss itinerary. Luzern also makes a fine home base for exploring the surrounding Central Switzerland region (known as Zentralschweiz).

PLANNING YOUR TIME

Luzern is worth at least a full day and two nights. To get the most from a full day in Luzern, begin with the TI's two-hour walking tour, or follow the self-guided walk in this chapter. Then hit the museums that interest you most. In the early evening, take a peaceful boat trip on Lake Luzern, then wander the town's scenic bridges at sunset.

With more time, consider one of the many fun and well-coordinated excursions within easy reach: boating on Lake Luzern, riding cog railways to mountain summits—the world's steepest, up Mount Pilatus, and Europe's oldest, up Mount Rigi—and exploring Swiss military history at Fortress Fürigen.

Luzern

Luzern (loot-SAIRN, "Lucerne" in English) is Switzerland's touristic darling—an urban hub for visitors seeking easy access to the Alps. Famous for its historic wooden bridges, the city grew up around a monastery and is said to have been founded here because an angel shone a heavenly spotlight on the site (the name "Luzern" is derived from *lucerna*, Latin for "lamp").

Today Luzern is a compact, charming, well-organized destination. It boasts an atmospheric old town of vividly decorated buildings, more than its share of watch and pocketknife shops, and a variety of exceptional museums: Art buffs flock to the Rosengart Collection for its Picasso exhibit; historians enjoy the History Museum; and gearheads have a ball at the Swiss Transport Museum. All in all, Luzern is a delightful place. Just be prepared to share it—the city (and its nearby mountaintops) are jammed with visitors from every corner of the globe. Make a point to find a quiet little corner of Luzern all to yourself...in this fine city, it's not hard to do.

Orientation to Luzern

Midsize Luzern has about 80,000 residents (and a metropolitan area sprawling to more than 200,000). It sits where the Reuss (pronounced "royce") River flows out of Lake Luzern (a.k.a. Vierwaldstättersee). South of the river is the train station and the bustling new town (Neustadt), and north of the river is the quaint, traffic-free old town (Altstadt). The river is spanned by a series of pedestrian bridges, including two classic wooden ones: the Chapel Bridge, with its famous stone Water Tower, and the Mill Bridge. Museums, restaurants, and hotels are scattered on both sides of the river.

TOURIST INFORMATION

Luzern's helpful, modern TI is inside the train station (Mon-Fri 8:30-19:00, Sat 9:00-19:00, Sun 9:00-17:00, shorter hours off-season, Zentralstrasse 5, tel. 041-227-1717, www.luzern.com). Pick up the free, informative *City Guide*. The TI sells the Swiss Travel Pass, public transport tickets, and tickets to activities around town, such as boat trips.

Sightseeing Passes: The **Swiss Travel Pass** covers most of Luzern's attractions. Without it, consider the **Lucerne Museum Card,** sold only at the TI, which covers entry to all Luzern museums over a two-day period (36 CHF); it pays for itself if you visit the Swiss Transport Museum and at least one other museum.

When you check into your hotel, get your free **Visitor Card,**

Luzern and Central Switzerland at a Glance

▲▲**Luzern** Pretty, pristine lakeside city boasting excellent museums, painted bridges, and a handful of historic sights. See page 58.

▲▲**Lake Luzern** Irregularly shaped lake at the very heart of Switzerland, traversed by vintage steamships and surrounded by steep hillsides, gravity-defying villages, and snowy peaks. See page 77.

▲▲**Mount Pilatus** Craggy peak hunkering south of Luzern, with sublime views, luge ride, ropes course, and a range of hiking options. See page 85.

▲**Mount Rigi** Mountain mass across the lake and east of Luzern, famous for its sunrise vistas and Europe's first cogwheel train. See page 95.

▲**Fortress Fürigen** Underground bunker southeast of Luzern giving you a peek at Switzerland's hidden defense system. See page 92.

LUZERN

which covers all in-city transit and provides 10-20 percent discounts at most Luzern sights and activities (including some lake boats and mountain lifts). Some Airbnbs also provide Visitor Cards.

ARRIVAL IN LUZERN

Luzern's waterfront, three-level **train station** is user-friendly. The tracks are on the middle, street level; the TI is along track 3, as are pay lockers. Upstairs you'll find the SBB ticket counters—take the escalator by track 10 (Mon-Fri 7:00-21:00, Sat-Sun until 20:00; international-travel windows close two hours earlier); a serene Tibits vegetarian cafeteria overlooks the tracks. Most other important services are downstairs in the underground RailCity shopping mall. There you'll find pricey WCs (with showers), ATMs, and shops and eateries (including a Co-op grocery store)—particularly convenient on Sundays, when many shops are closed.

From the bustling plaza directly out front (with the historic arch), buses fan out in every direction; Luzern's lake-boat dock is at the far end of this area.

For a quick exit on foot to the old town and Chapel Bridge, with the tracks to your back, go downstairs and head to the far end of the underground shopping zone, then escalate up—you'll pop out close to the river and main Seebrücke bridge.

HELPFUL HINTS

Medical Help: Permanence MedCenter is a welcoming drop-in clinic located downstairs in the train station (daily 7:00-23:00, tel. 041-211-1444, www.medcenter.ch).

Festivals: Central Switzerland's biggest Mardi Gras celebration, **Luzerner Fasnacht,** begins on the Thursday before Ash Wednesday (exact date depends on Easter, https://luzernerfasnacht.ch). The biggest parades are that day (called Dirty Thursday), but things stay noisy and busy well into the morning of Ash Wednesday. Book accommodations well in advance for this time.

The **Lucerne Festival** draws classical musicians and fans each year from mid-August to mid-September (www.lucernefestival.ch).

Markets: On Tuesdays and Saturdays, a farmers market borders both sides of the river near the main Seebrücke bridge (7:00-12:00). On Saturdays from May through October, a flea market stretches along the river from the Jesuit Church to the Mill Bridge, and on the first Saturday of the month, craft stalls set up on Weinmarkt in the old town.

Laundry: Jet Wasch is a 10-minute walk from the train station (full service only; Mon-Fri 8:00-12:00 & 14:00-18:00, Sat 9:00-16:00, closed Sun, Bruchstrasse 28, tel. 041-240-0151, www.jetwasch.ch). They can pick up or deliver to your hotel for an extra fee. For location, see the "Luzern Hotels & Restaurants" map, later.

Bike Rental: You can rent bikes at the train station and enjoy Luzern's delightful lakeside cycling paths (27 CHF/half-day, 35 CHF/day, discount with Eurail Global Pass or Swiss Travel Pass; inquire at SBB ticket office upstairs in station and ask for bike-route map; www.sbb.ch/mobilitaet).

Parking: The best downtown parking garage is **Parkhaus Kesselturm** at Burgerstrasse 20 (25 CHF/day if you prepay, choose "season ticket" on payment machines, tel. 041-240-3255, www.parking-luzern.ch). Avoid the train-station garages, which are much more expensive.

Water Fountains: Luzern is proud of its clean drinking water and its more than 200 public fountains—each with a fun design—that spout potable water. Take full advantage of these fountains to refill water bottles.

GETTING AROUND LUZERN

Except for the Swiss Transport Museum, most of Luzern's attractions are within an easy walk of the station. However, buses can be handy time-savers.

All public transit is included in a Swiss Travel Pass. If you're

staying at a Luzern hotel, you'll get a
Visitor Card that covers transit in the
city center (zone 10—this includes
everything in this chapter except the
train to Alpnachstad, with the Pilatus cogwheel train). Otherwise, you'll
need either a short-stretch ticket
(*Kurzstreckebillet*, 2.50 CHF, good for
up to 6 stops), a single ticket (*Einzelbillett*, 4.10 CHF, good for one hour), or a
day pass (8.20 CHF). Buy tickets from
machines at stops or at the TI. Transit
info: www.vbl.ch.

Tell-Pass: If you're home-basing
in Luzern for several days without a rail pass, consider the Tell-
Pass. It covers up to 10 consecutive days of free rides on lifts, boats,
and several area train lines (180 CHF/2 days, 210 CHF/3 days,
more for longer durations, cheaper Nov-March when schedules are
sparser; buy at TIs, train stations, and boat docks, www.tellpass.
ch).

Tours in Luzern

Walking Tour: A two-hour English-only tour is offered every
morning in summer. It covers the same route as my "Reuss River
Stroll" (see below), but with more stories (20 CHF, discount with
Visitor Card, departs from TI at 9:45, daily May-Oct).

Local Guide: Ursula Korner is a good guide (200 CHF/2
hours, mobile 079-479-8261, ursula.korner@ko5ive.com). If Ursula is busy, she'll help you find a replacement; the TI also has a
list of other guides.

Tourist Train: This tacky little train does a 40-minute circuit
of the city's sights, departing from Hotel Schweizerhof (12 CHF,
runs daily April-Oct, June-Aug hourly 11:00-19:00, less frequent
in spring and fall, www.citytrain.ch).

Boat Tours: For details on boat tours on Lake Luzern, see
page 77.

Reuss River Stroll

This self-guided orientation walk, worth ▲▲, gives you a brief
overview of the town. You'll walk up along the Reuss River, see
both of Luzern's famous wooden bridges, and wander through the
old town with its colorfully painted buildings. It takes about an
hour at a leisurely pace.

• *Begin at Bahnhofplatz, the busy zone between the lake and the train*

Luzern

200 Meters
200 Yards

OLD TOWN WALLS

ALTSTADT

MILL BRIDGE

HISTORY MUSEUM

Mühlen-platz

Weinmarkt

Korn-markt

Hirschen-platz

Falken-platz

Schwanen-platz

WALK ENDS

MANOR DEPT. STORE

Kapell-platz

ST. PETER'S CHAPEL

TOWN HALL

RATHAUS BRIDGE

WATER TOWER

CHAPEL BRIDGE

Reuss River

OPUS BAR

JESUIT CHURCH

THE BOX

THEATER

NEUSTADT

ROSENGART COLLECTION

POST

#1 Bus To Kriens

PED BOAT REN

station. Stand in front of the big stone arch.

❶ **Bahnhofplatz:** This is the transportation hub of Luzern—and all of Central Switzerland. From the area in front of the station, buses zip you anywhere in town. And underneath you is the extensive RailCity

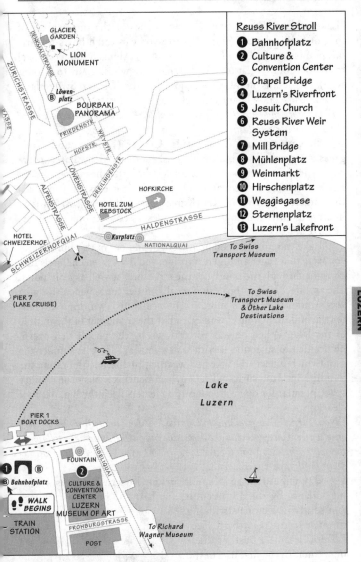

shopping mall, honeycombed with pedestrian passageways leading to different parts of town.

The big stone **arch** was the entrance of the venerable old train station—built in the late 19th century when Switzerland became a top tourist spot, thanks to the advent of steam-powered trains (and a stay by Queen Victoria). But it burned down in 1971 and was replaced with the modern station.

Cross the street to the lakefront, where you'll reach **Pier 1.** (German-speaking Swiss call the lake the Vierwaldstättersee—

"Lake of Four Forest States," since it lies at the intersection of four of Switzerland's cantons.) Here you can catch boats to various points around Lake Luzern, including Alpnachstad (cogwheel train to Mount Pilatus) and Vitznau (cogwheel train to Mount Rigi). For details on these excursions, see the "Central Switzerland Day Trips" section later in this chapter.

• *Turn right, and—with the lake on your left—stroll a few steps toward the huge modern building with the big overhanging roof. This is the...*

❷ **Culture and Convention Center (Kultur- und Kongresszentrum):** This building, finished in 1998 by Parisian architect Jean Nouvel, features a concert hall that hosts the Luzern Festival, one of Switzerland's biggest music events. It also holds the **Luzern Museum of Art** (Kunstmuseum Luzern), which is of interest mainly to serious art lovers (described later, under "Sights in Luzern").

Lake water is pumped up, through, and out of this building; if you were to wander around its far side, you'd see open channels that go right through the middle of the structure, as well as a big pond. The architect claims the design recalls earlier times, when this area was swampland...but it more likely recalls his own original plans for the building. Nouvel wanted to put the center out in the middle of the lake. When he was voted down by the people of Luzern, he decided to surround it with water anyway. The plaza under the roof (which reflects the lake and weather, further incorporating the building into the surrounding environment) is a busy community space popular for open-air concerts. Heaters keep the big, flat roof clear of snow.

• *Now turn 180 degrees and follow the lakeshore away from the conference center. Carry on straight across the busy street, and keep following the waterline. Soon you'll have magnificent views of Luzern's most famous landmark, the wooden...*

❸ **Chapel Bridge (Kapellbrücke):** Luzern began as a fishing village. By the 13th century, with traffic between northern and southern Europe streaming through nearby Gotthard Pass, Luzern became a bustling trading center. In the first half of the 14th century, this covered bridge was angled across the river as part of the town's medieval fortifications. Originally this wooden gallery stretched from the Jesuit Church and St. Peter's Chapel all the way to the pointy twin steeples of the Hofkirche, far to the right. The octagonal stone **Water Tower** (Wasserturm, pictured here), built around 1300, also housed a prison—in the below-water-level cellar.

In the 17th century, the bridge was decorated with paintings depicting the development of the town, starring its two patron saints—St. Leodegar and St. Mauritius. In 1993, a leisure boat moored under the bridge caught fire, and before long, Luzern's wooden landmark was in flames. (A plaque before the start of the

bridge tells the story.) The bridge was painstakingly rebuilt—when you venture onto it, you'll notice the lighter colored, newer wood in the middle. But many of its famous paintings were lost. Those still remaining under the wooden roof at the ends

of the bridge are restorations of the 17th-century originals; those in the middle were in storage at the time of the fire and therefore spared. Some burnt and charred paintings are still in their original spots. Boats are no longer allowed under the bridge, it's now strictly nonsmoking, and tiny security cameras are everywhere.

• *Wander out onto the bridge.*

Study the colorful **paintings** overhead. Coats of arms on the paintings tell you which aristocratic families sponsored them. Painting #1—immediately above the stairs as you enter—features a legendary and formidable giant, an icon of Luzern. This big boy (sometimes called the Wild Man) dates back to the Middle Ages, when mammoth bones discovered locally were mistakenly identified as the remains of a 15-foot-tall human giant.

Painting #2 shows an angel shining a divine light on the place where the town would be born, and where, in the eighth century, a monastery was founded. Painting #3 shows Luzern circa 1400—see how the bridge was already part of the city fortifications. Painting #6 shows a bigger city, as it looked in 1630. Paintings #9 and #10 remain charred black—a reminder of the bridge fire. In the middle of the bridge (just after the shop), a painting features St. Mauritius, (a plaque mid-bridge, near #48, tells why he matters to Luzern).

As you stroll, notice that the "window" openings facing the lake are smaller than those on the inland side. As part of the city defensive system, this design gave defenders more cover from lakeside attacks.

• *Head back over the bridge the way you came, and turn right along the water. Very soon you'll reach another bridge (with great views of the Chapel Bridge). Step out onto this bridge and take a look around at...*

❹ **Luzern's Riverfront:** You're surrounded on all sides by Luzern's colorful town center, its beautiful river, and the grand hotels that line its banks. The stately stone building at the end of this bridge is Luzern's historic town hall (Rathaus), dating from the early 1600s.

Look out to the Chapel Bridge, with the mountains just beyond. It's clear that Luzern is supremely well-placed to be a launch pad for alpine adventures: It sits where the flat, easy-to-traverse central plateau of Switzerland meets the wild and woolly Alps.

But it wasn't until a very famous tourist came here that Luzern really took off. Turn 180 degrees—with your back to the Chapel Bridge—and look up to the fanciful castle-like building, Château Gütsch, on the ridge above. Just to the right is a much lower-profile gray building. This was where a grief-stricken Queen Victoria holed up for a month in 1868. She was still mourning her beloved Prince Albert—who had died seven years before—and came here partly to honor his memory (he had climbed Mount Rigi, the peak across the lake, in 1837, and one of Victoria's treasured keepsakes was a pressed rose he had collected there). Victoria and her ensemble determinedly reached the summit of area mountains by riding donkeys and ponies.

Victoria's subjects were inspired by their intrepid monarch, and English aristocrats began to plan their own trips to Luzern. Mark Twain followed (in 1878 and 1897). As Luzern became a magnet for international visitors, the lakefront promenade filled in and fancy resort hotels went up—giving the city the nickname "Monte Carlo of Switzerland."

• *Return to the train-station end of the bridge, turn right, and continue along the river. Pause at the big, white church.*

❺ **Jesuit Church (Jesuitenkirche):** This was the first major Baroque church in Switzerland, circa 1670 (free, Tue-Wed and Fri-Sun 6:30-18:30, Mon and Thu 9:30-18:30). It's dedicated to the great missionary Francis Xavier, a co-founder of the Jesuit order, who's shown in a niche on the **facade** blessing a convert. Although surrounded by Protestant strongholds Bern (to the west) and Zürich (to the east), Luzern withstood the Reformation and remains predominantly Catholic. (A local once asserted to me, "North of Luzern, everyone is Protestant all the way to Norway. South of Luzern, everyone is Catholic all the way to Rome.") Luzern's music school uses the church's pipe organ for practice—if you're lucky, you may catch an impromptu concert.

Step inside the church. Even though Luzern was a relatively small town in the 17th century, the pope wanted to establish a strong presence in Central Switzerland to empower the area's Catholics during the tense times following the Protestant Reformation. The **interior** of the church once dripped with Baroque stucco, but it's been redone in the lighter Rococo style (c. 1750). Rich as it looks, there's no real marble here—what you see on the altar, pulpit, and side-chapel altars is stucco made from ground-up marble laid smoothly and economically over wood.

The decorations on the **ceiling** celebrate the life (and afterlife) of Xavier. In the biggest, central panel, you see the missionary traveling heavenward, in an exuberant setting that depicts both this church and Luzern's landmark Chapel Bridge. The pope's representative and townsfolk gather to wish Xavier Godspeed. His cart is pulled by an elephant, leopard, and camel, recalling his mission trips to the exotic Far East.

In the second **side chapel** on the right, you can meet the only Swiss saint: Brother Klaus, a 15th-century hermit who lived in the nearby mountains. He was a great peacemaker between the cantons and is considered the original Swiss isolationist. Since Klaus' time, Switzerland has avoided entanglement in foreign squabbles (an ethic that continues today—see the "Swiss Military Readiness" sidebar, at the end of this chapter). The statue wears Klaus' original robe. His walking stick is in a case just over the altar.

Back **outside**, you'll likely see a huge, wooden structure to the side of the church. Called simply "The Box," this is a performance venue (and sometimes a café) for the local Luzern Theater (to see what's on, check www.luzernertheater.ch).

• *Continue strolling downriver toward Luzern's other wooden bridge, the Mill Bridge. You'll pass the recommended Opus wine bar/restaurant and an iron pedestrian bridge (at the narrowest crossing spot, marking the location of Luzern's first bridge in the 12th century). Carrying on about 50 more yards, stop at the spiky fence partially damming the river.*

❻ **Reuss River Weir System:** This big river flowing out of the lake may seem wild, but it's been tamed. Lake Luzern's main

source of water is snowmelt, which trickles in from streams coming off the surrounding mountains. The water drains from the lake here on its way to the Rhine. To prevent the flooding of lakeside villages, in the mid-19th century the city devised and built a simple yet ingenious dam (*Nadelwehr,* "spiked weir") to control the flow of water and the lake level. When the water is highest (in the spring), spikes are removed to open the flow; as the summer wears on and the water level drops, spikes are gradually added to keep the flow steady. In winter, the dam is closed entirely to keep the lake level high enough for boats. It's a dangerous process as workers, tethered by safety cables, hoist the spikes into position.

• *Continuing down the river, you'll pass the History Museum on your left (described later, under "Sights in Luzern") before coming to the wooden...*

❼ Mill Bridge (Spreuerbrücke): Unlike the rebuilt Chapel Bridge, this 16th-century bridge is original—and the city is deter-

mined to keep it that way. Before you cross the bridge, pause to appreciate the first of its fine 17th-century paintings, which shows Luzern's favorite giant again, with the blue-and-white city and cantonal banners under the double eagle of the Holy Roman Empire (of which the Swiss lands were a part during the Middle Ages). The flip side shows Judgment Day, with some going to heaven and others to hell.

As you cross the bridge, notice that each painting includes a Grim Reaper-like skeleton lurking near people in every walk of life. Townsfolk crossed the bridge daily, and these scenes, painted during a time of war and plague, and based on the medieval allegory called the *danse macabre*—or dance of death—provided vivid reminders that, regardless of social standing or status, we must all face death.

Midway across is a little 16th-century chapel, built to ensure divine protection against destruction by flood. A line of family crests on the door frame acknowledges the volunteers who, over the years, have kept the chapel decorated according to the season. Since 1987, this has been the work of Frau Segesser. While you're paused here, notice the serious woodwork of the bridge construction. Like the Chapel Bridge, this one was part of the city fortifications; its downstream defensive wall is higher.

The far end of the bridge was designed to accommodate wagons delivering grain or whatever else was to be milled. Once upon a time, three mills churned here—this was the medieval industrial center of Luzern. The *"Spreu"* in the bridge's name means "chaff" (the sheath surrounding the wheat), which was separated from the wheat at the mill. You can see sketches of the mills as you leave the bridge (on the red wall on the left). A turbine that generated power in 1889 sits quietly on the left, but the tradition of harnessing water power continues here. Beneath you, underwater, a modern hydro-electric plant creates enough power for 1,000 households.

• *After crossing the bridge, turn right to find yourself in...*

❽ **Mühlenplatz:** This traffic-free square marks the entrance to the old town. Riverside benches make a good place for a picnic lunch or snack. On the left side of the square, at #11 Fischer-Stube, a mural shows the city back when the water mills were hard at work.

• *At the top of the square (under the Swiss Marilyn Monroe), head right on Kramgasse, then take the first left onto Weinmarktgasse, which leads to...*

❾ **Weinmarkt:** As the name implies, in medieval Luzern, this square served as a marketplace for wine. The soldiers on the fine 15th-century fountain (which flies the blue-and-white flag of the Luzern canton) remind visitors that this town is tough and strong. Enjoy the fine painted facades all around—a typical feature of Luzern's medieval and Renaissance architecture. At the top end of the square (near where you entered) is the ornate facade of the Hotel Waage/Hôtel des Balances. This was once the court of justice (hence the "scales" theme); the condemned were hanged from a linden tree just in front (about where a contemporary replacement tree is today).

Head higher up in the square, past the fountain. At first glance, the big mural on the green building at the top of the square seems to depict the Last Supper, but it's actually the Wedding Feast at Cana, where Jesus turned water into wine. The wine theme continues on the left side of the square, where a secret message hides in the strange zigzags on the modern shutters of a building. Start at the top left and read: W-E-I-N-M-A-R-K-T.

• *Leave the square on the far left side, then walk several yards to...*

❿ **Hirschenplatz:** History lingers long after things change—especially on this square. Its namesake, the Hirschen ("Deer") Hotel, is gone but its elaborate golden sign will always hang here. Across from that, guess who used to have a shop in the big green building? Yep—the jeweler. (See all the rings?) Notice the until-death-do-us-part ring at far left, and that high above, Cupid has shot his arrow.

To the right of the jeweler, a painted inscription on the corner building declares *"Goethe logierte hier 1779."* Goethe—the "German Shakespeare"—visited Luzern and stayed in a hotel on this corner. It was the city's top hotel at the time...I bet it was named the Golden Eagle. To the left of the jeweler, the grand facade on the Dornach House, from 1899, celebrates the 400th anniversary of the last battle against the Habsburgs. Switzerland has enjoyed a durable understanding that it can have disagreements—but no wars—with its historically aggressive and militaristic neighbors.

Just down the little lane on the right, on the left side, notice the Rent-a-Box shop. A clever variation on a consignment store, the shop invites people to rent display boxes to try to sell old watches and jewelry.

Continue out of the square (diagonally opposite from where you entered) onto the busy ⓫ **Weggisgasse.** As you stroll, you'll pass many international chain stores. However, every building in the old town—whether new or rebuilt—is required to offer residential apartments to prevent this historic zone from becoming only office space and touristy shops. This street is a real community.

• *After two blocks, you'll come to the* **Manor** *department store, with the recommended, tasty, and convenient Manora self-service cafeteria on the top floor (with great, free city views from its rooftop terrace). Turn right after Manor and walk one block, then hook left around the corner to...*

⓬ **Sternenplatz:** This tiny square is dominated by the colorful facade of the Restaurant Fritschi. The paintings feature characters and symbols from Luzern's annual Mardi Gras (Fasnacht) celebration—the city's biggest event. Pictured near the top of the building are Mr. and Mrs. Fritschi—the festival cheerleaders, celebrating Fasnacht by wearing masks and throwing oranges. Flanking them are their trusty servants, a nanny and a jester. Below is the story of Fasnacht: The cock calls at 5:00 in the morning the Thursday before Ash Wednesday (on the left), and the people get up to frighten winter away. Mr. and Mrs. Fritschi arrive on their wagon to kick off the festivities (on the right). Flying around the scene are oranges—tradition-

ally tossed by the Fritschis to their adoring fans. Once rare here in winter, oranges are special to the festivities, as they mark the beginning of spring.

Continue down the street at the bottom of the square (Hans-Holbein-Gasse), and you'll come upon a colorful **fountain** with more Fasnacht fun. Notice the colorful masks...and the oranges. This is where the locals gather—often more than 10,000 strong—at five in the morning to kick off the biggest party of the year—six days long.

⓭ **Luzern's Lakefront:** Continue to the riverfront, walking around **St. Peter's Chapel,** traditionally the church for Luzern's poor. You're back at the wooden Chapel Bridge, having made the full circle. Enjoy the classic Luzern view: the Chapel Bridge and Water Tower, with Mount Pilatus hovering in the background. From here, cross over to the lakeside and stroll to the left.

Any swans out? Residents say they originated as a gift from French King Louis XIV in appreciation for the protection he got from his Swiss Guards. Today, local children (and tourists) make sure the swans get their daily bread.

• *Your town walk is finished. From here you have several options: You can catch the one-hour lake cruise (from Pier 7, described later under "On Lake Luzern—Boating Options"). You can cross the street and peruse ritzy Swiss watches at the flagship Bucherer store (selling envy since 1888). You can walk along the lake to the Swiss Transport Museum. Or you can cut inland to the Lion Monument. Everything is described in the next section.*

Sights in Luzern

If you'll be doing a lot of sightseeing here, first review your options for saving money on admissions (see "Tourist Information—Sightseeing Passes," earlier).

MUSEUMS IN THE CENTER
Luzern is charming enough that simply strolling its streets and bridges and cruising the lake is enough for a happy day of sightseeing. But the city also offers some fine museums, all of which are within walking distance.

▲Rosengart Collection (Sammlung Rosengart)
In the 1930s and 1940s, wealthy resident and art dealer Siegfried Rosengart palled around with all-star modern artists, financing and collecting their works. At an early age his daughter Angela took an interest in her father's work and eventually became his business partner. This museum displays the fruits of their labor. Angela, now approaching 90, visits the museum daily and still has an art gallery in town. Worth ▲▲▲ for art lovers, this may be Switzerland's most user-friendly collection of modern art.

Cost and Hours: 18 CHF, covered by Swiss Travel Pass, daily April-Oct 10:00-18:00, Nov-March 11:00-17:00, mandatory bag check; well-written little 2.50-CHF English booklet—or borrow the excellent English descriptions when you buy your ticket; a few blocks from the train station in the new town up Pilatusstrasse at #10, tel. 041-220-1660, www.rosengart.ch.

Visiting the Museum: The building's three floors boast works from the big names of the late 19th and early 20th centuries, with an emphasis on the art of Pablo Picasso and Paul Klee. The ground and first floors feature an extensive **Picasso** collection focusing on his later works, including 32 paintings and some 100 drawings, watercolors, and graphic and sculptural works. Rosengart was Picasso's leading Swiss art dealer and helped place a number of works in national and international museums.

On the upper floor are black-and-white candid photographs of Picasso (from a rotating collection of 200) by American **David Douglas Duncan.** Documenting the last 17 years of Picasso's life, Duncan's intimate photos of the artist and his family capture the very human personality of this larger-than-life genius, while providing insight into his artistic process and lifestyle. The first floor also has some Impressionist and Modernist works by Braque, Monet, Renoir, Miró, Chagall, Cézanne, Matisse, Modigliani, and Pissarro.

Don't miss the basement, which displays 125 small works by **Paul Klee,** displayed chronologically so you can follow the evolution of his career. Watch as Klee discovers colors and blossoms from a doodler and, at times, watercolor artist into a mature painter.

▲History Museum (Historisches Museum)

This cluttered old museum is a repository for the accumulated bric-a-brac of Luzern's past. It's housed in one of the town's oldest surviving buildings, which was long used to store military weapons and uniforms. The exhaustive collection is displayed on three crowded floors, in an approach reminiscent of a 21st-century cabinet of curiosities. You'll wander through shelves of old weapons, stained-glass windows, church paintings and sculptures, costumes from Baroque times up to the present, folk art, and old-fashioned tourism posters. Each shelf (sometimes each item) has a barcode—use your scanner (included with entry) to learn more. Don't miss the modern and chilling guillotine on the ground floor—last used in 1940.

Cost and Hours: 10 CHF, covered by Swiss Travel Pass, Tue-Sun 10:00-17:00, closed Mon, Pfistergasse 24, tel. 041-228-5424, www.historischesmuseum.lu.ch.

Luzern Museum of Art (Kunstmuseum Luzern)

Located in the lakefront cultural center by the train station, this museum features ambitious special exhibits of contemporary art as well as displays drawn from its permanent collection, which focuses on historical and contemporary works by Central Swiss artists.

Cost and Hours: 15 CHF, covered by Swiss Travel Pass, Tue-Sun 10:00-17:00, closed Mon, Europaplatz 1, tel. 041-226-7800, www.kunstmuseumluzern.ch.

LÖWENPLATZ

North of the old town, Löwenplatz was a big deal back in the Romantic Age of tourism, when its three main sights (the lion sculpture, Bourbaki Panorama, and Glacier Garden) made it a destination. It remains a bucket-list stop for tour groups but has the tired air of a tourist trap. Drop by for a peek at old-time tourism here; behind the tacky souvenir shops, the sights do retain some of their Victorian-era charm.

Getting There: It's a 10-minute walk from the old town or a short bus ride across the river from the station (take bus #1, #6, #19, or #23 north from the train station to the Löwenplatz stop). Across from the bus stop is the round Bourbaki Panorama. The lion and the Glacier Garden are one long block farther up the hill.

▲Lion Monument (Löwendenkmal)

This free, famous monument remains an essential stop if you're visiting Luzern—if only because when you get back home, every-

one will ask you, "Did you see the lion?" Open from sunrise to dusk, the huge sculpture (33 feet long by 20 feet tall) is carved right into a cliff face, over a reflecting pool in a peaceful park—the site of a sandstone quarry when it was carved in 1821. Though it's often overrun with tour groups, a tranquil moment here is genuinely moving: The mighty lion rests his paws on a shield, with his head cocked to one side, tears streaming down his cheeks. In his side is the broken-off end of a spear, which is slowly killing the noble beast. (Note the angle of the spear, which matches the striations of the rock face, subtly suggesting more spears raining down on the lion.)

The lion memorializes a 1792 episode from the French Revolution, during which more than 600 Swiss Guards—hired to protect the French king—were killed or massacred when revolutionaries stormed the Tuileries Palace (the king managed to escape...for a while). The inscription reads, *Helvetiorum fidei ac virtuti*—"To the loyalty and bravery of the Swiss." While a local artist carved it in 14 months, it was designed by the great Danish Neoclassical sculptor Bertel Thorvaldsen.

Bourbaki Panorama

Here's your chance to get right in the middle of a great painting—literally. In the 19th century, before the dawn of cinema, modern people were hungry for visual entertainment. Panorama theaters like this were built all over Europe and hosted various gigantic paintings, which were rolled up and taken on road trips.

This 360-degree painting (a 33-foot-tall wraparound canvas with a circumference of 360 feet) tells the story of one of the culminating events of the 1870/71 Franco-Prussian War, during which French forces—routed by the Prussians—withdrew over the Swiss border.

Cost and Hours: 12 CHF, covered by Swiss Travel Pass; daily April-Oct 9:00-18:00, Nov-March 10:00-17:00; Löwenplatz 11, tel. 041-412-3030, www.bourbakipanorama.ch. A free booklet explains it all and makes for a good souvenir.

Visiting the Panorama: Upon arrival at the panorama, borrow the tablet guide (to zoom in and identify details) and ask them to play the English version of the historical soundtrack (10 minutes). Spend your waiting time enjoying the first-floor background exhibit. When the English narration starts, be on the second-floor viewing platform to savor all 360 degrees of drama.

After Prussia prevailed, some French soldiers were determined to surrender to the neutral Swiss rather than the enemy. For three days in February 1871, a hungry, weary 87,000-man army led by the panorama's namesake, General Charles-Denis Bourbaki, trudged through the snow and across the Swiss border, near Neuchâtel. Once in Switzerland, they gave up their weapons and surrendered to the Swiss—who, the story goes, took excellent care of them, nursing them back to health before sending them home with a hefty bill for their stay. Edouard Castres, who painted the panorama, actually witnessed the retreat as a Red Cross volunteer.

Glacier Garden (Gletschergarten)

This complex is a strange sort of miniature theme park with an eclectic hodgepodge of exhibits, most loosely relating to alpine geology. They are wrapping up an extensive renovation, likely in 2021, so expect changes.

Cost and Hours: 15 CHF (cheaper during renovation, when not all exhibits are open), covered by Swiss Travel Pass, daily April-Oct 9:00-18:00, Nov-March 10:00-17:00, Denkmalstrasse 4, tel. 041-410-4340, www.gletschergarten.ch.

Visiting the Garden: You'll walk through the **glacier-grinded grounds** that give the garden its name. While geologists might get a thrill out of this, it was just a bunch of holes to me. Then you can visit the **museum,** with exhibits about glacial processes and huge 3-D reliefs of late-18th-century Luzern, the Alps, and the lakes of Central Switzerland. The **Amrein's House** is an old chalet with some original furnishings and models of traditional Swiss buildings. From near here, a tunnel leads to a staircase or elevator up the steep **Tower Walk,** which leads to another old chalet and an observation tower.

You'll finish with the **Hall of Mirrors.** Made in 1896 for a national exhibition in Geneva, it's a delightfully low-tech fun house. You'll grope your way through twisting corridors—with mirrors on all sides—decorated like a Disneyfied Alhambra. It's confusing, dizzying, and claustrophobic, but goofy fun. As you run into yourself (literally) again and again, you'll lament the poor sap who has to clean the smudge marks off all those mirrors. As you leave, giggling and nauseated, you may find yourself wondering, "So, what exactly did that have to do with glaciers?"

FARTHER FROM THE CENTER
▲Swiss Transport Museum (Verkehrshaus)

This "Swiss Smithsonian," across the lake from the train station, includes hundreds of hands-on, kid-friendly exhibits in an enormous complex, cover-

ing virtually all modes of transportation. It's pricey and a little overwhelming, but it's an amazing display of Swiss ingenuity and craftsmanship. If you're in Luzern for only one day, skip this and enjoy the museums and ambience in the old town. But with a second day or younger kids in tow, or if you're obsessed with trains, planes, and automobiles, this museum is worth ▲▲▲—and hours of entertainment.

Cost and Hours: 32 CHF, 12 CHF for kids 6-15, free under 6, half-price with Swiss Travel Pass; more for planetarium, IMAX cinema, and chocolate exhibit (described at end of this listing); daily April-Oct 10:00-18:00, Nov-March until 17:00, café, Lidostrasse 5, tel. 041-375-7575, www.verkehrshaus.ch.

Getting There: From downtown, it's a 30-minute **walk** to the museum, most of it along a beautiful promenade (described earlier, under "Luzern's Lakefront"). To make a beeline to the museum, take **bus** #6, #8, or #24 from the station and get off at the Verkehrshaus stop. For a more scenic approach in summer, catch a **boat** in front of the train station (direction: Verkehrshaus, 1-2/hour, 10 minutes, 6 CHF).

Visiting the Museum: The museum's five main halls are arranged in a circle around a huge central plaza, with full-size airplanes and other attractions. Pick up a map and use the white line on the floor to navigate the full clockwise loop through the complex. Most exhibits are at least partly translated into English.

LUZERN

As you enter, check the schedule of demonstrations (ranging from car-crash tests to airport X-ray machines; usually in English on request).

The first building is a long shed packed with train engines and tram cars. You'll learn that hydropower generates 90 percent of the electricity for Swiss trains, and you'll appreciate the evolution of Swiss trains and tunnels over the last century.

The second hall is a car enthusiast's dream, with two floors devoted to road transport. One wall is stacked floor to ceiling with 80 vehicles dating from 1860 to 2005, mostly cars and motorcycles. Interactive screens let you zoom in on any vehicle for insights into its design and history.

The third building covers boats and submarines on the lower two floors and shows off some Swiss cable cars. Be sure to seek out (on the top floor) the "**Livemap Switzerland**"—an enormous (more than 2,000 square feet), up-to-date aerial photograph of Switzerland. Spread out on the floor like laminated linoleum, this photo map is detailed enough to show virtually every single building within the country's borders. Slide on the Swiss-flag slippers, borrow a map and magnifying glass, and glide across Switzerland, looking for the places you've visited so far.

The next hall is the Hans Erni Museum, showcasing works of a well-known local 20th-century painter and illustrator (they have nothing to do with transport, but are worth a quick peek).

The fifth and final building covers flight (airplanes below, space travel above). The helicopter and airplane simulations are included in your entry price (expect lines). There's also a relaxing parasailing simulator, where you can lie on a smoothly gliding platform and peer down at the countryside below.

Two vintage Swissair planes are parked in the central courtyard (a DC-3 and a Convair 990). You'll also find a miniature train that little kids can ride (small fee), and a high-tech swing set. Simulators, games, giant slides, and interactive exhibits can easily keep children busy all day.

More Sights: Three other attractions share the same grounds and hours as the Transport Museum: a planetarium, the Swiss Chocolate Adventure, and the IMAX Filmtheater. Each costs 16 CHF to enter (or get the 56-CHF ticket that covers everything; see website for showtimes). The Swiss Chocolate Adventure, a chocolate museum structured as a 20-minute amusement-park ride, is entertaining for chocoholics.

Richard Wagner Museum

This museum is about a 30-minute walk along the lakefront, south of the train station and housed in a building where the 19th-century German composer once lived. It's worth a visit only for enthusiasts.

Cost and Hours: 10 CHF, covered by Swiss Travel Pass, April-Nov Tue-Sun 11:00-17:00, closed Mon and Dec-March, café, Richard Wagner Weg 27, tel. 041-360-2370, www.richard-wagner-museum.ch.

ON LAKE LUZERN

Encircled by mountains, the almost fjord-like Lake Luzern is the most touristed in Switzerland, with great scenic variety. With many

boat routes and destinations (35 stops in all), you can take a spin around the lake any time of the year. Cruises range from a one-hour sampler tour (around Luzern's "harbor") to a full-blown, 5.5-hour exploration (to Flüelen, at the far end of the lake, and back). Some routes are round-trip dinner or sightseeing cruises, but most boats have scheduled stops and are designed for you to get out, explore, and then take the next boat back. Romantics will want to hitch a ride on one of the old-fashioned paddleboat steamers.

All boats are operated by the Lake Lucerne Navigation Company (tel. 041-367-6767, www.lakelucerne.ch). Buy tickets from the dockside offices (Piers 1 and 7) or the Luzern TI. Either can offer advice on which trip best fits your schedule and current weather conditions. Tickets can be purchased onboard as well.

Regular departures are free with a Swiss Travel Pass and half-price with a Eurail Global Pass (it can be smart to do the lake cruise on the day you arrive or depart—when you're already using a flexi-day for your train transportation). Skip a lake cruise if you're planning to take the Gotthard Panorama Express to Lugano (see page 369): You'll be boating the entire length of the lake, so there's little point in doing another lake excursion.

Boating Options

Quick Sightseeing Trip: The panorama yacht *Saphir* goes on a villa-and-castle cruise worth ▲, making a lazy one-hour, picturesque sightseeing loop around the lake with a well-done audio tour (27 CHF; discount with Visitor Card, Eurail Global Pass, or Swiss Travel Pass; buy tickets as you board; daily June-mid-Sept, departs every 75 minutes 10:15-19:00, fewer cruises mid-Sept-May; snack bar onboard and picnics welcome; departs from Pier 7 in front of the Hotel Schweizerhof).

Scenic Round-Trip: For more dramatic scenery, sail an hour across the lake on the scheduled boat to Weggis or Vitznau (where the Mount Rigi ascent starts), then back to Luzern (39 CHF round-trip to Weggis, 48 CHF to Vitznau, departs from Pier 1 in front of the train station). For most, a two-hour circle is enough lake scenery.

Full-Day Option: Sail from Luzern to Flüelen (3 hours, departs from Pier 1 in front of the train station), then catch the hourly train from there to Arth-Goldau, where you can ride the cogwheel train to the Rigi summit on your way back to Luzern.

Pedal Boats: You can also get out on the lake under your own power. Pricey pedal boats can be rented at Schwanenplatz, just across the bridge from the Luzern train station (20 CHF/30 minutes, 30 CHF/hour; 5 CHF more on weekends).

Sleeping in Luzern

Luzern is busiest—and most expensive—in summer. Spring and fall bring lower prices, and winter has rock-bottom rates. Air-conditioning is rare; to sleep with the window open but avoid nighttime street noise, ask for a room high up.

IN THE CENTER

$$$$ Hotel Wilden Mann, a local institution near the river on the new town side, fills a characteristic old house with 48 colorful rooms, each one different. While the prices are high, guests come here for the warm welcome and the history rather than cookie-cutter comfort (air-con in some rooms, elevator, Bahnhofstrasse 30, tel. 041-210-1666, www.wilden-mann.ch).

$$$ Hotel des Alpes is a good bet if you want to sleep right on the river in the old town, next door to Luzern's iconic Chapel Bridge and Water Tower. The 45 classic rooms are bright and well equipped; pricier riverfront rooms, some with balconies, come with beautiful views. The reception entrance is on the back of the building, or you can enter through the contemporary restaurant on the promenade and ride up the elevator (fans, Furrengasse 3, tel. 041-417-2060, www.desalpes-luzern.ch, info@desalpes-luzern.ch).

$$$ Hotel Continental Park, facing a park alongside the train station, feels fresh and stylish, with prices to match. Its 92 rooms sit over an appealing contemporary lobby and a restaurant featuring Ticinese cuisine—from the Italian-speaking part of Switzerland (air-con, elevator, Murbacherstrasse 4, tel. 041-228-9050, www.continental.ch).

$$$ Hotel Waldstätterhof fills a fine 19th-century building across the street from the train station. Its 96 bright, spacious, and modern rooms have all the amenities, and its rates are reasonable for the level of comfort (can be noisy—ask for a quieter courtyard room, family rooms available, elevator, pay parking—reserve ahead, Zentralstrasse 4, tel. 041-227-1271, www.hotel-waldstaetterhof. ch, info@hotel-waldstaetterhof.ch).

$$$ Hotel Zum Rebstock, a bit simpler, sits a bit farther from the river—on the way to Löwenplatz, across the lake from the train station, at the base of the steps to the twin-spired Hofkirche. Its 32 idiosyncratic rooms come with artistic flourishes (elevator, St. Leodegarstrasse 3, tel. 041-417-1819, www.rebstock-luzern.ch).

$$$ Schlüssel Hotel, well run by Marija, offers 10 tastefully decorated rooms with personal touches that make you feel at home. This recently renovated building, first opened as a hotel in 1545, takes pride in its long history. It's well located on a small square near the river and houses several restaurants (discount if you skip breakfast, family rooms, a few rooms have balconies, elevator, Franziskanerplatz 12, tel. 041-210-1061, www.schluessel-luzern. ch, welcome@schluessel-luzern.ch).

$$ Stern Luzern, located in the old shell of a building over a popular restaurant, is a solid value, offering 15 small and basic rooms. They also have eight newer, pricier rooms in an annex closer to the river (family rooms, tiny elevator, check-in at restaurant entrance at Franziskanerplatz 4, tel. 041-227-5060, www.sternluzern. ch, info@sternluzern.ch).

OUTSIDE THE CENTER
$$ Ibis Styles Luzern City has 115 modern rooms with colorful accents. It's near the action, but away from much of the noise (family rooms, elevator, Friedenstrasse 8, tel. 041-418-4848, www.ibis. com, h8549@accor.com). It's a 15-minute walk from the train station, or take bus #1—direction: Maihof, get off at Löwenplatz and walk down Friedenstrasse; the hotel faces the Bourbaki Panorama.

$ Hotel Alpha, once a convent-run boarding house for village girls, is now a respectable hotel for value-minded travelers who don't mind being away from the center. It offers 47 big, bright, dorm-style rooms, most with the toilet down the hall, though some have private baths. It's located in a nice residential area but has some street noise from the nearby school and playing field (many doubles are twins, family rooms, elevator, fans available, comfy lounges and TV room, pay parking—reserve ahead, Zähringerstrasse 24, at intersection with Pilatusstrasse, tel. 041-240-4280, www.hotelalpha.ch, info@hotelalpha.ch). It's a 10-minute walk or an easy two-stop bus ride from the train station: Take bus #12 or #18, get off at Pilatusplatz, and continue down Pilatusstrasse.

$ The Bed and Breakfast, lovingly run by Isabelle in her

Luzern Hotels & Restaurants

grandmother's former home, offers 13 bright, spacious rooms—three with private bathrooms. This is a perfect spot for those looking for a more personal experience and who don't mind being a bit away from the center. The kind staff and cozy garden will make you wish you were staying longer (closed Nov-Feb, family rooms, Taubenhausstrasse 34, tel. 041-310-1514, www.thebandb.ch, info@thebandb.ch). It's a 15-minute walk from the train station, or take bus #1—direction: Kriens-Obernau, get off at Eichhof and walk 100 yards down Taubenhausstrasse.

$ Ibis Budget Luzern City's 128 tight, cookie-cutter rooms are worth considering if you're on a budget and don't mind a soulless neighborhood near the train tracks. You get a narrow double bed, sometimes with a bunk bed above it, plus an opaque shower cabinet that opens straight into the room (air-con, breakfast extra, pay parking, Kellerstrasse 6, tel. 041-367-8000, www.ibis.com, h6782@accor.com). It's a 10- to 15-minute walk from the train station, or take bus #4 three stops to Brünigstrasse.

¢ Backpackers Luzern is calm and well run, sharing a mod-

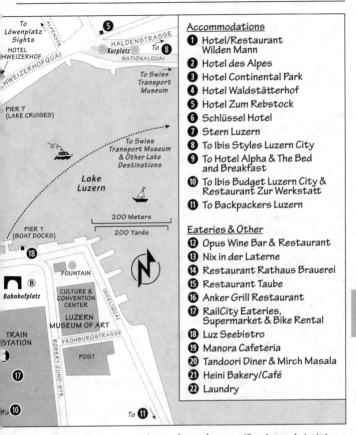

Accommodations
1 Hotel/Restaurant Wilden Mann
2 Hotel des Alpes
3 Hotel Continental Park
4 Hotel Waldstätterhof
5 Hotel Zum Rebstock
6 Schlüssel Hotel
7 Stern Luzern
8 To Ibis Styles Luzern City
9 To Hotel Alpha & The Bed and Breakfast
10 To Ibis Budget Luzern City & Restaurant Zur Werkstatt
11 To Backpackers Luzern

Eateries & Other
12 Opus Wine Bar & Restaurant
13 Nix in der Laterne
14 Restaurant Rathaus Brauerei
15 Restaurant Taube
16 Anker Grill Restaurant
17 RailCity Eateries, Supermarket & Bike Rental
18 Luz Seebistro
19 Manora Cafeteria
20 Tandoori Diner & Mirch Masala
21 Heini Bakery/Café
22 Laundry

LUZERN

ern, blocky building with student dorms *(Studentenheim)* in a peaceful residential area a 15-minute walk south of the train station. The place has 30 rooms (each with a balcony), shared toilets and showers, two guest kitchens, a welcoming lounge, and no curfew. The walk to the center is mostly along the lake, through pretty parks and next to a fine beach (no breakfast, elevator, full-service pay laundry, reception open 7:30-10:00 & 16:00-23:00, Alpenquai 42, tel. 041-360-0420, www.backpackerslucerne.ch, info@backpackerslucerne.ch). By bus, take #6, #7, or #8 from the station four stops to Weinbergli, then walk left five minutes to the hostel.

Eating in Luzern

Eateries along the river are pricey and a bit touristy, but that's where you'll make the best memories. Reservations are smart. A good way to eat well but affordably here is to visit a high-end restaurant for lunch, when you can get a filling multicourse meal for around 20-25 CHF (typically weekdays only). For a memorable evening on a budget, consider catching the last one-hour sightseeing boat on the lake (19:00) and enjoying a picnic dinner while you cruise.

NEAR THE RIVER

$$$ Opus, next to the big Jesuit Church, is both a trendy wine bar and a good restaurant. Pair your wine with meat, fish, pastas, and vegetarian dishes with Italian and international flair; the lush and varied "antipasti buffet"; or your choice of dried meats and cheeses (sold by weight). They always have a couple dozen bottles of wine open and available by the glass. Sit in the upscale, colorful interior; in the extremely romantic wine cellar with candlelight reflecting in the bottle-lined walls; or out front, under the church and next to the river (daily 9:00-24:00, Bahnhofstrasse 16, tel. 041-226-4141, www. restaurant-opus.ch).

$$$ Nix in der Laterne has a romantic, dressy interior and great outside seats right on the fast-rushing river. Nikki is Swiss-Austrian, and so is his cuisine. Daily options are listed on a chalkboard; their budget option is *tarte flambée*—a savory tart with mix-and-match toppings. Their nice variety of 22-CHF weekday lunches attracts a sophisticated local business crowd. This is a fine spot in a central location that thrives even without tourists (daily 11:30-24:00, Reusssteg 9, tel. 041-240-2543, www.nixinderlaterne. ch).

$$$ Wilden Mann, the recommended hotel in a historic building just off the river, has two very different restaurants, each serving well-regarded food in atmospheric surroundings. The very traditional, wood-clad **Burgerstube** offers traditional Swiss cooking, while **Sauvage,** filling a nondescript dining room and a delightful winter garden, is a more French/Mediterranean experience. The menus overlap—review both before choosing (daily 11:30-14:00 & 18:00-22:00, Bahnhofstrasse 30, tel. 041-210-1666, www.wilden-mann.ch).

$$ Restaurant Rathaus Brauerei is a lively microbrewery on the river under the Town Hall. While the beer hall is plain, there are plenty of outdoor seats—both under arches and on the river. It's a local favorite for its unfiltered, cloudy Seidel Rathausbier, which you can only get here. Special seasonal brews are on the menu board, along with salads, "gourmet" pretzel sandwiches (a light and affordable option), and Germanic main dishes (daily 9:00-24:00, Unter der Egg 2, tel. 041-410-6111, www.rathausbrauerei.ch).

$$$ Restaurant Taube, popular for serving "grandma's cooking," is known for its ham-and-cheese *Rösti*. The food is fine, and the interior is a simple, cozy cellar, but I'd eat here mostly to take advantage of their amazing riverside seating (22-CHF two-course weekday lunches, daily 11:30-14:00 & 17:30-22:30, Burgerstrasse 3, tel. 041-210-0747, www.taube-luzern.ch).

IN THE NEW TOWN

These places are in a more workaday district, closer to the train station than the river and away from the tourist zone. Each is patronized by a smart local clientele.

$$$$ Restaurant Zur Werkstatt is a fun, inventive approach to eating. The seating is communal and the 58-CHF three-course dinner *menu* changes each week (48-CHF vegetarian option). The open kitchen allows you to watch the action and take in the enticing aromas. It's a suitable splurge for the adventurous eater (also 25-CHF lunch specials, Mon-Sat 11:30-13:30 & 17:00-24:00, closed Sun, Waldstätterstrasse 18, tel. 041-979-0303, www.zurwerkstatt.ch).

$$$ Anker Grill Restaurant fills an old ballroom of the once-venerable Hotel Anker with an eclectic blend of old and new—mixing crystal glassware with exposed concrete, hip music, and low lighting. It's a fun and youthful place with an open kitchen and a diverse menu focused on fresh, local ingredients, tasty grilled meats, and pastas (25-CHF two-course weekday lunches, daily 11:30-10:00, Pilatusstrasse 36, tel. 041-220-8800, www.hotel-restaurant-anker.ch).

FAST AND AFFORDABLE

In the Train Station's "RailCity": As in every big Swiss city, Luzern's train station comes with a mall bursting with bright, efficient chain eateries. Near the TI, a **Migros Daily** serves prepared food (daily 6:00-22:00). Just down the escalator you'll find a string of creative **fast-food places** with small standup tables (kebabs, salads, burgers, and currywurst) and a big **Co-op supermarket** (daily 6:00-22:00). Upstairs is **$$ Tibits Vegetarian Restaurant,** a self-serve salad bar nestled in a modern, peaceful spot overlooking the tracks (daily 6:30-23:00).

On the Lakefront: $ Luz Seebistro, tucked between boat docks directly in front of the train station, has glassed-in indoor seating, a big deck out on the lake, and a takeout window. It's appealingly unpretentious and rough around the edges—a refreshing change in ostentatious Luzern. They serve drinks and a simple menu of burgers, sandwiches, *Flammkuchen* (flatbreads), and salads (daily 7:30-23:00, Schifflandungsbrücke 1).

Self-Service Cafeteria: $ Manora, a cafeteria on the fifth floor of the Manor department store in the old town, is ideal for a tasty, efficient self-serve lunch. In good weather, climb the stairs to the outdoor terrace, with great views over the rooftops of Luzern to the lake and Mount Pilatus. This place can get crowded during peak times—eat early or late, and send your travel partner up top to claim an outdoor table while you buy the food (Mon-Wed 9:00-18:30, Thu-Fri 9:00-21:00, Sat 8:00-16:00, closed Sun, Weggisgasse 5).

Indian Food: In the old town **$ Tandoori Diner** sells budget Indian meals (meat or vegetarian; chose one of eight combos—see photos and they'll dish it up immediately, Mon-Sat 11:30-21:30, closed Sun, Löwengraben 4, tel. 041-340-5296). **$$ Mirch Masala,** two doors away and run by the same folks, is a bit more elegant (17-CHF lunch buffet, pricier à la carte dinners, Mon-Sat 11:30-14:00 & 17:30-22:30, Sun 16:30-22:30, Löwengraben 8, tel. 041-410-6308).

Bakery: $ Heini Bakery/Café, on Falkenplatz a half-block down from the Manor department store, is popular with the local lunch crowd for its weekday salad bar, sandwiches, quiches, and delectable pastries. There are two sprawling indoor seating areas, plus outdoor tables in good weather (Mon-Fri 7:00-18:30, Sat until 17:00, Sun 9:00-17:00, Hertensteinstrasse 66, tel. 041-412-2020).

Luzern Connections

Luzern is well situated, with convenient connections to anywhere in the country. Note that Luzern is on both the Golden Pass and the Gotthard Panorama Express scenic rail routes (see the Scenic Rail Journeys chapter). Train info: www.sbb.ch.

From Luzern by Train to: Zürich (2/hour direct, 1 hour), **Zürich Airport** (hourly direct, 1 hour, more with change at Zürich main station), **Bern** (2/hour direct, 1 hour, more with transfer), **Interlaken** (3-4/hour, 2.5 hours, 1-3 changes), **Lausanne** (hourly direct, 2 hours, more with transfers), **Appenzell** (2-3/hour, 3 hours, change in Herisau, more with additional transfers), **Lugano** (2/hour, 2 hours, some with transfer), **St. Moritz** (1-2/hour, 4.5 hours, at least 2 changes; 6.5 hours via Glacier Express route, 2-5 changes including Göschenen and Andermatt), **Zermatt** (1-2/hour, 3.5 hours, 2 transfers).

Central Switzerland Day Trips

Perched on the edge of its scenic lake and ringed by family-friendly mountain peaks, Luzern is a perfect springboard for alpine excursions. Three side trips are especially popular and worthwhile: two famous and accessible mountains—Mount Pilatus and Mount

Rigi—and the hidden military fortress of Fürigen. All three can be reached by boat and mountain lifts from Luzern.

Planning Your Time

Mount Pilatus is a jagged pinnacle with a "top of the world" feeling that makes for a fun, relaxed day (especially in good weather). Mount Rigi, sitting a bit lower, is more enveloped in scenery and has a range of good trails. For either peak, allow the better part of a day for your round-trip.

Note that Fortress Fürigen is open only on weekends from April through October. It's possible to combine Mount Pilatus and the fortress into one jam-packed day trip, although it requires a bit of backtracking (or a taxi)—get an early start to fit it all in.

For any of these side trips, you can go out and back by train, or travel one way by boat. The boat is slower (and more expensive), but adds a scenic, romantic component to your day.

The connections outlined below are well coordinated but don't always leave lots of time between legs; confirm all schedules and logistics locally before embarking. For details on boat connections, see page 77; for various passes, see "Getting Around Luzern," earlier.

MOUNT PILATUS

Looming behind Luzern, Pilatus (7,000 feet), worth ▲▲, is a dramatic backdrop to the city and an enjoyable destination. While leg-

end dictates that it's named for Pontius Pilate—whose body is supposedly in one of its lakes, kicking up a fuss if disturbed—it more likely comes from a Latin word meaning "cloudy." It's also said to be infested with dragons (which local marketing relies on heavily—you'll see red dragons everywhere). Pack a picnic before leaving town, and spend a glorious day here with the marmots and ibex for company.

Ascending Mount Pilatus

There are two approaches from the base of the mountain to the summit, called Pilatus Kulm. A cogwheel train runs up to the top from the town of Alpnachstad, on the south side of the peak. The other ascent—by gondola and then cable car—runs from Kriens up the north side, with a chance to stop for a luge ride or the ropes course at Fräkmüntegg.

Lake Luzern Area

To Zürich

A-2   To Basel   Reuss R.   A-14

Luzern
See detail map

SWISS TRANSPORT MUSEUM

BUS CONNECTION

Kriens

KRIENSEREGG

FRÄKMÜNTEGG

Kastanien-baum

Lake

PILATUS-KULM

Mt. Pilatus

Hergiswil

Kehrsiten   Bürgen-stock

FORTRESS FÜRIGEN

Stansstad   Ennet-burger

Aemsigen

Alpnachstad

A-8

Stans

A-2

Sarnersee

Stanserhorn

Golden Pass Route to Interlaken

To Interlaken over Brünigpass

To Engelberg & Mt. Titlis

For maximum views, go up one way, down the other—in good weather, the view's spectacular on both sides in both directions. I'd take the cogwheel train up (the uphill ride is a bit more dramatic), and the gondola ride down (to catch more afternoon light).

However you travel, figure at least 4-5 hours for the total round-trip from Luzern (more for serious hikers)—though when it's busy, you may lose some time waiting for the various connections. Leave yourself enough time if you want to do the luge at Fräkmüntegg on the way down.

Cost: 72 CHF round-trip, whether by cogwheel train or gondola/cable car (does not include transportation between Luzern and the mountain). Swiss Travel Pass and Eurail Global pass holders get a 50 percent discount. Keep track of your ticket, as you'll need to scan it several times, up and down, until you exit at the last station.

Two **combo-tickets** cover all transportation, including between Luzern and the mountain: the Golden Round Trip (using a boat for the first leg) and the Silver Round Trip (using a train). These tickets don't save money, but they do simplify your journey with just one ticket.

LUZERN

Crowd-Beating Tips: The top of Mount Pilatus is popular and very crowded in summer and on sunny spring and fall weekends. You may have to wait to go up (between 9:00-12:00) and to get back down (15:00-closing time). Reservations are not available.

Information: www.pilatus.ch.

By Cogwheel Train from Alpnachstad: The cogwheel train, with old wooden cabins and red-velvet seats, leaves from the lakeside town of Alpnachstad. To reach Alpnachstad from Luzern, take either the **S5 train** (2/hour, 20 minutes, 7.80 CHF one-way, part of this journey not covered by the Visitors Card—before boarding, buy a 3.70-CHF ticket to cover the stretch from Hergiswil to Alpnachstad) or the **boat,** which leaves from

Pier 1 opposite the train station (7/day, 1-2 hours, 27 CHF one-way). The cogwheel train runs mid-May-mid-Nov only (daily, 30 minutes up, 40 minutes down; first train up at 8:10; last train up at 17:10, last train down at 17:45; longer operating times late June-late Aug, shorter operating times in Nov, does not run in off-season).

The ride up is dizzying—you'll be keenly aware that this is the steepest cog railway in the world (the grade, marked by signs, maxes out at 48 percent). For the best views, take a downhill-facing seat with your left shoulder against the window. You'll slowly trundle up through thick forest on a skinny stone track, with peek-a-boo views of the lakes below, occasionally passing through chunky-walled tunnels. The train stops halfway up at Aemsigen to let other trains pass—stay on board.

By Gondola/Cable Car from Kriens: The gondola/cable car combination to Pilatus starts from Kriens, a suburb of Luzern.

To reach Kriens, catch city bus #1, which departs frequently from the Luzern train station; the stop is on the other side of the street from where most of the bus platforms are located (15-minute ride, direction: Kriens, stop: Zentrum Pilatus). Exiting the bus in Kriens, cross the busy street and follow *Pilatus* signs 10 minutes uphill to the gondola station. (To return to Luzern from the gondola station, carefully follow blue-and-white signs for *Luzern bus Nr. 1* downhill for several minutes through a pleasant residential area to find bus #1; you don't want the bus stop in front of the gondola terminal.)

The **gondola** runs continuously from Kriens to Fräkmüntegg (30-minute trip; stay on the gondola at the Krienseregg midstation). At Fräkmüntegg, leave the gondola and line up for the **cable car** to the summit (7 minutes, 4/hour). The gondola and cable car run year-round, except for two weeks' maintenance in fall (first ascent from Kriens at 8:30, April–mid-Oct last descent from Pilatus at 17:30, off-season last descent at 16:30).

At the Pilatus Summit

The centerpiece of the Pilatus-Kulm summit—where both cable cars and cogwheel trains arrive—is a vast, underground visitors center. Here you'll find a good information office, souvenir shop, snack bars, and, at busy times, long lines of people waiting to head back down the mountain.

Get oriented by heading out to the big **panoramic terrace**, filling the area between the round, modern Hotel Bellevue and the old-school Hotel Pilatus-Kulm. (The visitors center is beneath your feet.)

Head over to the north (Luzern) side, overlooking the cable car. You're looking at Switzerland's vast central plateau, where more than two-thirds of the Swiss people live (many in the cities of Luzern, Zürich, Bern, and Basel). Immediately below, you can see the city of Luzern clustered around its little corner of the meandering, multifingered Lake Luzern (Vierwaldstättersee). For an even better view over the lake, go to the little gap between the boxy cable-car station and Hotel Bellevue. (The trail up to Esel—described later—begins right here.) Notice how Pilatus forms the first high, jagged peak of the mountains that fan out to the south.

Speaking of which...cross the terrace to the cogwheel-train side, and survey the cut-glass peaks of the Swiss Alps—which stretch from this point all the way to Italy. Looking out over this impenetrable wall of granite, it's easy to understand how Switzerland planned to essentially seal off its mountainous interior in case of invasion during World War II. Pilatus and the nearby peaks mark the boundary of the high-altitude fortress system called the Swiss National Redoubt. Exploring the Pilatus area, you'll see signs of hidden Swiss military installations, and the tourable stronghold of Fortress Fürigen is nearby (described later in this chapter).

Sleeping and Eating at the Summit

Sleeping: Two hotels at the summit offer a total of 50 rooms; the information office in the visitors center serves as the reception desk for both. The hotels book as "half-board," meaning room rates include breakfast and dinner. **$$$$ Hotel Pilatus-Kulm** is in a historic building from 1900; the modern **$$$$ Hotel Bellevue**

LUZERN

Luge Lesson

Taking a wild ride on a summer luge is a quintessential alpine experience. In German, it's called a *Sommerrodelbahn* ("summer toboggan run"). To try one of Europe's great accessible thrills, take the lift up to the top of a mountain, grab a wheeled sled-like go-cart, and scream back down the mountainside on a banked course. Then take the lift back up and start all over again.

Luge courses are highly weather-dependent, and can close at the slightest hint of rain. If the weather's questionable, call ahead to confirm that your preferred luge is open. Stainless-steel courses are more likely than concrete ones to stay open in drizzly weather.

Operating the sled is simple: Push the stick forward to go faster, pull back to apply brakes. Even a novice can go very, very fast. Most are cautious on their first run, speed demons on their second... and bruised and bloody on their third. A woman once showed me her travel journal illustrated with her husband's dried five-inch-long luge scab. He had disobeyed the only essential rule of luging: Keep both hands on your stick. To avoid a bumper-to-bumper traffic jam, let the person in front of you get as far ahead as possible before you start. You'll emerge from the course with a windblown hairdo and a smile-creased face.

Key Luge Terms

Lenkstange	lever
drücken / schneller fahren	push / go faster
ziehen / bremsen	pull / brake
Schürfwunde	scrape
Schorf	scab

is clean and bright, with Nordic-style furniture. The hotels share contact information: Tel. 041-329-1212, www.pilatus.ch, hotels@pilatus.ch.

Eating: Inside the visitors center is a basic **$ self-service cafeteria**; outside you'll find the cheaper **$ Panorama Grill**. The table-service **$$ restaurant** at the Hotel Pilatus-Kulm has both indoor and outdoor dining areas.

Hiking on Mount Pilatus

Many hiking opportunities—from easy to challenging—lead from the summit to great viewpoints. Review your choices below, and stop by the information office to pick up a map. For a representative sample, I'd ascend Esel, then head up to Oberhaupt and down around the other side.

Easy Hikes: From the outdoor terrace, the peak called **Oberhaupt** (marked with a cross) looms above you and is just a five-minute climb. Those with a bit more energy cancontinue on a 15-minute loop that goes along the ridge above Hotel Pilatus-Kulm (toward the biggest radar station in Switzerland, housed in an off-limits military zone), down some steep stairs, and around to the other side of the mountain. From here, you'll follow the "Dragonpath"— carved through tunnels and viewpoints in the rock—and eventually return to the visitors center. On the way, you'll look out over a tiny church (and its graveyard) clinging to the sharp crest of a ridge—this is the Klimsenkapelle, built in 1861.

On the other side of the platform, a steep 10-minute hike above Hotel Bellevue takes you up to **Esel** ("Donkey," commemorating the days before cable cars, when Queen Victoria came up to Pilatus on the back of a donkey). From up here, savor 360-degree views over the entire area. Below Esel hides an impressive part of Switzerland's anti-aircraft defense system. Patches of imitation rock in the mountainside hide modern missiles that point to the skies.

Harder Hikes: Hiking to **Tomlishorn** (35 minutes one-way), you'll spot more camouflaged military installations. Stop at the yellow *Echo* sign and shout your message out to the world. Somebody out there keeps yelling it back.

A 1.5-hour hike leads to the 6,700-foot cross-capped summit of **Matthorn** (not Matterhorn). This hike is moderately strenuous—generally uphill, with lots of ups and downs. A visitors' book invites you to sign and leave your impressions on this breathtaking spot.

Activities at Fräkmüntegg

This spot, on the north slope of Pilatus, is a summer-fun zone. If the weather's good, stop here to zip down the nearly mile-long Fräkigaudi, Switzerland's longest **luge ride** (8 CHF/ ride, daily mid-April- late Oct 10:00-17:00, closed if rainy, mandatory bag check, expect lines on sunny weekends, a 5-minute walk below the cable-car station, www. rodelbahn.ch).

At the fun **Suspension Rope Park** (Seilpark), you can test your agility on 10 ropes courses with varying degrees of difficulty (28 CHF includes instruction and three hours on the courses, family discounts—separate course for kids under age 8; late April-mid-Oct daily 10:00-17:00, until 17:30 July-Aug; next to the cable-car station, www.pilatus.ch).

FORTRESS FÜRIGEN

Fortress Fürigen (Festung Fürigen), built during World War II when Hitler threatened Switzerland, shows you another face of the country. Part of the reason Switzerland has been able to remain peaceful and neutral is its elaborate and secret system of defensive bunkers and fortresses. This fascinating exhibit, worth ▲ (or ▲▲▲ for military history buffs) is open only on weekends, April through October. Visitors explore the facility with the help of

audioguides, interactive displays, and short films. It's even possible to fiddle with—and even aim—heavy guns, knowing the ammo is now imaginary.

Cost and Hours: 7 CHF, cash only, covered by Swiss Travel Pass, April-Oct Sat-Sun 11:00-17:00, closed Mon-Fri and Nov-March, tel. 041-618-7340, www.nidwaldner-museum.ch (click on "Festung Fürigen").

Getting There: Fortress Fürigen is just outside the lakefront town of Stansstad, not far from Luzern. It's an easy trip from Luzern on the S4 **train** (2/hour, 17 minutes). From the train station in Stansstad, walk 15-20 minutes, following brown signs to *Festungsmuseum* or yellow hiking signs to *Kehrsiten* (down Bahnhofstrasse to Stanserstrasse, cross and follow signs, turn right on Achereggstrasse—where you'll pass a grocery and bakery that are handy for lunch—and then go left on Kehrsitenstrasse). You'll wind up walking along the lakefront, passing through a nice little park with free WCs and a beach, then cutting inland to circle behind the Aiola restaurant and a marina. Finally, you'll wind along the lake, on the shoulder of a narrow road, under cliffs for a few hundred yards. Watch for the low-profile shed burrowed into the cliff on your right: That's the entrance.

You can also get to Stansstad from Luzern by **boat** (7/day, 1 hour). From Stansstad's boat dock, walk 10 minutes up to the main street (Achereggstrasse) and keep left, following the brown signs for *Festungsmuseum*.

Drivers arriving in Stansstad should follow white signs to *Kehrsiten* and the lakeside parking lot. From here it's a 5-minute

Swiss Military Readiness

Strolling through the charming pastoral greenery of a peaceful Swiss village, my friend walked with me to the door of a nondescript barn. He said, "Stand here," and slid open the door to reveal a solitary, mighty gun—pointing right at me. Crossing a field, kicking a stray soccer ball back to a group of happy grade-schoolers, we came to another barn. This time I noticed the "wooden" door was actually metal, with a clever paint job. Inside was a military canteen, now selling snacks to civilians, and a steel ladder leading down into a military-gray world that felt like a vast submarine. A network of passages, just big enough for heavily armed soldiers to race down single file, led to a series of gun barns and subterranean command rooms.

Switzerland may be famous for its neutrality, but it's anything but lax defensively. Travelers marvel at how Swiss engineers have conquered the Alps with the world's most-expensive-per-mile road system. But no one designs a Swiss bridge or tunnel without also designing its destruction. Each comes with built-in explosives, so, in the event of an invasion, the entire country can be blasted into a mountain fortress.

Even today, you can't get a building permit without an expensive first-class bomb shelter worked into the plan. Old tank barriers (nicknamed "Toblerones" for their shape) stand ready to be dragged across the roads to slow any invasion. Sprawling hospitals are dug into mountains, still ventilated to be kept dry and ready for use. And halfway up alpine cliffs, Batcave-type doors slide open to allow fighter jets to zoom into action from hidden airstrips cut out of solid rock.

The end of the Cold War in 1989 brought changes even to neutral Switzerland. With deep cuts in its defense budget, Switzerland closed many of its 15,000 hidden fortresses. Some of the forts, such as Fürigen, are now tourist attractions that are no more formidable than medieval castles.

LUZERN

walk along the lake (behind the marina and along the cliffs) to the museum entrance.

Combining the Fortress with Mount Pilatus: The fortress is in the same direction from Luzern as Mount Pilatus, making it possible to combine both sights in one well-organized day. Stansstad (where you'll walk to the fortress) and Alpnachstad (where you'll take the cogwheel train to Pilatus) are on different rail lines, which fork at Hergiswil, so you'll have to backtrack there to change trains. Or consider taking a 10-minute taxi between the fortress and Alpnachstad for about 30 CHF (call Taxi Nidwalden, based near the fortress, tel. 041-620-0303).

Background

Fortress Fürigen was built in 1941, at a time when Switzerland found itself surrounded by hostile enemies: Nazi Germany, Nazi-controlled France, and Mussolini's Italy. The Swiss saw themselves as hedgehogs—if threatened, they were ready to curl up into a ball, spines out. In case of an invasion, the Swiss government would retreat to a secret bunker near Brünig in the Berner Oberland, and Swiss troops would abandon the central plateau (and the cities of Luzern, Zürich, Basel, and Bern) and fall back around the alpine stronghold known as the Swiss National Redoubt. The fortress at Fürigen, located at the boundary of that fortified zone (and one of nine such fortresses that ringed Lake Luzern), was meant to protect roads and rail lines that led from Luzern and Zürich along the lake into the mountains. This fortress came equipped with two cannons that could hurl huge artillery shells in the direction of Mount Pilatus. Fürigen (the name comes from a village and former grand hotel on top of the cliff) was one of the smaller fortresses of its type.

After World War II, these fortresses were retooled with a new focus: the threat of the Soviet Union and nuclear war. Fürigen could house and feed 100 people for three weeks. But in 1990, with the end of the Cold War, the practical Swiss decommissioned the fortress, refit it with vintage WWII and early Cold War gear, and opened it to the curious public. It's now administered by the local historical museum.

Visiting the Fortress

The fortress consists of an underground bunker that's invisible from the outside. Enter through an innocent-looking wooden shed. At the entrance, ask for the brochure (with map) and included English audioguide (which tells the story well). The bunker is always chilly (about 55 degrees Fahrenheit), but no worries: Visitors without jackets are loaned original Swiss Army coats. Allow an hour to visit the various parts of the bunker.

Just inside the entrance, you'll pass a machine-gun emplacement—aimed right at the front door. Then make your way down the 200-yard-long main tunnel. You'll pass the radio room—located near the entrance to assure clear reception—and reach a second machine-gun emplacement, guarding the inner door. Soon after, a detour leads to one of the two heavy artillery emplacements. The giant cannons, each operated by a half-dozen troops, could launch shells more than six miles. You can grab the wheels to aim the massive gun.

Continue deeper down the main tunnel, through heavily fortified doors, to the fresh-air tunnel, which provided exactly that—

creating a buffer in case of atomic attack (you can see the "atom filter" installed in 1960). Beyond that is the second big artillery emplacement. The main tunnel ends at the engine room, which provided electricity and ventilation for those stationed inside, even when shut off from the outside world.

On your way back out the main tunnel, two more worthwhile detours are on the left. First are the living quarters for the troops stationed here. Step into the WC (to see the one shower shared by all 100 men), then into the dining hall, kitchen, and storage rooms. Nearby is the hospital and a rack of guns, all lined up and ready to grab. Upstairs is the big bunk room for the enlisted men (their standard-issue gear is displayed in the cabinets), and the more private officers' quarters and offices.

Farther along—on the way out—step into the former munition magazine, which now houses a well-presented small museum. You'll see one of those huge shells that the big cannons could fire, and watch an informative video about the Swiss plan to use their National Redoubt in case of invasion. Nearby, a cheery cartoon implores homemakers to stockpile food—since they could never be sure when it might be cut off.

MOUNT RIGI

This long, shelf-like mountain, across the lake from Luzern, pro-

vides sweeping views of Central Switzerland (and, on a clear day, Germany and France, too). Even though it's at a lower altitude (5,900 feet) than Pilatus, this so-called Queen of the Mountains boasts the oldest cog railway in

Europe (from 1870) and claims to offer the best vistas in the area. Like Pilatus, the top can be busy between 10:00 and 15:00—especially in summer and on good-weather weekends.

Ascending Mount Rigi

You can reach the top of Rigi, called Rigi Kulm, from either its "front" (west, lake-facing) or "back" (east) side. Hourly cogwheel trains chug up to the summit from base stations on both sides (hikers can hop off partway up or down). The west side also has a cablecar option to the lakefront.

The schedules and prices listed here are for April through mid-October (boats and the Vitznau-Rigi Kulm train run less frequently in winter). Trains run hourly, so a missed connection can be a big waste of time; check schedules locally before you go.

Cost: 117 CHF round-trip—that's 45 CHF for the boat ride, and 72 CHF for the cogwheel train and cable car. With a Swiss Travel Pass, the entire trip is free; with a Eurail Global pass, it's half-price (but you'll have to use one of your flexi-days). To simplify things, buy your Rigi Kulm ticket at the boat dock.

Information: www.rigi.ch.

From the West: From Luzern, coming up the west side makes the most sense, as it gives you an excuse to take a scenic boat ride

to the base of the mountain. My recommended round-trip from Luzern: Boat to Vitznau; cogwheel train to Rigi Kulm; mountaintop fun up top; cable car back down to Weggis; boat back to Luzern. You could do it the other way around—cable car up, cogwheel train back—but the train is more impressive on the way up, and doing it this way lets you walk downhill from the cable car to the boat. Figure 5-6 hours for the total round-trip from Luzern (travel between Luzern and the summit alone takes about 1.5 hours one-way).

From Pier 1 in front of Luzern's train station, hourly **boats** leave for Weggis (45 minutes), then continue to the cogwheel train station at Vitznau (one hour). At Vitznau, the **cogwheel train** chugs to the summit (hourly, 30 minutes up, 40 minutes down, daily 9:15-19:15, June-early Sept until 22:05). The train departs from right in front of the boat dock. For the best views up, sit on the side closest to the station, ideally facing downhill. The train makes several stops on the way up, including Rigi Kaltbad (with the cable-car station to Weggis). Stay on the train until it reaches the top, **Rigi Kulm.** There you'll find a small information office, souvenir shop, snack bar, and WCs.

Have fun up top! Enjoy the views, maybe go for a hike (for details, see later). When you're ready to head back, make your way to **Rigi Kaltbad** (a one-hour downhill hike or quick train ride).

From Rigi Kaltbad, the **cable car** (just toward the lake from the train station) carries you down in 10 minutes to Weggis on the lakefront (2/hour, Mon-Fri 6:45-19:10, Sat-Sun from 8:10). From here you'll walk about 10 minutes downhill to the **boat dock** (follow *Schiffstation* signs) for your cruise back to Luzern (hourly, 45 minutes). In summer, the last boat departs at 20:57 (earlier off-season); if you miss it, you can get back to Luzern by taking the bus to Küssnacht, then the train to Luzern from there.

From the East: If you're visiting Rigi from Zürich, Lugano, or other points to the north, east, and south, it makes sense to ascend the "back" side of the mountain from the town of Arth-Goldau, on Switzerland's main rail line. From Arth-Goldau, a cogwheel train takes you up to the summit (hourly, daily 8:00-17:10, July-Aug until 18:10, 45-minute ride).

Sleeping and Eating at the Summit

Stay overnight and watch the sun rise, accompanied only by the sounds of the wind and the ringing of a few cow bells.

$$$ Rigi Kulm Hotel is set just below the summit, with 33 rooms, stunning views, and a basic **$ cafeteria** and pricier restaurant (tel. 041-880-1888, www.rigikulm.ch, hotel@rigikulm.ch, Käppeli family).

$$$ Rigi Kaltsbad Mineral Bath & Spa, between Vitznau and Rigi Kulm, has 52 rooms and is a nice place to rejuvenate with its indoor and outdoor pools and bathing areas (tel. 041-399-8181, www.hotelrigikaltbad.ch, info@hotelrigikaltbad.ch).

Hiking on Mount Rigi

The mountain is laced with more than 60 miles of hiking trails and other attractions to while away an afternoon. All are well described in the *Rigi Explorer Guide,* available at Luzern's TI, at lift and cogwheel train stations, and on the Rigi website.

Easy Summit Hike: The obvious choice is the easy, uphill hike to the **summit at Rigi Kulm** (5,899 feet), at the base of a giant Swisscom communications tower. It's directly above the Rigi Kulm station, about 10 minutes if you huff up the steep path, or 20 minutes if you loop around on the more scenic, gentler path (both paved). Up top, you have sweeping views in every direction. The big lake below you is the Zugersee, with the town of Zug on its right side (behind the hill). In the opposite direction the snow-covered peaks of the Swiss Alps recede and overlap all the way to Italy.

Classic Rigi Kulm to Rigi Kaltbad Hike: The lovely downhill ramble from the summit at Rigi Kulm to the cable-car station at **Rigi Kaltbad** takes about one hour. You can also go partway, to the scenic Staffel train station (about 20 minutes), and take the train from there.

If you opt for the whole hike, carry on past Staffel, following the blue *Staffelhöheweg* signs along the train tracks—enjoying a slow-motion look at the same grand views you saw from the train. At the fork, stay right for the 30-minute route to Rigi Kaltbad (the left fork takes 50 minutes). When you reach the next little station, at Staffelhöhe, keep along the trackside trail another 15 minutes to Rigi Kaltbad.

Chänzeli Detour: This detour from the station at Staffelhöhe adds 10 minutes to your Rigi Kaltbad travel time but is well worth it: From the station, veer off to the right, hiking out along one last ridge—flanked by fingers of Lake Luzern and with vistas in all directions. After passing a hilltop crucifix, you'll twist down on switchbacks to the concrete Chänzeli viewpoint (4,800 feet), with excellent views over Pilatus and Luzern. From here it's an easy and level 10-minute walk to Rigi Kaltbad's cable-car station.

Alpkäserei Chäserenholz Route: With a little more time, consider the fun Alpkäserei Chäserenholz (alpine dairy) route from Rigi Kulm down to Rigi Kaltbad (about 1.5 hours), which offers a chance to sample some mountain cheese at a working farm. From the Rigi Kulm train station, walk in the opposite direction from the restaurant—alongside the long barn-like structure at the head of the tracks. From here, follow the unpaved road steeply downhill about 15 minutes, following *Alpkäserei Chäserenholz* signs.

You'll reach a fork in the road, pointing right to the Staffel train station, or left down to the cheese hut. The alpine dairy has a simple menu of drinks and cheese specialties—which taste that much better a mile high, where they're made (cash only, usually open daily in season 9:00-18:00—off-season, confirm it's open before hiking down; tel. 041-855-0206, chaeserenholz@bluewin.ch). After visiting the hut, hike a steep 5-10 minutes back up to the crossroads, and turn left, following *Staffel* signs another 20 minutes to Staffel—on a gravel road, passing through bucolic farmland with mountain views. At the big white tents, fork off to the right to head up to the Staffel station. From here, you can either hop on the train, or walk the rest of the way to Rigi Kaltbad and the cable car station (follow directions above, under **"Classic Rigi Kulm to Rigi Kaltbad Hike"**). If you're ambitious, add in the Chänzeli detour from Staffel on your way back to the cable car.

Alpkäserei Chäserenholz Extension: For a longer hike from the alpine dairy, continue down Rigi's "back" ridge to the alpine hut **Obere Schwändihütte,** then across the mountain to the Klösterli stop, where you can visit the cute Chapel of Maria-of-the-Snow before hopping on the cogwheel train (1.5 hours from the summit to Klösterli stop). You can also hike along sections of the Mark Twain trail, which traces his route up the mountain (as described in *A Tramp Abroad*), with excerpts from his account signposted along the way.

BERN & MURTEN

Enjoy urban Switzerland in the charming, compact capital of Bern. Ramble the ramparts of Murten, Switzerland's best-preserved medieval town, and resurrect the ruins of an ancient Roman capital in nearby Avenches.

PLANNING YOUR TIME

On a quick trip, big Bern and little Murten—about a half-hour apart by train or car—are each worth a half-day. Either makes a fine day trip or overnight stop. Murten, while easy by train, is even better by car.

Bern is a convenient stop between other Swiss destinations (such as going from the Berner Oberland to Murten, Luzern, or Zürich). But a short taste of Bern may leave you wanting more. Consider spending a night (or two) to linger, explore, and savor its livability.

If you're day-tripping, stick your bag in a locker at the Bern station, spend a few hours taking my self-guided "Heart of Bern" walk and visiting some museums, then catch a late-afternoon train to your next stop. You could combine the destinations in this chapter by ending your busy Bern day in Murten, where you can spend the evening wandering the walls and savoring a lakeview dinner. In the morning, linger in Murten or move on to your next destination.

Bern

Stately but human, classy but fun, Switzerland's de facto capital is the most rewarding place to experience Swiss urbanity. Window-shop along streets lined with cozy, covered arcades, people-watch in the lively market square, and sip from your choice of colorful, historic fountains. Enjoy Bern's excellent museums, quaint-for-a-capital ambience, and delightful river scene. In this city (and canton), look for flags "bear-ing" the symbol of the local mascot: a roaring bear.

The city, founded in 1191, managed to avoid war damage and hasn't burned down since a great fire swept through in 1405. After the fire, wooden buildings were no longer allowed, and Bern took on its gray-green sandstone complexion (using stone quarried nearby). During its 12th- and 13th-century growth spurt, the town grew through two walls. Looking at the map of the city—contained within a bend of the Aare River—you can see how Bern started with a castle at the tip of the peninsula and expanded with a series of walls, each defending an ever-bigger city from its one land-accessible side. The clock tower marks the first wall (1218). A generation later, another wall was built (in 1256, at today's prison tower). The final wall—where today's train station sits—was built in 1344.

In 1353, the surrounding canton (also called Bern) became the eighth to join the Swiss Federation. Today, Canton Bern is Switzerland's second-largest, both in area (after Graubünden) and population (after Zürich). Since 1848, the city of Bern has been Switzerland's seat of government. It's small for a capital (140,000 people, or 360,000 with the suburbs—two-thirds Protestant and one-third Catholic). Though firmly German-speaking, it's strategically located near French-speaking regions, and you'll also hear French around town.

Bern's pointy towers, sandstone buildings, colorful fountains, and riverside setting make it one of Europe's finest surviving medieval towns. Albert Einstein, artist Paul Klee, and a trio of real, live mascot bears are among the famous Bernese who've contributed to the inviting character of this wonderfully livable small city. And more than 18,000 students help keep Bern young and frisky, despite all the government ministries and bureaucrats.

Orientation to Bern

User-friendly Bern is packed into a peninsula bounded by the Aare River. The train station is located where the peninsula connects to the mainland. From there, a handy main drag leads gradually downhill, straight through the middle of town past most of the major sights, to the tip of the peninsula (then across a bridge and finally to the Bear Park and a hilltop rose garden). Allow a leisurely 30 minutes to walk from the station to the Bear Park following my self-guided walk, later in this chapter.

Tourist Information: The main TI is on the ground floor inside the **train station** (daily 9:00-19:00, Sun until 18:00, tel. 031-328-1212, www.bern.com). A second TI is near the **Bear Park,** inside the Old Tram Depot (unpredictable hours but likely daily 11:00-16:00, Nov-March Fri-Sun only). If you don't have a Swiss Museum Pass and plan to do some serious sightseeing, ask at a TI about the Museum Card, which covers the main sights in town (28 CHF/24 hours, 35 CHF/48 hours).

ARRIVAL IN BERN

By Train: Bern's bustling train station is a thriving three-story mall. The trains almost get lost. The lower level—where the trains arrive—has pay WCs (with showers), a Co-op grocery store, a big Migros takeaway deli, and lots of other long-hours, takeout eateries. The ground floor has the TI, train ticket office (Mon-Fri 6:45-21:00, Sat-Sun until 20:00), and lockers (down a corridor behind the TI). And on the upper level, you'll find another Migros grocery store and a long-hours pharmacy (daily 6:30-22:00).

On arrival, follow signs to exit to *Bahnhofplatz.* Trams and buses fan out from under the glass canopy on this square (use the electronic board and posted maps to find the correct lettered stall—or *perron*—for your bus or tram). While most of my recommended sights and accommodations are within walking distance, hopping a bus or tram can be smart (and, with the Bern Ticket provided by your hotel, it's free; your lodging confirmation serves as your transit ticket until you get the card at check-in).

By Car: The old town is essentially car-free (only service vehicles and public transit allowed), so leave your car outside of town. While expensive, the most convenient place to park is at the huge garage behind the station: From the A-1, exit for *Bern Zentrum* signs, then follow *Bahnhof* and *Bahnhof Parking* (3 CHF/hour, 36 CHF/day, www.parking-bern.ch). From here, you're just an elevator ride away from the TI and the start of my self-guided walk. For cheaper parking (especially if staying longer), consider the park-and-ride at the Neufeld exit (2 CHF/hour, 18 CHF/day, includes bus ride to the station). Another affordable option—if you're day-tripping to Bern and want to visit the Paul Klee Center—is to park there all day (until midnight) for 7 CHF, then hop on bus #12 into the town center.

HELPFUL HINTS

Blue Monday: Most of Bern's museums are closed on Mondays. But you can still follow my self-guided walk, tour the cathedral (and climb its tower), tour the Zytglogge-Turm, watch the parliament in action (generally possible Mon afternoons), ogle the beasts at Bear Park, and go for a swim in the river.

Market: An outdoor market with clothes, gifts, and other merchandise fills Waisenhausplatz at the north end of Bärenplatz several times per week (Jan-Nov Tue 9:00-18:00 and Sat until 17:00, plus April-Oct Thu 9:00-18:00, www.marktbern.ch).

Bookstore: A block from the train station, **Stauffacher** is huge, with an entire floor of English books, including a fine selection of writing on Switzerland, and a café (Mon-Fri 9:00-19:00, Thu until 20:00, Sat until 17:00, closed Sun, Neuengasse 37—for location see the "Bern Hotels & Restaurants" map, later, tel. 031-313-6363, www.stauffacher.ch).

Laundry: A five-minute walk from the train station, **Wash Bar** is a trendy bar that also has self-service laundry machines (daily 9:00-23:30, Schanzenstrasse 1, tel. 031-310-0666). **Jet Wash,** another self-service launderette, is a three-stop bus ride from the train station (Mon-Sat 7:00-21:00, Sun 9:00-18:00, take bus #20 from platform G in front of station to the Lorraine stop, then find Dammweg 43 on the left, mobile 077-417-9502, www.jetwash.ch). For locations, see the "Bern Hotels & Restaurants" map, later.

GETTING AROUND BERN

The city is walkable, though its buses and trams can be handy. For short rides of up to five stops—such as between the train station and Bear Park—buy a *Kurzstreckebillet* (short-stretch ticket, 2.60 CHF). For longer journeys—such as going all the way out to the Paul Klee Center—you'll need an *Einzelbillett* (standard single ticket, 4.60 CHF). A day pass is 13 CHF (buy tickets from touch-screen machines at stops, credit cards accepted, info at tel. 031-321-8844, www.bernmobil.ch). All public transit in Bern is also covered by the Swiss Travel Pass. And if you're overnighting here, your hotel or hostel will give you a Bern Ticket that covers local transit. Be sure to ask for it at check-in.

Tours in Bern

Walking Tours

These leave daily from April through October at 11:00 from the TI at the train station (off-season Sat only, 1.5 hours, 25 CHF, call the day before to confirm schedule and ensure the guide speaks English). The TI also offers a four-hour **iPod audioguide** (18 CHF). Both tours are half-price with a Swiss Travel Pass.

Local Guide

Marie-Therese Lauper is a charming and hardworking independent guide who offers special rates for individuals and small groups (mobile 079-700-0880, www.bern-guide.ch).

Denise O'Gorman Abersold is another excellent guide (book through Bern TI and request her, 300 CHF/2-hour tour, info@bern.com).

Heart of Bern Walk

Follow this self-guided walk to explore central Bern. You'll start at the train station and finish at the Bear Park at the far end of town, where you can catch a bus back to the station. Along the way, visit a bakery or supermarket to put together a picnic, which you can eat at a terrace behind the cathedral or near Bear Park. (I'll point out a good cheese shop, too.)

❶ Train Station

The station is essentially a bright and airy shopping mall, with a TI and all the shops you could need. For a grand perch, ride the escalator to the top floor directly above the red circle benches. The huge board listing departures illustrates why so many Swiss urbanites choose not to own a car.

With your back to the big departures board, step outside onto the big square called Bahnhofplatz. The old town was sealed off here with a fortified wall, which was replaced in the 19th century by the train station.

Cross the street to the big glass canopy. Bern's vision is to create a carless city. The striking glass-topped transit hub, designed by renowned Spanish architect Santiago Calatrava, makes riding the bus or tram a bit more elegant.

On the left of the square stands the **Holy Ghost Church** (Heiliggeistkirche). Notice the gray-green Bernese sandstone, used for the church and surrounding buildings. Because this stone is porous and easily eroded by water, Bern's buildings are designed with characteristic oversize eaves. To maintain architectural harmony, even newer buildings (like these) are required to be built with the same local stone (though generally just a thin veneer).

• *Turn left onto the street that runs in front of the church, called Spitalgasse. This marks the start of one long street (with four names). The spine of both the peninsula and our walk, this street rambles downhill through the heart of town to the bridge and Bear Park.*

About 100 yards down the street, you'll reach the first of Bern's 11 Renaissance **fountains,** the Bagpiper. These colorful 16th-century fountains—mostly by the same artist—are Bern's trademark. The city commissioned them for many reasons: to brighten the cityscape, to show off the town's wealth, and to remind citizens of great local heroes and events. The fountains also gave 16th-century artists something to work on after the Reformation deprived them of their most important patron, the Catholic Church. Evenly spaced throughout town, the fountains naturally became community gathering places—the spot to get the latest neighborhood news and gossip.

Shopping opportunities abound under the more than three miles of arcades that line Bern's lanes. Stores run the gamut from affordable to high-end (generally open 9:00-18:30, Thu until 21:00, Sat until 16:00, closed Sun). In German, the slang for the corridor under these arcades is *Rohr* (pipe). To stroll through the town is to *rohren* (go piping).

• *Continue* "rohren" *down Spitalgasse until you reach...*

❷ Bärenplatz

The street runs under the **Prison Tower** (Käfigturm)—once a part of the city wall (c. 1256). Renovated in the 1640s, the tower served as a prison until 1897 (*Käfig* means "cage"). Notice how the hand on the clock really is a hand—and how it was built in a slower-paced era, when just an hour hand told time precisely enough. The bears on the tower are part of Bern's coat of arms (with the double-eagle reminder that Bern was part of the Holy Roman Empire in

Bern

KULTURZENTRUM REITHALLE

MUSEUM OF FINE ARTS

Aare River

Grosse Schanze

WALK BEGINS

TRAIN STATION ❶

MAIN POST

#12 Ⓑ Bahnhof-platz

HOLY GHOST

NEUENGASSE

GENFERGASSE

HODLERSTR

AARBERGERG.

Waisen-haus-platz

FRANZ.-KIRCHE

CAFE DES PYRÉNÉES

ZEUGHAUS

PASTRIES

KNIFE SHOP

CHEESE SHOP

BRUNNGA

Kornhaus-platz ❻

SPITALGASSE

Bubenberg-platz

LOEB DEPT STORE

Bären-platz

MARKTGASSE

PRISON TOWER ❷

ZYTGLOGGE (CLOCK TOWER) ❼

MÜNSTERGASS

Bundes-platz

AMTHAUSGASSE

KOCHERGASSE

PARLIAMENT ❸

ROOFS HERREN-

CASIN ❺

SCHANZENSTR.

LAUPENSTR.
← To Murten & Lausanne

HIRSCHEN-GRABEN

BUNDESGASSE

LAUPENSTR.

❹

KIRCHENFELD BRIDGE

FUNICULAR BUNDESBAHN

WEIHEGASSE

DALMAZI BRIDGE

KUNSTHALL MUSEUM

Helvetia-platz

ALPINE MUSEUM

HISTORICA EINSTEIN MUSEUM

MARZILI

SULGENECKSTRASSE

MARZILISTRASSE

BRÜCKENSTRASSE

AEGERTENSTR.

MARZILIBAD (POOL & RIVER BATHS)

NATIONAL HISTORY MUSEUM

To start of swim ↓

the early Middle Ages). You'll see many, many bears, depicted all throughout this walk—and live bears await you at the end.

As each of the town's successive walls and moats was torn down, Bern was left with an elongated swath of land that's now a people-friendly "square" like this one. **Bärenplatz** is a top place to be seen in the evening. It was named for the bear pits that filled a ditch here, back when this was beyond the town center.

Head to the left 50 yards to find the **Dutch Tower** (Holländerturm). Swiss soldiers were famous mercenaries—guns for hire

Heart of Bern Walk

1 Train Station
2 Bärenplatz
3 Parliament
4 Terraces
5 Kirchenfeld Bridge
6 Kornhausplatz
7 Zytglogge-Turm

8 Kramgasse Shops & Einstein House
9 Bern Cathedral
10 Münsterplattform
11 Junkerngasse
12 Nydegg Bridge
13 Bear Park
14 Old Tram Depot

who fought all over Europe. Returning from a battle in the Netherlands, the soldiers brought back the habit of smoking. But in the 18th century, smoking tobacco was forbidden within the city walls of Bern, so they hid in this tower to smoke discreetly. Locals joke that now that a new, modern-day smoking ban has come to Bern, this tower may regain its historic function.

Farther along, about 100 yards down at the far end of the square, find the modern, mossy **fountain** by the Swiss surrealist Meret Oppenheim. Made in 1983, it symbolizes growth and life, and is supposed to demonstrate communication between an object of art and the beholder. It worked well...too well, in fact, as most citizens immediately communicated their dislike and wanted it destroyed. But Bern's politicians proved braver than expected, and the fountain survived. Time has transformed Oppenheim's gray concrete column into a multicolored pillar decorated with moss, grass, and flowers. Residents do like it in the winter, when it's covered with ice. The grand building beyond the fountain—once the city orphanage—is the police station.

At the end of the square near the fountain, notice lots of public seating, as well as ping-pong tables and a piano available to play. Bern is working hard to make its stately streets more inviting—partly to encourage tourists like you to visit for more than just a few hours. On the nearby corner (with Zeughausgasse), look for the **Glatz** pastry shop; they invented their own local cookie, the *Berner Mandelbärli* ("Bern Almond Bear").

Art lovers can detour just a couple of blocks to the left (as you face the fountain) to reach Bern's concise **Museum of Fine Arts,** with one or two quality paintings by virtually all of the great European masters...plus some Swiss artists mixed in (described later, under "Sights in Bern").

With your back to the modern fountain, stroll a few blocks back down to the south end of Bärenplatz. Most mornings except Sunday, this area thrives with market stalls selling local produce, bread, flowers, sausages, cheeses, and other goodies. Farther down, closer to another fountain, are some tempting food carts. Brick-and-mortar restaurants also line the square (see "Eating in Bern," later). Old-timers play giant chess under the trees, and a massive underground parking lot hides under your feet.

• *Just past the end of Bärenplatz looms a giant building. This is the...*

❸ Parliament (Bundeshaus)

You may brush elbows with some high-powered legislators, but you wouldn't know it—everything looks very casual for a national capital. Like so much else in Bern, the parliament building is made of that distinctive green-gray sandstone; because it's recently been cleaned, this gives you a look at the color in its purest form. When Switzerland became a modern nation in 1848, Bern became the seat of government for two main reasons: It straddles the German and French parts of the country, and the city offered to build all of the necessary buildings. Look right.

Look left. This entire chunk of Bern's hilltop is federally owned—including the super-swanky, five-star Bellevue Palace Hotel just up the street to the left, where visiting dignitaries stay. (Legally, Switzerland does not have a "capital"—Bern is simply the seat of government, and the de facto "Federal City," or *Bundesstadt*. But that's a whole other story...)

Check out the building's **statuary:** The woman on the top of the building represents political independence, the one on the left (under the *1291*—when the first three cantons bound together to found the nucleus of Switzerland) stands for freedom, and the one on the right (under *1848*—when the people got their constitution assuring democracy) symbolizes peace.

Switzerland's bicameral system was inspired by the US Constitution, with one big difference: Executive power is shared by a committee of seven, with a rotating ceremonial president and a passion for consensus. This is a mechanism to avoid power grabs by any single individual...a safeguard that the Swiss love (and enjoy bragging about lately).

The fine granite **plaza** in front of the parliament (built in 2004 to replace a parking lot) is a favorite spot for demonstrations and markets. On Tuesday and Saturday mornings, it hosts a higher-end market than the one we just saw on Bärenplatz—where the choosiest chefs come to source their ingredients. Hidden in the pavement is a 26-squirt fountain (one for each canton)—a real kid-pleaser (and makes for fun photos) on a hot summer day. On the left is the Swiss National Bank—this country's Fort Knox, with half the Swiss gold stock buried under the square (the rest is in Zürich).

Touring the Parliament: When parliament is in session, the **galleries** are open to the public, so you can watch the action (free; generally Mon afternoon, Tue and Thu mornings, and all day Wed; leave ID at entrance, lines can be long, no photos). When parliament is not in session, you can take a free, guided, hour-long **tour** of the building (English tours normally mid-July-mid-Aug Mon-Sat at 14:00, Sat only off-season, no tours early Sept-early Oct; reserve up to 3 days ahead at www.parlament.ch—click "Services" then "Visiting the Parliament Building," tel. 058-322-9022). To enter for either of these, find the entrance around back of the building, from the terraces.

• *Walk through the passageway to the right of the parliament. You'll pop out overlooking Bern's outskirts from a series of...*

❹ Terraces

From here, you have a commanding view over the outskirts of Bern. Below you flows the Aare River—fed by glaciers, which give it its bright-blue sheen. On a hot day, the river is speckled with locals doing the "Bern float." On the right side of the river, look for

Bern's biggest swimming pool, the **Marzilibad.** Just this side of the pool complex, notice the canal that cuts away from the river. This was dug recently to allow a safer exit for swimmers floating down the river (before, they had to grab for a pole along the riverbank as they floated past).

Just above the river is Bern's own little "mountain," the **Gurten** (with the view tower poking up above its forested summit). The Gurten is the city's favorite recreation spot, offering a luge ride and music festivals in summer and modest skiing opportunities for children in winter. To frolic with the Bernese, you can either hike up or ride a little funicular to the summit (take tram #9 to Wabern/Gurtenbahn, then ride the funicular from there).

Pan to the left, where, on a clear day, you can see the mirage-like outlines of the **Eiger, Mönch, and Jungfrau**—the highest peaks in the Berner Oberland. (The prickly, chalet-style building just in front of these peaks holds Bern's Albert Einstein Museum and its Historical Museum—described later.) They're easily reached on the opposite side of the bridge we're about to visit.

Before moving on, look back at the rounded end of the Parliament building; up high, see the colorful seals of the 26 cantons of Switzerland.

• *Turn left and stroll along the terrace walls a few hundred yards to...*

❺ Kirchenfeld Bridge

Walk out to the center of the bridge for great views back on Bern's cathedral and town center—lined up along its promontory, and hemmed in by the Aare River. Directly below, notice the security nets. The bridge used to be the favorite place for suicides—to the terror of people living below. Bern has many high bridges, and you'll see this safety netting on all of them.

Look down at the **dam** that runs across the river below you. (Wait—is that a bear out on the dam?) The waterfall here was natural, but a system of modern sluices better controls the flow. Even so, Bern was deluged with dangerous floods until 2005, when a new canal was built upriver—allowing high waters to be diverted harmlessly. Just this side of the dam is the recommended **Schwellenmätteli Restaurant lounge,** where a trendy local crowd enjoys cocktails over the rushing river on nice days. By the way, the Aare begins in the mountains and flows through Interlaken; after leaving Bern, it continues north and joins the Rhine in Basel.

If you continued along this bridge to its far end, you'd reach a sprawling complex of museums (described later, under "Sights in Bern"); if you're planning to visit any of them, you can do it now.

Otherwise, turn around and head back the way you came. At the base of the bridge, the **Casino** isn't for gamblers—it's the home of Bern's Symphony Orchestra, and also hosts graduation ceremonies and wedding receptions. Step into the lobby, then bear right to ogle the vast, opulent café that fills a newly restored Neoclassical gallery. The outdoor terrace here serves coffee for not much more than other local cafés.

• *Leaving the bridge and the river behind you, follow the tram tracks around the left side of the handsome sandstone house up to another swath of land created by the removal of a city wall—to Theaterplatz, and then to...*

❻ Kornhausplatz

This square is ornamented by the colorful fountain of an **Ogre** (*Chindlifresser,* "child-eater"). Two legends try to explain this gruesome sight. It's either a folkloric representation of the Greek god Chronos, or a figure that was intended to scare children off the former city walls.

Kornhausplatz is a major hub for **tram** traffic—which ground to a halt in the summer of 2019, when record-high temperatures actually warped the tram tracks, making them unsafe. Living in a mountain nation of receding glaciers, rockslides, and avalanches, the Swiss feel the tangible, everyday effects of climate change. Climate issues are huge in Swiss politics. The country has several environmental parties, and in October 2019 elections, they combined to win an unprecedented 20 percent of available parliament seats. Meanwhile, Switzerland's far-right, nativist movement has faltered because they've been caught flat-footed on climate issues. (Apparently, even Swiss racists have a soft spot for the environment.)

The building behind the Ogre, on the left, used to be the granary and now houses the modern public library and the huge recommended **Kornhauskeller** restaurant. If the restaurant is open, wander down the stairs and head inside—even if you're not eating here, you must take a peek at this magnificent subterranean place. Once the vast city wine cellar—now a recommended restaurant—this space was built in high Baroque style (1718) and renovated with paintings inspired by the Pre-Raphaelites in 1897. The 12 columns (in the upper level) show traditional costumes of Bernese women. Across the street from the Kornhauskeller, notice the **Café des Pyrénées**. This was a hotspot for Bern's avant-garde in the 1960s; the gray-ponytail crowd still hangs out here today.

Head up the little street next to the café, Rathausgasse, to reach two quality shops selling classic Swiss items (both on the left). First up, at #84, **Klötzli Messerschmiede** sells a wide range of top-quality **knives**—from touristy Swiss Army models, to heirloom-quality pocketknives, to professional chef's knives. Tucked behind the cash register is a special room with a suit of armor and real swords.

Next door at #82, **Zur Chäshütte** is a classic Swiss village cheese shop—smack-dab in the big city. Step inside, take a big whiff of the funky aroma, and peruse the well-stocked display case. With more than 150 types of cheese, you may want to buy a few slabs for your picnic. Rezent means strong, pungent, and well-aged, while mitte is a bit milder. Consider buying a combination: a hard, aged cheese (their "house cheese"—Hauskäse—is aged in the cellar below your feet); a more typical, semi-mild Swiss cheese (such as Gruyère, Emmentaler, or the more intense Appenzeller); a goat-milk cheese (Geiss); or perhaps a softer, French-style, brie-like cheese. They also sell yogurt, honey, and jam.

• *Just past the cheese shop, turn right one short block down Zibelegässli. You'll run right into Bern's main landmark...*

❼ Zytglogge-Turm

Bern's famous clock tower was part of the original wall marking the first gate to the city (c. 1250). The clock, which dates back to 1530, performs four minutes before each hour: The happy jester comes to life, Father Time turns his hourglass, the rooster crows (in German, that's "kee-kee-ree-kee" rather than "cock-a-doodle-doo"), and the golden man on top hammers the bells. Apparently, this little spectacle was considered quite entertaining five centuries ago. The word *Zytglogge* is local dialect. The Standard German equivalent, which doesn't actually exist, would be *Zeitglocke* (literally "time bell").

To pass the time waiting for the action, read the plaque explaining what's so interesting about the fancy old clock (for example, the golden hour hand is an hour behind for half the year because of the modern innovation of Daylight Saving Time). You can determine the zodiac, today's date, and the phase of the moon—look at the black-and-gold orb.

Inside the tunnel under the clock are the old regional measurements (Swiss foot, the bigger Bernese foot, and the *Elle*, or "elbow," which was the distance from the elbow to the fingertip) and the official meter and double meter. It took a strong leader like Napoleon to bring consistency to measurements in Europe; he replaced the many goofy feet and elbows of medieval Europe with the metric system used today (c. 1800).

Touring the Tower: Enthusiasts can tour the medieval internal mechanics—early Swiss engineering at its best—and see the bellows that enable the old rooster to crow (20 CHF, half off with

Swiss Travel Pass, 50-minute tour, April-Oct daily at 14:30, off-season Sat only, buy ticket at the door).

• *With the clock at your back, continue your stroll down the main drag. At this point, you enter the oldest part of town, where bigger department stores are replaced by quainter shops and galleries on...*

❽ Kramgasse

Bern has wide streets like this one, but not many true squares. In the Middle Ages, craftsmen exhibited their goods on the side-

walks under simple roofs. Eventually, these were formalized, buildings were expanded, and arcades evolved. Today, though the **arcades** are privately owned, owners must keep them clean and allow public access. Then as now, the main activity here is shopping—*kramen* means, roughly, to shop for an assortment of items ("rummage" would be the closest translation). Pop-up stores are popular in Bern—up-and-coming vendors can lease a space for six months to test the market.

Most shops are underneath the arcades, but don't miss the ones in the **cellars** that you can access only from the main road. The cellars, marked by old-time hatches, were originally for storing household goods, and later, wine. The city's water was often contaminated, so people mixed water with wine—or drank only wine. The wine was produced in Lausanne on Lake Geneva, which was then controlled by Bern—so they sent ample amounts of wine here as tribute. People said "merry Bern" was floating on wine, just as Venice was floating on water. The merry times ended in 1798, when Napoleon's army moved in (and drank all the wine). The cellars were once again used for household goods, and the city got a new nickname: "sad Bern." Napoleon's soldiers also looted Bern's tremendous treasury, and Napoleon used money from Bern to finance his Egyptian crusade.

In the middle of the street is the **Zähringen Fountain.** It's named for the German duke, Berthold V, the Duke of Zähringen, who founded Bern in 1191. Legend says he couldn't decide on the name, so he went hunting, proclaiming that he'd name the city for the first animal he killed. It was, of course, a *Bär* (bear)—and Bern had its name. Notice the armor-clad bear is holding a flag not of a bear, but of a lion—the family crest of the Zähringers.

Directly in front of and behind the fountain, a **grate** reveals a bit of the canal that used to flow open down the middle of the peninsula, providing people with a handy disposal system, place to wash, and the medieval equivalent of a fire hose. Today, the water that pours from the fountains' spouts is perfectly potable—locals love to brag about the quality of their water. Fill up your bottle and save a few francs.

By the way, although this feels like a pedestrian zone, buses and occasional cars do tend to sneak up on distracted tourists—stay alert. The bus that uses this street—#12—is practically made for visitors, connecting the train station to the Paul Klee Center by way of the main drag...handy to hop on and off at will.

• *Now head down Kramgasse. On the right at #73, chocolate lovers will want to peek into* **Confiserie Tschirren**—*the top-end chocolatier and pastry shop in Bern.*

Keep going. About 200 yards down, on the right at #49, is the home of a very smart man.

The apartment that Albert Einstein called home between 1903 and 1905—the years when he formulated his special theory of relativity while working in obscurity at the Patent Office—is now the **Einstein House** museum (6 CHF; daily 10:00-17:00, closed late Dec-Jan; tel. 031-312-0091, www.einstein-bern.ch). Einstein and his wife Mileva welcomed their first child in this one-bedroom apartment, and shared a kitchen and bathroom with the neighbors. Inside, you can see period furniture, including Einstein's Patent Office desk, and a few photos and manuscripts. Another apartment one floor up has been turned into an informative—if dry—exhibit on Einstein's life. This quick, inexpensive visit (well-described in English with a few historic artifacts and a 20-minute video—request English) is just about the right amount of Einstein for most visitors. It doesn't do much for me, but I guess everything's relative.

If this little exhibit piques your interest, consider also visiting the Einstein Museum's far more extensive exhibit (triple the price but free with Swiss Travel Pass), located within Bern's Historical Museum (see "More Sights in Bern," later in this chapter).

A bit farther down, you reach the **Samson fountain.** In the statue on top, notice the donkey's jawbone tucked into Samson's waistband. This is the symbol of the butcher's guild, which was located just to the left, in what is today the music conservatory. Notice how close this fountain is to the previous one. It's believed that the butchers financed this fountain specifically to have one next to their slaughterhouse.

Near the fountain on the right, in the cellar of #37, is **Hanftheke Bern** (*hanf* means hemp), a marijuana shop. In Switzerland, marijuana with less than 1 percent THC (the psychoactive component of cannabis) is legal. This strain is high in cannabidiols, which make you very relaxed...but you can't get high on it. The person behind the counter is happy to explain the local approach to pot.

• *Twenty yards below the Samson fountain, at #29, turn right through the narrow tunnel-lane, Münstergässchen, to the...*

❾ Bern Cathedral (Berner Münster)

Bern's 15th-century Catholic-turned-Protestant cathedral is capped with a 330-foot-tall tower, the highest in Switzerland (finished in 1893). The late-Gothic church was dedicated to St. Vincent of Zaragoza.

Before heading into the church, if it's Tuesday or Saturday, head up the street to your right (Münstergasse) to find a thriving market—this one specializing in meat. At #41 (on the left), look way up high to see a rusted-metal sculpture sticking out from the roofline. This is called **Roofspit,** and it shoots a spurt of water down onto the street below a few times each minute (it's turned off during the market). Notice the 5-CHF coins permanently stuck in the pavement where the water splashes, luring suckers to bend over to grab a coin—and get wet. Who says the Swiss don't have a sense of humor?

Return to the cathedral, and get up close to the **main portal,** with its striking gold-leaf highlights. This seems pretty un-Protestant; it probably survived because its theme, the Last Judgment, showed that no matter how rich you are or what rank you have in Church hierarchy, anyone can end up in hell (an idea Protestants dug). Condemned people are popping in the flames like lottery balls. Notice the humorous details in the commotion of people heading to hell (especially what the little green devil is doing to the sinful monk). Just below on the left are statues of the virtuous virgins (dressed like Bern burghers), while on the right are the foolish virgins who squandered their oil (dressed like the city's historic rivals, the Burgundians).

Cost and Hours: Free to enter cathedral; Mon-Sat 10:00-17:00, Sun from 11:30; mid-Oct-April Mon-Fri 12:00-16:00, Sat 10:00-17:00, Sun 11:30-16:00; audioguide-5 CHF, tel. 031-312-0462, www.bernermuenster.ch.

Visiting the Church: Step inside and grab a pew in the nave. The plain interior was once adorned with 26 separate little chapels and altars dedicated to Mary and various saints. An ornate screen separated the priests from the worshippers. But when the Reformation came to town in 1528, all this was swept away. The iconoclasts believed that images distracted worshippers from focusing on God, so they destroyed the distasteful decoration. The new center of attention was the pulpit, where Protestant preachers shared the word of God—not in Latin, but in the people's language.

Those Protestant iconoclasts didn't manage to trash the church's precious painted keystones. Look up to the ceiling, where you can see giant, colorful coats of arms. These don't honor saints,

Albert Einstein in Bern

The man who changed how we see our universe made his greatest discoveries during the eight years he lived in Bern (1901-1909).

Raised in Germany, Albert Einstein (1879-1955) went to college in Zürich, hoping to land a job teaching math and physics. But the young grad's GPA and résumé were mediocre, so instead he took a job in Bern's Patent Office, inspecting and registering inventions.

Twenty-three-year-old Albert and his new bride Mileva (his brainy college sweetheart) rented a second-floor apartment at Kramgasse 49 (today's Einstein House), where Mileva soon gave birth to their first son, little Hans Albert. Einstein punched the clock at the Patent Office and spent his spare time reading, hiking the Bernese countryside, and thinking. At night, he'd join with his mates—the self-named "Olympia Academy"—to smoke, drink beer, and talk math and philosophy. Outwardly, he led an ordinary life, but his thoughts were always on science's Big Questions. At home, in pubs, or at work he'd scribble down equations and ideas, filing them in his self-described "Department of Theoretical Physics"—a desk drawer in his office.

Then, one warm spring day, as Einstein walked on the outskirts of Bern, it all started coming together. So began his *annus mirabilis*—the miracle year of 1905—in which the 26-year-old amateur physicist wrote five papers that would shock and perplex the world. Published in a major physics journal, they touched on subjects such as how molecules move and how light can appear as either a wave of energy or as a beam of tiny particles.

The most famous and unsettling paper, his theory of special relativity, described a world in motion. A person on a moving train and someone who's stationary see the world from different perspectives—that's the classic principle of relativity described by Galileo and Newton. But Einstein said there's an exception to the rule—light, whose speed remains constant whether it's on a moving train or on the ground. So a person on a moving train and one at rest won't agree on what they see...yet they're both right. The

but prestigious Bernese families. Notice that this church isn't a "Cathedral" (that's in Lausanne), but a *Münster*. The local burghers actively discouraged having their church be named a cathedral, because then they'd have a bishop in town, bossing them around. The Bernese burghers remained independent; this church was sometimes called the people's church *(Leutkirche)*.

For another bit of decoration that the iconoclasts missed, head discrepancies only become obvious as the train travels close to the speed of light. Then, while the person on the train thinks everything is normal, the one on the ground sees the train shrink, train clocks slow down, and the person on the train stops aging!

Einstein's papers initially drew little interest and a measure of skepticism. But over time, other physicists grasped the significance of Einstein's work, seeing how he took earlier findings, wove them together, and did the math that explained it all. Subsequent experiments proved that even Einstein's most bizarre assertions were correct. Time on a fast-moving jet really does slow down (hence, those interminable intercontinental flights).

Einstein was invited to lecture at the local university, though he was still working nine-to-five at the Patent Office. In his spare time, he worked on his next project, general relativity. He theorized that gravity is not a force that attracts things but a curving of space—like a bowling ball on a soft mattress—that affects the motion of nearby objects. In 1909, Einstein's growing reputation won him a job offer to teach in Zürich, and he quit the Patent Office and left Bern for good.

Einstein would never again approach the creative level of his days in Bern. (In 1922, he won the Nobel Prize for his work done during the 1905 *annus mirabilis.*) Albert and Mileva split, and he married a cousin. When Hitler took power in Germany (1933), Einstein—a pacifist and a Jew—left Europe for America. His curly black hair had turned white, and his aging face later became a pop-culture icon of genius—complete with pipe, moustache, basset-hound eyes, and halo of frizzy white hair (which he backcombed in order to look sufficiently unkempt).

In 1939, Einstein wrote a letter to President Franklin Delano Roosevelt warning that scientists (including some in Germany) could soon discover a way to release an enormous amount of energy. The research was based on a principle he'd outlined back in 1905—that energy is equivalent to mass times the speed of light squared (a very big number). And so, $E = mc^2$ became the principle behind the atomic bomb—a very big bang from an idea hatched in the pubs and arcaded streets of Bern.

To learn more, visit the Einstein House in the town center and the Einstein Museum just across the river (both described in this chapter).

to the third glassed-in chapel on the right. High on the far wall (to the left of the window), you can see a bit of an angel's halo; just to the left of this, you can very faintly see an image of Mary kneeling. This was likely a scene of the Annunciation. Historians are using modern technology to uncover pre-iconoclasm art like this.

Continue on to the end of the right aisle, and look right for a beautiful, colorful, highly entertaining stained-glass window (from the 1760s) illustrating the "dance of death"—the idea that no matter who you are, no matter how powerful or wealthy, death will still come for you. Spend some time appreciating each of the scenes of a macabre skeleton harassing a Bernese person.

Now head to the giant, black-marble altar under the transept. Look toward the apse; the three stained-glass panels on the left are original, from 1441. Now look up to the ceiling over the choir, where you'll see another 78 colorful keystone decorations, featuring saints and other Christian VIPs.

Climbing the Tower: You can pay 5 CHF to huff up the spiral staircase (over 300 steps) to a viewpoint at the base of the lacy see-through steeple (same hours as cathedral). From this 210-foot-high vantage point, you enjoy a behind-the-scenes look at the varied courtyards and rooftop gardens hidden behind the conformist building facades. Don't forget to turn around to appreciate an up-close look at the tower's carved figures. On the way down, peek at

the cathedral's **bells**—including the largest bell in Switzerland, a 10.5-ton beauty cast in 1611 and called Susanne (named by a bellringer after his sizeable girlfriend). This bell was so heavy that it took eight men to swing her. If you're up here when the Prayer Bell rings, you may feel the tower sway.

• *Head behind the cathedral to a terrace overlooking the river, the...*

⑩ Münsterplattform

Starting in the 14th century, this terrace was built from all kinds of "recycled" stones from older buildings. Archaeologists have even unearthed some heads of statues that were victims of Reformation iconoclasts.

Look out over the edge of the terrace for another view of the dam in the Aare below you. The base of the terrace, once overgrown, has recently been reclaimed and spiffed up to host many sweet little community gardens.

Twin 18th-century **pavilions** grace the square. On the right is a tiny branch of the city library (providing park-goers with books, *boules,* and table tennis). And in the far left is a café offering a scenic spot under a chestnut tree for a bite or a drink on a sunny day. Behind the café, the elevator (a "vertical tram") has been carrying passengers up and down since 1896 (1.20 CHF).

• *With your back to the river, exit on the right. Walking past the end of the cathedral, turn right and walk down...*

❶ Junkerngasse

Still the most expensive street to live on in Bern, this sleepy lane was lined with the mansions of the wealthy burghers of Bern—mostly on the right, facing out over the river. But you'd never know it since these mansions blend in with the simple townhouses nearby. The Bernese value thrift and hard work, and pride themselves in not showing off wealth ("That's for Zürich!" they snort).

At the end of the first block on the right is the **Erlacherhof**—a particularly fancy mansion, known as the only house in Bern with a courtyard. Today it's the mayor's residence.

Just past the building, on the right, notice the **stairs** leading through the wall and down to the river (marked *Bubenbergrain*). Historically, the lower-lying, riverside part of Bern was home to tradespeople: fishermen, tanners, and traders. But they needed to bring their wares up to market in the town, so several of these staircases were built. Notice that the steps are long and shallow—easier to traverse while hauling a big load.

A few steps past the Erlacherhof (and the fountain nearby), watch on the left for the tiny lane marked *Ob. Gerechtigkeitsgasse,* with a big sign for *Spysi*. Head down this little lane and look for a door halfway down on the right. This is **Spysi,** a sort of soup kitchen that was established during the Industrial Revolution. Many of the tradespeople who used the steps we just saw were replaced by modern factory jobs, leaving them poor and destitute. Spysi (from *speisen,* "to eat") offered them a very cheap meal. To this day, from November through April, down-on-their-luck Bernese people can get a big bowl of soup and a hunk of bread here for a few coins. Just past Spysi, notice the *pissoir*—a discrete public urinal for men.

At the end of the little lane, you pop out back on Bern's main drag—now called Gerechtigkeitsgasse. You're greeted by the **Fountain of Justice,** a blindfolded figure who triumphs over the mayor, pope, sultan, and Holy Roman Emperor. (Notice that Bern's mayor is depicted as being of equal status with these European powers.)

Turn right and carry on down the main drag, noticing that—as the terrain changes—the houses get narrower, and the cellar doors are vertical rather than horizontal. Remember that as you walk, you're going back in time, getting closer to the original (and oldest) core of town. The cellars along this stretch are a little less big-corporate and more funky and colorful, from the "Cave of Tango" to the "Seamen's Club."

Near the end of the street on the left, look for the Café Restaurant Treff. Notice the three **gutters** immediately in front—just like the channels we've seen all through town. Except...do you notice anything strange about this one? The middle one is running backward—uphill. This is an elaborate (but very subtle) prank: A hid-

BERN & MURTEN

den pump pushes the water backward, just to, y'know, mess with people. (Swiss humor strikes again!)

At the end of the street on the right, just before the bridge, look for the red *nette Toilet* **sign** on the window of the Junkere Café-Bar. The city government pays local bars to let the public use their WCs—so feel free to pop in and use the toilet.

• *From here, you reach...*

⑫ Nydegg Bridge

Head partway out onto the bridge and look left, where a church sits on the site of the original town castle. Notice the curve of the streets in this part of town: The outer curve follows the path of the original city wall, while the inner curve traces the wall that surrounded the castle. The small bridge below is the oldest in Bern (and, until 1844, was the only bridge crossing the Aare here). High on the ridge, just above the tollbooth's pointy spire, is the Rosengarten—a delightful garden with a grand view over Bern and a recommended restaurant (described in "Eating in Bern," later).

Now cross the bridge and look upstream. On the side of the tall white building, you can (barely) pick out the words *Fabrique de Chocolat W. Lindt*—the original Lindt chocolate factory, evoking an age when this stretch of river was lined with mills powering the industrial zone of Bern—tanneries, shipyards, lumber mills, and so on. As you look upstream, notice the peaceful path along the left bank, a nice place for a walk.

• *Continue across the bridge, bear right, and look over the railings into...*

⑬ Bear Park (BärenPark)

The symbol of Bern is the bear, and some lively ones frolic along this terraced hillside, to the delight of locals and tourists who crowd along the rails. From 1857 to 2009, Bern housed its mascot bears in two big, barren, concrete pits *(Bärengraben)*. But thanks to the agitation of the B.L.M. (Bear Liberation Movement), the city government was forced to replace the pits with posher digs. The last of the pit bears died in 2009, and later that year, three-year-old brown bears Finn (a male from Finland) and Björk (a female from Denmark) moved to the big enclosure between the old pits and the river. Soon they welcomed their female cubs, Ursina and Berna. This ursine family enjoys much better conditions than their fore-bears, including a private fishing channel next to the river. In 2013, the surly teenager Berna was sent to a preserve in Bulgaria due to irreconcilable differences with her mother. Today Bern's bear family is happy, and Berna is shacked up with a new boyfriend in Bulgaria.

The two historic pits are still there. The first one is used from time to time to hold the bears while their enclosure is cleaned. You can visit the second one—find the concrete stairs leading down to the Bären Bistro, a bear-themed bar (for more info, see www.tierpark-bern.ch).

• *Above Bear Park is the...*

⑩ Old Tram Depot (Altes Tramdepot)

This used to be the garage for trams that ran across the bridge from the old town. Now the depot hosts a brewery restaurant/café with a lively beer garden and terrace, as well as a TI, nice public WC, and Eiswerkstatt, a popular ice cream shop.

To continue this walk, you could take a seven-minute hike up the moderately steep, cobbled pathway to the left (with your back to the river). This takes you to the city's delightful **rose garden** (Rosengarten)—a manicured, picnic-perfect park with inviting benches, a fun kids' play area, and the best viewpoint in town for watching the sunset. It's also home to the recommended **Restaurant Rosengarten,** which offers a grand city view and grand prices.

Alternatively, you could turn right and walk along the river, then return to the center via either Kirchenfeld or Dalmazi bridge.

Or, to return directly to the **train station,** jump on bus #12 (every 6 minutes, get ticket from machine, covered by Swiss Travel Pass or hotel-issued Bern Ticket). For that matter, you could take bus #12 in the opposite direction to head out to the **Paul Klee Center**—just a few minutes' ride.

Wherever you wander in Bern, be sure to get off into the quieter side lanes, which have a fascinating and entertaining array of shops and little eateries.

More Sights in Bern

▲▲The Berner Float and Marzilibad

For something to write home about, join Bern's merchants, students, and carp in a float down the Aare River. The Bernese, proud of their very clean river and their basic ruddiness, have a tradition—sort of a wet, urban *paseo*. On summer days, they hike upstream 5 to 30 minutes, then float back down to the excellent (and free) riverside baths and pools (Marzilibad) just below the parliament building. The water—which originates in an alpine glacier—is clean, vivid blue, and very cold (it maxes out at about 65 degrees Fahrenheit, even in summer).

The process is simple: Hike up the paved riverside sidewalk as far as you like, then take the steps leading into the water whenever you want to "put in." As you approach Marzilibad, be ready to paddle your way over to the canal just beyond it—designed to catch floaters completing their trip. You can also try to grab one of the several poles placed to help people exit the river. The locals

make it look easy, but it can be dangerous—the current is swift. If you miss the last pole, you're history. The TI warns that this experience is only for strong, experienced swimmers.

If a float down the river is a bit much for you, simply enjoy the Marzilibad, a well-equipped public swimming pool and park with picnic spots, restaurant, lockers, wading pools, games, and more.

▲Museum of Fine Arts (Kunstmuseum Bern)

Featuring 800 years of art, this three-story museum shows off quality European and Swiss art, plus temporary exhibits. While the specific canvases can change, you'll typically find old masters from the 13th to 19th century (including Fra Angelico and Filippo Lippi); 19th-century Impressionist and Post-Impressionist art by Manet, Monet, Cézanne, Van Gogh, and Toulouse-Lautrec; and 20th-century works by Dalí, Picasso, and Miró. Each artist is represented by one or two fine pieces.

But the stars of the show are the lesser-known Swiss artists, who are mixed in among the big names as if to assert their worthiness on the global stage. Be sure to tune into some of these names: You'll find Paul Klee (1879-1940), of course, with his vivid, almost childlike works. But you'll also discover Adolf Wölfli (1864-1930), who did intricate collages with pencil on paper; Alberto Giacometti (1901-1966), who sculpted rough-textured figures; Ernst Ludwig Kirchner (1880-1938), whose big, colorful, sloppy canvases are reminiscent of Cézanne; Ferdinand Hodler (1853-1918), whose serene landscapes evoke Van Gogh, with bold lines and soothing colors; Pierre Bonnard (1867-1947), an Impressionist with a love of color and a Renoir-like flair; and Johannes Itten (1888-1967), who was influential in the Bauhaus movement and made huge strides in exploring the harmonious use of colors.

Cost and Hours: 10 CHF, extra for some temporary exhibits, covered by Swiss Travel Pass, Tue 10:00-21:00, Wed-Sun until 17:00, closed Mon, no English descriptions—rent the worthwhile English audioguide (6 CHF), café, 4 blocks north of station and just off the top of Bärenplatz at Hodlerstrasse 8, tel. 031-328-0944, www.kunstmuseumbern.ch.

BERN & MURTEN

▲▲Paul Klee Center (Zentrum Paul Klee)

With his wavy building mirroring the wavy landscape of the Bern countryside, Italian architect Renzo Piano celebrates the creative

spirit of the Swiss-born artist. Paul Klee wasn't just a great painter—he was an interdisciplinary explosion of creative energy. The center, which fosters music and theater as well as the visual arts, has a mission: to bring art to the people. For example, a huge zone is devoted to a children's creative workshop that includes painting and a shadow theater.

While it owns about 4,000 Klee works, the center has no permanent exhibit; rather, it curates engaging temporary exhibits that pull from its Klee collection—sometimes heavily, sometimes tangentially. (But the curators always make sure there are at least a few Klee pieces on display.) It's the best place in the world to experience and learn about this modernist painter of lively, almost childlike art. Artistically, you can't put Klee in a box. His paintings—mostly from the 1920s and 1930s—are playful yet enigmatic. His art is full of symbolism...or maybe we just think so. Kids love Klee, and they always teach the art snobs a thing or two with their interpretations.

You'll find the main exhibition space (with two large halls) in the middle of the three wings; the left wing has cafés, an art database, a movie about building the museum, a cozy hangout, and the children's workshop.

Cost and Hours: 20 CHF, covered by Swiss Travel Pass, Tue-Sun 10:00-17:00, closed Mon, heavily academic audioguide-6 CHF, pick up free English-language booklet for each exhibit, mandatory lockers, cafés, Monument im Fruchtland 3, tel. 031-359-0101, www.zpk.org.

Getting There: From the train station, ride frequent bus #12 (usually from platform L, at the far end of the Bahnhofplatz canopy on the right) for 15 minutes to its last stop, Zentrum Paul Klee, then walk five minutes up the path.

Parking: Museumgoers can park all day (until midnight) for 7 CHF—a great deal if you combine the museum visit with a trip into town afterward. Buy the ticket inside, at the ticket desk.

Children's Workshops: 15 CHF for 1-hour workshop (age 4 and older, Mon-Fri at 14:00 and 16:00, Sat-Sun also at 12:00, no reservations taken).

BERN & MÜRTEN

▲Einstein Museum (at Bern Historical Museum)

Fans of the genius will want to visit this museum devoted to Einstein and his times. For those with a keen interest in Einstein or his theories, it's worth ▲▲. This museum is far more engaging than the Einstein House downtown, and has many more artifacts from Einstein's life. But it's also very expensive—so unless you're a serious Einstein fan, or have a Swiss Travel Pass, it may not be worth the money. The Einstein exhibit fills the second floor of Bern's Historical Museum, the big, prickly, chateau-style Romantic building just across the Kirchenfeld Bridge from the old town. The rest of the museum—included in your ticket whether you want it or not—is an afterthought to the Einstein section (and skippable).

Cost and Hours: 18 CHF, covered by Swiss Travel Pass, Tue-Sun 10:00-17:00, closed Mon.

Getting There: It's across the Kirchenfeld Bridge from parliament at Helvetiaplatz 5—take tram #6, #7, or #8, or bus #19, or walk a scenic 10 minutes; tel. 031-350-7711, www.einsteinmuseum.ch.

Visiting the Museum: Buy your ticket and head up to the second floor. The final ascent—through a mirrored stairway—prepares your brain to expand your ideas about space and time. The exhibit uses photos, displays, and artifacts to thoughtfully trace Einstein's entire life span—from his birth in Germany, to his education in Zürich and early work life in Bern, to his professional success in Berlin, to his exile at Princeton after the rise of the Nazis. The museum explains Einstein's accomplishments and complicated personal life, details his travels after leaving Bern, and places him in historical context, with special emphasis on his Jewish identity (which for Einstein was more cultural than religious). Einstein's concepts are nicely illustrated by video presentations, and everything is well-explained in English (the audioguide is not necessary). You'll learn fascinating details, like the fact that Einstein's second wife was his cousin, and that he was offered the presidency of Israel in 1952, but turned it down.

Other Bern Museums

The Historical Museum and its Einstein exhibit are part of a larger ensemble that includes Alpine, Communication, Natural History, Rifle, and Kunsthalle (contemporary art) museums. All appeal mainly to visitors with specific interests. The Natural History Museum is fun for kids. The TI has a helpful pamphlet describing the museums (all covered by Swiss Travel Pass except Rifle Museum, most open Tue-Sun 10:00-17:00, closed Mon; see "Getting There" for Einstein Museum, above; www.museen-bern.ch).

Bern's Edgy Alternative Zone

To see a funky side of staid Switzerland, head to the counterculture art settlement called the Kulturzentrum Reithalle (named for the former "Riding Hall" that's part of the complex, sometimes also called the Reitschule). You'll find graffiti, wood-pallet furniture, stacked containers, skate ramps, drug deals, and other facets of real-life Swiss society that many visitors miss entirely. (Heidi and cowbells it ain't.) The complex is tucked along the train tracks north of the station, near the river—you'll see it as you come in on the train from Interlaken.

Sleeping in Bern

As Switzerland's capital, Bern hosts not only tourists but also waves of businesspeople and politicians, keeping room rates rather high throughout the year. In general, prices rise during the week and drop on weekends; however, street noise (mostly revelers out late) also increases on weekends. Frequent conventions and other events can drive demand and prices radically higher. Sleeping within walking distance of the train station is convenient and puts you in the endearing heart of the city, but can be pricier. If you don't mind a short tram ride, you can find lower-priced lodgings in the neighborhood across the river to the north. Many Swiss hotels don't have air-conditioning, and don't appreciate Americans complaining about it being too hot. Make sure you get your free Bern Ticket city transport pass at check-in.

DOWNTOWN BERN, NEAR THE STATION

These places are within a 5- to 10-minute walk from the train station. The first four hotels have rates that can skyrocket due to conventions, but can drop to tempting lows on weekends and at slower times, making a high-end splurge suddenly affordable—check around to find the best rates for your dates. Especially on weekends, light sleepers should be sure to request a quiet back-facing room.

$$$$ Hotel Savoy is a pricey, business-class place located super centrally, just off the main drag near the station. It has a sterile lobby and 63 solid, business-class rooms (air-con, elevator, Neuengasse 26, tel. 031-328-6666, www.hotelsavoy-bern.ch).

$$$ The Bristol is well-located, on a quieter side street near the station, and well-priced for what you get. It feels young and playful, and tries hard to have a Monty Python-esque sense of humor (with a plaid color scheme and oddball art in the lobby). Its 100 rooms are modern, solidly built (back rooms are pin-drop quiet), and well-equipped, but lack plush business-class touches (air-con, elevator, gym, Schauplatzgasse 10, tel. 031-311-0101, www.thebristol-bern.ch).

$$$ Hotel Kreuz rents 97 good rooms filling a beautiful his-

Bern Hotels & Restaurants

KULTURZENTRUM
REITHALLE

To **7**

MUSEUM OF
FINE ARTS

Aare River

Grosse
Schanze

TRAIN
STATION

MAIN
POST

HOLY
GHOST

PRISON
TOWER

FRANZ.-
KIRCHE

CAFE DES
PYRÉNÉES

Kornhaus-
platz

MARKTGASSE

ZYTGLOGGE
(CLOCK TOWER)

Bundes-
platz

PARLIAMENT

CASINO

KIRCHENFELD-
BRIDGE

FUNICULAR

KUNSTHALLE
MUSEUM

MARZILI

ALPINE
MUSEUM

Helvetia-
platz

HISTORICAL
EINSTEIN
MUSEUM

MARZILIBAD
(POOL & RIVER BATHS)

NATIONAL
HISTORY
MUSEUM

To start
of swim

toric building a few steps off the lively Bärenplatz (air-con, elevator, Zeughausgasse 41, tel. 031-329-9595, www.kreuzbern.ch).

$$$ Hotel Goldener Schlüssel is the oldest inn in downtown Bern, but it's been nicely renovated. Its 34 small, Euro-style rooms are fitted with prefab bathroom pods. The quieter, high-ceilinged back rooms are worth reserving in warm weather, as the rooms facing Rathausgasse get café and disco noise from across the street. Rates are high for what you get (RS%, family rooms, elevator,

200 Meters
200 Yards

To Zürich & Luzern
via A-1

ROSE GARDEN

#10 **B**

LAUBEGGSTRASSE

AARGAUERSTALDEN

17

TENBERGSTRASSE

UNTERTOR BRIDGE

HASPEL-GASSE

To Paul Klee Center

POSTGASSHALDE

NYDEGG-KIRCHE

RATHAUSGASSE

GERECHTIGKEITS.

B #12

NYDEGG BRIDGE

GASSE

EINSTEIN

JUNKERNGASSE

MATTE

BEAR PARK

ster-atz

ERLACHERHOF

CATHEDRAL

BUBENBERG-GRAIN

GERBERNGASSE

16

OLD TRAM DEPOT

inster-attform

SCHIFFLAUBE

AARSTRASSE

DAM

Aare River

GR. MURISTALDEN

OBSTBERG

SCHLOSSHALDENSTR.

To Interlaken via A-6

BEAR STATUE

Accommodations

1 Hotel Savoy
2 The Bristol Hotel
3 Hotel Kreuz
4 Hotel Goldener Schlüssel
5 Backpackers Hotel Glocke
6 Bern Youth Hostel
7 To Hotel Marthahaus & Jet Wash Launderette
8 To Ibis Hotels

Eateries & Other

9 Restaurant Lötschberg
10 Restaurant Harmonie
11 Gourmanderie Moléson
12 Mishio

13 Ristorante Luce
14 Kornhauskeller
15 Entrecôte Café Fédérale
16 Altes Tramdepot & Eiswerkstatt
17 Restaurant Rosengarten
18 Schwellenmätteli Restaurant
19 Bärenplatz Food Carts
20 Bread à Porter
21 Manora Cafeteria
22 Supermarket/Cafeteria (2)
23 Tibits Cafeteria
24 Mekong & Bread à Porter
25 Meet Point
26 Stauffacher Bookstore
27 Wash Bar Launderette

Rathausgasse 72, tel. 031-311-0216, www.goldener-schluessel-bern.ch, info@goldener-schluessel-bern.ch).

¢ **Backpackers Hotel Glocke** rents the cheapest beds in the old town. It's a mixture of small dorms and (on two upper floors) basic but adequate **$** private rooms (some with private bathrooms). All the rooms are stacked directly above a nightclub (the reception desk provides free earplugs, but light sleepers may be happier elsewhere). The pleasant common room has a nice view over the bustling city-center streets below (no breakfast, elevator, no curfew, reception open 8:00-12:00 & 15:00-22:00, 10-minute walk from station or take tram #9 to Zytglogge stop, Rathausgasse 75, tel. 031-311-3771, www.bernbackpackers.ch, info@bernbackpackers.ch).

¢ **Bern Youth Hostel,** below the parliament building near the river, is well-run and welcoming even to people who don't often stay in youth hostels. In addition to dorm beds, they have en suite private rooms, making this an affordable alternative to expensive downtown hotels (elevator, affordable dinners, pay parking, Weihergasse 4, tel. 031-326-1111, www.youthhostel.ch/bern, bern@youthhostel.ch). To reach the hostel, walk three blocks south from the train station and take the Marzilibahn funicular down to Weihergasse (1.40 CHF, free with hostel confirmation or Bern Ticket, runs until 21:00, after that use bus #30, www.marzilibahn.ch).

NORTH OF THE RIVER

These listings are an easy bus or tram ride from the center.

$$ Hotel Marthahaus is a better value than downtown hotels. Located two bus stops from the train station (walkable without luggage) in a quiet, elegant residential neighborhood north of the river, it's run as a fundraiser by a charitable organization that helps young people and seniors. Half of the 40 bright, simple rooms have shared bathrooms (family rooms, elevator, guest kitchen; take bus #20 from platform G at station to the Gewerbeschule stop, walk up the street to Wyttenbachstrasse and follow the yellow signs two short blocks to Wyttenbachstrasse 22a, tel. 031-332-4135, www.marthahaus.ch, info@marthahaus.ch).

Two **$ Ibis** hotels are in a big metallic building at the Bern Convention Center: **Ibis Bern Expo** (breakfast extra, tel. 031-335-1200, www.ibis.com) and **Ibis Budget Bern Expo** (breakfast extra, pay parking, tel. 031-335-1212, www.ibisbudget.com). From the station, take tram #9 for 10 minutes to the Guisanplatz Expo (direction: Wankdorf Bahnhof, hotels are at Am Guisanplatz 2).

Eating in Bern

IN THE OLD TOWN

$$ Restaurant Lötschberg, a local favorite with a fun and youthful vibe, serves old-style Swiss cuisine in a modern space. One long wall is lined with a large variety of Swiss wines (Mon-Sat 10:00-24:00, Sun 11:00-23:00, Zeughausgasse 16, tel. 031-311-3455). They also have a less-expensive **takeaway window** at the front of the restaurant, with affordable salads and sandwiches to go.

$$ Restaurant Harmonie, just off Kornmarkt, feels cozy and classic. The interior has hard-backed wooden tables filled mostly by locals, and there's a small outdoor terrace draped in ivy. The menu is classic Swiss with some international flourishes—including a variety of burgers (Mon-Fri 11:00-23:00, closed Sat-Sun, Hotelgasse 3, tel. 031-313-1141).

$$$ Gourmanderie Moléson feels refined, high-end, and posh. It's a long, skinny, classy bistro serving healthy and classic dishes with a French flair, including fondue and *tartes flambées* (like pizza without tomato sauce—known as *Flammkuchen* in German). It has a dressy and very Swiss interior with tables that tumble out onto the street (Mon-Sat 11:30-14:30 & 18:00-23:30, closed Sun, Aarbergergasse 24, tel. 031-311-4463, www.moleson-bern.ch).

$$ Mishio is a mod pan-Asian place worth considering. The interior has an open kitchen, noisy acoustics, and plain furnishings. The trick here is to get an outside table on the terrace, which overlooks the lively Bärenplatz (Mon-Sat 11:00-22:00, closed Sun, Bärenplatz 2, tel. 031-313-1121).

$$ Ristorante Luce brings the cooking of Italy's Emilia Romagna region (with lots of pastas and pizzas) to Bern. Choose between a venerable dining hall and great seating out on lively Bärenplatz (daily 11:30-14:00 & 18:00-23:00, reservations smart, Zeughausgasse 28, tel. 031-310-9999, www.ristoranteluce.ch).

$$$ Kornhauskeller, in the palatial cellar of the old granary originally built to house the state's wine cellar, has vaulted archways decorated with colorful murals. This dressy, pricey Mediterranean (Swiss, French, Italian) place offers a fine antipasto bar: Make a meal out of the 19-CHF or 27-CHF plate, telling the man behind the buffet exactly what you'd like (daily 11:45-14:30 & 18:00-23:00, Kornhausplatz 18, tel. 031-327-7272).

$$$$ Entrecôte Café Fédérale is a dressy and traditional bistro with a reputation for great steak. It sits at the bottom of Bärenplatz, with tables under trees facing the parliament building. Very old-school urban Swiss, it's a quiet place with more local politicians than tourists (daily 11:00-23:00, Bärenplatz 31, tel. 031-311-1624, www.entrecote.ch).

ACROSS THE RIVER, WITH VIEWS

$$ Altes Tramdepot, in the Old Tram Depot above Bear Park, offers seating in its big, boisterous microbrewery (which was once the tram shed), or on a leafy *Biergarten* terrace with a postcard view of the old town's skyline. It's popular, serving good-time food and Swiss specialties (*Rösti* and wurst plates, fast and healthy weekday lunches, also wok dishes). They have "flight" taster boards for those who want to sample several of their brews (daily 11:00-24:00, reserve in evening for outdoor view seating, bus #12 to Bärengraben stop, tel. 031-368-1415, www.altestramdepot.ch).

$$$ Restaurant Rosengarten, perched at the edge of the city's rose garden atop the hill above the Bear Park, **enjoys com-**

manding city views—especially at sunset (when you should reserve ahead). During the day, come for lunch, or for tea and cake amidst grannies (24-CHF weekday lunch specials). At night, you'll dine with couples enjoying the fresh seasonal menu. While the interior feels upscale (and has the best views), there's also a more casual yet still high-end *Biergarten* (daily 9:00-24:00, Alter Aargauerstalden 31b, a moderately steep walk up from the Bear Park—or take tram #10 from the old town, tel. 031-331-3206, www.rosengarten.be).

$$ Schwellenmätteli Restaurant is a chance to join trendy locals for a meal or drink while sitting directly over the river, next to the roar of water racing over the dam. The inside section is peaceful and open all year. The outside, open only in good weather, is loud—not good for conversation—but fun: At the tip of the platform is a lounge complete with sofas, mattresses, and a glass floor that lets you see the river racing underneath. This mod restaurant/lounge has a Swiss-Mediterranean menu (burgers, *Flammkuchen,* veggie dishes, and weekday lunch specials)—but you're here for the setting, not the food (daily 9:00-24:00; reservations smart for dinner, Dalmaziquai 11, cross Kirchenfeld Bridge from downtown and take path downhill to your left, or a pleasant 15-minute riverside stroll from Bear Park, tel. 031-350-5001, www.schwellenmaetteli. ch).

CHEAP EATS

While Bern has its share of affordable eateries, many are closed at dinnertime; you'll find the best selection of budget takeaway dinner fare at the train station.

$ Bärenplatz Food Carts: For lunch, drop by the food carts that cluster around the parliament end of Bärenplatz (Mon-Sat mornings). The assortment often includes an organic sausage-and-falafel wagon, tacos, Asian fast food, and more. Grab what looks good and enjoy it on the bench under the Prison Tower. On the north end of Bärenplatz, consider the cheap takeout window for the recommended Lötschberg restaurant (described earlier).

Bakeries: Bern is very picnic-friendly. For a budget alternative to formal restaurant eating, small bakeries are all around town. One good option is **Bread à Porter,** which offers fresh sandwiches, quiches, salads, and usually a few small tables or stools at a bar (Mon-Fri 6:30-18:30, Sat until 16:00, closed Sun, Kornhausplatz 11 and Münstergasse 74).

Supermarkets: Two large supermarkets are in the center—Co-op (Aarbergergasse 53, in the basement) and **Migros** (Marktgasse 40, ground floor). Both are open standard shop hours and closed Sun. Early, late, or on Sunday, visit one of the midsize supermarkets in the **train station** (Migros on the upper level, daily 8:00-21:00; Co-op on the lower level, daily 6:00-23:00). You'll get a solid value on takeout food from the two **Migros Takeaway** supermarket delis (bottom level of the train station and at Marktgasse 40). The staff will pack you up a hot lunch or dinner to take away for 10-15 CHF. Portions are big—often enough for two—and there are always several options on offer (such as lasagna with side salad or bratwurst with potatoes and veggies), as well as pizzas, quiches, and salads.

Self-Service Restaurants: For fine views at budget prices, **$ Manora** restaurant at the Manor department store has a self-service cafeteria with hot meals, pastas, pizzas, paninis, and a salad bar. Choose and pay for your meal, then head to the rooftop (Mon-Wed 9:00-19:00, Thu until 21:00, Fri until 20:00, Sat 8:00-17:00, closed Sun, Marktgasse 10). The downtown **Co-op** and **Migros** supermarkets both run fine self-service restaurants with similar offerings. Both also have Asian food counters and kids' play zones. Co-op's cafeteria has a nice glassed-in terrace, while Migros has a by-weight buffet and free tap water (hidden next to the tray-return conveyor belt). **$$ Tibits**, a busy buffet chain on the ground floor of the train station, offers a huge variety of vegetarian-only salads and sandwiches, plus two different hot dishes. Help yourself to a plate and pile it on. You'll pay by weight: An average helping will cost you about 20 CHF (free water, Mon-Sat 6:30-24:00, Sun 8:00-23:00, Bahnhofplatz 10, tel. 031-312-9111).

Global Food: A few cheap takeout places hide deep under the arcades in the old town. **$$ Mekong**, tucked down a nondescript passage between the Zytglogge-Turm and Kornmarkt, is packed with value-conscious Bernese enjoying quality Asian cooking. While pricier at dinner, they have 15-CHF lunch specials—a bit cheaper for takeaway (Mon-Sat 11:30-14:30 & 17:30-22:00, Sun 18:00-22:00, Kornhausplatz 7, look for sign off Zibelegässli, tel. 031-311-2600). **$ Meet Point**, a Middle Eastern takeout counter with a couple of stools, sells cheap *döner kebabs* (Mon-Sat 9:30-21:00, closed Sun, Neuengasse 17).

Bern Connections

From Bern by Train to: Murten (hourly direct, 35 minutes, more with transfer), **Avenches** (6/day direct, 40 minutes, more with transfers), **Lausanne** (2/hour, 1 hour), **Interlaken** (2/hour, 1 hour, a few change in Spiez), **Luzern** (2/hour direct, 1 hour, more with transfer), **Zürich** (4/hour direct, 1-1.5 hours, more with transfers), **Zürich Airport** (2/hour, 1.5 hours), **Zermatt** (1-2/hour, 2 hours, transfer in Visp), **Montreux** (2/hour, 1.5 hours, transfer in Lausanne), **Lugano** (1-4/hour, 3.5 hours, 1-3 transfers), **Appenzell** (3/hour, 3 hours, 1-2 transfers), **Frankfurt** (4/day direct, 4 hours, more with change in Basel). Train info: Toll tel. 0900-300-300 (1.20 CHF/minute) or www.sbb.ch.

ROUTE TIPS FOR DRIVERS

Interlaken to Bern: From Interlaken, catch the autobahn (direction: Spiez, Thun, then Bern). Circle Bern on the autobahn, taking the fourth Bern exit, *Neufeld Bern*. Signs to *Bern Zentrum* take you to Bern Bahnhof (train station). Turn right just before the station into the Bahnhof Parkplatz (described earlier, under "Arrival in Bern").

Bern to Murten: From the station, drive out of Bern following signs for *Lausanne*, then follow the green signs to *Neuchâtel* and *Murten*.

Murten

The finest medieval ramparts in Switzerland surround the old town of Murten (pop. 8,000; pronounced MOOR-ten; if you say MURR-ten, you get a quizzical look). You're on the linguistic cusp of Switzerland: 25 percent of Murten speaks French; a few miles to the southwest, nearly everyone does (French-speakers call the town Morat).

Murten's old center is endearing. Its lively streets include a nicely arcaded main drag with breezy outdoor cafés and elegant shops (many closed Mon). Its castle is romantic, overlooking Lake Murten and the rolling vineyards of gentle Mont Vully in the distance. Spend a night here and have a local Vully wine (white, red, or rosé) with dinner. Murten is touristed, but mostly by locals, and never to the point of feeling overrun.

Make time for nearby Avenches (see end of chapter). Though sleepy today, the town was once a powerful Roman capital—as its ruins attest.

Orientation to Murten

TOURIST INFORMATION

Murten's TI is just inside the city walls at the far end of town from the train station (April-Sept Mon-Fri 9:00-12:00 & 13:00-18:00, Sat-Sun 10:00-12:00 & 13:00-17:00; Oct-March shorter hours and closed Sat-Sun; Französische Kirchgasse 6, tel. 026-670-5112, www.regionmurtensee.ch).

ARRIVAL IN MURTEN

By Train: The train station is a five-minute walk from the center, and has a ticket office, free WC, and small pay lockers—the ticket office can store bigger bags (Mon-Fri 6:50-18:30, Sat 7:50-18:00, Sun 7:50-12:00 & 13:00-17:00). To reach the town from the station, exit to the right, take the first left, and walk uphill on Bahnhofstrasse, then turn right through the town gate. Murten's old center is tiny, and a delight on foot.

By Car: If you're overnighting here, get parking advice from your hotelier. You can park overnight in the old town for free (19:00-8:00). During the day, don't park inside the gates; metered prices are steep and there's a strict 75-minute time limit. Instead, park in the lot near the castle and Co-op supermarket or near the clock tower (2 CHF/hour, pay at machine).

HELPFUL HINTS

Local Guide: American **Mary Brunisholz,** who married into this part of Switzerland, is an excellent guide with a car (300 CHF/half-day, mobile 078-601-7040, mary.brunisholz@vtxnet.ch). The TI has a list of other guides.

Events: The town's **Youth Festival** commemorates the anniversary of the Battle of Murten each June 22. The **Murten Classics** music festival takes place in August and September, and the **Licht Festival** lights up the town and the lake in mid-late January.

Murten Walk

This self-guided introductory walk will give you the lay of the land and a lesson on the historic 15th-century Battle of Murten.

• *Start your walk just outside the town's main gate and TI, in front of the public school, where you see a statue of the feisty town hero...*

Adrian von Bubenberg

Burgundy was the aggressive power of the day, and this Murten native stopped a 15th-century Burgundian power grab by beating Charles the Bold. Adrian von Bubenberg (sent by Bern to hold

Murten

To Praz,
Biel & Neuchâtel

Lake Murten

BOAT DOCK

Harbor

BOAT TICKETS

To Praz,
Mont Vully
via path

Pantschau Park

To Praz & Mont Vully

RYF

LÄNGMATT

WALK BEGINS

ADRIAN VON BUBENBERG STATUE

To Bern via A1 & 11

BERN STR.

RAFFOR

FRENCH CHURCH

CLOCK TOWER (BERN GATE)

GERMAN CHURCH

RYF

STAIRS

TOWN HALL

HAUPTGASSE

KREUZGASSE

DEUTSCHE KIRCHGASSE

CASTLE

RATHAUSGASSE

To Pool

MUSEUM

WATER-WHEEL

WALK ENDS

SCHLOSSGASSE

WEAPONS SHOP

SCHULGASSE

CINEMA

TOWN GATE

TÖRLIplatz

BIG TOWER

TOWER

MEDIEVAL WALLS

CATHOLIC CHURCH

To Bern

LAUSANNESTRASSE

BUDENBERGSTRASSE

BAHNHOFSTRASSE

FRÄLICHSTRASSE

POST

MEYLANDSTRASSE

FREIBURGSTRASSE

TRAIN STATION

ALTE FREIBURGSTRASSE

PRA PURY

WILERWEG

To Avenches

VISSAULASTR.

N

50 meters

50 yards

Accommodations
1 Hotel/Restaurant Murtenhof & Krone
2 Hotel Ringmauer

Eateries & Other
3 Restaurant Eintracht
4 Restaurant Anatolia
5 Ristorante l'Italiano & La Botega Italiana Deli
6 Chesery

7 Pizzeria Taverna Italiana
8 Züger Bakery
9 Adler Hotel & Pub
10 Bar Cave in Blue
11 To Hotel Murten Bar
12 Supermarket
13 Steps to Lake
14 Access to Ramparts (2)

the line against the expansionist Burgundians) stands here, looking across the lake at the distant peaks of the Jura Mountains—the historic border between the Swiss and the French (more on the battle a little later).

The earliest Swiss clockmakers were from those Jura Mountains. Look at the **clock tower**—where's the minute hand? As part of its lease, the restaurant below takes responsibility for hand-winding the clock each day, as it has since 1712. That's the Bern gate—so called because it opens up onto the road to Bern.

• *Rather than enter the gate, go right instead (hugging the outside of the wall, not downhill). Head around the first turret, and look up at the cannon-balls, left in the wall from the 1476 Battle of Murten to remind towns-folk of their incredible victory over the Burgundians—like an Alamo with a happy ending. Turn the corner onto the...*

Lakeview Terrace

Across the way is Mont Vully (mohn voo-YEE)—one big vineyard and a mecca for lovers of Swiss wines. The lowlands to the right—a rich former lakebed—are the heart of the fertile Three Lakes Region (Lakes Biel, Neuchâtel, and Murten). The lush farmland is called the "vegetable garden of Switzerland" for its soil, which yields more than 60 varieties of produce.

The ancient Celtic Helvetii tribe settled here and took advantage of the fertility of this land. The Romans located their capital nearby (at Avenches) when they took over the region and established their colony of Helvetia (named after the Celtic tribe—the same word is the Latin origin of Switzerland's official name, Confoederatio Helvetica).

• *Behind you, check out the small...*

French Church

Foreseeing a showdown with Burgundy, Adrian von Bubenberg had the town walls strengthened. As three-quarters of the townspeople were German-speaking, they took a vote and decided to tear down the French church to get more stones. (This little church was rebuilt for the French-speaking community six years after its big one was demolished.)

• *Circle round the church, and if it's open, go inside.*

As the Calvinist Reformation swept through Catholic Switzerland in the early 16th century, churches like this were stripped of their rich paintings, sculptures, and stained glass. Elaborate altars were replaced with simple, Bible-topped tables, and pulpits became the focus. The emphasis was teaching the word of God. In this church, about the only exceptions to the "no distractions" rule are the tiny stained-glass coats of arms—heraldry of the wealthy families who helped fund its construction. The church, still Protestant and serving its French community, is open sporadically.

• *From here, leave the church and head straight toward the pointy spire of the German church across town. Walk along Französischer Kirchgasse past the TI and the clock tower, and go up the lane to #26 (on left). This is one of few Murten buildings that survived a 15th-century fire that destroyed the then-wooden town. Stand in the doorway and remember that people during the Middle Ages were much shorter. Before the fire, most houses looked like this one. After the fire, building was limited to the characteristic yellow Jura stone (like the former library, across the street, at #31). Continue straight ahead to the...*

German Church

Murten's German church is also post-Reformation Protestant simple. Inside, in the center of the ceiling, notice the big stucco relief with two seals: the bear for Bern and the three castles for Fribourg. As the town is on the border between two cantons (Bern and Fribourg), for 400 years its rule was shared: Every five years, it would flip between cantons. Around 1800, when Switzerland was reorganized under Napoleonic rule, Murten became firmly a part of Fribourg.

The Protestant passion for Bible study is also evident in this church. Explore the choir (two rows of seats on each side for big shots) behind the altar. Find Adrian von Bubenberg's seat. (Hint: The window above shows the war hero in red, with his victorious local yokels in their alpine red-knit hats...underdogs whupping the Burgundians.) The old pulpit was carved in 1460 from a single oak tree. Notice the two prime seats on either side of the altar; the one to the preacher's right was for the leader of Bern or Fribourg—depending on who happened to be ruling that year. The front window (crucifixion) dates from 1926.

• *Leaving the church, hook left around the back. Finger the limestone and sandstone tombstones, quarried from Mont Vully for noble families. Then climb the two flights of creaky stairs and start walking along the...*

Ramparts

Strolling Murten's ramparts is a must (free, open daily until dusk). Survey the town, and note the uniformity of its architecture. Paint your place the wrong color, and you may be instructed to redo the job—at your own expense. Scanning the countless chimneys and beavertail ceramic roof tiles, think of the enforced conformity that comes with living in a small town (and look to see if there are any oddballs). Telephone and electricity wires are all underground, as in Europe generally. Look back at the roof of the German church. The six-sided "star of David" isn't a Jewish symbol in this case, but recalls the star that guided the wise men to Bethlehem on the first Christmas.

• *Continue 50 yards to the **tower with the steep staircase**. Climb the steps for a commanding town and lake view.*

Enjoy perhaps the ultimate view. The Jura Mountains in the distance (at the border with France) peek above vine-laden Mont Vully. On the right is the German church, Bern Tower, and French church. And to the far left is the castle tower—flying the black-and-white flag of Fribourg Canton—where this walk finishes.

With your back to the lake, look inland and imagine the action on June 22, 1476. Mighty Charles the Bold, with his 20,000 well-armed Burgundians, was camped on the hill (the one with the divided forest) for 10 days, laying siege to the town of 2,000. Runners were sent out from the town to gather help. A makeshift army of about 10,000 villagers gathered on the hills to the left. Just as George Washington attacked when the Redcoats were celebrating Christmas, the Swiss swooped in as the Burgundians were still hungover from a big Midsummer Night's Eve bash. The Battle of Murten was fought in pouring rain—a muddy, bloody mess. More than 10,000 Burgundians were slaughtered—many driven into the lake with their armor to drown (try swimming in a coat of mail). For centuries, French bones would wash ashore. Charles the (no-longer-so-) Bold barely got away on a very fast horse.

This victory demonstrated to the Swiss the advantages of *E Pluribus Unum,* and the gradual unification of the many still-fiercely independent Swiss cantons into the Helvetic Confederation snowballed. In this sweet little corner, an influential battle in European history had been fought. Burgundian power ebbed, and Europe got to know a new nation...Switzerland.

• *Walk a bit farther along the wall and descend at the next tower (across from Hotel-Restaurant Ringmauer).*

At the bottom of the stairs, study the fine old **clock** mechanism from 1816. It once powered the big clock in the City Hall tower. Later, it spent decades in a to-be-assembled pile, gathering dust in an attic. Finally, in 1991, a town resident—recognizing a

BERN & MURTEN

good challenge—reassembled it into perfect working order. Notice how the gearbox powers three clock faces (as the tower had), and how the old hand crank raises the stones that power the clock, which rings on the quarter-hour. The white face displays the clock's time.

• *Step outside the wall, where you'll see the Catholic church (1886), private gardens along the wall, and evidence of how the wall was constructed in several distinct stages.*

The first phase was built with large river stones, some arranged in a neat fishbone pattern. Later, the town ran out of money, and the next stage shows pebbles and rubble mixed with a rough concrete. And finally, when the town prospered again, they finished the wall with finely cut sandstone. The former dry moat is now individual private gardens.

• *Walk back into town, stopping on the first corner at the fire station-turned-community-cinema.*

Contributors are thanked with their names on the **cinema** door. Notice what's playing tonight (in Switzerland, movies are subtitled, not dubbed, to accommodate a two-language audience). At this corner, spin slowly, admiring the town's fine shutters.

• *Then, continue a block (noticing again that most buildings were stone—built after a fire) to the...*

Main Street (Hauptgasse)

In the 19th century, Murten's townsfolk got their water from the three fountains on this street. Turn left along the street and enjoy the colorful store signs—they still hang out their shingles in the traditional fashion. Bakery and *pâtisserie* competition on this street is fierce. Drop into one for regional specialties: *Nidlechueche,* a sweet, doughy cream tart; and *Seeländer Zwetschgen,* a chocolate-covered prune with liqueur.

Near the top of the main street, **Simonet Weapons** sells all the latest products from Victorinox, origi-

nator of the Swiss Army knife. There's the green "stay-glow," and even a model with a USB flash drive for the outdoorsman with a laptop (closed Sun-Mon). At the top of the street (#16), Murten's oldest house has fine paintings under its eaves.

• *Farther to the right, at the top of town, step into...*

Murten Castle and Town Museum

The town castle, which houses the police station in its former prison (tower open to the public), shows off an impressive cannon from 1882. A plaque on the nearby overlook helps you identify the villages on the other side of the Murtensee.

The town museum, just down the hill, is a humble collection earnestly showing off the town history (6 CHF, generally Tue-Sun 14:00-17:00, closed Mon and Dec-mid-March, described in German and French only—borrow English booklet). It fills an old mill with modern displays and lots of artifacts. Outside is a functioning water mill, a WC, a lane leading down to the lake, and an elephant.

An elephant? Yes, in 1866 an elephant escaped from a traveling American circus. It rampaged through Murten and was killed. To this day, one lane is nicknamed Elephant Alley.

Our walk ends here, but you can backtrack to the Town Hall (past the Hotel Murtenhof & Krone) and descend the steps nearby for some more fine lake views.

Activities in Murten

Lake Activities

To get to Murten's lazy lakefront, you can take the steps by the Town Hall (noted above). Or go out the gate by the TI and take a left down the hill. You'll see the boat dock first. Just beyond the grassy breakwater and the small-boat harbor is a big park flanked by handy eateries. There's mini golf, windsurfing/paddle boarding gear rental and instruction, a snack bar, and a fine lakeside promenade with benches made for sunset views.

Lake Murten Cruises

Boats do a **75-minute loop cruise** at 12:00, 14:15, and 15:40. Consider stopping in a small town (Praz or Môtier) on the French-speaking shore. From there you could hike through vineyards up Mont Vully—where a pretty lake and Alp views await—and return on the lake with your same ticket. Or you can walk back to Murten, clockwise around the lake (about 1.5 hours from Praz) or meet the train at Sugiez in Bas-Vully. Ask the TI for the *Vully Les Vignerons* map to help you make a plan and for information on wine tastings in the area.

Another option is the **Three Lakes cruise,** which covers all three of the region's lakes—connected by canals—and stops at several medieval villages on the way to the town of Biel (Bienne in

French). The boat leaves Murten at 9:50, arrives in Biel at 14:05, then turns around and heads back along the same route, leaving Biel at 14:45 and arriving in Murten at 18:55. You can condense this full-day trip by taking the boat to Biel and a train back to Murten (1 hour).

Cost and Hours: 75-minute loop cruise—22 CHF; boat from Murten to Praz or Môtier—14.20 CHF; half-day Three Lakes cruise—61 CHF one-way, 69 CHF round-trip; all covered by Swiss Travel Pass and discounted 50 percent with Eurail Global Pass, ask TI about boat-trip discount vouchers; buy tickets on board or at the kiosk at pier 1; boats run daily late May-late Sept, Fri-Sun only in off-season, no boats in winter but see website for special Licht Festival trips; tel. 032-729-9600, www.navig.ch.

Swimming Pool

The Olympic-size public swimming pool is outside of town next to the lake, just past the castle (8 CHF; indoor pool Mon 14:00-21:00, Tue-Fri 9:30-21:00, Sat-Sun until 18:00; outdoor pool daily in summer; Lausannestrasse 2, tel. 026-672-3636, www.schwimmbad-murten.ch).

Biking

The Three Lakes region has 100 miles of signposted bike paths. Pick up a free map at the TI. The best easy ride circles the lake and Mont Vully (through vineyards and, if you like, to the summit for a good view). As elsewhere in Switzerland, you can pick up rental **bikes** at train-station ticket counters (online reservations required; for rates and specifics, see page 448).

Nightlife in Murten

Movies

Murten's cute little community co-op theater plays movies nightly (16 CHF, Schulgasse 18, www.kino-murten.ch). Movies are shown in their original language (capital letter indicates the soundtrack language, small letters indicate subtitles—for example, "E/fd" means "English with *français* and *Deutsch* subtitles").

From early July to early August, Murten hosts an open-air film festival (outside wall, past TI, details at www.open-air-kino.ch, then select "Murten").

Pubs

There are a few options for nightlife. The **Adler Hotel & Pub** sells drinks and tasty *Flammkuchen* in a fun and welcoming interior or lively exterior facing Murten's main drag (daily 11:00-24:00, Hauptgasse 45, tel. 026-672-1920). **Bar Cave in Blue** on the main street is popular with the late-night crowd (daily from 21:00, Schlossgasse 4, tel. 026-670-1901). The **Hotel Murten** bar just outside the clock tower is another good place for drinks (daily 15:00-late, at Bernstrasse 7, tel. 026-678-8181; don't confuse this with the Hotel Murtenhof & Krone within the walls).

Sleeping in Murten

This adorable town is no secret. The peak time is May through mid-September (especially on weekends)—make a reservation and expect maximum prices. The nearest youth hostel is in Avenches (see the end of this chapter).

$$ Hotel Murtenhof & Krone offers elegance at fair-for-Switzerland prices in 57 nicely appointed rooms—each a stylish mix of old and new. There's a wide range of sleeping accommodations, so email them your needs in terms of size, view, and price (RS%, some rooms with air-con, family rooms, elevator, pay parking, next to castle at Rathausgasse 3, tel. 026-672-9030, www.murtenhof.ch, info@murtenhof.ch, well-run by brothers Marc and Ariste Joachim). They have the best lakeview restaurant in town (described later, under "Eating in Murten").

$$ Hotel Ringmauer (Ramparts) sits just under the wall in the quiet corner of town farthest from the lake. It rents 14 small, simple rooms (family rooms, discount if you skip breakfast, attached restaurant, Deutsche Kirchgasse 2, tel. 026-670-1101, www.restaurantringmauer.ch, restaurantringmauer@bluewin.ch, Padmakumara Nawarathna and family).

Eating in Murten

Eating in Murten is a joy. I'd stroll the main drag up one side and down the other to survey the action before making a choice. For elegance and a lake view, it's the restaurant at Hotel Murtenhof & Krone. There are several good options right on the lake a 10-minute walk down from the town center. Budget eaters can assemble a picnic at the Co-op grocery. Bakeries make good sandwiches, but they close by about 18:00.

RESTAURANTS

Anything called *Seeländer* or mentioning "three lakes" is typical of this Three Lakes region. Traditional restaurants serve *Egli-Filets*, the very popular perch "from the lake" (these days caught in the Bodensee—Lake Constance in English—up by the German border). As this is the "vegetable garden of Switzerland," restaurants pride themselves on offering good produce. You'll want a glass of smooth and refreshing Vully (voo-YEE) wine with your meal (about 5 CHF/glass).

$$$ Hotel Murtenhof & Krone's restaurant is perched high above the lake in the old town. Its covered terrace gives diners a comfortable and classy lake view regardless of the weather. Sipping a glass of local wine with the right travel partner, while gazing across the lake at hillside vineyards as the sun sets, is one of Europe's fine moments. Choose from "updated Three Lakes cuisine" and several vegetarian options. Reserve ahead for their limited lakeview seating (Tue-Sun 11:00-23:00, closed Mon and Dec-Feb, tel. 026-672-9030, www.murtenhof.ch).

$$$ Restaurant Eintracht serves good-value, local cuisine from a fun and unpretentious menu, including old-time chef specials—even horsemeat (18-CHF lunch specials include soup and main course, half-portions available, healthy specials, generally 7:30-23:30, Sun until 18:00, closed Wed, streetside seating under arcades, Hauptgasse 19, tel. 026-670-2240, Ramseier family).

$$$$ Restaurant Anatolia features quality Turkish dishes made from fresh ingredients by the welcoming owner, Mehmet. Dine indoors with the fine mural of Istanbul, or watch the main-drag action from an outside table (daily 10:00-23:00, shorter hours and closed Wed off-season, Hauptgasse 45, tel. 026-670-2868, www.anatolia.ch).

$$$ Ristorante l'Italiano is the town choice for authentic Italian cuisine. The Prozzillo family emphasizes gastronomic simplicity. As its menu makes quite clear, they don't serve pizza (Tue-Sat 9:00-14:00 & 17:00-23:00, closed Sun-Mon; outdoor seating, Hauptgasse 11, tel. 026-672-2212). **La Bottega Italiana**, a deli next door, is owned by the same family.

$$ Chesery is a café (with regional cheese plates, quiches, and other light meals), wine bar, and elegant secondhand store with indoor and outdoor seating. This quirky spot is worth a peek even if you're not eating (20-CHF lunch specials, daily 11:00-22:00, Rathausgasse 28, tel. 026-670-6577).

$$$ Pizzeria Taverna Italiana is one of two pizzerias in Murten's old town. The one on the main street has better views, but townsfolk say Pizzeria Taverna Italiana is a better value (daily 10:30-14:00 & 17:00-23:00, closed Feb-April, near Hotel Murtenhof at Kreuzgasse 4, tel. 026-670-2122).

CHEAP EATS

The main street has four **bakeries**, all with ample charm. **Züger** has indoor and outdoor seating, an inviting pastry and confectionary counter, and delicate open-face sandwiches typical of the region. This is the perfect place to try the local *Nidlechueche* (11.50-CHF breakfast combo—coffee, croissant, and roll; generally 7:30-18:30, closed Tue, Hauptgasse 33, tel. 026-670-2253).

The Co-op **supermarket** towers between the train station and city center (Mon-Sat 7:00-20:00, Sun 8:00-18:00).

BERN & MURTEN

Murten Connections

From Murten by Train to: Avenches (1-2/hour, 7 minutes, direction: Lausanne), **Bern** (hourly direct, 35 minutes, more with change in Kerzers), **Lausanne** (5/hour, 1.5-2 hours), **Zürich** (3/hour, 2 hours, 1-2 transfers). Train info: Toll tel. 0900-300-300 (1.20 CHF/minute) or www.sbb.ch.

ROUTE TIPS FOR DRIVERS
Murten to Lake Geneva (50 miles): The autobahn from Bern to Lausanne/Lake Geneva makes everything speedy (see the Lake Geneva & French Switzerland chapter). Murten and Avenches are 10 minutes off the autobahn; Broc, Bulle, and Gruyères are within sight of each other and the autobahn. It takes about an hour to drive from Murten to Montreux. The autobahn (direction: Simplon) takes you high above Montreux (pull off at great viewpoint rest stop) and Château de Chillon. For the castle, take the first exit east of the castle (Villeneuve); signs direct you along the lake back to the castle.

Near Murten: Avenches

Avenches, four miles south of Murten, was once Aventicum, the Roman capital of Helvetia. Today, it's a quaint little French-speaking town with an ancient amphitheater taking a bite out of it. Below the town spreads a vast field of sparse Roman ruins.

With a pleasant, small-town French ambience, Avenches (ah-VAHNSH) is much quieter than Murten, and its old walls are mostly gone. Just a few minutes away by train, it makes an easy half-day trip. From the unstaffed Avenches train station, it's a seven-minute, somewhat steep walk to the town, amphitheater, and Roman museum. Exploring more of the ruins requires some outdoor walking. The **TI** is on the town's main square (Mon-Fri 8:30-12:00 & 13:30-17:30, Sat 9:30-12:30, closed Sun; Sept-April also closed Sat; Place de l'Eglise 3, tel. 026-676-9922, www.avenches.ch).

Sights in Avenches

Roman Avenches
Aventicum was a Roman capital, with a population of 20,000. The Romans appreciated its strategic crossroads location, fertile land, and comfortable climate (in modern times, it's been voted the "most livable place to retire"). While the population of today's Avenches could barely fill the well-worn ruins of their Roman amphitheater, Aventicum was once one of the largest cities of the Roman Em-

pire. Everything sits on Roman ruins, which were quarried nearly to oblivion over several centuries; the scant remains were finally spared in the 19th century, and today, things are carefully preserved. Metal detectors must be registered here. Mothers, knowing that turning up anything ancient will bring on the archaeologists, yell at their kids, "Don't dig!" Even the benches on the main street are bits of a 2,000-year-old temple cornice.

The town has five Roman sights: the amphitheater, a lone tower, a sanctuary and a theater in a field outside of town, and a museum. While you'll pay to enter the museum, the ruins are free and always viewable.

The **amphitheater,** or arena, which once seated 18,000, is the largest Roman ruin in Switzerland (free, always open). There's no more gladiator action, but it's busy with an annual opera festival and other musical events. At the top of the amphitheater (just past the museum entrance), scan the surrounding countryside. The Roman town filled the low area in front of you (now partly farmland; Avenches' medieval residents retreated to the more easily defensible hilltop). The **tower** on the ridge (on left)—the only one remaining of the original 73 towers—marks where the wall once stood. In the middle, past the lone standing column of the **sanctuary,** you can see the small **theater** ruins (described later).

The **Roman museum,** next to the amphitheater, fills a medieval tower with three floors of Roman artifacts—such as gravestones, mosaics, glass, and fishing spears—which afford a fairly intimate look at domestic life back then. There's no English posted on the ground floor displays, so good students borrow the extensive English catalog. Upstairs, don't miss the "gold" bust of Marcus Aurelius (AD 80) found in an old Roman sewer in 1939—it's actually a plastic copy; the original is in a bank in Lausanne (free, more for temporary exhibits, covered by Swiss Travel Pass; Tue-Sun 10:00-17:00, closed Mon except in June, shorter hours off-season and closed Tue Nov-Jan; tel. 026-557-3300, www.aventicum. org).

Perhaps the best Aventicum experience is to spend some quiet time at sunset pondering the evocative **Roman theater** (Théâtre Romaine) and **sanctuary** in the fields, a half-mile walk out of town (free, always open, tiny free car park at the site). The single column marks "Du Cigognier"—nicknamed the "stork sanctuary" (c. 1700) for the stork nest it supported. The site was a quarry until the 19th century, so almost nothing remains.

Sleeping in Avenches

Sleeping in little Avenches is the Murten area's best option for travelers on a tight budget. Coming here works best by car. It's not impossible by train, but schedules are sparse and hauling your bags uphill from the train station is a chore. For other accommodation options, see the town website at avenches.ch.

¢ The Avenches **IYHF hostel** fills a traditional building in a quiet setting on the far side of town. It's a 15-minute walk from the train station if you take the stairs—longer route possible for those with wheeled bags. Run by the Dhyaf family, it has a homey TV room and a big backyard (private rooms available, dinner available, no curfew, reception open 7:00-10:00 & 17:00-22:00, pay parking, closed late Oct-March, Rue du Lavoir 5, tel. 026-675-2666, www.youthhostel.ch/avenches, avenches@youthhostel.ch).

BERNER OBERLAND

Interlaken • Schilthorn • Jungfrau

Rather than tackle a checklist of famous Swiss mountains and resorts, choose one region to savor: the Berner Oberland. Here you can frolic and hike high above the stress and clouds of the real world. Take a vacation from your busy vacation. Recharge your touristic batteries high in the Alps, where distant avalanches, cowbells, the fluff of a down comforter, the whistle of marmots, and the crunchy footsteps of happy hikers are the dominant sounds. If the weather's good (and your budget's healthy), ride a cable car from your home-base village to a hearty breakfast at the revolving Piz Gloria restaurant, on top of the 9,748-foot Schilthorn peak. Linger among alpine whitecaps before riding down to the towns of Mürren, Gimmelwald, or Lauterbrunnen. Tunnel through the Eiger mountain on a train ride to the "top of Europe" at 11,333 feet—Jungfraujoch, the saddle between the Jungfrau and Mönch peaks—for exhilarating panoramas, glacier views, and fun snow activities.

Your gateway to the rugged Berner Oberland—the mountainous part of the canton of Bern—is the old resort town of Interlaken. Near Interlaken is Switzerland's open-air folk museum, Ballenberg, where you can climb through traditional houses gathered from every corner of this diverse country.

Ah, but the weather's fine and the Alps beckon. Head deep into the heart of the Alps, and ride a lift to a stop just this side of heaven. For me, that stop is the village of Gimmelwald.

PLANNING YOUR TIME

Prime time in this region is about late May until early October (though weather can be iffy on the fringes). Spring is not a good time to visit if you plan on dramatic hikes, as many trails are still snow-covered. And many hotels, restaurants, and shops are closed between the skiing and hiking seasons: from late April until late May, and again from mid-October to mid-December.

Interlaken is the region's administrative headquarters, transportation hub, and tackiest tourist town. Use it for business—banking, laundry, shopping—and as a springboard for alpine thrills... but ideally, not for spending the night.

If the weather's decent, explore the two areas that tower above either side of the Lauterbrunnen Valley, south of Interlaken: On

one side is the summit of Jungfrau (and beneath it, the tiny settlement of Kleine Scheidegg), and on the other is Schilthorn (overlooking the villages of Gimmelwald and Mürren).

Ideally, spend three nights in the region, with a day exploring each side of the valley. For accommodations without the expense and headache of mountain lifts—and equally handy to both sides of the valley—consider the valley-floor village of Lauterbrunnen. But for the best overnight options, I'd stay on the scenic ridge high above the valley, in the rustic hamlet of Gimmelwald or the resort town of Mürren. I've also listed a few options in other nearby mountain villages.

If your time is very limited, consider a night in Gimmelwald, breakfast at the Schilthorn, an afternoon doing the Männlichen-Kleine Scheidegg hike, and an evening train out. What? A nature lover not spending the night high in the Alps? Alpus interruptus.

The highest-altitude lifts are very expensive, and it only makes sense to splurge if you have a good chance of seeing an alpine panorama instead of fog or clouds. Let your plans flex with the weather. If it's good—go! Ask at your hotel or the TI for the latest info or check www.jungfrau.ch, www.schilthorn.ch, or www.meteo.search.ch. Webcams showing live video from the famous (and most expensive-to-reach) peaks play just about wherever you go in the area.

For a summary of the wildly scenic activities this region has to offer (from panoramic train rides and lifts to spectacular hikes and mountain biking), see "Activities in the Berner Oberland" on page 198.

GETTING AROUND THE BERNER OBERLAND

For more than a century, this region has been the target of nature-worshipping pilgrims. And Swiss engineers and visionaries have made the most exciting alpine perches accessible.

By Lift and Train

Part of the fun here—and most of the expense—is riding the many mountain trains and lifts (gondolas, cable cars, and funiculars).

Trains connect Interlaken to Wilderswil, Lauterbrunnen, Wengen, Kleine Scheidegg, and the Jungfraujoch, and also to Grindelwald. Lifts connect Wengen to Männlichen and Grund

Berner Oberland Transport Time/Cost

Code:
1st # = Approx. 2nd class one-way
cost in Swiss francs (CHF)

2nd # = Duration of trip in minutes

Notes:
Confirm prices locally.
Round-trip fares can be cheaper.
Most lifts run twice hourly.

Swiss Passes cover travel to Wengen and Mürren; Eurail/other int'l passes
cover travel only to Interlaken. (Passes offer discounts beyond these points.)

BERNER OBERLAND

(near Grindelwald); Grindelwald to First and Männlichen (and
to Eigergletscher by 2021); Lauterbrunnen to Grütschalp (where a
train connects to Mürren); and the cable-car station near Stechelberg to Gimmelwald, Mürren, and the Schilthorn.

For an overview of your many options, study the "Berner
Oberland Transport Time/Cost" map and the "Berner Oberland at
a Glance" sidebar in this chapter. Lifts generally go at least twice
hourly (sneak preview: www.jungfrau.ch or www.schilthorn.ch).
While train and bus schedules are stable, lift schedules flex with
demand, doubling their scheduled departures when necessary.

Train Station Ticket Offices: Ticket offices typically close at

Berner Oberland at a Glance

Towns, Villages, and Resorts

▲▲▲**Gimmelwald** Wonderfully rustic time-warp village—and a good home-base option—overlooking the Lauterbrunnen Valley. See page 179.

▲▲**Mürren** Pleasant resort town near Gimmelwald, midway up the Schilthorn cable-car line; a good high-mountain home base for those who find Gimmelwald too small and rustic. See page 188.

▲▲**Kleine Scheidegg** Small resort area with breathtaking views of Eiger, Mönch, and Jungfrau peaks; hotels and restaurants (see page 223); and train station for ride to the high-altitude Jungfraujoch (see page 202).

▲**Lauterbrunnen** Small town in the middle of the Lauterbrunnen Valley. From here, a cable car goes up to Grütschalp (with connections to Mürren and Gimmelwald), a train runs up to Wengen (with connections to Kleine Scheidegg and the Jungfraujoch), and the PostBus goes to Stechelberg (near the Schilthornbahn lift). See page 171.

▲**Interlaken** Big town between Lake Brienz and Lake Thun, at the "entrance" to the Berner Oberland. See page 154.

Top Lifts and Trains

▲▲▲**Schilthornbahn** Cable car soaring from Stechelberg in the Lauterbrunnen Valley to the 9,748-foot Schilthorn peak, with Piz Gloria revolving restaurant, James Bond exhibit, and stupendous views. Stops at Gimmelwald, Mürren, and Birg along the way. See page 198.

▲▲▲**Jungfraubahn** Train running from Kleine Scheidegg station and through tunnel inside Eiger and Mönch mountains to 11,333-foot Jungfraujoch saddle, with observation deck, shops, tip-top views, and snow activities. See page 202.

Walks and Hikes

▲▲▲**Männlichen-Kleine Scheidegg** Easy, mostly downhill ridge hike from cable-car station at Männlichen to Kleine Scheidegg, with spectacular views of Eiger and more. See page 215.

▲▲**Cloudy-Day Lauterbrunnen Valley Walk** Easy trails and pleasant walks along valley floor, plus short trail to Staubbach Falls at upper end of town. See page 207.

▲▲**North Face Trail** Relatively easy, view-filled hike from top of Allmendhubel funicular to villages of Mürren and/or Gimmelwald, passing farms with food service, Sprutz waterfall, mountain huts, and meadows. See page 209.

▲▲**Schynige Platte to First** Demanding, all-day ridge walk from Schynige Platte train station to gondola station at First. Fabulous views of Jungfrau-area peaks and Lake Brienz. See page 217.

▲▲**Birg to Gimmelwald via Bryndli** High, scenic, difficult hike from Birg cable-car station below Schilthorn summit to Gimmelwald. Trail winds past knobby summit of Bryndli, with nonstop views. See page 220.

▲**Mürren to Gimmelwald** Super-easy, paved, entirely downhill 30-minute stroll. See page 213.

▲**Sefinen Valley to Kilchbalm** Easy trail from village of Gimmelwald up Sefinen Valley to dramatic Kilchbalm, a glacier-carved bowl with streams, waterfalls, and meadows. See page 208.

▲**Allmendhubel to Grütschalp** Fairly easy walk from Allmendhubel down to Grütschalp, with views of the Jungfrau. See page 211.

▲**Gimmelwald-Tanzbödeli-Obersteinberg-Stechelberg/Gimmelwald** Difficult yet highly rewarding all-day hike offering spectacular views and relative solitude (aside from goats, cows, chamois, and a cheesemaker). See page 218.

▲**Sprutz Waterfall** Moderately difficult hike from Gimmelwald up to and behind the waterfall (also a good stop on a hike down from Allmendhubel). See page 219.

▲**Grütschalp to Mürren** Super-easy, family-friendly stroll along the ridge with grand views of the Eiger, Mönch, and Jungfrau. See page 212.

More Sightseeing Options

▲▲**Ballenberg** Open-air folk museum near Interlaken, on Lake Brienz. See page 162.

▲**Trümmelbach Falls** Lauterbrunnen Valley's most powerful falls, accessed via elevator ride up into the mountain and dramatic walk through several wet caves. See page 174.

▲**Harder Kulm** Easy funicular ride from Interlaken up to a historic restaurant with a grand view. See page 164.

19:00 or 19:30. You'll find ticket machines on the platforms, but if you need to talk to a real person, don't wait too late in the day.

Passes and Deals: Trains and lifts can get expensive here—consider money-saving passes. If you have a **Eurail Global Pass,** trains and lifts beyond Interlaken are 25 percent off (doesn't require a flexi-day); with the **Swiss Travel Pass,** they're covered up to Wengen (above Wengen, pass holders get 25-50 percent off) and up to Mürren (ascending from there to the Schilthorn is 50 percent off). While those two passes are the best option for most Swiss trips using public transportation (both described starting on page 443), there are a few others to consider: The **Berner Oberland Regional Pass** covers most trains, buses, and lifts in this area (and all the way to Bern, Luzern, Gstaad, and Birg) but costs about the same as the more versatile Swiss Travel Pass (www.regionalpass-berneroberland.ch). The **Jungfrau Travel Pass** is more limited in scope, covering transportation on the east side of the valley, plus from Lauterbrunnen to Mürren via Grütschalp; it's worth considering only if you're focusing exclusively on the Wengen-Kleine Scheidegg-Jungfraujoch area (3-8 day versions available, from 180 CHF, www.jungfrau.ch). And the **Junior Travelcard,** valid across Switzerland for families traveling with children, lets kids ages 5-16 travel free with at least one parent (children under age 5 already travel free; 30 CHF/one child, 60 CHF/two or more children, buy at Swiss train stations).

Individual lifts offer a changing assortment of discounts—ask about deals for early-morning and late-afternoon trips, youths, seniors, families, groups (assemble a party of 10 and you'll save about 25 percent), and special promotions. Generally, round-trips are double the one-way cost, though some high-up trains and lifts are 10-20 percent cheaper when you buy a round-trip. It's possible to buy a package covering all of your planned lifts at once, but you'll lose the flexibility to change with the weather.

By Car

Interlaken, Lauterbrunnen, and Stechelberg are accessible by car. You can't drive to Gimmelwald, Mürren, Wengen, or Kleine Scheidegg, but don't let that stop you from *staying* up in the mountains: Park your car and zip up on a lift. For the lift to Gimmelwald, Mürren, and the Schilthorn, use the pay parking lot at the cable-car station near Stechelberg. For the train to Wengen or Kleine Scheidegg, use the pay parking garage behind the train station in Lauterbrunnen.

By Bus

The handy PostBus connects points along the valley, from Lauterbrunnen to Trümmelbach Falls to the Schilthornbahn cable-car station at Stechelberg (4.40 CHF, 2/hour, about 20 minutes from

Lauterbrunnen to the cable car, covered by many transit passes, www.postauto.ch).

HELPFUL HINTS IN THE BERNER OBERLAND

Closed Days: On Sundays and holidays (including lesser-known religious holidays), small-town Switzerland is quiet. Lifts and trains run, but many stores are closed.

Visitor Cards *(Gästekarten):* Hotels issue free Visitor Cards (paid for by your room tax) that include small discounts on some sights, as well as other perks that vary by town, such as free bus service in Interlaken.

Money: Interlaken, Lauterbrunnen, and Wengen have plenty of banks and ATMs, but there is no bank or ATM in Gimmelwald and only one ATM in Mürren. Plan accordingly.

Rainy-Day Options: When it rains here, locals joke that they're washing the mountains. If clouds roll in, don't despair. They can roll out just as quickly. With good rain gear, proper shoes, and the right choice of trail, you can thoroughly enjoy a hike in the rain, with surprise views popping out all around you as the clouds break. Some good bad-weather options are the North Face trail (but avoid the steep-and-slippery detour to Sprutz waterfall), the easy downhill amble from Mürren to Gimmelwald, the walk from Mürren/Allmendhubel to Grütschalp, the Sefinen Valley hike, and the Lauterbrunnen Valley walk. Also consider a visit to Trümmelbach Falls, the Swiss Open-Air Museum at Ballenberg, or the Lauterbrunnen Valley Folk Museum.

Local Guidebook: For in-depth information on the area's history, folk life, flora, fauna, and hiking options, consider Don Chmura's *Exploring the Lauterbrunnen Valley* (sold at Lauterbrunnen TI).

Local Hiking Guide: Licensed private hiking guide **Doris Schmied** knows local flora, fauna, and culture (around 400 CHF/day, mobile 079-689-9816, www.doris-hike.ch).

Skiing and Snowboarding: This is a great winter-sports destination, with good snow on higher runs, nice variety, relatively reasonable prices, and a sense of character that's missing in swankier resort areas. You can even swish with the Swiss down the world's longest sledding run (9 miles long, out of Grindelwald, open only when snow's good). Three ski areas cluster around the Lauterbrunnen Valley: Mürren-Schilthorn (best for experts), Kleine Scheidegg-Männlichen (busiest, best variety of runs), and Grindelwald-First (best for beginners/intermediates, but lower elevation can make for iffier snowpack). For info, see www.jungfrau.ch/winter. For more tips, see the Switzerland in Winter chapter.

Interlaken

When the 19th-century Romantics redefined mountains as something more than cold and troublesome obstacles, Interlaken became the original alpine resort. Ever since, tourists have flocked to the Alps "because they're there." Interlaken's glory days are long gone, its elegant old hotels eclipsed by newer, swankier alpine resorts. Today the town center has been re-envisioned for the needs of mass tourism. It's an alpine gateway town with shops filled with chocolate bars, Swiss Army knives, trinkets, lots of tour guides squeezing their groups into trains and gondolas, and plenty of sunburned backpackers nursing an adrenaline hangover.

Efficient Interlaken (pop. 5,500) is, above all, a good administrative and shopping center. Its streets are a strange combination of faded grand hotels, adventure-travel companies, and curry houses. While handy, it's too bustling and touristy to provide a real mountain experience. Take care of business, give the town a quick look, and view the webcam coverage (at the TI) of the weather higher up...then head for the hills.

Orientation to Interlaken

Interlaken straddles the Aare River, which connects two alpine lakes: Lake Brienz and Lake Thun. The older part of town (called Unterseen) is on the right bank of the Aare and has pockets of charm and a cute village square. The newer section (Interlaken proper), with most services and both train stations, is on the river's left bank.

TOURIST INFORMATION

A small TI operates at the Interlaken Ost train station in summer and is convenient if you're arriving there (daily 8:30-18:30, though hours may vary; closed Oct-May).

Interlaken's Latest Tourism Boom

While the Swiss Alps are now passé for European jet-setters, Interlaken is cashing in on huge group-travel interest from Asia and the Arab world. It's a tourism trend across Switzerland: In 2018 international arrivals from Asia were up 6 percent and from the Middle East up 10 percent (US visitors were up 3 percent).

Tourists from India come to this region to escape their monsoon season—especially in April and May—and to visit romantic places they've seen in Bollywood movies. (The Alps often stand in for Kashmir, which is less accessible to film crews.) There's even a restaurant called "Bollywood" atop the Jungfraujoch. Interlaken is also popular with tour groups from China; the Schilthornbahn marketing department recently opened an office in Shanghai. And tourists from the hot and arid Arabian Peninsula—who grew up visiting cafés adorned with faded wallpaper depicting dreamy alpine scenes—visit to photograph their children frolicking in chilly mist and fog. (Some vacation packages even offer a refund if all they get is sunshine.) Every expectation is that Asian tourism will continue to grow, and this corner of the Swiss Alps will become ever more international—and crowded.

If you prefer to avoid the congestion caused by mass-tourism crowds, sleep in the high country (instead of Interlaken), hike away from the towns, and be active early and late.

Otherwise, visit the main TI, located by the post office at Marktgasse 1 (Mon-Fri 8:00-18:00—until 19:00 July-Aug, Sat-Sun 9:00-17:00; shorter hours and closed Sun Oct-May; tel. 033-826-5300, www.interlaken.ch). Pick up the timetable and the hiking guide published by the Jungfraubahn mountain railway (both include a good map of the area). The TI sells tickets for the Swiss rail system, the various mountain trains and lifts, and adventure sports.

ARRIVAL IN INTERLAKEN

Interlaken has two train stations: Ost (East) and West. Major trains generally stop at both stations, but for ease and economy, confirm which station you want when buying your ticket.

Interlaken Ost is the transfer point for narrow-gauge trains to the high mountains (to Lauterbrunnen, Gimmelwald, Jungfraujoch, etc.) and to Luzern. Use this station if you're headed to those destinations or staying at the recommended Interlaken Hostel (next door). Interlaken Ost has free WCs, lockers, ticket counters, and a summer-only branch TI.

Interlaken West is closer to most of my listed hotels and downtown shopping and services. All trains from western Switzerland—Bern, the Golden Pass, Basel—stop at Interlaken West, and then continue to Interlaken Ost. Interlaken West has WCs, lockers (by track 1), and ticket counters.

From Interlaken East to Interlaken West: It's a pleasant 30-minute walk between the West and Ost train stations. Otherwise, pay a few francs for the easy 3-minute trip by train (3/hour) or 10-minute trip on any of several local buses (free with Visitor Card; #21, #102, #103, or #104).

HELPFUL HINTS

Laundry: Tiny self-service **Wäscherei** has a change machine, soap, English instructions, and a handy riverside location (daily 7:00-22:00; Beatenbergstrasse 5, steps from Unterseen's main square, tel. 033-822-1566).

Bike Rental: The Interlaken West train station participates in the Swiss rail system's bike-rental scheme (see page 448). **Flying Wheels,** a short walk from the Ost train station, is a hip, well-organized, family-friendly outfit that specializes in electric bikes and guided bike tours. Its English-speaking staff give tips on where to go and can help you pick the right bike (bikes-30 CHF/half-day, 35 CHF/day; electric bikes-45 CHF/half-day, 55 CHF/day; includes helmet, daily May-Sept 9:30-20:00 in good weather, shorter hours off-season, across street from northeast corner of Höhematte Park at Höheweg 133, tel. 033-557-8838, www.flyingwheels.ch). For info on their tours, see "Adventure Sports," later.

A short walk from the West train station, you can also rent a bike at **Eiger Sport** (bikes-20 CHF/half-day, 30 CHF/day; electric bikes-49 CHF/half-day, 60 CHF/day; helmets extra, Mon-Fri 8:30-12:00 & 13:30-18:30, Sat 8:30-16:00, closed Sun; from the West train station, cross the river—it's on the left at Bahnhofstrasse 2, tel. 033-823-2043, www.eigersport.ch).

"Free" Walking Tours: "Free" tours are actually "pay what you think it's worth" tours—you'll be hit up for a tip at the end. Though light on sights and history, they offer a fun city overview and a chance to join a smart local student on a stroll through his or her hometown (likely Mon, Wed, and Sat at 18:00 from Outdoor Interlaken Höheweg Shop at Höheweg 95, tel. 033-826-7719, www.interlakenfreetour.com).

BERNER OBERLAND

Interlaken Walk

Most visitors use Interlaken as a springboard for high-altitude thrills (and rightly so). But the town itself has history and scenic charm, and is worth a short walk. This 45-minute stroll circles from the West train station, down the main drag to the big meadow, past the casino, along the river to the oldest part of town (called Unterseen—historically a separate town), and back to the station.

• *With your back to the West train station, turn left and walk along...*

Bahnhofstrasse: This main drag, which turns into Höheweg as it continues east, cuts through the town center from the West train station to the Ost train station. The best souvenir shopping is along this stretch (finer shops are on the Höheweg stretch, near the fancy hotels). Looking high up to the top of the cliff on your left, notice the pointy dome of Harder Kulm—the historic restaurant at the "Top of Interlaken" (described later).

Just past the unfortunately named Hotel Krebs, set back from the street is a handy Co-op grocery store. Free (and futuristic) WCs are inside the round structure at the end of this strip. Continuing on the main drag, it changes names to Höheweg; on the right at #2, the TV in the window of the Schilthornbahn office shows the weather up top.

At the end of the street looms **Metropole Hotel** (a.k.a. the "concrete shame of Interlaken")—at 18 stories, by far the town's tallest building. Step right into the main lobby (through the second set of doors) and ride the elevator to the top for a commanding view of the "inter-laken" area, and gaze deep into the Jungfrau region to the scenic south. A meal or beverage here costs no more than one back on earth. Consider sipping a drink on the outdoor view terrace (or come back tonight—it's open late).

"Fancy Hotel Row": The Metropole marks the beginning of Interlaken's strip of high-end, Romantic Age hotels. Hotels like the Victoria-Jungfrau harken back to the late-19th-century days when Interlaken was *the* top alpine resort. The first grand hotels were built here to enjoy the views of the Jungfrau in the distance. Today, the *junge Frauen* getting the most attention are next door, at Hooters.

In fact, the odd placement of that restaurant is rooted in local politics. Most of the tourism industry here is locally owned—which is a good thing. But the downside is that local big shots are not above petty village bickering. In this case, the guy who owned this patch of land in front of the classiest hotel in town lost an argument with the hotel's owner...so, he put up a tacky, low-rise Hooters chain restaurant. That'll teach him. Meanwhile, the CEOs of the two dominant mountain lifts (Jungfraubahn and Schilthornbahn)

BERNER OBERLAND

Interlaken

UNTERSEEN

BERNER OBERLAND

POOL

CASI

KURSA

BEATENBERGSTR.

SEESTRASSE

17 2

SPIELMATTE

MUSEUM OF TOURISM

16

18

AUF DEM GRABEN

FREIHOFSTR.

UNTERE GASSE

3

HAUPTGASSE

MÜHLEGASSLI

AARESTRASSE

VICTORIA JUNGFRAU

HARDERSTR.

14

9

HÖHE WE

SCHELDSTRASSE

15

22

BAHNHOFSTRASSE

Marktplatz

11

POST

Co-op

19

JUNGFRAUSTR.

13

12

CENTRALSTRASSE

21

SEESTRASSE

HELVETIASTR.

4

AARMÜHLESTR.

8

BOAT DOCK

Bahnhof-platz

WALK BEGINS & ENDS HERE

Aare River

WEST STATION

NIESENSTR.

13

10

1

GUISANSTR.

BEKNASTR.

ROSENSTR.

WYCHEL

Ship Canal

RUGENPARKSTRASSE

WALDEGGSTRASSE

To Lake Thun

To N-18 Autobahn (Bern & Luzern)

SEILPARK

GOLDSWIL

To Brienz & Luzern

To Lake Brienz

Funicular to Harder Kulm

BOAT DOCK

OST (EAST) STATION

Aare River

UNTERE BÖNIGSTRASSE

Private Trains to Jungfrau Region

BIG, RITZY HOTELS

MONASTERY SITE

LINDENALLEE

Höhematte Park

MATTEN

To N-18 Autobahn (Bern & Luzern) & Lauterbrunnen Valley

400 Meters

400 Yards

Accommodations
1. Hotel Lötschberg
2. The Aarburg & Launderette
3. Hotel Rössli
4. Adventure Guesthouse
5. Interlaken Hostel
6. Backpackers' Villa Sonnenhof
7. Balmer's Herberge & Metro Bar
8. Happy Inn Lodge & Brasserie 17

Eateries, Nightlife & Other
9. Metropole Hotel's Top o'Met
10. Migros Cafeteria & Supermarket
11. Confiserie Rieder Tea Room
12. Velo Café
13. Global Cuisine Strips (2)
14. Biryani House
15. Restaurant Bären
16. Città Vecchia Ristorante & Pizzeria
17. Benacus
18. Stadthaus
19. Restaurant Schuh
20. Supermarket
21. K44 Climbing & Vertical Sport
22. Bike Rental (2)

don't play well together. There's little coordination, and the map for one system treats the other's lifts like they don't exist.

• *Now turn your attention to the big field across from those hotels.*

Höhematte Park: This "high meadow"—or *höhe Matte* (but generally referred to simply as "the park")—originated as farmland belonging to the monastery that predated the town (marked today by the steeples of both the Catholic and Protestant churches, just beyond the far end of the park—neither are of sightseeing interest). The actual **monastery site** is now home to the courthouse and county administration building. With the Reformation in 1528, the monastery was shut down, and its land taken by the state. Later, as developers started to eye the parkland, the town's leading hotels and business families bought it and protected it from commercial use (a very early example of smart town planning). Today, this is a fine place to stroll, hang out on the park benches or at Restaurant Schuh, and watch the paragliders gracefully land.

• *But for now, we'll take a detour toward the river. After the Victoria-Jungfrau Hotel, follow the passage on your left (through a shopping arcade) into the grounds of the…*

Casino Kursaal: The venerable old Kursaal, originally a kind of 19th-century weight-loss retreat, is now a convention center and casino (passport but no tie required to enter). In the garden, at the top of each hour, dwarves ring the toadstools on the flower clock. And, all day long visitors from India pose at the bronze-colored statue of Yash Chopra—the Steven Spielberg of India, who shot many romantic scenes for his Bollywood films here.

• *Circle around the left side of the Kursaal to the river (note the huge public swimming pool across the river—an inviting complex that also has a water slide). Turn left and walk downstream along the riverside path for a few minutes, passing under the train bridge, and cross the pedestrian bridge, stopping in the middle to enjoy the view.*

Aare River: This short stretch of Switzerland's longest river connects Lake Brienz and Lake Thun (with an 18-foot altitude difference that's controlled by sluices—notice it has quite a flow). From Lake Thun, it heads for Bern and ultimately into the Rhine. In the distance (looking downstream), a church bell tower marks a different parish and the technically separate town of Unterseen, across the river—we're headed there next. Behind the spire is the pointy summit of the Niesen (like so many Swiss peaks, capped with a restaurant and accessible by a lift).

Cross the rest of the way over the bridge, turn left, and stroll downstream along the far side of the river, toward the church spire. Watch on your left for one of those old wooden sluices that help control the river flow. The delightful, tree-lined riverside walk is fronted by fine residences. Notice that your Jungfrau view now includes the Jungfraujoch observation deck (the little brown bump in the ridge just left of the peak).

• *At the next bridge, turn right and walk a half-block up into the old town square, lined with 17th-century houses on one side and a modern strip on the other.*

Unterseen: This was a town when Interlaken was only a monastery, and today it preserves a little of its medieval layout and streetscape. Three recommended restaurants face this square.

In the upper part of the square (behind the big building), the big *Tourismuseum* sign marks the worthwhile—but generally empty—**Museum of Tourism** (grandly named, but really a local history museum), which shows off three floors of classic posters, fascinating photos of the construction of the Jungfraujoch, and exhibits on folk life, crafts, and winter sports (8 CHF, covered by Swiss Travel Pass, Wed-Sun 14:00-18:00, closed Mon-Tue, Dec-April open only Wed and Sun 14:00-18:00, Obere Gasse 28, tel. 033-826-6464, www.touristikmuseum.ch).

From the little square, retrace your steps and continue straight across the big bridge, carrying on straight on Spielmatte. From the bridge, watch on your right for another one of those antique sluices.

Soon you'll reach a second bridge. On the left is yet another old sluice. If you look closely, you'll notice two heraldic emblems, each featuring an ibex, a wild mountain goat: a yellow one on the left, and a silver one on the right. This marks the border between the two towns/parishes. You're leaving Unterseen and returning to Interlaken.

Back to the Train Station: You're just a five-minute walk from the main drag, and a 10-minute walk from the West station where we began. Carry on straight past the second bridge, crossing the train tracks. After about three blocks, a little restaurant-lined square called Marktplatz opens up on your left. The river originally ran through here, and the settlement on this side of the river was called "Aarmühle" (mill on the Aare), after the mill that was here. But in the 19th century, town fathers mindful of the English tourists flocking here made a key marketing decision: They ditched the difficult-to-pronounce "Aarmühle" and changed the town's name to the romantic "Interlaken" (between the lakes). Judging from the throngs of tourists on the main drag, that was a smart decision.

BERNER OBERLAND

• *Continuing straight ahead, you'll run into Bahnhofstrasse/Höheweg. Turn right to head back to the West station—or turn left to go back toward Höhematte park and, beyond it, the Harder Kulm funicular and the Ost station.*

Sights and Activities near Interlaken

For hikes and walks in the Berner Oberland, see page 206.

EASYGOING EXCURSIONS

▲▲Swiss Open-Air Museum at Ballenberg

At the far end of Lake Brienz from Interlaken, the Ballenberg open-air museum is a rich collection of more than 100 traditional and historic buildings brought here from every region of the country. All the houses are carefully furnished, and many feature traditional craftspeople at work. The sprawling 50-acre park, laid out roughly as a huge Swiss map (Italian Swiss in the south, Appenzell in the east, and so on), is a natural preserve providing a wonderful setting for this culture-on-a-lazy-Susan look at Switzerland.

Ballenberg has entrances at either end (east and west, about a mile apart, each served by the local bus). If you start in the east and go west, it's a generally downhill stroll. Pick up a daily craft-demonstration schedule at the entry, and the free map/guide. There are daily events and demonstrations, hundreds of traditional farm animals (like very furry-legged roosters, near the merry-go-round in the center), and a chocolate shop (under the restaurant, just outside the park, on the east side).

There are more historic buildings than you can see in a single visit. Survey your map, note where the demonstrations are happening, and make a smart plan. Buildings I particularly enjoy are: #1361 (cheese upstairs, cow bells you can ring downstairs); #911 (a big Appenzell house); #611 (barbershop museum upstairs); #321 (sausages hanging from the ceiling); and #221 (a house and farm designed for hands-on fun).

Cost and Hours: 28 CHF, covered by Swiss Travel Pass, houses open daily mid-April-Oct 10:00-17:00, grounds and restaurants 9:00-18:00, tel. 033-952-1030, www.ballenberg.ch.

Eating: Along with several eateries, picnic tables and grills with free firewood are scattered throughout the park.

Getting There: The trip from Interlaken to Ballenberg takes about 20 minutes by car (pay parking at either entrance), 50 minutes by train and bus, or 2 hours by boat and bus. By public transport, you'll first go to Brienz by train or boat, then from Brienz to Ballenberg by local bus. Trains for Brienz leave from the Interlaken Ost train station (2/hour, 15-20 minutes). Boats to Brienz leave from a dock just behind the Ost train station (every 1-2 hours, 1.25

hours, early April-late Oct only, tel. 058-327-4811, www.bls.ch). From the Brienz station or boat dock, catch local bus #151 to either museum entrance (hourly, 20 minutes). Use the online timetables at www.sbb.ch to plan your trip, and check bus return times carefully—after 18:00, buses back to Brienz leave only from the park's west entrance. Without a rail pass, ask for the Ballenberg combo-ticket when buying your train or boat tickets: This covers the complete round-trip from Interlaken (or beyond), and saves about 10 percent off your fare and park entry.

Boat Trips

"Interlaken" is literally "between the lakes" of Thun and Brienz, and you can explore these lakes on a lazy boat trip. While more relaxing than exciting—I'd rather spend a sunny day on a high-mountain lift—a lake-boat cruise can be a scenic way to slow your pulse (free with Swiss Travel Pass or Eurail Global Pass but uses a flexi-day, 5/day July-Aug, 2-4/day spring and fall, tel. 058-327-4811, www.bls.ch). You can pay extra for the "first class" top deck, but most people crowd the lower decks; the front deck is smaller but quieter and comes with a nice breeze. The ride begins by heading up a long, dull canal—but then, when the boat reaches the lake, the scenery opens up. From there, boats slowly hopscotch their way up the lake, stopping at middle-of-nowhere docks and offering pleasant views of little shoreline communities and cottages. Returning by train makes for a good plan, as the boats are slow and run only a few times a day.

Lake Thun: Departing from just behind the West train station (follow signs for *Pier One*), boats on Lake Thun make stops including the St. Beatus caves (30 minutes from Interlaken, 16.60 CHF, described next) and two visit-worthy towns: Spiez (80 minutes, 29 CHF) and Thun (2.25 hours, 45 CHF). Consider riding as far as one of these two towns, then zipping back on the train. Note: If disembarking in Spiez, the train station is a dull uphill hike away, but a bus stop is near the boat dock. Buses meet some boats and zip passengers right up to the train station (confirm with boat crew that your boat is coordinated with the bus).

The **St. Beatus caves,** named after a legendary medieval monk, can be visited either on your own or with a 1.25-hour guided tour (18 CHF, tours depart every 45 minutes, mid-March-mid-Nov daily 9:45-17:00, closed off-season, tel. 033-841-1643, www.beatushoehlen.swiss). To avoid the hike up from the lakeshore, try this plan: Catch bus #21 from either Interlaken station (5.20 CHF, about 2/hour, 15-25 minutes, direction: Thun), get off at the Beatushöhlen stop; tour the caves; take the short, steep hike down to the lake; and return to Interlaken by boat.

Lake Brienz: Departing from behind the Ost train station, boats on Lake Brienz are a fun way to get to the town of Brienz (32 CHF, 1.25 hours, get off here for the Ballenberg open-air museum); there's also a stop at the super-cute village of Iseltwald on the way.

▲Harder Kulm (Harderbahn)

Standing like a pointy little crown on a forested bluff high above Interlaken is a Romantic Age view restaurant that has rewarded a century of visitors with commanding views of Interlaken, the lakes, and the Berner Oberland peaks. While some make the steep climb up from town on foot, most just catch the Harder Kulm funicular—marketed as the "Top of Interlaken"—which leaves from just over the river from Interlaken Ost train station. It's easy and very scenic, but it's still a "Berner Oberland Lite" experience, with cut-glass peaks farther away than they are from the many grand lifts near the Lauterbrunnen Valley. I'd go up Harder Kulm only if you're a mountain-lift completist, or if you're quickly passing through Interlaken without time to delve deeper. On a nice day, be prepared for lines going up—and going down.

Cost and Hours: 32 CHF round-trip, half-price with Swiss Travel Pass, smaller discount with Interlaken Visitor Card, at least 2/hour, daily mid-April-late Oct 9:10-20:55, in winter until 17:55, operated by Jungfraubahn—www.jungfrau.ch.

Visiting the Mountaintop: You'll ride up in eight minutes, in a glass-roofed funicular. From the top station, you'll walk about

five minutes along a ledge to reach the restaurant and nearby viewpoint (at 4,337 feet)—cantilevered to jut out toward the mountain vistas, with Interlaken at your feet. Visitors crowd around on the platform to pose with props: a Swiss flag and a life-size plastic cow.

For a slightly more relaxed experience, hike up the little trail just before the restaurant (marked *pavilion*). Just a few steps takes you above the hubbub, to similar views but without the crowds (and with a few benches for lingering).

The **$$ restaurant** itself has indoor and outdoor seating—all with grand views—and a predictable menu of Swiss and international standards. Some tables are for the little self-service **$ snack bar.** In peak season, there's frequently live folk music out on the terrace.

ADVENTURE SPORTS

High-Adrenaline Trips

For the thrill-seeker with money, several companies offer trips such as rafting, canyoning (rappelling down watery gorges), bungee jumping, and paragliding. Costs range from roughly 150 CHF to 200 CHF—higher for skydiving and hot-air balloon rides. Interlaken's two dominant companies are **Alpin Raft** (tel. 033-823-4100, www.alpinraft.ch) and **Outdoor Interlaken** (tel. 033-826-7719, www.outdoor-interlaken.ch). Other companies are generally just booking agents for these two outfits. For an overview of your options, study the racks of brochures at most TIs and hotels.

Indoor Climbing

K44 is a breathtaking indoor climbing facility. The 21-CHF entry fee lets you climb as long as you like (includes equipment but not instruction, family deals; daily 8:30-22:00; next to—and run by—**Vertical Sport,** at the back of the park across from Hotel Savoy at Jungfraustrasse 44, tel. 033-821-2821, www.kletterhalle-interlaken.ch). I find just watching the action is thrilling. While not designed for public viewing, they may let you in as a spectator if you have a special interest and ask politely.

Rope Courses

Outdoor Interlaken's Seilpark offers eight rope courses of varying difficulty and height, giving you a treetop forest adventure through a maze of rope bridges and zip lines.

Cost and Hours: 39 CHF, family deals, must weigh between 44 and 264 pounds; June daily 10:00-18:00, July-Aug until 20:00; April-May and Sept-Oct Mon-Fri 13:00-18:00, Sat-Sun from 10:00; closed Nov-March; last entry 2 hours before closing time; from Interlaken's West train station, it's a 15-minute walk—head right up Rugenparkstrasse and into the park, then look for signs; tel. 033-826-7719, www.outdoor-interlaken.ch (select "Summer," "Earth Activities," then "Adventure Park").

Bike Tours

Flying Wheels offers bike tours of varying length and difficulty, including a tour of the Lauterbrunnen Valley (189 CHF, 6 hours, includes picnic and Trümmelbach Falls visit; 249 CHF for 7-hour version that adds a mountain lift and a downhill ride from Mürren to Gimmelwald). For contact info, see page 156.

CASTLES

Three impressively well-kept and welcoming old castles in or near the town of Thun are worth considering for day trips (30 minutes from Interlaken by train or car, or about 2 hours by scenic boat ride).

BERNER OBERLAND

Thun Castle (Schloss Thun)

Built between 1180 and 1190 by the Dukes of Zähringen, this castle in the center of Thun houses a five-floor historical museum offering insights into the cultural development of the region over some 4,000 years. From the corner turrets of the castle, you're rewarded with sweeping views of the city of Thun, the lake, and the Alps.

Cost and Hours: 10 CHF, daily 10:00-17:00, shorter hours off-season, Nov-Jan Sun only, tel. 033-223-2001, www.schlossthun.ch.

Hünegg Castle (Schloss Hünegg)

Located in Hilterfingen (on the outskirts of Thun), this castle-museum exhibits furnished rooms from the second half of the 19th century. The castle is situated in a beautiful wooded park by the lake, not far from the Hilterfingen boat dock and the #21 bus from Interlaken or Thun.

Cost and Hours: 10 CHF, Tue-Sat 14:00-17:00, Sun from 11:00, closed Mon and mid-Oct-mid-May, tel. 033-243-1982, www.schlosshuenegg.ch.

Oberhofen Castle (Schloss Oberhofen)

A 20-minute walk along the lake from Hünegg Castle, this castle is set in a beautifully landscaped park with exotic trees. The castle's museum explores domestic life in the 16th to 19th centuries, including a Turkish smoking room and a medieval chapel.

Cost and Hours: Gardens—free, April-late Oct daily 9:00-20:00, until 21:00 in summer; museum—10 CHF, mid-May-late Oct Tue-Sun 11:00-17:00, closed Mon; both closed off-season, by Oberhofen am Thunersee boat dock or take bus #21, tel. 033-243-1235, www.schlossoberhofen.ch.

Nightlife in Interlaken

Lively Nightlife: A young frat-party dance scene rages at the **Metro Bar** bomb-shelter disco, with cheap drinks and a friendly if loud atmosphere (at Balmer's, Hauptstrasse 2 in Matten). **Brasserie 17** is a more local scene with craft beers on tap and a down-and-dirty pub/sports bar ambience. On game nights sports play on the big screen, and Thursday evenings often feature live music (burgers, ribs, wings, and other bar food until 21:30, open nightly until 24:00, in the Happy Inn Lodge hostel at Rosenstrasse 17, tel. 033-822-3225). And if you're into **Hooters,** you won't have a hard time finding it.

Mellow Nightlife: To nurse a drink with a park view, the outdoor tables at **Restaurant Schuh** (on the edge of Höhematte

Park) are convenient—if you don't mind the schlocky music. The **Top o'Met** restaurant in the Metropole Hotel skyscraper has great indoor and outdoor view seating with reasonable prices, 18 floors above everything else in town (open nightly until late, see "Eating in Interlaken," later). While the interior is lit like a grocery store, the outdoor seating is particularly nice on a warm evening.

Or you could just stroll the main street and marvel at the shops filled with tourists buying watches on their blitz tours.

Sleeping in Interlaken

Interlaken is not the Alps. I'd sleep in Gimmelwald, Mürren, or at least Lauterbrunnen (20 minutes away by train or car). In ski season, however, prices go down in Interlaken, while they shoot up at most mountain hotels. Price ratings given here are for summer; they drop a bit in spring and fall, and plunge from November to March.

Hotels and Guest Houses

$$ Hotel Lötschberg has a sun terrace and 18 rooms just a three-minute walk from the West train station, but it's still residential and quiet. They have a lounge with microwave, fridge, and free tea and coffee (closed Jan-mid-April; from the West train station turn right, after Migros at the circle go left to General-Guisan-Strasse 31; tel. 033-822-2545, www.lotschberg.ch, hotel@lotschberg.ch).

$$ The Aarburg offers nine plain, peaceful rooms over a restaurant in a traditional, beautifully located building just steps from the charming main square of Unterseen, a 10-minute walk from the West train station. Rooms are small, but guests can enjoy the shared lounge (check-in 16:00-21:00—make arrangements for other times, Beatenbergstrasse 1, tel. 033-820-4460, www.theaarburg.ch, well-run by Tim and Kat).

$$ Hotel Rössli, across the river from the West train station in Unterseen, is nicely located, if a bit dated. Their 35 rooms include "economy" rooms with a private bath down the hall and "budget" rooms with shared facilities (closed Dec-mid-Jan, elevator, comfy lounge, Hauptstrasse 10, tel. 033-822-7816, www.roessli-interlaken.ch, info@roessli-interlaken.ch).

$ Adventure Guesthouse, owned by a nearby hostel, is a cheery, family-friendly, nine-room place in a quiet residential neighborhood (family rooms, patio; from West train station exit left and take first bridge to your left, after crossing two bridges turn left on Helvetiastrasse and go 3 blocks to #29; mobile 077-456-2338, www.adventure-guesthouse.ch, info@adventure-guesthouse.ch).

Hostels

Interlaken is a prime destination for hostels—with something for every taste, from efficient and institutional to family-friendly and hotelesque to more party-oriented.

¢ **Interlaken Hostel** is very convenient—right next to the Ost train station in a big, sterile modern building, full of daylight and with plenty of amenities (private rooms available, bike rental, game room, check-in 15:00-24:00, Untere Bönigstrasse 3, tel. 033-826-1090, www.youthhostel.ch/interlaken, interlaken@youthhostel.ch). Their modern, welcoming, self-service **restaurant** is open to the public and popular with locals for its good value.

¢ **Backpackers' Villa Sonnenhof** is a creative, prizewinning guesthouse affiliated with the Methodist church. Wholesome without being restrictive, it's fun, colorful, and great for families and travelers of all ages (private rooms, family rooms, view rooms have balcony and WC but shared shower, half-board dinner at nearby restaurant, kitchen, elevator, garden, movies, small game room, free entry to public swimming pool and tennis courts, reception open 7:00-23:00; across park from the main drag at Alpenstrasse 16—a level 15-minute walk from either train station, or take bus #102 to Sonnenhof stop; tel. 033-826-7171, www.villa.ch, mail@villa.ch).

¢ **Balmer's Herberge** is high-energy, youthful, and very social. This 200-bed Interlaken institution is many people's idea of backpacker heaven, with movies, table tennis, bar, restaurant, tiny grocery, kitchen, hot tub, swapping library, excursions, and friendly, hardworking staff. It can feel like a frat party, especially on summer weekends (reserve far in advance for private rooms; 20-minute walk from either train station at Hauptstrasse 23, in Matten, tel. 033-822-1961, www.balmers.com, mail@balmers.com). More-expensive rooms in an adjacent building come with semiprivate kitchens and fewer beds per WC.

¢ **Happy Inn Lodge,** above the lively, noisy Brasserie 17 pub, has 16 cheap, conveniently located backpacker rooms, plus two basic doubles with private baths. It's a decent option for the young and scrappy (5-minute walk from West train station at Rosenstrasse 17, tel. 033-822-3225, www.happyinn.com, info@brasserie17.ch).

Eating in Interlaken

In the Heart of Interlaken

$$ **Metropole Hotel's Top o'Met** café/restaurant, capping Interlaken's 18-story aesthetic nightmare, actually serves good traditional and modern food at down-to-earth prices, with no gouging on drinks. For 5 CHF, you can enjoy a glass of Swiss wine and awesome views from an indoor or outdoor table. You can see both lakes

and the Jungfrau at the same time and watch the paragliders swoop gracefully by (daily 25-CHF deals for lunch or dinner include 2 courses plus water and coffee—you may need to request it specifically for dinner, 50-CHF fondue for two; daily 8:00-23:00, Oct-May 10:00-22:00; hot food served 11:30-14:00 & 18:00-21:30, Höheweg 37, tel. 033-828-6666, Marco).

$ Migros is a great bet for a fast, inexpensive, self-service meal (if you don't mind eating in a cafeteria). You dish up what looks good, pay by the weight, and enjoy nice seating with a local crowd. As they strive to sell out, hot food dwindles in the last hour (Mon-Thu 8:00-20:00, Fri until 21:00, Sat until 18:00, closed Sun, in a modern mall across the street from the West train station at Rugenparkstrasse 1, tel. 058-567-8131).

$ Confiserie Rieder Tea Room—on the charming Marktplatz square just off the main drag—is a sweet bit of local elegance tucked away in all the modern tourism. Along with homemade pastries (their favorite is the chocolatey truffle cake), they serve light meals of quiche, toast, and salads (Tue-Sun 8:20-18:30, closed Mon, Marktgasse 2, tel. 033-822-3673).

$ Brasserie 17 is a sloppy bar with sloppy bar food (burgers, salads, ribs and wings) to complement its craft beer on tap (food served daily 11:30-13:30 & 18:00-21:30, open until 24:00, at the Happy Inn Lodge at Rosenstrasse 17, tel. 033-822-3225).

Quality Coffee Shop: $ Velo Café, tucked deep in urban streets in the heart of the city, is Interlaken's hipster coffee joint, with a variety of quality coffee drinks and healthy, hit-or-miss light meals. Choose between the stay-awhile hangout interior, or the streetside terrace out front (daily 9:00-22:00, Unionsgasse 10, tel. 079-902-1626).

$ Global Cuisine: An abundance of restaurants caters to Interlaken's many international tourists. Two good zones to explore are next to the West train station on **Rugenparkstrasse,** where you'll find Chinese (Asia Garden), Arab (Royal Döner), and Italian (West End); and **Jungfraustrasse,** a pedestrian street in the center with Indian, Arab, Chinese, and Mexican eateries. For something a notch above, locals recommend **$ Biryani House,** tucked away from its flashy competitors on a quiet back street behind the Metropole Hotel. It's nondescript but high quality, specializing in biryani—a sort of fried rice dish (daily 12:00-22:00, Blumenstrasse 16, tel. 076-784-5040).

Supermarkets: For picnic supplies, handy options include **Migros** (described earlier) and a big **Co-op** supermarket, which also has a good cafeteria, across the street from the Ost station (similar hours except Co-Op cafeteria is open Sun, Untere Bönigstrasse 10). You'll find smaller grocery stores scattered around town, including one open late inside each train station (daily until 21:00).

BERNER OBERLAND

In Unterseen

This sleepy, old-fashioned district—just a short walk from the tourist chaos—is a fine place for a good meal. These spots are about a 10-minute stroll from the West train station. The last three places are all within a few steps on Unterseen's extremely charming main square—a characteristic corner of Old Interlaken.

$$ Restaurant Bären fills a classic low-ceilinged gingerbread house with cozy indoor and fine outdoor seating. Lovingly run by Hans-Peter and his family, this is my choice for a traditional dinner. It's a solid value for *Rösti,* fondue, raclette, fish, traditional sausage, and salads. Their chicken cordon bleu is popular (Tue-Thu 17:00-23:00, Fri-Sun 10:00-23:30 or later, closed Mon, Seestrasse 2, reserve in advance at tel. 033-822-7526).

$$ Città Vecchia Ristorante and Pizzeria serves decent Italian (actually, Sardinian—the operating family's heritage) with classy indoor seating or outdoors on Unterseen's leafy main square. Rinaldo and Theresa offer an extensive menu. It's top end for an Italian joint so a bit pricey (lunch specials, daily 12:00-14:00 & 18:30-22:00, Untere Gasse 5, tel. 033-822-1754).

$$$ Benacus, run by Wilderswil-born celebrity chef René Schudel, is where Swiss urbanites come for a quality meal when they're slumming it in the mountains. It has a seasonal menu of quality international fare in an upscale atmosphere, plus a few tables out on the square. This is the place to splurge with class (Tue-Sat 17:00-24:00, closed Sun-Mon, Kirchgasse 15, tel. 033-821-2020).

$$ Stadthaus, a big, high-energy eatery just across the square, is also owned by René Schudel. The concept here is classic Swiss dishes done in a quality way, but without pretense (for example, a variety of *Rösti*), plus some international meals. Local appreciate this place because it's priced on par with touristy eateries on the main drag, but offers higher quality and more authentic cooking. There's a big, inviting, covered terrace and an interior space that feels like an upscale beer hall (daily 9:00-24:00, Untere Gasse 2, tel. 033-822-8689).

Interlaken Connections

Interlaken is connected to Montreux (on Lake Geneva) and Luzern via the Golden Pass scenic rail route (see the Scenic Rail Journeys chapter). Interlaken, Bern, Basel, and Frankfurt are linked by an express train, but for most other destinations you'll change in Bern. Train info: www.sbb.ch.

From Interlaken Ost by Train to: Bern (2-3/hour, 1 hour), **Zürich** (2-3/hour, 2 hours, 1-2 changes), **Zürich Airport** (2-3/hour, 2.5 hours, 1-3 changes), **Luzern** (3-4/hour, 2.5 hours, 1-3 changes), **Lugano** (1-2/hour, 5 hours, 2 changes, more with additional transfers), **Zermatt** (1-2/hour, 2 hours, change in Spiez and Visp), **Lausanne** (at least 2/hour, 2 hours, change in Bern and sometimes Spiez; longer scenic route via Golden Pass—see the Scenic Rail Journeys chapter).

From Interlaken to the Lauterbrunnen Valley: Note that trains to Lauterbrunnen are covered by the Swiss Travel Pass (or discounted 25 percent with a Eurail Global Pass). **Trains** to **Lauterbrunnen** depart from Interlaken Ost (1-2/hour, 20 minutes). You can **drive** to Lauterbrunnen or Stechelberg, but not to Gimmelwald (park at the cable-car station near Stechelberg and ride up on the lift; see page 177) or to Mürren, Wengen, or Kleine Scheidegg (park in Lauterbrunnen and take the cable car to Mürren or the train to Wengen or Kleine Scheidegg). For more details, see "Lauterbrunnen Valley Connections" on page 177.

By Car: For a scenic drive from Interlaken to Montreux, Chamonix, or Zermatt, see my recommended driving route on page 311.

Lauterbrunnen

BERNER OBERLAND

Lauterbrunnen is the valley's commercial center and transportation hub. It's what locals call a "street town"—with all its commercial businesses lined up along one long street. Sitting under sheer cliffs at the base of its namesake valley, with its signature waterfall spurting mightily out from the cliff (floodlit at night), Lauterbrunnen is a fine springboard for Jungfrau and Schilthorn adventures. As such, it's a bit of a bottleneck, and the train-station area can be congested—even chaotic—during peak season. For that reason, I still prefer overnighting in Gimmelwald or Mürren, perched on the ledge above the valley.

Orientation to Lauterbrunnen

In addition to its train station and cable car, the town is just big enough to have all the essential services (grocery, bank, bike rental, launderette, and so on)—plus several hotels and hostels. It's idyllic, in spite of the busy road that slices it in two.

Tourist Information: Stop by the friendly TI to check the weather forecast, find out about guided walks and events, and buy hiking maps or regional train or lift tickets (daily 8:30-12:00 & 14:00-18:30; Oct-May Tue-Sat 9:00-12:00 & 13:30-17:00, closed Sun-Mon; on the main street a few houses up from the train station, tel. 033-856-8568, www.lauterbrunnen.swiss).

Arrival in Lauterbrunnen: The small, modern **train station** has a ticket office, a few small lockers (hiding just to the right of ticket office; check larger bags at ticket desks), and free WCs. Across the main street is the cable-car station; up the ramp to the right is the stop for the PostBus up the valley; and a giant parking garage is on the opposite side of the tracks. Go left as you exit the station to head up the main drag (toward the gushing waterfall) and find the TI and my recommended hotels and eateries. **Drivers** can pay to park in the large multistory lot behind the station.

HELPFUL HINTS

Medical Help: The **Care Mate clinic** (with pharmacy) is near the Jungfrau Hotel (look for *Arzt* sign, English spoken, tel. 033-856-2626, answered 24/7).

Money: Several ATMs are along the main street, including one immediately across from the train station.

Laundry: The **Valley Hostel** has coin-op machines (daily 9:00-21:00, Wi-Fi, tel. 033-855-2008).

Bike Rental: You can rent mountain bikes at **Imboden Bike** on the main street (bikes-28 CHF/4 hours, 38 CHF/day; electric bikes-38 CHF/4 hours, 50 CHF/day; RS%, includes helmet, Mon-Fri 8:30-18:30, Sat-Sun 9:00-17:00—until 18:30 June-mid-Sept, tel. 033-855-2114, www.imboden-bike.ch).

Sports Gear: Rent hiking boots, skis, and snowboards at the **Alpia Sports/Intersport** shop (daily 8:00-12:30 & 14:00-18:30, longer hours in winter, closed during Easter holiday, at Hotel Crystal, tel. 033-855-3292, www.alpiasport.ch).

Activities in and near Lauterbrunnen

For hikes and walks from Lauterbrunnen, including the "Cloudy-Day Lauterbrunnen Valley Walk" that links Lauterbrunnen to Staubbach and Trümmelbach falls, see page 207.

Lauterbrunnen

To Trümmelbach Falls, Schilthorn Cable Car (to Gimmelwald & Mürren) & Stechelberg Village via Road

To Trümmelbach Falls, Schilthorn Cable Car (to Gimmelwald & Mürren) & Stechelberg Village via Trail

Staubbach Waterfall

Weisse

FOLK MUSEUM

To Wengen, Kleine Scheidegg & Jungfraujoch

Lütschine

To Wengen

MAIN DRAG

To Grütschalp & Train to Mürren

To Grütschalp & Train to Mürren

POST

TRAIN STATION

CABLE-CAR STATION

To Isenfluh

River

To Interlaken & Grindelwald

Not to Scale

Note: Train station to church is a 5-min. walk

BERNER OBERLAND

Accommodations
1 Hotel Restaurant Silberhorn
2 Hotel Staubbach
3 Hotel Restaurant Oberland
4 Valley Hostel/Laundry
5 Chalet im Rohr
6 Camping Jungfrau & Weidstübli Restaurant

Eateries & Other
7 Airtime Café
8 Flavours Café
9 Horner Pub
10 Supermarket
11 Bike Rental
12 Alpia Sports Shop

Staubbach Falls

The second highest waterfall in Switzerland (nearly 900 feet) is literally in Lauterbrunnen's backyard—just follow the trail past the church toward the sound of rushing water. Its spray looks like falling dust—*Staub*—hence the name. A trail cut into the cliff takes visitors up "behind" the falls (in winter, it's closed due to the danger of rockslides).

▲Trümmelbach Falls

Sneak a behind-the-scenes look at the valley's most powerful waterfall, Trümmelbach Falls. Ride the elevator up through the

mountain, climb up to the upper falls, and then hike down through several caves (wet, with lots of stairs, and claustrophobic for some). You'll see the melt from the Eiger, Mönch, and Jungfrau grinding like God's band saw through the mountain at the rate of up to 5,000 gallons a second. The upper area is the best; if your legs ache, skip the lower falls and ride down on the elevator. A café (with WC) is directly across from the bus stop. The falls ticket kiosk is a short walk beyond the café.

Cost and Hours: 11 CHF, daily April-Oct 9:00-17:00, July-Aug until 18:00, closed Nov-March, opening date varies with ice conditions, tel. 033-855-3232, www.truemmelbachfaelle.ch.

Getting There: The falls are about halfway between Lauterbrunnen and the Schilthornbahn cable-car station; from either, it's a short ride on the PostBus or a 45-minute walk. Or combine a visit to Trümmelbach with a walk on the valley floor; see page 207.

Hang Out with BASE Jumpers

The Lauterbrunnen Valley has become an El Dorado of BASE jumping (the name stands for the four fixed objects parachuters jump from: building, antenna, span, and earth—in this case, cliffs). The world BASE jumping championships are held here. BASE jumpers hike to the top of a cliff, leap off—falling as long as they can (this provides the rush)—then pull the ripcord to release a tiny parachute, hoping it will break their fall and a gust won't dash them against the walls of the valley. The Lauterbrunnen jumps are considered too tough for beginners—anyone considering BASE jumping should have extensive skydiving experience. Driving up the valley, you'll see windsocks in fields marking landing places. (For a fascinating look at this sport, search for "BASE jumping Lauterbrunnen" on YouTube, and read the FAQ at www. swissbaseassociation.ch.)

BERNER OBERLAND

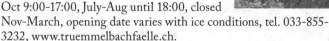

To learn more about BASE jumping, talk with the jumpers themselves. They congregate at the ¢ **Horner Pub,** at the upper end of Lauterbrunnen (near the waterfall). This is the grittiest place in town, providing cheap beds and filling meals for BASE jumpers, with five beers on tap. Locals, jumpers, and stray tourists gather here in the pub each evening—it's the town's only real after-dark scene (daily 12:00-23:00, dorm beds in 9 rooms, apartments available, no breakfast, disco Fri-Sat from 22:00 upstairs, tel. 033-855-1673, www.hornerpub.ch, mail@hornerpub.ch, run by Charlotte).

Lauterbrunnen Valley Folk Museum
(Talmuseum Lauterbrunnen)
This interesting museum shows off the region's folk culture and two centuries of mountaineering from all the towns of this valley. You'll see lace, old tools, exhibits on cheese and woodworking, cowbells, classic old photos, and a brass bell—carried from the next valley in 1497—that rang at the church until 1952 (another bell is outside the neighboring village church). Request an English translation booklet.

Cost and Hours: 5 CHF, free with hotel Visitor Card, mid-June-early Oct Tue and Fri-Sun 14:00-17:30, closed Mon and Wed-Thu year-round, closed off-season, over bridge and below church at the far end of Lauterbrunnen town, tel. 033-855-3586, www.talmuseum-sagenwelt-lauterbrunnen.ch.

Sleeping in Lauterbrunnen

The price ratings given are typical for high summer (July-Aug). Expect lower prices off-season (when many hotels close). Free parking is easy to find. For more peace, choose Gimmelwald or Mürren.

$$ Hotel Silberhorn is a family-run, formal, 40-room hotel. It's in a very convenient location—a hundred yards uphill from the train station on a quiet side street. Almost every double room comes with a fine view and balcony; you can pay more for waterfall-view rooms clad in warm, knotty-pine woodwork (closed late Oct-mid-Dec, lots of stairs, dinner available, tel. 033-856-2210, www.silberhorn.com, info@silberhorn.com).

$$ Hotel Staubbach, a big, creaky Old World place, is one of the oldest hotels in the valley (1890), with 33 simple rooms. Rooms that face up the valley have fabulous waterfall views, though you may hear the happy crowd across the meadow at the Horner Pub or the church bells chiming on the hour (closed mid-Nov-March, elevator, 10-minute walk up from station on the left, tel. 033-855-5454, www.staubbach.com, hotel@staubbach.com).

$$ Hotel Oberland is smack-dab in the center of town, with 28 tidy rooms, most with balconies and views of the Staubbach waterfall or Jungfrau (closed mid-Oct-mid-Dec, family rooms and apartments available, 5 rooms are in nearby Crystal Hotel annex, popular with my tour groups, 5-minute walk up from station on the right, free parking, tel. 033-855-1241, www.hoteloberland.ch, info@hoteloberland.ch, Bev works the front desk).

¢ **Valley Hostel** is practical and comfortable, offering inexpensive beds for quieter travelers of all ages, with a pleasant garden (private rooms, family rooms, reception open 8:00-12:00 & 15:00-22:00—shorter hours off-season, 5-minute walk up from train station, tel. 033-855-2008, www.valleyhostel.ch, info@valleyhostel.ch, Abegglen family: Stefan and Fränzi).

¢ **Chalet im Rohr**—a creaky, flower-draped, woody firetrap of a place—has oodles of character—and lots of paragliders and BASE jumpers (cash only, private rooms, family rooms, common kitchen, across from church on main drag, tel. 033-855-2182, www.chaletimrohr.ch, info@chaletimrohr.ch, Hans and Elsbeth von Allmen-Müller).

¢ **Camping Jungfrau,** a five-minute drive south of town, provides beds in dorms, two- to six-bed bungalows, and cabins, along with spots for campers. This can be a good deal for families (or small groups) traveling by car who want to stay a few days and cook for themselves. It's romantically situated along the small lane beyond Staubbach Falls, huge, and well-organized by Hans. Ample facilities include a recommended restaurant, grocery store (open daily), communal kitchen, lounge, ATM, and playground (tel. 033-856-2010, www.campingjungfrau.swiss, info@campingjungfrau.ch).

Eating in Lauterbrunnen

$$ Hotel Restaurant Oberland, along the main drag a few minutes up from the station, serves good-value meals including traditional Swiss dishes and pizzas. It's a high-energy place with lots of tourists and a huge front porch good for lingering into the evening. As it's quick to fill with its own hotel guests, reservations should be considered required (daily 11:30-21:00, dinner seatings at 18:00 and 20:00, tel. 033-855-1241, www.hoteloberland.ch).

$$ Hotel Restaurant Silberhorn, with an elegant dining room, is the local choice for a fancy dinner out. Prices are reasonable, and they have all of the Swiss standards, plus good wood-fired pizzas. Call to reserve a view table (lunch specials, daily 18:00-21:00, classy indoor and outdoor seating, above the cable-car station, tel. 033-856-2210).

$ Airtime Café feels like a hipster alpine Starbucks with hot drinks, homemade treats, breakfast, and simple lunches (sandwiches, meat pies, soup, homemade sourdough bread). They have

Wi-Fi, an English-language swap library, and can help you book adventure-sport activities (daily 8:30-18:00, kitchen until 16:00, closed Nov, tel. 033-855-1515, Annette and Fred).

$ Flavours, a café without a hint of yodeling or cowbells, serves up full breakfasts, burgers, focaccia sandwiches, fresh-squeezed juices, and gelato (takeaway available, daily 9:00-18:00, kitchen until 15:00, shorter hours off-season, closed Nov-April, tel. 033-855-3652).

$ Horner Pub, at the upper end of Lauterbrunnen near the waterfall, focuses on beer (see "Activities in and near Lauterbrunnen," earlier), but their kitchen cranks out alpine shepherd's macaroni, cheap pastas, burgers, and raclette (daily 12:00-23:00, tel. 033-855-1673).

$ Weidstübli Restaurant, at **Camping Jungfrau** near the waterfall, has earned a reputation in the valley as a great place for dinner (closed Mon-Tue and Nov-mid-Dec, tel. 033-856-2010).

Supermarket: The small but well-stocked **Co-op** is on the main street across from the station (Mon-Fri 8:00-18:30, Sat until 17:00, closed Sun). The smaller grocery at **Camping Jungfrau** is usually open daily (call tel. 033-856-2010 to check before heading out).

Lauterbrunnen Valley Connections

The valley-floor towns of Lauterbrunnen and Stechelberg have connections by mountain train, bus, and cable car to the traffic-free villages, peaks, and hikes high above. Prices and trip durations given are one-way and per leg unless otherwise noted.

Getting from Lauterbrunnen to Gimmelwald or Mürren

To reach the mountain villages of Gimmelwald and Mürren, you have two options:

Schilthornbahn Cable Car: This is the most direct way to Gimmelwald, the easiest option if you're packing heavy, and the most sensible choice for drivers (cheaper parking, direct connection). First, by car (10 minutes) or by PostBus (2/hour, 20 minutes, departs 5 minutes after trains arrive), head to Stechelberg at the far end of the valley. From here, ride up on the Schilthornbahn cable car—first stop Gimmelwald (5 minutes), change there for Mürren (5 minutes more). The total bus-plus-cable car cost to Gimmelwald is 10.40 CHF; to Mürren is 11.20 CHF.

From Stechelberg, the cable car runs at least twice hourly (at :25 and :55 past the hour, more frequently during peak season). It runs late into the night (Mon-Fri until 23:45, Sat-Sun until 24:55), but after 20:00 it's just once hourly. Note: Above Mürren, the cable car stops running much earlier. (Be aware that the Schilthornbahn cable car is closed for servicing for a week in late April or early May and three weeks from early November through early December. During these times, a cargo cable car from the valley floor goes up to Mürren, where a small bus shuttles travelers down to Gimmelwald.)

Grütschalp Cable Car and Mürren Train: This is the more scenic route. From the Lauterbrunnen train station, ride the cable car across the street up to Grütschalp, where you'll immediately transfer to a tiny train. Sit on the left as the train rolls you along the incredibly scenic cliffside to Mürren, looking across to the Eiger, Mönch, and Jungfrau panorama (the total trip takes 20 minutes). The total cost to Mürren is 11.20 CHF; add 6 CHF to ride the Schilthornbahn down to Gimmelwald. Compared to the Schilthornbahn, this option is approximately as convenient to Mürren, but longer for those headed to Gimmelwald (you'll have to walk through Mürren—about 15 minutes—then take the cable car down in 5 minutes, or hike down in 30).

Trains to Interlaken, Wengen, Kleine Scheidegg, and Jungfraujoch

Lauterbrunnen's train station has slick trains to Interlaken Ost (1-2/hour, 20 minutes, 7.60 CHF, covered by Swiss Travel Pass, 25 percent discount with Eurail Global Pass). From here, cute, old-fashioned, yellow-and-green Wengernalpbahn trains head up the steep cogwheel track twice hourly to **Wengen** (15 minutes, 6.80 CHF) and **Kleine Scheidegg** (45 minutes, 30.80 CHF; change here for the **Jungfraujoch**—see page 202). Note that the Swiss Travel Pass covers train travel only up to Wengen; buy any supplementary tickets before boarding the train in Lauterbrunnen (or pay a 10-CHF surcharge to buy on board). For the best views, sit on the right side—and be ready after the many short tunnels, just before Wengen, for grand views down over the Lauterbrunnen Valley. Feel the cogwheel gripping the tracks as you work your way up the steep incline. In Wengen, you can walk a few minutes up through town to the cable car up to **Männlichen**, where the spectacular hike to Kleine Scheidegg begins.

BERNER OBERLAND

Gimmelwald

Saved from developers by its "avalanche zone" classification, Gimmelwald was (before modern tourism) one of the poorest places in Switzerland. Its traditional economy was stuck in the hay, and its farmers—unable to make it in their disadvantaged trade—survived only on a trickle of visitors and Swiss government subsidies (and working the ski lifts in winter). For some travelers, there's little to see in such a village. Others (like me) enjoy a fascinating day sitting on a bench and learning why they say, "If heaven isn't what it's cracked up to be, send me back to Gimmelwald."

Take a walk through the town. The huge, sheer cliff face that dominates your mountain views is the Schwarzmönch (Black Monk). The three peaks above (or behind) it are, left to right, the Eiger, Mönch, and Jungfrau. Although Gimmelwald's population dropped in the last century from 300 to about 100 residents, traditions survive. Most Gimmelwalders have one of two last names: von Allmen or Feuz. They are tough and proud. Raising hay in this rugged terrain is labor-intensive. One family harvests enough to feed only about 15 cows. But they'd have it no other way, and, unlike the absentee-landlord town of Mürren, Gimmelwald is locally owned. (When word got out that urban planners wanted to develop Gimmelwald into a town of 1,000, locals pulled some strings to secure the town's bogus avalanche-zone building code. Today, unlike nearby resort towns, Gimmelwald's population is the same all year.) Those same folks are happy the masses go to commercialized Grindelwald, just over the Kleine Scheidegg ridge. Don't confuse Gimmelwald and touristy Grindelwald—they couldn't be more different.

Tourist Information: Thanks to local schoolteachers Olle and Maria and their son Sven, Gimmelwald has a helpful little website (www.gimmelwald.ch) where you can check out photos of the town in different seasons, get directions for 11 of the best hikes from town, and see all the latest on activities and rooms for rent. For more on hikes from Gimmelwald, see page 208.

Getting There: See "Lauterbrunnen Valley Connections" on page 177.

Gimmelwald Tours: In addition to my self-guided "Gimmelwald Walk," you can download the free Schilthorn Explore App,

Gimmelwald

To Gimmeln & Mürren

To Mürren (30-min. Uphill Hike)

To Sprutz Waterfall, Spilboden, Bryndli, Rotstockhütte & Schilthorn

PAVED ROAD

BENCHES

To Mürren (5 min.) & on to Schilthorn (30 min.) via lift

FIRE STN.

❺

FORMER SCHOOL

VIA FERRATA SUSPENSION BRIDGE

❷

BENCHES

❶

❸

❹

CABLE-CAR STATION

Cliffs

To Sefinen Valley

Cliffs

Not to Scale

To Stechelberg (1-Hour Hike)

To Schilthornbahn Valley Station, Bus Stop & Car Park

❶ Olle & Maria's B&B

❷ Esther's Guest House

❸ Pension Gimmelwald & Honesty Shop

❹ Mountain Hostel

❺ Cheese Hut

BERNER OBERLAND

which includes a Gimmelwald Audio Village Tour (find it under "Trip Suggestion" in the app). It describes Gimmelwald's past and present in some detail at each of the eight stops along its route. To read the tour instead, look for binders attached to benches around the village. For a bit of Christmas-in-Gimmelwald fun, go to https://classroom.ricksteves.com and search for "Christmas Gimmelwald."

Gimmelwald Walk

Gimmelwald, though tiny, with one zigzag street, offers a fine look at a traditional Swiss mountain community.

• *Start this quick self-guided walk at the...*

Cable-Car Station: When the lift came in the 1960s, the village's back end became its front door. As you walk out of the station, pause at the big Infopoint map to orient yourself. Then turn right (uphill).

Gimmelwald was, and still is, a farm village. As you start up the street, you'll see a sweet little hut on the right. Set on stilts to keep out mice, the hut was used for storing cheese (the rocks on the rooftop here and throughout the town are not decorative—they keep the shingles on through wild storms). Behind the cheese hut stands the former village schoolhouse, long the largest structure in town. (In Catholic Swiss towns, the biggest building is the church; in Protestant towns, it's the school.) Gimmelwald's students now go to school in Lauterbrunnen, and the building is used as a chapel when the Protestant pastor makes his monthly visit. The little gray tower-like structure on the roof is the town fire siren. Now

turn around: On the other side of the street, next to the little playground, is a bench with a nice view, and just beyond it is the recommended Mountain Hostel.

• *Walk up the lane 50 yards to Gimmelwald's...*

"Times Square": The yellow alpine "street sign" shows where you are, the altitude (1,370 meters, or 4,470 feet), how many hours and minutes it takes to walk to nearby points, and which tracks are serious hiking paths (marked with red and white, and further indicated along the way with red and white patches of paint on stones). You're surrounded by buildings that were

built as duplexes, divided vertically right down the middle to house two separate families. Look for the Honesty Shop at Pension Gimmelwald, which features local crafts and little edibles for sale (summer only).

Behind the street sign, the lettering high up on the post office building is a folksy blessing: "Summer brings green, winter brings snow. The sun greets the day, the stars greet the night. This house will protect you from rain, cold, and wind. May God give us his blessings." Small as Gimmelwald is, it still has daily mail service. The postman comes down from Mürren each day to deliver and pick up mail. The date on this building indicates when it was built or rebuilt (1911). Gimmelwald has a strict building code: For instance, shutters must be of wood and can only be painted certain colors.

• *From this tiny intersection, walk away from the cable-car station and follow the town's...*

Main Street: Walk up the road past the garden-gnome greeting committee on the right. Generations ago, Gimmelwald had

Swiss Cow Culture

Traditional Swiss cow farmers could make more money for much easier work in another profession. In a good year, farmers produce enough cheese to break even—they support their families on government subsidies of about $5,000 per cow. (Throughout the Alps, various governments support traditional farming as much for the tourism as for the cheese.) But these farmers have made a lifestyle choice to keep tradition alive and live high in the mountains.

The cows' grazing ground can range in elevation by as much as 5,000 feet throughout the year. In the summer (usually mid-June), the farmer straps elaborate ceremonial bells on his cows and takes them up to a hut at high elevation. The cows hate these big bells, which weigh upward of 10 pounds and can cost more than 2,000 CHF apiece—a proud investment for a humble farmer. When the cows arrive at their summer home, the ornamental bells are hung under the eaves and the cows get more practical bells.

These high-elevation summer stables are called "alps." Try to find some on a Berner Oberland tourist map (such as Wenger-

more than twice the population and needed to produce more food. The terracing above was originally for potato patches, now gone wild. All along this walk you'll also see private garden patches. Until recently, most locals grew their own vegetables, often enough to provide most of their family's needs. Today, while still widespread, most gardening is a hobby.

On the left, notice the announcement board, with notifications such as deals on chainsaw sharpening, upcoming shooting competitions, and news on community projects. Cross the street and admire the big barn, dated 1995. At the far front corner is a cow-scratcher. Swiss cows have legal rights (for example, in the winter they must be taken out for exercise at least three times a week). This big barn is built in a modern style. Traditionally, barns were small (like those on the hillside high above) and closer to the hay. But with trucks and paved roads, hay can be moved more easily, and farm businesses need more cows to be viable. Still, even a well-run big farm hopes just to break even. The industry survives only with government subsidies (see sidebar).

Ahead you can see a barn with cowbells and milk canisters. A nalp, Grütschalp, or Schiltalp). The cows stay at the alps for about 100 days (roughly from June 10 to September 21). The farmers hire a team of cheesemakers to work at each alp—mostly hippies, students, and city slickers eager to spend three summer months in mountainous solitude. Each morning, the hired hands get up at 5:00 to milk the cows; take them to pasture; and make the cheese, milking the cows again when they come home in the evening. In the summer, all the milk is turned into alp cheese (it's too difficult to get it down to the market in liquid form). In the winter, with the cows at lower altitudes, the fresh milk is sold as milk.

Meanwhile, the farmers, glad to be free of their bovine responsibilities in summer, turn their attention to making hay. The average farmer has a few huts at various altitudes, each surrounded by small hay fields. The farmer follows the seasons up into the mountains, making hay and storing it above the huts. In the fall, the cows come down from the alps and spend the winter in the village, eating the hay the farmer spent the summer preparing for them.

Throughout the year you'll see farmers moving their herds to various elevations. If snow is in the way, farmers sometimes use tourist cable cars to move their cows. Every two months or so, Gimmelwald farmers bring together cows that aren't doing so well and herd them into the cable car to meet the butcher in the valley below.

century ago the village had 55 households, and 43 of them lived on farming. Today, just a few working farms survive.

• *Go just beyond the next big barn. On your right is a...*

Water Fountain/Trough: This is the site of the town's historic water supply—still perfectly drinkable. Village kids love to bathe and wage water wars here when the cows aren't drinking from it.

• *Detour left down a gravel path (along a wooden fence). First you'll pass (on your left) the lovingly tended pea-patch gardens of the woman with the best green thumb in the village. Continue along the path 50 yards or so to the corner. Notice the small barn ahead on the left. It's an 18th-century work of wooden art—cows downstairs and hay upstairs. Just to the right is another water trough in front of a house called...*

Husmättli: This is the oldest building in town, from 1658.

BERNER OBERLAND

(There are more 17th-century buildings on the road that zigzags down from Gimmelwald into the Sefinen Valley.) Study the log-cabin construction. Many old houses were built without nails. The wood was logged up the valley and cut on the water-powered village mill (also in the Sefinen Valley). Gimmelwald heats with wood, and since the wood needs to age a couple of years to burn well, it's stacked everywhere.

From here (at the water trough in front of Husmättli), look up to find a house with 10 solar panels on the roof—it belongs to teachers Olle and Maria. As part of a green energy policy, a Swiss building code requires that new structures provide 30 percent of their own power. Switzerland is gradually moving away from nuclear power; its last reactor is supposed to close in 2034. The panels you see heat the water that Olle and Maria use for bathing and home heating; they fire up their furnace only from November to February.

• *Return up the gravel path to the main paved road, turn left, and continue.*

Twenty yards along, on the left, look for the house with the *Self Service* sign. Climb the ramp, open the door, and you'll find a refrigerator with local cheese sold on the honor system by the Rubin family. (Villagers generally see no need to lock their doors.) Just outside the door, in the summer months, you may see a bunch of scythes hanging above a sharpening stone. Farmers pound, rather than grind, the blade to get it razor-sharp for efficient mowing on slopes too rocky or steep for machines or grazing animals. Feel a blade...carefully.

A few steps farther, notice the cute **cheese hut** on the right.

This is where the cheese you saw on sale was produced (thousands of pounds turned and salted). The hut's front wall is an alpine art gallery with nail-shoes used as flower pots. Nail shoes grip the steep, wet fields—this is critical for a farmer's safety, especially when carrying a sharp scythe. Even today, farmers buy metal tacks and fasten them to boots. The hut is full of strong cheese—up to three years old.

Look up. In the summer, a few goats are kept here behind the hut (rather than at a high alp) to provide families with fresh milk (about a half-gallon per day per goat). The farmers fence the goats in so they eat only this difficult-to-harvest grass.

On the left (at the *B&B* sign; see page 186) is Olle and Maria's home. Proprietors of a popular B&B, they ran the local school until it closed in 2010; now they both commute to teach at schools in other villages. (Check out Maria's cute "Amazing Window Store.")

• *Fifty yards farther along on the right is the house called...*

Alpenrose: This is the old village school building, in use from about 1810 to 1930. Now it's a family home. You might see big ceremonial cowbells hanging under the eaves on the uphill side. These swing from the necks of cows during the procession from town to the high Alps (mid-June) and back down (mid-Sept).

• *At the end of town, pause at the tiny viewpoint just before where a lane branches off to the left, leading into the dramatic...*

Sefinen Valley: At the bottom of this wild valley is a stream that rushes down toward Stechelberg. All the old homes in town are made from wood cut from the left-hand side of this valley (shady side, slow-growing, better timber) and milled on the valley floor. The info binder chained to the bench is part of the town's guided tour app (see "Gimmelwald Tours," earlier).

• *A few steps ahead, the road switches back at the...*

Gimmelwald Fire Station *(Feuerwehrmagazin)*: Peer through the windows in the bottom-floor door at the tractor-like engines.

Then walk up around the hairpin bend to the notice board on the side of the building. The *Föhnwacht-Reglement* sheet explains rules to keep the village from burning down during the Föhn season, a period of fierce dry winds. During this time, there's a
24-hour fire watch, and even smoking cigarettes outdoors is forbidden. Mürren was devastated by a Föhn-caused fire in the 1920s. Villagers in Gimmelwald—mindful of the quality of their volunteer fire department—are particularly careful. The town hasn't had a terrible fire in its history (a rare feat among alpine villages).

Check out the other posted notices. This year's Swiss Army calendar tells reservists when and where to go (in all four official Swiss languages). Every Swiss male does a 22-week stint in the military, then serves three weeks a year in the reserves until age 34. The *Schiessübungen* poster details the shooting exercises required this year.

• *Unless you're really pooped, continue uphill along the road.*

High Road to More Views: The resort town of Mürren hovers in the distance. And high on the left, notice the hay field. This field is a festival of alpine flowers in season (best at this altitude in May and June).

• *In a couple of minutes, you'll reach a peaceful set of benches, off the lane on the downhill side (just before the now-closed Hotel Mittaghorn and just steps from where you started). Grab a bench. Take a moment to relax and savor the view. For three decades, this has been a favorite place of mine to sit quietly, appreciate the Alps, and be thankful that I can travel and experience such wonders.*

Sleeping in Gimmelwald

Gimmelwald is my home base in the Berner Oberland. To inhale the Alps at 4,593 feet and really hold them in, you'll want to sleep high in Gimmelwald, too. Poor and pleasantly stuck in the past, the village has only a few accommodations options—all of them quirky and memorable. The Visitor Card that comes with your hotel stay gives you free entry to the public swimming pool in nearby Mürren (at the Sportzentrum—see page 189).

Be warned: You'll meet a lot of my readers in this town. This is a disappointment to some; others enjoy the chance to be part of a fun extended family.

$$ Olle and Maria's B&B rents Gimmelwald's most expensive and comfortable rooms. The Eggimanns' quirky but alpine-sleek house, where they raised three kids, offers visitors an intimate peek at this community. Two rooms with shared bath are upstairs, while the "double" with private bath is a ground-level studio apartment with a kitchenette and a private entrance (family room available, breakfast extra, 3-night minimum, cash or PayPal only, nonrefundable 50 percent deposit via PayPal required, pay laundry service; from cable car, continue straight for 200 yards along the town's only road, look for *B&B* sign on left; tel. 033-855-3575, www.olleandmarias.ch, oeggimann@bluewin.ch).

$$ Esther's Guest House, overlooking the village's main intersection, rents seven clean, basic, and comfortable rooms. Three rooms have private bathrooms, and all share a generous lounge and kitchen (10 percent cheaper for 3 nights or more, family rooms available—one sleeps up to 6, breakfast extra, sack lunches available, low ceilings, tel. 033-855-5488, www.esthersguesthouse.ch, info@esthersguesthouse.ch). Tobias and Franziska also rent two five-person **apartments** with kitchenettes next door.

$ Pension Gimmelwald is an old, low-ceilinged farmhouse converted into a family-style inn, with 10 simple shared-bath rooms, 2 rooms with private bath, a six-bed family room, a restaurant, and a cozy bar. Its generous restaurant terrace, overlooking the Mountain Hostel, has gorgeous views across the valley (breakfast extra, dinner available, open late May-mid-Oct and late Dec-March, 2-minute walk up from cable-car station, tel. 033-855-1730, www.hotel-pensiongimmelwald.ch, welcome@hotel-pensiongimmelwald.ch, Englishman David and Sabine).

¢ **Mountain Hostel** is a beehive of activity, as clean as its guests, cheap, respectable, and friendly. The 40-bed hostel has low ceilings, bar, pool table, and healthy plumbing. It's mostly a college-age crowd; families and older travelers will probably feel more comfortable elsewhere. Petra Brunner, who lines the porch with flowers, runs this relaxed hostel. Read the signs, respect

Petra's rules, and leave it tidier than you found it (closed Nov, from the lift station it's 20 yards up the path to the left, tel. 033-855-1704, www.mountainhostel.com, info@mountainhostel.com).

Eating in Gimmelwald

$$ **Pension Gimmelwald Restaurant** is the only place to eat in town. Each night at 19:00 they serve a maximum of 30 people one 30-CHF three-course meal (you have no choices). During the day they serve drinks, soup, and simple meat-and-cheese board-type dishes. You can eat in their rustic indoor dining room or on a jaw-dropping view terrace. David proudly serves their award-winning, very smooth Schwarzmönch dark beer. The atmosphere here is jazz-and-blues mellow (reservations required for dinner, daily late May-mid-Oct and late Dec-March 12:00-15:00 & 18:00-21:00, bar open until 22:00, closed off-season, tel. 033-855-1730, www.hotel-pensiongimmelwald.ch).

Picnics: Consider packing in a picnic meal from the larger towns. Mürren, a five-minute cable-car ride or a 30-minute hike up the hill, has a grocery store and good restaurants (see "Eating in Mürren," later). If you need a few groceries and want to skip the hike to Mürren, you can buy the essentials—noodles, spaghetti sauce, and candy bars—at the little Honesty Shop at Pension Gimmelwald (closed off-season). Farmers post signs to sell their produce. The Rubin family sells cheese and eggs in their house on the town's main street (see "Gimmelwald Walk," earlier). There might be something to eat at the hostel.

Nightlife: For after-dark entertainment in Gimmelwald, **Pension Gimmelwald** offers a mellow scene with an old-time bar,

BERNER OBERLAND

cozy lounge, and view terrace. And from almost anywhere in Gimmelwald, you can watch the sun tuck the mountaintops into bed as the moon rises over the Jungfrau. If that's not enough nightlife, stay in Interlaken.

Mürren

Pleasant as an alpine resort can be, Mürren is traffic-free and filled with cafés, souvenirs, old-timers with walking sticks, and snap-happy tourists. Its chalets are prefab-rustic. With help from a cliffside train, a funicular, and a cable car, hiking options are endless from Mürren. Sitting on a ledge more than 2,000 feet above the Lauterbrunnen Valley (total altitude: just over a mile high), surrounded by a fortissimo chorus of mountains, the

town has all the comforts of home without the pretense of more famous resorts.

Mürren dates from 1384, but its historic character has been overwhelmed by development (unlike Gimmelwald). Still, it's a peaceful town, with 400 permanent residents—and dropping. There's no full-time doctor, no police officer (they call Lauterbrunnen if there's a problem), and no resident priest or pastor. (The Protestant church—up by the TI—posts a sign showing where the region's roving pastor preaches each Sunday.) There's not enough business to keep a bank, butcher, or proper bakery open (the last place for provisions is the Co-op grocery store). Depending on the time of year, Mürren is either lively (winter and summer, when the population swells to 4,000) or completely dead (spring and fall).

Getting There: See "Lauterbrunnen Valley Connections" on page 177.

Orientation to Mürren

Mürren perches high on a ledge, overlooking the Lauterbrunnen Valley. You can walk from one end of town to the other in about 15 minutes.

Tourist Information: Mürren's TI, inconveniently located in the sports center at the top end of town, is a wealth of information (June-Oct and mid-Dec-April daily 8:30-19:30, off-season 8:30-12:00 & 13:00-17:00, free WCs and Wi-Fi, follow signs to *Sportzentrum* on the upper road—behind the giant old Hotel Alpin Palace, tel. 033-856-8686, www.muerren.swiss, Sam). Pick up the flier that lists a slew of weekly activities, including a town walking tour (1/week June-Oct and Dec-April, free with your hotel's Visitor Card, otherwise 20 CHF).

HELPFUL HINTS

Money: The only ATM in town is at the cable-car station.

Laundry: Hotel Bellevue has a little self-service launderette in a shed on the side of the hotel (open 24/7, but you must buy tokens at the bar inside).

Bike Rental: You can rent mountain bikes at **Stäger Sport** (30 CHF/half-day, 40 CHF/day, includes helmet, daily 9:00-18:00, closed late Oct-mid-May, in middle of town, tel. 033-855-2355, www.staegersport.ch). There's a bigger bike-rental place in Lauterbrunnen (Imboden Bike, described on page 172).

Sports Center: The slick **Sportzentrum** that houses the TI offers a world of indoor activities, including table tennis, a fitness room, sauna, hot tub, and steam bath (each with its own charge; most services open same hours as TI—see above). A **$ café** offers a reasonably priced, basic menu, with indoor and outdoor seating (daily 8:00-18:00). The indoor pool is free with the Visitor Card given out by hotels and hostels (otherwise 12 CHF, daily 13:00-20:00, until 21:00 in winter, tel. 033-856-8686, www.sportzentrum-muerren.ch).

Yoga: Denise (proprietor of the recommended Chalet Fontana) offers yoga classes at the sports center on Tuesdays in summer (€12, mobile 078-642-3485).

Skiing and Snowboarding: The Mürren-Schilthorn ski area is the Berner Oberland's best place for experts, especially those eager to tackle the famous, nearly 10-mile-long Inferno run. The runs on top, especially the Kanonenrohr, are quite steep and have predictably good snow; lower areas cater to all levels, but can be icier. For rental gear, try the friendly, convenient **Ed Abegglen** shop (best prices, next to recommended Chalet Fontana, tel. 033-855-1245), **Alfred's Sporthaus** (good selection and decent prices, between ski school and Sportzentrum, tel. 033-855-3030), or **Stäger Sport** (in the town center, tel. 033-855-2330). For more info on snow sports, see the Switzerland in Winter chapter.

Mürren Walk

Mürren has long been a top ski resort, but a walk across town offers a glimpse into a time before ski lifts. This stroll takes you through town on the main drag, from the train station (where you'll arrive if coming from Lauterbrunnen) to the cable-car station.

• Start at the...

Train Station: The first trains pulled into Mürren in 1891. A case inside the station displays an original car from the narrow-gauge, horse-powered line that rolled fancy visitors from here into town. The current station, built in 1964, comes with impressive engineering for heavy cargo. This is the "port" of Mürren. Look out back, where a small truck can be loaded up, attached to the train, and driven away.

• Wander into town along the main road (take the lower, left fork) for a stroll under the...

Alpin Palace Hotel: This towering place was the "Grand Palace Hotel" until it burned in 1928. Today they're planning an ambitious renovation (in the meantime, it houses a "pop-up lodge," described later). The green meadow below the station on the left is a popular hangout for wild mountain goat and chamois (the animals,

To Birg & Schilthorn

LMENDHUBEL

To Grütschalp

FUNICULAR

SPORT-ZENTRUM

TRAIN STATION

To Grütschalp & Lift Down to Lauterbrunnen

TENNIS COURTS

Cliffs

Note: Cable-car station to train station = 10-min. walk

Not to Scale

❶ Hotel Eiger & Eiger Guesthouse/Restaurant
❷ Hotel/Restaurant Edelweiss
❸ Hotel/Restaurant Bellevue & Launderette
❹ Hotel Jungfrau
❺ Pop-Up Lodge Mürren
❻ Hotel/Restaurant Blumental
❼ Hotel Regina
❽ Chalet Fontana
❾ Stägerstübli Restaurant
❿ Café Liv
⓫ Supermarket
⓬ Stäger Sport

not the rags) that seem to understand that they can't be hunted so close to residences. At the corner, the two benches make goat watching more comfortable.

• Carry on past the hotel for a...

Cliffside Stroll: Just ahead, the small wooden platform cantilevered over the cliff is where snow-removal trucks dump their loads in the winter. Just beyond, on the right (across from Hotel Alpina), you can fill your water bottle with sweet spring water from the Alps high above. Farther down, Hotel Edelweiss' restaurant terrace comes with breathtaking views (overhanging a sheer cliff).

A few houses beyond, the vacant lot offers the same views stretching from the big three: Eiger, Mönch, and Jungfrau—plus the Schwarzmönch looming in the foreground. Panning right, you'll see waterfalls gushing from the cliffsides (especially after a good rain), and eventually a cattle farm in the high alp. There were plans for a big apartment-hotel to be built here, but the community said no. Now the lonely tree stump is a popular place for Instagram photos.

Farther along, you'll pass the inviting outdoor seating of the recommended Café Liv—the closest thing to a Starbucks in town.

• Just after the café, detour from the main street out to the cliff-hanging

BERNER OBERLAND

tennis court. Pause at the far corner of the first court, step up to the small arch, and look down.

Via Ferrata: Directly below, at the base of the modern wall, is the start of the 1.5-mile *via ferrata*, a "trail" with a steel-cable guide that mountaineers use to venture safely along the cliff all the way to Gimmelwald (see page 194). The steel cable disappears over the cliff and ends at the Gimmelwald lift station (which you can see in the distance). On hillside above and behind you may see parasailers taking off from above the Schilthorn lift station. Track their flight as they expertly catch the valley updraft (feel it on your face). Farther to the right, the Allmendhubel funicular trundles visitors up to some of the best views in the region—and the start of some glorious hikes (described later). Listen for the river, waterfalls, and avalanches on the far side.

• *Backtrack the way you came, then turn left at the Stäger Sport onto the main street to reach...*

"Downtown" Mürren: At the main intersection, a small service road leads down to Gimmelwald. Stay right (following *Schilthornbahn* and *Mürren* signs) and enter the main drag. Here you'll find my favorite restaurant in town (Stägerstübli), the only grocery store (Co-op), and the best souvenir shop (Abegglen).

A bit farther on, past the faded old Hotel Regina, the tiny fire barn on the right (labeled *Feuerwehr*) has a list showing the leaders of the volunteer force and their responsibilities. The old barn behind it on the right evokes the time, not so long ago, when the town's barns housed cows. Imagine Mürren with more cows than people, rather than more visitors than residents.

Across from the fire barn is the town bulletin board—with notices targeting both visitors and locals.

About 60 feet beyond the fire barn (across the street from and just before the old schoolhouse—*Altes Schulhaus*), detour right uphill a few steps into the oldest part of town. Explore the windy little lanes, admiring the ancient woodwork on the houses, 400-year-old timbers that could tell a story, Swiss precision in firewood stacking, and cute little pea patches. Arc your way up and around to the left, eventually returning to the main drag at the Hotel Alpenruh.

• *Back on the main drag, continue to the far end of Mürren, where you come to the...*

Cable-Car Station: The larger cars that dock in the back of the station take hikers and skiers up to the Schilthorn and run down to the valley via Gimmelwald. The smaller cable car out front goes directly to the valley floor. This was the main route down to Stechelberg until 1987, but today it is only for cargo, garbage, and backup passenger service in spring and fall when the newer cars are closed for maintenance. With ever-larger crowds of tourists blitzing from the valley floor to the Schilthorn and back, plans are in the works for a new, bigger cable car to replace this service lift.

• *From here you can hike or catch the lift (5 minutes) down to Gimmelwald. Or, hike back into town along the high road, where you'll pass Mürren's two churches, the Allmendhubel funicular station, and the Sportzentrum (with swimming pool and TI).*

Activities in Mürren

During ski season and in the height of summer, the Mürren area offers plenty of activities for those willing to seek them out. In spring and fall, Mürren is pretty quiet. For hikes from Mürren, see page 209.

Allmendhubel Funicular (Allmendhubelbahn)

A surprisingly rewarding funicular (built in 1912, renovated in 1999) carries nature lovers in less than four minutes from Mürren up to Allmendhubel, a 6,257-foot perch offering a Jungfrau view that, though much lower, rivals the Schilthorn (without all of the James Bond kitsch). Consider mixing a mountain lift, grand views, and a hike with your meal by eating at the restaurant on Allmendhubel (good chef, open daily until 17:00).

Allmendhubel, with a huge playground, is particularly good for families. This is also the departure point for the North Face hike and walks to Grütschalp (see page 211). While at Allmendhubel, consider its Flower trail, a 20-minute loop with nice mountain views and (from July through Sept) a chance to see more than 150 different types of alpine flowers in bloom. At a minimum, simply climb the steep hill behind the playground to reach a stunning viewpoint, with benches looking out over the little restaurant facing all that big scenery.

Cost and Hours: 8.80 CHF one-way, 14 CHF round-trip, half-price with Swiss Travel Pass, early June-mid-Oct daily 9:00-17:00, runs every 20 minutes, tel. 033-855-2042 or 033-856-2141, www.schilthorn.ch.

Tandem Paragliding

If you've ever wondered what it's like to soar like an eagle, a tandem paragliding flight will give you a pretty good idea. Two companies offer guided flights that take off just above the Mürren cable-car station and end near the Stechelberg cable-car station. After your pilot rigs you into the tandem harness and gives you a few brief instructions, he'll take you on a short run downhill and then you're both up, up, and away—flying gracefully over the Lauterbrunnen Valley, along cliff faces, past waterfalls, and over treetops. Flights last around 15 to 20 minutes...God willing.

Cost: 180 CHF for Mürren-Stechelberg flight, transport to Mürren not included; other flight options available, no experience necessary. Airtime Paragliding is based at the recommended Airtime Café in Lauterbrunnen (tel. 079-247-8463, https://airtime-paragliding.ch). Paragliding Jungfrau offers similar tandem flights at similar prices (tel. 079-779-9000, www.paragliding-jungfrau.ch).

Mürren *Via Ferrata* (Klettersteig Mürren)

Mountaineers and thrill-seekers can test their nerves on this 1.5-mile trail along the cliff running from Mürren to Gimmelwald. A *via ferrata* ("way of iron" in Italian) or *Klettersteig* ("climbing path" in German) is a cliffside trail made of metal steps drilled into the mountainside with a cable running at shoulder height above it. Equipped with a helmet, harness, and two carabiners, you are clipped to the cable the entire way.

The journey takes about three hours (one-way only, dry weather only). While half of the route is easily walked, for several hundred yards (across what's called "The Hammer Corner") you are literally hanging over a 2,400-foot drop. I did it, and through the most horrifying sections, I was too scared to look down or take pictures. Along with ladders and steps, the trip comes with three thrilling canyon crossings—one by zip line (possible with guide only), another on a single high wire (with steadying wires for each hand), and a final stint on a terrifying suspension bridge (which you can see from the Schilthorn cable-car—look for it just above or below Gimmelwald). For a peek at what you're considering getting yourself into, search for *"Via Ferrata* Mürren Gimmelwald" on YouTube.

On Your Own: Experienced mountaineers can rent gear (25 CHF from the Gimmelwald hostel, or at Mürren's Stäger Sport) and do it independently; others should hire a licensed mountain guide.

With a Guided Tour: The most practical way to experience the *via ferrata* is to join a guided group tour (135 CHF, includes gear and donation to the Mürren Via Ferrata Association, tours go daily from Stäger Sport in Mürren, June-mid-Oct at 9:10 and 14:10, weather permitting, hiking boot rental-20 CHF, small groups of 4-8, reserve by phone, tel. 033-854-1280, www.klettersteig-muerren.ch).

Nightlife in Mürren

Mürren has several lively, atmospheric places for a drink after dinner (for details on these recommended spots, see "Sleeping in Mürren" and "Eating in Mürren," next). The three top choices are **Eiger Guesthouse** (with a popular sports bar-type hangout with pool tables, games, and Wi-Fi), **Tächi Bar at Hotel Eiger** (classy, boomer-friendly cocktail bar with dancing), and **Hotel Blumental's Bliemlichäller Bar** (a lively characteristic cellar, dancing Fri-Sat at 21:30). For a simpler bar-and-view scene, **Hotel Bellevue** has elegant alpine-lounge ambience and a great terrace. In July and August, you can enjoy occasional folkloric evenings (free, Wednesdays, at Sportzentrum).

Sleeping in Mürren

Mürren is just over a mile high, so if you sleep here you may feel the altitude. These price rankings are based on summer room rates; they often rise during the ski season. Except where noted, all hotels and restaurants listed here close in spring (anywhere from Easter to early June) and again in fall (sometime between mid-Oct and mid-Dec). Half-board, if available, can be a good idea in Mürren.

$$$ Hotel Eiger, a four-star hotel dramatically and conveniently situated just across from the tiny train station, is a good but expensive bet. Family-run for four generations, Adrian and Susanna Stähli offer all the services you'd expect in a big-city hotel (plush lounge, elegant dining rooms, original art on the walls, indoor swimming pool, exercise room, and saunas) while maintaining an Old World, woody elegance in its 50 business-class yet charming rooms. Their "unique" suites, while pricey, include two double rooms and can be a good value for groups of four or five (grand breakfast, discounts for stays of 3 nights or more, email for best deals, elevator, tel. 033-856-5454, www.hoteleiger.com, info@hoteleiger.com).

$$ Hotel Edelweiss is all about the location—convenient and literally hanging on the cliff with devastating views. It's a big, modern building with 30 straightforward rooms (some with balconies) and a busy, recommended restaurant that's well-run by hardworking Sandra and Daniel Kuster-von Allmen (closed Nov-mid-Dec, elevator, piano in lounge, self-serve pay laundry, tel. 033-856-5600, www.edelweiss-muerren.ch, info@edelweiss-muerren.ch).

$$ Hotel Bellevue feels country-upscale and authentically Swiss, with a homey lounge, solid woodsy furniture, a great view terrace, the recommended hunter-themed Jägerstübli restaurant, and 19 comfortable rooms—most with balconies and views. It may be under new management in the near future, so some details could change (discount if staying 2 nights or more in June or Oct, self-serve pay laundry, tel. 033-855-1401, www.bellevuemuerren.ch, bellevue@muerren.ch, Ruth and Othmar Suter).

$$ Hotel Jungfrau has a classic exterior and a modern interior—with 29 rooms plus two apartments for up to six people (email for best deals, elevator, pay laundry service, close to TI/Sportzentrum on the upper road, tel. 033-856-6464, www.hoteljungfrau. ch, mail@hoteljungfrau.ch, Martin and Connie).

$$ Pop-Up Lodge Mürren is a fun concept: The giant, hulking Hotel Alpin Palace looms at the train-station end of town, awaiting a massive renovation. In the meantime, they're renting dated, charmless, but clean and well-equipped rooms to travelers. It's attached by a long walkway to the Sportzentrum and the TI, which is where you'll check in (includes full access to Sportzentrum, tel. 033-856-8686, www.popuplodge.ch, info@popuplodge. ch). For budget travelers, they're also renting basic rooms with shared bathrooms inside the old **$ Sport Lodge** by the tennis courts (the former hotel staff house)—book and check in through the TI.

$$ Hotel Blumental has 14 rooms with woody accents and down comforters, a recommended restaurant in the main building, plus six modern rooms of equal quality in the chalet out back (half-board available, tel. 033-855-1826, www.blumental-muerren. ch, blumental@muerren.ch).

$ Eiger Guesthouse offers 12 good, small, budget rooms—including some great bunk-bed family rooms—across from the train station, above an easygoing ground-floor pub. Four of the rooms share three sets of bathroom facilities, while the rest are en suite. Ema—born in Portugal but a longtime Switzerland resident—is your host (RS%, closed Nov, lots of stairs, game room, view terrace, tel. 033-856-5460, www.eigerguesthouse.com, info@ eigerguesthouse.com).

$ Hotel Regina, once a luxury hotel catering to posh English holiday-goers, may be a faded beauty but still has plenty of charm. It has 50 basic rooms (most with shared toilets and showers) and is conveniently located at the cable-car end of town. Management continues to revive the place bit by bit. For solo travelers, the single rooms are a decent value (family deals, tel. 033-855-4242, www. reginamuerren.ch, info@reginamuerren.ch).

$ Chalet Fontana, run by charming Englishwoman Denise

Fussell, is a fine budget option, with five simple, crispy-clean, and comfortable rooms (cash only, closed late Oct-April, fridge in common kitchen, across street from Stägerstübli restaurant in town center, mobile 078-642-3485, www.chaletfontana.ch, chaletfontana@gmail.com). Denise also rents a family apartment with kitchen, bathroom, and breakfast (in a separate building with a mountain view).

Eating in Mürren

Outside of summer and ski season, only a few places remain open.

$$ Hotel Edelweiss offers lunch and dinner with the most cliff-hanging dining in town, with Swiss specialties, burgers, pizzas, salads, and daily specials. It's family-friendly, the views are incredible, and the prices are good (daily 11:00-20:30, tel. 033-856-5600).

$$ Eiger Guesthouse Restaurant, a busy local hangout with a relaxed pub atmosphere, has long hours and a mostly Italian menu (pizzas, meal-sized salads). They also serve fondue, raclette, *Rösti*, inexpensive house wine, and proudly local beers (Wi-Fi and game room, daily 8:00-22:00, closed Nov, tel. 033-856-5460).

$$$ Stägerstübli, serving big portions of *Rösti* and meat dishes in the town center, is in a 1902 building that was once a tearoom for rich tourists. Locals were limited to the room in the back—which is now the nicer area to eat (look for grizzled regulars indoors). Sitting on its terrace, you know just who's out and about in town (Thu-Mon 11:30-20:30, closed Tue-Wed, tel. 033-855-1316, Lydia).

$$ Hotel Blumental's restaurant (called La Grotte) specializes in typical Swiss cuisine, but also serves fish, international, and vegetarian dishes in a stony and woody dining area. It's one of Mürren's most elegant, romantic settings (cheese fondue served for one or more, daily from 14:00, tel. 033-855-1826).

$$$ Hotel Bellevue's restaurant is atmospheric, with three dining zones: a spectacular view terrace, a sophisticated indoor area, and the *Jägerstübli*—a cozy, well-antlered hunters' room guaranteed to disgust vegetarians. This is a good bet for game, as they buy chamois, wild boar, and deer directly from local hunters (meatless dishes available, daily 11:30-14:00 & 18:00-21:00, tel. 033-855-1401).

$ Café Liv is a mod, hip, and youthful coffee shop with light lunch plates, smoothies, pastries, and quality coffee, including takeaway (Mon-Thu 12:00-18:00, Fri-Sun from 10:00, in town center on the main street, across from tennis courts, tel. 076-213-7305).

BERNER OBERLAND

Supermarket: The **Co-op** has good picnic fixings and sandwiches (Mon-Fri 8:00-18:30, Sat until 18:00, Sun 11:00-17:00, can be closed Tue-Thu afternoons off-season). Given restaurant prices, this place is a godsend for those on a tight budget.

Activities in the Berner Oberland

Scenic Rides on Lifts and Trains

The Berner Oberland is famous for its high-altitude thrill rides. I've described the best of them here. A nice hot chocolate at 10,000 or even 11,000 feet on a sunny day surrounded by the heart of the Swiss Alps is pretty hard to beat. And those on a tight budget can enjoy the same majesty by taking advantage of much less expensive lifts and hiking (see "Hiking and Biking," later).

THE SCHILTHORN AND PIZ GLORIA

The Schilthornbahn cable car carries skiers, hikers, and sightseers effortlessly to the nearly 10,000-foot summit of the Schilthorn, where the Piz Gloria cable-car station awaits, with its solar-powered revolving restaurant, shop, and panorama terrace. At the top, you have a spectacular panoramic view of over 100 peaks—starring the Eiger, Mönch, and Jungfrau mountains, all lined up on the horizon. The entire experience is worth ▲▲▲.

Cost: You can ride to the Schilthorn and back from several points—the cable-car station near Stechelberg on the valley floor (105 CHF), cliff-hanging Gimmelwald (94.60 CHF), or the higher Mürren (82.60 CHF).

Hours: Starting from Stechelberg, the ride requires three changes on the way up: at Gimmelwald (5 minutes), Mürren (5 minutes), and Birg; the entire ride, from valley floor to mountaintop, takes about 35 minutes (or about 25 minutes from Mürren). The first Schilthorn-bound lifts leave Stechelberg at 7:25, Gimmelwald at 7:30, and Mürren at 7:35; last lift from Stechelberg at 16:25 (17:35 in July-Aug), last return from Schilthorn at 17:55 (18:55 in July-Aug). Note that the Stechelberg-Gimmelwald-Mürren segment runs far longer hours than the Mürren-Birg-Schilthorn segment. Lifts run all year, except during maintenance closures (a week in April and three weeks in Nov-Dec).

Discounts: With a Swiss Travel Pass, you ride free to Mürren, then pay half-price to the top; if you have a Eurail Global Pass, you get 25 percent off any ride. Special promotions can save you even more (including a good-value early-morning breakfast deal)—check the website or ask when buying tickets.

Information: See www.schilthorn.ch or call 033-826-0007 for more details and current weather conditions.

Avoiding Crowds: Crowds are a big problem in peak season, especially on weekends (the worst bottleneck is in Mürren). Groups have priority access. Beat the hordes by catching an early lift—preferably before 9:30. It can also make sense to ascend later—it's quieter after about 14:30 (and the mountains across the valley are bathed in late-day sunlight). You can also reserve a specific lift departure time online 24 hours in advance (5 CHF extra); this commits you before you know the weather, but you have the option to use the ticket at another time without a reserved spot.

Planned Changes: To alleviate congestion at Mürren, plans call for a second lift to be built between Mürren and Birg. Phase two will add a direct lift between Stechelberg and Mürren (skipping Gimmelwald) to serve visitors ascending directly from the valley floor. (When? Good question. This initiative is called "Project 20XX" to emphasize its open-endedness.) Because of this work, at some point in the future, the Piz Gloria station up top may be closed for as long as a year.

Visiting the Schilthorn

Ascending the Schilthorn: As the cable car floats up the first stage of the ascent, from Stechelberg to Gimmelwald, you'll see sweet little farms dotting the valley, the paved trail along the river, a line of tour buses foretelling how many groups are above you, and the treacherous metal bridge marking the end of the *via*

ferrata cableway hike. On stage two—Gimmelwald to Mürren—you'll sail above the rooftops of Gimmelwald. You'll also see fields of wooden tripods, which serve two purposes: They stop avalanches and shelter newly planted trees. Made of wood, they're designed to eventually rot when the tree they protect is strong enough to survive the winter snowpack. On the third stage, just above Mürren on the way to Birg, look right to see a reservoir building that powers grey shower posts that make snow—a necessity these days for the local ski industry. Keep an eye on the altitude meter.

You'll change cable cars at Birg. While Birg has the thrilling Skyline Walk (described next), if the weather is good, continue directly to the summit—you'll come back down through Birg later anyway.

Birg Station and Skyline Walk: The Birg station (8,784 feet) has a handy **$ café** with basic food (bratwurst, soup) and glorious outdoor seating; nearby is the breezy (and free) **Skyline Walk** viewing platform that juts out over the cliff face. With more time, it's worth hiking down to the **Thrill Walk**—a free 600-foot-long catwalk bolted to the cliffside. If walking the see-through metal catwalk seems tame to you, along the way you

can choose to tightrope across a cable bridge (there's a net below), cross a section of glass flooring, and crawl through a chain-link tube—all with airy views to the valley far below (both experiences are free with cable-car ticket).

Schilthorn Summit Exterior: Remember, you're here for the view—and it can disappear for the rest of the day in minutes. (The Schilthorn peak doubles as an ideal cloud-catcher.) If it's sunny when you arrive, ignore the indoor attractions—head outside on the deck and luxuriate in the vistas until you're satiated.

Upon arrival, head up two escalators to the **Skyline View Platform** (or go to the right out of the lift to zip up on the eleva-

tor). Outside, information boards identify the peaks, and directional signs point hikers toward some seriously steep downhill climbs. There are plenty of James Bond-themed photo ops. The big, round viewing scopes identify each peak as you survey the panorama; the pink scopes magnify. Note that the classic "Eiger, Mönch, Jungfrau" panorama is on the opposite side from the big platform. Watch paragliders set up, psych up, take off, and fly with the birds. In summer, live folk musicians often perform here (typically June-Aug 11:00-15:00).

Find the stairs near the big platform to walk along the ridge out back—the **007 Walk of Fame,** where cast and crew members from the film have left their handprints and personal messages. At the end of this is the Piz Gloria view platform, offering great views back at the revolving restaurant with the mountains beyond. If you dare, let yourself through the gate by the platform and walk carefully along a gravelly, vertiginous trail (with no railings)—to leave the crowds behind and really feel rugged. This is a great place for a photo of the mountain-climber you. There's also an opportunity to "touch the snow"—a novelty for visitors from warm climates.

Schilthorn Summit Interior: Back inside, consider a drink or a bite at the **$$ 360° Restaurant** (up the stairs). In this revolving

restaurant, you're invited to sit and slowly spin— viewing all the scenery from the comfort of your chair. The restaurant serves drinks (including hot cocoa), salads, soups, and main dishes all day at prices that surprisingly don't rise with the altitude. Or consider the 35-CHF James Bond Brunch, with breakfast foods 8:00-11:00, then soups, salad bar, and warm dishes until 14:00 (after that, it's à la carte only). If you're heading up for an early breakfast, mention it when you buy your ticket down below to save 11 CHF on the buffet before 9:00. There's a cheaper **$ snack bar** on the main level.

Then head down the stairs and follow the maze that leads to the **Bond World 007** exhibit and cinema. This interactive exhibit, well-signed in English, is worth a few minutes for even non-Bond fans. It takes you behind the scenes of the 1969 James Bond movie, *On Her Majesty's Secret Service,* which used the Schilthorn as one of its major locations (and financed the complex's completion). Step into the role of James Bond and try your hand at flying a helicopter to Piz Gloria or bobsledding down the Alps in the simulators. Even the prizewinning WCs are Bond-themed—a sign in the men's room urged me to "Aim Like James."

At the end of the exhibit, the Bond World 007 **cinema** shows a 20-minute video on a continuous loop that highlights the area's natural wonders and activities (including racing down the famous

Inferno ski run), briefly shares the story of the Schilthornbahn lift itself, and shows a substantial clip from *On Her Majesty's Secret Service*.

Finished? You can hike down from the Schilthorn, but it's tough. (Hiking *up* is easier on your knees...if you don't mind a 5,000-foot altitude gain.) For information on **hikes** from lift stations along the Schilthorn cable-car line, see "Hiking and Biking," later. My favorite "hike" from the Schilthorn is simply along the ridge out back, to get away from the station and be all alone on top of an Alp. (But if you need company, both Birg and the Piz Gloria have Wi-Fi.)

JUNGFRAUJOCH

A literal high point of any trip to the Swiss Alps is the Jungfraubahn train ride through the Eiger mountain to the Jungfraujoch (the saddle between the Mönch and Jungfrau mountains)—an experience worth ▲▲▲. At 11,333 feet, it's Europe's highest train station. (If you have a heart or lung condition, you may want to check with your doctor before making this ascent.) Keep in mind that you can enjoy the Berner Oberland without tak-

ing this trip—it's long, slow, expensive, crowded, and cold. But if the weather's perfect and you have a spare day and spare cash, the views are exhilarating and it's fun to be up on a snowy glacier in midsummer.

Cost and Hours: Round-trip fares are 211 CHF from Interlaken Ost, 190 CHF from Lauterbrunnen, 176 CHF from Wengen, and 128 CHF from Kleine Scheidegg. The train runs about twice hourly year-round. The last train back down departs the Jungfraujoch at 17:43 and Kleine Scheidegg at 18:30 (one hour later July-Aug); for first departures see next.

Discounts: From May to late October, a "Good Morning Ticket" saves you 25 percent on the 6:35/7:05 departures from Interlaken Ost, the 7:07/7:37 departures from Lauterbrunnen, and the 8:00/8:30 departures from Kleine Scheidegg. To get the discount you must leave the top by 13:00. Eurail Global pass holders get 25 percent off and can't combine discounts, so they should go whenever they want. The same goes for Swiss Travel Pass holders, who travel free as far as Wengen (with a 25 percent discount beyond)—buy your supplementary ticket before boarding, or pay a 10-CHF surcharge to buy it on board. The Jungfrau Travel Pass offers discounted tickets but it's usually hard to make it pay off (see page 152 for details).

Information: Visit www.jungfrau.ch or call 033-828-7233.

Crowd-Beating Tips: At peak periods (especially July-Aug), trains are standing-room only. During peak times, reserve a seat at a fixed time the day before (5 CHF extra for each leg—up and down; allow about two hours up top). The Jungfraujoch platforms can be jammed and chaotic. Without a reservation, you may have to wait in line (potentially an hour or more) both to get up, and to get back down.

Weather: Don't bother coming all the way up here if it's cloudy. But be aware that even when it's socked in down in the valleys, it can still be gloriously sunny up top—check the webcams and weather forecast at www.jungfrau.ch before committing.

Planning Your Trip: Visiting the Jungfraujoch takes most of a day. The trip up from Lauterbrunnen takes a little under two hours each way, with a change of trains halfway at Kleine Scheidegg. If you're coming from Interlaken, Gimmelwald, or Mürren, add another half-hour. You'll want at least 1.5 hours at the top—more if you eat, hike, or sled. Expect outdoor temperatures to be around freezing in summer—so if you plan to go outside, bring a hat and gloves, shoes with good traction, sunglasses, and sunscreen. Even if you stay inside, the train is chilly, and you'll need a jacket. To minimize altitude sickness, local guides recommend drinking a half-liter of water as you ascend on the train.

Ultimate Alpine Combo: For a thrilling day of alpine scenery, try this plan: Ride the train to Wengen, ride the cable car up to Männlichen, hike from there to Kleine Scheidegg (about 1.5 hours, easy), then catch the train up to the Jungfraujoch.

Eating: You'll find a variety of eateries in the main Jungfraujoch building (see "Shops and Services," later), but it's all overpriced and poor quality; I'd eat before or after my visit, or bring a picnic.

Planned Changes: A **"V-Cableway"** (V-Bahn) lift from Grindelwald directly up to the Eigergletscher stop on the Jungfraujoch line is slated for completion in December 2020. While this 15-minute Eiger Express ride will dramatically save time for people coming from Grindelwald, it makes little difference for those coming from the Lauterbrunnen Valley.

Visiting the Jungfraujoch
Ascending the Jungfraujoch

From Lauterbrunnen or Wengen, you'll board a characteristic little yellow-and-green Wengernalpbahn train to get as far as Kleine Scheidegg. There, you'll transfer to the Jungfraujoch train. The platform can be a bit hectic—take a calming breath and find your

BERNER OBERLAND

way to the end of the correct line: green if you've reserved, yellow if you haven't.

The 35-minute ride from Kleine Scheidegg to the top is mostly in a tunnel, with just a couple of stops. The first one, after 5 minutes, is at **Eigergletscher**—a high-altitude junction with the Eiger Express funicular (expected in late 2020) along with glimpses of a glacier. Stay on the train, and you'll soon enter the tunnel in which you'll travel through the Eiger to the Jungfraujoch. After 11 more minutes, you'll stop for 5 minutes at **Eismeer**, where you can enjoy glacier and mountain views from an amazing perch (10,368 feet). Look out the windows and marvel at how people could climb the Eiger—and how the Swiss built this train track more than a hundred years ago. From there, you'll ride up through darkness—watching video screens explaining all your sightseeing options up top—to the **Jungfraujoch**.

At the Top

Once you reach the top, breathe deep, take it easy, and move slowly—you're way high up and your body isn't used to such altitudes. Study the map to see your options. Or just go with the flow—big, blue *TOUR* signs lead you on a loosely one-way route through the complex, with several optional stops and shortcuts. I'll explain your options so you can decide as you reach each fork in the road.

Jungfrau Panorama: To get ahead of the crowds, upon arrival, muscle your way through the congested shopping zone, bearing left for the *TOUR* signs. You'll follow a tunnel to the Jungfrau Panorama, a 360-degree video that's pleasantly distracting while you wait in line for the elevator that rockets you up to the observation deck.

Sphinx Observation Deck: Head up the stairs and out onto the platform; at 11,782 feet, the views are truly astounding. Use the **orientation panels** to get your bearings: You're between the Mönch and the Jungfrau (the Eiger is hidden, behind the Mönch). Looking toward the Mönch, notice the fun snow area below you, and the trail snaking across the snow to the Mönchsjochhütte (both described later). Looking left, you're gazing

(north) down on the Lauterbrunnen Valley area: Kleine Scheidegg, Gimmelwald, and in the distance, Interlaken. Try to spot
the Schilthorn cable-car station. Farther to the left looms the giant
Jungfrau. And left of that spreads the Aletsch Glacier—Europe's
longest, at nearly 11 miles (or a bit less, by the time you read this).
The silver-domed building above you is a scientific measurement
station (from 1930). Scared of heights? Whatever you do, don't look
down through the floor grates. The Sphinx has a tiny snack stand
and a few benches where you can sit to munch a sandwich.

Ride the elevator back downstairs, where you'll find a small
exhibit with interesting statistics on recent climate warming and
the recovery of the ozone layer. From here, you have two choices:
Turn right to go outside and walk on the glacier (described next);
or turn left to head (slowly) back toward the train.

Outdoor Attractions: You'll find a **Snow Fun Park** set up on
the Aletsch Glacier, offering skiing and snowboarding (35 CHF),

sledding (20 CHF), and a
zip line (25 CHF—prices
include equipment; 45
CHF for all three activi-
ties, mid-May-mid-Oct).
The ticket desk also sells
hot, cold, and hard drinks
to enjoy in a sling-backed
chair on the snow. To get
away from the Jungfrau-
joch crowds, you can hike an hour across the ice to **Mönchsjochhütte** (a mountain hut with a small restaurant). While this can be
a highlight, you need good shoes—when it's slushy, you'll end up
with wet feet.

Indoor Attractions: Back inside—or if you skip the outdoor
area—you'll head through a passage called **Alpine Sensation,**

draped in light-up edelweiss and Swiss
kitsch. Eventually you'll arrive at another fork: Turn right to return to the
train station, or left for more amuse-
ments.

Turning left, next you'll come to
the **Ice Palace** (Eispalast), a very slippery tunnel with walls and floors made
of ice, with a few modest ice carvings.
Gripping the handrail as you scramble
around on sheer ice, ponder how much
less litigious Swiss society is.

Jungfraujoch View: Next you'll
ride an elevator (or hike up a few flights

of stairs) to another outdoor experience: the **Plateau**, where you can walk out on the snow toward the Jungfrau, and look back at the classic Jungfraujoch view—with the Sphinx's glittering silver dome capping a sheer cliff.

Shops and Services in the Berghaus: From here, head back to the main building (Berghaus), with the train station on the ground level. To get there, you'll walk down past several levels of shops (including the **Lindt Swiss Chocolate Heaven,** a candy store with a brief exhibit about Swiss chocolate making); the pricey **$$$ Restaurant Crystal;** the self-service **$ Aletsch** cafeteria; and a basic **$ coffee bar** on the main level, near the doors to the train station.

Returning to Lauterbrunnen: Trains depart twice hourly (at :13 and :43 past the hour); unless you've reserved a seat, you may have to wait in line to board a train back down to earth. In Kleine Scheidegg, you'll change to the Wengernalpbahn line back down to Lauterbrunnen.

Hiking and Biking

This area offers days of possible hikes. Many are a fun combination of trails, mountain trains, and cable-car rides. The information below can help you decide which hike to tackle, but isn't intended as a turn-by-turn guide. Good hiking maps and more detailed trail descriptions than what I've provided here are essential and available from area TIs and hotels. Before setting out on any hike, check locally to be sure you've made the best match between your skills, gear, and trail conditions (snow can persist on trails even into summer). Every year, tourists die doing stupid things in the Alps. Respect the risks or you could end up as a sad memory marked by a cross at the side of a trail.

EASIER HIKES

Hikers' Loop: If you're staying in Lauterbrunnen, are in good shape, and have only one full day here, consider this ambitious day plan: Ride the cable car to Grütschalp, walk along the ridge to Mürren, take the cable car up to the Schilthorn and back down to Mürren, ride the funicular up to Allmendhubel, hike the North Face trail to Gimmelwald, take the lift down to the Schilthornbahn station near Stechelberg, catch the PostBus to Trümmelbach Falls, visit that, and walk through the valley back into Lauterbrunnen. Make it more or less strenuous or time-consuming by swapping lifts and hikes (all described in this chapter). Or rent a mountain bike and do a wheeled variation on this (parking your bike in Mürren for the Schilthorn trip).

On the Valley Floor
▲▲Cloudy-Day Lauterbrunnen Valley Walk

Try the easy trails and pleasant walks along the floor of the Lauterbrunnen Valley. You don't ever need to (and shouldn't) walk along the main road, which parallels the river. A fine, paved, mostly vehicle-free farm lane (great for walkers, runners, bikers, and people with strollers) goes all the way along the valley on the opposite side of the river from the main road, from the town of Lauterbrunnen to the top of the valley (Stechelberg). Small bridges let you cross from the lane to the main road at various points. The local PostBus runs the entire length, with stops along the way, twice an hour.

For a smell-the-cows-and-flowers lowland walk—ideal for a cloudy day, weary body, or tight budget—try this three-mile, basically level ramble from Lauterbrunnen to Stechelberg. While you could go either way, I'd go upstream (very gradually uphill) to walk toward the grandest mountain views.

At the edge of Lauterbrunnen town is the Horner Pub (described on page 177). Just beyond that, hike up the (free and slippery) gallery for a close-up view of mighty **Staubbach Falls.** Staubach is one of 72 waterfalls in this "Valley of Loud Fountains" (as *lauter Brunnen* means). Fact-filled information posts accompany each waterfall. Notice the cone-like mound of earth piled against the side of the cliff—formed by centuries of rocks hurled by the river. You'll see mounds like this (and often "ice caves" formed by the constant mist) all along the valley.

Follow the river up the valley. Along the way, you may see **BASE jumpers**—parachutists who leap from cliffs (or helicopters looking for their bodies). Wind socks in fields mark landing spots. Lauterbrunnen Valley is the BASE jumper's mecca.

About 45 minutes after leaving town, you can cross the river for an optional side trip to **Trümmelbach Falls** (described on page 174). After seeing the falls, you can catch the PostBus in either direction—back to Lauterbrunnen, or on to Stechelberg. Or keep walking: From the falls, walk uphill on the main road about five minutes, then cross through the Breithorn Campsite and over the river to return to your trail.

After walking about half an hour farther upstream, you come to a fine picnic stop at the base of **Mürrenbach falls,** where the water enjoys a 1,400-foot free fall. Just beyond is the **Schilthornbahn cable-car station.** From here you can ride the lift up; catch the PostBus back to Lauterbrunnen; or walk another half-hour to the top of the valley. At the top, just before the end of the trail, a five-minute side trip takes you over a bridge and to one final waterfall, **Sefinenfall.** Next to Hotel Stechelberg, where the road ends, you'll find another stop for the PostBus back to Lauterbrunnen.

Gimmelwald Area Hikes

① Sefinen Valley to Kilchbalm
② North Face Trail
③ Allmendhubel to Grütschalp
④ Allmendhubel to Grütschalp via Winteregg
⑤ Grütschalp to Mürren
⑥ Mürren to Gimmelwald
⑦ Gimmelwald-Tanzbödeli-Obersteinberg-
   Stechelberg/Gimmelwald
⑧ Sprutz Waterfall
⑨ Birg to Gimmelwald via Bryndli

Alternate Route via Gimmelwald: If you're staying in Gimmelwald, try this plan: Take the Schilthornbahn lift down to the station near Stechelberg (5 minutes), then walk 1.5 hours along the river to Lauterbrunnen (side-tripping to Trümmelbach Falls about halfway). To return to Gimmelwald from Lauterbrunnen, take the cable car up to Grütschalp (10 minutes), then either walk to Gimmelwald (1.5 hours) or take the train to Mürren (10 minutes). From Mürren, it's a downhill walk (30 minutes) to Gimmelwald. (This loop trip can be reversed or started at any point along the way—such as Lauterbrunnen or Mürren.)

From Gimmelwald
▲Sefinen Valley to Kilchbalm
The trail from Gimmelwald up the Sefinen Valley (Sefinental) is easy and a good rainy-weather hike, as you can go as far as you like. After two hours and a gain of only 800 feet, you hit the end of the

trail at Kilchbalm, a dramatic bowl of glacier fields. Snow can make this route unsafe, even into the summer, so confirm conditions locally before setting out. There's no food or drink along the way.

From the Gimmelwald fire station, walk about 100 yards down the paved road, following *Stechelberg* signs. Turn onto the dirt Sefinental road, which becomes a lane, then a trail. You'll cross a raging river and pass a firing range where locals practice their marksmanship (some Fri and Sat evenings; the *danger of fire* sign refers to live bullets). Follow signs to Kilchbalm into a forest, along a river, and finally to the glacier fields.

From Mürren
▲▲North Face Trail

This pleasant, fairly easy, 2.5-hour, four-mile hike offers excellent views, flowery meadows, mountain huts, and a dozen information boards, describing the fascinating climbing history of the great peaks around you. You'll also pass a few farms (technically "alps," as they are only open in the summer) that serve meals and drinks. You'll begin at 6,385 feet and finish at 5,375 feet; while it's mostly downhill, there's one uphill stretch that can be challenging if you're not in shape. The trail is well-signed and easy to follow, but it's wise to get a trail map from the Mürren TI or the cable-car station and confirm the route. The signed route loops counterclockwise around to Mürren; near the end, at Spilboden, you can drop straight down into Mürren, or opt to extend the hike and descend into Gimmelwald via the Sprutz waterfall. This final, optional stretch is the most challenging—very steeply downhill, with uneven footing, followed by an uphill (and dizzying) hike back up from the waterfall, and finally back down into Gimmelwald. To keep things easy, skip Sprutz.

To begin the hike, ride the Allmendhubel funicular up from Mürren (good restaurant at top—see page 193). Leaving the funicular, look for the children's play area and a blue *North Face Trail* sign. Follow the path uphill, skirting to the right around the play area, passing through small cattle gates, and past the chairlift station. From here, follow the blue signs down into the valley toward Sonnenberg. (Along the way, you'll see yellow directional signs pointing toward *Sonnenberg, Suppenalp,* and *Schiltalp,* as well as blue *North Face Trail* signs.)

You'll head over a little ridge and drop into lovely **Blumental** ("Flower Valley," under the Schilthornbahn cable-car line), which is hopping with marmots (see the "Hiking in the Berner Oberland" sidebar for more on these rodents and other animals you may see).

Following the trail down into the valley, you can make a brief detour to the left to the remote and quirky pension/restaurant **Sonnenberg;** they were allowed to break the all-wood building code with concrete for protection against avalanches.

From here, follow the paved trail across the meadow, then hook left to the quainter **Suppenalp.** Lean against the house with a salad, soup, or sandwich, and enjoy the view (closed Mon-Tue). Notice how older huts are built into the protected side of rocks and outcroppings, in anticipation of avalanches.

From here, you'll head uphill on the gravel path—directly toward the looming, craggy Schwarzmönch peak. You'll gain altitude as you curve around the ridge (called **Schiltgrat**), directly under the tourists gliding in cable cars up to the Schilthorn. In spots where the path is not clearly defined, look for white-and-red stripes painted on rocks. Watch on your left for great views down over Mürren. Going through a small alpine forest, more peaks come into view. You'll emerge at a broad, grassy **meadow** high over Gimmelwald, where the views open up. Look high on the right for

both the Birg and Piz Gloria stations on the Schilthornbahn.

After strolling blissfully through high alpine meadows, you'll finally come to a group of huts called **Schiltalp** (with a romantic farm setting and good self-service food and drink). At Schiltalp,

if the poles under the eaves have bells, the cows are up here. If not, the cows are at the lower farms. Half the cows in Gimmelwald (about 100) spend their summers here. In July, August, and September, you can watch cheese being made. Thirty years

ago, each family had its own hut. Labor was cheap and available. Today, it's a communal thing, with several families sharing the expense of a single cow herder. Cow herders are master cheesemakers and have veterinary skills, too.

From Schiltalp, the trail winds gracefully downhill, where you'll cross the bridge to pick up the trail to Spilboden—another rustic alp settlement. At Spilboden, you have two choices. To finish the North Face trail, head left through meadows and the hamlet of Gimmeln, then back to Mürren. Or—for a more dangerous and demanding option—cut off to the right, descending steeply through a thick forest and under the dramatic Sprutz waterfall into Gimmelwald. This is much steeper and requires a bit more uphill hiking. If you're up for it, get details for Sprutz waterfall under "More Difficult Hikes," later.

▲Allmendhubel to Grütschalp (a.k.a. Mountain View Trail)

For a not-too-tough two-hour walk with great Jungfrau views, ride the funicular from Mürren to Allmendhubel and walk to Grütschalp (a drop of about 1,500 feet), where you can catch the train back to Mürren. You'll see this route clearly marked as the "Mountain View trail" on maps and brochures.

Hiking in the Berner Oberland

This region is a wonderful place to hike. I've listed my favorite excursions in this chapter. The super-scenic walk from Männlichen to Kleine Scheidegg is the best of all worlds: It's both dramatic and relatively easy (but doesn't open until June). Other relatively easy hikes include the North Face trail from Allmendhubel; various walks from Mürren or Allmendhubel to Grütschalp; the Sefinen Valley hike from Gimmelwald; and the stroll along the Lauterbrunnen Valley floor. More challenging routes include the spectacular hike from Schynige Platte to First and the hike from the Birg cable-car station down to Gimmelwald (including the Sprutz waterfall).

To do any serious hiking, invest in a good hiking map at any TI, and ask about current weather and trail conditions. For easy hikes, it's usually enough to use the 3-D maps in the free brochures (called *Wandern/Hiking*) published by the Schilthornbahn (for the west side of the valley) and the Jungfraubahn (for the east side); they're available at stations, hotels, and TIs. These overview maps of the mountainsides also make attractive souvenirs.

Don't forget a water bottle and some munchies. In addition to a good map, for serious hikes it's wise to carry sun protection, an extra layer of clothing, and basic first-aid supplies. Know when the last lifts run in the afternoon. Trails are well-marked, with yellow signs listing destinations and the estimated time it'll take you to walk there; some trails are also marked with red-and-white stripes painted on rocks and trees.

Electric Fences: The many working farms in this area contain their livestock with solar-powered electric fences (which look like plastic tape strung between thin metal poles). You can't tell

▲Grütschalp to Mürren

For a family-friendly, super-easy panorama stroll with grand views, walk either direction between Mürren (5,381 feet) and Grütschalp (4,879 feet)—roughly following the scenic train line between the same points. You'll enjoy the best Jungfrau views walking from Grütschalp to Mürren. The trail from the tiny station at Grütschalp to Winteregg (5,177 feet) is a 30-minute scenic walk mostly through cow country with an accompaniment of tinkling bells on a gravelly lane. The trail between Winteregg and Mürren mostly parallels the train track—also scenic and gravelly, but less interesting. The highlight, along with the dramatic views of the Eiger, if they're turned on without touching a wire—but it's much better not finding out. On certain trails (for example, at several points on the North Face Trail), hikers may need to let themselves through gates in the electric fences. In some, a long, plastic, pointy pole sticks out horizontally and pivots like a door—just walk on through (if there's tape on the pole, touch it only on the tape). At other gates, you'll need to grab a plastic handle, unhook it, and rehook it—again, being careful not to touch the wires.

Weather Concerns: Clouds can roll in anytime, but on warm summer days, skies are usually clearest in the morning. Locals always seem to know the weather report (as much of their income depends on it). All over the region, TV sets are tuned to the local weather station, with real-time views from all the famous peaks. You can also check weather reports and view live webcams at www.jungfrau.ch and www.schilthorn.ch. For more detailed weather reports in English, visit www.meteoswiss.admin.ch.

Snow can curtail your hiking plans, even in July. Before setting out on any hike, get advice from the TI or a knowledgeable local. The high trails (Männlichen to Kleine Scheidegg, Schynige Platte to First, and anything from Schilthorn or Birg) are typically passable only from June into October.

Wildlife: As hunting is not allowed in the vicinity of any lifts, animals find safe havens in places you're likely to be. Keep an eye out for chamois (called *Gemsen* here)—the sure-footed "goat antelopes" that live at the top of the tree line and go a little lower when hungry. Spotting an ibex—a wild goat with horns, scrambling along the rocky terrain—is another Berner Oberland thrill. You'll also encounter marmots—big alpine rodents (like 2-pound squirrels) that get fat each summer, then sleep underground for six months through the winter. These burrowing critters are fun to watch, and if you sit still, they don't see you. You'll hear them whistle. The best viewing place is above Allmendhubel, in the meadow above the highest hut in Blumental.

For general tips about hiking in Switzerland's mountains, see page 238.

BERNER OBERLAND

Mönch, and Jungfrau, is the wonderful restaurant/playground/cheese farm midway at Winteregg. (The Grütschalp-Mürren train also stops here.) The Alpkäserei Staubbach offers windows to peer into the cheese-making action (before 11:00), and sells fresh yogurt and cheese. The Winteregg Restaurant has a dramatic view terrace and an extensive alp-happy playground.

▲Paved Downhill Bliss from Mürren to Gimmelwald

This super-easy, super-scenic stroll drops you down on a paved road from Mürren to Gimmelwald in about 30 minutes. While there's about an 800-foot elevation drop, it's all smooth and easy—doable for any fitness level, or even with a stroller (and more interesting than the 5-minute cable-car ride). It's simple—just stay on the same paved path the whole way down—but I've noted a few things to look out for.

In **Mürren,** take the trail down between the cable-car station and Hotel Alpenruh, following *Wanderweg* signs through the lower levels of town. When you reach the wider, paved road, turn right and continue downhill—this is the "road" to Gimmelwald, so keep an eye out for vehicles (cars, mini trucks, tractors, and bikes blazing downhill). Crossing under the first set of overhead cables (for the service lift from the valley floor up to Mürren), look high on the right for the Birg cable-car station. As the road bends left, you'll pass some "tripods" on your right—these provide structure for new trees being planted as an avalanche barrier (around the time the trees are big enough to do the job on their own, these supports will simply rot away naturally).

Enjoy the grand alpine views across the valley. You'll cross the little **Mürrenbach stream** as it churns downhill; on the right, look for the flood gates used to control its flow, and on the left, watch it tumble down into the valley. Continuing farther, down in the valley below you'll see some of the houses of Stechelberg—the end-of-the-valley community. Crossing under the second set of cable-car cables, visually trace them downhill toward Gimmelwald's station—the end point of this walk, and the starting point of my self-guided "Gimmelwald Walk" (see page 180).

A bit farther along, you'll see steep **switchbacks** snaking down below you. Head on down. At the second switchback are more of those avalanche tripods. After the third switchback, the road straightens out, following the cable cars all the way into town. You'll pass through a small forest, cross the little Wyenbach waterfall, then reach the outlying houses of **Gimmelwald.** One of the first buildings you'll pass is the now-closed Hotel Mittaghorn; just past this, signs on the left point steeply down toward *Pension Gimmelwald, M-Hostel,* and the cable car—take this route for the quick route to the village center. Or, for a commanding "aerial view" over Gimmelwald, carry on farther to the four benches positioned perfectly over town. Lounge here as long as you like, with alpine cliffs in your face, a real Swiss mountain farming community all around you, and a charming village at your feet. (You could also follow my "Gimmelwald Walk" in reverse as you stroll through the town to the lift station; see page 180).

From Lauterbrunnen/Wengen
▲▲▲Männlichen-Kleine Scheidegg Hike

This is my favorite easy alpine hike (2.5 miles, about 1.5 hours, 900-foot altitude drop to Kleine Scheidegg). It's entertaining all

the way, with glorious mountain views. If you missed the plot, it's the Monk (Mönch) protecting the Young Maiden (Jungfrau) from the Ogre (Eiger). The trail usually opens sometime in June and closes due to snow in October. Ask about conditions and get a map at the lift stations or at TIs; there are also useful webcams at www.maennlichen.ch and www.jungfrau.ch.

Ascending to Männlichen: If the weather's good, start off bright and early. From the Lauterbrunnen train station, take the little mountain train up to **Wengen.** Sit on the right side of the train for great valley and waterfall views. In Wengen, buy a picnic at the Co-op grocery across the square from the station, walk a couple of blocks into town, and catch the lift to Männlichen, located on top of the ridge high above you (23 CHF one-way, half-price with Swiss Travel Pass, 3/hour, 6-minute trip, mid-May-mid-Oct first ascent at 8:30, at 8:10 July-mid-Sept, last ascent at 16:50, somewhat shorter hours off-season, tel. 033-855-2933, www. maennlichen.ch). Couch potato thrill-seekers can pay 5 CHF extra for the "Royal Ride" to climb the spiral stairs and enjoy an open-air rooftop perch. This lift may run even when the trail is closed; if the weather is questionable, confirm that the Männlichen-Kleine Scheidegg trail is open before ascending. If it's sunny, don't waste time in Wengen—you can linger back here after your hike.

Riding the gondola from Wengen to **Männlichen,** you'll go over the old lift station—built in 1978, then inundated by a 1999 avalanche that buried a good part of Wengen (notice there's no development in the "red zone" above the tennis courts). Farms are built with earthen ramps on the uphill side in anticipation of the next slide. The forest of avalanche fences near the top was re-inforced after that 1999 avalanche. As you ascend, you can also survey Wengen—the bright red roofs mark new vacation condos, mostly English-owned and used only a few weeks a year.

When you get to the station at the top of the Wengen-Männlichen lift (7,313 feet, WCs), check inside to see if they have any free "king for a day" Männlichen Experience envelopes; these fun souvenirs open up to make a panoramic crown that names the mountains you're seeing.

Männlichen Gipfel Detour ("The Royal Walk"): Before your easy hike, consider a steeper detour that'll give you an easy king- or queen-of-the-day feeling: Turn left from the Wengen-Männlichen lift station, and hike uphill to the little peak you see up ahead, topped with a crown-shaped viewpoint (Männlichen Gipfel, 7,687 feet). Marked as "The Royal Walk," this path gains more than 350 feet of elevation; if you're in decent shape,

it takes about 20 minutes up, then 10 minutes back down. The last stretch is thin-air-sucking steep, with ropes you can grab onto for added confidence; even Coloradans get a bit winded. But once at the **summit,** you're rewarded with 360-degree views. Beneath you, look for avalanche barriers—both directly below the viewpoint, and striping the cliffs across the valley. Looking back at the cable car, you'll see the Eiger, Mönch, and Jungfrau; in front of them, the pointy Tschuggen peak indicates the location of the Jungfraujoch station. Stretching to the right of those peaks is the Lauterbrunnen Valley; on the far ridge, try to spot the Birg and Schilthorn cable-car stations. On the left side of the three big peaks is the Grindelwald Valley, a parallel universe of alpine villages, lifts, and hikes. And in the opposite direction from the big peaks, the knobby ridge straight ahead is Schynige Platte, with Interlaken on the valley floor beyond and below.

Easy Hike to Kleine Scheidegg: Back at the lift station, enjoy the walk—facing spectacular alpine panorama views—to Kleine Scheidegg for a picnic or restaurant lunch. To start the hike, leave the Wengen-Männlichen lift station to the right. Ahead of you in the distance, left to right, are the north faces of the Eiger, Mönch, and Jungfrau; in the foreground is the Tschuggen peak, and just behind it, the Lauberhorn. This hike takes you around the left (east) side of this ridge. Simply follow the signs for *Kleine Scheidegg,* and you'll be there in about 1.5 hours—allowing extra time for gawkers, picnickers, and photographers. (Speed demons without cameras can make it in an hour.)

Walk a few minutes to the second Männlichen lift station (with free WCs; these lifts go to Grindelwald, the touristy town in the valley to your left). Nearby is the Berghaus Männlichen restaurant (wait for better options later), a great kids' play area, and a landing pad for helicopter sightseeing flights.

From here, carry on along the path as it curls around the left

(Grindelwald-facing) side of the ridge. From time to time, you might have to tiptoe through streams of melted snow—or some small snow banks (with ropes to hang onto for safety), even well into the summer—but the path is well-marked, well-maintained, and mostly level all the way to Kleine Scheidegg.

About two-thirds of the way through the hike, you'll curve around the bend and arrive at a cluster of benches and a shelter with incredible unobstructed views of all three peaks—the perfect picnic spot.

About 15 minutes later, you'll reach the first sign of civilization: the recommended **Restaurant Grindelwaldblick** (the best lunch stop up here—less crowded, more Swiss and friendly than Kleine Scheidegg options, described on page 224). Hike to the restaurant's fun mountain lookout to survey the Eiger and look down on the Kleine Scheidegg (rated ▲▲ for its spectacular panoramic mountain view).

From the Grindelwaldblick, it's a steep 10-minute hike down to the Kleine Scheidegg train station, with plenty of lesser lunch options (described on page 224).

Optional Add-Ons: From Kleine Scheidegg, you can catch the train up to "the top of Europe" (see Jungfraujoch listing, earlier), take the train back down to Wengen (note that your Swiss Travel Pass doesn't cover you until Wengen; buy a supplementary ticket before boarding, or pay a 10-CHF surcharge to buy on board), or hike downhill (gorgeous 30-minute hike to the Wengernalp station, a little farther to the Allmend stop; 60 more steep minutes from there into Wengen—not dangerous, but requires a good set of knees). The alpine views might be accompanied by the valley-filling mellow sound of cow bells, alphorns, and distant avalanches. If the weather turns bad or you run out of steam, catch the train at any of the stations along the way. The boring final descent from Wengen to Lauterbrunnen is knee-killer steep—catch the train instead.

MORE DIFFICULT HIKES
Above Interlaken
▲▲Schynige Platte to First

The best day I've had hiking in the Berner Oberland was on this demanding seven-hour ridge walk, with Lake Brienz on one side and all that Jungfrau beauty on the other. Start at the Wilderswil train station (just outside Interlaken), and catch the little train up to Schynige Platte (6,454 feet; 32 CHF one-way, goes every 40 minutes and takes about an hour, runs late May-late Oct). Catch the early 8:05 train to have time for Faulhorn and get to First before it closes. The high point on the trail is Faulhorn (8,790 feet, with a famous mountaintop hotel—from 1832, the first mountain hotel in Switzerland and its character survive). From here, hike on to First (7,110 feet), where you ride a small gondola down to Grindelwald (33 CHF; runs continuously—until at least 17:00 in summer) and catch a train back via Zweilutschinen to wherever you're staying.

You can also do this hike in reverse, which means less climbing, from First (7,113 feet) to Schynige Platte (last train down at 17:53). The TI produces a great Schynige Platte map/guide narrating the train ride up and describing various hiking options from there (available at Wilderswil train station).

At the Schynige Platte station, look for a promotional booth run by Lowa, a local manufacturer of top-end hiking boots. They provide free loaners (already broken in) to hikers who'd like to give their boots a try.

Easier Options at Schynige Platte: For a shorter (3-hour) ridge walk, consider the well-signposted Panoramaweg, a loop from Schynige Platte to Daub Peak.

The alpine flower park at the Schynige Platte station offers a delightful stroll through several hundred alpine flowers (free, late May-late Oct daily 8:30-18:00, www.alpengarten.ch), including a chance to see edelweiss growing in the wild.

From Gimmelwald

▲Gimmelwald-Tanzbödeli-Obersteinberg-Stechelberg/ Gimmelwald

This six-hour, 11-mile hike can be extremely rewarding, offering perfect peace, very few people, traditional alpine culture, and spectacular views. Allow eight hours if you include the Busenalp side trip.

Prepare ahead; this demanding hike requires serious shoes and is best done with a good, locally purchased map. There's no food or drink for five hours, so pack accordingly.

About 100 yards below the Gimmelwald firehouse, take the **Sefinental** dirt road (described earlier, in the Sefinen Valley to Kilchbalm hike). As the dirt road switches back after about 30 minutes, take the right turn across the river and start your ascent, following signs to *Obersteinberg*.

After two hours of hard climbing, you have the option of a 30-minute (each way) side-trip to **Busenalp**. This is fun if the goat-and-cow herder is there, as you can watch traditional cheesemaking in action. (He appreciates a bottle of wine from hikers.) Trail markers are painted onto rocks—watch carefully. After visiting Busenalp, return to the main path.

At the *Obersteinberg 50 Min/Tanzbödeli 20 Min* signpost, head for **Tanzbödeli** ("Dancing Floor"). This is everyone's favorite alpine perch—great for a little romance or a picnic with breathtaking views of the Obersteinberg valley. From here, you enter a natural reserve, so you're likely to see chamois and other alpine critters. From Tanzbödeli, you return to the main trail (there's no other way out) and continue to **Obersteinberg.** You'll eventually hit the Mountain Hotel Obersteinberg (see "Sleeping in Obersteinberg," later; American expat Vickie will serve you a meal or drink, and loves to show off her cheese cellar).

From there, the trail leads to another mountain hotel at **Tschingelhorn** (www.tschingelhorn.ch). About an hour later, you hit a fork in the trail and choose where you'd like your hike to end: back to Gimmelwald (2 hours total) or Stechelberg (near the bottom of the Schilthornbahn cable car, 1.5 hours total).

▲Sprutz Waterfall

The forest above Gimmelwald hides a powerful waterfall with a trail snaking behind it, offering a fun gorge experience. The waterfall itself is not well-signed, but it's on the Gimmelwald-Spilboden trail. It's steep, through a forest, requires climbing up and down stairs that are carved into the rock without handrails, and can be very slippery when wet—but the actual crossing under the waterfall is just misty. The sun has the most fun with the cascading water between 12:00 and 14:00.

The hike up to Sprutz from Gimmelwald isn't worth the trip in itself, but the trail is handy when combined with the hike down from Birg and Bryndli (described on the next page) or the North Face Trail (see earlier, under "Easier Hikes"). As you descend on either of these hikes, the trail down to Gimmelwald splits at Spilboden—to the right for the forest and the waterfall; to the left for more meadows, the hamlet of Gimmeln, and then gracefully back into Gimmelwald (or Mürren).

If taking the **Sprutz route,** you'll head downhill and enter a thick forest, where several sharp switchbacks appear below you. Make your way down this trail, watching your footing on the uneven path (with rocks and roots). There are a few forks in the path—just follow the red-and-white stripes (and occasionally yellow *Bergwanderweg* signs). You'll begin to hear the **waterfall**, and finally you'll see it—and the steps carved into the rock to either side. Make your way down carefully, and cross under the falls (you'll crouch a bit under the rock). On the other side, start back uphill, at first on steep steps with no railings. (If you're fearful of heights, this is an adrenaline rush, but not actually difficult; there's a cable in the cliff wall to steady yourself.) Head back up out of the **gorge,** watching for the red-and-white trail markers at a sharp left turn. At the two benches just above, turn right (following signs toward *Gimmelwald*), continue through the forest, then pop out at the meadows high above Gimmelwald. From here, you'll follow narrow, rutted trails cut into the grass as you descend very steeply to **Gimmelwald.**

From Mürren

To arrange a guide for the white-knuckle, cliff-hugging *via ferrata* trail near Mürren, see page 194.

From the Schilthorn

Several tough trails lead down from the Schilthorn (there's a reason that virtually all visitors take the cable car down). Only a serious, experienced hiker should consider walking all or part of the way back into Gimmelwald. Proper shoes and clothing (weather can change quickly) and good knees are required. Don't attempt to hike down unless you've confirmed that the trail is clear of snow. While it's possible to make the steep descent directly from the top of the Schilthorn, I prefer the less strenuous (but still challenging) hike from the intermediate cable-car station at Birg.

▲▲Birg to Gimmelwald via Bryndli

You can combine this difficult downhill hike (4-5 hours) from the Birg cable-car station with a visit to the Schilthorn by buying the round-trip excursion early-bird fare (it's cheaper than the Gimmelwald-Schilthorn-Birg ticket). Visit the summit first, then descend to Birg to hike down.

The most interesting trail from Birg to Gimmelwald is the high one via Grauseeli lake and Wasenegg Ridge to **Bryndli,** then down to Spilboden and the Sprutz waterfall. Warning: This trail drops 4,500 feet, is quite steep and slippery in places, and can take over four hours. Locals take their kindergarteners on this hike, but Americans unused to alpine hikes shouldn't attempt it.

From the **Birg lift station,** hike toward the Schilthorn, taking your first left down and passing along the left side of the little Grauseeli lake. From the lake, a gravelly trail leads down rough switchbacks (including a stretch where the path narrows and you can hang onto a guide cable against the cliff face) until it levels out. When you see a rock painted with arrows pointing to Mürren and Rotstockhütte, follow the path to **Rotstockhütte** (traditional old farm with light meals and drinks), traversing the cow-grazed mountainside.

The safer, well-signposted approach to Bryndli is to drop down to Rotstockhütte, then climb back up to Bryndli. Thrill-seekers instead follow **Wasenegg Ridge**. It's more scary than dangerous if you're sure-footed and can handle the 50-foot-long "tightrope-with-handrail" section along an extremely narrow ledge with a thousand-foot drop. This trail gets you to Bryndli with the least altitude change. A barbed-wire fence leads you to Bryndli's knobby little summit, where you'll enjoy an incredible 360-degree view and a chance to sign your name on the register stored in the little wooden box.

From **Bryndli**, a steep trail winds directly down toward Gimmelwald and soon hits a bigger, easier trail. The trail bends right (just before the farm/restaurant at Spilboden), leading to Sprutz. Walk under the Sprutz waterfall, then follow a steep, wooded trail that deposits you in a meadow of flowers at the top side of Gimmelwald. (For details on the hike from Spilboden down to Sprutz and Gimmelwald, see earlier.)

MOUNTAIN BIKING

Mountain biking is popular and accepted, as long as you stay on clearly marked mountain-bike paths. You can rent bikes in Mürren (Stäger Sport, see page 189) or in Lauterbrunnen (Imboden Bike, see page 172). The Lauterbrunnen shop is bigger, has a wider selection of bikes, and is likely to be open when the Mürren one isn't. But if you pick up a bike in Mürren, you may be able to drop it at the Lauterbrunnen train station (ask at Stäger Sport). Some hotels also rent or loan mountain bikes.

As with any activity in the mountains, get maps and seek advice locally before venturing out. I've outlined some of the most popular bike rides next.

Lauterbrunnen to Interlaken: This is a gentle downhill ride on a peaceful bike path across the river from the road (don't bike on the road itself). You can return to Lauterbrunnen by train (you'll have to buy a regular ticket for the bike). Or rent a bike at either Interlaken station, take the train to Lauterbrunnen, and ride back. Ask at Interlaken's Flying Wheels about their partnership in Lauterbrunnen, allowing a one-way rental (see page 156).

Lauterbrunnen Valley (between Stechelberg and Lauterbrunnen town): This delightful, easy bike path features plenty of diversions along the way (same as "Cloudy-Day Lauterbrunnen Valley Walk" on page 207).

Mürren to Winteregg to Grütschalp and Back: This fairly level route takes you through high country, with awesome mountain views (see description of this walk earlier).

Mürren to Winteregg to Lauterbrunnen: This scenic descent (steep, with four miles of switchbacks), on a service road with loose gravel, takes you to the Lauterbrunnen Valley floor.

Mürren-Gimmelwald-Sefinen Valley-Stechelberg-Lauterbrunnen-Grütschalp-Mürren: This is rewarding but very demanding—with one very difficult stretch where you'll likely walk (or carry) your bike down a steep gulley for 500 yards. While you'll be on your bike most of the time, to complete the loop take the cable car from Lauterbrunnen up to Grütschalp and then bike back to Mürren.

More Berner Oberland Towns

I'd sleep in Gimmelwald, Mürren, or Lauterbrunnen, but you could also consider overnighting in the following places.

Sleeping and Eating in Wengen

Wengen—a bigger, fancier Mürren (pop. 1,300) on the east side of the valley at 4,180 feet—has plenty of grand hotels, restaurants, shops, diversions, and terrific views...though it lacks the soul of the towns I've described earlier. This mostly traffic-free resort is an easy train ride above Lauterbrunnen and halfway up to Kleine Scheidegg and Männlichen. From Wengen, you can catch the Männlichen lift (www. maennlichen.ch) up to the ridge

and take the rewarding, view-filled, nearly downhill Männlichen-Kleine Scheidegg hike (described on page 215).

Wengen's **TI** is a two-minute walk from the station. When you get off the train, look for the big map and bear left up to the main drag (Dorfstrasse). This strip is lined with big hotels on the left; on the right are a playing field, the bottom station for the

Männlichen cable car, and the TI (Tourist Center Wengen, daily 9:00-18:00, July-Aug until 21:00, closed Sat-Sun off-season, tel. 033-856-8585, https://wengen.swiss).

The good-sized **Co-op grocery,** across the square from the train station, is great for picnic fixings (daily 8:00-18:30; closed Sun off-season). The small **Dorflade Wengen** grocery store on the main street (near the cable-car station) is open until 21:30.

Above the Train Station: $$$$ Romantik Hotel Schönegg, at the top end of Wengen's main road, is a centrally located splurge exuding a warm and woody ski-lodge ambience, with a generous view terrace out front. Its 20 rooms are designed in a cozy alpine style, all with balconies and great views (family room with fireplace, elevator, sauna, half-board in good restaurant with big terrace available, tel. 033-855-3422, www.hotel-schoenegg.ch, mail@hotel-schoenegg.ch).

$$$ Hotel Berghaus, in a quiet area facing a pasture, is a five-minute uphill walk from the main street (about 10 minutes from the station). This sedate old place offers 19 rooms above a fine restaurant specializing in fish (family rooms, elevator, open June-Sept and mid-Dec-early April, tel. 033-855-2151, www.berghaus-wengen.ch, info@berghaus-wengen.ch, Fontana-Fuchs family). At the train station, dial #25 on the hotel phone to request a free pickup (until 18:00, reserve in advance). Or, to walk to the hotel from the main drag, head up the street across from Hotel Bernerhof, bear right at the fork, go 200 yards more (past the church), and it's on the left.

Below the Train Station: $$ Bären Hotel, run by friendly Therese and Willy Brunner, offers 17 tidy rooms with modern new bathrooms (rates include half-board in their restaurant—or opt out to save money, family rooms, elevator, kids' playroom, table tennis, closed mid-Oct-mid-Dec, tel. 033-855-1419, www.baeren-wengen.ch, info@baeren-wengen.ch). Their **$$$ restaurant** is the best option in town for a quality, memorable meal. It feels professional, with sharp service, but still bright and inviting. They try to locally source their ingredients and enjoy crafting seasonal specials (lunch specials, dinner reservations wise, daily 11:30-14:00 & 18:00-22:00). From the station, cross the street to the Co-op grocery, turn right and go under the rail bridge, and follow the road down the hill—the hotel will be on your right.

Sleeping and Eating at or near Kleine Scheidegg

This high settlement above the timberline (6,762 feet) is as close as you can stay to the Jungfraujoch. All of these places serve meals and let you sleep face-to-face with the Eiger. Confirm prices and availability before ascending. Note that the last train down to Lauterbrunnen leaves Kleine Scheidegg at 18:30 (19:30 in July-Aug).

$$$$ Hotel Bellevue des Alpes, lovingly maintaining a 1930s elegance, is a very expensive but potentially worthwhile splurge. Since the 1840s, five generations of von Allmens have run this classic old 60-room alpine hotel (subsidized by the family income from Trümmelbach Falls). Every detail has been preserved, and filmmakers often use the hotel as a set for pre-WWII period shoots. The hallway is like a museum lined with old photos (breakfast and sumptuous four-course dinner included, four floors and no elevator, no TVs, closed mid-April–mid-June and mid-Sept–mid-Dec, tel. 033-855-1212, www.scheidegg-hotels.ch, welcome@scheidegg-hotels.ch).

¢-$ Bergrestaurant Kleine Scheidegg is a handy, basic lodge in the train-station building. It has 17 rooms with shared bath, plus dorm beds (includes breakfast, dinner extra, open year-round, tel. 033-828-7828, www.bergrestaurant-kleine-scheidegg.ch). The **$$ restaurant** has a predictable menu of basic Swiss and international food.

¢-$ Restaurant Grindelwaldblick, a 10-minute hike up along the path toward Männlichen and visible from the train station, is more charming, romantic, and remote than **Bergrestaurant Kleine Scheidegg**. You can't get wheeled luggage up along the path by yourself, but for 10 CHF they'll bring it up for you (private rooms, family room, closed Nov and May, tel. 033-855-1374, www.grindelwaldblick.ch, grindelwaldblick@grindelwald.ch). The **$$ restaurant,** with a great sun terrace and a cozy interior, sells good three-course lunches and dinners, including a cheesy *Rösti* (food served daily 11:00-20:00, drinks until 22:00).

Sleeping in Stechelberg

Stechelberg, at 3,025 feet, is the hamlet at the end of the road up the Lauterbrunnen Valley; it's about a mile beyond the Schilthornbahn lift that goes up to Gimmelwald, Mürren, and the Schilthorn. From the lift station, it's a five-minute ride on the same PostBus that comes from Lauterbrunnen (2/hour) or a 20-minute walk. Beyond Stechelberg lies the rugged upper end of the Lauterbrunnen Valley, which is mostly a nature reserve with only a few scattered huts and a narrow service road.

$ Hotel Stechelberg, at road's end, is surrounded by waterfalls and vertical rock, with a garden terrace, a good restaurant, and 16 quiet rooms—half in a functional old building, half in a concrete, no-character new building (free parking, bus stops right in front, hotel closed in Dec, restaurant closed Mon-Tue off-season, tel. 033-855-2921, http://hotelstechelberg.tcnet.ch, hotel@stechelberg.ch, Marianne and Otto).

¢ The **Alpenhof** fills a former "Nature Friends' Hut" with 44 cheap beds. Creaking like a wooden chalet built in 1926 should, and surrounded by a broad lawn, it provides a good, inexpensive base for drivers and families (each group gets a private room, breakfast extra, open nearly year-round, kitchen, no Wi-Fi, free parking, tel. 033-855-1202, www.alpenhof-stechelberg.ch, alpenhof@stechelberg.ch, Diane and Marc from England). From Hotel Stechelberg, head up the paved path, go right at the fork, and cross the river; it's on your left.

Sleeping in Obersteinberg

Here's a wild idea: ¢ **Mountain Hotel Obersteinberg** is a mile-high, working alpine farm with cheese, cows, a mule shuttling up food once a day, and an American (Vickie) who fell in love with a mountain man. It's a 2.5-hour hike from either Stechelberg or Gimmelwald. They rent 12 primitive rooms and 30 loft beds. There's no shower, no hot water, and no electricity. Bring a battery-powered lamp; otherwise, candles light up the night. Ask for a hot-water bottle to warm your bed; first come, first served (sheets extra, breakfast and dinner included, discount if you go without meals; closed Oct-May, tel. 033-855-2033, more info under "Mountain Hotels" at www.stechelberg.ch). The place is filled with locals and Germans on weekends, but it's all yours on weekdays. Why not hike here from Gimmelwald and leave the Alps a day later?

ZERMATT & THE MATTERHORN

There's just something about the Matterhorn, the most recognizable mountain on the planet. Anyone who says, "You've seen one mountain, you've seen them all" hasn't laid eyes on this pointy, craggy peak. Just seeing the Matterhorn is a great experience, but hiking with that iconic pinnacle as a backdrop is even better.

Oh, and there's a town, too. Zermatt, a little burg of about 5,800 people, might well be the most touristy resort in Switzerland. While the village has pockets of traditional charm, virtually everyone you meet in Zermatt earns a living one way or another from those who flock here for a peek at the peak. Aside from the stone quarries you'll pass on the way into town, tourism is Zermatt's only industry.

With the first ascent of the Matterhorn in 1865 and the arrival of trains, Zermatt found itself on the Grand Tour of Europe. Over time its residents learned it was easier to milk the tourists than the goats, and mountain tourism became the focus. Today the town is a collection of over a hundred modern chalet-style hotels with a well-organized and groomed infrastructure for summer and winter sports with no gas engines—only electric cars slalom between the pedestrians. Sure, there are fabulously wealthy visitors, but locals like to say that the "traffic-free" nature of the town is a great equalizer. With only pedestrians and the golf-cart-style shuttles on the lanes, "you have no idea who owns a Ferrari."

Many visitors find Zermatt too touristy and overrated, especially considering its inconvenient location (at the dead-end of a long valley in the southwest corner of the country). And if you make the long trek and find only cloudy weather, you may end up shopping for a T-shirt that reads, "I went all the way to Zermatt and didn't even see the lousy Matterhorn." But in sunny weather, riding the high-mountain lifts, poking through lost-in-time farm hamlets, and ambling along on scenic hikes are even more enjoyable with that classic triangular summit nodding its white head in the background.

GETTING TO ZERMATT

Zermatt is barely two hours from Bern and Interlaken by train, thanks to the Lötschberg Base Tunnel. It's also easy to reach from Zürich or Lausanne (about 3 hours). Another popular way to reach Zermatt is from St. Moritz on the Glacier Express, an all-day ride on a historic narrow-gauge line that cuts across the country (see the Scenic Rail Journeys chapter). You can also do just half of this route by connecting Zermatt with Luzern or Lugano (changing in Andermatt).

PLANNING YOUR TIME

High summer into early fall is the best time to come to Zermatt. On a two-week trip in Switzerland, I'd suggest two nights and the better part of two days here—if the weather's good. Spring is a bad time to visit as most trails, lifts, and restaurants are closed.

Zermatt has earned its reputation for untrustworthy weather—the valley can get completely socked in at any time of year. While two good-weather days are enough to experience the highlights, add at least one buffer day, if you can, as insurance against rain. For the latest weather report, check the webcams and forecast at www.zermatt.ch. In clear weather, you'll want to spend your daylight hours up above town.

With One Day: If you have just one good day in Zermatt in high season (when all the lifts are running), buy the Peak2Peak ticket that covers the necessary lifts and do this: Catch the first train up to the high Gornergrat ridge. On the way down, do the gentle-but-gorgeous Riffelseeweg hike that connects the Rotenboden and Riffelberg train stops. From Riffelberg, take a gondola over and down to the stop called Furi, and, depending on your timing and interest, ride all the way up to the Matterhorn Glacier Paradise station at the Klein Matterhorn summit, then return via the Schwarzsee ridge (and perhaps hike part of the way back to Zermatt). To visualize this plan, see the "Zermatt Area" map, later.

With a Second Day: If it's clear, I'd head up to the Rothorn summit, or at least to the midpoint lift station at Blauherd for the walk to the restaurant at Fluhalp, and then do one of the hikes from the Sunnegga ridge.

Other Options: If the Rothorn excursion sounds more appealing than the Matterhorn Glacier Paradise, start with the two-hour Naturweg hike from Sunnegga to Riffelalp (better Mat-

ZERMATT

terhorn views than if done in reverse). Then take the train to Gornergrat and, on the way back down, get off at Rotenboden and hike to Riffelberg. From there, you can either keep walking or take the train back to town. If Mother Nature cooperates, you can do the Matterhorn Glacier Paradise and/or hikes from Schwarzsee on a second day.

Orientation to Zermatt

Zermatt (elevation 5,265 feet) lies at the end of the Nikolaital valley, in the shadow of the mighty Matterhorn (14,690 feet, "Cervin" in French, "Cervino" in Italian).

The train station is at the north end of the town's shopping zone, a few steps from the main drag, Bahnhofstrasse. As you stand in front of the station with the tracks at your back, the heart of the village is to your right. Lifts to thrilling Matterhorn viewpoints leave from near the train station: The cog railway up to Gornergrat leaves from across the street, the Sunnegga-Rothorn station for the funicular/gondola/cable car to Rothorn is a few blocks ahead along the river, and the gondola/cable car up to the Matterhorn Glacier Paradise (aside the Klein Matterhorn peak) is at the upper (southern) end of the village (about three-quarters of a mile away).

Zermatt bans cars within the town limits and brags that its streets are traffic-free. Well, not quite. Electric cars (resembling big golf carts) buzz around the streets like four-wheeled Vespas. Half of these cars are owned by hotels, which use them to shuttle guests and luggage to the train station; the other half operate as taxis.

In this small town, locals don't bother much with street names and house numbers. To find your hotel, use the map in this chapter or pick up a free map from the TI.

TOURIST INFORMATION

Zermatt's TI is right at the train station (daily 8:00-20:00, tel. 027-966-8100, www.zermatt.ch). The unstaffed lobby stays open later and has all the essentials (maps, brochures, etc.).

The TI sells lift passes/tickets and is well-versed in helping visitors weigh their options given current weather, time constraints, budgets, and hiking interests. They also offer several free resources: an extremely detailed village map, the *Adventure in the Mountains* booklet with lift schedules/prices and information on year-around activities, and a panoramic hiking map. The region's trail signs can be confusing; the hiking map, which outlines the distance and difficulty level of the most popular hikes, can help you avoid taking a longer or steeper route than you intended. More detailed maps are available for free on the TI's website.

ZERMATT

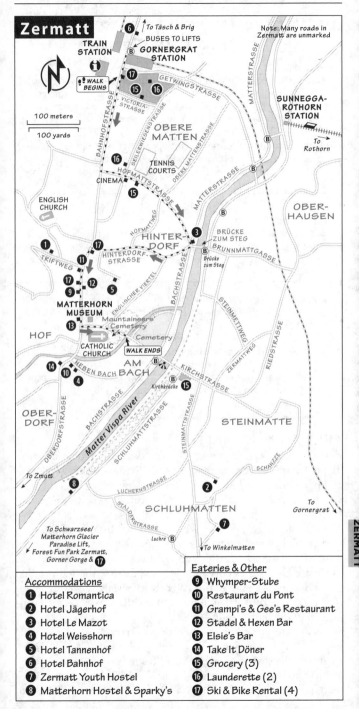

Zermatt

Note: Many roads in Zermatt are unmarked

100 meters
100 yards

To Täsch & Brig
TRAIN STATION
BUSES TO LIFTS
GORNERGRAT STATION
WALK BEGINS
GETWINGSTRASSE
OBERE MATTEN
VICTORIA-STRASSE
BAHNHOFSTRASSE
SEILERWIESENSTRASSE
SUNNEGGA-ROTHORN STATION
To Rothorn
MATTERSTRASSE
TENNIS COURTS
OBERE MATTENSTRASSE
HOFMATTSTRASSE
CINEMA
ENGLISH CHURCH
OBER-HAUSEN
HOFMATTWEG
HINTER DORF
BRÜCKE ZUM STEG
BRUNNMATTGASSE
Brücke zum Steg
TRIFTWEG
HINTERDORF-STRASSE
ENGLISCHER VIERTEL
BACHSTRASSE
STEINMETTWEG
RIEDSTRASSE
MATTERHORN MUSEUM
Mountaineers' Cemetery
Cemetery
WALK ENDS
HOF
CATHOLIC CHURCH
AM BACH
KIRCHSTRASSE
ZERMATTWEG
STEINMATTSTRASSE
STEINMATTE
NEBEN BACH
Kirchbrücke
OBERDORFSTRASSE
OBER-DORF
BACHSTRASSE
Matter Vispa River
SCHLUHMATTSTRASSE
SCHANZZE
To Zmutt
LUCHERNSTRASSE
STALDERSTRASSE
SCHLUHMATTEN
To Gornergrat
Luchre
To Winkelmatten
To Schwarzsee/
Matterhorn Glacier
Paradise Lift,
Forest Fun Park Zermatt,
Gorner Gorge &

ZERMATT

Accommodations
1 Hotel Romantica
2 Hotel Jägerhof
3 Hotel Le Mazot
4 Hotel Weisshorn
5 Hotel Tannenhof
6 Hotel Bahnhof
7 Zermatt Youth Hostel
8 Matterhorn Hostel & Sparky's

Eateries & Other
9 Whymper-Stube
10 Restaurant du Pont
11 Grampi's & Gee's Restaurant
12 Stadel & Hexen Bar
13 Elsie's Bar
14 Take It Döner
15 Grocery (3)
16 Launderette (2)
17 Ski & Bike Rental (4)

Zermatt at a Glance

In Zermatt

▲▲**Matterhorn Museum** Underground museum resembling archaeological dig covers history of Zermatt and its magic mountain. **Hours:** Daily 11:00-18:00 in summer, Oct-June open afternoons only, closed Nov-mid-Dec. See page 235.

▲**Town Wander** Orientation stroll, from the train station, through the attractive old Hinterdorf quarter, with antique chalets and traditional *mazots* (shacks on stone stilt), to the cemetery. See page 233.

Lifts and Trains

▲▲▲**Matterhorn Glacier Paradise Summit** Europe's highest cable-car station (12,739 feet), with jaw-dropping Alps view, year-round snow, and a "palace" carved into ice (but no hikes). See page 242.

▲▲▲**Sunnegga Viewpoint** Best mountain destination for budget travelers, offering the ultimate Matterhorn views (7,506 feet). See page 247.

▲▲**Gornergrat Top Station** Viewpoint (10,270 feet), reached by a cogwheel train, that hovers above the Gorner Glacier with fantastic views of the Matterhorn and Switzerland's tallest mountain—Monte Rosa (15,200 feet). See page 244.

ARRIVAL IN ZERMATT

Zermatt's small **train station** is located in the middle of town. The ticket office is beside the tracks (daily 7:00-19:00); a free WC and pay lockers are downstairs. The TI is immediately to the right as you leave the tracks, and lines of electric taxis wait right out front.

All the hotels I list are within walking distance of the train station, though the two hostels are far enough away that you might want to take a taxi or the bus (see individual listings for directions). There are also free airport-style luggage carts at the train station (5-CHF deposit)—useful if it's a fairly level walk to your hotel (or if your car is parked at Täsch, you can use them to wheel your baggage onto the shuttle train—see next).

Cars are not allowed in Zermatt. **Drivers** can park in the huge lot at Täsch, a few miles before Zermatt (16 CHF/day), then take the shuttle train into town (runs every 20 minutes until about 22:00, less frequent after that, 8.40 CHF one-way, www. matterhornterminal.ch). Täsch has many parking options, but

▲▲**Rothorn Summit** Cable-car station at 10,180 feet with sweeping views of the Matterhorn and its valley. See page 246.

▲**Schwarzsee Ridge** Hillside midpoint (8,474 feet) directly under the Matterhorn, with a lovely picnic spot and a jumping-off point for hikes. See page 243.

Walks and Hikes

▲▲▲**Riffelseeweg Hike** Easy, mostly downhill walk with nonstop scenery between two mountain stations. See page 245.

▲▲▲**Blauherd-Fluhalp Hike** Mostly level walk from the Blauherd lift station past a picturesque glacial lake (and great Matterhorn views). See page 246.

▲▲**Matterhorn Trail Hike** Deservedly popular trail from the Schwarzsee gondola station back to Zermatt. See page 243.

▲▲**Hikes from Sunnegga** Long, mostly gentle trail (Gourmetweg) back down to Zermatt, mixing hillside hamlets and lush forest, or a moderately strenuous walk (Naturweg) across to the Gornergrat's Riffelalp station. See page 247.

▲**Furi to Zermatt Hike** Steep hour-long hike past cute hamlets and down into town. See page 243.

the big modern lot at the station is most convenient. With 4,000 spots, it's rarely full (look for the big sign: *Matterhorn Terminal Täsch*). Park (you'll pay when you leave) and hop on the next shuttle train—it's very slick.

GETTING AROUND ZERMATT

Even though Zermatt is "traffic free," your feet aren't your only transportation option. Buses are useful for hauling luggage to more distant lodgings or for saving the 20-minute walk between the station and the Matterhorn Glacier Paradise lifts. Buses depart across from the train station to the Matterhorn Glacier Paradise lifts at the top of town and make several stops along the way, including at the Sunnegga-Rothorn lift (about 3/hour, last buses leave around 18:00 or 19:00). The green Bergbahnen line goes more directly (2.50 CHF); the red line takes a more roundabout route via the Winkelmatten neighborhood. Both routes are covered by same-day mountain-train/lift tickets, the local Peak Pass, and the Swiss Travel Pass (but not the Eurail Global pass),

ZERMATT

and charge extra for large luggage. Ask the TI for a timetable or check www.e-bus.ch.

You can also hire an **electric taxi** from in front of the train station (about 12 CHF for a short ride in the heart of town, extra charge for greater distances, luggage, and rides at night, tel. 027-967-3333).

HELPFUL HINTS

Festivals: Folk troupes from all over western Switzerland converge on Zermatt for the **Folklore Festival,** usually on the second weekend in August. Sunday afternoon features a parade through town followed by free performances.

Goat Parade: Every day in summer (July-mid-Aug, at about 9:00 and again at 16:30), a small flock of furry "blackneck" goats are herded through the center of town (down the length of Bahnhofstrasse) on the way to and from the pasture. They're unique to the surrounding Upper Valais region, with a black head and shoulders, a white rear end, and long horns. (Babies that don't fit the proper color scheme are immediately butchered, ensuring the herd evolves as expected.) Keep an eye out for this charming and unusual parade.

Laundry: Waschsalon Doli is nice and central (drop-off service only, Mon-Sat 8:30-12:00 & 14:00-19:00, closed Sun, tel. 027-967-5100). To find it from the station, take the first left past McDonald's, turn right at the tennis courts, and go down the steps at their sign. **Womy Express** is in the Viktoria Center mall across from the train station (drop-off service only, Mon-Fri 8:30-12:00 & 13:30-18:30, Sat 8:30-12:00, closed Sun, tel. 027-967-3242).

Cinema: The **Vernissage Cinema,** oddly located in the Backstage Hotel, plays a rotating schedule of historical Matterhorn-centric films and some first-run features in the evening during peak season (Hofmattstrasse 4, tel. 027-966-6970, www.backstagehotel.ch).

Ski and Mountain Bike Rental: For equipment rental in town, try **Matterhorn Sport** (branch near Sunnegga-Rothorn lift, another at Bahnhofstrasse 78, tel. 027-967-2956, www.matterhornsport.ch), **Bayard Sports & Fashion** (branches on Bahnhofplatz and at Bahnhofstrasse 35, tel. 027-966-4960, www.bayardzermatt.ch), and **Dorsaz-Sport** (near Matterhorn Express lift, tel. 027-966-3810, www.dorsaz-sport.ch).

ZERMATT

Sights in Zermatt

Consider the following options for when the weather is not cooperating with an alpine adventure. Besides the sights listed below, other bad-weather options include walking up and out of town until you hit the cloud cover (the small hamlet of Winkelmatten is a pleasant 20-minute stroll from the Catholic church), catching a movie, and/or taking a dip in one of the big hotel pools (nonguests can enjoy for a fee; get advice from TI).

▲Town Wander

Zermatt is charming enough, despite its single-mindedness about catching the tourist dollar. The streets may be lined with chalet after chalet, but all the dark wood and overflowing flower boxes lend this super-touristy town an authentic charm. Here's a simple walk to orient you:

Train Station Square (Bahnhofplatz): Zermatt entertains two million guests a year and, as there's only one way into town, they all arrive here. While skiing is the big draw in winter, this is a popular terminal in summer for the scenic Glacier Express—the eight-hour train ride connecting Zermatt and St. Moritz each day (see the Scenic Rail Journeys chapter). The first train arrived here in 1891 (and the first winter train in 1928). Across the street is the station for the cogwheel train to Gornergrat (at an altitude of more than 10,000 feet), which opened in 1899.

The town is committed to its car-free environment. Listen to the sounds of a traffic-free city. Locals who own cars have to park them at a garage at the south end of town. Electric shuttles, like golf carts, move people to and from hotels and serve as taxis. (The first Zermatt bus ran on gas...it lasted about one day after locals put sugar in the tank. City leaders got the message.)

Here at Bahnhofplatz, you'll find the TI and the big Co-op supermarket (the budget-friendly depot for most shopping needs).

Bahnhofstrasse and Hofmattstrasse: Stroll up Bahnhofstrasse, the town's main street, toward Hotel Pollux. You'll notice even bikes are forbidden—this street is only for people and the twice-daily parade of goats. Bahnhofstrasse is lined with shops, restaurants, and hotels. Zermatt strives to be a high-class mountain resort...but for active guests.

After 250 yards take the first left, just before Hotel Pollux, and stroll down Hofmattstrasse until you reach the little bridge over the river. This is a practical street with a sports arena (its tennis courts freeze over and become ice rinks for curling and hockey in the winter), indoor golf, the cinema, and the Migros supermarket.

Little Bridge and the Old Town: For centuries Brücke zum Steg has bridged the Matter Vispa River. Two hundred years ago this was a humble wooden crossing just strong enough to support a cow. The embankment containing the river was built after World War II to contain floods (once common with the spring and summer melts). This is the practical spine of Zermatt, with a shuttle bus running along the riverbank. Higher buildings are connected to this street by a clever system of tunnels and elevators (handy in the snowy winter).

Notice the many small hotels. Hotels in Zermatt are generally family owned and run. Local inheritance laws—which require that all relatives who own a stake in a plot of land agree to any sale— have prevented big chains from infiltrating the town.

While hotel owners may be local, hotel staffers are typically not Swiss. Zermatt may look quintessentially Swiss, but most of the workers who keep the hotels, restaurants, and lifts going are from other parts of Europe, particularly Portugal. In Täsch, the next village down the valley (with more affordable housing than Zermatt), the majority of residents are Portuguese. While some Swiss feel that the current policy of free movement between Switzerland and the rest of Europe should be curtailed, no one has figured out how to square that vision with the needs of the hospitality industry. Here, as elsewhere, immigrants get the job done.

Imagine standing on the old wooden bridge in 1800. Ahead of you is the Hinterdorf quarter—then the core of the Zermatt village. Narrow lanes are lined with traditional wooden buildings called *mazots,* built between the 16th and 18th centuries. Stroll slowly up Hinterdorfstrasse, taking a slight right turn at the fountain, which honors mountaineering legend Ulrich Inderbinen (for more on Inderbinen, see the Matterhorn Museum listing, next). Along the way, you'll notice several buildings labeled according to their former purpose. Before the tourism boom, you'd have seen houses built with hand-hewn larch trees. Foundations were made by stacking local quarried stone, set on stilts with "plate stones" to keep rodents out of storage huts (filled with tasty corn, cheese, and meat). Staircases were on the outside to save space on the heated inside. (You'll also see several *mazots* perched around Hotel Romantica, and on the walk up to—and around—the Winkelmatten area.) The valley's best and most scenically situated clusters of *mazots* are in the hamlets of Blatten and Zum See, just below the Furi gondola station, and in Zmutt below the Schwarzsee gondola station (see the "Zermatt Area" map, later).

Walk uphill until you reach busy Bahnhofstrasse again, turn

ZERMATT

left as the street narrows, and pass through Zermatt's nightlife district until you reach a square next to the big church.

Church Square: Notice the two grand 19th-century hotels. Monte Rosa Hotel was Zermatt's first (1838). The Grand Hotel Zermatterhof was built a few decades later. Locals thought early tourists would appreciate big, modern, city-type buildings like these. Only later did they realize people came here to escape the urban environment and enjoy chalet-type hotels, as is now the standard.

The plaque on Monte Rosa honors the Englishman Edward Whymper. He fell in love with the Matterhorn and, in 1865, set out from this hotel for the first ascent of that mountain. On the way down, four of Whymper's party of seven fell to their deaths. (You'll see their names listed on bronze markers along Bahnhofstrasse.) The news put Zermatt on the map and mountain lovers soon followed. Now, each year several thousand attempt to climb the iconic mountain. While most make it, about a dozen each year die trying.

The Matterhorn Museum fills the sunken building in the middle of the square next to Zermatt's beloved marmot fountain. Beyond the square is the city hall *(Gemeindehaus).* And just beyond that are three community information boards that illustrate how, behind the crowds of tourists, a real community lives and works here. Check out the boards—they list anything from report dates for military reserve training to upcoming ballot measures (the Swiss love participating in their democracy) to childcare services. While it's a little old fashioned, it's a far cry from the days when such news would be hollered from the steps of the city hall by the local herald.

At the corner of the church (across from the Matterhorn Museum), notice the standard yellow signpost, which you'll find at every trail intersection in the high country, telling the altitude (1,616 meters) and how long it takes to hike to nearby points.

Mountaineers' Cemetery: Finish this walk by turning right and wandering into the little cemetery just below the church. It's dedicated to great climbers and mountain guides, many of whom died on the mountain (and many of whom were English). It's worth a thoughtful wander. The lovingly tended graves (here and across the lane in the bigger cemetery) are adorned with flowers and lit by glowing votive lanterns at night. Look for "the tomb of the unknown climber." A few steps farther along is a bridge famous for Matterhorn selfies.

▲▲Matterhorn Museum

This fun and interesting museum is the town's best indoor activity, and worth at least an hour of your time, especially on a rainy day. Most of the museum is underground—the idea is that it's like an archaeological dig where you can unearth the history of Zermatt and its famous mountain. It brings you back to the 19th century, when Zermatt saw the advent of mountaineering and the Golden Age of tourism. Quite suddenly, what had been a tiny, backwater village became a major destination, known worldwide.

Cost and Hours: 10 CHF, covered by Swiss Travel Pass; daily 11:00-18:00 in summer, Oct-June open afternoons only, closed Nov-mid-Dec; audioguide-5 CHF (or download their free app), under glass dome at Kirchplatz 11, across from Catholic church, tel. 027-967-4100, www.zermatt.ch/museum.

Efficiency Tip for Glacier Express Travelers: In summer, when the early Glacier Express arrives in Zermatt at 16:10, consider going straight to the museum on arrival for an hour's visit before heading to your hotel (let your hotel know in advance as many have no evening reception). Leave your bags in the museum's free lockers.

Visiting the Museum: Pick up the free English flier, and consider paying for the excellent audioguide, which lets you hear Zermatt's history from two perspectives: that of native Zermatt alpinist Hannes Taugwalder or British mountaineer Edward Whymper. Then head downstairs.

The museum's main hall is filled with little *mazots* (those stone-roofed huts you've seen all around town). Each hut houses an exhibit. There are also reproductions of an old hotel and church from Zermatt's past. About half of the museum shows typical village furnishings, tools, and stuffed alpine fauna, and tells about the local prehistory and geology.

The rest of the museum focuses on Zermatt's mountaineering history. Reliefs of the Matterhorn (and the surrounding region) offer a helpful topographic overview. In the mountain guides' hut, press the buttons to see the different routes up the Matterhorn. Consider that even now, only about half the people who attempt this climb make it to the top. Find the picture of local hero Ulrich Inderbinen, who climbed the Matterhorn more than 370 times, the last when he was—no kidding—90 years old. (Inderbinen died in 2004 at age 104; a fountain in the Hinterdorf area of town honors him.)

Another hut displays artifacts found after deadly accidents, with a room dedicated to July 14, 1865—the day the Matterhorn was finally conquered by a team of seven climbers. (Four of them died on the descent, when the least-experienced among them fell, dragging three others to their deaths; you can see the snapped rope in a glass case.) Short movies play in the "hotel." Don't miss the display case (in the hall with the WCs) that holds a collection of Matterhorn memorabilia and products.

Forest Fun Park Zermatt

This high-ropes park, located right under the gondola line to Furi (about 10 minutes past the Matterhorn Express station), has zip lines and a good range of ropes courses at various difficulty levels. Since it's open in all weather, the park is a great way to enjoy active fun on a rainy day.

Cost and Hours: 35 CHF, 25-29 CHF for kids, daily 10:00-19:00, shorter hours or closed off-season, Zen Stechenstrasse 110, tel. 027-968-1010, www.zermatt-fun.com.

Gorner Gorge (Gornerschlucht)

This deep, narrow, and dramatic gorge is lined with a skinny wooden walkway over its river so hikers can enter at one end and walk about 15 minutes (past a waterfall and whirlpools) to the other. You can enter and leave at either end or just go in and out from the bottom. It's about 15 minutes beyond the top end of Zermatt and on the path down from the Furi gondola station. Consider this if hiking to or from Furi (well signed, right under the gondola). Wear sturdy shoes as the visit (allow 15-20 minutes) involves steep stairs and potentially slippery walkways.

Cost and Hours: 5 CHF, June-mid-Oct daily 9:15-17:45, closed off-season, tel. 027-967-2096, www.gornergorge.ch.

High-Mountain Activities in Zermatt

Think of the Zermatt region's many lifts and hikes in terms of the three high-mountain summit stations to which they're linked: **Matterhorn Glacier Paradise** (closest to the Matterhorn), **Gornergrat** (the historic train that goes to 10,000 feet), and **Rothorn** (farthest up the valley from the Matterhorn). While prices are steep, the community has invested hundreds of millions of dollars in their mountain lifts in recent years. They're absolutely state of the art, and experiencing them is unforgettable. Strategies for enjoying each of these are laid out below.

Weather Watch: Whichever excursions you opt for, pay close attention to the weather—the lifts aren't cheap, and none of them is worth it if the Matterhorn is completely socked in. If the weather's iffy, confirm that the entire route is open before you buy a summit ticket—upper segments can close if it's too windy (though the Gornergrat train and some Klein Matterhorn lifts usually keep running). That said, don't wait for perfectly clear skies to head into

The Lowdown on High-Altitude Hiking

Here are some tips for staying safe and getting the most out of your Swiss mountain adventure:

- A waterproof/windproof outer layer will protect you from the Alps' unpredictable weather, and hiking boots are a must for navigating the rocky terrain. No matter how warm it might be in the valley, take extra layers for cold weather at the top.
- June through September are the best months for hiking in the Alps, though at high altitudes snow can make hiking difficult any time of year.
- The weather can be unpredictable, but locals can give you a general idea of what to expect. You can find weather reports in English at www.meteoswiss.admin.ch. It's also smart to check live webcams such as the ones at www.zermatt.ch.
- Know the symptoms of altitude sickness: shortness of breath, headaches, fatigue, and—in serious cases—confusion and ataxia (not being able to walk straight). Having plenty of water is a must, and ibuprofen, acetaminophen, or aspirin can combat headaches.
- A network of huts throughout the Swiss Alps provides meals and a place for hikers to sleep (see www.sac-cas.ch). But watch out, as they can be pricey.
- Many trails cross through fields of cattle. Hikers are expected to close gates after passing through. It's best to keep your distance from cows, especially if calves are nearby. If they're in your way, try to pass without making any sudden movements or loud noises.

the hills—even in bright, sunny weather, the Matterhorn loves playing peek-a-boo behind the clouds. If it's at least sunny-ish, get up the mountainside.

Be Prepared: Even when it's balmy in the valley, take cold-weather gear if you're heading up the mountainside. It's cold up there (even at the lower elevations)—and can be windy to boot.

Passes and Tickets: It can be tricky figuring out the best ticketing option for your excursion. Consult the TI to determine whether you should buy a pass covering multiple lifts, or individual tickets. They expertly grapple with these questions every day on behalf of travelers.

A **Peak Pass** gives you unlimited access to all lifts in the area, bike transport, and use of the local bus (1 day-175 CHF, 2 days-195 CHF, 3- and 5-day nonconsecutive passes available; prices are about 40 percent cheaper in late spring and late fall; 5-CHF refundable card deposit, www.matterhornparadise.ch). You can

ZERMATT

purchase the pass online or in person at the Zermatt TI, the train station in Täsch, or the base stations for all three lifts/trains.

Another pass option is the **Peak2Peak** ticket: a one-day pass covering the trains/lifts for the Matterhorn Glacier Paradise and the Gornergrat, as well as the Riffelberg Express gondola that connects them (172 CHF, half-price with Swiss Travel Pass; available July-mid-Aug and Dec-mid-April).

Even with the freedom and ease of a pass, it pays to consider **individual tickets** (lift prices are listed later). Keep in mind that Swiss Travel Pass holders pay half-price on full-fare individual tickets, but get only a 25 percent discount on the Peak Pass. All three mountain excursions offer ticket-buyers some kind of discount in the later afternoon (though the Swiss Travel Pass discount beats these).

Connecting the Mountainsides: I've described the three main excursions as separate experiences, but they can easily be combined to get the most out of a sunny day. The Gornergrat railway connects to the Klein Matterhorn hillside/Matterhorn Express lifts via the **Riffelberg Express** gondola, running between Riffelberg and Furi. It operates only at the height of summer (24 CHF, half-price with Swiss Travel Pass; July-mid-Aug 8:30-16:30, last descent at 16:45). If you're riding the Riffelberg Express to connect the Matterhorn Glacier Paradise and the Gornergrat on the same day (and don't have a Peak Pass), you may save money with the Peak2Peak ticket (see earlier).

Hikers can connect the Gornergrat hillside with Sunnegga, on the slopes of the Rothorn, via the moderately strenuous two-hour Naturweg hike (described later, under "Hikes from Sunnegga").

MATTERHORN GLACIER PARADISE

An excursion to what's branded as Matterhorn Glacier Paradise (the summit station for the Klein—"Little"—Matterhorn) has three main highlights: the summit (with views across the top of the Alps and a few fun indoor/outdoor activities), the halfway point at Schwarzsee (a nice spot to bask in Matterhorn views), and hikes down the mountainside (including my favorite, the Matterhorn Trail, from Schwarzsee). Note that you won't find any hiking paths from the very top of the Klein Matterhorn, since it's covered with snow year-round.

If you've visited the Berner Oberland's Schilthorn and/or Jungfraujoch (or France's Aiguille du Midi) in clear weather, the expensive trip up to this summit might not be worth it. But you should still consider the ride up to the Schwarzsee midpoint, with its lovely views and great hikes.

Lift Stages: Lifts go about six times per hour and the various segments take six to eight minutes each. The upward trip starts

ZERMATT

Zermatt Area

Klein Matterhorn 12,739'

MATTERHORN GLACIER PARADISE

Monte Rosa 15,200'

Gorner Glacier

Theo

Findel Glacier

Gornergrat 10,270'

Riffelsee

ROTENBODEN

Rothorn 10,180'

FLUHALP

Ober-rothorn

Stellisee

RIFFELBERG

GREAT HIKE

Grünsee

BERGHAUS GRÜNSEE

Riffelberg Express

Naturweg

RIFFELALP

BLAUHERD 8,435'

Leisee

FINDELN

FURI

FINDEL-BACH

ZUM SEE

SUNNEGGA 7,506'

Gourmetweg

WINKEL-MATTEN

BLATTEN

FOREST FUN PA

TIEFMATTEN

GORNER GORGE

RIED

To Täsch, Visp & Brig

ZERMATT 5,265'

To Trift

with a gondola ride over glacier-carved foothills to **Furi.** Depending on the time of year, you may be able to transfer at Furi for the cable car to **Trockener Steg**—if the weather's great, take this cable car, as it gets you to the summit faster (you can return via Schwarzsee). Otherwise, stay on the gondola and ride it to the scenic ridge at **Schwarzsee.** From Schwarzsee, a second gondola dips down to the Furgg intermediary station, then soars up to Trockener Steg. From Trockener Steg, a cable car takes you to the summit, with great views on the left side over glaciers and across to the Gornergrat train station.

Cost: A peak-season (July-Aug) round-trip ticket between Zermatt and the Matterhorn Glacier Paradise summit costs 110 CHF; Zermatt to Schwarzsee is 55 CHF round-trip (35 CHF one-way). All tickets are about 10 percent less in spring and fall, and half-price with the Swiss Travel Pass. An afternoon discount for the summit (beginning at 13:30) is available from mid-May through mid-Oct. Thrill seekers ask about the extra "crystal ride" cabins with a transparent floor, only available on the last leg of the journey.

Hours: The Klein Matterhorn lifts are open daily year-round. In summer (May-mid-Oct) they generally start running at 8:00,

ZERMATT

Note:
This bird's eye view
looks south

Not to Scale

with the last ride up between 16:00 and 16:30, and the last ride down at 16:15-16:30 (from the summit) and 17:35-18:00 (from Furi). Note that the two stretches of gondola (from Furi to Schwarzsee, and from Schwarzsee to Trockener Steg) only run late June to mid-Oct, and the cable car between Furi and Trockener Steg runs all day only in spring (May-mid-June) and late summer (mid-Aug-mid-Oct); at the height of summer it runs only in the early morning. The Riffelberg Express gondola—a spur line connecting Furi up to Riffelberg, on the Gornergrat hillside—runs only in midsummer (see "Connecting the Mountainsides," earlier).

Information: For detailed schedule and price info, go to www.matterhornparadise.ch.

Getting There: The Matterhorn Express base station for the gondola to Furi (and Schwarzsee) is about a mile upriver from the Zermatt train station: Walk up Bahnhofstrasse to the Catholic church, cross the bridge, and follow the river or catch a bus (see "Getting Around Zermatt," earlier).

Trip Tips: It's always frigid at the summit and often windy—take cold-weather gear no matter how pleasant it might be in the valley. Since the area around the summit stays snow-covered all year long, you can even get in some summer skiing, but rent your

ZERMATT

gear in town—there are no rentals up top. Consider packing a lunch, as the summit's restaurant is expensive (picnicking is allowed on the summit's observation deck). And save money by using the free WCs at the Schwarzsee or Trockener Steg stations rather than the pay WCs at the summit.

▲▲▲Matterhorn Glacier Paradise Summit (12,739 feet)

To really get your high-altitude high, zip up to the highest cable-car station in Europe, the Matterhorn Glacier Paradise, on the side of the Klein Matterhorn. Be warned: Some visitors are disappointed by the view of the "real" Matterhorn from the summit, because it's not the classic postcard profile. (For views of the Matterhorn you imagined, visit the intermediate Schwarzsee stop.)

The best summit feature is the **observation deck** (or "Panorama Platform") with its stunning views (access by elevator, then 42 steps). On a clear day, you can see Italy and France (including Mont Blanc, Europe's highest peak), as well as the Berner Oberland's Jungfrau and Mönch peaks (which you'll be viewing from the "back").

Inside is a tunnel (which leads to other attractions) that's cut out of granite, similar to the surface climbers hang on to when they climb. Go ahead and grip it.

Find the low-profile entrance of the **Glacier Palace,** marked *Gletschergrotte* (free with Peak Pass or full-price lift ticket, 8 CHF with discounted Swiss Travel Pass lift ticket, July-mid-Aug daily 8:15-16:00, rest of year 9:30-15:45). This place brags that it's the "highest glacial grotto in the world"—a claim that must make other high-altitude glacial grottos seethe with envy. The "palace" is basically a big hole dug into the glacier, allowing you to walk deep inside. As you wander, you'll see ice sculptures and some lackluster exhibits about glaciers, local wines, and "glacier fleas" (a.k.a. "springtails," little bugs that live up here).

Outside, you can trot across the snow, and young kids can take a turn on a very tame snow-tubing slope (free). Near the cable car's docking point is a darkened hall showing a range of exciting short films about high adventure in the local mountains.

Picnickers can take advantage of the observation deck; otherwise, your food options are limited to the **$$$ restaurant** inside.

ZERMATT

▲Schwarzsee Ridge (8,474 feet)

Roughly halfway to the Klein Matterhorn summit is the gondola station of **Schwarzsee** (named for the alpine lake nearby). When the gondola's running, you can detour here on your way back down the mountain—or come from Zermatt without going on to the summit. Though much lower in elevation, this area is the closest you can get to the Matterhorn by lift. There's a lovely picnic spot near the station, making this a great place to pause on your way up or down the mountain. It's also the starting point for one of the best hikes in the area, including the Matterhorn Trail. Shorter walks back to town from the gondola station at Furi are also worthwhile.

▲▲Matterhorn Trail Hike (2-3 hours)

This moderately strenuous hike (#29 on local signs and maps) goes from Schwarzsee via Stafel to either Furi (2 hours), where you can ride the gondola back into town, or all the way to Zermatt (3 hours total), either via Zmutt or Furi. (From Schwarzsee, avoid the trail that leads directly down to Furi—it's much steeper than it is fun.)

From the Schwarzsee station, head down to the lake, then follow *Matterhorn Trail* signs to Stafelalp (the name of the hillside and the restaurant). A little farther down the path, ignore the red signs pointing to Stafelalp—red signs are for skiers—and stay on the main road. At the first major fork, about 30 minutes into your hike, a wooden sign off to the right points to the shortest path to Restaurant Stafelalp (20 minutes from here, near the mini village of Stafel), which takes you through a fascinating pocket of mossy hillocks, ponds, and bubbling streams.

From the restaurant, follow signs to Furi and Zmutt. After about 30 minutes you'll need to make a choice: Head downhill to cross over the Grande Dixence dam and on to the cute hamlet of Zmutt (25 minutes), or stay on the path to the gondola at Furi (which becomes hike #29a after the fork; about 40 mostly level minutes). I recommend taking the Zmutt fork, as it is a joy—an almost tourist-free time warp (with a restaurant or two as well as a fine cluster of traditional *mazot* buildings); from there, it's about an hour down to Zermatt.

▲Furi to Zermatt Hike (1 hour)

If returning to Zermatt via Furi, you can either take the gondola from Furi or hike a pleasant hour, past the adorable hamlets of Zum See and Blatten (and its restaurant) and the Gorner Gorge (see listing under "Sights in Zermatt," earlier). The trail is steep, stony, and stepped at times.

ZERMATT

GORNERGRAT

The Gornergrat is my pick if you can fit in only one high-mountain excursion. Located between the Klein Matterhorn and the Ro-

thorn, it's not inherently better than the neighboring peaks, but it's a best-of-all-worlds experience.

This cogwheel-train excursion (which has been wowing visitors since 1899) has two main highlights (aside from the train ride itself): the sweeping views from the top station, and the Riffelseeweg hike between the Rotenboden and Riffelberg stops.

Train Stations: A cogwheel train takes you from Zermatt steeply up to the Gornergrat summit (10,270 feet) in about 35 minutes, with stops at Findelbach, Riffelalp, Riffelberg, and Rotenboden. On the way up, sit on the right side for good Matterhorn vistas.

Cost: Peak-season (July-Aug) trips up to the Gornergrat station cost 57 CHF each way (49 CHF in May-June and Sept-Oct; no round-trip discount, half-price with Swiss Travel Pass). If going up in the late afternoon, get a discounted round-trip "Good Afternoon Ticket" (late April-Oct only, half-price with Swiss Travel Pass). If combining a Gornergrat trip and a Matterhorn Glacier Paradise visit on the same day via the Riffelberg Express, consider the Peak2Peak ticket (described earlier, under "Passes and Tickets").

Hours: Trains run daily year-round, departing 2-3/hour from early June to mid-Oct, with the first ascent at about 7:00 and the last descent at 20:00; fewer trains and last descent around 19:00 in off-season. The Riffelberg Express gondola runs only in midsummer; see "Connecting the Mountainsides," earlier.

Information: Tel. 0848-642-442, www.gornergratbahn.ch.

Getting There: The Gornergrat train station is right across the street from Zermatt's train station.

▲▲Gornergrat Top Station (10,270 feet)

From the train platform, walk to the main building, where an elevator brings you to the observation platform. You'll be presented with a sweeping panorama, including great views of the Matterhorn (though it's not *quite* the perfect profile that you see from the Rothorn) and lots of shopping opportunities. You're also up close to the *other* big mountain in the neighborhood, Monte Rosa, the highest point in Switzerland (15,200 feet). And from here you have the best possible look at the Gorner glacier, a thousand-foot sheer drop below the platform.

There's also a chapel and a hotel, with a **$$$$ restaurant** and a **$$$ self-serve buffet.**

▲▲▲Riffelseeweg Hike (1.5 hours)

Perhaps my favorite hike in the Zermatt region is the easy Riffelseeweg path (hike #21 on local signs and maps), which usually opens in late June. Take the train from the Gornergrat summit back down to the Rotenboden station. From there, follow the official Riffelseeweg trail (not the Swiss Topwalk labeled *#23* toward Riffelalp—don't confuse your Riffels!). Just down the hillside from the Rotenboden station, you can also enjoy the pretty lake called Riffelsee—and, if you're lucky, catch the Matterhorn's reflection on its surface. Eventually you'll come to a fork with unclear signage. Take the downhill trail to the left that gets you closer to the Matterhorn—the other path cheats you out of the nicest stretch of this walk.

The trail leads over some gorgeous topography, ending at the Riffelberg station. You can continue by train back into Zermatt, or disembark at any point to hike down—or cross over to Sunnegga, on the Rothorn side, via the Naturweg hike (described later). Or you can head over to the Matterhorn Glacier Paradise station via the Riffelberg Express gondola, which whisks you efficiently over and down to the gondola station at Furi (described earlier, under "Connecting the Mountainsides").

ROTHORN

Of the main mountain options in the area, the Rothorn (ROTE-horn) hillside offers *the* classic Matterhorn view. It's also less crowded than the Gorner-grat, has many good hiking options, and its first stage, at Sunnegga, offers the cheapest ride into the mountains—and arguably the single best Matterhorn vantage point anywhere.

The excursion has four main highlights: the view from the Rothorn summit, the hike from Blauherd to Fluhalp and back, the view from Sunnegga, and a variety of hikes from Sunnegga. The view from the summit is fantastic, but it's not that much better than what you see from Blauherd—if you don't have a Peak Pass, you might want to skip the summit and save your time and money for the lower stations.

Lift Stages: The lift system up to Rothorn has three parts: a frequent funicular (3-6/hour, 8 minutes) up to **Sunnegga,** a five-minute gondola ride to **Blauherd,** and, finally, a cable car (at least 3/hour) to **Rothorn.**

Cost: Peak-season (July-Aug) ticket between Zermatt and the Rothorn costs 74 CHF round-trip (49 CHF one-way); Zermatt to Blauherd is 53 CHF round-trip (33 CHF one-way), and Zermatt to Sunnegga is 27 CHF round-trip (18 CHF one-way). All full-fare tickets are about 10 percent less in spring and fall, and half-price with the Swiss Travel Pass. A round-trip ticket to the Rothorn summit is discounted after 14:00 (July-Sept only, no Swiss Travel Pass discount).

Tip: If you intend to tackle the Naturweg hike but don't have a Peak Pass, you'll save money by getting the **Naturweg combo-ticket** in advance to cover your one-way rides between Zermatt and Sunnegga, and between Riffelalp and Zermatt (35 CHF; half-price with Swiss Travel Pass).

Hours: Daily lifts to the summit operate seasonally: The lower-elevation Sunnegga funicular operates June-mid-Oct; the middle lift (Sunnegga-Blauherd) runs July-mid-Oct, and the top lift (Blauherd-Rothorn) goes from July until late Sept. From July to mid-Sept, the lifts start running at 8:00, with the last ride to the summit from Blauherd at 16:40, and the last ride down between 16:50 (from Rothorn) and 18:00 (from Sunnegga). Lifts operate on shorter schedules outside those months. Everything is open again for skiers in winter but closes entirely in the shoulder season.

Information: For detailed schedules and pricing, go to www.matterhornparadise.ch.

Getting There: The base station for the Sunnegga-Rothorn funicular is across the river from the Zermatt train station, just downstream from the Gornergrat train tracks.

▲▲Rothorn Summit (10,180 feet)

Atop the Rothorn, you have your choice of taking panoramic photos of the entire Matterhorn massif, watching paragliders step into thin air, eating at a fancy **$$$$ pizzeria,** and/or picnicking on the rocks. Far below you'll see the Grünsee (lake with restaurant, more easily hikeable from Sunnegga—you'll need strong knees to descend to the lake from here) and beyond it the Riffelalp station on the Gornergrat train line.

▲▲▲Blauherd-Fluhalp Hike (1.5 hours)

Perhaps the best hike on this mountainside is the easy, mostly level walk from the Blauherd station (8,435 feet) to the restaurant at Fluhalp, then back again (1.5 hours total). The start of the hike isn't well-signed: From behind the Blauherd station, walk up the gravel road in back of the "Blue Lounge" building. Continue for a few more yards toward the ski lift labeled *Hublot Express* to find a narrow hiking path on the right—look for the rock next to the path that's painted with an inconspicuous red-and-white trail marker. (You can also simply follow the road that curves to the right behind the Blue Lounge, but I prefer the smaller hiking path that parallels it.)

About 15 minutes into the hike, you hit its best part: the lake called Stellisee. It's pretty in its own right, but on calm days it becomes a reflecting pool for the Matterhorn—walk around to the far end to take in the view. If you're short on time, you can turn around here (which cuts the total hike time in half). Or push on to Fluhalp—the path climbs gently but steadily from here.

Note: From Blauherd, the 40-minute, 1,000-foot descent along the Murmelweg ("Marmot Path") to Sunnegga is a disappointment—just steep enough so you can't enjoy the view, and with no guarantee you'll see the elusive rodents.

▲▲▲Sunnegga Viewpoint (7,506 feet)

This stop, just uphill from Zermatt, at the end of the in-mountain funicular, is the cheapest of all the lifts from Zermatt, but it's quite possibly the best spot anywhere to enjoy the classic Matterhorn view. (It's also the starting point for several great hikes, described next.)

From the Sunnegga lift station, you can go through the tunnel (following the "Wolli" sheep signs) to take a free mini-lift down to a lakeside picnic-and-play area with nice views. Or you can eat at the self-service **$$$ buffet.**

▲▲Hikes from Sunnegga

Gourmetweg Hike (Sunnegga-Zermatt, 2.5 hours): This popular hike is mostly gentle, taking you through deserted villages, among larch forests, and past several restaurants. If you follow the official #6 path via the hamlet of Ried, it takes about 2.5 hours. You can cut the walk shorter by following signs off the route to steeper paths back to Zermatt.

The first part, leading through several sleepy hamlets, has fantastic Matterhorn views but is confusingly signed. Near the start of the hike, a fork points left (signed *Paradies*), but either path will take you to the same spot farther down the Gourmetweg trail. A little farther along (with the village of Findeln below you), a sign shows the Gourmetweg going downhill on a low road and also on a higher path—take the low road.

Not long after Findeln, with the ravine on your left, there are two spots where you can cut the walk short and hike steeply down into town via the Winkelmatten neighborhood (about 50 minutes

ZERMATT

to reach central Zermatt). If you continue on the Gourmetweg toward Ried, be warned that the trail turns into a relatively tedious forest walk, albeit over soft, fragrant pine needles. You have one last chance at a more direct route (via Tiefmatten) into town but after that, resist the urge to follow downhill paths off the main trail—some of these seeming shortcuts are knee killers, and ultimately won't save time.

Naturweg Hike (Sunnegga-Riffelalp, 2 hours): Level overall, but with enough up and down to get your heart pumping, the #19 Naturweg trail connects Sunnegga with Riffelalp. From the cute lake called Leisee, just under the Sunnegga station, go crosswise via the unremarkable Moosjisee, then up-up-up toward Grünsee. The path doesn't lead to the lake itself (though it's just a short detour off the trail), but rather to the pleasant Berghaus Grünsee restaurant and mountain refuge—perfectly placed for a well-earned break. From the refuge you're rewarded with an extra-scenic final stretch through forests and on to Riffelalp.

From Riffelalp you can either take the Gornergrat train back to town (25 CHF, half-price with a Swiss Travel Pass—or use the Naturweg combo-ticket described earlier, under "Cost"), or follow one of two good, relatively easy trails all the way into Zermatt (1.5 hours via the Arvenweg, hike #14, or 2 hours via the poorly signed Riffelalpweg, hike #20).

OTHER MOUNTAIN ACTIVITIES
Paragliding
Tandem paragliding down the mountainside is an expensive but unforgettable experience. You pick the altitude of your takeoff point and land back in Zermatt (about 170 CHF from Blauherd or Riffelberg, 220 CHF from Gornergrat or Rothorn; contact Air Taxi Paragliding, tel. 027-967-6744, http://airtaxi-zermatt.ch; or FlyZermatt, tel. 027-967-2100, www.flyzermatt.com).

Mountain Biking
The hills above Zermatt are laced with great mountain-bike paths, ranging from easy to difficult. Bikers can buy day passes or single-ride tickets for riding lifts and transporting bikes. For more information on trails and passes, or to connect with local guides, visit the TI and pick up the helpful bike map. Detailed info on individualized bike tours is available for free on the TI's website (www.zermatt.ch/en/bike).

Summer Skiing
Zermatt's high elevation and variety of runs—and, in winter, the chance to actually ski or snowboard from Switzerland to Italy—make this a popular skiing destination. Summer skiing is an option at Matterhorn Glacier Paradise (first lift starts at about 8:00,

last lift stops around 14:00—after that the snow's too slushy, late April-mid-Oct, limited area in midsummer). A one-day summer lift ticket will run you about 110 CHF; for specifics, see www.matterhornparadise.ch.

For equipment rental in town, see "Helpful Hints," earlier. For more tips, see the Switzerland in Winter chapter.

Sleeping in Zermatt

Little Zermatt has more than a hundred hotels. This is a resort town, plain and simple, where building after building is for guests (many who rent by the week). You'll pay less at most places early and late in the season (June and Oct), and more during ski season (Dec-late March/early April). Many hotels close in the off-season (early spring and late fall) and those listed below don't have a night reception. Let them know if you plan to arrive after 19:00.

$$ Hotel Romantica, a flower-dappled, four-story chalet located one scenic (and steep) block up from the main street, offers 13 cozy alpine rooms with balconies. It's lovingly run and decorated by the Cremonini family, who make you feel at home and provide all the modern conveniences. They also rent two tiny alpine cottages (family room, some minimum-stay requirements, elevator, closed May and Nov, Chrum 21, tel. 027-966-2650, www.romantica-zermatt.ch, info@romantica-zermatt.ch).

$$ Hotel Jägerhof has 48 homey rooms and 7 apartments with lots of rustic charm. It's a little farther from the center and across the river toward the Matterhorn Express lift, but they'll pick you up at the train station for no extra fee (use the designated phone at the station). The rustic lounge and restaurant—complete with mounted deer heads—are plenty cozy, and the rooms with balconies are worth the extra francs (family rooms, elevator, fitness room, bike rental, open year-round, Steinmattstrasse 85, tel. 027-966-3800, www.jaegerhofzermatt.ch, jaegerhof@zermatt.ch, Perren family). From the train station, walk to the Catholic church and take a left. Cross the river and walk up Kirchstrasse one more block, then hang a right onto Steinmattstrasse. Look for the small wooden *Hotel Jägerhof* sign on your left.

$$ Hotel Le Mazot has nine cozy-if-basic rooms with spacious bathrooms, in a quiet location next to the river. The four rooms with stunning Matterhorn-view balconies make this a good value (some shared baths, closed Nov and mid-April-mid-June, Hofmattstrasse 23, tel. 027-966-0609, www.bblemazot.com, bblemazot@mail.ch).

$$ Hotel Weisshorn offers 16 dated rooms over a restaurant, right in the heart of town. The rooms are nothing special and the common areas are threadbare, but it might do if everything else is

ZERMATT

full (some shared baths, closed May, Am Bach 6, tel. 027-967-1112, www.holidaynet.ch/weisshorn, welcome@weisshorn-zermatt.ch).

$ Hotel Tannenhof, run by hardworking Christiane, hides a few steps off the main drag behind a fancy hotel that steals the Matterhorn views. Its 19 rooms are small and don't have much character, but you can't beat the location (thin walls, closed Oct, Englischer Viertel 3, tel. 027-967-3188, www.rhone.ch/tannenhof, hotel-tannenhof@rhone.ch).

¢-$ Hotel Bahnhof is a respectable budget hotel and hostel in a remodeled building with four floors (but no elevator) across the street from the train station. There are 17 tidy, alpine-style rooms (those without bath have Matterhorn-view balconies) and three dorm rooms. The basement features a relaxing lounge, a dining room, and a large guests' kitchen. It's well-run, but management is offsite at night—so if the younger crowd comes back late after partying, you're on your own (family rooms, no breakfast, nice showers, closed May and Oct-Nov, Bahnhofplatz 54, tel. 027-967-2406, www.hotelbahnhofzermatt.com, welcome@hotelbahnhofzermatt.com, Lauber family).

¢-$ Zermatt Youth Hostel looks over town from a perch high above the river and offers views of the Matterhorn. The super-modern hostel offers dorm beds and private rooms, most with bathrooms—travelers of all ages will feel comfortable here (no curfew, reception open 7:00-10:00 & 16:00-22:00, Staldenweg 5, tel. 027-967-2320, www.youthhostel.ch/zermatt, zermatt@youthhostel.ch). From the station, walk 15 minutes uphill toward the end of town or take the red-line bus marked *Winkelmatten* to the Luchre stop; the hostel is 50 yards uphill from there (follow signs with international hostel symbol).

¢ Matterhorn Hostel has 56 rock-bottom beds—crammed into 10 dorm rooms—over Sparky's restaurant, just a 15-minute walk from the train station. It's hard to justify staying here if you can get a bed at the fine official youth hostel or Hotel Bahnhof (simple breakfast extra, sheets and towels extra, reception open 7:30-11:00 & 16:00-22:00, Schluhmattstrasse 32, tel. 027-968-1919, www.matterhornhostel.com, info@matterhornhostel.com). Take the green- or red-line bus to the Kirchbrücke stop, then follow Schluhmattstrasse upstream for a few minutes.

Eating in Zermatt

Zermatt's restaurants are very expensive. But affordable takeout-type places aren't too hard to find, and you can easily assemble a picnic at one of the town's bakeries or supermarkets.

$$$ Whymper-Stube, named for the first brave soul to conquer the Matterhorn, specializes in raclette and meat-and-cheese fondue. This cozy space with a friendly staff attracts some tourists, but local regulars warm six barstools in the corner. On evenings in peak season, reservations are smart (kitchen open daily 11:00-21:00 except no lunch service in winter, closed May and mid-Oct–mid-Nov, Bahnhofstrasse 80, across from the huge Zermatthof hotel, tel. 027-967-2296, www.whymper-stube.ch).

$$ Restaurant du Pont, the oldest restaurant in town, draws plenty of tourists photographing each other while eating fondue. Its low ceilings and folk sayings on the wall add to the ambience, but it feels a bit sloppy compared to other restaurants specializing in Swiss cuisine (kitchen open daily 9:00-21:30, on Bahnhofstrasse at end of square with big Catholic church, tel. 027-967-4343, Evelin Kalbematten).

$$$ Sparky's, in the same building as the Matterhorn Hostel, isn't very Swiss—Sparky himself is a friendly Brit who's lived in Zermatt for decades—but has a popular bar and serves Middle Eastern and Southeast Asian cuisine (kitchen open Tue-Sun 16:00-22:00, closed Mon and mid-Sept–mid-Nov, Schluhmattstrasse 32, tel. 027-968-1918).

$$$ Grampi's, located just above Gee's Restaurant & Bar on the main drag, is a bustling restaurant serving Italian specialties to locals and tourists. Try a pizza baked in their wood-fired oven or a healthy salad (daily 18:00-24:00, Bahnhofstrasse 70, tel. 027-967-7775).

$$$ Stadel can easily be overlooked, but this small restaurant with indoor/outdoor seating dishes up homemade Swiss specialties with a smile and at a fair price (daily 12:00-22:00, closed Nov, Bahnhofstrasse 45, tel. 027-967-3536).

Sandwiches and Kebabs: Smack in the middle of town you'll find several good bakeries that seem to have the budget eater in mind. A hearty sandwich, some yogurt, and juice is my fast-and-easy bakery lunch to go. Tucked away just uphill from the Catholic Church, **$ Take It Döner** sells kebabs (daily 11:00-21:00, Oberdorfstrasse 24, cash only).

Supermarkets: A large **Co-op** is in the little mall across from the train station, and **Migros** is across from the tennis courts on Hofmattstrasse. The small **Pam,** along the river at the corner of Kirchstrasse and Schluhmattstrasse, is convenient if you're staying at the upper end of town. All are open daily about 8:00-19:00.

After-Dinner Drinks: There are only a few parts of town dishing up after-dinner action. Along the main drag, **Gee's Bar & Restaurant** serves drinks and "street food" in a modern indoor/outdoor space with live music every night at 22:00. Across the street, the **Hexen Bar** caters to a crowd looking for something a bit more traditional. **Elsie's Bar,** located in a cozy building across from the Catholic church, oozes with character; the extensive list of wine and cocktails can be enjoyed inside or out.

Zermatt Connections

Zermatt is at the end of the Nikolaital valley, which is reached on the narrow-gauge Matterhorn Gotthard Railway (MGB, www.mgbahn.ch). Swiss Rail info: www.sbb.ch.

By Train: All these trains from Zermatt transfer in Visp. Some have multiple transfers. Trains from Zermatt go to: **Bern** (1-2/hour, 2 hours), **Zürich** (1-2/hour, 3.5 hours), **Montreux** (1-3/hour, 2.5 hours), **Lausanne** (2/hour, 3 hours), **Interlaken Ost** (1-2/hour, 2.5 hours, 2 transfers), **Luzern** (1-2/hour, 3.5 hours, 2 transfers).

By Glacier Express to Eastern Switzerland: This scenic train departs Zermatt (at least once daily through most of the year, more in summer) and arcs scenically on high-altitude tracks over the middle of Switzerland to the east. All of these Glacier Express trains go through **Chur** (6 hours), then continue either to **Davos** or **St. Moritz** (8 hours total to either). For details, see the Scenic Rail Journeys chapter.

APPENZELL

Appenzell • Ebenalp • Liechtenstein

Welcome to cowbell country. In the moo-mellow and storybook-friendly Appenzell region, you'll find the warm, intimate side of the land of staggering, icy Alps. With just one percent of Switzerland's territory and one percent of its population, the little canton of Appenzell stubbornly celebrates its way of life. You'll see its symbol everywhere: a scary bear walking upright, yielding its sharp claws and teeth. And yet the people here are welcoming. You'll savor Appenzell's cozy, small-town atmosphere—and if there's time, you can stop by one of Europe's smallest nations, Liechtenstein.

Appenzell is one of Switzerland's most traditional regions... and the butt of jokes because of it. Entire villages meet to vote in town squares such as Appenzell town's Landsgemeindeplatz (an event featured on most postcard racks). Until 1990, the women of Appenzell couldn't vote on local issues. But in a break from convention, in 2000 Appenzell's schools were the first in Switzerland to make English—rather than distant French—the mandatory second language.

A gentle beauty blankets this region of green, rolling hills, watched over by the 8,200-foot peak of Mount Säntis (Appenzell's highest point). As you travel, you'll enjoy an ever-changing parade of finely carved chalets, colorful villages, and cows mooing, "Milk me." While farmers' daughters make hay, old ladies with scythes walk the steep roads, looking as if they just pushed the Grim Reaper down the hill. When locals are asked about Appenzeller cheese, they clench their fists as they answer, "It's the best." (It is, without any doubt, the smelliest.)

If you're here in late August or early September, there's a good

Appenzell Region

Note: Not all rail lines are shown

10 Kilometers
10 Miles

GERMANY — To Munich (A-96)

Romanshorn • Lindau
Lake Constance
Rorschach
Bregenz
To Winterthur & Zürich (A-1, E-60)
Gossau
St. Gallen   St. Marg.
Herisau   Teufen
Stein   Stoss   Altstätten   Dornbirn
Gais   Oberriet
Jakobsbad (LUGE)   Gonten-bad   APPENZELL   Ranksweil
Urnäsch   Appenzell Town
Helmberg   (BAREFOOT TRAIL)   Brülisau   AUSTRIA
To Rapperswil & Luzern   Ebenalp   Wasserauen   Feldkirch
See Ebenalp detail map
▲ Mt. Säntis   To Innsbruck via Arlbergpass (A-14)
To Zürich & Luzern   Buchs • Schaan   Vaduz
SWITZERLAND   Sevelen   LIECHTEN-STEIN
(A-3)

╍╍╍╍ Appenzeller Bahnen
- - - - Other Rail

Sargans   Baby Rhine   To Chur & Pontresina

SWITZ.

---

chance you'll get to watch (or at least have to slow down for) the ceremonial procession of flower-bedecked cows and whistling herders in formal folk costumes. The festive march down from the high pastures is a spontaneous move by the herding families, and when they finally do burst into town, locals young and old become children again, running joyously into the streets.

PLANNING YOUR TIME

On a two-week trip through Switzerland, save a day for the Appenzell region. This pastoral area has its subtle charms—but it can be anticlimactic after the rugged Berner Oberland or Matterhorn. In the Appenzell region, I prefer overnighting in Appenzell town, which is a more efficient base for getting around the region; however, those up for a mountaintop retreat and rustic accommodations should consider Ebenalp. If you have only a week or less in Switzerland, skip the Appenzell region and head instead for the high mountains.

GETTING AROUND THE APPENZELL REGION

This area is a breeze by **car**—you could see everything in this chapter in one (very busy) day. Notice that the attractions in Stein and Urnäsch and the Kronberg luge ride form a handy little loop to the west of Appenzell town. The lift up to Ebenalp is just to the south.

The regional narrow-gauge **trains** are run by a private operator (Appenzeller Bahnen—Eurail Global Pass and Swiss Travel Pass are valid). A very handy train generally runs twice an hour (except after 20:00, when it's hourly), taking about 50 minutes to connect almost all of the destinations I describe. Starting up at Wasserauen (at the base of Ebenalp lift), it runs through Appenzell town, stopping at Gontenbad (one end of the Barefoot Trail), Jakobsbad (luge ride and other end of the Barefoot Trail), and Urnäsch (folk museum), and then going north to Herisau (change here to reach Luzern) and Gossau (change here to reach Zürich). A separate line runs from Appenzell to the city of St. Gallen.

The one destination in this chapter not well covered by public transportation is Stein (with its folk museum and tourable cheese factory). It is reachable by taxi (for details, see the listing later in this chapter).

Appenzell Town

The center of this authentically Swiss town is a painfully cute pedestrian zone lined with colorful, patterned house fronts (rather

than the white-painted or wooden facades favored elsewhere). This is a great spot to simply let your pulse slow and enjoy Swiss small-town life. The big square of Landsgemeindeplatz—near many of my recommended restaurants—is where residents gather on the last Sunday of each April to vote on local issues by show of hands. (The rest of the year, it's a parking lot.) A fountain on the square shows an Appenzeller raising his hand to be counted.

Appenzell town is touristy, sure. But from watching the locals robustly greet each other in the streets or laugh over a local beer in the pubs, it's clear this is also a real, living town.

Orientation to Appenzell Town

Appenzell town (pop. 6,000) clusters along its main street, Hauptgasse, which runs from the bridge over the Sitter River to the biggest square, Landsgemeindeplatz. From the middle of this colorful drag, Postgasse (which turns into Poststrasse) heads south to the train station. You can walk from one end of town to the other in about 10 minutes.

TOURIST INFORMATION

The helpful TI is on the main street at Hauptgasse 4 (generally daily 10:00-12:00 & 13:30-17:00, tel. 071-788-9641, www.appenzell.ch). Stop by on arrival to pick up maps and ask about special events in town.

If you stay at least three nights in the region, your hotel or pension will give you an **Appenzell Card.** This covers all local train trips (on trains operated by Appenzeller Bahnen, as far as St. Gallen), free rides on three different cable cars, free admission to local museums, a free ride on the Kronberg luge, a day's free bike rental, discounted PubliCar taxi service, and more. It can be worth extending a two-night stay to three just to get the card.

ARRIVAL IN APPENZELL TOWN

The cute **train** station has a ticket office (Mon-Fri 7:30-18:00, Sat-Sun 8:00-12:15 & 13:15-17:00), WCs, and small lockers (the ticket office and TI can store larger bags).

If arriving by **car,** ask your hotel about parking. If you're just day-tripping here, leave your car in the pay lot by the brewery just across the river from downtown. Walk across the bridge and veer right onto the main drag, Hauptgasse; the TI is just past the church, on your right.

HELPFUL HINTS

Blue Monday: Some of Appenzell's museums are closed on Monday, but hiking and biking are good any day the sun shines. The folk museum in Urnäsch, the cheese factory in Stein, and (unless it's raining) the Kronberg luge in Jakobsbad are other good Monday options—as is the folk museum in Appenzell town spring through fall.

When the Cows Come Home: If you're here at the right time of year, you might luck into seeing the festive procession of cows heading up to the high-mountain pastures (*Alpfahrt,* generally late May-early June) or returning from a summer high in the

Appenzell Town

Accommodations

1. Hotel Adler
2. Hotel/Restaurant Traube
3. Hotel Hecht Appenzell
4. To Haus Lydia & Gästehaus Koller

Eateries & Other

5. Restaurant Marktplatz
6. Gasthaus Hof
7. Café-Hotel Appenzell
8. To Hotel Freudenberg
9. Drei Könige
10. Lokal Gelateria
11. Bistro Appetito
12. To Supermarkets
13. To Bike Rental
14. To Wasserauen/Ebenalp Cable Car (by foot)
15. To Barefoot Trail, Kronberg Luge & Jakobsbad (by foot)

Alps (*Alpabfahrt*, generally late Aug–early Sept). Unfortunately, the cows don't give much advance notice—announcements of the event pop up around town just a few days ahead. There's also the one-day Appenzell cattle show in early October.

Bike Rental: The **train station** has a few electric bikes that can be reserved through the national rail system (see page 448), but don't forget the Appenzell Card (described earlier) includes a day's free bike rental. Some hotels rent bikes or can help you arrange a rental.

For mountain bikes, go to the garage of **Elmar Neff,** a five-minute walk beyond Landsgemeindeplatz (30 CHF/half-

APPENZELL

day, 40 CHF/day; Mon-Fri 7:30-12:00 & 13:15-18:30, Sat until 16:00, closed Sun, shorter hours off-season; Hauptgasse 58, tel. 071-787-3477, www.neff-zweirad.ch).

Sights in the Appenzell Region

The Appenzell region has three folk museums—one in Appenzell town, another in Stein, and a third in Urnäsch. All are good, and they're different enough that visiting all three is worth considering if you have ample time and interest. To be more selective, weigh these differences: Stein's is the biggest, most modern, and probably the best-presented (but also the most difficult to reach without a car); Urnäsch's is the most atmospheric, as it's in a creaky old house; and Appenzell town's is the most convenient, giving a good all-around look at the region (it's especially strong on local costumes) but lacking a bit of the charm of the other two.

APPENZELL TOWN
▲Appenzell Museum
This folk moo-seum, situated above the TI, provides a fine and efficient look at the local cow culture.

Cost and Hours: 7 CHF, covered by Swiss Travel Pass; Mon-Fri 10:00-12:00 & 13:30-17:00, Sat-Sun 11:00-17:00; Nov-March Tue-Sun 14:00-17:00, closed Mon; Hauptgasse 4, tel. 071-788-9631, http://museum.ai.ch.

Visiting the Museum: Buy your ticket, borrow the English translations, and ride the elevator five floors up. From the elevator, detour up the stairs to the attic for a collection of coins, measurement instruments, and torture devices. Check out the excellent collection of traditional costumes on the fifth floor, then work your way down, wandering through the rest of the exhibits as you go. You'll see old flags and banners, reconstructed rustic rooms, woodcarvings, 19th-century peasant art, handmade embroidery, and (oddly) an Egyptian coffin. One thought-provoking room displays boards called *Rebretter*, which were used to lay out the body of a recently deceased loved one. The boards were painted with the name and information of the deceased and, after the burial, displayed on the family's house.

APPENZELL

▲Folk Music

The accordion never really caught on here, making Appenzell's folk music, which still uses older instruments (violin, dulcimer), unique in Switzerland. Free concerts take place every Thursday (early-June-mid-Oct) at 18:30 in the City Hall; every Wednesday at 20:00 at the ritzy Hotel Hof Weissbad (about two miles out of town); and every Saturday (July-early Sept) at the Romantik-Hotel Säntis. The hotels require a reservation if you plan to eat dinner. If not, try to convince the staff to let you have a drink within earshot of the music. You can also ask the TI (or check their website) about live music options.

Modern Art Museums

Appenzell has a modern-/contemporary-art museum with two branches in great settings: **Kunstmuseum Appenzell** is a silver-clad modern building right behind the train tracks (Unterrainstrasse 5, tel. 071-788-1800), and **Kunsthalle Ziegelhütte** is a bit farther out (Ziegeleistrasse 14, tel. 071-788-1860).

Cost and Hours: 9 CHF each, 15-CHF combo-ticket covers both; also covered by Swiss Travel Pass; Tue-Fri 10:00-12:00 & 14:00-17:00, Sat-Sun 11:00-17:00, shorter hours Nov-March, closed Mon year-round; www.h-gebertka.ch.

HIKING

Appenzell makes a good home base for hiking, with gentle hills and pastoral scenery all around. The TI can suggest several easy walks in the region. I recommend two possibilities here.

Appenzell to Wasserauen

This two-hour walk, which takes you to the foot of the Ebenalp cable car (described later) begins near the parish church in Appenzell and leads you along a creek through meadows and forests. The path is well-marked. Once you reach Wasserauen, you can take the cable car up to Ebenalp, or simply hop on the train back to Appenzell.

Barefoot Trail (Barfussweg)

This 1.5-hour walk between Jakobsbad and Gontenbad offers a surprising and unusual experience...yes, with your shoes off. The trail leads over meadows, through creeks, and on stretches of asphalted road, in a tranquil valley roughly parallel to the Appenzell-Urnäsch road and rail line. Two specially designed fountains along the way will refresh your feet. The path was inspired by the philosophy of 19th-century therapist Sebastian Kneipp, who sought to treat medical conditions with water of different temperatures and pressures.

To get from Appenzell to the trailhead, take the train to Jakobsbad (1-2/hour, 8 minutes, trailhead right across the street from the train station and the Kronberg luge ticket office—described later), and do the barefoot walk to Gontenbad. From Gontenbad, you can ride the train back to Appenzell (4 minutes), or keep on walking (about another hour).

NEAR APPENZELL TOWN
▲Stein

The unassuming, hill-capping village of Stein has two worthwhile attractions, side by side: a cheese production facility with a visitors center, and arguably the region's best folk museum. If you don't have a car, use the subsidized taxi service, **PubliCar,** which takes passengers to Stein and other locations not serviced by buses (each passenger pays a distance-dependent fare plus a flat fee—about 12 CHF from Appenzell to Stein). To reserve, ask at the TI, or call 0848-553-060 (more info at www.publicar.ch).

Appenzeller Dairy (Appenzeller Schaukäserei)

This is one of several dozen dairies in the area where the well-known Appenzeller cheese is made, and it's set up to explain the process to curious visitors. It's fast, smelly, and user-friendly.

Cost and Hours: 9 CHF (includes small cheese tasting), 15 CHF combo-ticket also covers Appenzell Folklore Museum; daily 9:00-18:30, off-season until 17:30; tel. 071-368-5070, www.showcheese.ch.

Visiting the Dairy: As you enter, pick up the English description of the cheesemaking process ("From Milk to Cheese"), and ask about the next English showing of the 10-minute video (which treads a fine line between being informative and promotional).

Large, colorful displays trace the cheesemaking process, and you can peer down into the production facility (cheese is generally made 9:00-15:00—most interesting when they pour the contents of the giant vat into the long line of wheel molds). You'll learn how the special pungent flavor of Appenzeller cheese comes from an age-old, secret-recipe herbal brine mixture that's lovingly rubbed on each wheel as it ages. Down the long hallway, watch hundreds of wheels of cheese silently age. Then head into the tasting area, where you can nibble on the various types of Appenzeller-brand cheese. The ladies at the cheese counter love to cut it so you can sample it. Notice how the age affects the aroma and taste. The dairy also sells yogurt and cold drinks, and the restaurant serves powerful cheese specialties.

Appenzell Folklore Museum
(Appenzeller Volkskunde Museum)

This excellent museum offers a modern, well-presented look at the folk culture in these parts.

Cost and Hours: 7 CHF, 15 CHF combo-ticket also covers Appenzeller Dairy, covered by Swiss Travel Pass; Tue-Sun 10:00-17:00, closed Mon; tel. 071-368-5056, www.appenzeller-museum.ch.

Demonstrations: A visit to this museum is best on Saturdays and summer Wednesdays, when demonstrations are going on (cheesemaking starts at 13:00, most interesting around 14:45). Call ahead to confirm the schedule.

Visiting the Museum: Borrow the essential English translations at the entry, then explore the three floors of exhibits. The ground floor is dedicated to local customs and lifestyles. The replica of the alpine cheesemaking hut is occasionally used for live demonstrations. There's a huge collection of cowbells, which, according to the explanation, are used for various purposes: to scare off evil spirits, to make the lead cow easier to follow in processions, to more easily find a lost cow..."and anyway, cows like them."

Upstairs is an art collection titled "Peasant Painting 1600-1900," with everything from huge murals from the sides of barns to delicate oil paintings to miniature wood carvings—virtually all featuring pastoral countryside scenes of cheesemaking huts, cows, and rolling meadows. Each of the "naive" (untrained) artists who created these works is explained in a short bio, which brings the collection to life. You'll see great examples of the brightly painted traditional regional furniture (also easy to find in local hotels and restaurants).

The basement shows off more furniture pieces (in the replica of a traditional bedroom, notice how the colorful paint makes the furniture stand out from the plain wooden walls). But the focus here is on two other local crafts: weaving and embroidery. The exhibit explains how embroidery gradually evolved from being simple and handmade to machine-made, as it went from a craft to an industry. The rustic loom and the giant embroidery machine are sometimes used for demonstrations.

▲Urnäsch

This appealing one-street town has Europe's cutest museum. It's a 15-minute train ride from Appenzell.

Museum of Appenzell Customs (Appenzeller Brauchtumsmuseum)

Located on the town square across from the church, this museum brings this region's folk traditions to life.

Cost and Hours: 8 CHF, covered by Swiss Travel Pass; daily 9:00-11:30 & 13:30-17:00 except closed Sun morning, shorter hours in off-season; tel. 071-364-2322, www.museum-urnaesch.ch.

Visiting the Museum: Exhibits are displayed on four floors of two adjacent, different-as-day-and-night buildings. The new building is slick and mostly used for temporary exhibits. The 400-year-old, aptly named "Old House" has low ceilings, dramatically sloping funhouse floors, and lots of creaks. Warm and homey, it's a happy little honeycomb of Appenzeller culture—you'll feel like a local invited you over for a visit.

First ask to watch an English showing of the 20-minute movie that explains four of the major regional festivals. The most memorable is Silvesterchläus—the Appenzell New Year, celebrated on January 13 per the old Julian calendar. On this date, local men celebrate by putting on gigantic, cartoonish headdresses and giant cowbells. You'll see some of those costumes—and others—then twist your way up through the tiny halls and staircases, pausing to look at replicas of local rooms, collections of handicrafts and tools, and other slices of Appenzell life. On the top floor of the new building, don't miss the music room, where you can try your hand at traditional musical instruments, including a hammered dulcimer and a coin-in-a-bowl (which, in the right hands, is more musical than you might think). There's no English, and barely any German, but it's still fun to explore.

Kronberg Luge Ride (Bobbahn)

Between Appenzell and Urnäsch, in the village of Jakobsbad, you can enjoy a bobsled ride that runs on steel rails from April through November. Each sled has seatbelts and can carry two people. Two side handles allow you to control the speed: Respect the *Bremsen!*

signs—which suggest when to brake. The same entertainment zone includes a chairlift for hikes, as well as a high-ropes course.

Cost and Hours: 9 CHF per sled for adults—two adults can share one sled, 6 CHF per sled for kids—ditto, multiple-ride cards available and shareable; daily 9:00-18:00, shorter hours in spring and fall, closed Dec-March; no rides in rainy weather, tel. 071-794-1289, www.kronberg.ch.

Getting There: The luge is just across the tracks from the Jakobsbad station, which is an 8-minute train trip from Appenzell.

Sleeping in Appenzell Town

Sleep in touristy Appenzell town if you want comfort—or for a rustic, high-altitude thrill, opt for the low-tech, no-shower dorms at Ebenalp (listed later). Appenzell town is small, and the hotels are central. The *B&Bs* are a 10- to 20-minute hike from the town center.

HOTELS

$$ Hotel Adler rents 20 rooms in a building that dates from 1562 and boasts a historic fondue cellar (winter only). The hotel has two types of rooms: modern or traditional Appenzeller. Helpful Franz Leu, a seventh-generation innkeeper, decorates the halls with fun memorabilia (family rooms, elevator, pleasant garden lounge, small parking lot, closed Nov and Feb, Weissbadstrasse 2, between TI and bridge on Adlerplatz, tel. 071-787-1389, www.adlerhotel.ch, info@adlerhotel.ch).

$$ Hotel Restaurant Traube rents seven cozy, tastefully decorated, modern rooms in a very pretty building right in the center of town (Marktgasse 7, tel. 071-787-1407, www.hotel-traube.ch, info@traube-appenzell.ch).

$$ Hotel Hecht Appenzell rents 38 bright, updated rooms on the main drag, but without the family-run feel (elevator, quieter rooms in back, Hauptgasse 9, tel. 071-788-2222, www.hecht-appenzell.ch, info@hecht-appenzell.ch).

B&BS

To experience a pleasant Swiss residential neighborhood, consider the following B&Bs, just east of Appenzell's pedestrian zone. To reach them from the town center (TI/town church), cross the bridge and take a right on Eggerstandenstrasse. You'll reach **Gästehaus Koller** first (just a few houses down), then—after another 500 yards or so—Haus Lydia. To reach Haus Lydia by public transit, take the train to the Hirschberg station (2 minutes from Appenzell on the line to St. Gallen). From the station, it's a three-minute downhill walk following the tracks.

$ Haus Lydia has four guest rooms on the upper floors of a large, traditional home filled with tourist information and a woodsy folk atmosphere, plus a garden and a view of Ebenalp. The crisp, nicely decorated rooms are a good value if you have a car or don't mind a 20-minute walk from the town center (great breakfast, Eggerstandenstrasse 53, tel. 071-787-4233, www.hauslydia. ch, contact@hauslydia.ch, friendly Frau Mock-Inauen). She also rents two roomy apartments by the week (no breakfast).

$ At Gästehaus Koller, Stefan and Karin rent four comfortable rooms on the upper floor of their home. Stefan is a carpenter and did much of the woodwork, and his wife, Karin, makes traditional costumes (Eggerstandenstrasse 9, tel. 071-787-0222, www. gaestehaus-koller.ch, info@gaestehaus-koller.ch).

Eating in Appenzell

TRADITIONAL MEALS WITH TABLE SERVICE

Restaurants in Appenzell's old town cater to locals and day-trippers with classic Swiss-German menus and elaborate desserts. Almost every menu features (surprise) the heavenly but oh-so-smelly Appenzeller cheese. The Appenzeller beer is tasty, famous, and about the only thing cheap in the region. Many top restaurants cluster around the big main square (Landsgemeindeplatz). All of these places are open until about 23:00.

$$$ Restaurant Marktplatz is filled with locals playing cards in a genuine Appenzeller atmosphere among beautifully detailed inlaid tables and wood-carved wall panels. Armin, who grew up in Appenzell, serves seasonal specialties with class in a building that has been in the family for over a century (closed Sun-Tue, Kronengarten 2, tucked behind small parking lot across from Landsgemeindeplatz fountain, tel. 071-787-1204, www. marktplatz-appenzell.ch).

$$$ Gasthaus Hof, which feels particularly local, has a pleasant beer garden out back. The menu features a bewildering variety of specials, but they are most proud of their cheese dishes—the cozy dining room is filled with the unforgettable aroma of Appenzeller cheese (daily, Engelgasse 4, tel. 071-787-4030, www. gasthaus-hof.ch).

$$$ Café-Hotel Appenzell serves from a large menu (including salads and vegetarian dishes) in a genteel dining room and at a host of inviting outdoor tables. They also run a pastry shop in one corner of the building (daily, at corner of Landsgemeindeplatz closest to TI, tel. 071-788-1515, www.hotel-appenzell.ch).

With a View over Town: A steep 15-minute uphill walk or short drive from the town center, **$$$ Hotel Freudenberg** has reasonably priced meals and sweeping panoramas over Appenzell's rooftops from outdoor tables. If you'd like to dine with a view, it's worth the effort, but wear appropriate footwear for the steep climb up (closed Wed and Nov; go under train station, turn right, and follow yellow *Freudenberg* signs through a residential zone, then up through the hills; Riedstrasse 57, tel. 071-787-1240, www.hotel-freudenberg.ch). Drivers can follow the yellow *Freudenberg* signs from near the train station.

CHEAP EATS AND TREATS

$$ Drei Könige is clearly the local favorite serving coffee, delicious cakes, and light food in a cozy interior or on a sunny terrace (Wed-Mon 8:00-18:30, Sat-Sun until 17:00, closed Tue; Hauptgasse 26, tel. 071-787-1124).

$ Lokal Gelateria is a low-key café serving homemade gelato (made with milk produced just a few kilometers away), coffee, and alcoholic beverages. Their location, tucked behind an old saw mill along the banks of the Sitter River, makes this a nice place to retreat (Wed-Sun 14:00-18:00, closed Mon-Tue, in bad weather, and in winter; Weissbadstrasse 3a, tel. 071-787-0115).

$$ Bistro Appetito has good, inexpensive pizzas. Take out or eat in their small dining room just off Landsgemeindeplatz (closed Mon, Marktgasse 13, mobile 078/893-5676).

Supermarkets and Cafeterias: The **Migros** (with a self-service cafeteria) and **Co-op** supermarkets face each other along Zielstrasse, a five-minute walk downhill from Landsgemeindeplatz (both generally open Mon-Sat 8:00-19:00, closed Sun).

Appenzell Connections

For details on taking the train to nearby destinations, see "Getting Around the Appenzell Region," earlier. For connections beyond the Appenzell region, you'll generally change in either Herisau or Gossau.

From Appenzell Town by Train to: Zürich (3/hour, 2 hours, change in Gossau), **Chur** (2/hour, 2.5 hours, 1 or more changes), **St. Moritz** (1-3/hour, 4 hours, several changes), **Luzern** (2-3/hour, 3 hours, change in Herisau; more with additional changes), **Bern** (3/hour, 3 hours, 1-2 changes), **Interlaken** (3/hour, 4 hours, 1-3 transfers), **Lausanne** (2/hour, 4.5 hours, change in Gossau), **Munich** (2-3/hour, 4.5-6 hours, 1 change, more with additional changes). Train info: www.sbb.ch.

Ebenalp

This mountain features wonderful views and a cliff-hanging hut, providing a lofty "hills-are-alive" alternative to Appenzell town. From Wasserauen—five miles south of Appenzell town by road or rail line—ride the lift up to Ebenalp (5,380 feet), a high, rocky ridge that drops off to vertical cliffs on the southern side. On the way up, you'll get a sneak preview of Ebenalp's cave church and the cliffside boardwalk that leads to the restaurant (near the top, left side). From the top you'll enjoy a sweeping view north all the way to Lake Constance (Bodensee). Though this excursion is doable in so-so weather, clear skies really enhance the Ebenalp experience—ask in Appenzell before you head up to the mountain, or check the webcam at www.ebenalp.ch. In any weather, sturdy shoes and rain gear are recommended—the weather can change in the blink of an eye.

Getting There: First, a train takes you from Appenzell to Wasserauen (1-2/hour, 12 minutes). Then, across the road from the

Wasserauen station, the Ebenalp lift carries hikers to the summit and back every 15 minutes (20 CHF one-way, 31 CHF round-trip, half-price with Swiss Travel Pass, 6-minute trip, daily July-Aug 7:30-19:00, June and Sept until 18:00, May and Oct 8:00-17:30, mid-Dec-March 9:30-17:00, usually closed April and Nov-mid-Dec—call ahead, free parking, pick up free hiking map before you ascend, tel. 071-799-1212, www.ebenalp.ch).

Hiking from the Lift Station to Aescher-Gasthaus am Berg: Leaving the lift, look for *Wildkirchli* and *Aescher* signs pointing to the 15-minute hike down to the mountain hut. First you'll hike steeply down under the cables, then you'll hook right and venture downhill through a good-sized natural cave where archaeologists once found the bones of prehistoric bears. It's slippery, so watch your step and use the railing—trust me, you'll soon return to daylight. As you emerge into the light, you'll pass a tiny **museum** (free and always open; scan barcode with phone for English descriptions) in a hut built on the site where hermit monks lived from 1658 to 1853. Don't miss the 400-year-old **Wildkirchli church,** a few yards farther along the cliff, in a separate cave.

Next you'll follow the cliff-hugging path (not for those afraid of steep drop-offs, though there's a sturdy railing) to a 170-year-old, weathered-shingle hut sitting snugly against the mountain. Originally built to house farmers, goats, and cows, it evolved into a lodge for pilgrims coming to the monks for spiritual guidance. Today, the recommended **Aescher-Gasthaus am Berg** has just

one hiker hut for rent, but its restaurant welcomes hordes of tourists in search of a decent meal and great views (see listing, later).

From the guesthouse's sunny cliffside perch, you can almost hear the cows munching on the far side of the valley. Only the paragliders tag your world as 21st century. In the distance, nestled below Säntis peak, are the isolated Seealpsee (Lake-Alp Lake) and the recommended Berggasthaus Seealpsee.

Returning to the Ebenalp Lift: Retrace your steps through the cave (allow 25 minutes for this uphill hike). Or, for a different and more strenuous yet less-crowded return, you can hike up around the back of the mountaintop: As you leave Aescher-Gasthaus am Berg, continue straight on the path. At the fork, the path winds you steeply uphill, among goats and wildflowers, eventually arriving back at the top of the Ebenalp lift (allow 40 minutes).

Hikes from Aescher-Gasthaus am Berg: The trail beyond

Aescher-Gasthaus am Berg leads to a pair of rugged hikes that are worth considering: down to the alpine lake called Seealpsee (and eventually all the way down to Wasserauen), or up for a steep-but-scenic route back to the Ebenalp lift (described above).

APPENZELL

The hike down to **Seealpsee,** which takes a little over an hour, is steep but rewarding: Take a left at the first fork beyond Aescher-Gasthaus am Berg. After some initial knee-jarring switchbacks, the trail gets easier, and as it flattens out, a fork to the right leads in about 10 minutes to the lake. To reach Wasserauen (45 minutes) and the train back to Appenzell, retrace your steps till you reach the nearest fork, but this time take the other path (to the right), which turns into a narrow road.

Sleeping and Eating on Ebenalp

Sleeping: Although Appenzell town offers all the predictable comforts, hardy travelers enjoy overnighting on Ebenalp instead. The facilities are limited (only rainwater) and reaching any of these accommodations involves some steep hiking. Beyond these two options, the entire region is a hit with hikers, who can trek between as many as 24 mountain hotels, each a day's hike apart. All originated as alpine farms.

¢-$ Berggasthaus Seealpsee is on the idyllic alpine Seealpsee, most easily reached by an hour-long hike up a private road from the Wasserauen train station (private rooms available, includes sheets and showers, closed Nov-mid-April, tel. 071-799-1140, www. seealpsee.ch, info@seealpsee.ch, Parpan-Dörig family).

¢ Berggasthaus Ebenalp perches just a couple of minutes' steep walk up from the upper lift station (200-foot elevation gain). There's a paved path up, so it's actually doable with wheeled luggage. Its rooms are booked long in advance for Saturdays, but are otherwise empty (restaurant, coin-op rainwater shower, closed same months as lift—usually April and Nov-mid-Dec, tel. 071-799-1194, www.gasthaus-ebenalp.ch, infos@gasthaus-ebenalp.ch).

Eating: Built in 1805, **$$ Aescher-Gasthaus am Berg** is a memorable place to eat. The hut is actually built into the cliff; its back wall is the rock itself (see photo at the start of the Ebenalp section). The outdoor terrace and comfortable dining room are filled with happy hikers and plenty of tourists drawn by *National Geographic* publicity that labeled this a "destination of a lifetime." For a strenuous 45-minute pre-dinner hike, copy the goats: Take the high trail toward the lake, circle clockwise up toward the peak and the lift, then hike down the way you originally came (closed Nov-April, 15 minutes by steep trail below top of lift, tel. 071-793-9223, www.aescher.ch).

You can also eat at the restaurant of the **Berggasthaus Ebenalp,** listed earlier.

Liechtenstein

Appenzell is just an hour away by car from the tiny and touristy country of Liechtenstein. This quirky remnant of medieval feudal politics is truly landlocked, without a seaport, or even an airport. Liechtensteiners—who number about 37,000—speak German, are mostly Catholic, and have a stubborn independent streak. Women weren't given the vote until 1984.

Liechtenstein is not worth going out of your way for (unless you collect stamps—postal or passport), but it's a no-brainer detour if you happen to be driving south from Appenzell toward Chur or the Upper Engadine (Pontresina/St. Moritz).

Vaduz

Low-key Vaduz, with about 5,000 people, feels basically like a midsized Swiss town. Its pedestrianized main drag is lined with modern art and hotels bordering a district of slick office parks. Like other "micro-countries," Liechtenstein offers businesses special tax and accounting incentives. Many European companies establish their official headquarters here to take advantage of its low taxes.

Getting There: Heading south on the A-13 expressway from Appenzell, the road actually skirts Liechtenstein just across the Rhine (the border). For a 30-minute detour, exit at Buchs and turn toward Schaan. After crossing the border (without stopping, or likely even noticing), you'll wind up in the town of Schaan. Follow signs (south/right) toward Vaduz, the capital of the Principality of Liechtenstein (Fürstentum Liechtenstein, or FL for short on its sleek black license plates).

Visiting Vaduz: Various parking lots and garages are along the main street, Äulestrasse. Try to park directly under the looming castle. If you park at the Marktplatz garage, you can simply walk one block up to the pedestrian zone called Städtle, where you'll run right into the **TI** (at #39, tel. from Switzerland 00-423/239-6363, www.tourismus.li). The TI will stamp your passport for 3 CHF.

Go for a stroll along enjoyable Städtle street. Use Swiss francs or euros to buy a postcard and some Liechtenstein stamps to send to the collector in your life (but be sure to write and send it before leaving the country).

The prince's striking castle, a 20-minute hike above Vaduz, is closed to the public, but there's a fine view from the grounds (find the trail near Café Burg). The billionaire prince, who looks down on his six-by-twelve-mile country, wields more real political power in his realm than any other member of European royalty. The Liechtenstein family purchased this piece of real estate from the Holy Roman Emperor. In 1719, the domain was granted principality status, answering only to the emperor. In 1806, during the age of Napoleon, Liechtenstein's obligations to the Habsburg emperor disappeared, and the country was granted true independence.

The Liechtenstein princes, who lived near Vienna, saw their country merely as a status symbol, and at first didn't even bother to visit. In fact, it wasn't until the 20th century that the first Liechtenstein prince actually lived here. Later, after World War I, tough times forced the principality to enter an economic union with Switzerland. To this day Liechtenstein enjoys a very close working relationship with its Swiss neighbors—functioning in some ways like just another Swiss canton, with the same currency, international diplomacy, bus system, and even soccer league.

Leaving Vaduz: After visiting the castle grounds, you'll quickly run out of things to do. No problem—just head back to Switzerland. Continue south through town on Äulestrasse, turn right at the well-marked *Schweiz* sign, cross back over the Rhine, and you're back in Switzerland (and on the A-13 expressway)... having checked another country off your list. Or, if you're headed northeast toward Austria, drive back north through Schaan, then up to Feldkirch.

LAKE GENEVA & FRENCH SWITZERLAND

Lausanne • Château de Chillon • Montreux • Gruyères

Lake Geneva, in the southwest corner of the country, is the Swiss Riviera. Separating France and Switzerland, the lake is surrounded by Alps and lined with a collage of castles, museums, spas, resort towns, and vineyards. The elegant French-style villas that grace the lakeshore—with pastel colors, frilly balconies, and characteristic mansard roofs—give it an air of gentility. This area is so beautiful that Charlie Chaplin and Idi Amin both chose it as their second home.

French is the predominant language at Lake Geneva ("Lac Léman" in French, "Genfersee" in German). To establish a better

connection with the locals, see the "French Survival Phrases" in the appendix, *s'il vous plaît.*

Skip the big, dull city of Geneva; instead, sleep in fun, breezy Lausanne. Explore the romantic Château de Chillon and stylishly syncopated Montreux. It's also worth taking one day to delve into the French Swiss countryside, which offers up rolling green foothills topped with castles; chocolates, vineyards, and Gruyère cheese galore; a high-mountain excursion to give you a quick dose of the Alps; and picturesque towns tucked into the folds of the hillsides.

Lake Geneva and French Switzerland at a Glance

▲▲▲**Château de Chillon** Medieval castle perched romantically on eastern shore of Lake Geneva, with climbable ramparts, damp dungeons, and literary history. See page 295.

▲▲**Lausanne** Twisty, 3-D city stretching up a steep hill from the lakefront, with pleasant old town, plenty of sights—most notably the Olympic and Art Brut museums—and easy boat and train connections to the surrounding area. See page 273.

▲▲**Gruyères** Storybook small town overlooking dreamy countryside, with worthwhile nearby sights, including a folk museum, cheese- and chocolate-making factories, and a mini mountain with views of the Lake Geneva basin. See page 303.

▲**Montreux** Relaxed lakeside resort offering few sights—just sublime views of the misty lake and cut-glass peaks, and immediate access to the Golden Pass and Chocolate Train scenic rail lines. See page 300.

PLANNING YOUR TIME

On a quick trip, you can get a good overview of Lake Geneva's highlights in a day. Lausanne makes the best home base. Make a beeline for Château de Chillon in the morning, then do my self-guided "Old Lausanne Walk" in the afternoon.

With more time, lazily float your way between Lausanne and Chillon (2 hours) or other lakeside towns on a scenic boat cruise, and get lost in Lausanne's old town and unique museums (the Art Brut and Olympic museums). Or, for an action-packed day, consider my Chillon-Vevey-Vineyard day trip (described later).

Beyond Lausanne and Chillon, the French Swiss countryside to the east is not worth the trouble for most, but can be worth exploring if you have a third day—and a car. If you're heading to the Berner Oberland from here by car, carve out some time for the Gruyères region en route, or consider a longer detour via Les Diablerets. Without wheels, you can get a good, quick taste of the Gruyères region's sights and scenery on the convenient, if touristy, Chocolate Train, which departs from Montreux.

GETTING AROUND LAKE GENEVA

By Train: You can easily connect towns along Lake Geneva via train. Take a faster IR (interregional) train between larger cities, such as Lausanne or Montreux, or a slower "S" train (regional) if you're heading for a smaller destination, such as Château de Chillon.

By Boat: This region offers a dizzying array of boat routes. Daily boat trips connect Lausanne with Vevey (1 hour, 21 CHF),

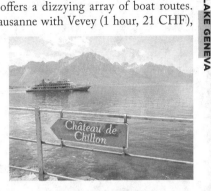

Montreux (1.5 hours, 26 CHF), Château de Chillon (2 hours, 29 CHF), and points in between. These run about four times per day in each direction (late June-early Sept, fewer in shoulder season, virtually none mid-Oct-mid-April). First class costs about 40 percent more and gets you passage on the deck up top, where you should scramble for the first-come, first-served chairs. You can sail free with a Swiss Travel Pass (using a travel day of a flexipass) or get 50 percent off with a Eurail Global Pass (does not use a day of pass); to avoid giving up a day just for the cruise, take an afternoon cruise on the same day you arrive by train in the morning.

Study the schedule (at www.cgn.ch, at TIs, and in boat ticket windows) to find a cruise that appeals to you. For just a quick hop on the water, the 15-minute cruise between Montreux and Château de Chillon is fun. The pretty town of Vevey, between Montreux and Lausanne, is enjoyable for a short stop and a visit to Charlie Chaplin's former home. A separate line runs from Lausanne directly across the lake to Evian-les-Bains, the French spa town famous for its mineral water (hourly, 35 minutes, passport required). Avoid calling the expensive info line (toll tel. 0900-929-929).

Lausanne

Lausanne is the most interesting city on the lake, proudly dub-

bing itself the "Olympic Capital" (it's been home to the International Olympic Committee since 1915). Amble along the serene lakefront promenade, stroll through the three-tiered, colorful old town, explore the sculptures at Olympic Park, and visit

French Switzerland

To Neuchâte

To Paris

FRANCE

Yverdon-
les-Bains

10 Kilometers

10 Miles

Vallorbe

SWITZERLAND

A-1

E-23

A-9

Lausanne

Ouchy

Nyon

Rolle

Cul

E-62

A-1

N-1

Lake Geneva

Evian-
les-Bains

FRANCE

Yvoire

Geneva

FRANCE

To
Lyon

Rhône R.

GENEVA'S
EAUX-VIVES
STATION

A-40

A-40

A-41

A-40

To
St. Gerv
les-Bai
& Chamo

To Lyon

To Annecy

the remarkable Art Brut museum. Take a peek at the Gothic cathedral, and climb its tower for the view.

The Romans founded Lausanne on the lakefront—but with the fall of Rome and the rise of the barbarians, the first Lausanners fled for the hills, establishing today's old town. The Roman site was abandoned (scant ruins survive), but in the age of tourism, the waterfront—a district called Ouchy—was revived. The city thus has a design problem that goes back 1,500 years: two charming zones separated by a nondescript residential/industrial section. Thankfully, the waterfront and the old town are easily linked by a steep, handy Métro line.

Lausanne has the energy and cultural sophistication of a larger city, but is home to only about 130,000 people (350,000 in the greater area). A progressive city government that subsidizes art and culture and a university with plenty of foreign students carbonate the place with a youthful spirit.

Orientation to Lausanne

The tourist's Lausanne has two parts: the lakefront **Ouchy** (oo-SHEE), with a breezy resort ambience and the Olympic Museum; and the **old town,** with creaky Old World charm and fine museums, directly uphill from the lake. The old town district is divided roughly into two adjacent parts: the true old town, or *vieille ville* (vee-yay veel), near the cathedral; and the city center, or *centre-ville,* with my favorite hotels and restaurants. The train station is located between Ouchy and the old town, and it's all connected by the slick Métro.

Walking around Lausanne's old town feels like a life-size game of Chutes and Ladders. Two-dimensional maps don't do justice to the city's bridges, underpasses, stairways, hills, and valleys. Even the Métro trains and platforms are on an incline. Expect to be confused by the street plan at first. The model of old Lausanne in the City History Museum helps you understand how it developed.

Be careful to pronounce Lausanne correctly (loh-zahn), and don't confuse it with Luzern.

TOURIST INFORMATION

Lausanne has two full-service TIs: One is at the train station's main entrance, and the other is at the lakefront Ouchy Métro stop (both daily 9:00-19:00, Sept-May until 18:00, tel. 021-613-7373, www.lausanne-tourisme.ch).

At the TI, ask about multilingual **walking tours** (15 CHF, pay guide directly, Mon-Sat usually at 10:00 and 14:30, 2 hours, no tours Oct-April, meet in front of Town Hall at Place de la Palud, www.lausanne-a-pied.ch). The language situation is potluck, depending on the guide and the tourists who show up. Most guides speak English, but not all; the TI has a list, so check with them in advance, or directly with Lausanne-à-Pied at tel. 021-320-1261. (If there's no English tour, my self-guided "Old Lausanne Walk," later, will probably be more informative.)

Be sure to ask about concerts (free and otherwise)—especially organ concerts at the cathedral. If you're here between mid-June and mid-September—prime time for cultural events—pick up the TI's free *L'Agenda Culturel Et Gratuit De L'Eté* program.

ARRIVAL IN LAUSANNE

By Train: The train station, with lockers, WCs, a ticket office (Mon-Fri 6:30-20:00, Sat-Sun 7:00-19:30), late-night groceries, and a Métro stop, is midway between the old town and the lakefront. This sounds inconvenient, but the **Métro** takes you either up to the Old Town or down to the lake in less than five minutes, with

LAKE GENEVA

Lausanne

PALAIS DE BEAULIEU

COLLECTION DE L'ART BRUT

HERMITAGE

BOIS DE SAUVABELIN

See Lausanne City Center detail map

CASTLE

Ripponne-M. Béjart

VIEILLE

VILLE

Place de la Riponne

CENTRE-VILLE

CATHEDRAL

CITY HISTORY MUSEUM

FLON

MERC.

Bessières

HIGH PED. BRIDGE

PONT BESSIÈRES

Lausanne-Flon

Place de l'Europe

Place St. François

Parc Mon-Repos

TRAIN STATION

POST

Lausanne-Gare

AVE. DU THÉÂTRE

AVE. STE. LUCE

AVE. DE LA GARE

Grancy

GRANCY

400 Meters

400 Yards

Crêt de Montriond

Délices

Metro Line #2

Jordils

OUCHY

Parc Olympique

AVE. DE L'ÉLYSÉE

| Metro Line |
| .... Boat |

OLYMPIC MUSEUM

Ouchy

FOUNTAIN

OLYMPIC PARK

Parc du Denantou

To Geneva

AVE. DE RHODANIE

HOTEL CHÂTEAU D'OUCHY

Place du Port

QUAI D'OUCHY

To Pully, Vevey, Chaplin's World & Montreux

BOAT TICKET OFFICE

Lake Geneva

To Geneva

To Evian, France

To Montreux & Château de Chillon

1 Fleur de Pains Bakery
2 Café du Vieil-Ouchy
3 Supermarket
4 Boat Rental

constant departures. A **taxi** from the train station to your hotel runs a steep 15 CHF, and the Métro is probably faster anyway.

By Car: Driving is tricky in this nearly vertical city—especially in the twisty old town. Consider leaving your car at a park-and-ride (labeled *P+R*); several flank the city and are well-connected by Métro to the old town (16 CHF/day covers parking and transit into center). If you're coming on the freeway from the north (such as from Bern), exit at *Vennes* and use the covered park-and-ride garage by the Vennes Métro stop. Or stay on the freeway as it loops down to *Lausanne Sud,* ending near the Ouchy park-and-ride, close to the base station of the Métro. If you're approaching on the lakeside road from the east (such as from Montreux), follow blue signs along the lakeshore directly to Ouchy. For more information, go to www.lausanne.ch/stationnement.

By Boat: From the dock, veer left toward the plaza with the flagpoles. Across the street is the TI and Métro station.

By Plane: Lausanne and the Lake Geneva area are served by the Geneva airport, at the lake's southwest corner. The airport sits on the western edge of Geneva, straddling the French border. For more on the airport, and how to get to town from there, see "Lausanne Connections," later.

HELPFUL HINTS

Sunday Closures: Sundays are pin-drop quiet; many shops and restaurants are closed.

Market Days: On Wednesday and Saturday mornings, produce stands fill the pedestrian streets of the old town. On Saturday there's a small flea market on Place de la Riponne.

Laundry: Quick-Wash, well-run and handy, is just behind the train station (self-service, daily 8:00-22:00, below station at Boulevard de Grancy 44, mobile 079-449-3761).

Bike Rental: A bike is worthless in this steep city, but can be great for exploring the lakefront, vineyards, and nearby villages. It's a three-hour waterfront pedal from Ouchy to Montreux and back. Ask the Ouchy TI for bike-rental options.

GETTING AROUND LAUSANNE

By Public Transport: Lausanne's nifty **Métro** and **bus** network makes it easy to get around. For transit info, visit www.t-l.ch.

The Métro has two lines (converging at the Lausanne-Flon stop in the city center), but only line #2 is useful for travelers. Using it is simple: up (direction: Croisettes) or down (direction: Ouchy/Olympique). This inclined 14-stop line (which is completely automated—don't try to delay the doors from closing) climbs up from the lakefront to the Old Town, then all the way up to the freeway. The key stops are Ouchy (at the lakefront); Lausanne-Gare (at the train station); Lausanne-Flon (at the bottom end of the old town—exit into Place de l'Europe, ride the elevator up to the pedestrian bridge on Rue du Grand-Chêne, then stroll straight into the town center); and Riponne-M. Béjart (at the top end of the old town, on Place de la Riponne). You're unlikely to need the bus, except to reach the Art Brut museum.

If you're sleeping in Lausanne, your hotel should give you a Lausanne Transport Card, which covers local transit and is paid for by your hotel tax. Otherwise, unless you have a Swiss Travel Pass, you'll need to buy tickets from the friendly ticket machines (with English instructions). Tickets are valid on both Métro and buses (short-ride ticket-2.30 CHF, valid 30 minutes, up to three stops; single ticket-3.70 CHF, valid one hour; all-day ticket-9.30 CHF, valid 6:00-24:00). Almost everything in this chapter is in the central zone 11. But the Lausanne Transport Card will take you well into the countryside and to some lakeside villages.

By Taxi: Cabs are pricey—figure 15 CHF for a short ride.

Old Lausanne Walk

There's no way to see this town without lots of climbing. Locals are used to it (try to keep up). This self-guided stroll introduces you to both parts of Lausanne's charming old town, starting in *centre-ville* near the Church of St. Francis and ending in *vieille ville* near the cathedral.

❶ Lausanne-Flon Métro Station
This is where you're most likely to arrive in town.
• *From the Métro stop, ride the elevator up to the high pedestrian bridge (Passerelle du Flon). Orient yourself from midway across the bridge, which leads to the city's main thoroughfare. Start by looking west (toward the solitary gray skyscraper)...*

❷ Passerelle du Flon View
Below you stretches Flon (the "Quartier du Flon")—once a ravine of the Flon River, then a down-and-dirty industrial zone, and now—so typical of post-industrial 21st-century Europe—a thriving people zone. Its old warehouses come alive at night with trendy bars, restaurants, theaters, and nightclubs. The recommended Vinothèque Nomade bar/restaurant is immediately

Lausanne City Center

LAKE GENEVA

Hotels, Eateries & Services

9 Hôtel des Voyageurs
10 Hôtel Régina
11 Hôtel du Marché
12 To Hôtel Lausanne by Fassbind
13 Hôtel Elite
14 Café Romand
15 Café du Grütli
16 Brasserie Le Vaudois
17 The Great Escape
18 Inglewood Hamburger
19 Manora Cafeteria
20 Traiteur Bosphore
21 Restaurant à l'Etage
22 Vinothèque Nomade
23 Supermarket (2)
24 Launderette
25 Bus #2 to L'Art Brut (2)

Old Lausanne Walk

1 Lausanne-Flon Métro
2 Passerelle du Flon View
3 Place St-François & Rue de Bourg
4 Pont Bessières
5 Lausanne Cathedral
6 Esplanade de la Cathédrale
7 Place de la Palud
8 Place de la Riponne

100 meters
100 yards

below. The only reminder of the mills that once churned here is the name of the hottest nightclub in town: MàD (which stands for "Moulin à Danse" or "Dance at the Mill;" it's just out of sight at Rue de Genève 23). The Bel Air Tower (to the right) is famous as the country's first skyscraper (1932). The more elegant building, far to the left in the trees, was the 19th-century home of the Swiss Supreme Court.

Turn around and look down on the green rooftop of the Métro station (where different local plants grow all year). Scan this human coral reef of a city. Look for the viaduct, built in the 19th century as a double set of arches to cross the ravine. Now, as the city has evolved, only the top set of arches is visible.

· *Walk to where the pedestrian bridge hits the busy street, Rue du Grand-Pont. Head right toward the green copper spire of the Church of St. Francis. As you walk along Rue du Grand-Pont, enjoy lovely views of the cathedral on your left and the grassy Métro station on the right, with its vertical garden. You'll soon reach...*

❸ Place St-François & Rue de Bourg

The Church of St. Francis marks the town's center and transportation hub. Across the busy street stands the grand post office, a belle époque building from the days when post offices were a big deal. It's flanked by two also-grand banks (still a big deal in Switzerland). The church is Gothic, founded by Franciscans in the 13th century. But in 1536, it went Protestant—and was gutted of decorations. Later, a grand Baroque organ was installed. The church's locally quarried stones, laid 500 years ago, cleaned up quite nicely. Near the fountain, the brass plaques in the pavement feature the names of children born in the city hospital on full-moon nights in the year 1998. These plaques celebrate the creation of the rustic fountain that replaced a much larger horse trough (this was once the wagon entry point of town).

As you leave the square, heading up the pedestrianized Rue de Bourg, the multiethnic makeup of today's Switzerland (one of the most multicultural countries in Europe) is on parade. At the first corner (Rue St. François), glance downhill—it's lined with circa-1960 St. Francis signposts. Rue de Bourg is lined with top-end shops. Blondels (on the left) is still hand-making chocolate in this location after 150 years. Notice the fine architecture above the noisy storefronts. On Wednesdays and Saturdays this street is filled with market stalls.

· *When the street ends, turn left (onto Rue Caroline), continuing uphill and over the large bridge toward the cathedral.*

❹ Pont Bessières

Pause mid-bridge and enjoy the view—similar to the earlier Passerelle du Flon view but higher up. Find the skyscraper, the court-house, and the Jura Mountains in the distance (border of France). And notice how the old river valley below is built over. The railing you may be leaning on is designed to discourage suicidal people from leaping. While Switzerland seems to have it all, its mindset can be conservative, and the orderliness can be stressful. For what-ever reason, Switzerland illustrates how money doesn't always buy happiness.

Walking toward the cathedral, you'll notice that Lausanne's old town—filling the highest hill in town with administration buildings, offices, schools, and apartments—is subdued compared to the commercial center.

• *Climb up, with the patch of grass on your left, past the City History Museum to the cathedral. We'll enjoy the view terrace in a bit. But first, check out the biggest church in the country.*

❺ Lausanne Cathedral (Cathédrale de Lausanne)

Lausanne's cathedral is an Evangelical Reform Church, meaning that it belongs to the tradition of the early Protestant reformer John Calvin. Iconoclasm, the removal of religious symbols, suited the Calvinists well. The once-ornate cathedral, originally dedicated to Mary, was cleared of all its statues and decorations. Its fres-coes were plastered over, and its colorful windows were trashed and replaced by plain ones. But, thankfully, there's still a lot to see.

Cost and Hours: Free, daily 9:00-19:00, Oct-March until 17:30; www.cathedrale-lausanne.ch.

Concerts: Organ concerts here take place on some Friday eve-nings in peak season (check the schedule at www.grandesorgues.ch, or ask at the cathedral welcome center or TI).

Visiting the Church: Inside, the **pipe organ** above the main door is American-made (by Boston-based company Fisk) and was installed in 2003. Locals love their organ and figure its cost (four million CHF) was money well spent. Look back at its 7,000 pipes: The "stiletto in Oz" design represents the wings of angels.

Admire the **stained glass.** The **rose window** in the south (right) transept has the church's only surviving 13th-century glass. The rest of the glass dates from the early 1900s. Don't miss the bold and clearly labeled scenes in the apse. The north (left) transept has some dreamy blue Art Nouveau scenes.

The **Mary Chapel,** below the rose window (and just to the

left), was the most elaborate chapel in the church. In 1536, it was scraped clean of anything fancy or hinting of the Virgin Mary. Look at the bits of surviving original paint, and imagine the church in its colorful glory six centuries ago. Also notice the stamp for the "pilgrims' passport." This church is a stop on one of the many pilgrimage routes across Europe that funnel hikers to the Camino de Santiago in northern Spain. If you're on a pilgrimage of any sort, take a stamp. But a much better pilgrim's experience is in the adjacent painted portal.

The **painted portal** (on the right side of the nave, as you face the altar) was the church's main entrance in the Middle Ages.

Today, it's glassed in to protect its remarkable painted Gothic statuary. Imagine being a pilgrim approaching this beautifully painted main entrance to one of the great churches of Europe: On the left are six Old Testament prophets and on the right are six apostles—all standing upon symbols of evil and welcoming you with benevolent smiles. High above you, Jesus is about to crown Mary "Queen of Heaven." And then you step inside.

The Tower: In the back-right corner of the church you'll find a small **TI/welcome center** and gift shop, and the entrance to the tower climb (224 steps, grand lake views, lots of Alps, 5 CHF).

Since the Middle Ages, a **night watchman** has lived in the church's tower. As the city was originally built of wood, fire was a constant fear. His job: to watch for fires and to call out the hours. The city is made of stone today—so there's little danger of fire—and people wear their Swiss timekeepers on their wrists. Nevertheless, Lausanne's night watchman, the last one of his kind in Switzerland, still calls out the hours. Every night on the hour, from 22:00 to 2:00 in the morning, he steps onto his balcony and hollers. His first announcement: "I am the watchman. I am the watchman. We just had 10 o'clock. We just had 10 o'clock."

• *Back outside, belly up to the fine viewpoint immediately in front of the cathedral.*

❻ Esplanade de la Cathédrale

On a clear day, look beyond the spire of the Church of St. Francis to see the French Alps (Chamonix and Mont Blanc, over there somewhere, are just out of sight). Evian-les-Bains, the famous French spa town, is immediately opposite Lausanne. On the right, the soft, rolling Jura Mountains, which mark the border of France and Switzerland, stretch all the way from Lake Geneva to Germany.

• *Across the square from the cathedral is the* **City History Museum** *(described later, under "Sights in Lausanne"). Now might be a good time to visit.*

A covered wooden staircase (**Escaliers du Marché**) leads down from the cathedral's front door. At the top of the stairs, a sign points to **Chemin de St. Jacques** (indicating that you're on "The Way of St. James"—look for the stylized seashell icon of the Camino de Santiago pilgrimage near the next set of stairs). Head through the tunnel under the busy road (note the fine view back at the cathedral from just after the tunnel). Continue down the covered steps, pass the recommended Café du Grütli, and land on a long and narrow cobbled square.

❼ Place de la Palud

This square is marked by its colorful Fountain of Justice. Since 1585 this blindfolded figure of Justice, holding her sword and scales, has commanded fairness as she stands triumphantly over kings and bishops. Imagine the neighborhood moms sending kids here to fetch water in the days before plumbing. Behind the fountain is a mechanical clock, with animated figures that perform with recorded French narration every hour, on the hour (daily 9:00-19:00). The Town Hall at the bottom of the square dates from 1685.

• *Uphill from Town Hall, Rue de la Madeleine leads to the vast and modern…*

❽ Place de la Riponne

The Palais du Rumine (former university), overlooking the square, now houses a collection of museums (all of which are skippable). The recommended **Great Escape**, a fun hamburger bar with a nice selection of beers, fills the terrace a few steps above (between the square and the cathedral tower). There's a free WC on the first floor of the Palais du Rumine.

• *Our tour is over. To reach the **Collection de l'Art Brut**, walk northwest about 10 minutes or catch bus #2 from Rue Neuve (a block west of Place de la Riponne, across the street from the blocky church). To head down to the lakefront **Ouchy district**, ride the Métro from this square (the Riponne-M. Béjart stop). Or simply enjoy poking around more of the old town's twisty lanes.*

Sights in Lausanne

IN AND NEAR THE OLD TOWN

▲City History Museum (Musée Historique de Lausanne)

This museum, housed in what was the bishop's residence (facing the cathedral), has nicely presented displays that trace life in Lausanne from Roman times to the present.

Cost and Hours: 8 CHF, covered by Swiss Travel Pass, Tue-Sun 11:00-18:00, closed Mon except July-Aug, bags must be checked in lockers, Place de la Cathédrale 4, tel. 021-315-4101, www.lausanne.ch/mhl.

Visiting the Museum: The highlight for many is the 1:200-scale model of Lausanne in the 17th century (when you enter the museum, request to hear the 8-minute recorded English commentary on the model). Head upstairs and follow the one-way route of "Lausanne, The Exhibition."

The model, in the first room, is based on an engraving from 1638 (see copy on wall). It will give you a feel for how this hilly city and its quirky street plan developed. You're viewing the town from the perspective of the lakefront district of Ouchy, with the Church of St. Francis in the foreground. You can see river valleys that have since been built over by the modern city. The little water mills mark the birthplace of industrial Flon. Though the city's walls are long gone, its vineyards survive.

The adjacent room shows how the city tackled urban planning and the construction of the Grand-Pont. Downstairs are rooms dedicated to the economic, social, and cultural history of Lausanne: Bernese epoch (Protestant, 1536-1798), Lausanne silver from the 18th century, a collection of musical instruments, memorabilia from the Grand Tour, which brought money and the first tourists to Lausanne, and an exhibit about the beginnings of the modern era. The final display features holograms of locals describing what their hometown means to them.

▲▲Collection de l'Art Brut

This well-displayed, evocative collection shows art produced by untrained artists, many labeled (and even locked up) by society as "criminal" or "insane."

Cost and Hours: 10 CHF, covered by Swiss Travel Pass, Tue-Sun 11:00-18:00, closed Mon except July-Aug, bags must be checked in lockers, Avenue des Bergières 11, tel. 021-315-2570, www.artbrut.ch.

Getting There: From the Old Town, the museum is an easy 10-minute walk (west from Place de la Riponne) or bus ride (#2 to the Beaulieu-Jomini stop, direction: Désert, frequent service from Place St-François or from Rue Neuve near Place de la Riponne). From the train station, take bus #3 or #21 (also very frequent, direction: Bellevaux or Blécherette).

Visiting the Museum: In 1945, artist Jean Dubuffet began collecting art he called "Brut"—created by untrained, highly original individuals who weren't afraid to ignore rules. In the 1970s, he donated his huge collection to Lausanne, and it has now expanded to 60,000 works by hundreds of artists—loners, mavericks, fringe people, prisoners, and mental-ward patients. Dubuffet said, "The art does not lie in beds ready-made for it. It

runs away when its name is called. It wants to be incognito."

The works are displayed (perhaps fittingly) without much rhyme or reason on four floors. About 800 works are on display at any given time. Read the posted thumbnail biographies of these outsiders, and then enjoy their unbridled creativity. As you tour the thought-provoking collection and learn about the artists, ponder the fine line that separates sanity and insanity when it comes to creative output.

IN OUCHY, LAUSANNE'S WATERFRONT

The lazy resort charm of Lausanne lies on its lakefront. The place is lively from Easter through October, and dead otherwise. Start at Ouchy's **Riponne-M. Béjart stop,** connected by Métro with the train station and the old town every few minutes.

Before you leave the Métro, notice the parade of Olympic athletes literally hanging from the ceiling. Walk straight out (past the TI) to the main road, **Quai d'Ouchy.** Several restaurants are a block to the left. Also to the left, across the street, notice the grand Hotel Château d'Ouchy. It was built around a 13th-century tower—a reminder of Lausanne's importance in the Middle Ages. Before the hotel gates is an Olympic countdown clock (marking the days, and even seconds, remaining until both the next winter and summer games). Continuing past the hotel, you'll pass an elaborate kids' playground on the left and a sprawling festival zone on the right before reaching the **lakefront.** Environmentalism is popular in this city, which boasts 300 square feet of green space per inhabitant—more than nearly any city in Europe.

Straight ahead, the big C-shaped **weathervane** stands on the breakwater, indicating to sailors if the wind is *vaudaire* (roughly southeast, over the lake from Montreux), *bise* (northerly), *joran* (northwest), or *vent* (southwest). It's a puzzle, as the "C" is designed to line up with the semicircle cutouts in the four strangely placed stone pillars. Crouch down, match the "C" with the pillar that creates an "O," then look down at the pavement for the corresponding name of today's wind.

At the **harbor,** you'll find the departure docks for various boat cruises (see next). A five-minute stroll farther along the lake takes you to Ouchy's main attraction, the Olympic Museum and Park (described later).

Boat Rides

Several boat cruises leave from the harbor at Ouchy. Solar-powered **Aquarel tour boats**—quiet, smooth, slow, and green—run on the hour (12 CHF, 40-minute tours in good weather, no narration, June-Sept Wed-Sun 14:00-19:00, mobile 079-754-0535, www.lesaquarelsduleman.ch). Lake Geneva **cruise boats** operated by CGN leave from the piers just to the left (see "Getting Around Lake Geneva," earlier). Stop by dock 3, next to the main boat-ticket office, for information on the lake's still-steaming historic paddleboats (1904-1927).

▲▲▲Olympic Museum and Park (Le Musée et Parc Olympique)

This museum celebrates the colorful history of the Olympic Games. It's set in a beautiful lakeside park where the Olympic flame flick-

ers between editions of the games. The exhibits and park celebrate the ideals of Pierre de Coubertin, who in 1894 founded the International Olympic Committee and restarted the games after a 1,500-year lapse. Coubertin acknowledged that to ask nations to love one another was naive, but to ask them to respect one another was a realistic and worthy goal.

The museum is a thrill for Olympics buffs—and plenty of fun for those of us who just watch every two years. This is your chance to see Jesse Owens' spiked jumping shoes, Katarina Witt's red skating dress, a basketball signed by the 1992 American "Dream Team," and Cathy Freeman's running shoes. The exhibits are lively (with fun, interactive stations designed to keep kids' attention), and plenty of seating to let you rest your feet while listening to the audioguide.

Cost and Hours: 18 CHF, family deals, free with Swiss Travel Pass; daily 9:00-18:00, mid-Oct-April Tue-Sun 10:00-18:00, closed Mon; worthwhile audioguide-5 CHF, Quai d'Ouchy 1, tel. 021-621-6511, www.olympic.org/museum.

Getting There: From the Ouchy Métro stop, turn left and walk five minutes along the water to the big, white fountain, then walk up the stairs. On the way, you'll pass the Beau-Rivage Palace, Lausanne's venerable belle époque hotel, which, since 1857, has hosted a glamorous guest list that includes Winston Churchill, Woody Allen, Charlie Chaplin, Dizzy Gillespie, Liz Taylor, and, uh, Richard Nixon.

Visiting the Museum: Entering the building, you'll pass under a high-jump bar set at the current Olympic record level. Imagine trying to clear it yourself—these are no average feats.

The exhibits span three levels. Start on the upper floor, **The Olympic World,** which covers the history of the games and their organization. You'll learn how the Olympics were born in ancient Greece, then reconceived by French aristocrat Pierre de Coubertin (1863-1937). Coubertin, a progressive thinker with socialist leanings, believed that strict French schools needed more physical education. He looked to British traditions as a model, and worked with British and Greek educators to hold the first modern games in Athens in 1896. Fourteen nations participated (more than 200 competed in Rio in 2016). The exhibit covers the different host cities since then, the complex politics involved, the tradition of the torch, and the games' planning and organizational challenges. You'll see past Olympic flags, torches, and mascots, and an audiovisual display of opening ceremonies throughout the years.

One level down, on the ground floor, **The Olympic Games** covers the winter, summer, and Paralympic games. Displayed are uniforms, shoes, and other personal memorabilia of competitors through the decades. Sit riveted in the circular projection theater, which serves up a medley of dramatic replays of competition highlights.

The basement exhibit, **The Olympic Spirit,** is about athletes' lives in the Olympic village—what they eat, where they live, drug tests and anti-cheating measures, and the "Olympic Truce" that athletes from hostile nations commit to observe. Interactive displays allow you to try your hand at Olympic sports and a thought-provoking body-image wall shows the diverse bodies of Olympic athletes and how little they resemble fashion-model stereotypes. The exhibit concludes with a room of shiny replica medals from each of the modern games.

The museum's top-floor **café** has nice views and just-tolerable prices. Outside, in the park, there's a full-scale track on which you can measure your pace against the performance of Olympic athletes.

LAKESIDE AND VINEYARD EXCURSIONS NEAR LAUSANNE

Promenade Stroll to Pully

A delightful promenade stretches in both directions from the Ouchy Métro stop. From here, you can walk along the lakeshore until the Swiss cows come home. The best easy walk is east to Pully (left as you face the lake, about 1 hour). Along the way you'll meet locals strolling and jogging, and see birds and boats bobbing on the lake. At Pully, you can catch the train back to Lausanne (2/hour, 5 minutes).

Lavaux Wine Country

Beyond Pully are the terraced vineyards of the Lavaux wine country. These dreamy terraced banks—with farms and villages, winding lanes, and glorious mountain and lake views—are the quintessence of Lake Geneva's charms.

Hiking trails snake from Pully all the way to Montreux (a very full day's walk). The best stretch is between Lutry and Vevey. Parts of the trails are marked with plaques that explain in English the grape-growing process, as well as the local flora, fauna, and culture. There are countless options to mix and match boat rides, train rides, and scenic hikes here. Your Lausanne Transport Card (from your hotel) covers public transit as far as Epesses (zone 19). Trains generally go twice an hour. The TI is your best source for information and adept at reviewing options. Stop by, get their advice, and pick up the *Montreux Riviera Walks* map, which shows the various hiking routes. For tips on seeing this area by car, see "Route Tips for Drivers," later.

Chexbres-Village to St-Saphorin Hike: For a short and easy walk (less than an hour) that offers a superb sampling of the glories of the Lavaux region, take the hike from Chexbres-Village to St-Saphorin. From Lausanne, ride the train to Chexbres-Village (30 minutes, change in Vevey). At Chexbres, find the light-blue sign across the street from the TI pointing to St-Saphorin. You'll first wind down some village streets (following the blue signs), before being directed onto a concrete promenade that snakes scenically through the vineyards. It's all downhill from here, with gorgeous views of vineyards and villages, Lake Geneva, and France beckoning from across the water. At St-Saphorin, you can pause to sample some wines, then catch a train back to Lausanne.

Lavaux Express Tourist Train: A kitschy tourist choo-choo makes a one-hour loop, affording you an up-close look at the vineyards. Half the departures are from the boat dock at Lutry and half from the dock at nearby Cully—in both towns the boat dock is a short walk from the train station (15 CHF; Wed and Sat-Sun at 13:30, 15:00, and 16:30; also Sat-Sun at 10:30; 25-CHF wine-tasting trip Fri-Sun evenings at 18:30, includes visit to a wine-cellar *cave;* no service Nov-March; tel. 0848-848-791, www.lavauxexpress.ch).

Bike to Morges

The best bike path goes west (after sharing with cars for a half-mile, the trail leaves the road and hugs the shoreline all the way to Morges). You'll pass Vidy (with its Roman ruins—just foundations, free), the headquarters of the International Olympic Committee (not open to the public), lots of sports facilities, and finally, just peaceful lakefront parkland stretching to Morges (about 6 miles away, easy return by boat or train).

Chillon-Vevey-Vineyard Day Trip

With a full day and plenty of energy, consider this busy itinerary: Start early and catch the train from Lausanne to Montreux (30 minutes), then walk or bus to Château de Chillon (see "Getting There" on page 296). After visiting the château, enjoy a picnic with views of the castle, then board a bus (20 minutes) or boat (35 minutes, check schedules at Montreux TI) to Vevey. In Vevey, walk towards the train station (15 minutes) to find the post office, where you'll catch a bus to Chaplin's World (10-minute ride; see "Getting There" on page 302). After visiting Chaplin's World, head back the way you came and take the train from Vevey to Chexbres-Village (10 minutes). From there, follow my recommended hike to St-Saphorin (described earlier) before returning to Lausanne by train (30 minutes).

Nightlife in Lausanne

Trendy **Quartier du Flon,** Lausanne's old industrial district, is a ghost town by day and thriving entertainment area at night. With a beach bar in summer and skating in winter, it's well worth a peek.

From the Flon Métro station, the main drag Voie du Chariot leads to the central Flon square (following what was the original train line serving the warehouses). You'll pass Vinothèque Nomade (described next), lively cocktail bars, and a trendy restaurant row lining the Main Square. Flon's central square also has bowling, a cinema (multiplex; "VO" means it's playing in the original language), and **MàD** (an iconic nightclub with four floors of dancing and pricey cover, starting well after my bedtime).

$$$ Vinothèque Nomade is where locals sip wine or famous cocktails and hang out on the big, modern sun terrace or in the more formal dining room inside. They serve tapas and beautifully presented European and Mediterranean dishes (Mon-Sat 12:00-22:00, closed Sun, across from Flon Métro stop, Place de l'Europe 9, tel. 021-320-1313).

Sleeping in Lausanne

Lausanne hotels are priciest between April and October, but with a summer lull in July and August. Prices also fall on weekends, as the city gets more business than leisure travelers. Courtesy of Lausanne's tourist tax, along with your hotel room you'll get a Lausanne Transport Card, which gives you free access to the city's public transportation (plus discounts at many recommended museums) for the duration of your stay. Ask for yours when you check in.

IN THE OLD TOWN

To find Voyageurs and the Régina (which are across the street from each other), take the Métro to the Lausanne-Flon stop, ride the elevator up to the pedestrian bridge, cross Rue du Grand-Pont, walk up Rue Pichard, and take the first right. For the Marché, continue one more stop up on the Métro to Riponne-M. Béjart, then walk five minutes up Rue Pré-du-Marché. Because the Régina and Voyageurs are buried in Lausanne's old town, they can be challenging for drivers. You're allowed to drive through the pedestrian zone to your hotel to drop off your things, but you'll have to park the car at a nearby garage. Get careful instructions, or leave your car at a park-and-ride and arrive by Métro.

$$$ Hôtel des Voyageurs rents 35 classy, Swiss-modern rooms with all the conveniences (noisy rooms facing the pedestrian street, elevator, Rue Grand Saint-Jean 19, tel. 021-319-9111, www.voyageurs.ch, hotel@voyageurs.ch).

$$ Hôtel Régina, immersed in Old-Town charm on a steep pedestrian street, is a find: 35 comfy rooms, hardworking hosts (Michael and Dora), and a great location (RS%, family rooms, ceiling fans, elevator, Rue Grand Saint-Jean 18, tel. 021-320-2441, www.hotel-regina.ch, info@hotel-regina.ch).

$$ Hôtel du Marché offers 40 nice, modern rooms (a dozen with dated private baths) and a few studios in an inviting, quiet neighborhood close to the center. A few rooms serve as a permanent residence for locals. It's a five-minute walk from Place de la Riponne in the Old Town, on the way to the Art Brut museum (family rooms, nice breakfast extra, elevator, Rue Pré-du-Marché 42, tel. 021-647-9900, www.hoteldumarche-lausanne.ch, info@ hoteldumarche-lausanne.ch).

$ Hôtel Lausanne by Fassbind is a modern 54-bed hotel on the edge of the old town, just a few minutes' walk from the Bessières and Ours Métro stops. It's simple, but a good value with nice amenities when compared to other options in this price range. Some rooms have a view of Lake Geneva or the cathedral, and top-floor rooms come with balconies (family rooms, lounge, breakfast extra, pay laundry, elevator, Rue Marterey 15, tel. 021-601-8000, www.byfassbind.com/hotel/lausanne, l@byf.ch).

NEAR THE TRAIN STATION

This hotel is easier for drivers and offers rooms with lake views (unlike most hotels in the Old Town).

$$ Hôtel Elite, run by the Zufferey family, is on a quiet, leafy, residential street just above the train station. Its 33 dated rooms are pleasant without being plush—a few have balconies (elevator, free parking; from station, cross the street and go uphill around McDonald's, take first right to Avenue Sainte-Luce 1; tel. 021-320-2361, www.elite-lausanne.ch, info@elite-lausanne.ch).

Eating in Lausanne

By Swiss standards, you can eat well and affordably here. Lausanne restaurants typically offer a weekday lunch deal for about 20 CHF (sometimes on Saturday, too). This usually just means a main course, perhaps with a side salad or coffee thrown in.

OLD TOWN
Restaurants with Table Service

$$ Café Romand is a venerable, moderately priced restaurant (with a small outdoor terrace) filled with natives enjoying hearty Swiss home cooking—one of the last old-time brasseries still in business. The city's students, pensioners, and professionals sit under old-time photos in this characteristic yet simple eatery like they own the place (Swiss wines by the glass, Mon-Sat 11:45-23:00, closed Sun, Place St-François 2, tel. 021-312-6375).

$$$ Café du Grütli, named for the meadow south of Luzern where Switzerland was born, offers typical French Swiss cuisine near Place de la Palud. While they have outside tables on a cozy cobbled lane, I prefer their 1850s-era dining room. It's a bit touristy, but the Prutsch family (Willi, Heike, and Vanessa) is hands-on, the food's fresh, and the service is very good. The family is into hunting, so you'll find game on the menu as well as an award-winning fondue (Mon-Sat 10:00-14:30 & 18:00-23:30, closed Sun, Rue de la Mercerie 4, tel. 021-312-9493).

$$$ Brasserie Le Vaudois is a classic old-school brasserie, with charming seating inside and out, serving all the traditional French and Swiss dishes (long hours daily, Place de la Riponne, tel. 021-331-2222).

Burgers

$$ The Great Escape is a happening local spot in good weather. The fun-loving crew cranks out great burgers and a few other bar-food-type options on nights and weekends (order inside), but offers a few nicer options and table service for lunch (weekdays only). The restaurant is like a big woody pub (with classic rock playing, one screen showing sports, and a long bar), but I prefer the rickety tables outside on the gravelly square. When it's busy, people perch throughout the small park with their little Great Escape trays (you'll pay a 2-CHF deposit for your tray—don't forget to turn it in and get your coin back). While quiet early, it gets loud and crazy late—but remains welcoming for all ages (daily 11:00-23:00, Place de la Madeleine, above the Métro stop on Place de la Riponne, tel. 021-312-3194).

$$ Inglewood Hamburger is a thriving joint with friendly service in the old center near Place de la Palud. Happy locals munch creative burgers on the small terrace or within the quaint interior (beer on tap, Mon-Sat 18:30-21:30, closed Sun, Rue St. Laurent 14, tel. 021-323-6388).

Self-Service and Cheap Eats

$$ Manora cafeteria, on the seventh floor of the downtown Manor department store, offers a quick and healthy series of lunch buffet lines where you can grab what looks good, including salads, hot meals, fancy fruit juices, desserts, and so on (Mon-Fri 9:00-19:00, Sat until 18:00, closed Sun, hot food served until 15:00, air-con, free Wi-Fi, Rue St-Laurent 7). For even cheaper Manor eating, their food hall in the basement has a selection of ready-to-eat picnic meals.

$ Traiteur Bosphore, a cleaner and brighter-than-average kebab shop, is a good option for a quick and inexpensive takeaway lunch or early dinner. There's no seating—stand at the back counter or walk to the nearby Place de la Louve and find a bench (Mon-Fri 10:00-18:45, Sat until 17:00, closed Sun, Rue de la Louve 7).

Supermarket: The **Co-op** department store, in the center, has a big supermarket in the basement (there's also a lunch cafeteria upstairs; store open Mon-Fri 8:30-19:00, Sat until 18:00, closed Sun, Rue St-Laurent 24).

OUCHY

The lakeside Ouchy district is the place to relax. Immediately in front of the Métro stop is a fun zone with fountains, parks, playgrounds, promenades, and restaurants.

$$ Café du Vieil-Ouchy, charming and reasonably priced, seems a bit out of place among all the fancy, expensive restaurants. It offers traditional Swiss cuisine, including the local filet of perch, cheese fondue, and various versions of *Rösti* (outdoor seating, main courses listed on chalkboard, daily 12:00-22:00, Place du Port 3, tel. 021-616-2194).

Picnics: The most affordable option is a picnic with the local office gang on any of the many inviting benches or scenic lakeside perches. Leaving the Métro station, head left one block to Avenue d'Ouchy, where you'll find several eateries including a **Co-op** supermarket (at #70, daily 6:00-22:00) and **$ Fleur de Pains,** a bakery offering sandwiches, quiche, tarts, and a few humble tables (daily 6:00-19:00, at #73).

NEAR THE TRAIN STATION

$$ Restaurant à l'Etage, owned by hardworking Hari, who came to Switzerland from Nepal, serves Indian and Nepali meals inside the Lausanne train station, overlooking the grand hall (enter up a stairway along track 1, Sun-Fri 11:30-14:00 & 18:30-22:00, closed Sat, Place de la Gare 9, tel. 021-311-3911).

Supermarkets: The train station has two **Co-op** grocery stores with long hours (daily 5:30-24:00).

Lausanne Connections

By Plane: If arriving by plane, you'll land at Geneva airport (airport code: GVA, www.gva.ch). It's straightforward and easy to manage. Exiting from baggage claim, you're met by various local TI desks. To the left is a bank of ATMs and beyond that, the airport's train station, with handy connections to points all over Switzerland. Trains leave for Lausanne about every 20 minutes (27 CHF, 50 minutes—much faster than driving). Geneva's city-center train station is the first stop on any train departing from the airport; you can get a free ticket for this short hop in the baggage-claim area (before customs—look for machines).

From Lausanne by Train to: Montreux (5/hour, 30 minutes), **Château de Chillon** (hourly, 35 minutes, station name: Veytaux-Chillon, more with change in Montreux or Clarens), **Gruyères** (2/hour, 1.5 hours, 2 changes), **Geneva** (7/hour, 45 minutes), **Geneva Airport** (at least 4/hour direct, 50 minutes), **Bern** (3/hour, 1.5 hours), **Murten** (hourly direct, 1.5 hours, more with changes), **Interlaken** (at least 2/hour, 2 hours, change in Bern and sometimes Spiez; or go by Golden Pass scenic route—see the Scenic Rail Journeys chapter), **Luzern** (3/hour, 2.5 hours; or go by Golden Pass scenic route—see the Scenic Rail Journeys chapter), **Zürich** (2/hour direct, 2 hours, more with change in Bern or Yverdon-les-Bains), **Zermatt** (2/hour, 3 hours, change in Visp), **Lyon** (hourly, 3 hours, 1-2 changes), **Chamonix** (hourly, 2.5 hours, 3 changes), **Paris** (5/day direct, 4 hours, more with changes). Train info: toll tel. 0900-300-300, www.rail.ch.

By Boat: For boat connections from Lausanne, see "Getting Around Lake Geneva" near the beginning of this chapter.

ROUTE TIPS FOR DRIVERS

If connecting the Lake Geneva sights by car, note the various routes. The expressway high above the lake zips you quickly between Lausanne and Montreux; although slower, the lakeside road provides great lake-and-vineyards views for about half of the drive (but also passes through several congested towns along the way).

For an even slower but more scenic approach, consider detouring to the **Corniche de Lavaux.** This rugged, sometimes frightening Swiss Wine Road swerves through picturesque towns and the stingy vineyards that produce Lake Geneva's tasty but expensive wine. It lies roughly between Lausanne and Montreux; to get a taste, detour from the lakeside road between Cully (near Lausanne) and Vevey (near Montreux). Going in either direction, follow signs for Chexbres to find the wine road. The Route de la Corniche between Chexbres and Cully is particularly well known. Note that this isn't a tidy, straightforward route; expect lots of exploring on twisty vineyard roads. Getting lost is the point.

Château de Chillon

This medieval castle, set wistfully at the edge of Lake Geneva on the outskirts of Montreux, is a ▲▲▲ joy. Because it's built on a rocky island, it has a uniquely higgledy-piggledy shape that combines a stout fortress (on the land side) and a residence (on the lake side).

Remarkably well-preserved, Château de Chillon (shee-yohn) has never been damaged or destroyed—always inhabited, always maintained. Today it's Switzerland's best castle experience. Enjoy the château's tingly views, dank prison, battle-scarred weapons, simple Swiss-style mobile furniture, and 800-year-old toilets. Stroll the patrol ramparts, then curl up on a windowsill to enjoy the lake.

GETTING THERE

The castle sits at the eastern tip of Lake Geneva, about 20 miles east of Lausanne and about 2 miles east of Montreux. From Lausanne, you can connect to the castle using a combination of methods. For a memorable outing, consider mixing and matching these options.

By Train Plus a Short Walk: The S2 regional train (7.40 CHF one-way, hourly, 30 minutes, direction: Villeneuve) takes you to the station at Veytaux-Chillon, a 10-minute walk along the lake (ideal for picnicking) from the castle.

By Train Plus a Bus Ride or Hike: The faster, more frequent IR (interregional) train whisks you to Montreux (14.80 CHF one-way, 2/hour, 20 minutes), where you transfer to a bus that takes you straight to the castle. From the Montreux station, escalate down to Avenue des Alpes, cross the street, and go down the stairs to Grand-Rue (or take the elevator down, marked *Ascenseur public Grand-Rue*). Cross the street and find the blue bus stop on your right, where you can hop bus #201 to Château de Chillon (3.50 CHF, 6/hour, less frequent after 19:00 and Sun, 10 minutes, direction: Rennaz Village, stop: Chillon; buy tickets from machines—coins only, covered by Swiss Travel Pass, www.vmcv.ch). You can also walk the two miles from Montreux to Château de Chillon (figure about 45 minutes one-way).

To return to Lausanne, simply reverse the above directions (catch the regional train from the Veytaux-Chillon station back to Lausanne—trains leave hourly at :21 past the hour—or hop the bus from Château de Chillon to Montreux, direction: Vevey, stop: Escaliers de la Gare).

By Boat: A slower but more scenic route to Château de Chillon is to cruise there from Montreux (15 minutes), Vevey (30-60 minutes), or even Lausanne (2 hours). For details, see "Getting Around Lake Geneva," near the beginning of this chapter.

ORIENTATION TO CHATEAU DE CHILLON

Cost and Hours: 12.50 CHF, 6.25 CHF with Riviera Card (see "Sleeping in Montreux," later), free with Swiss Travel Pass, 29-CHF family ticket, daily 9:00-19:00, March and Oct 9:30-18:00, Nov-Feb 10:00-17:00, last entry one hour before closing, tel. 021-966-8910, www.chillon.ch.

Parking: There's free, easy parking along the road above the castle, but you'll need a blue cardboard clock (the ticket desk can give you one).

Tours: My self-guided tour hits all the highlights, but for more depth, rent the excellent 1.5-hour audioguide (6 CHF, leave ID as deposit) or download the audioguide app (3 CHF) from the château's website.

Baggage Storage: The castle has free lockers (1-CHF deposit, off the first courtyard in the room with vending machines). The Veytaux-Chillon train station and boat dock don't have lockers, but the Montreux station has a few.

Eating: Consider bringing a picnic to enjoy outside the castle on benches by the lake. Food at the garden **$$ café** next to the castle is expensive, but there are few other options nearby.

BACKGROUND

The aristocratic Savoy family (their seal is the skinny red cross on the towers) enlarged Château de Chillon to its current state in the 13th century. From the outside, the castle has looked pretty much the same for 800 years. The only major difference: In the Middle Ages, it gleamed with a bright whitewash.

This was the Savoys' fortress and residence, with four big halls (a major status symbol) and impractically large lake-view windows (because their powerful navy could defend against possible attacks from the water). But when the Bernese invaded in 1536, the castle was conquered in just two days, and the new governor made Château de Chillon his residence (and a Counter-Reformation prison). With the help of French troops, the French-speaking Swiss on Lake Geneva finally kicked out their German-speaking Bernese oppressors in 1798. The castle became—and remains—the property of the canton of Vaud. It's been used as an armory, warehouse, prison, hospital, and tourist attraction. Jean-Jacques Rousseau's writings first drew attention to the castle, inspiring visits by Romantics such as Lord Byron, Goethe, and Victor Hugo, plus other notables, including Dickens and Hemingway.

⊙ SELF-GUIDED TOUR

When you buy your ticket, ask for the free English brochure and map (there's also a kids' version). The numbers in my tour correspond to those in the brochure, on the audioguide, and posted at the site.

You'll cross a natural moat (the château is built on an island) and enter the **first courtyard** (#3, with handy fountains for your water bottle). In the room marked #4, you can pick up an audio-guide and get oriented with a good model of the castle (if the audioguide desk isn't open, check the gift shop—Room 2).

• *Start by heading down the stairs marked 5/9 to a series of...*

Cellars: You can see how the castle was built upon a foundation of jagged natural stone. In Room 8, find the hidden water gate—a secret escape route for the castle lord, who could (and did, in 1536) hightail it into a waiting boat when the Bernese invaded. Room 9 is **Bonivard's Prison,** named for a renegade Savoyard who was tortured here for six years (lashed to the fifth column from the entrance). When the Romantic poet Lord Byron came to visit, Bonivard's story inspired him to write *The Prisoner of Chillon*, which vividly recounts a prisoner's dark and solitary life ("And mine has been the fate of those / To whom the goodly earth and air / Are bann'd, and barr'd—forbidden fare"; full text available in the gift shop). You can still see where Byron scratched his name in a column (third from entrance, covered by glass).

• *Head back out the way you came in and turn left through the big gate into the **second courtyard** (#12), dominated by the towering keep (more on that later). Just before the keep, on the left, go into the...*

Constable's Dining Room (#13): This is one of the château's finest halls. Look up to the six-centuries-old wooden ceiling. The gigantic fireplace was used to roast large animals (including bears and boars) for feasts. The opposite wall has the first of many grand lake-view windows you'll see in the castle. From here the lords of Savoy had a view of all their land holdings.

• *Climb up the spiral staircase to the...*

Aula Nova (#14): This room has a striking barrel-vaulted ceiling that was restored in the 1920s. The collection of mobile furniture recalls a time when nobility traveled throughout their realm (and took their belongings with them) to keep an eye on things and collect taxes. In fact, in many European languages, the word for "furniture" implies that it's mobile—German *Möbel*, French *mobilier*, and so on. Enjoy the ornate decorations on each traveling chest.

• *Continue up to the...*

Private Quarters (#15-17): The **bedroom** (#16) has a short bed—only about five and a half feet long. Not only were people shorter back then, but they also slept half-upright, propped up on pillows. The **coat-of-arms hall** (#18) is usually filled with temporary exhibits. The walls are lined with the family crests of some 50 "bailiffs" who governed this territory during Bernese rule. Capping this hall is another great wooden ceiling reminiscent of a waffle.

• *Exit at the far end of the hall, and turn right into the...*

Camera Domini (#19): This was the bedroom of the master of the house. Its location—at the farthest end of the castle from the entrance—was particularly secure. In the corner, notice the spiral stairs (closed to the public) that the lord could use to scamper down to Mass in his private chapel, or up to the ramparts. Under a sumptuous fleur-de-lis ceiling, wall paintings (imitating tapestries) illustrate various animals, including a camel, lion, griffin (with the body of a lion and the head and wings of an eagle), and the trademark Bernese bear. Study the model in the middle of the room, which helps you imagine what this room looked like in all its original colorful splendor.

• *Exit the room and turn right (following the 20/24 sign). In Room 21, make sure to see the* **medieval latrines,** *a feature that aims to please a certain class of traveler. Take the narrow stairs down and pass through Room 22. You'll end up in a* **small courtyard** *(#23), where stairs lead up to an observation post with good views. From the courtyard, squeeze into that* **private chapel** *(#24) where the lord's staircase ended up. Leave this room following the signs for 26, and you'll wind up in the...*

Third Courtyard (#25): Notice that the courtyard's irregular shape causes the angled walkways to focus your attention on the grand window of the master's bedroom—the *camera domini* we visited earlier. There's no question who was king of this castle.

• *Go in the door marked 26/33. The* **aula magna** *(#26) is yet another grand hall—this one for banquets—with spectacular (for their time) lake-view windows. Proceed through a few more rooms (including more latrines, #29) to the...*

Domus Clericorum (#31): In this "house of the clerks," the castle bean-counters kept meticulous records of all money and goods that passed through here, creating an invaluable historical record. In Room 32 a series of **models and illustrations** explain the gradual construction of the château over time.

• *Climb back up into the third courtyard again, then pass through to the...*

Fourth Courtyard (#34): From this vantage point you can see how the entire defensive system of the castle developed over the years. The first phase was the steep ramp, followed by the thick walls, and finally the semi-circular towers with just enough of an opening to attack invaders below. This is quite a contrast to the grand windows on the other side of the castle, where the lake served as a natural defense.

• *Now's the time to scramble along the…*

Sentry Walk: As you pass through various indoor rooms and outdoor galleries (marked 38/46), pretend that you're defending the château from invaders. Enjoy the castle courtyard and lake views. Circle all the way around, finally squeezing through the archway (rather than going down the wooden stairs) into the…

Keep (#42): This was the last line of defense and final refuge in the event of a siege. To climb to the top of the eight-story tower, you can scale 76 claustrophobic steps for views over the castle, lake, and surrounding mountains. From here you can see France (across the lake) as well as three different Swiss cantons.

• *Our tour is over. You may scramble the ramparts, enjoy the lake views, and play king (or queen) of the castle at will.*

Montreux

This expensive resort—primarily famous for its jazz festival each July—doesn't offer much to see, but its laid-back vibe and lakeview accommodations help you remember that you're on vacation. About five miles to the northwest, the town of Vevey is home to the worthwhile Chaplin's World museum.

The Montreaux **train station** (with a few storage lockers by track 1) is one steep block uphill from the main waterfront road. Exit the station via the escalator down to Avenue des Alpes. Then walk left 200 yards and cross the street by the post office to the stairs *(escalier)* and elevator *(ascenseur)* down to Grand-Rue, where you'll find the TI, boat dock, and my recommended hotel.

The Montreux **TI** has extensive information about the region and possible excursions (Mon-Fri 9:00-18:00, Sat-Sun until 17:00; shorter hours off-season; Place de l'Eurovision, tel. 0848-868-

484, www.montreuxriviera.com). In spring and summer it offers a two-hour walking tour of the city, though it's not always offered in English (15 CHF, Wed-Sat at 10:00, no tours Oct-March, meet in front of TI, call TI to confirm language).

Visiting Montreux: The lakeside promenade takes you along parks, palm trees, *crêperies*, ice-cream stands, modern sculptures, and the Friday produce market. In the center, meet the statue of Freddie Mercury, who had strong bonds with Montreux (his band, Queen, bought the local Mountain Recording Studios here in 1978).

For an easy way to see several sights in the French Swiss countryside, including the town of Gruyères and the chocolate factory in Broc, take a ride from Montreux on the **Chocolate Train** (described later, under "Getting to Gruyères").

Sleeping in and near Montreux: All hotel guests receive a free Riviera Card, which covers public transit and provides discounts on boat cruises and museum entries. **$$$ Hôtel Splendid** has genteel public spaces; it's worth paying extra for a bigger lakeview room (5-minute walk from train station, across the street from TI at Grand-Rue 52, tel. 021-966-7979, www.hotel-splendid.ch). The institutional **¢ Montreux Youth Hostel** is nicely situated near a lakeside park in the village of Territet (private rooms available; actually closer to Château de Chillon than to Montreux, and easily reachable by frequent buses; closed mid-Nov-March, Passage de l'Auberge 8, tel. 021-963-4934, www.youthhostel.ch/montreux). On the main square of nearby Vevey, the **¢-$ Vevey Hotel and Guesthouse** offers "chic and cheap" beds in a 19th-century townhouse on the lake (private rooms available, 3-minute walk from train station—cross Avenue de la Gare and head to the left of the big yellow building down Avenue Paul Cérésole to Place du Marché 5, tel. 021-922-3532, www.veveyhotel.com).

Montreux Connections: Trains go from Montreux to **Lausanne** (4-5/hour, 30 minutes), **Vevey** (5/hour, 10 minutes), **Gruyères** (2/hour, 1-2 hours, 1-3 changes), **Bern** (3/hour, 2 hours, change in Lausanne, more with additional changes), **Geneva** (2-3/hour direct, 70 minutes, more with change in Lausanne), **Zermatt** (1-2/hour, 2.5 hours, change in Visp). Montreux is also the first/last stop on the Golden Pass route to Interlaken and Luzern (see Scenic Rail Journeys chapter); note that the trip to Interlaken or Luzern on regular trains (changing in Visp or Lausanne, respectively) is faster, if less scenic.

Bus #201 goes from Montreux to Chillon and Vevey (for the Chaplin's World museum). Catch it on Grand-Rue; facing the lake, the Chillon bus (direction: Rennaz Village) is headed to the left, and the Vevey bus to the right (6/hour, 3/hour after 19:00 and on Sun morning, 10 minutes to Chillon, 20 minutes to Vevey). The

boat connecting Montreux to Lausanne, Château de Chillon, and several other Lake Geneva destinations departs from the big park next to the TI (see "Getting Around Lake Geneva," earlier).

NEAR MONTREUX
▲▲Chaplin's World

This museum explores the colorful life of actor and filmmaker Charlie Chaplin (1889–1977), who relocated here in 1952 after being denied re-entry into the US for his outspoken political beliefs. Although a bit out of the way, Chaplin's World is worth a visit—even for those with no prior interest in Chaplin or his films. The museum (and Chaplin's former home) sit on 10 acres surrounded by landscaped gardens with expansive views. With film clips, recreated film sets, and tons of memorabilia, the three-part visit (studio/museum, house, and gardens) celebrates Chaplin's groundbreaking career and provides insight into the man behind *The Tramp*.

Cost and Hours: 25 CHF; daily 10:00-18:00, June-Aug from 9:00, Oct-March 10:00-17:00; Route de Fenil 2, tel. 0842-422-422, www.chaplinsworld.com.

Getting There: From the Vevey train station, take bus #212 (departs in front of the post office, 3 CHF, 2/hour, 15 minutes, direction: Fenil, stop: Chaplin, buy tickets from machines, coins only, covered by Swiss Travel Pass). Drivers should take the A9 to the *Vevey* exit. There is easy pay parking at the museum.

Eating: The estate's former barn is now **$$ The Tramp** café, a nice place for a light snack or drink.

Visiting the Museum: Your visit starts just beyond the gift shop with a short biographical film. Then, you're invited into the studio-like "Chaplin's World." The first room covers Chaplin's early years in Victorian-era London (after his father's death, his mother was committed to a psychiatric hospital). Young Charlie and his brother took odd jobs to survive, and at age nine, Chaplin joined a dance and comedy troupe, touring the UK and eventually the US.

His big break came in 1912 when he was "discovered" by a US film producer. Re-created film sets highlight Chaplin's rise to stardom, from *The Immigrant (1917)* to *Gold Rush* (1925; be sure to test the movable cabin—constructed on rockers to make it sway). By 1923 Chaplin had starred in more than 70 films and started his own movie company (United Artists, based in the heart of Hollywood). The final room houses treasures from Chaplin's career, including an Honorary Academy Award (bestowed in 1929, at the inaugural award ceremony) and the oversized shoes, signature derby hat, and cane he used in character as the mustachioed, sure-footed Tramp.

Next you can walk through Chaplin's former **home,** the Manoir de Ban, for a closer look at his life in Vevey and his role as a husband and father. The first floor focuses on the controversies that led Chaplin to settle in Switzerland at the age of 63. You'll explore memorabilia-strewn reconstructions of Chaplin's library, living room, and dining room, where you can imagine Chaplin's bilingual family gathering for dinner (while his eight children primarily spoke French, Chaplin insisted they speak English at dinner). The second floor highlights Chaplin's encounters with celebrities from Albert Einstein to Mahatma Gandhi. You'll see Chaplin's bedroom, with numerous family photos. The last room—wife Oona's bedroom—displays home movies filmed here.

Outside, the manicured **gardens** are great for roaming. Picture Chaplin and Oona playing with their children on the lawn. You're encouraged to do the same.

French Swiss Countryside

The sublime French Swiss countryside is sprinkled with crystal-clear lakes, tasty chocolates, fragrant cheese, and sleepy cows. Those

with a car will enjoy twisting and turning through this idyllic corner of the Swiss Alps. (For most, it's not worth the trouble by public transit.)

The Gruyères area, just north of Lake Geneva, is particularly handy if you're traveling between Lake Geneva and points north (e.g., Bern, Murten, or the Berner Oberland). The town of Gruyères, famous for cheesemaking, is charming but touristy; nearby, you can visit two very different cheesemakers, a chocolate factory, an appealing little mountain with surprisingly big views, and a workaday town with a fine folk museum. East of Lake Geneva are even more cute villages that can be laced together with a scenic drive.

Southeast of the lake is the mountainous Diablerets region, highlighted by a picturesque hillside village and a lift up to an icy peak.

Gruyères

This ultratouristy town, a household name because of its cheese, fills its fortified hilltop like a beautiful bouquet—but when you get up close, you realize the flowers are fake. Gruyères' ramparts are now a park, and its ancient buildings serve only tourists. Everything is expensive, from museums to food, and it seems the cafés work to ensure there's nowhere free to sit. But even with those downsides, the charming townscape and gorgeous setting make Gruyères worth a visit.

GETTING TO GRUYÈRES

The larger town of Bulle is the area's transit hub, with direct trains from Bern and easy connections from Lausanne (both about an hour away). From Bulle, local trains and buses connect easily to Gruyères (trains run hourly, 7 minutes).

Chocolate Train: To fit a visit to Gruyères and the Cailler Chocolate Factory into an easy all-day side-trip by public transit from Lake Geneva, hop on the Chocolate Train in Montreux. With either panoramic or old-time belle époque coaches, the train leaves Montreux shortly before 9:00. You'll be served coffee and a croissant while enjoying the scenic ride. At 10:00, the train lets you off in Gruyères for a visit to the Maison du Gruyère cheese factory near the train station. An hour later, a bus drives you up to Gruyères' picturesque old town to explore and pause for lunch. At about 14:00, the bus brings you downhill to Broc for a visit/tasting at the Cailler Chocolate Factory; then you board the train back to Montreux, arriving around 16:15 (99 CHF, first class only; 59 CHF with first-class Swiss Travel Pass or Eurail Global Pass, 69 CHF with second-class pass; runs July-Aug daily, May-June Mon-Thu and Sept-Oct Mon, Wed, and Thu only, none Nov-April; tel. 021-989-8190, www.mob.ch).

Orientation to Gruyères

Tourist Information: The TI is at the town entrance (daily 9:30-17:30, shorter hours Nov-April, Rue du Bourg 1, tel. 0848-424-424, www.la-gruyere.ch/gruyeres).

Arrival in Gruyères: The town's **train station** *(gare)* is at the foot of the hill, a steep 15-minute hike up to the village itself. A bus meets each train (just outside station shack, check timetable at www.rail.ch, 3 minutes, 3 CHF, covered by Swiss Travel Pass, get off at first stop: Gruyères Ville).

Drivers should follow signs up to town and shoot for a spot in the P1 lot (2 CHF/hour). On your way uphill you'll pass P3 on the right, then P2 on the left—parking in either saves you a few francs but requires a longer walk up into town.

Festivals: The town center hosts a one-day cheese festival on the first Sunday in May, and over a weekend in late June the castle goes full medieval with the midsummer festivities of La Saint-Jean. The region's most colorful autumn cow processions *(désalpes)* are in nearby Charmey, Albeuve, and Jaun (www.la-gruyere.ch). If you're here on a summer weekend, you might happen to catch a free alphorn concert on the main square (about a dozen performances a year, mostly Sat or Sun, some on Thu, always 15:00-17:00).

Sights in Gruyères

Gruyères' main attraction is the charming town itself. You'll see the town symbol—the crane *(grue* in French)—everywhere.

Wander around the manicured main square, which feels like a movie set. The big square dominates the fortified town center. And while overtaken by tourism, it still offers hints of the hard life of centuries past. Imagine the jubilation in 1755 when the fountain (with its wooden pipes) first brought the town running water. And nearby, you'll see hollowed out stones—once ancient measuring bins used by merchants when a lively market occupied this square. Crowning the town is its castle, built in the 13th century and once the fortified home of a leading medieval Swiss noble family: the counts of Gruyères. Don't skip the castle's ramparts, which are free—you can walk all the way around to enjoy sweeping views of the surrounding countryside.

The following town center sights are all covered by the Swiss Travel Pass. Combo-tickets can save money if you visit more than one sight.

Castle

Gruyères' castle is nicely restored and works to illustrate its long history. A one-way route takes you through rooms that cover three eras: the 13th century (counts of Gruyères), the 16th century ("bailiffs" period, when financial ruin put the castle under the control of a neighboring state), and the 19th century (the Romantic Age). Later rooms feature both Romantic paintings and contemporary fantasy paintings. Admission in-
cludes a dull 18-minute audiovisual show about the town's history, heavy on myths and legends.

Cost and Hours: 12 CHF, daily 9:00-18:00, Nov-March 10:00-17:00, tel. 026-921-2102, www.chateau-gruyeres.ch.

H. R. Giger Museum

A spooky contrast to idyllic Gruyères, this museum is dedicated to the Swiss artist who designed the monsters in the *Alien* movies. Not for young kids or the easily creeped out, this museum shares those movies' dark aesthetic. It also displays temporary exhibits by other surrealist artists.

Cost and Hours: 12.50 CHF; daily 10:00-18:00, shorter hours and closed Mon Nov-March; below the castle in the Château St. Germain, tel. 026-921-2200, www.hrgigermuseum.com.

Tibet Museum

This museum displays an offbeat but genuinely interesting collection of art and artifacts—statues, paintings, and other objects—from the top of the world. These prized Tibetan possessions of a Swiss collector are thoughtfully displayed inside a former church, making it feel as though the Tibetan deities are squatting in Jesus' old house. Dim lighting and mood music add to the mellow ambience. It's very small—especially considering its high price—but might interest anyone who enjoys Tibetan culture. Ask for the English booklet for an explanation of the exhibit.

Cost and Hours: 10 CHF; daily 11:00-18:00, Nov-Easter shorter hours and closed Mon; 4 Rue de Château, tel. 026-921-3010, www.tibetmuseum.ch.

NEAR THE TRAIN STATION

▲La Maison du Gruyère Cheese Factory

Gruyères is justifiably famous for its Gruyère cheese (no "s" at the end when it's the cheese itself). The cheese is an A.O.C. *(appellation d'origine controlée)* product, meaning that to be called Gruyère, it must be made right here, according to exacting standards.

This modern cheese-production center at the foot of Gruyères is handy for train travelers (it's right across from the station). To see the same cheese made in a more traditional setting, head to the hillside *fromagerie* in Moléson (described later). Admission here includes a sample of three varieties of Gruyère cheese (aged different lengths of time), plus a cheesy cow-narrated audioguide, essential for understanding the otherwise sparse exhibits.

Cost and Hours: 7 CHF, 12-CHF family ticket, covered by Swiss Travel Pass; daily 9:00-18:30, Oct-May until 18:00; restaurant, well-stocked gift shop also serves as a decent minimart for travel essentials; straight ahead as you come down the road from Gruyères' hilltop, tel. 026-921-8400, www.lamaisondugruyere.ch.

Visiting the *Fromagerie:* A cow consumes 220 pounds of grass and 22 gallons of water each day to produce 6 gallons of milk, while 100 gallons of milk goes into making one 77-pound wheel of cheese. You'll come across these fun cheese facts and more en route to the viewing area. Smell the various alpine flowers and plants— see if you can discern the subtle flavors they lend the cheese—and hold some cheesemaking tools in your hands. Above the production floor, big windows give you a view down into the milky vats (most interesting when cheese production is going on, generally 9:00-11:00 and 12:30-14:30)—watch as the curds are pulled from the vats. Even if cheesemakers aren't working during your visit, videos show the process. The finale is the cellar (near the ticket desk), where long rows of cheese wheels age. Watch a robot cheesemaker move up and down the aisles, lovingly flipping and rubbing each wheel just right. And if you want even more, a 15-minute video is on a loop in the theater.

Sleeping and Eating in Gruyères

Sleeping: $ Hotel le Saint-Georges is ideal if you want to sleep right on the main square. It has 14 comfortable, traditionally outfitted rooms above a restaurant (Rue du Bourg 22, tel. 026-921-8300, info@lesaintgeorges.ch, www.lesaintgeorges.ch).

$ La Ferme du Bourgoz, a quaint farmhouse midway between the walled town and the train station, is a B&B with 3 homespun rooms and a big family room (Chemin du Bourgo 14, tel. 079-252-7451, www.lafermedubourgoz.ch, info@lafermedubourgoz.ch, Eliane).

Eating: Gruyères' main square is surrounded by eateries serving (guess what?) all manner of Gruyère cheese dishes. These places are more or less interchangeable; pick the spot that looks best. A less romantic but perhaps more practical option is the cafeteria/restaurant at the cheese factory (described earlier).

Near Gruyères

The following worthwhile sights are just a short hop from Gruyères in the towns of Moléson-sur-Gruyères, Bulle, and Broc. Bulle and Broc have train stations; Moléson is served by bus. The sights are just minutes apart by car and clearly sign-posted. Drivers can link them with one of my scenic countryside drives through this region, both of which include a stop to summit 10,000-foot Les Diablerets.

Moléson-sur-Gruyères

The sleepy vacation-home village of Moléson-sur-Gruyères, about five miles from Gruyères, is basically a big parking lot with a bundle of condos on one side and three attractions on the other: a mountain lift, the luge ride, and an old farmhouse that offers a cheesemaking demo. The village has a **TI** (tel. 026-921-8500, www.moleson.ch), plenty of free parking, and hourly bus service from Gruyères.

▲▲Le Moléson Mountain

The verdant hills and pastures immediately surrounding Gruyères are beautiful but relatively undramatic, with one exception: the rocky-headed Moléson massif, which stretches up into the air over the hills behind Gruyères. At 6,678 feet, it's not much by Swiss standards, but its solitary prominence makes for impressive 360-degree views from its summit.

From the parking lot, a funicular takes you to the Plan-Francey transfer point (4,987 feet), where you can catch a cable car to the mountaintop perch. From the top of the lift, you can climb to its rooftop viewing platform—or, for a grand king-of-the-mountain climax, hike 10 minutes up a long set of stairs to the actual summit. From there (weather permitting) you can see Lake Geneva, Mont Blanc, and even some peaks of the Berner Oberland.

The mountain's hiking options include the 2.5-hour, not-as-steep-as-it-looks Panoramic Trail from the summit to Plan-Francey via Gros-Plané—get details and free hiking maps from the Moléson TI before heading up. There's a good self-service restaurant at the top of the lift.

Cost and Hours: 35 CHF round-trip to summit, 46 CHF day-ticket covers unlimited funicular and cable-car rides plus the summer luge (described later), no discounts with Swiss Travel Pass or Eurail Global Pass; lifts run daily 3/hour until 18:00 (last descent at 17:40), also Fri-Sat June-Oct 2/hour 18:00-23:00 for stargazing from observatory, closed Nov-mid-Dec and April-mid-May, www.moleson.ch.

▲Fromagerie d'Alpage du Moléson

Each morning at 10:00, the traditional old Fromagerie d'Alpage du Moléson hosts a small group of visitors for a cheesemaking demonstration. In stark contrast to the sterile Maison du Gruyère's cheese factory, this rustic 17th-century farmhouse gives you an intimate look at the traditional, smelly method of crafting cheese in a huge cauldron over an open fire.

Cost and Hours: 5 CHF for 45-minute cheesemaking demonstration, daily at 10:00, closed Oct-April, lunches served in restaurant; at Place de l'Aigle 12—from the main Moléson parking lot, hike about 5 minutes up to the *fromagerie*.

Reservations: Space at the demos is limited to 50 people, so it's wise to reserve a slot the day before. Use the email link from their website, or call (tel. 026-921-1044, www.moleson.ch, Sophie).

Visiting the *Fromagerie:* A slow-moving video (with some English captions) traces the entire process. Then they repeat the whole thing in the flesh: First the milk is brought to the proper temperature and consistency. Then the cheesemaker skims out the curds with a cloth and packs it into a frame to drain and compress. Finally, he chops it into blocks and separates it into smaller circular frames that will turn it into wheels of cheese. Visitors are offered cups of the cheesemaking leftovers (milk minus curds, a.k.a. whey) to taste—it's like sweet skim milk. Then the cheesemaker takes buckets of whey out to feed to the

pigs. Unfortunately, there's not a word of English during the presentation, but even for non-Francophones, it's still memorable.

Summer Luge

On the hillside adjacent to the *fromagerie* is a low-key luge ride—not Switzerland's best, but worthwhile for kids, luge aficionados, and anyone with the Moléson day-ticket, which covers unlimited rides (6 CHF/ride, daily 11:00-18:00, closed Nov-May and in bad weather).

Bulle

The small town of Bulle (pronounced "bool") has its charms, but is most worthwhile for the Musée Gruèrien folk museum. The train station is just two blocks from the central square and its castle (closed to the public); the museum is just beyond the castle. Between the castle and train station is a regional **TI** (closed Sun, Place des Alpes 26, tel. 0848-424-424, www.la-gruyere.ch). The museum has a small parking lot, and there's plenty of street parking (free if you have a blue cardboard clock to set on your dashboard).

On Thursday mornings, a produce-and-craft **market** fills the center of town—it's particularly big and colorful at the height of summer, when many vendors wear traditional costumes and sell handmade crafts (and when most stalls stay open until 14:00).

▲Musée Gruèrien

Bulle's refreshing, cheery folk museum teaches you all about life in these parts and leaves you feeling good (if a little frustrated that there are no English descriptions). A two-minute walk behind the castle, the museum is located in the basement of the modern library, with thoughtfully displayed cheesemaking and cow-culture artifacts and fine 19th-century photographs of village and folk life. In this cheese-crazy region, cows are key—notice the many cowbells and the panels from barns painted with murals of the cows' twice-yearly procession up and down the Alps.

Cost and Hours: 12 CHF, covered by Swiss Travel Pass; Tue-Sat 10:00-17:00, Sun from 13:30, Oct-May closes Tue-Fri 12:00-13:30, closed Mon year-round; Rue de la Condémine 25, tel. 026-916-1010, www.musee-gruerien.ch.

Broc

The sweet-smelling town of Broc (pronounced "broh") is 30 minutes from Gruyères by an hourly train—which takes you right to the chocolate factory (use the Broc-Fabrique stop). By car, just follow the signs once you get to Broc and park for free in the big square, a 5-minute walk from the factory entrance.

Cailler Chocolate Factory

This factory's fun "Maison Cailler" visitors center features exhibits about the production and shipment of chocolate, a collection of old chocolate molds, and vintage films about chocolate production. Unlike the Alprose factory near Lugano, here you only get a glimpse of the production process.

Cost and Hours: 15 CHF, daily 10:00-18:00, Nov-March until 17:00, last entry one hour before closing, at Rue Jules Bellet 7, follow signs to *Nestlé* and *Broc Fabrique,* tel. 026-921-5960, www.cailler.ch. Try to visit in the morning, when it's less busy. On weekends and in summer, the wait can be up to three hours (they'll give you an estimated entry time when you arrive).

Visiting the Factory: Tours depart every five minutes. With a small group, you'll walk through a series of rooms hearing a goofy history of chocolate. Then you enter a zone where you actually learn about Switzerland's chocolate industry. You'll taste almonds and hazelnuts, crumble a cocoa bean in the palm of your hand, and touch a block of cocoa butter. Peek into the actual working factory, as video screens explain the process. In the tasting room, friendly employees are happy to answer questions as visitors sample creations from elegant trays. Your tour ends in the chock-full-of-chocolate gift shop.

▲▲Scenic Drives in Les Alpes Suisses

Many rent a car in Switzerland simply to better experience the country's dramatic scenery. And the French-speaking Alps put the "joy" in joyride. In this part of the Swiss Alps east of Lake Geneva, narrow but smooth roads wind past grand old working farms, antique shops, cheesemakers, hilltop churches, lots of lumber industry, and romantic covered wooden bridges. I've outlined two scenic driving routes that offer a taste of the area's remote and pristine landscape. While you can rely on GPS or buy a map, most tourist offices have a free "Grand Tour de Suisse" map that provides the same detail. Before setting out, plot your route by the series of towns and villages you'll lace together. A highlight of both drives is the most impressive Glacier 3000 mountain lift up Les Diablerets.

Valley Loop Drive from Gruyères (or Bulle)

To see how your car does on steep inclines—and how your travel partner does with carsickness—consider this half-day (three-hour) loop from Gruyères through the Simmental Valley to the town (and cable car) of Les Diablerets. You'll cover about 80 miles in all, making a tidy little loop around this scenic region. You can also do this loop from Bulle; just follow signs to Broc, then pick up my driving route below.

From **Gruyères,** head northeast, following signs to *Broc* (with its chocolate factory, described earlier), then *Charmey.* The stretch between Gruyères and Broc has fantastic views back to Gruyères town (on the right). From **Broc,** you'll follow a tiny road over 4,951-foot Jaun Pass, leaving the French-speaking region for the German-speaking zone. Then you'll descend scenically into the **Simmental Valley** (famous for its cows and richly ornamented farmhouses). About 45 minutes into your drive, you'll reach a fork in the town of Boltigen. Turn right (following the sign to *Zweisimmen*) to head south on highway 11 through **Zweisimmen** and Saanen. (From here you could cut the loop short by staying on highway 11 and going directly to Château-d'Œx.) For the full loop, leave highway 11 at **Saanen,** head straight through two roundabouts, and follow the smaller road south. Continue to resorty **Gstaad,** pass through idyllic farm country to the cute little hamlet of Gsteig, go over the 5,072-foot pass at Col du Pillon (consider stopping here for its famed **Glacier 3000** lift), and arrive at the town of **Les Diablerets.** Continue west for about six miles to **Le Sépey,** then head north over the pass called Col des Mosses. At **Château-d'Œx,** head west and then north (perhaps side-tripping to the scenic village of Grandvillard) back to Gruyères.

From Interlaken to Montreux, Chamonix, or Zermatt

The touristy town of Interlaken (see the Berner Oberland chapter) is a handy base for joyriding through the mountains to other

Swiss and French alpine destinations. Drivers leaving Interlaken for Zermatt (with its crowd-pleasing Matterhorn), Montreux (on Lake Geneva), or Chamonix (in France), can spend a couple hours exploring the region en route. Though most of the drive is the same for all three destinations, expect a total drive time of 2.5 hours to Montreux (80 miles), 3 hours to Chamonix (115 miles), and 3.5 hours to Zermatt (150 miles). (There's a faster, 70-mile, 2.5-hour route from Interlaken to Zermatt but it misses the charming towns and sights I describe below.)

From **Interlaken,** head southwest on highway 11, hugging the south side of Lake Thun. When you reach the town of **Spiez,** take exit 19 (continuing on highway 11) and drive for about 30 miles (roughly an hour) through the pastoral **Simmental Valley.** At **Saanen,** head straight through two roundabouts and drive about 12 miles (20 minutes) on a smaller road south through the famed mountain resort of **Gstaad,** the cute village of Gsteig, and on to Col du Pillon (with the fun **Glacier 3000** lift). Next, you'll pass through **Les Diablerets,** where you'll take the fork south (signed *Rue des Ormonts*) and drive 33 miles (about an hour), climbing over the 5,833-foot pass at Col de la Croix to the delightful little village of **Gryon** before winding down about 25 minutes to the autobahn (A9/E62) that cuts across southwest Switzerland. From the autobahn, it's an easy drive to **Montreux** (20 minutes), **Chamonix** (1 hour), or **Zermatt** (1.5 hours).

▲▲▲Diablerets Summit (Glacier 3000)

For a grand alpine trip to the tip of a 10,000-foot peak, take a cable car from Col du Pillon pass to the top of the Diablerets massif, high above the town of Les Diablerets. Up top you'll enjoy views of peaks all around, a vast glacier slowly oozing down below you, and some fun mountaintop diversions. While similar lifts in the Lauterbrunnen Valley and Zermatt area are more thrilling, this is French Switzerland's answer to high-altitude fun. Allow two hours to get your money's worth.

Cost and Hours: 80 CHF round-trip, 40 CHF with Swiss Travel Pass or Eurail Global Pass; 3/hour early May-early Oct 9:00-16:50, tel. 024-492-3377, www. glacier3000.ch.

Getting There: It's about a 1.5-hour drive from Gruyères to the pass called Col du Pillon, where you'll find free parking at the base of the Les Diablerets cable car. By public transit, catch the train to the town of Les Diablerets; from here public buses connect to the lift (hourly, 10 minutes).

Ascending Diablerets: At **Col du Pillon** you'll load into the cable car, ride five minutes up, switch to another car (follow *Glacier 3000* signs), then ride another five minutes to the summit. In just 15 minutes total, you're standing on a perch overlooking a glacier, with panoramic alpine views.

The top of the lift is called **"Glacier 3000"** (as it's at nearly 3,000 meters). At your feet sprawls a glacier filled with skiers from fall through spring. I remember summer skiing here—but, with climate change, those days are over. From the top of the cable car you'll find an elevator (the air is thin so you'll appreciate the lift), gift shop, view terrace, cafeteria, and restaurant. To summit the peak called Scex Rouge (which is actually two peaks), climb 100 steps to a viewing platform. From there, walk the thrilling Peak Walk suspension bridge, which stretches 100 yards to the second peak (with the best viewpoint). Free telescopes have built-in labels identifying the peaks around you. You can see the Matterhorn, Jungfrau, and a bit of Mont Blanc, the Alps' highest peak.

High-Altitude Luge: From the top of the lift you can ride the "alpine coaster"—the world's highest summer luge course, perched on a rocky bluff (9 CHF/ride). You'll sit on a plastic sled and shoot down a 3,000-foot-long metal rail, with twists and turns that feel like they're about to send you over the edge (pull back on your handles to brake). At the end, you and your sled are pulled safely back up to the top.

Chairlift: A chairlift (included in your lift ticket) takes you down to the glacier itself. From here, a level but slushy walk across the ice field leads (for about an hour) to a bowling-pin-like rock called Quille du Diable ("pin of the devil"), where you'll find a restaurant with a terrace and more grand views.

Town of Les Diablerets

The pleasant if scruffy and modern-feeling town of Les Diablerets is 10 minutes from the base of the cable car. The town makes a good overnight stop for drivers seeking an evening surrounded by dramatic and snowy mountain views (**TI** open daily, tel. 024-492-0010, www.villars-diablerets.ch). For public-transit travelers just passing through, Les Diablerets offers bus connections for destinations not served by trains.

My favorite place to stay is **$$ Auberge de la Poste**, offering

10 comfortable rooms with plenty of rustic flavor despite its location in the center of town. Alex Pichard is the latest in a line of Pichards since the French Revolution who've run this creaky, low-ceilinged coaching inn (two blocks from the station, just past the TI at Rue de la Gare 8, tel. 024-492-3124, www.aubergedelaposte. ch, info@aubergedelaposte.ch). Their **$$ restaurant** is a reliable choice for an affordable dinner (daily 18:30-21:00).

LUGANO

Lugano, the leading city of the Italian-speaking Swiss canton of Ticino, gives you Switzerland with an Italian accent. The town (population 60,000; metropolitan area 140,000) sprawls luxuriously along the shores of Lake Lugano. Just a short, scenic train ride over the Alps from the German and French regions of Switzerland, Lugano has a splashy, zesty, Mediterranean ambience. It attracts vacationers from the rainy north with its sunshine, lush vegetation, inviting lake, and shopping. While many travelers come here for the fancy boutiques, others make this a base for hiking, cruising the lake, and passing lazy afternoons in its many gardens. Its mountains aren't mighty, its beaches are lousy, and the cityscape is nothing thrilling, but Lugano is the best spot to enjoy palm trees in Switzerland, and its charm merits at least a short visit.

PLANNING YOUR TIME

Lugano lies conveniently at the intersection of the Gotthard Panorama Express and the Bernina Express—two of Switzerland's more scenic train rides. Blitz sightseers arrive along the Gotthard Panorama route one day and take off on the Bernina Express the next.

If relaxing is on your itinerary, spend two nights and a full day here, arriving and departing on the scenic trains. With a day, spend the morning exploring the old town with my self-guided walk, then do a boat cruise and ascend a mountain lift in the afternoon. If looking for something a bit more active, consider my half-day Gandria and Monte Brè plan. Any extra time you have can be spent relaxing in the gardens and along the lakefront.

Orientation to Lugano

The old town is on Lake Lugano, which is bordered by promenades and parks. A funicular connects the old town with the train station above. Nearly everything in this chapter (with the exception of the mountain lifts) is within a five-minute walk of the base of the funicular. The town of Lugano fades into other, smaller waterfront communities all around the lake (much of which lies in Italy).

Italian is the language of Lugano and its region (Ticino), which is surrounded on three sides by Italy (see "Italian Survival Phrases" in the appendix). In this corner of Switzerland, a *Strasse* (street) becomes a *Via*, and a *Platz* (square) becomes a *Piazza*.

TOURIST INFORMATION

Lugano's main TI is in the **Town Hall** building, by the lakefront (Mon-Fri 9:00-18:00, Sat until 17:00, Sun 10:00-16:00; shorter hours and closed Sun in off-season; Palazzo Civico, Riva Alber-tolli, tel. 058-866-6600, www.luganoruismo.ch). There's also a branch at the **train station** (Mon-Fri 9:00-18:00, Sat until 13:00, closed Sun, shorter hours in off-season). If you arrive here, stop by the TI to pick up a city map, a bus and boat schedule, and to inquire about any special events.

The TI offers a free **city walk** (Mon from the main TI, Sat from the train station branch, departs at 10:00, 2 hours). The TI also offers different **excursions,** such as to the fishing village of Gandria; to the top of San Salvatore; and to the top of Monte Brè, including a short boat ride (all tours well described on the website). Excursions run once a week in two languages at the same time, and depending on who signs up, may lean much more heavily toward one or the other (tours cost 10 CHF and include transport or lift tickets worth much more, reservations required, all tours leave from the TI).

Ticino Ticket: All Lugano hotel guests get a free Ticino Ticket, which covers all public transit in the city and entire Ticino region for the duration of your stay (plus other worthwhile discounts). This opens up many fun options.

ARRIVAL IN LUGANO

The train station is on a hill above downtown. It has pay lockers (in the underground passage), WCs, a ticket office (daily 7:00-19:00), ATMs, a convenient small grocery (open long hours daily), a surprisingly genteel restaurant (Buffet della Stazione, with affordable pizzas and a salad bar), and a helpful branch TI.

The easiest way to get to the town below is by **funicular** (look for *funicolare* sign—it's by track 1 in the middle of the station, departs every 5 minutes, daily 5:00-24:00, 1.30 CHF, free with Ticino Ticket or Swiss Travel Pass). The funicular deposits you right in the heart of the old town, at Piazza Cioccaro, also the start of my self-guided Lugano walk. You can also **walk** (but not with wheeled luggage) down the hill.

HELPFUL HINTS

Laundry: Il Girasole is a self-service launderette with English instructions a 15-minute walk away from the lake—or take bus #7 (direction: Pregassona) three stops from Lugano Centro to Piazza Molino Nuovo, then walk a block onward (daily 7:00-22:00, Via Giuseppe Bagutti 8, tel. 091-922-9900, mobile 076-503-7964, www.lavanderiaselfservice.ch).

Local Guide: Lovely **Christa Branchi** teaches enthusiastically about her city and its history (180 CHF/1-3 hours, 220 CHF/half-day, 330 CHF/day, mobile 079-413-6402, christabranchi@hotmail.com).

LUGANO

Lugano Center

Accommodations
1 To Hotel Int'l au Lac
2 Hotel Pestalozzi Lugano
3 Hotel San Carlo
4 Albergo Stella
5 Hotel & Hostel Montarina

Eateries & Other
6 La Tinera
7 Bottegone del Vino
8 La Cucina di Alice
9 Pizzeria Tango & Piazza della Riforma Eateries
10 Il Fermento Pub
11 Manora Cafeteria
12 Co-op Cafeteria
13 Grand Café al Porto
14 To Launderette
15 Paddleboat Rental (2)
16 Buses to Malpensa
17 Buses to Tirano & St. Moritz

GETTING AROUND LUGANO

The town center is easily walkable, and the two nearby hilltop excursions, San Salvatore and Monte Brè, start from funicular stations that are each a 20-minute lakeside stroll (in opposite directions) away from the center.

Buses can save time, though. All lines converge at the Lugano Centro terminal on the north edge of downtown. Bus #2 (2-4/hour) is the one to know: It conveniently links the Paradiso neighborhood (for San Salvatore), the train station, Lugano Centro, Cassarate (for Monte Brè), and Castagnola (where the path to Gandria starts). Buses are free with the Ticino Ticket you'll receive upon check-in at your hotel. Otherwise, buy bus tickets from the English-speaking touchscreen machines at most bus stops (2.30-CHF regular "Area 100" ticket valid for one hour; 4.60-CHF day pass—to buy, touch "Further Tickets," then "Day Pass," then select "Lugano"; also covered by Swiss Travel Pass, www.tplsa.ch).

Lugano Walk

Resorty Lugano hides some interesting history, but let's face it: You're here to relax. Consider taking this short self-guided stroll to get yourself oriented...or just grab a gelato and wind your own way through the city center's arcades and lakeside promenade.

Start on Piazza Cioccaro, at the base of the funicular that connects the train station with the town center.

• *With your back to the funicular, go down the narrow street to the right*

of the building at the bottom of the square.

Via Pessina: In this tangled, colorful little corner are several small delicatessen-type shops run by Signor Gabbani. Venture in if you'd like to be tempted by some of the best local cheese, bread, salami, and/ or wine.

• *Bear right (at the Gabbani salamis), and on your right, at Via Pessina 3, find the...*

Grand Café al Porto: This venerable, elegant institution is the most historic café in town. The *1803* above the fireplace is the date it opened—and also when Ticino joined the Swiss Federation. Once a convent (notice the fine *sgraffito* facade), the café evokes the 19th-century days when Giuseppe Mazzini and fellow Italian patriots would huddle here—safely over the border—planning their next move to unify Italy. Much later, as World War II wound down, US intelligence officer Allen Dulles (future head of the CIA) met right here with Nazi and Italian representatives to organize a graceful end to the war and prevent the Germans from ruining Italy with a scorched-earth retreat. And in more carefree times, this is where Clark Gable and Sophia Loren dipped cookies in their coffee.

• *Just past Grand Café al Porto, take a left at the fountain into...*

Piazza della Riforma: This square is Lugano's living room. With geraniums cascading on all sides, the square hosts an open-

air cinema, markets (Tue and Fri mornings), and local festivals. The stately yellow building is the City Hall (*municipio*, with TI).

• *Facing the City Hall, make a 90-degree left turn and walk (between the* farmacia *and the white bank building) down...*

Via Canova: This street leads directly to the city park. Follow it for a few blocks, watching for the elegant gallery that burrows through a block (on your left after the second crosswalk). Just after that, on your right, you'll pass the **Lugano Art Museum of Italian Switzerland** (MASILugano), which displays ever-changing exhibits of primarily 19th- and 20th-century art (main collection-8 CHF, covered by Swiss Travel Pass, Wed-Sun 10:00-17:00, Tue from 14:00, closed Mon, Via Canova 10, http://masilugano.ch).

Next is the creamy little **Church of San Rocco.** Its rich frescoes celebrate the saint responsible for protecting the city from the plague.

A block beyond the Church of San Rocco (on your left) is the parklike **Piazza Indipendenza.** The giant head on its side is the work of Polish sculptor Igor Mitoraj, who has decorated squares all over Europe with similar sculptures. On your right is the vast, sterile **casino** building.

• *Continuing straight across the street from Piazza Indipendenza, pass through the gate to come face-to-face with the pink palace in the...*

City Park (Parco Civico Villa Ciani): The park's centerpiece, the Villa Ciani, houses a fine-arts museum. Sprawling from here

along the lake is a lush park filled with modern art and exotic trees from around the world. Its water gate evokes the 19th century, when this was the private domain of aristocrats. The flower beds are organized to show off maximum color all year long. If the weather's nice, stow your guidebook and remember you're on vacation as you explore this ingeniously landscaped, people-friendly space. It's lit at night and particularly good for a late, romantic stroll (open long hours daily).

• *From the city park, walk back to the town center along the...*

Waterfront: This lovely promenade gets even nicer on Friday and Saturday evenings from June through August (after 20:30), when the busy street is closed off to traffic and you'll find concerts and other events in full swing.

On the right, the casino's top-floor restaurant overlooks the lake. If it's open, ride the glass *elevatore* up and down for a fun and free view. Then continue strolling through the arcade or under the mulberry trees (a favorite of silk worms, dating from the time when silk was a local industry) until you reach the **TI** and the **boat dock** (for details on lake cruises, see "Cruising Lake Lugano," later). On the way, you'll pass a wonderful, recommended bar (**Il Fermento,** with Ticino craft beers and a fun ambience inside) and several places to rent paddleboats (8 CHF/30 minutes).

Look across the lake for the village clustered around a huge, blocky, sand-colored building (lit up in bright colors at night). That's the Casinò di Campione, the largest casino in Europe, which enjoys special legal privileges, granted by Mussolini when he saw what casino tourism had done for nearby Lugano. The casino dominates **Campione d'Italia**—a tiny enclave of Italy that's surrounded by Switzerland on all sides; residents use Swiss francs, have Swiss phone numbers and license plates, and pay Swiss taxes...but carry Italian passports.

• *Back at the yellow City Hall building, cross the busy road. A block inland from the TI is Piazza della Riforma again. The first left off the square is...*

Via Nassa: This is one of Lugano's main shopping streets. For the next several blocks, just enjoy the wandering, window shopping, and people-watching along this gauntlet of boutiques and jewelry shops under typical Lombardi arcades. On the right, at #22, the Co-op department store has a good selection of chocolates (just inside the door on the left), a basement supermarket, and a handy top-floor cafeteria.

• *Follow Via Nassa until it dead-ends at the small but historic...*

Church of St. Mary of the Angels (Chiesa Santa Maria degli Angioli): This lakefront church, which dates from 1499, was part of a monastery (next door). Inside the church are the city's best frescoes.

The Passion and Crucifixion of Christ, the artistic highlight of all Ticino and the finest Renaissance fresco in Switzerland, is on the wall that separates the nave from the altar area. Milanese Bernardino Luini, who painted it in 1529, is sometimes called the "Raphael of the North" for the gentle expressions and calm beauty of his art. Follow the action as the scenes from Christ's passion are played out, from Jesus being crowned with thorns (left) to the doubting apostle Thomas touching Jesus' wound after his Resurrection (right). The central dominating theme is the Crucifixion. The work is full of symbolism. For instance, at the base of the cross, notice the skull and femur of Adam, as well as his rib (from which Eve was created). Worshippers saw this and remembered that without Adam and Eve's first sin, none of the terrible action in the rest of the fresco would have been necessary. Luini spent a decade working on this fresco, applying his paints day by day, a section at a time, over thin layers of wet plaster.

Facing the giant fresco, look to your left to find the three smaller frames. This is Luini's *Last Supper,* which was sliced off a wall of the monks' dining hall and put on canvas to be hung here.

Finally, wander up to the front of the church. The altar is rich and unusual with its wooden inlay work.

• *Along the lakefront across from the church begins the...*

Giardino Belvedere: This delightful little garden park is an

The Story of Lugano

Lugano's history is tied to its strategic position: where the Italian world is pressed up against the Alps, and just below the most convenient alpine passes. The Celts crossed the Alps here and left their mark. The ancient Romans were here, too—the oldest sacred building in Switzerland is an early Christian baptistery on Lake Lugano.

In 1220, when the first road over the Gotthard Pass was built, the Swiss took an interest in acquiring the Italian-speaking region of Ticino, leading to a three-century-long battle for control. Several castles in the nearby town of Bellinzona recall a pivotal Swiss victory in 1513. With this success, the Swiss gained a toehold south of the Alps. At first, Ticino was ruled from farther north, as a sort of colony. But in 1798, after French troops invaded Switzerland and proclaimed the Helvetic Republic, locals stood up to Napoleon by creating an independent Republic of Ticino. The Ticinese couldn't rule themselves peacefully, though, and five years later (in 1803) they joined the reestablished Swiss Federation as a regular canton, on the same footing as the rest of Switzerland.

In the 19th century, Lugano—Italian-speaking, just a short trip from Milan, yet safely over the border in Switzerland—provided a refuge and staging ground for intellectual Italian revolutionaries. They'd meet here to plan the Risorgimento, the struggle for Italian unification (c.1840-1869). Later in the 19th century, tourism arrived, and the grand lakefront hotels were built.

Today, Lugano is second among Swiss cities only to Zürich in its number of banks. It's easy for Italians and others with suitcases of hard cash—black money—to swing by and take advantage of the secret bank accounts. But the mentality here remains Italian. Rather than the Zürich model ("live to work"), the people of Lugano brag that they work to live.

open-air modern-art museum. The building facing it was once a monastery, then the Grand Hotel Palace. This first grand hotel on the lake was radical in that it actually faced the lake. From here, survey the scene. Paradiso, the big hotel zone with its 80-foot-high fountain, is a 15-minute walk along the lakeside. From there, the San Salvatore lift zips sightseers to the summit. The ridge across the lake marks the border of Italy.

• *Our walk is finished. The big and bold* **Lugano Art and Cultural Center** *(LAC, contemporary art exhibits, 20 CHF, Tue-Sun 10:00-18:00, closed Mon, www.luganolac.ch) faces the lake here. If you've got energy left, continue along the lakefront on the pleasant path to Paradiso; there you can summit San Salvatore, hop on a lake cruise, or do both.*

Sights near Lugano

MOUNTAIN LIFTS

Two handsome mountains (San Salvatore and Monte Brè) flank Lugano's city center, and you can conquer either one, sweat-free, by lifts. At about 3,000 feet, Lake Lugano's mountains are unimpressive compared with the mightier Alps farther north; if you've done some of the higher lifts in the Berner Oberland or Zermatt regions, nothing here will thrill you. Still, the commanding mountaintop views over the lake are enjoyable. Doing more than one is overkill. San Salvatore is best and relatively handy to Lugano town; Monte Brè works better with a Gandria visit. Monte Generoso is a higher mountain that's a little farther from town.

▲San Salvatore

The easiest and most rewarding peak on the lake, thanks to its fine panoramic views, San Salvatore (2,990 feet) rockets up from the Lugano suburb of Paradiso. You can reach it by funicular.

Cost and Hours: 30 CHF round-trip, half-price with Swiss Travel Pass, 2/hour—departs on the hour and the half-hour, 12-minute ride, transfer to another funicular midway up; daily mid-July-Aug 9:00-23:00; rest of year 9:00-18:00, Fri-Sat until 22:00, closed Nov-mid-March; these are last-ascent times—last descent generally 30 minutes later; tel. 091-985-2828, www.montesansalvatore.ch.

Getting There: To reach the base of the funicular, either walk along the water (about 20 minutes south of the city center; keep

your eye out for brown *funicolare* signs), or take bus #2 (direction: Paradiso, get off at Paradiso/Geretta stop, rather than staying on until the Funicolare San Salvatore stop).

At the Summit: You'll find good viewpoints, a playground, and a restaurant (reasonably priced if you buy the daily special with your funicular ticket—menu posted at valley station, food served 11:00-15:00, in high season also 19:00-23:00).

From the lift, be sure to climb five more minutes to the actual summit. On the way up, pop into the Salvatore Museum, with its small collection of religious art and exhibits on local geology (included in funicular ticket, closed Mon-Tue). At the top of the mountain, there's a small church surrounded by a view terrace. For the best panorama, climb to the rooftop of the church (entrance around the right side) for a sweeping, nearly 360-degree view. Unfortunately, the bay directly in front of Lugano is just about the only thing you can't see from up here.

▲Monte Brè

Departing from the other end of Lugano, in the suburb of Cassarate, this funicular takes you to arguably the best view down on Lugano itself (3,005 feet).

Cost and Hours: 25 CHF round-trip, 16 CHF one-way, discount with Ticino Ticket, half-price with Swiss Travel Pass, 2/hour—generally at :05 and :35 after the hour, 15-minute trip, transfer to another funicular partway up where you buy your tickets; lift runs daily June-Oct 9:05-19:05 plus July-Aug Fri-Sat until 23:05, off-season until 17:05, closed Jan-Feb; these are last-ascent times—last descent generally 30 minutes later, tel. 091-971-3171, www.montebre.ch.

Getting There: From Lugano's old town, you can take bus #2 (direction: Castagnola) to the Cassarate/Monte Brè stop. Getting off the bus, walk a little farther along the water, then follow brown *funicolare* signs uphill to the right. Don't dawdle—the automatic turnstile gate closes with little warning shortly before the funicular departs. You can also reach Cassarate via the lake boat from downtown Lugano.

At the Summit: You'll find two restaurants good for a drink or a snack up top, but Ristorante Vetta, farther down from the lift station, has better views and a nice shaded playground nearby (daily 10:00-19:00, until 23:00 Fri-Sat—reservations required, tel. 091-971-2045, www.vetta.ch).

Monte Generoso

The tallest mountain but farthest from Lugano, Monte Generoso (5,590 feet) is high enough that you can see some of the more distant cut-glass peaks. A cogwheel train climbs up from the station at Capolago (at the south end of Lake Lugano) in 40 minutes, leaving you at Generoso Vetta, a 10-minute walk below the summit.

Cost and Hours: 54 CHF round-trip, half-price with Swiss

Travel Pass, June-Sept roughly hourly 9:25-16:35, off-season until 15:35, few or no trains Nov-March, tel. 091-630-5111, www. montegeneroso.ch.

Getting There: From Lugano, take a regular train (15 minutes) to Capolago. You can also get there by boat, though it's slower and only runs once a day at 10:15.

CRUISING LAKE LUGANO WITH A STOP IN GANDRIA

Lake Lugano is made to order for a boat trip. The lake boats serve as regular public transport to a couple of car-free spots on the lake. You can either ride the boat around the lake or hop on and off the boat to explore. There's also a dizzying array of more elaborate excursions to choose from (such as a lunch trip, a grand tour, a shopping excursion into Italy, and an evening dinner cruise).

Boats and Schedules

The basic one-hour boat cruise does a loop from Lugano. It stops at a few desolate restaurants and hamlets along the far side of the lake, visits Gandria (a peaceful and picturesque little fishing town with several romantic view restaurants), then returns to Lugano (27.40 CHF round-trip including stopovers, 16.60 CHF for one segment, free with Swiss Travel Pass).

You can get off at any point, look around, and wait for a later boat; from Gandria, you can also return to Lugano by foot or bus (explained later). Note that if you're hopping on and off the boat, you'll actually cobble together the trip from various longer cruises, each with different itineraries. Some circle the lake clockwise, others counterclockwise, and not every boat makes every stop (the boat serves only those parts of the lake within Swiss borders). Pick up the boat schedule *(orario)* or find it online (www.lakelugano.ch, tel. 091-222-1111). Study it carefully to note when the next boat comes and exactly where it stops. The schedule can be confusing, so ask at the TI or one of the boat docks if you need planning help. If planning on spending all day on the water, consider the day pass (49 CHF, 20 percent discount with Ticino Ticket).

Stops on the Lake

If you want to get off the boat, consider one of the following stops.

LUGANO

On the Far Side of the Lake

The best place to break your journey is at the adjacent stops of **Cantine di Gandria** and **Museo Doganale,** which are a quick walk from each other (boats dock at just one of these stops, not both). Cantine di Gandria has two traditional trattorias and wine grottos—great for a rustic meal or just a snack and a drink (daily 11:30-21:00, closed Oct-April, Grotto Teresa: tel. 091-923-5895, Grotto Descanso: tel. 091-922-8071). A five-minute walk from Cantine di Gandria takes you to the bright orange **Museo Doganale,** right on the Italian border, with underwhelming exhibits on customs and smuggling (5 CHF, no English but worth a quick visit, daily 13:30-17:30, closed mid-Oct-March, tel. 079-512-9907, www. zollmuseum.ch).

Gandria

This town, on the Lugano side of the lake, is the most popular stop. A dense cluster of houses hangs over the lake with a few lazy, romantic hotels and several inviting restaurants. The only "streets" are stairways and cool, narrow passageways between the lake below and the road above. Either of the two restaurants by the boat dock will do for a meal or drink (**Ristorante Roccabella:** tel. 091-971-2722; and just up the stairs to the left, **Ristorante Antico:** tel. 091-971-4871). For something more memorable, it's worth seeking out **\$\$\$ Locanda Gandriese,** which has better food and a smaller, quieter terrace (pasta and polenta dishes, daily 11:30-10:00; a short walk farther into town past Ristorante Antico, just below the church; tel. 091-971-4181).

Reaching Gandria by Bus: You can also connect Gandria and downtown Lugano by minibus (#490, about hourly Mon-Fri, fewer on weekends, 4.60 CHF, timetables at www.lakelugano.ch). The bus stop in Lugano, called Al Forte, is across the street from Lugano Centro bus station, in front of Via Giovanni Nizzola 2. In Gandria, buses drop and pick up at the parking lot above the car-free village.

Returning to Lugano from Gandria: You can **walk** back to Lugano along a scenic, mostly lakeside path, through restored olive groves, with multilingual signposts telling you all about olive cultivation (follow signs for *Sentiero dell'Olivo*). The old olive press makes for a good starting point. From there, walk to the main upper road, take a left and climb the stairs to an overlook (signposted *9*). Then follow the well-signed path (1 hour). Along the way you'll pass the inviting **Lido San Domenico** (6 CHF)—a nice place for a swim and a snack. Eventually you'll stray from the lake and intersect with a parking lot. Take the stairs up, up, up past some private homes to the town of Castagnola, a suburb of Lugano. From the Castagnola post office, catch **bus #2, #11, or #12** back into Lugano. It's also possible to **walk** another 40 minutes back to town and the Monte Brè **funicular**—simply continue down busy Via Rivera. After crossing a bridge, you'll see brown signs pointing to the *funicolare* on the right.

You can also return from Gandria to Lugano via **boat** or the **minibus** described above. Note that the last boat and bus depart from Gandria around 18:05 (confirm locally). If you miss these, you'll have to walk or pay about 50 CHF for a **taxi.**

▲▲Half-Day Gandria and Monte Brè Plan

A pleasant way to spend half of your Lugano day is this fun, active circuit: Catch the boat to Gandria and have lunch. Then hike from there on the olive grove trail (*Sentiero dell'Olivo*, 1.5 hours) back to Lugano's Monte Brè funicular (described above). Ride the lift to Monte Brè, where you can enjoy the summit and an *aperitivo* at the terrace restaurant. Then, with the playground to your left and the lake to your right, follow the wooden fence into the shaded forest—within 20 minutes you'll reach the tiny village of Brè. Wander through the town and then ride bus #12 from the parking lot next to the church back to Lugano Centro (20 minutes).

CHOCOLATE EXCURSION
Alprose Chocolate Factory

A visit to this factory in Caslano, a small town near Lugano, makes a fun excursion. Alprose is one of Switzerland's smaller, less-well-known chocolate producers, but their factory is geared up for visitors and generous with free samples.

Cost and Hours: 5 CHF, daily 9:00-17:00, Via Rompada 36, Caslano, tel. 091-611-8856, www.alprose.ch.

Getting There: The S60 suburban train runs from Lugano to Caslano (Mon-Fri 4/hour, Sat-Sun 2/hour, 20 minutes, direction: Ponte Tresa, covered by rail passes). The train leaves from the cute yellow antique train station across the street from Lugano's main station (marked *Ferrovie Luganesi;* go down the stairs). Machines and windows sell tickets (13.20-CHF day pass covers your return). From Caslano station, cross the tracks and go one block downhill along Via Stazione, then turn right on Via Rompada (passing *Museo del Cioccolato* signs).

Visiting the Factory: The machines are in operation Monday to Friday from 9:00 to 14:00, but you're always allowed a look at the factory. An elevated, enclosed, air-conditioned walkway lets you watch as big dollops of chocolate are dropped into plastic molds, cooled and popped out onto a conveyor belt, wrapped (mechanically), and packed (manually) into boxes. Next to the factory is a modest museum. A 10-minute film describing the chocolate-making process runs continuously (ask for the English soundtrack). The shop sells fresh factory seconds for a reduced price.

Sleeping in Lugano

Demand for hotel rooms in Lugano is more even than in other Swiss destinations, but prices are generally at their highest between April and October. Hotels in the city center are easily reachable by a funicular from the train station to Piazza Cioccaro.

IN THE CITY CENTER

$$$$ Hotel International au Lac is a classic, elegant hotel with 74 rooms, old-school furnishings, some Lake Lugano views, and even a "museum" of relics from the hotel's Victorian past. It's conveniently and scenically located where pedestrian-only Via Nassa hits the lake. Four generations of Schmids have maintained the early-20th-century ambience since 1906, with old photos, inviting lounges, antique furniture, and, it seems, many of their original guests (family-friendly, air-con, elevator, cozy bar with fun view seats on balcony, swimming pool, pricey parking, closed Nov-March, Via Nassa 68, tel. 091-922-7541, www.hotel-international.ch, info@hotel-international.ch). From the station take the funicular down and walk (5 minutes), or take bus #4 (direction: Lugano Centro) four stops to Piazza Luini, right at the hotel's front door.

$$$ Hotel Pestalozzi Lugano, near the city park, is plain and vaguely institutional (it's run by a nonprofit foundation). It offers 54 fresh but somewhat sterile rooms—some with lake views. Though it's a bit farther from the train-station funicular, this hotel is a better value (family rooms, some rooms with lake view and/or air-con—ask when you reserve, elevator, tel. 091-921-4646, www.pestalozzi-lugano.ch, info@pestalozzi-lugano.ch). From the station, you can reach the hotel quickly by taking bus #2 (direction: Castagnola) four stops to Palazzo Congressi.

$$ Hotel San Carlo, also on the pedestrian-only shopping street, is conveniently close to the train-station funicular, but the

20 rooms are small and dated. It's a poor value for the price (thin walls, elevator, no air-con but fans, skimpy breakfast, Via Nassa 28, tel. 091-922-7107, www.hotelsancarlolugano.ch, sancarlo@ticino.com).

NEAR THE TRAIN STATION

$$$ Albergo Stella, a wonderful little oasis, offers 14 rooms between slick office buildings just behind the train station. Owners Daniel and Alexandra Hahne are caring, hands-on, and committed to giving guests a great experience. Enjoy the garden and the tiny swimming pool (RS%, some rooms have terraces, air-con, lots of stairs, Via Francesco Borromini 5, tel. 091-966-3370, www.albergostella.ch, info@albergostella.ch). From the station, find track 4 and walk to the end of the platform (keeping the station building on your right), turn left to cross the street by the big willowy tree, head uphill for a few yards, then turn left up Via Francesco Borromini.

$$ Hotel & Hostel Montarina, a creaky pink mansion in a palm garden overlooking the lake, has to be one of Europe's most appealing hostels, with 124 cheap dorm beds. It's a great hotel option as well, with 24 private rooms; half of these are antique rooms with classic furniture and shared bathrooms, and the other half are modern "comfort" rooms, with private bathrooms and air-conditioning. Surrounded by lush tropical gardens and an extremely inviting swimming pool, and with a helpful staff, this place is well worth considering, even for those who usually don't stay in hostels (breakfast buffet extra, reception open 7:30-23:00, late-night train noise, lockers, small kitchen, pay laundry, free parking, closed Dec-Jan, Via Montarina 1, tel. 091-966-7272, www.montarina.ch, info@montarina.ch). At the train station, head to track 4, then walk along the platform with the station and lake on your left, and go through the parking lot toward the *Continental Parkhotel* sign. Just before the sign and a stone wall, take the sharp uphill turn to the right; halfway up the hill, go left through the gate marked *#1*.

Eating in Lugano

My recommended restaurants are all in the old town. You'll pay a premium to dine on Piazza della Riforma, but it can be worth the expense. Lugano is not the best place for lakeside dining—instead, cross the lake to the remote little grotto restaurants, or visit the town of Gandria (both options described earlier, under "Cruising Lake Lugano"). Good news for the wine-curious: You'll pay the same per liter for the little one-deciliter (about 3.5 oz) glasses as you do for the big half-liter (about 17 oz) carafes—so go with the small glasses and try several different wines. Experiment. The Ticino merlot is great. This is the only corner of Switzerland that embraces the Italian *aperitivo* ritual—so keep an eye out for places with that happy-hour tradition of offering a small plate of meats and cheeses with your drink in the early evening.

IN THE OLD TOWN

$$ La Tinera, beloved by locals, serves affordable, traditional Ticinese cuisine with seasonal and nightly specials (such as *bollito misto,* a beef stew offered every Tuesday). It's tucked away in an old wine cellar, with heavy wooden furniture and decorated with wine bottles and antique copper cookware (air-con, Mon-Sat 11:30-15:00 & 18:30-23:00, closed Sun, Via dei Gorini 2, just a block behind Piazza della Riforma, tel. 091-923-5219).

$$$ Bottegone del Vino is a quality wine bar with indoor and outdoor ambience and a small but enticing menu (just a few top-end dishes). Sitting here, you feel in the know—but order carefully, as prices really add up (Mon-Sat 11:30-24:00, closed Sun, a block off Piazza della Riforma at Via Magatti 3, tel. 091-922-7689).

$$$ La Cucina di Alice is a rare find with personality and lakeside dining. They take food seriously and it shows in their professionalism, seasonal menu, and creative presentation (daily 12:00-22:00, Riva Vela 4, tel. 091-922-0103).

Around Piazza della Riforma: Various restaurants offer decent but pricey food and great people-watching from outdoor tables on Lugano's main piazza. The ambience here is delightful at twilight. At **$$$ Pizzeria Tango,** a helpful waitstaff serves Italian cuisine with a Ticino influence. While many of its tables face the busy main piazza, its interior and the tables facing a

quiet little square in the back are also inviting (daily 11:00-23:00, Piazza della Riforma, tel. 091-922-2701).

Facing the Lake: $$ Il Fermento Pub was named Switzerland's bar of the year in 2017 and when you immerse yourself in its fun and welcoming ambience you'll understand why. It's rock n' roll rather than hip-hop, the staff enjoy their work, and the seven

Ticino craft beers on tap are great. Peanuts in the shell are free and if you're here for a meal it's *Flammkuchen* (German-style pizzas, both savory and sweet) and salads (daily 12:00-24:00, ask for a quieter table outside, facing the lake at Via Marconi 91, tel. 091-923-4545).

CHEAP EATS

Self-Service Cafeterias: Part of a chain, **$$ Manora** offers affordable, healthy food—a salad bar, pasta bar, main-dish counter where meat or fish is cooked in front of you, and lots more. Sit inside or outside on the covered terrace (with a playground). As it has its own entrance (on Salita Chiattone, up the stairs 100 yards from the bottom of the train-station funicular), it stays open later than the Manoras in other Swiss cities. During business hours, you can also enter via the bridge from the third floor of the Manor department store (daily until 22:00, last orders at 21:00, Piazza Dante 2).

The **Co-op's fourth-floor cafeteria,** midway along the Via Nassa pedestrian mall, has a pretty rooftop terrace, but is otherwise a poor second to Manora, with a smaller selection and shorter hours (Mon-Sat 11:00-15:00, closed Sun, Via Nassa 22).

Supermarkets: Try the midrange **Co-op** on Via Nassa, or the more upscale **Manor** off Piazza Dante. Both share the same hours (Mon-Sat 8:15-19:00, Thu until 21:00, closed Sun) and are in the basements of their similarly named department stores. On Sunday, your only option is the small **Piccobello** at the train station (daily 6:00-22:00).

Lugano Connections

The opening of the world's longest railway tunnel—the over 35-mile-long **Gotthard Base Tunnel**—has shortened travel times between Lugano and Zürich, Luzern, and the rest of northern Switzerland.

If you're not in a hurry, though, knit Lugano into your Swiss itinerary with **scenic trains**—take the 5.5-hour **Gotthard Panorama Express** train-and-boat combination to Luzern, or the **Bernina Express** bus-and-train combination to eastern Switzerland. More details about these trips are in the Scenic Rail Journeys chapter. Train info: Toll tel. 0900-300-300, www.rail.ch.

Long-distance **buses** leave Lugano from various points around the train station. The Bernina Express and St. Moritz buses leave from the restaurant end of the station building (away from the lake), while airport buses leave from narrow streetside parking spaces at the end of track 4 (also going away from the lake). Allow extra time when departing, as you might need to ask for help, and bus stop locations may change due to construction work.

From Lugano by Train to: Luzern (2/hour, 2 hours), **Zürich** (1-2/hour, 2.5 hours), **Interlaken Ost** (1-2/hour, 5 hours, 2 changes, more with additional transfers), **Bern** (1-2/hour, 3.5 hours, 1-3 transfers), **Milan** (at least hourly, 2 hours).

From Lugano by Bus and Train to the Upper Engadine: The **Bernina Express** bus (#731) leaves from outside Lugano's train station at 10:00 (daily April-late Oct only), connecting in Tirano with trains heading over the scenic Bernina Pass to Pontresina, Samedan, St. Moritz, and Chur (reservations required, tel. 081-288-6565, www.berninaexpress.ch; see the Scenic Rail Journeys chapter). A less scenic but quicker option with no changes is the **Palm Express** bus to St. Moritz (#631), which leaves Lugano's train station at 15:31 daily in peak season (mid-June-mid-Oct, 4 hours to St. Moritz; reservations required, tel. 058-341-3492, www.postauto.ch, use webcode 10037 to reserve; bus from St. Moritz to Lugano runs Fri-Sun in off-season). You can always reach St. Moritz from Lugano via **regular train** to Bellinzona, then bus to Thusis, then train to St. Moritz (almost hourly, 4 hours total).

From Lugano by Bus to Italy's Lake Como: An Italian-run local bus (#C12) goes from Lugano to Menaggio on Lake Como (nearly hourly, fewer on Sun, 1 hour, www.asfautolinee.it). From Menaggio, you can take a ferry across the lake to Varenna. This bus leaves Lugano from Stazione Nord near the train station and, less frequently, from a stop on Via Campo Marzio, by the corner of Via Pietro Capelli. This is near the Lido stop of bus #2, in the Cassarate neighborhood a little east of downtown. Tickets are sold at the Lucini Store a few minutes' walk from the park (at Viale Carlo Cattaneo 21) or by the driver for a surcharge.

From Lugano to Milan's Airports: The closest major airports to Lugano are actually in Italy, near Milan: Malpensa Airport and Linate Airport (www.sea-aeroportimilano.it). The handiest way to reach Malpensa is to use the direct buses that leave from Lugano's train station—there are three competing operators, with stops right next to each other at the far end of track 4 (www.malpensaexpress.ch, www.jetbus.ch, and www.luganoservices.ch, about hourly, 80 minutes, 25 CHF, smart to reserve ahead). Alternatively, you can take the one-hour train to Milan's Central Station, from where a train (Malpensa Express) and/or shuttle buses leave frequently for Malpensa and Linate.

UPPER ENGADINE

Pontresina • Samedan • St. Moritz

Pontresina, Samedan, and St. Moritz are a trio of towns that anchor the Upper Engadine region, tucked away in an intriguing and picturesque fringe of Switzerland. Here you can ride a vintage funicular to a scenic hike along a mountain ridge, explore the unique townscapes of an exotically remote mountain valley, gaze on a local virtuoso's paintings that capture the region's grandeur, and hear enticing snippets of the obscure Romansh language.

Nestled in the southeast corner of the country, the time-passed Upper Engadine (Engiadin Ota in Romansh, Oberengadin in German) is arguably less thrilling—and certainly more difficult to reach—than the mountain resorts of the Berner Oberland and Zermatt. But this region, wedged in the Alps between Italy and Austria, offers rough-around-the-edges mountain culture that feels far from Germanic influence, and closer to the Latin roots that run deep beneath this part of Switzerland. It's also a more rugged landscape—less groomed by humanity, with more wildlife than you'll see elsewhere in Switzerland (the area is home to the largest colony of ibex in the Alps). And for train travelers riding the scenic Bernina Express or Glacier Express, or drivers keen to experience the country's most exciting roads, this area is an easy stopover.

Celtic people inhabited this region centuries before Christ, and the hillsides are still terraced, recalling the hard work that came with farming up here in ancient times. Like French and Spanish, Romansh evolved from the Latin that arrived with Roman soldiers and settlers, who moved here as Rome expanded. Town names date back to various invaders. For instance, "Pontresina" comes from "Bridge of the Saracens."

Two valleys meet here, carving out a picturesque region dominated by three very different towns that form a convenient little triangle, each about 10 minutes apart by train or bus. The most famous is the ritzy ski resort of St. Moritz, where even summertime prices are unreasonably high (and the town's charm disappointingly low). Pontresina is a lower-key resort town with more than a few vestiges of its high-society past. Its relatively reasonable prices and proximity to my favorite hike make it an ideal base for the region. And humble Samedan, with its cobbled lanes and cluster of lovingly painted facades, hoards most of the village charm (though there's little to do). If you can ignore the jet set comparing tans in St. Moritz, the Upper Engadine feels like a place where normal Swiss people go to find some high-altitude fun.

PLANNING YOUR TIME

Compared with the other high-mountain areas I recommend in this book (especially the Lauterbrunnen Valley and Zermatt), the Upper Engadine is pretty ho-hum. But *getting here* is anything but: Whether by a scenic rail journey or over some of Europe's most otherworldly mountain-pass roads, the trip alone—though time-consuming—makes a visit here worthwhile. And the free transit pass for overnight guests makes it worth staying two to three nights (see the "Engadin Card" sidebar, later). The chance to experience Switzerland's overlooked Romansh corner is a cultural bonus.

Conveniently, you can use the Upper Engadine to link two scenic rail trips: the Bernina Express and the Glacier Express (see the Scenic Rail Journeys chapter). And drivers should note that the valley lies right at the end of the stunning Julier Pass, a high-alpine wonderland of waterfalls and green ridges (take routes via Tiefencastel).

If staying two nights, with one full (good-weather) day, I'd do the Muottas Muragl panoramic hike to Alp Languard (above Pontresina) in the morning, head over to St. Moritz for a joyride up to Piz Nair, stroll Samedan in late afternoon, and, if it's still nice out, maybe head back up to Muottas Muragl to watch the sunset. (If the weather's bad, hit the Bellavita spa in Pontresina.) With two full days, you could do the Muottas Muragl hike one day, and hike around on Piz Nair the next (or take the Morteratsch glacier trail near Pontresina if it's cloudy), leaving you time to visit the Segantini Museum in St. Moritz before taking a leisurely wander around Samedan.

Like other mountain resort areas, this region has two distinct tourist seasons: summer (June-mid-Oct) and winter (Dec-March). Outside of these seasons, many places are closed and the area can feel dead.

GETTING AROUND THE UPPER ENGADINE

Pontresina, Samedan, St. Moritz, and Punt Muragl (the base of the funicular to Muottas Muragl) are all less than 10 minutes apart and well-connected by **bus** (about 2/hour, 5.60 CHF per trip, 11.20 CHF for 24-hour ticket). You can also take the **train** between towns (runs about hourly, same price), but the much more frequent buses take you up into each village center and save you the walk up from the train station down below. Bus rides within a town (such as between St. Moritz Bad and St. Moritz Dorf) cost 3 CHF. All local transport is covered by the Engadin Card and Swiss Travel Pass.

Pick up the bus schedule *(Fahrplan/Urari)* at a TI, and study your options with the help of the map. Pay attention to which stop to use. For example, Pontresina Bahnhof is at the bottom of town, while Pontresina Post is near my recommended hotels. St. Moritz's most useful stops are Schulhausplatz (town center, near the Piz

Allegra (Welcome) to Graubünden

Pontresina, Samedan, St. Moritz, and the rest of the Upper Engadine belong to Switzerland's biggest canton, Graubünden. Isolated by high mountain ranges, this canton is also one of the country's most conservative. The name Graubünden goes back to 1395, when a group of farmers wearing gray clothes organized themselves in the "Gray League" to fight for their autonomy. This fiercely independent region didn't join the Swiss Confederation until 1803.

People in Graubünden believe the best way to control nature is to obey it. Passionate about their environment, they purify all dirty water before returning it to the rivers. Engineers are currently going through the expensive process of removing canals (built to direct streams and rivers) and once again allowing the water to choose its own course. The natives love their beautiful countryside and cherish their customs—consistently voting against EU membership, immigration, and other issues that might compromise Swiss neutrality and self-determination. Many urban Swiss see this conservatism as narrow-minded and harmful to the country's economy, and support a more open, European Switzerland.

Graubünden cuisine is hearty. Try *Pizokel*, a *Spätzle*-like creation of cheesy flour dumplings. In fall you might find *Pizokel* made from chestnut flour and served with wild mushroom stew. Graubünden's air-dried beef, *Bündnerfleisch*—very expensive and sliced paper-thin—is popular throughout Switzerland. *Capuns* are cabbage leaves stuffed with a mix of dough, leeks, bacon, onion, and air-dried beef. *Bündner Gerstensuppe* is a creamy barley-and-vegetable soup. For a Graubünden dessert, it's got to be *Nusstorte*, a rich walnut cake.

Graubünden has three official languages: German, Italian, and Romansh (a descendant of Latin with its own independent history). You'll overhear conversations where one person speaks Italian, the other replies in German, a third butts in with Romansh...and everybody understands each other. On trains and buses, the announcements are in German and Romansh (which sounds a bit like Italian).

Most tourists here speak German (others Italian, others English), but if you'd like to please your Romansh hosts, try these phrases:

English	Romansh
Welcome.	*Allegra* (ah-LEY-grah)
Hello (Good day).	*Bun di.* (boon dee)
Good evening (after 17:00).	*Buna saira.* (BOO-nah SIGH-rah)
Please.	*Per plaschair.* (pehr plah-ZHAIR)
Thank you very much.	*Grazcha fich.* (GRAHTS-chah feech)
Goodbye.	*Arevair.* (ah-reh-VAIR)

Nair funicular station) and Bahnhof (train station). In Samedan, the Chesa Planta stop is more central than the Bahnhof. If you're going, say, from St. Moritz to Samedan, save time by making sure you're not on a bus that travels via Pontresina. Bus info: Tel. 081-837-9595, www.engadinbus.ch.

Considering the cost of parking, and the frequency of buses and trains, it makes little sense to drive between towns, especially with the Engadin Card.

HELPFUL HINTS

Altitude Alert: Even the valley floor here is at a high elevation (more than 6,000 feet), and you might feel dizzy and tired, especially on your first day. Top athletes from all over the world come here for altitude training before the Olympics.

Hiking Tips: Hikers should bring appropriate gear, including solid shoes, sun protection, windbreaker, hat, and water (for more hiking tips, see the sidebar on page 238). Even in summer, chill winds blow down from the snow-capped mountains, and it can get cold—especially on chairlifts. Here, and across the region, trails are marked according to their difficulty. Yellow signs indicate easy hikes and walks. White-and-red signs signal more demanding hikes, where real hiking boots are in order. Blue signs are for alpine routes that require serious gear (these trails can be treacherous and include rock climbing and glacier crossings).

Keep in mind that in the Alps, some flowers are protected; pick one, and you may be fined. Some meadows are also protected for haymaking. Signs ask you to stick to the trails, as trampled grass is hard to cut.

Winter Activities: If you want to ski some of the most famous slopes in the world, head for Corviglia, the largest ski area in the region. It offers varied terrain, mostly intermediate runs, and good snowboarding (convenient from St. Moritz, or a bus ride from Pontresina). Other areas to consider are Corvatsch-Furtschellas (great views) and Diavolezza-Lagalb (smaller, less crowded, great for nonskiers who want views). Both cater mainly to intermediate and expert skiers. See www.engadin.ch/en/bergbahnen for more information and to buy lift tickets in advance. The area also has more than 100 miles of cross-country skiing trails, great sledding, Nordic walking, and spectator sports such as polo in the snow (horses and all). Ask at any TI for information; for more tips, see the Switzerland in Winter chapter.

Essential Brochures: Any TI can give you the local bus schedule (*Fahrplan/Urari*); their *Information for Visitors* guide includes a panoramic foldout map showing the lifts and hiking trails.

Pontresina

A popular winter and summer mountain resort with about 2,000 residents, Pontresina ("Puntraschinga" in Romansh) makes a good Upper Engadine home base. At 6,000 feet above sea level on a wind-protected terrace overlooking the Bernina Valley, Pontresina faces southwest and enjoys plenty of sunshine. Popular trails through its larch forests offer spectacular views of the 13,000-foot Piz Bernina peak and the immense Morteratsch glacier.

Pontresina's first tourists, mostly German and British, arrived in the 1850s. For a while, it was a summer-only destination. But by the early 1900s, the Muottas Muragl railway was inaugurated, the first grand hotels were built, and tourists began showing up in winter, too. Although a bit sterile and resorty—with not quite enough local charm or character—Pontresina offers more activities and services than Samedan, without being as glitzy as St. Moritz. This makes Pontresina the best compromise home base in this region.

Orientation to Pontresina

Pontresina sits on a ledge overlooking the confluence of two mountain streams, which then flow together across the valley to join the Inn River. Virtually everything of interest is along Via Maistra (may-strah)—Romansh for "Main Street." My recommended hotels are at the top end of Via Maistra, and the TI is near the bottom end. The train station sits in the valley floor a 10-minute walk below.

Tourist Information: The TI is in the heart of town in the slick Rondo Culture and Congress Center, right on Via Maistra. The staff is happy to suggest hikes and mountain lifts (Mon-Sat 8:30-18:00, Sun 16:00-18:00; shorter hours and closed Sun in off-season, tel. 081-838-8300, www.pontresina.ch).

Engadin Card

Many tourist regions offer guest cards that grant discounts to overnighting tourists, but the Upper Engadine offers summer visitors something better: a guest card that covers all transportation in the region, including the pricey mountain lifts. In the rest of Switzerland, you have to factor in the price of a lift ticket when planning alpine excursions, even with a Swiss Travel Pass. Here, with an Engadin Card (Engadin is the German spelling), you can ride lifts to your heart's content, and it's free.

The pass is free (with a 10-CHF deposit) for anyone who stays at least two nights in a participating hotel in summer (May-Oct). The most common version is the "mountain railways inclusive" card, which covers local public trains and buses, mountain lifts, and even some guided hikes (see www.engadin.ch; select "Mountain Railways Included"). Most hotels in the region offer the pass, including those I recommend in Pontresina. However, not all hotels offer the pass, and some offer different versions of the card: Before you book, it's worth asking whether the pass is included, and which version you'll get. Versions include a card that covers just local transit, but not lifts (which is essentially useless); the "mountain railways all-inclusive" card (which lets you take a bike on board at no extra cost); and a card that covers all the mountain lifts, but not public transit between towns (not a big deal since local transit is pretty reasonable).

ARRIVAL IN PONTRESINA

The train station lies at the foot of the town, and has lockers and a ticket office. You can walk about 10 minutes steeply uphill to the town center, following the white signs to *Pontresina*. Or take bus #1 or #2 to Pontresina Post, near my recommended hotels (2-3/hour, buy ticket at counter inside train station or on bus, free with Swiss Travel Pass). To get straight to the TI, get off at Pontresina Rondo or Pontresina Punt Ota Sur. Walking the 10 minutes from Pontresina back down Via da Mulin to the train station offers dramatic gorge views.

All my recommended hotels (except the hostel) offer free or discounted parking, but drivers who aren't spending the night should head for one of the hourly pay garages, either near the uphill end of Via da Mulin or near the TI.

HELPFUL HINTS

Music: Free summer classical music concerts are offered in the Tais Forest across the river, and (on rainy days) in the Rondo Cen-

Pontresina

200 Meters
200 Yards

To Muottas Muragl
Viewpoint &

To Samedan
& St. Moritz

Bernina River

To Alp Languard,
& Trail to Muottas Muragl

ALP LANGUARD CHAIRLIFT

ST. MARY

BELLAVITA POOL & SPA

VIA CRUSCHEDA

ALPINE MUSEUM

SPANIOLA TOWER

PONTRESINA TRAIN STATION

VIA DA LA STAZIUN

VIA DA MULIN

VIA DA BERNINA

Tais Forest

POST

GIARSUN

To Bernina Pass

Roseg River

CONCERTS

SUROVAS TRAIN STATION

To Roseg Valley

VIA MAISTRA

UPPER ENGADINE

Accommodations
1. To Romantik Hotel Muottas Muragl
2. Hotel Bernina
3. Chesa Mulin Hotel
4. Hotel Engadinerhof & Ristorante Nostra Pizzeria
5. Pontresina Youth Hostel & Bike Rental

Eateries & Other
6. Colani Stübli
7. Grond Café
8. La Trattoria Restaurant
9. Kronenstübli
10. To Bock auf Alp Languard
11. Grocery
12. Rominger Möbel Furniture Shop
13. Ski Rental
14. Bike Rental

ter or in the church next door (daily at 11:00, mid-June–mid-Sept, confirm and get details at TI).

Ski Rental: Try **Gruber Sport** (at Via Maistra 190, across from Hotel Schweizerhof, tel. 081-842-6236, www.gruber-sport.ch).

Shopping: Furniture and housewares store **Rominger Möbel** has an upstairs showroom that's like a modern Engadine home show: Walking among hand-carved beds, tables, and dressers—all made from the fragrant Swiss pine unique to this region—gives you a sense of good living high in this remote corner of Switzerland. You can find good souvenirs here (Mon-Fri 8:30-12:00 & 14:00-18:00, Sat until 17:00, closed Sun, Via Maistra 246, at the top end of town 5 minutes past Pontresina Post bus stop, tel. 081-842-6263, www.rominger.ch).

Sights and Activities in Pontresina

CHURCHES AND MUSEUMS
Church of St. Mary (Begräbniskirche Sta. Maria)
Above town, just beyond the five-sided, 13th-century Spaniola Tower, stands this remarkable little church. Inside, the wooden ceiling is entirely original. Faded 13th-century, Byzantine-inspired frescoes survive on the west wall (to the left as you enter). The other walls and ceiling were richly decorated by an Italian workshop (1497). The frescoes depict the legend of Mary Magdalene and (above) the story of Lazarus' resurrection. Imagine this church five centuries ago, packed with illiterate villagers who worshiped by following along with the pictures.

Cost and Hours: Free entry, but limited hours: generally opens Mon, Wed, and Fri at 14:30 or 15:30 and closes at 16:00 or 17:30; also open Tue and Thu in summer; closed altogether in off-season. For more information, contact the Pontresina TI.

Hiking Back to Town: For a quick (10-minute) hike, walk down from the church a different way: Follow the yellow sign for *Las Blais*, which takes you under the chairlift. Signs along the way share interesting facts on ibex, which you may see from here if you look up the hillside. Eventually, head down to the left following the *Puntraschigna-Laret* sign; you'll come back into town near the TI.

Alpine Museum (Museum Alpin)
This little museum is worth a quick visit—it was founded by the local mountain guides' association. The exhibits fill three floors of an old Engadine town house, covering the development of alpine mountain climbing and skiing, the regional mining industry (with plenty of mineral samples), hunting, local animals, and replicas of traditional rooms (bedroom, kitchen, living room). About 130 of the 250 bird species found in the Upper Engadine are shown here. Listen to the recorded songs of 60 different birds on the primitive aviary jukebox. Find the slideshow room, where you can choose from four themes (mountains, flowers, butterflies, and a changing theme)—the mountain slides will make you feel like a wimp. Rounding out the space are temporary exhibits. Be sure to pick up the brief English descriptions when you enter.

Cost and Hours: 8 CHF, covered by Swiss Travel Pass, Mon-

Sat 15:30-18:00, closed Sun and in off-season, Via Maistra 199, tel. 081-842-7273, www.pontresina.ch/museumalpin.

LIFTS AND HIKES

Pontresina is a hiker's paradise. The town boasts one of Switzerland's largest mountaineering schools and has a good reputation for adventure sports. Shops lining Via Maistra rent and sell all kinds of sports gear. The TI will help you find the right hike. Their great, free foldout *Panorama* map is marked with hiking trails and lists details about each one. They also hand out a leaflet describing a few popular routes. (Most hikers agree that the Muottas Muragl-Alp Languard panoramic route is tops.) For a fee, you can hire an English-speaking mountaineer through the TI.

▲▲Muottas Muragl Viewpoint (8,105 feet)

This impressive alpine perch isn't as high as other spots mentioned in this chapter (Piz Nair, Diavolezza), but it's my favorite for its spectacular views over Pontresina and Samedan, and far away to the valleys and lakes beyond St. Moritz. To reach the viewpoint, ride the cute 1907 funicular from the Punt Muragl valley station. At the top of the funicular, you can rent a deck chair, have a meal, do an easygoing loop hike, or start a hike over to Alp Languard (described later). And since the funicular runs till late in the evening, it's the perfect place to watch the sunset. A pricey-but-good restaurant on the terrace is open late daily.

Getting There: Catch the funicular from the **Punt Muragl** valley station (25 CHF one-way, 35 CHF round-trip, 15 CHF after 18:00, covered by Engadin Card; runs early June-mid-Oct 2/hour 8:00-23:00—round-trip ticket lets you return on this funicular or on the Alp Languard lift described later; also runs late Dec-March; same contact info as recommended Romantik Hotel Muottas Muragl: tel. 081-842-8232, www.muottasmuragl.ch).

To reach the valley station from Pontresina, take bus #1 (in either direction—the bus stops at Punt Muragl both on the way into and out of town) or #2 (direction: Maloja). You can also catch the train between Pontresina and Samedan and get off at Punt Muragl (by request only—press the green button, or the train won't stop). You can park here for free—but if you're hiking to Alp Languard, it makes more sense to take the train or bus, as the hike ends back at Pontresina.

▲▲▲Muottas Muragl Panoramic Hike

This fantastic hike over to Alp Languard, directly above Pontresina, comes with grand views the entire way and a gradual descent of about 400 feet. Midway, there's a great soup or coffee-and-cakes stop (ask for the WC key for a fun alpine memory). Keep your eyes open for ibex, bighorn stags, and marmots.

It's about four hours round-trip from Pontresina, including three hours of easy to moderately strenuous hiking. Leave Pontresina by 13:30 if you want to catch the chairlift down from Alp Languard. For extra credit, consider the more challenging upper route (the "Climate Trail") that climbs the mountainside above the main route

via the Chamanna Segantini hut (adds about an hour to the hike).

▲▲Alp Languard Viewpoint (7,710 feet)

At Alp Languard, hovering right over the center of Pontresina, you can head out on a loop hike, bask in a lounge chair, unwind after your hike from Muottas Muragl, let the kids loose in the play area, and enjoy an affordable lunch with unbeatable views at the **$$ Bock auf Alp Languard** chalet (early June-mid-Oct daily 9:00-17:00, tel. 079-719-7810).

Getting There (and Back): A six-minute chairlift runs continuously between Alp Languard and a station a few minutes uphill from central Pontresina (early June-late Oct 8:30-17:30, 16.50 CHF one-way, 24 CHF round-trip—or, if coming from Muottas Muragl, use the return part of the round-trip ticket you bought there, covered by Engadin Card, tel. 081-842-6255). Don't worry if you arrive here after the lift's stopped running: It's only a 45-minute hike back into town. Where the path splits, take the left fork (the "Röntgenweg") for an easier descent on a zigzag path through the trees.

Morteratsch Glacier Walk

A popular, inexpensive excursion from Pontresina is by train to Morteratsch, partway up the Bernina Pass. From Morteratsch, an easy trail leads up-valley for 50 minutes to the tongue of the Morteratsch glacier, with signposts marking the glacier's reach in past decades. It's also a pleasant walk on a cloudy day. The whole round-trip from Pontresina is about two hours by train.

Following the glacial stream gently uphill, you first pass a field of dramatically lumpy glacier-hewn rocks. Farther along, you get the sense you're hiking on the bottom of a drained swimming pool—it's amazing (and alarming) to see, high up on the hillsides, the obvious former extent of the glacier (it hit the upper line in 1850). At the top of the trail, you're eye-to-eye with the snout of the glacier. Keep in mind that much of what looks like rock here is actually dirty ice. To extend the hike, you can scramble over the rock field past the end of the official path for a more up-close look, but be careful—the ground is very unstable beyond the groomed path.

Back at the trailhead, you can eat at the restaurant near the train stop, and also visit a traditional cheesemaker (also near train stop, mid-June-early Oct only, tel. 081-842-6273, www.alp-schaukaeserei.ch).

Getting There: The train drops you off right at the foot of the trail (hourly, 8 minutes from Pontresina, 5.60 CHF without Engadin Card). From the highway, drivers should follow signs for Morteratsch to the large parking lot at the end of the road (pay at machine). Walk from the lot toward the white Morteratsch Hotel, and then past it (with the hotel on the right) to the trailhead.

Diavolezza Peak (9,930 feet)

The 15-minute cable-car ride up to the peak called Diavolezza—the "she-devil"—takes you over an otherworldly green landscape of babbling brooks, then past stark rock and ice to a ridgetop station. There you'll find a restaurant and terrace with expansive views of the top of the Morteratsch glacier. To turn this into a hiking excursion, return to the valley on foot (2 hours on a moderately difficult trail via Lake Diavolezza, or 3.5 hours on an easier trail past Lake Collinas).

Getting There: To reach the lift station from Pontresina, either take the train 10 minutes beyond Morteratsch to the Bernina Diavolezza stop or drive 12 minutes toward the Bernina Pass (free parking). The cable car is covered by the Engadin Card (otherwise 26 CHF one-way, 36 CHF round-trip, 3/hour, daily 8:30-17:00, tel. 081-838-7373, www.diavolezza.ch).

Roseg Valley Stroll

You can hike two easy hours up the Roseg Valley, directly opposite Pontresina (look for the trailhead behind the Pontresina train station) and marvel at its glacier (from a distance). Consider taking the fun **horse-drawn omnibus** back to Pontresina—or take the omnibus up and hike back (reservations required, June-Oct departures at fixed hours, 20 CHF one-way, 32 CHF round-trip, mobile 078-944-7555, www.engadin-kutschen.ch). You can also rent a private carriage (120 CHF one-way for up to 4 people, 220 CHF round-trip includes 1.5 hours for exploring; several coachmen offer this—try the Costa family, tel. 081-842-6057, www.stalla-engiadina.ch, office@stalla-engiadina.ch).

OTHER ACTIVITIES

▲Bellavita Pool and Spa

This delightful pool complex is an ideal place to relax in any weather. The fun indoor-outdoor swimming-pool complex includes an enclosed, 250-foot-long spiral waterslide, an outdoor pool that stays at 93 degrees Fahrenheit year-round, and an indoor water playground for kids. There's also a spa (nudity required) with a series of saunas, steam baths, and more. (The spa is usually mixed-gender and adults-only, but it's women-only Mon 13:00-17:00 and Thu after 17:00; kids ages 6-15 allowed with parents Sat-Sun 12:00-16:00.)

Cost and Hours: Pool only—11 CHF, pool and spa—26.50 CHF; pool open Mon-Fri 10:00-22:00, Sat-Sun until 21:00, spa open similar hours; in the middle of town at Via Maistra 178, tel. 081-837-0037, www.pontresina-bellavita.ch. You can rent a swimsuit for a few francs, or buy one in the shop.

Biking

Several sports stores rent bicycles, easy-to-use electric-powered bikes, in-line skates, tennis rackets, and other gear. Riding the train to the Bernina Pass and biking nine miles back into town is just one of many fun biking options. In the town center, **Fähndrich Sport** rents good mountain bikes (25-38 CHF/half-day, 35-50 CHF/day, the higher price is for a full suspension) and electric bikes (39 CHF/half-day, 54 CHF/day; includes helmets, cheaper for multiple days; Mon-Fri 8:00-12:00 & 14:00-18:30, Sat until 17:00, closed Sun except July-Aug and Dec-March, closed most of May; Via Maistra 169, tel. 081-842-7155, www.faehndrich-sport. ch). Across the street from the train station, in the lower level of the big youth hostel building, **Bikezentrum Pontresina** rents a huge selection of bikes (mountain bikes-31 CHF/half-day, 43 CHF/day; electric bikes-39 CHF/half-day, 54 CHF/day; includes helmets; daily 8:30-12:00 & 13:30-18:00, closed Oct-mid-June; tel. 081-838-8388, www.pontresina-sports.ch).

Sleeping in Pontresina

The Romantik Hotel Muottas Muragl is perched on an alpine ledge above (and just barely outside) town—see listing for directions. The other hotels listed here are within steps of Pontresina Post, the town's most convenient bus stop. All of these hotels, including the hostel, offer the Engadin Card free to guests staying at least two nights (see the "Engadin Card" sidebar, earlier in the chapter).

$$$ Romantik Hotel Muottas Muragl offers a secluded overnight high in the Alps, with 16 elegant-rustic rooms furnished in the local Swiss pinewood. When the funicular takes the last tourist down, things become as peaceful as the Alps can be (cheaper for 3 or more nights, price includes funicular ticket, open mid-June-mid-Oct and mid-Dec-March only, free parking at base of funicular, tel. 081-842-8232, www.muottasmuragl.ch, info@ muottasmuragl.ch).

$$$ **Hotel Bernina,** a well-run and woody three-star place, picks up guests at the Pontresina station for free (let them know what time you'll arrive). Its 41 tidy, attractive rooms can be a fine value for this area, and come with nice touches (sauna, good restaurant serving Engadine specialties, Via Maistra 207, tel. 081-838-8686, www.hotelbernina.ch, info@hotelbernina.ch).

$$ **Chesa Mulin Hotel,** below the main street, offers 30 modern, bright, and comfortable rooms, most with nature-based themes. The inviting sitting area with open fireplace and library makes bad weather tolerable. The friendly Isepponi-Schmid family takes good care of their guests (discounts sometimes available in shoulder season for guests over age 60, elevator, sauna, sundeck, free access to Bellavita pool and spa with 2-night stay, limited free parking, Via da Mulin 15, tel. 081-838-8200, www.chesa-mulin.ch, info@chesa-mulin.ch).

$$ **Hotel Engadinerhof,** while less cozy, can be a good value. The hotel preserves a pre-WWII ambience, and its 88 rooms gather around a sprawling and classic Old World lounge. The three-night minimum is waived when business is slow. Cheaper sink-only rooms ("Category A") are clean and have well-preserved furniture from the 1930s. "Category B" offers the same old-fashioned rooms, plus antique bathrooms, and "Category C" gets you modern rooms (family deals, elevator, free pickup from train station if staying at least 3 nights, pay parking, Via Maistra 203, tel. 081-839-3100, www.engadinerhof.com, info@engadinerhof.com).

¢ **Pontresina Youth Hostel,** across the street from the train station, rents 120 beds. There's no curfew, and guests have 24-hour access (though check-in times are limited; includes sheets and lockers, discount at Bellavita spa, four-course dinner available, pay laundry service, game and TV room, limited pay parking, closed early April-early June and mid-Oct-early Dec, Via da la Staziun 46, tel. 081-842-7223, www.youthhostel.ch/pontresina, pontresina@youthhostel.ch).

Eating in Pontresina

Virtually all restaurants in Pontresina are part of a hotel, apart from a few bakeries that serve reasonably priced meals. Except for the Grond Café, all the restaurants listed below are closed off-season, generally from early April to early June and again from mid-October to mid-December. The Muottas Muragl and Alp Languard viewpoints (both described earlier) also have good eating options (though Alp Languard's closes before dinnertime).

$$ **Ristorante Nostra Pizzeria** serves wood-fired pizzas as well as some local dishes in two pleasantly low-key rooms on the ground floor of Hotel Engadinerhof (pastas, meat dishes, fondue

for two, daily 11:00-14:00 & 18:00-22:30, only pizza after 21:30, Via Maistra 203, tel. 081-839-3333, www.engadinerhof.com).

$$$ Colani Stübli, a cozy, elegant eatery, serves regional and seasonal specialties, including meat dishes and local starchy dishes such as *Krautpizokel* and *Capuns* (67-75-CHF fixed-price meals, daily 12:00-14:00 & 18:00-21:00, limited menu available 14:00-18:00 and after 21:00, at Hotel Steinbock, Via Maistra 219, tel. 081-839-3626, www.hotelsteinbock.ch).

$ Grond Café is a bakery with great desserts, plus sandwiches and takeaway lunches (daily 7:00-18:30, Via da Mulin 29, tel. 081-838-8030).

$$ Pontresina Youth Hostel, by the train station, welcomes nonguests for its hearty four-course self-serve dinner (20 CHF includes soup, salad, main course, dessert, and tap water; daily 18:30-19:30, vegetarian option, reservations appreciated, Via da la Staziun 46, tel. 081-842-7223, www.youthhostel.ch/pontresina, pontresina@youthhostel.ch). They also serve a 12-CHF breakfast year-round and a 15-CHF, three-course lunch in winter (daily Dec-March 11:00-14:00).

$$$$ Elegant Five-Star Hotel Dining Rooms: Pontresina's two top hotels have wonderful restaurants in sumptuous dining rooms. **La Trattoria,** in the fanciful faux-castle Hotel Walther at the top end of town, serves straightforward yet inventive Italian cuisine (daily 18:30-20:00 in summer, off-season closed Sun-Mon, Via Maistra 215, tel. 081-839-3636, www.hotelwalther.ch). **Kronenstübli** is in the Grand Hotel Kronenhof, which dominates the bottom end of town and has public rooms fit for a Viennese palace. It's less accommodating to anyone concerned about price, but if you've got francs to burn, its five-course fixed-price meal is a memorable splurge (also has three-course meals, Tue-Sat 19:00-21:30, closed Sun-Mon, Via Maistra, tel. 081-830-3030, www.kronenhof.com).

Supermarket: Picnickers seek out the **Co-op** grocery, just below Via Maistra on Via da Mulin (Mon-Fri 8:00-19:00, Sat-Sun until 18:00).

Samedan

Tiny Samedan (sah-MAY-den, population 3,000) is the prettiest—and sleepiest—town of the three described in this chapter.

The historic capital of the valley, it's stuffed with traditional Engadine architecture, and Romansh remains strong here. Though charming, Samedan is also humble, workaday, and even a bit rough around the edges. Aside from the grand Hotel Bernina, the town seems almost untouched by the era of belle époque tourism. It was primarily the region's transportation hub back then, when horse-drawn carriages met arriving train passengers to cart them off to fancy hotels in St. Moritz and Pontresina—and today it still feels like the backwater cousin of its ritzy neighbors.

There's not much to do here after an hour or two, but it's worth popping over from Pontresina for a quick taste of untouched Engadine-village beauty.

Orientation to Samedan

Samedan is gently spread along the slope of a hill that rises from the Inn River. The train station is at the bottom of town; the town center clusters just above. The main street, called Plazzet, runs through the middle of town parallel to the river (it's closed off on market day—Tue, June-early Oct). All the streets seem to converge at the main square, called Plaz, with its tall Protestant church.

Tourist Information: Samedan's TI is at Plazzet 3, by the Chesa Planta bus stop (Mon-Fri 9:00-12:00 & 15:00-18:00, Sat from 10:00, closed Sun year-round and Sat off-season, tel. 081-851-0060, www.engadin.ch/en/samedan).

Arrival in Samedan: Whether you come by **bus or train,** you'll stop at the train station, which has lockers, ticket windows, and a free WC. Most buses do go up into the town itself after a short wait (ask the driver); if you stay on, you'll want to get off in two stops, at Chesa Planta. Or, from the train station, just hike up the hill, bearing left on Via Mulin to reach the main square. **Drivers** who are here for just a quick visit can park free for one hour in the big garage just off the roundabout into town (past the Co-op and before the station). Pay street parking is usually easy to find (maximum 2 hours within the town center or 12 hours at the top of town); pay parking is also available at the train station.

Helpful Hints: If looking for a sit-down meal, **$$$ Restaurant 1865,** in the grand Hotel Bernina, is a decent value, with pizzas, calzones, and main courses (daily 18:00-22:00, Plazzet 20, tel. 081-852-1212).

Sights in Samedan

Samedan Town Walk

Samedan offers few activities other than relaxing and enjoying the town. For a start, follow this pleasant, self-guided stroll with nice views. The route described here takes you steeply up through town to a perch overlooking Samedan's magnificent setting, and offers a look at the local architecture.

Begin at the **main square** (Plaz), where all of Samedan's cobbled streets meet. Just downhill, the blocky, modern building with the colorful tiled window frames is Samedan's **"vertical spa,"** with several levels of pools (more expensive and less extensive than Pontresina's spa, www. mineralbad-samedan.ch).

From the square, walk uphill on Surtuor (leaving the steeple behind you on the left) to the fork in the road, and take the lane on the left, following the white sign for *Kath. Kirche.* Continue straight up the hill for a block to find (on the right) a 13th-century, castle-like **stone tower** that was the private tower of a noble family. From its wooden balcony, they'd oversee festivities in their little domain. It's now used for changing museum exhibits (www.latuor.ch).

Next door, the house at **#12** dates from 1656. The extended roof beams form an X-shaped St. Andrew's cross. This was a popu-

lar way to bless homes here. Notice the sturdy beam ends—roofs were built to support heavy stones and snow. Houses in the region are known by Romansh names: For example, you'll see houses marked *Chesa Juzi* (Juzi's House) and *Chesa dals 3 Frers* (House of the Three

Traditional Engadine Architecture

Samedan and Pontresina both have fine old traditional houses. A short stroll in either town shows plenty of traditional elements and medieval ingenuity intended to keep inhabitants

warm in the harsh mountain weather. Walls are thick—typically two feet—for insulation. Notice how windows are like the narrow end of a funnel—originally covered with animal skin rather than glass. Bay windows gathered maximum precious light and came with built-in seats where women sat to do handwork.

Even though they're thoroughly modernized, the structural essence of these grand farmhouses survives. You can still see the big lower door for animals and the big upper door for hay and the carriage—with a smaller door built into it for people to get in and out while minimizing heat loss. People had the animals sleep below in the hope their rising body heat would warm the living space above. Proud noble-family coats of arms still decorate buildings; many local families can trace their heritage to the Middle Ages.

Look for the traditional Engadine *sgraffito* ornamentation on exterior walls. To make *sgraffito,* facades are covered with a layer of dark plaster, which is then covered with white or colored plaster. Before the white plaster dries, decorative designs are scratched into it, so that the dark background appears. These rustic and crude decorations—much more durable than painted facades—look modern, but have a long history.

Brothers). A little farther up, across the street, look between Chesa Manzoni and Chesa Sleim to see an interesting modern house that's influenced by old local styles.

Continue uphill to the **Catholic Church** (Neo-Romanesque from 1910, with a bell dating back to 1505), at the top of the town. From here, survey the surrounding slopes and their ancient terracing, a vestige from Celtic peoples.

Carry on uphill, passing the ski lift. Yes, you can do it. Where the road swings right, pause at the wooden bench for the gorgeous **view.** Samedan overlooks the point where the Inn River (coming from St. Moritz) is joined by the Flaz (coming from Pontresina and the Bernina Pass). From here, the Inn continues through Innsbruck in Austria before joining the Danube.

Huff and puff the thin air (you're at 6,000 feet) to the dramatically situated Protestant **Church of St. Peter.** The Romanesque bell tower (c. 1100) predates today's late Gothic church (c. 1480; now a burial church, generally closed to tourists). Benches line the cemetery walls and offer sunny, wind-protected picnic spots. Beneath you stretches the highest-altitude airport in Europe, a favorite place to fly gliders (launched by a yellow truck with a huge winch). When you've had your fill of the views, continue around the far side of the church, where the paved path leads quickly back down into town—steer for the tall steeple.

Chesa Planta

This interesting old mansion, just a block from the main square, shows off upper-crust lifestyles of the 18th and 19th centuries. This former residence of the wealthy local Planta family is preserved just as it was when they lived here. It's rarely open, but the fascinating interior makes it worth considering if you happen to be here at the right time. You'll see some gorgeous wood-carved rooms, a beautifully painted dining room, original granite slab floors, and fancy ceramic stoves. Upstairs, the same building houses a Romansh library *(biblioteca rumauntscha)*, where scholars collect Romansh literature. A copy of any new book published in the Romansh language is sent to this library.

Cost and Hours: 10-CHF German tour (with an English handout), covered by Swiss Travel Pass, 1.5-hour tour runs Thu at 16:30 in Jan-early April and July-mid-Oct; may open other weekdays and/or offer self-guided visit with tablet—check; tel. 081-852-1272, www.chesaplanta.ch.

St. Moritz

The oldest and perhaps best-known winter resort in the world, St.

Moritz has long been the winter haunt of Europe's rich and famous. It's said that in 1864, St. Moritz hotel pioneer Johannes Badrutt invented winter tourism in the Alps. To allay his British guests' skepticism, he offered them free accommodations if the winter weather was bad. They came and enjoyed fine weather. He liquored them up, they had fun...and they brought their friends along the next year. St. Moritz hosted the Winter Olympics in 1928 and 1948.

Although St. Moritz might have been a real town once, today it's little more than a charmless cluster of luxury hotels and de-signer boutiques. (Think of it as the anti-Gimmelwald.) For the jet set, winter is prime time in St. Moritz, when celebrity-spotting and prices are at their peak. In summer, however, it's pretty quiet, and mostly attracts sporty Swiss vacationers of means who come for active recreation (in-line skating, polo, golf, paragliding, horseback riding, lake strolling, etc.).

For the rest of us, the town has little to offer—I don't recom-mend overnighting here (though nightlife seekers will find it live-lier here than in surrounding towns). But those with the Engadin Card should consider a visit for the fun cable-car ride up to Piz Nair and its views, a hike or bike on the mountainside above town, and a quick look at the Segantini Museum.

Orientation to St. Moritz

The older section of St. Moritz (known as the "Dorf") sits on a steep slope above the lake. The train station *(Bahnhof)* is next to the

lake at the base of the hill. The main bus stop (called Schulhausplatz) is at the top. Schulhausplatz is of-ficially called "Plazza da Scoula" in Romansh (but you won't hear much Ro-mansh in German-speak-ing St. Moritz).

From the center of town, the busy Via dal Bagn runs downhill to the modern suburb of St. Moritz Bad, which sprawls on a level plain at the far end of the lake. St. Moritz Bad has some sports facilities (covered pool, tennis courts, ice-skating hall, horseback riding, and so on) and a one-block shopping district (Via Salet), but it's mostly a characterless concrete town. Aside from its proximity to the lake, St. Moritz Bad is pretty, well, bad.

Tourist Information: The über-slick and helpful TI is along the main drag (Via Maistra) in the old center, a block from the main bus stop at Schulhausplatz. Swing by to get personalized advice on walks and hikes, check their cheap posters (see "Helpful Hints," later), and grab a free town map (Mon-Sat 9:00-18:30, closed Sun, Via Maistra 12, tel. 081-837-3333, www.stmoritz.ch). There's also a tiny branch TI next to the ticket office at the train station (daily 10:00-14:00 & 15:00-18:30).

UPPER ENGADINE

ARRIVAL IN ST. MORITZ

St. Moritz's **train station** is near the lake, just below the Dorf. The station has lockers, ticket windows, a baggage-storage desk, an inexpensive café, and a branch TI.

The town center towers above the station. You can simply **walk** uphill for 15 minutes, but it's more fun (and less work) to head up via the Serletta parking garage: Exit the station to the left (look for *Zentrum/Dorf* signs with an escalator icon) and cross the footbridge into the garage. Inside, find the art-lined escalator (Switzerland's longest) that zips you up next to the Palace Hotel. Even ritzier, to enjoy your own private Swiss mountain lift for a couple of minutes, ride the elevator that runs next to the escalators (enter underneath the first stage). From the top, it's a relatively quick walk up to the center. To avoid walking from the station, hop on **bus** #3 up to Schulhausplatz (4/hour, 3 CHF, covered by Engadin Card).

If arriving by **car,** you can pay to park at the Serletta garage (near the train station) or at the more central Quadrellas garage (on Schulhausplatz). Street parking is a little cheaper.

HELPFUL HINTS

Winter Activities: Ender Sport is one of many ski-rental shops (winter hours: Mon-Sat 8:00-19:00, Sun 10:00-13:00 & 15:00-18:00, just uphill from TI and recommended hotels at Via Maistra 26, tel. 081-833-3536, www.endersport.com). For a thrilling splurge you can take a ride—between a professional pilot and brakeman—on the mile-long Olympic **bobsled** course from St. Moritz to Celerina...in 75 seconds (250 CHF, open late Dec-early March, reserve ahead, www.olympia-bobrun.ch).

Bike Rental: To rent an e-bike or mountain bike, contact the St.

Moritz sailing club, on the lakeshore just below the town center (helmets provided, open June-Oct, mobile 079-209-3899, www.scstm.ch). Mountain bikes are also rentable at the Chantarella funicular station above town.

Posters: St. Moritz's tourist board offers pre-WWII tourism posters for 5 CHF each. Buy from the main TI or order online (https://shop.stmoritz.ch).

Sights and Activities in St. Moritz

MUSEUMS

While the Berry Museum is just downhill from the center's pedestrian zone, the others are a 10- to 15-minute walk from the center of town, with the Segantini perched directly uphill from the Engadiner Museum. A steep, woodsy path connects the two—look for the path directly across the street from the Segantini Museum; leaving the Engadiner, head to the right to start the walk up.

▲▲Segantini Museum

This museum is dedicated to the ultimate painter of alpine life. Giovanni Segantini (b. 1858) came here to get away from the misty air of Milan, and to live more cheaply (in those days, Switzerland was a low-budget destination). The crisp alpine atmosphere was great for capturing the bright, sharp, crystal-clear mountain light. Painting in the open air with brushstrokes that invigorated his fascinating scenes, Segantini created works reminiscent of the French Impressionists. The tiny museum, which looks like a Neo-Byzantine church, is based on Segantini's design for the Swiss Pavilion at the 1900 World's Fair in Paris—but made of local stone rather than the originally intended steel. Segantini died young (at age 41, in 1899), and money ran out before this grandiose pavilion could be built. Segantini's masterpiece, the *Alpine Triptych*, was also painted for the World's Fair, but not quite completed. Segantini's vision—both his pavilion and his life's major work—lives on here, near where he settled in his 30s.

Cost and Hours: 10 CHF, not covered by Swiss Travel Pass; Tue-Sun 10:00-12:00 & 14:00-18:00, closed Mon and in off-season; worthwhile 30-minute audioguide-3 CHF, Via Somplaz 30, tel. 081-833-4454, www.segantini-museum.ch.

Getting There: To reach the museum on foot you can simply follow signs along Via Somplaz, but for a nicer stroll, look for the "Segantiniweg" path that cuts through the woods just above the road. (Or take bus #2 or #5 one stop from Schulhausplatz to the Segantini Museum stop.) Drivers will find metered roadside parking just before the museum.

Visiting the Museum: The paintings are displayed on two floors. Begin by climbing the stairs to the round room on the top floor, where you can view the haunting *Alpine Triptych:* three paintings representing (left to right) life, nature, and death. Notice how, even in the death scene—as the body of a newly deceased loved one is brought out to a horse cart while mourning women look on—there's a glimmer of hope and faith in the swirling clouds above. Segantini even designed the *Triptych*'s frames, ornamented with the local five-needled Swiss pine.

Then head back to the entry level, and spend some time with the many smaller canvases here. Particularly notable is *Ave Maria at the Crossing*, where a man rowing a simple boat—laden with a flock of sheep and a mother and baby—pauses to pray at sunset as the church bells toll.

Engadiner Museum (Museum Engiandinais)

This four-story Engadine-style house, built in 1905 to house this museum, displays a collection of lovingly reassembled living areas *(stüvas)* from the region's surviving patrician houses of centuries past. Most of these interiors are entirely paneled in wood, much of it elaborately carved (especially in the Stüa de Gros). Following the well-done tablet guide (included with entry), you can also peek at a smoky farm kitchen and a nightmare-inducing four-poster bed that's overseen by a painted skeleton, just in case life in medieval Switzerland didn't provide enough reminders of one's mortality.

Cost and Hours: 13 CHF, covered by Swiss Travel Pass; Wed-Mon 10:00-18:00 in summer, 14:00-18:00 in winter, Thu until 20:00, closed Tue year-round, also closed in off-season; Via dal Bagn 39, walk 10 minutes downhill from town center, tel. 081-833-4333, www.museum-engiadinais.ch.

Berry Museum

Dedicated not to delicious little fruits, but to local painter Peter Robert Berry (1864-1942), this museum introduces visitors to another talented alpine artist. While Berry enjoyed neither the talent nor the fame of Segantini, and the entry price is steep, this is a suitable rainy-day activity for art lovers (and anyone with a Swiss Travel Pass).

Cost and Hours: 15 CHF, covered by Swiss Travel Pass, includes audioguide; hours uncertain but likely open in summer and winter Wed-Mon 10:00-18:00 with a midday break, closed Tue; also closed in spring and fall, confirm exact times locally; just below the center of St. Moritz Dorf at Via Arona 32, tel. 081-833-3018, www.berrymuseum.com.

LIFTS AND HIKES
▲▲▲Piz Nair (10,030 feet)

With an Engadin Card, the trip up to the Piz Nair station (at 9,915 feet) is the best reason to visit St. Moritz in the summer. (Without the card, your money's better spent on a visit to Muottas Muragl/Alp Languard—and I'd skip St. Moritz altogether.) The ride up is a treat, and from the top you get a sprawling, nearly 360-degree view across the region's rugged mountain rooftop and down to the lakes and valleys below. The view restaurant offers pleasant indoor and outdoor seating.

The ride up to Piz Nair has three stages: two funiculars, then a cable car, all of which leave every 20 minutes. From a station just uphill from Schulplatz, in the middle of St. Moritz Dorf, ride the first funicular to Chantarella (8:20-17:00, last ascent to Piz Nair at 16:00, last descent at 17:20). At Chantarella (6,578 feet), change to a second funicular up to Corviglia (aim for a seat on the left, 8:30-16:50, last descent at 17:10). At Corviglia (8,156 feet), switch to the cable car for the last leg up to Piz Nair (8:45-16:25, last descent at 16:45). The entire ride up takes 30 minutes; riding all the way down can take a little longer, as the funicular isn't timed for the convenience of descending passengers.

The mountain's footpaths and bike trails are well-maintained. Experienced hikers up for a steep challenge can walk back to town in about four to five hours. For a much easier descent, ride the cable car down to the Corviglia ridge, then enjoy great views while hiking from there back into town (2 hours via Marguns—which also has eating options, fairly easy walk most of the way but with steep parts at the start and end). Corviglia is a lovely spot to hang out before heading down, with an alpine hut serving food (a short uphill walk from the station), and the absurdly swanky, crassly promotional Quattro Bar (as in the Audi model it's hyping), which perfectly captures the whole St. Moritz vibe. An even less strenuous walking option is "Heidi's Flower Trail," a relatively level one-hour loop through wildflower fields from the Chantarella funicular station.

Cost: 12.60 CHF for each leg, 69-CHF round-trip ticket, covered by Engadin Card. If you're taking a mountain bike, check your Engadin Card—if it's "all-inclusive," it includes the cost of the bike transport; otherwise it's 17.30 CHF for a day pass for the bike (cyclists without an Engadin Card pay 69.20 CHF for a day pass). Tel. 081-83-5020, www.mountains.ch.

UPPER ENGADINE

Walk Around the Lake

The charming lake below St. Moritz is a delightful place for a stroll—especially on sunny summer days, when it's filled with sailboats. It takes about an hour to walk all the way around.

Eating in St. Moritz

As in Pontresina, most of St. Moritz's restaurants are in hotels.

$$$ Restaurant Hauser is the standard stop for locals who know where to find the best-value sit-down restaurant meal in town. Centrally located, this place has everything—restaurant, café, pastry shop, indoor and outdoor seating, and a vast menu—and you'll find everyone here (weekday lunch specials, sandwiches to go, daily 7:00-21:00, below Hotel Hauser at Via Traunter Plazzas 7, tel. 081-837-5050).

$ Buffet Espresso café at the train station is a rare budget option in this pricey town, serving a couple of hot dishes daily until 17:00, as well as good Italian-style sandwiches (daily 6:00-20:00, tel. 081-834-4105).

Supermarket: There's a small, basic **Co-op** grocery right on the main square (Mon-Fri 8:00-19:00, Sat-Sun until 18:00, Schulhausplatz/Plazza da Scoula 12).

In St. Moritz Bad: $$$ Veltlinerkeller, decorated with a huge stuffed moose head, is a casual-feeling eatery—with the grill right in the dining area—that serves a variety of Italian specialties, including pastas and grilled meats (Mon-Sat 9:00-14:00 & 17:00-22:30, closed Sun in fall and spring, Via dal Bagn 11, 20-minute walk from St. Moritz Dorf or take bus #3 from Schulhausplatz to the Via Salet stop, tel. 081-833-4009, www.veltlinerkeller-stmoritz.ch).

A larger **Co-op** supermarket at Via dal Bagn 20 has a small, basic top-floor café with a limited menu and view terrace. It offers the cheapest meals in town (Mon-Fri 8:00-19:00, Sat-Sun until 18:00; 15-minute walk downhill from town center, just before you reach the St. Moritz Bad shopping street—get off bus #3 at the Via Aruons stop).

Upper Engadine Connections

BY TRAIN

From Pontresina to: Chur (hourly, 2 hours, change in Samedan), **Zürich** (hourly, 3.5 hours, change in Samedan and Chur or Landquart), **Luzern** (hourly, 4.5 hours, 3 changes), **Appenzell** (hourly, 5 hours, 3 changes), **Zermatt** (every 2 hours, 7 hours, several changes).

From St. Moritz and Samedan to: Chur (hourly direct, 2

hours, more with change), **Zürich** (1-2/hour, 3.5 hours, change in Chur or Landquart), **Luzern** (1-2/hour, 4.5 hours, several changes), **Appenzell** (1-3/hour, 4 hours, several changes), **Zermatt** (1-2 direct Glacier Express trains/day, 8 hours), **Tirano** (hourly, 2.5 hours), **Milan** (hourly, 5 hours, 1-2 changes).

For details on the Bernina Express to Tirano and the Glacier Express to Zermatt, see the Scenic Rail Journeys chapter. Train info: Toll tel. 0900-300-300, www.rail.ch.

BY BUS

The Palm Express bus offers a connection-free trip over the Maloja Pass to **Lugano** once a day in summer (departs St. Moritz train station at 12:20, stops at Menaggio on Italy's Lake Como en route, arrives at Lugano's train station at 16:20; daily mid-June-mid-Oct, Fri-Sun only mid-Oct-mid-June, reservations required at least 4 hours ahead, tel. 058-341-3492, www.postauto.ch, use Webcode 10037 to reserve, consider the audioguide—available via free Post-Auto app). Otherwise, connect via train to Thusis, then bus to Bellinzona, then train to Lugano (hourly, 4 hours). To **Milan,** the quickest route is by bus from St. Moritz to Chiavenna in Italy, then onward by train (every 2 hours, 4.5 hours).

UPPER ENGADINE

SCENIC RAIL JOURNEYS

Golden Pass • Gotthard Panorama Express •
Bernina Express • Glacier Express • Chur

 Switzerland has one of the world's best rail networks, and many of its tracks run through dramatic and beautiful scenery. While just about any train ride in Switzerland is photogenic, four are aggressively marketed as the most spectacular: Golden Pass, Gotthard Panorama Express, Bernina Express, and Glacier Express. If you're looking for a scenic day enjoying the Alps from the window of your train, and would like to do it in a "panoramic" car (with huge windows that sweep halfway across the ceiling), these journeys can be great experiences. Though they aren't quite as "fantastic with countless highlights" as they're advertised to be (the high lifts in the mountains themselves are much higher and more breathtaking), the trains are a fun way to do some sightseeing while getting from point A to point B.

This chapter provides you with all the logistical, nuts-and-bolts information you'll need to splice each journey into your itinerary. Keep this in mind as you plan: You don't need to take a special train to enjoy the routes described in this chapter. Regular nonpanoramic trains also run along all these scenic routes. They go more frequently and cost less, but don't come with the expansive windows, special meals, and souvenirs that the scenic trains advertise.

I've described highlights along each route, written in the direction that most travelers are likely to go. If you travel in the opposite direction, the same information still applies—just hold the book upside-down.

This chapter also includes information about Chur, a town that's not really worth a visit, except that it lies on both the Bernina Express and Glacier Express routes and can be handy for a pit stop

Scenic Swiss Rail Routes

GERMANY

• Zürich

FRANCE

AUSTRIA

Luzern •

BOAT

TRAIN • Flüelen

• Wassen

Chur

Inter-
laken •

Davos

Spiez •

Disentis

• Filisur

St. Moritz

Lausanne •

• Zweisimmen

Andermatt •

• Airolo

Gstaad •

• Brig

Pontresina

Montreux •

Poschiavo

• Visp

Geneva •

• Bellinzona

Tirano

Zermatt •

Lugano •

• Sorico
Menaggio

BUS

ITALY

------- Golden Pass

------- Glacier Express

———— Gotthard Panorama
Express

———— Bernina Express

or an overnight (especially if you're connecting to or from Zürich or Appenzell).

TICKETS

Schedules Can Change: In this chapter, I've listed specific departure and arrival times, but these schedules are always subject to change, so it's essential to confirm the times before you travel. Timetables for most of these trains appear on the Swiss Rail website (www.sbb.ch) and Germany's all-Europe rail site (www.bahn.com or their helpful DB Navigator app), but neither has Swiss price information. Avoid calling the expensive Swiss Rail info line (tel. 0900-300-300). Any train station in Switzerland can provide free schedules. Each scenic rail line also operates its own website, with even more details.

Buying Tickets: You can purchase tickets and reservations for all these scenic rail lines at a train station in Switzerland, but do this in advance if traveling during peak season. Station staffers are familiar with the scenic routes and can help you sort through your options. These trips are covered by both Swiss Travel Passes and the Eurail Global Pass, though reservations (required on some trains) cost extra.

You can also buy tickets in advance via the Swiss Rail website or each scenic rail website. Or book via the North American-friendly RailEurope.com (online or through your travel agent)—but you'll pay a substantial markup.

Seat Reservations: Some scenic trains require seat reservations. Reservations are essentially scenic-train supplements that happen to come with a reserved seat. Be warned that many sell out several days ahead in high season. Reservations are required for all classes of the Glacier Express and Gotthard Panorama Express, the panoramic cars in all classes on the Bernina Express, and the bus segment of the Bernina Express. Reserve for the Golden Pass train between Zweisimmen and Montreux if you want a front-row VIP seat and during peak season. These options are explained in each section later.

If you're set on taking a panoramic train and your itinerary is already fixed, it makes sense to book your scenic-train seats as soon as you can. On most routes at most times, however, individual travelers usually book just a few days in advance—usually after they've seen a weather report. If your itinerary is flexible, I'd recommend you do the same: Keep an eye on the weather, pick a good travel day, and then reserve your seats at any train station. Only from mid-July to mid-August do trains (especially the über-promoted Glacier Express) tend to book up further ahead.

Rail Passes: Swiss Travel Passes and the Eurail Global Pass cover travel on all four scenic trains. Seat reservations, though, always cost extra. You can skip reservations if traveling scenic routes on standard regional trains, rather than on the designated tourist departures.

When buying your ticket or making reservations, be sure the ticket agent understands what type of rail pass you have and exactly what trip you're taking. (Pass coverage varies on boats, buses, and mountain lifts, and is subject to change.) Confirm that you've purchased all of the reservations and other tickets you need to complete your trip.

TRAIN TYPES

Various types of trains, with various types of cars, run these routes. Here are the key distinctions to look for:

Classes: Most trains have both first- and second-class cars. The difference between the first- and second-class cars is generally the same on tourist trains as on standard trains (first class has somewhat wider seats, a little more legroom, and fewer passengers; second-class cars offer the same scenery, go just as fast, and usually still have plenty of room). If you have a second-class rail pass, you can always pay extra to sit in first on any given train. In bigger train stations, a digital panel on the tracks indicates departure time, destination, and at which part of the platform you'll find the first- or second-class cars.

Standard vs. Tourist Trains: Used by local commuters, standard trains may stop at more stations along the route than the designed-for-tourists panoramic trains. Many travelers enjoy the flexibility of following the scenic route

on standard trains, enabling them to hop off and explore a village, then hop on the next standard train that comes through (reservations are not necessary on standard domestic trains).

Panoramic vs. Standard Cars: All the tourist trains on the routes in this chapter offer special panoramic cars, usually in both first and second class, so there's no need to splurge for first class. Panoramic cars have huge windows that curve back into the roof of the train car, allowing you to view high mountains from a wider angle than in a normal train car. The Golden Pass trains are one notch above: The driver sits in a little bubble upstairs, leav-

ing the very front of the train open for VIP seating with unobstructed views of what's coming up. The windows in the panoramic cars generally can't open, meaning that photographs often suffer from glare, and there are no window shades, so the interior can heat up on sunny days even with air-conditioning. Bring sunglasses and a hat.

Since nonpanoramic cars have a smaller field of vision than the panoramic cars, these require a little more bobbing and weaving to enjoy the views. Aside from being cheaper, the chief advantage of standard cars is that the windows generally can be opened, for cool air and better photos. Passengers in panoramic cars are free to walk to the standard cars to open a window and snap a photo.

Golden Pass

The exceptionally picturesque Golden Pass train route cuts a swath diagonally across the pristine center of the country, connecting Luzern with Lake Geneva, and German Switzerland with French. Of all the rail journeys in this chapter, it's the one you're most likely to take, as it's central and laces together many of Switzerland's top sights.

ROUTE OVERVIEW

The Golden Pass officially runs between Luzern and Lake Geneva's Montreux in about five hours. The route has three distinct segments (Luzern-Interlaken Ost, Interlaken Ost-Zweisimmen, and Zweisimmen-Montreux). Because the tracks change from narrow to standard gauge to narrow again, you'll switch to a different train (waiting across the platform) at Interlaken Ost and Zweisimmen. You can lengthen your stop in Interlaken if you'd like to eat lunch there or walk around town.

The best stretch of the route is between Zweisimmen and Montreux. To enjoy just this part of the route, start in Interlaken (or in Bern—changing trains in Spiez). This is the stretch most likely to fill up, so it's worth reserving a seat, especially in summer.

The three trains that make up the full route are run by different companies and have different services. Here's the breakdown.

Luzern to Interlaken Ost: Regular trains, all with semi-panoramic windows (hourly, 2 hours).

Interlaken Ost to Zweisimmen: Regular trains (roughly hourly, 1 hour, sometimes with a change in Spiez).

Zweisimmen to Montreux: Specially designed tourist trains (8/day, 2 hours). Of the daily departures, four are panoramic trains, two are panoramic trains with VIP seats, and two are "classic" trains with vintage rail cars.

PLANNING YOUR TIME

Because it connects so many knockout Swiss destinations, the Golden Pass can be spliced into your itinerary in many different ways. I'd focus on the best stretch, using it to connect Interlaken and Lake Geneva (sleeping on the Lake Geneva end in either Montreux or Lausanne). Check schedules for the Zweisimmen-Montreux leg to pick the departure with your preferred type of train car. If you can avoid having to change trains in Spiez, that's a minor plus.

To go all the way from Luzern to Lake Geneva, here's a sample day plan: Take the 8:06 train from Luzern to Interlaken Ost (arriving at 9:55), wander Interlaken and have a quick lunch, catch the 13:08 train to Zweisimmen (arriving at 14:20), then change to a panoramic train and arrive in Montreux at 16:13.

You could also easily make a fuller day of the Golden Pass—starting in Zürich and ending in Lausanne—by tacking on standard trains from Zürich to Luzern, and from Montreux to Lausanne.

For onward train connections from major Golden Pass stops, see the Connections sections for Luzern (page 84), Interlaken Ost (page 170), and Montreux (page 300).

ORIENTATION TO THE GOLDEN PASS

Cost: The Golden Pass trip from Luzern to Montreux costs 76 CHF second class; the "best of" segment from Interlaken to Montreux is 53 CHF. The entire ride is covered by the Global or Swiss Travel passes. Reservations cost about 9 CHF extra and while not required, are recommended for the stretch from Zweisimmen to Montreux for summer departures and the super-scenic front seats (more details under "Seating," later).

Information: The three rail companies that operate the route (MOB, BLS, and the Zentralbahn) run an office and a website that can answer your questions (tel. 021-989-8190, www.goldenpassline.ch). A free booklet available on the train describes the route and includes a schedule.

Seating: Between Zweisimmen and Montreux, two panoramic trains have special VIP seats in the first car. On these trains, the driver sits in a little domed area upstairs—leaving both the front and back of the train open for passengers. The first two rows of VIP seats offer an unobstructed view of the pristine alpine scenery coming right at you, but they usually book up fast (and overall there may be fewer VIP seats available in the future—check).

Eating on the Golden Pass: The Luzern-Interlaken stretch is the only section with a restaurant car, but it may be closed on trains running early or late in the day. Snacks and bar service may be available between Zweisimmen and Montreux, but the menu is limited and pricey. Save your money by packing a picnic.

SCENIC RAIL JOURNEYS

⊙ SELF-GUIDED TOUR

This tour briefly outlines the first stretch of the five-hour Golden Pass journey, then focuses on the *crème de la crème*—the two hours between Zweisimmen and Montreux (described from north to south), the best and most visually exciting part of the trip.

As you leave Luzern (sit on the right side), you'll go along the lake to Alpnachstad, the starting point for the cogwheel train that climbs to the top of Mount Pilatus (the massive bulk on the right). Then the train follows the Sarner Aa River through farmland, passing through the town of Sarnen and running along Lake Sarnen. Beyond the end of the lake is the town of Giswil, where the train begins its gradual ascent to the **Brünig Pass.** Eventually the train runs above the beautiful turquoise waters of the Lungernsee reservoir. After passing the resort of Lungern, the train climbs gradually through the forest to the summit station of Brünig-Hasliberg (keep an eye out for fake animal cutouts—lynx, ibex, deer—placed whimsically in the woods at eye level). After cresting the pass, the train descends to the Aare River valley, with its sheer cliffs and waterfalls. The arrow-straight river channel, straightened by the ever-efficient Swiss, slices through the broad valley and on to Meiringen. (Sir Arthur Conan Doyle chose Meiringen and nearby Reichenbach Falls as the setting for the death of Sherlock Holmes.) The train then follows the river to beautiful **Lake Brienz** (Brienzersee; a bus runs from the town of Brienz to the remarkable open-air museum at Ballenberg).

Beyond Brienz, the train follows the lakeshore to **Interlaken** ("between the lakes"), where the town sits between the big lakes of Thun and Brienz. As the train pulls out of Interlaken, you cruise along the south bank of **Lake Thun** (Thunersee). Before long, at the town of Spiez, you'll split off and head southwest to Zweisimmen—squeezing between two mountainsides and into the rolling, cow-speckled **Simmental** valley.

At **Zweisimmen,** you'll change to a panoramic train and continue through the Simmental, famous among American farmers for its top-end cows. Big farmhouses lie scattered in the lush meadows—an indication that the farmland is good here. The large wooden buildings are typical of Bernese farm architecture: housing the barn, sheltering the crops, and storing agricultural machines, all under one huge roof. Farming is heavily subsidized in Switzerland, and farmers form the strongest economic lobby. Trying to increase their income, many farmers have added exotic crops (like melons) or animals. Ostriches, yaks, bison, and highland cattle have become a common sight in the Swiss Alps lately.

Between Saanenmoser and Schonried, the train reaches its highest point (about 4,000 feet) and stops at the famous resort town of **Gstaad.** Although known as a favorite hangout for well-known rustic mountain folk such as Julie Andrews, Monaco's Princess Caroline, and Roman Polanski, the town doesn't offer much in the way of sights. In winter, its modest ski slopes are less crowded than the town's flashy nightspots. Sipping their cocktails, the *après*-skiers eye each other and discuss the latest trends in ski fashion. In summer, Gstaad hosts the Swiss Open tennis, polo, and golf tournaments, as well as high-quality music festivals.

Just south of Gstaad, say *auf Wiedersehen* to the German-speaking part of Switzerland and *bonjour* to **French Switzerland.** The mountains are jagged. In fact, many are called *dents,* French for "teeth." With the change in language comes a change in culture and architecture. French-style gray stone houses start to replace half-timbered, woody, German-style chalets. The mountain airstrips—generally made for the Swiss Air Force during World War II—are used today for sightseeing flights around the Alps. The cute village of Rougemont, with its fine church and traditional houses, is famous among the Swiss as the place where the wealthy send their girls to boarding school.

Happy **cows** spend their summers on the Alps, wandering freely and munching the fragrant herbs of these lush alpine meadows. The resulting milk is the secret ingredient for tasty Gruyère cheese. On steep hillsides here, the grass is still cut by hand. It dries in the summer sun, then is collected and stored in the barns to serve as cow salads through the winter.

You might consider interrupting your journey in **Château-d'Œx,** known for its Hot-Air Ballooning Week (last week of January). Bertrand Piccard and Brian Jones took off from here on March 1, 1999, and sailed their balloon all the way around the world. Below the train station, Le Chalet restaurant gives insight on Gruyère cheese production.

South of Château-d'Œx, the valley narrows to a deep gorge. The hillsides above were devastated by the 1999 **Lothar** winter storm. Entire forests were leveled, aggravating an already precarious avalanche situation. Trees on steep slopes stop snow from sliding down and burying the villages, but once the trees are gone, artificial avalanche barriers need to be erected. Landslides and floods have been relatively common in recent years—an unfortunate consequence of deforestation and the construction of vacation homes in areas that traditionally served as pastures and forestlands.

The small **lake** is dammed and used for hydroelectric power. Switzerland makes good use of its Alps, with their fast-flowing streams. Although it has some nuclear power plants, 60 percent of Switzerland's energy is hydroelectric. The country exports its electricity to France and Italy.

Montbovon is the place to change trains if you're going to Bulle or Gruyères (see page 303). After the first tunnel, an inscription on the barn to the right welcomes you to the Gruyère region: *La Gruyère vous salue.*

The train winds its way uphill with more curves and tunnels than before. Passing through the **Jaman Tunnel,** you're engulfed in nearly two miles of darkness. When you emerge, you're in another world—you've left the feudal Middle Ages and entered the 19th-century belle époque. At the village of Les Avants, one of Switzerland's oldest winter resorts, the first glimpses of Lake Geneva sprawl deep underneath you. Beginning a steep descent, the train passes through a series of sharp bends in tunnels before delivering you from the mountains to lake level.

The architecture has even more of a French flair now that you've entered the **"Swiss Riviera."** Palm trees, vines, and many sanatoriums indicate that this is a warmer climate. You're surrounded by the vineyards of the Lavaux region, famous for its white wine. The view broadens to include the French Alps of Savoy across the lake, the lakeshore of the Swiss Riviera to the west, and the broad Rhône Valley to the east. As you approach Montreux—with its grand hotels—the train meanders its way intimately through private gardens.

Montreux is one of the only train stations in Europe with three different rail gauges: regular, narrow (which you're on), and very skinny (for the Rochers de Naye train, taking sightseers to a nearby peak with views less exciting than those you've just enjoyed).

From here, it's an easy train trip to Lausanne, or a quick bus ride or about a two-mile lakefront hike to Château de Chillon (covered in the Lake Geneva & French Switzerland chapter).

Gotthard Panorama Express

The journey marketed as the Gotthard Panorama Express is half by boat and half by train, from Luzern to Lugano in the Italian-speaking region of Ticino. The boat ride passes the place where the first Swiss cantons pledged "all for one and one for all," the birthplace of the Confoederatio Helvetica in 1291.

Don't go out of your way to do this trip. The boat ride is more pastoral than thrilling, and the train ride is more interesting as a lesson in Swiss engineering than impressive for its views. (Because the train cuts through the highest mountains inside the old Gotthard Tunnel, it only reaches 3,600 feet above sea level.) But if you're connecting Luzern and Italian Switzerland in high season and have the time, this 5.5-hour boat-train combination is undeniably scenic.

However, if you're in a hurry to get between Luzern and Lugano, it's possible to do the whole trip by train in only 2 hours via the new, 30-mile-long Gotthard Base Tunnel, which allows full-size freight trains to traverse the Alps and permits passenger-train speeds of up to 150 miles an hour. Most train schedules will route you through the new tunnel; to take the more scenic route, look for regional trains that require a transfer in Erstfeld.

Note that if you've already taken a boat trip on Lake Luzern, you won't see much more by taking the Gotthard Panorama Express boat. Conversely, if you're planning on doing the whole Gotthard Panorama trip, don't bother doing a boat trip while in Luzern.

ROUTE OVERVIEW

The Gotthard Panorama Express begins with a slow boat trip along the length of Lake Luzern from the city of Luzern to Flüelen (3 hours). There you'll switch to the train, and cut down into the Italian-speaking canton of Ticino (2.5 hours).

The boat trip from Luzern to Flüelen is lazy and very pretty. As the traditional steamer blows its old-time horn, you glide by idyllic lakeside resort towns and under mighty peaks. In Flüelen, you leave the boat and board the train.

If you want to skip the reserved panoramic train, standard regional trains (without panoramic cars) make the scenic Luzern-Lugano trip with more options (2.5 hours total, 2-3/hour with 1-2 transfers, avoid nonstop trains if you want the scenic route).

For onward train connections, see the Connections sections under Luzern (page 84) and Lugano (page 332).

SCENIC RAIL JOURNEYS

Gotthard Panorama Express

ORIENTATION TO THE GOTTHARD PANORAMA EXPRESS

Cost: The Gotthard Panorama Express trip costs 150 CHF for first class or 127 CHF for second-class boat ride (second-class bookings not available on train segment). You'll also pay a seat reservation fee of 16 CHF (required for all train passengers except kids under 6 who don't need their own seat). There are no seat reservations for the boat.

All rail passes cover the regular train ticket value in the same class of service (but not the seat reservation fee). With a second-class pass, the train upgrade to first class adds 17.50 CHF. The Swiss Travel Pass covers lake boats while the Global Pass gives you half off boat rides on Lake Luzern, so the discounted boat ticket costs 23 CHF.

Schedule: The official package runs once daily except Mon in each direction between mid-April and mid-October. Going from north to south, you'll leave Luzern on the 11:12 boat; after it docks in Flüelen, you have 15 minutes before the 14:10 train leaves for Lugano. The total trip takes about 5.5 hours. Going from south to north, you leave Lugano at 9:22 to make a Flüelen-Luzern boat departing at 12:00.

Information: The boat and train companies both have brochures and websites about the Gotthard Panorama Express (boat: tel. 041-367-6767, www.lakelucerne.ch; train: www.sbb.ch, choose "Leisure & Holidays," then "Travel in Switzerland," then "Panorama Trips"). Download the free Gotthard Panorama Express app.

Boarding the Boat and Train: If you're doing the full Gotthard Panorama Express route, board the boat at pier 1 across from the Luzern train station. Present your ticket. There's no real baggage check on the boat; travelers just stack their backpacks and suitcases in a corner.

As the train approaches the platform in Flüelen, watch for the car that corresponds to your reservation (the official Gotthard Panorama Express packet includes a sheet showing where to stand for your car).

◐ SELF-GUIDED TOUR

Here's what you'll see if you're doing the entire Gotthard Panorama Express route. If you're taking only the train, skip to that section.

Boat Trip

The boat crisscrosses the **Vierwaldstättersee** (the "Lake of Four Forest Cantons"—let's call it Lake Luzern). The trip is popular with the older generation of European tourists, who eat and drink their way through the lazy route. On a sunny day, you can sit on the deck and enjoy the mountain views. Survey the boat before you settle on a seat—consider sun, shade, and wind.

After two hours, you sail into the **canton of Uri,** and the landscape gets rougher, the slopes steeper, and the villages fewer and more rustic. Swiss patriots get excited as the boat approaches **Rütli.** The meadow above is the birthplace of the Swiss Confederation. In 1291, representatives of the three founding cantons met here and swore allegiance to each other, against their oppressive neighbors. More than 700 years later, Switzerland is still a confederation—but now its cantons number 26.

You may see hikers disembark at Rütli and head for the mystical meadow marked by a big Swiss flag. Then they follow the **Weg der Schweiz** ("Path of Switzerland"), a trail leading around the lake. Along the way, they contemplate stone signs representing each of the 26 cantons in the order they joined the union. The canton markers are spaced according to each canton's population (the 20-mile-long trail is designed to have exactly 5 millimeters for each Swiss citizen).

Later, the boat stops at **Tellskapelle.** This 16th-century frescoed chapel marks another legendary spot—where Swiss hero William Tell jumped ship on the way to prison and swam to freedom.

The last stop is **Flüelen,** where the panoramic train awaits.

Train Trip

From Flüelen, the train climbs from 1,540 feet up to 3,600 feet at the old Gotthard Tunnel—once the primary north-south transportation route through the Alps. You enter a classic alpine world of snowcapped mountains towering above wild valleys, with narrow gorges carved over eons by angry white water. Wooden chalets, pine forests, and lush meadows dotted with munching cows complete this image of picture-perfect Central Switzerland.

The train tracks are protected from avalanches, landslides, and waterfalls by concrete galleries. Gazing out the window, you'll see some of the greatest accomplishments of Swiss road-and-railroad engineering. **Wassen,** marked by its striking chapel, is the climax for trainspotters—it once had more trains passing per minute than just about anywhere else. First, the chapel is on your right. Then the train loops around the tiny town, and the chapel is on your left. Your train disappears into a tunnel, and when you emerge, the same chapel is still there. The train actually spirals up the slopes. Bring a compass and you can watch it spin 360 degrees.

Göschenen is the last stop before the 9.5-mile-long **Gotthard Tunnel.** After 10 minutes of rocketing through darkness, you emerge in a whole different world—a different climate (warmer), canton (Ticino), and language (Italian). Since the 13th century— long before this tunnel was built—the Gotthard Pass has been *the* major trade route over this part of the Alps, connecting northern and southern Europe. The trade continues to rumble under rather than over the pass, now by high-speed rail through the much longer Gotthard Base Tunnel.

Welcome to **Ticino,** Switzerland's botanical garden. While the weather around Lake Luzern is often iffy, Ticino feels Mediterranean—warm and southern—making it a favorite weekend destination for the Swiss. Rather than cuckoo-clock-like chalets, the houses are now plain, square, and made of stone. Instead of conifers, the forests are full of chestnut trees. You'll see vineyards, oleander, and even palm trees. And the upcoming train stops are announced in Italian now: *"Prossima fermata..."*

While life seemed almost too good in the pristine and touristic Lake Luzern region, here in the valley of **Leventina,** the economy is tougher. Unemployment rates are high, young folks have to commute into the cities farther south for a job, houses and roads aren't as well maintained, and window boxes no longer come with so many flowers. On either side of **Faido,** the train goes through several more tunnels—including the 10-mile-long Ceneri Tunnel (opening in 2020); before you know it you'll arrive in Lugano.

Bernina Express

The Bernina Express is one of the more exciting rides through the Swiss Alps, thanks to its diversity: starting with the sunny, palm-tree ambience of Lugano, getting a taste of Italy along beautiful Lake Como, climbing up and over the twisting Bernina Pass, and seeing mountain towns like Pontresina before finishing up in eastern Switzerland. The first half of the trip is by bus; the second by rail. The little

red train with panoramic cars spirals up to 7,380 feet, passing steep mountains and cliffs, glaciers, waterfalls, and a wild, rugged landscape.

ROUTE OVERVIEW

The Bernina Express combines a bus trip through Italy with a train ride up and into the mountains. The bus begins in Lugano, but soon crosses the border to run along the west side of Italy's Lake Como, eventually arriving at Tirano, where passengers change to a train. From Tirano, the train crosses back into Switzerland and twists

Bernina Express

Note: Bernina Express & Glacier Express share the same route between Chur & St. Moritz

north up the steep mountainside, mastering a very steep grade on regular tracks (no cogwheels) en route to the most spectacular stretch: over the Bernina Pass. Then the train winds back down the other side and finally deposits you in one of several eastern Swiss towns, such as Pontresina, St. Moritz, Samedan, and Chur. (In summer, you can also finish in the resort town of Davos.)

The route can be reversed (Chur or Pontresina to Tirano by train, then bus to Lugano). In fact, this way arguably provides an even better scenic experience.

PLANNING YOUR TIME

The trip between Pontresina and Lugano takes about six hours. Starting or finishing in Chur makes for a very long day (8-9 hours). If you want to travel the whole route, split it up and do the Pontresina-Chur stretch on the way to destinations such as Zürich or Appenzell, or as part of the Glacier Express (which overlaps with the Bernina Express on this segment).

If you have more time, consider taking a standard regional train along the Pontresina-Tirano route (rather than the official

Bernina Express train with panoramic cars). That way, you can get off as you like to hike and explore (see "Skipping the Official Panorama Train," later).

Also remember that you don't have to start or end the trip in Lugano. You could use the Pontresina-Tirano train as a way of connecting to Milan or Lake Como (see "Connecting to Towns in Italy," below). You could also make a day trip out of the Bernina Express, leaving Pontresina in the morning, exploring over the pass to Tirano (2.5 hours by train), then heading back.

Don't worry too much about which of the Upper Engadine towns your train stops in (Pontresina, St. Moritz, or Samedan)— the three towns are within 10 minutes of each other by local bus or train.

For onward train connections from the major Bernina Express stops, see the Connections sections for Lugano (page 332) and Chur (at the end of this chapter).

ORIENTATION TO THE BERNINA EXPRESS

Cost: A one-way trip on the Bernina Express from Lugano to Pontresina costs 84 CHF second class, 105 CHF first class. Lugano to Chur costs 117 CHF second class, 165 CHF first class. St. Moritz is a few francs more expensive than Pontresina. The official Bernina Express trip requires a reservation for both the bus (14 CHF) and the panoramic train (14-16 CHF, 10 CHF in winter). The entire trip (including the bus) is covered by the Swiss Travel and Global passes, but passholders have to pay for reservations (10 CHF for train and another 10 CHF for the bus).

If you don't have a reservation for the bus, you may be allowed to board and pay if there's room, but there are no guarantees; if you don't have a reservation for the panoramic cars on the train, you can sit in the nonpanoramic cars without a reservation.

Schedule: The bus from Lugano to Tirano leaves daily at 10:00 (April-late Oct only) from outside Lugano's train station. Facing the lake with the Lugano station at your back, walk about 100 yards to the left to find the stop (look for yellow signs saying *Tirano, St. Moritz,* and *#731*).

About 13:00, you'll arrive in Tirano. Here, you'll board a panoramic train that continues north over the mountains. In summer, one train leaves Tirano at 14:07 and arrives in Pontresina at 16:10 and St. Moritz at 16:19; another leaves Tirano at 14:25 and arrives in Pontresina at 16:15 and Chur at 18:19. All trains follow the same tracks for most of the trip before fanning out at the end to different destinations.

If you're doing it the other way around, the train from

St. Moritz leaves at 9:30, stops in Pontresina at 9:47, and arrives in Tirano at 12:00. From Chur, the train departs at 8:32 and stops in Pontresina at 10:22, arriving in Tirano at 12:49. The bus from Tirano leaves at 14:20 and arrives in Lugano at 17:30. Remember to confirm all times.

In winter (late Oct-March), the bus service stops, but the Bernina Express panoramic trains still run over the pass to Tirano a couple of times a day.

Information: The Bernina Express is operated by the Rhätische Bahn (RhB, tel. 081-288-6565, www.berninaexpress.ch). You can buy an English guidebook about the Bernina Express on the train or at gift shops along the way, or pick up the free "panorama map" at the train station. Recorded English commentary plays on the train's loudspeaker, but the interactive Bernina Express app provides more information.

Bring Food: Your time between bus and train in Tirano may be brief (especially if the bus is running late), so it's smart to pack a lunch. There aren't any convenient grocery stores or takeaway options near the Tirano station.

Bus Tips: There are no WCs on the bus, but it stops for a WC break in Sorico, Italy (Swiss francs accepted). Bags can be put under the bus. The bus trip is almost entirely through Italy. If many people reserve the trip, a second bus may be added.

Train Tips: Once you reach Tirano, you'll switch to a train. For the first part of the ride, views are somewhat better on the right (though the left is better for seeing the train curve around the famous spiral viaduct at Brusio). After Poschiavo, views are better on the left.

Topless Trains: If traveling in July and August, ask about sitting in the yellow "convertible" train cars with flip seats and no roof (but be aware that these go only on certain segments of the trip). The railway decides the day before—depending on the weather—whether to add these cars to the train (available in both first and second class). Bring a jacket, hat, and sunscreen. If you get cold, you can move into a regular car when the train stops.

Skipping the Official Panorama Train: The train segment of the Bernina Express can be done on a standard regional train (with smaller windows that open, and possibly a car with larger-view windows). These trains stop at all stations along the line, giving you more options to hop off and walk around in the beautiful surroundings. (The regular Bernina Express only stops at three important stations—Poschiavo, Alp Grüm, and Ospizio Bernina.) On a standard train, you can get off at Poschiavo for a quick visit, at the Bernina Pass for hiking, or at Diavolezza to do a cable-car trip. Alp Grüm and Ospizio Bernina are starting points for several great hikes (at Ospizio Bernina, you can leave your bags at the restaurant near the station). Take advantage of the frequent and easy train connections to make as many short stops as time and interest allow. Not only do you save yourself the panoramic train supplement, but you have the flexibility of traveling without a seat reservation. The panoramic cars are indeed great—and this stretch is particularly well-suited for a panoramic car—but the trip is still very rewarding on a standard train.

Connecting to Towns in Italy: There are many other ways to reach Tirano than by bus from Lugano. For example, inexpensive, direct, hourly trains run to Tirano from both Milan (2.5 hours) and Varenna, a favorite stop on Lake Como (1.5 hours).

History Exhibit in St. Moritz: A small, free exhibit on the history of the Bernina Express rail line, including an English film, is in the St. Moritz train station. It's worth a look, though not a special trip.

◐ SELF-GUIDED TOUR
Bus Trip

The bus trip is more scenic than relaxing. Lakes Lugano and Como are almost fjord-like, lined with little Italian getaways. For the best views, sit on the right-hand side (if your reserved seat is on the left, change once the bus is under way).

At first, the bus takes you around Lake Lugano on narrow, winding roads, frequently honking its horn to warn oncoming traffic at tight passages. Leaving Lugano, you'll pass the town of Gandria (fun to visit from Lugano by boat and described in that chapter). Shortly after Gandria, you cross the border into **Italy** (no need to show passports). You may notice changes in architecture and design: Whereas the Swiss love meticulously manicured gardens, painstakingly renovated houses, and clean, uncluttered lines, the Italians take things a bit easier.

Once the bus leaves Lake Lugano, the road broadens and takes you through modern Italian villages before hitting picturesque **Lake Como** (Lago di Como). Tunnels occasionally disrupt your views, but you can catch glimpses of the lush lakefront. Above the town of Menaggio are your first views of the lake. The village across the lake on the right (by the funny hump of land) is the *real* Bellagio. At the nearby village of Dongo, the Italian fascist dictator

Mussolini was captured at the end of World War II. In Gravedona, the street narrows, and getting the bus through is a tight squeeze. Posh private villas and gardens line the street; look for the 12th-century Romanesque Church of Santa Maria del Tiglio. From here, the trip takes you to the tiny harbor town of Domaso, a touristy area with plenty of campgrounds, hotels, and swimming pools.

Shortly before noon, the bus stops for 15 dull minutes in **Sorico,** at the northern tip of Lake Como (no view). You'll have a chance to use the WC and buy a snack or drink (Swiss francs accepted).

The bus then crosses the **"Pian di Spagna"**—famous for a tense standoff between Spanish and Swiss troops during the religious wars of the Counter-Reformation. The trip continues up the fertile **Valtellina Valley,** where some of northern Italy's white wine is produced. The sunny slopes on the left side are reserved for vineyards, the right lower slopes are for woodland, and the bottom of the valley is occupied by apple plantations. For centuries (from 1512 until Napoleon in 1797) this region belonged to Switzerland's largest canton, Graubünden. This region is Italian today, but many Swiss are still nostalgic for the valley (called the *Veltlin* in German) and its wines. The white Grüner Veltliner grape is named after the valley, though it isn't actually grown here. In Tresivio (just after Sondrio, toward the end of the bus ride) you'll notice the creamy white, brown-trimmed 17th-century Baroque pilgrimage church of Santa Casa on the hill to your left.

Tirano is our last stop in Italy. In the old town, the bus passes an impressive Renaissance church (Madonna di Tirano, on the left) before arriving at the Italian Railways train station. Now you'll need to cross under the tracks to the separate, narrow-gauge, Swiss rail station. Go down the ramp or the stairs and through the tunnel, following *Retica* signs into the Swiss station building (which is still on Italian territory but inside the Swiss customs zone). You'll pass by a customs office, which will normally show no interest in you.

You may have time for lunch and some sightseeing in Tirano before hopping on the official Bernina Express trains. To cram in more sightseeing, take an earlier departure from Tirano on a regional train to gain time for a stopover in the fine town of Poschiavo (described later), and catch another train onward from Poschiavo.

Train Trip
Part One: Tirano to Poschiavo
From Tirano, the train rolls streetcar-style through the center of town, crosses the Italian-Swiss border, and then climbs up to **Brusio.** Here the train swirls up a circular viaduct—an ingenious construction allowing the train to reach higher altitudes without the

help of a cogwheel mechanism. As the train spirals up, you can see the front and back cars curving in front of and behind you, riding over the viaduct.

Sit back and enjoy the most scenic part of the trip. You'll pass dark old pine forests with needle-and-moss-covered boulders. Chestnut forests, tobacco plantations, and vineyards contribute to the lush tableau. Wildflowers along the track include bright-orange lilies and mountain azaleas. The train slaloms up the steep mountain and offers more and more views of waterfalls, steep cliffs, and the Poschiavo valley and lake far below you.

If you're not stopping in Poschiavo, skip down to "Part Two."

Poschiavo

If you detour for a quick break in this cute town, check the time of the next train (posted on the wall) before you leave the station.

Deposit your bags at the station's luggage counter (small fee), just beyond the TI, where you can pick up a free map and the English translation for a short orientation walk (TI tel. 081-839-0060, www.valposchiavo.ch).

The best quick visit to Poschiavo includes a stroll to the main square (Piazza Comunale), with the Museo Casa Console and near the town's main church (St. Ignazio). From the station, walk straight out and down the main street until it ends at the river, then turn left, following signs for *Museo Casa Console*. Cross the river over the pedestrian bridge and continue left, then right, then left, following the *Museo* signs.

The main square, **Piazza Comunale,** is lined with Neoclassical and Neo-Gothic buildings, including an impressive Catholic church (Chiesa di San Vittore Mauro). A church stood here as early as 703, but the building has been rebuilt and renovated several times: The bell tower dates from 1202, and the Baroque front door was carved in the 1700s. Don't miss the little yellow building just before the church, with the intricate wrought-iron grills. Have a peek inside, and don't be startled by the skulls lining the walls—you're standing in front of the local ossuary.

If you have a Swiss Travel Pass, find the tiny **Museo Casa Console** in the old Town Hall, below the 12th-century church tower. It has a nice collection of Romantic-era paintings of this region—the sort that helped kick off the tourism boom and, in a sense, brought you here. Before becoming glamorized in the Romantic era, mountains were seen more as obstacles than objects of beauty (free with pass, otherwise overpriced at 10 CHF, Tue-Sun 11:00-16:00, closed Mon and Nov-mid-Dec, tel. 081-844-0040, www.museocasaconsole.ch).

Go from the main square a block north and find the **Church of St. Ignazio.** It's ironic that this Protestant church's namesake, St. Ignatius of Loyola, was the founder of the militant Jesuit order, whose main purpose was to fight "heretic" Protestants. Notice the inscription above the central pulpit, which is fervently Protestant: *Chiesa cristiana vangelica riformata da gli errori e superstizioni umane* ("Christian evangelical church, reformed from human errors and superstitions").

Then it's back to the station...you've got a train to catch.

Part Two: Poschiavo to Pontresina

Thirty minutes after leaving Poschiavo, just before the Alp Grüm station, you'll spot the first glacier, **Palü Gletscher** (on the left, above the little lake of Palüsee). It lies nestled between the peak of Piz Varuna (11,330 feet) on the left and the eastern summit of Piz Palü on the right (12,790 feet).

The screeching of the wheels is a reminder that this is the only train that crosses over the Alps without any tunnels. It goes right over the top. The **Ospizio Bernina** station marks the Bernina Pass and the highest point of this trip (7,380 feet, above the tree line). Next to the station, you'll see the White Lake (Lago Bianco), whose color comes from the snowmelt, also called "glacier milk." At the end of the lake, look to the left for a watershed sign that explains that this is a European continental divide: From here, rivers flow either north (toward the Inn and Danube rivers, and finally to the Black Sea) or south (to the Adriatic Sea via the Adda and Po rivers).

Behind the White Lake, you can see the glaciers of **Sassal Masone** and **Piz Cambrena.** This mountain pass separates not only European drainage basins, but also cultures. In earlier decades, the train line was more susceptible to bad-weather closures. The Italian-speaking valley of Poschiavo was often cut off from Switzerland in the winter, and better connected to the valleys across the border in Italy.

The train crosses the barren landscape and descends into the **Engadine** valley. Tourists and convalescents discovered this part of

Switzerland at the end of the 19th century. Imagine the gorgeous skiing here in the winter, which still attracts the rich and famous. After the railroad opened this secluded valley to the world, the first hotels and sanatoriums were built (the air and sunshine supposedly helped cure diseases like tuberculosis). Poets found their muse in the wild, romantic landscape, while painters flocked in, attracted by the quality of the light. Keep an eye out for typical Engadine architecture—small windows set in thick walls, etched *sgraffito* decorations, and carved wooden doors.

The **Montebello curve** offers you the best views over the **Morteratsch** glacier on the left, with impressive peaks in the background. From left to right: the Bellavista Range (12,770 feet), Crest Agüzza (12,690 feet), and the highest peak in the canton, **Mount Bernina** (13,280 feet). Mount Bernina was first climbed in 1850 by a team led by rangers from the village of Schanf. Their gear consisted only of thick woolen pants, a shirt and jacket, hobnailed shoes, and a hat with a black veil to shade them from the strong sunshine.

As you continue, the tracks are lined by more and more larch trees. The milky-white waters from Lago Bianco and the Morteratsch glacier run wild in a broad riverbed alongside the tracks, as satisfied cows chew away in the meadows while waterfalls tumble down the cliffs. From the Morteratsch station, there's a fine one-hour hike to the edge of the glacier, past posts tracking the glacier's recent retreat.

Next stop: **Pontresina.** This town is a good place to break the journey (see the Upper Engadine chapter). Consider spending a night or two in Pontresina, exploring the quaint village of Samedan, visiting the glitzy resort of St. Moritz, and maybe doing some hiking before continuing on your way.

If you're going to **St. Moritz,** your train trip is nearly over (about 10 minutes after Pontresina). If you're continuing to **Chur** (or, in summer, to Davos), there's more to see.

Part Three: Pontresina to Filisur

Although you're leaving the glaciers behind, your trip will still lead you through magnificent mountain scenery, with steep cliffs and deep gorges. (Note that from here on, the trip overlaps with the Glacier Express.)

First, you'll slide through the broad and mellow valley around Samedan, following the shortest river in Switzerland, the Flazbach. On the right, look for the funicular heading up to **Muottas Muragl,** a viewpoint overlooking the valleys that come together in Samedan (described in the Upper Engadine chapter). Samedan is home to Europe's highest airport. It serves glider enthusiasts and vacationers in St. Moritz.

SCENIC RAIL JOURNEYS

After Samedan, in **Bever,** the train leaves the Inn River valley and climbs to another spectacular leg of its journey. The section between Bever and Bergün boasts amazing engineering work. Technicians from all over the world come here to admire the diversity of spiral tunnels, looping viaducts, galleries, and bridges that span the Albula Gorge.

The train works its way up along a cheerfully splashing mountain creek, between the Swiss pine and larch trees and some isolated farmhouses. The **Albula Tunnel,** the highest subterranean alpine crossing in Europe, takes you up to 5,970 feet (it will soon be replaced by the Albula Tunnel II, set to open in 2021). This pass serves as another barrier between cultures and climate—it takes you from the valley of the Inn River (part of the Danube watershed) to the valley of the Albula, a tributary of the Rhine, and the weather is often quite different on either side of the tunnel.

From **Preda,** the train loops down through five spiral and two straight tunnels, crosses nine viaducts, and goes under two galleries—it's considered the most ingenious railway line ever built. It covers almost eight miles and descends more than 1,365 feet in altitude. The village of **Bergün** will be visible three separate times as you loop around the valley. Bergün greets you with a modern, public open-air swimming pool and an onion-shaped 17th-century "Roman tower." As the train continues winding down the pretty valley, you may be able to see other parts of the track below or next to you. Every winter, the street along the tracks above Bergün is closed to cars, and 100,000 sled enthusiasts enjoy the ride of their lives on a winding three-mile stretch.

You'll pass through **Filisur,** where summer Bernina Express trains to Davos split off. If you're continuing to Chur, read on.

Part Four: Filisur to Chur

After Filisur, the train enters a tunnel, and an announcement reminds you to ready your camera and position yourself on the left side. Just after the tunnel, you'll cross the famous **Landwasser viaduct.** A masterpiece of engineering, its pillars were built without scaffolding. Iron towers, which formed the center of each pillar, were built first. With the help of cranes set up atop each pillar, materials were hoisted up and the brick was laid. The 425-foot-long viaduct curves elegantly in a radius of 330 feet. Below, the wild Albula River carves the dramatic gorge; above, your train's panoramic windows allow you to see the steep, rugged cliffs looming over the tracks (a particularly beautiful stretch is right after Solis). Notice how nicely the dark limestone masonry matches the surrounding landscape (it was quarried right here).

Thusis is the commercial hub of the broad and lush Domleschg valley. The trip takes you down along the Hinterrhein

("Back-Rhine") River. Notice the many fortresses, castles, towers, and ruins along the river, a reminder that taxes were levied on the traders traveling this major route between northern and southern Europe. The 13th-century castle above the town now belongs to a local chemical company.

Reichenau marks the confluence of two arms of the Upper Rhine (the Hinterrhein and the Vorderrhein—"Front-Rhine"). This town became wealthy from the taxes it got from the passing merchants. The 17th-century Reichenau Castle, right where the rivers converge, was once used as a school, but is now a hotel.

The train follows the Rhine at the foot of Calanda Mountain to our final stop, **Chur.** You can catch the Glacier Express (explained next) from Chur or from St. Moritz.

Glacier Express

This most promoted of the Swiss scenic rail routes travels between Zermatt in the southwest of Switzerland and the best-known resort towns in eastern Switzerland (St. Moritz and Davos). If you stay on for the whole ride, you'll spend more than eight hours crossing 291 bridges, going through 91 tunnels, and reaching an altitude of 6,670 feet.

While it's an impressive and famous journey, the Glacier Express is not necessarily the be-all and end-all of Swiss rail trips. Much of the journey is down in valleys (as opposed to along the sides of cliffs), meaning that high-altitude views are a little lacking. And doing the whole route makes for a longer day than some wish. But the stark landscape, carved by the glaciers that gave the train its name, is striking. The trip offers a dramatic way to connect eastern Switzerland with tucked-away-in-the-mountains Zermatt.

ROUTE OVERVIEW

"Glacier Express" is a misnomer—you'll only glimpse glaciers at the two ends of the route, and it's hardly an express. Not only does it take its time (traveling at about 20 mph to make the full trip in 8 hours), but it also makes plenty of stops along the way. The route cuts along the southern part of Switzerland, between St. Moritz/Davos (in the east) and Zermatt (in the west). You can ride in either direction.

PLANNING YOUR TIME

Eight hours on a winding, jolting narrow-gauge train is a long time. If you don't want to commit to the whole eight hours, keep in mind that the most distinctive stretch of the trip is the high-mountain pass between Disentis and Brig. The stretch between St. Moritz and Filisur (which is also part of the Bernina Express route) is also a highlight. There are several ways of doing just a part of the route, though none is an obvious winner. Consider doing just St. Moritz to Chur (2 hours), then continuing to Zürich or Appenzell; St. Moritz to Brig (6.5 hours), then branching off to Interlaken, Bern, or Lausanne; Luzern or Lugano to Zermatt, connecting at Göschenen (6 hours); Luzern to St. Moritz, connecting at Andermatt (6.5 hours, see "**Luzern to St. Moritz Option**" later); or Lugano to Bern, via Göschenen and Brig (5.5 hours).

ORIENTATION TO THE GLACIER EXPRESS

Cost: You'll pay 152 CHF for second class, or 268 CHF for first class, between St. Moritz and Zermatt (prices include seat reservation fees). The entire trip is covered by the Swiss Travel and Global passes except the required reservation fee (23-44 CHF, price depends on the season, cheaper if you don't do the whole route). Those with a second-class rail pass will need to pay an additional fee to upgrade to first class. If you're riding the full length of the Glacier Express *sans* rail pass, the cost is high enough to warrant a look at the Swiss Half-Fare Card, which can quickly pay for itself (see page 445).

All Glacier Express trains have panoramic first- and second-class cars with air-conditioning, headsets for commentary, and the option of an in-seat meal. Second-class seating can get extremely crowded in summer, so consider splurging on first class.

Schedule: The Glacier Express train runs at least once daily in each direction, *except* from mid-October to mid-December (when local trains are your only option). Going from east to west, the train begins in St. Moritz at 9:15 and arrives in Zermatt at 17:10. Going from west to east, the train departs Zermatt at 8:52 and arrives in St. Moritz at 16:38. Those overnighting in Davos need to change trains in Filisur. In summer, one or two extra departures per day are added, an hour earlier and later than the times above. Confirm all times before your trip.

Information: The Glacier Express is operated jointly by the Matter-horn Gotthard Bahn (MGB), based in Brig (tel. 084-864-2442, www.glacierexpress.ch or www.matterhorngotthardbahn.ch), and the Rhätische Bahn (RhB), based in Chur (tel. 081-288-6565, www.rhb.ch). For more detail than found here or in the headset narration, consider picking up a guidebook before you board, or buy the (overpriced) official guide on board.

Picking the Best Seat: For most of the trip—including the most dramatic stretch, between Disentis and Brig—it's slightly pref-

erable to sit on the south-facing side of the train (generally seat numbers ending in 1 or 2 in both classes face south on this stretch; in second class, seats ending in 3 or 8 are along the aisle on the south-facing side). Coming from the east, even-numbered seats face forward for most of the trip. Keep in mind: Trains change directions in Chur—so if you start on the right side facing backward in Davos, Samedan, or St. Moritz, you'll be on the (slightly preferable) left side facing forward for most of the trip. Conductors take reserved seat numbers seriously, but may allow you to switch into an unoccupied seat if you prefer.

Luggage: You'll keep your luggage with you (they don't check it through)—just slip it between the backs of the seats.

No-Show Bridges: Most promotional materials show the Glacier Express train venturing across ancient aqueducts and old stone bridges. It makes for picturesque publicity. But realize that you can barely see these bridges from the train itself...because you're on them.

Taking Regular Trains: This is the one scenic train where following the same route on regular trains is not a good option.

Glacier Express Elevations

ZERMATT 5,263'
ANDERMATT 4,711'
OBERALP PASS 6,670'
DISENTIS 3,707'
BRIG 2,202'
REICHENAU 1,981'
CHUR 1,919'
ST. MORITZ 5,824'
ELEVATION IN FEET

The train takes 8 hours to travel 180 miles (290 kilometers), going through 91 tunnels and crossing 291 bridges.

SCENIC RAIL JOURNEYS

While it can be done, and does save the seat reservation fee, you'll need to change three times rather than enjoying the convenience of staying in one car the whole way. Regular trains are, however, the only option in late fall, when the express doesn't run.

Luzern to St. Moritz Option: An alternative, convenient way to connect visits to the Berner Oberland and the Upper Engadine regions is to go by train from Luzern to St. Moritz on a route that covers some of the nicest portions of the Glacier Express trip. Two trains leave Luzern every morning for St. Moritz with changes in Erstfeld, Göschenen, and Andermatt (see www.sbb.ch for schedules).

Eating on the Glacier Express: The train has a fancy restaurant car that offers a **$$$$ lunch,** which is handy if you're in for the full trip. The 45-CHF fixed-price meal includes a salad (summer) or soup (winter), a main dish, and a dessert (drinks cost extra). Their trademark gizmo is a tilted wine glass—appropriate since lunch is generally served when the train is going up a steep incline (11:00-13:30).

To save a few francs, it's fine to bring your own **picnic,** and most seats have tables—perfect for a grocery-store feast.

◑ SELF-GUIDED TOUR

All Glacier Express trains—whether they begin in St. Moritz or Davos—go through Chur. I'll describe the route starting at Chur and heading toward Zermatt. (For details on the trip from St. Moritz to Chur, see parts three and four of the Bernina Express self-guided tour, earlier.)

Just outside Chur (near where the St. Moritz train line hits the Chur line), you'll be following the **Vorderrhein Gorge**, nick-named "the Swiss Grand Canyon." It was carved by the Rhine River (though this little "Front-Rhine" is not navigable). After about nine miles, the train diverges from the Rhine and enters a pastoral region called **Surselva**, centered on the town of Ilanz. This is Romansh country, where the fourth official language of Switzerland is kept alive—barely—in communities like this one. Keep an eye out on the right side of the train for three doors, under small brown roofs, tucked into a stone wall beneath a road along the bottom of the hillside. They're part of Switzerland's military defenses; access to this pass can be blown up on short notice. From this valley (**Reichenau**, roughly 2,000 feet above sea level and the lowest altitude of the route), the big climb begins.

As you approach **Disentis**, the tracks begin to twist along the edge of a canyon—making the scenery more dramatic (a taste of what's to come). Thirty years ago, those mountains above you were covered in snow year-round—but no longer. You'll pull into Disentis, with its big 17th-century Benedictine monastery looming in your window (first on the left side, then on the right). Your car will jiggle as a cogwheel engine (a.k.a. rack-and-pinion drive) is attached. This locomotive has gears that can lower to latch onto the cogs of an extra rail with grippable teeth. At a 10 percent incline (that's 100 meters of gain per kilometer, or about 500 feet per mile), conventional train wheels start to slip.

You'll work your way up the mountain alongside the Vorderrhein River. Just west of **Sedrun** was the staging ground for the

excavation of the Gotthard Base Tunnel, which runs 30 miles under the mountain from Erstfeld to Bodio. Beyond Rueras, the track steepens and the train slows to allow its gears to latch into the cog rail. After Tschamut, the last inhabited place before Oberalp Pass, you enter a long series of snow sheds—designed to protect the tracks (and trains) in case an avalanche strikes.

You'll emerge from the sheds at **Oberalp Pass**, the literal high point of this journey (6,670 feet), and glide along the Oberalp Lake. Notice the extensive network of avalanche fences high above you—a reminder of the many generations of Swiss farmers who have learned to live on the land. The reddish streaks you might see on the snow? Believe it or not, that's sand from the Sahara Desert.

SCENIC RAIL JOURNEYS

It gets caught up in high-altitude winds and carried all the way to the Swiss Alps.

As you descend from the pass, you'll travel through the town of **Andermatt,** which is rebranding itself as a luxury ski resort. Deep below you is the older, 9.5-mile-long Gotthard Tunnel, which takes trains unscenically from Göschenen to Airolo. The huge boulders seen throughout this desolate terrain were deposited by glaciers.

Soon after, you'll go through the 9.5-mile-long Furka Base Tunnel. While it might seem like a view killer, realize that this tunnel—finished in 1982—makes it possible for the Glacier Express to continue running through the winter. Automobiles are allowed onto the train to ride smoothly and safely between Realp and Oberwald. This is especially handy in the winter, when the road is closed.

You'll emerge into the region of **Goms,** with its pretty villages. The up-close view of the village of **Reckingen** is particularly fun as the train snakes through a narrow passage between the dark-wood houses. Along this stretch, the train joins up with another of Europe's great rivers, the **Rhône.** Just a bubbly little mountain stream here (originating from the once-mighty Rhône Glacier nearby), the Rhône flows all the way to Marseille, France, where it meets the Mediterranean. Some of the construction you may see in this area is part of a project to "correct" (channel and control) this upper stretch of the powerful river, which has a long history of flooding the valley.

As the valley gets rockier, consider that you're on the "back" side of the Berner Oberland. If you climbed up high enough to the north, you'd see the Jungfrau, Mönch, and Eiger mountains (from the village of Fiesch/Kühboden you can do just that, with the help of a cable car up to Eggishorn, which boasts views of the Matterhorn and Mont Blanc to boot).

Finally, you'll arrive at **Brig,** an ugly industrial town with good connections to other train lines (transfer here if you're not continuing to Zermatt). From Brig, it's 25 miles to Zermatt and the Matterhorn, following the craggy **Nikolai Valley.** You'll feel the tug as the train's cogwheel attaches again for another steep climb. Keep an eye out for vineyards—the highest in Europe. We're out of milk country and into wine country. Along this section, the route closely follows the **Vispa River** as it scenically tumbles along. Shortly before the village of **Randa,** you pass a cone of rubble left by a huge avalanche that wiped out two miles of road and track here in 1991.

At **Täsch,** vast parking lots mark the end of the road for drivers. From here it's train-only into the traffic-free terminus of this line, Zermatt. Think about how much the terrain has changed

SCENIC RAIL JOURNEYS

since you started the trip: from remote valleys to fertile farmlands, to tundra above the tree line, to this rough and rocky terrain.

As you continue along the valley lined with quarries, you'll begin to get your first glimpses (provided the weather's clear) of the unmistakable shape of the **Matterhorn**—a fitting exclamation point marking the end of this long journey. **Zermatt**—with its bunker-like, avalanche-proof train station—lies just around the bend.

GLACIER EXPRESS CONNECTIONS

If you're not going all the way to St. Moritz or Zermatt, Chur and Brig are handy places to bail out of the Glacier Express.

From Brig by Train to: Bern (2-3/hour, 1-2 hours direct), **Lausanne** (2/hour, 2 hours direct), **Interlaken Ost** (1-2/hour, 70 minutes, change in Spiez), **Luzern** (1-2/hour, 2.5 hours, change in Bern and sometimes Olten), **Zürich** (hourly, 2 hours, more with change in Bern).

For Chur connections, see the next page.

Chur

The routes of the Glacier Express and the Bernina Express both pass through Chur—supposedly Switzerland's oldest and warmest town. Fanning out over the foothills from the Rhine River, Chur is a handy transportation hub for these two scenic train lines and has a charming-enough old town. Overall, Chur (pronounced "khoor") is just a typical Swiss burg—fine for passing through, but not worth a detour.

Visiting Chur: Chur's train station is at the bottom (north end) of the town center, where it sits atop a long underground concourse housing the **TI** (tel. 081-252-1818, https://chur.graubuenden.ch), a ticket office, the handy Bahnhofplatz parking garage, and a Co-op supermarket. To get to the old town, follow *Stadtzentrum* signs up the escalator, then walk straight up Bahnhofstrasse. In two blocks, you'll reach the big roundabout at Postplatz. The old town is straight ahead.

Public **WCs** are next to the cathedral. If you've got time to kill, you can wander up through the cobbled old town to two big churches (the Romanesque cathedral and the Gothic Church of St.

Martin), some remains of the medieval city wall, and the town museum (Rätisches Museum, www.raetischesmuseum.gr.ch). Follow the handy red signs pointing you toward the attractions.

Sleeping in Chur: Sleep in Chur only if you must, in order to connect to one of the scenic rail lines. Here are three moderately priced places in the atmospheric old town, an easy 10- to 15-minute walk from the train station: **$ Hotel Restaurant Rebleuten** (overlooking a quiet little square a block off Kornplatz at Pfisterplatz 1, tel. 081-255-1144, www.rebleutenchur.ch); **$$ Hotel Freieck** (with a mod lobby and 39 rooms over a low-key café, Reichsgasse 44, tel. 081-255-1515, www.freieck.ch); and charming **$$ Hotel Franziskaner** (with rooms above a popular restaurant, Kupfergasse 18, tel. 081-252-1261, www.hotelfranziskaner.ch).

Chur Connections: In addition to being a key stop for the Glacier Express and the Bernina Express, Chur also offers speedy, frequent connections to **Zürich** (3/hour, 2 hours), **Luzern** (3/hour, 2.5 hours, 1-2 changes), and **Appenzell** (2/hour, 2.5 hours, 1 or more changes).

SWITZERLAND IN WINTER

One of my favorite Swiss memories happened one winter night on the snowy slopes of the Berner Oberland. My friend Walter (who ran the old Hotel Mittaghorn in Gimmelwald) and I, warmed by hot chocolate laced with schnapps, decided to go sledding between mountain-high villages. We strapped flashlights to our heads, miner-style, and zoomed through the crisp, moonlit night.

That said, this is a summertime book. I've included plenty of tips on hiking, while mostly ignoring the winter-sports scene. But winter activities are an important part of the Swiss culture (and tourist industry).

Just a century ago, clever entrepreneurs in the Swiss Alps realized that skiing (which began as a method of wintertime transportation in Scandinavia 4,000 years ago) could be a profitable extension of their resorts' spring and summer seasons. Telemark (cross-country) skiing came first, then alpine (downhill) skiing, and, more recently, snowboarding. Generations of Swiss skiers have honed their skills on these slopes. Big names include Erika Hess, Vreni Schneider, Wendy Holdener, Carlo Janka, and the venerable 1948 Olympic champion Karl Molitor (whose family currently runs a ski-rental shop in Wengen, in the Berner Oberland).

You don't have to be a skier or snowboarder to enjoy Switzerland in the winter. Ski resorts offer plenty of other activities, including snowshoeing, sledding, ice skating...and shopping. Or just ride up a lift, rent a chair in the sun, and warm up with a glass of *Pflümli* (plum liqueur).

TOP WINTER DESTINATIONS

The winter-sports season begins in early December and runs through Easter. Peak time hits at Christmas and New Year's—during this period, hotel prices in resort towns surpass summer highs.

While Switzerland's resorts vary greatly, they share a rich ski culture, an astounding variety of terrain, relatively mild temperatures (compared to many American destinations), and a lively *après*-ski scene. For those who can afford them, the best winter activities are in the Berner Oberland (Mürren, Wengen, Grindelwald, and Gstaad); the southern canton of Valais (Zermatt, Saas-Fee, Crans-Montana, and Verbier); and the eastern canton of Graubünden (St. Moritz, Davos, Klosters, and Arosa).

The **Berner Oberland** offers the ultimate diversity of terrain and character, as well as great sledding and stellar views (see the Berner Oberland chapter). The

cliff-hanging town of Mürren is relatively uncrowded and a good home base for expert skiers, with the 10,000-foot Schilthorn peak as the backbone of its ski area. Across the valley, Wengen offers skiing for all skill levels, fine accommodations, and shopping, with a complex lift system connecting it to Kleine Scheidegg, Männlichen, and Grindelwald. Grindelwald, a little closer to Interlaken, is a bit pricier, but has the world's longest sled run and easy access to more than 100 miles of downhill trails, including the area's best range of beginners' runs. For more on these ski regions, see the Jungfrau Region tourism website (www.jungfrauregion.swiss).

The canton of **Valais** is known for its excellent winemaking (in the Rhône River valley) as well as its ski slopes (www.valais.ch). Connected to Italy by several high-mountain passes, Valais is home to Switzerland's best-known sight: the Matterhorn (see the Zermatt & the Matterhorn chapter). The area around the Matterhorn, including the villages of Zermatt and Saas-Fee, enjoys high elevation and good skiing.

The canton of Graubünden (www.graubuenden.ch) is home to **St. Moritz,** a resort town so well known that it's a registered trademark (see the Upper Engadine chapter). St. Moritz offers designer boutiques, luxury accommodations, a natural mineral-spring spa... oh, and ski slopes, too (www.stmoritz.ch). In addition to skiing, winter visitors to St. Moritz play polo and cricket on snow, go bobsledding on natural ice, or try "skijoring"—skiing while being pulled by riderless horses.

TIPS FOR WINTER SPORTS

Expect to spend 60-80 CHF a day on lift tickets. You may find cheaper prices in the off-peak season (before mid-Dec and after Easter), if you buy a multi-day pass, or if you have a Swiss Travel Pass. Prices may also be lower for seniors, teenagers, and kids (exact age cutoffs vary). Most ski areas offer half-day afternoon passes.

Rental prices are a bit higher than what you'd find in the US. Depending on the fanciness of the gear, you'll pay 50-80 CHF per day for skiing or snowboarding equipment. If you haven't packed ski wear, you'll pay about 50 CHF per day to rent ski pants, a jacket, and gloves.

Many rental shops in Switzerland belong to the Intersport rental network (www.intersportrent.ch), which sets fairly high standards for its member shops. Places outside this network can be cheaper, but Intersport shops are generally a safe bet and offer useful bonuses: You can reserve gear online at a discount, and many network shops let you pick up rental gear at one ski area and drop it off at another in the region for no charge (an especially handy option in the Berner Oberland).

Always ask your hotelier if they've arranged any special rental deals through local shops. Rental prices don't vary much (since so many shops are part of the Intersport network), so choose a place that's close to your hotel or convenient for getting up the mountain.

Swiss ski resorts are deservedly popular, and slopes can get crowded. Peak crowd times are Christmas, New Year's, mid-February to mid-March (when European school holidays hit), and Easter. The Berner Oberland also fills up in mid-January for world-class racing. Hit the slopes as soon as they open—the hordes don't usually arrive until 10:00 or later. This is especially true in swankier resorts, where well-heeled tourists enjoy long nights and short ski days.

For more in-depth information on the winter scene, see the winter sports section of the Swiss tourism website (www.myswitzerland.com).

CHRISTMAS CELEBRATIONS

Switzerland is an ideal place to celebrate the winter holidays. Imagine spending your days exploring Christmas markets in cozy Swiss cities, sipping hot mulled wine *(Glühwein)*, picking out your favorite handmade ornaments, then relaxing at night in a warm little chalet, making figure-eights with your cube of bread through a steaming pot of cheese fondue.

Swiss Christmas markets are a treat, whether in big cities (such as Bern, Zürich, and Basel) or smaller towns (Interlaken, Appenzell, Chur, and many others). While some of the bigger markets start at the beginning of December and run through Christmas Eve, smaller towns host markets for just one week or weekend. Check the Swiss Tourist Board's website for dates (www.myswitzerland.com/christmas).

You'll find all cities festively decorated, but Zürich's remarkable display of tasteful, twinkling lights is arguably Switzerland's

best. This being the land of Calvin—the most austere of Protestant Reformers—most Christmas decorations are relatively understated here, but they're still charming.

In the village of Gimmelwald, residents in each home adorn a window for Advent. Just as children open a different little paper window each day on an Advent calendar, Gimmelwald residents reveal a new decorated window on a different house each day. The debut of a new Advent window often comes with a party. Under a cold sky, with stars reflecting off the snow and the moon inside a halo, the village gathers. In a kind of roving block party, neighbors emerge to meet friends and enjoy grilled sausages, hot mulled wine, and folk music on the accordion. Men take sections of logs (the size of a four-foot chunk of telephone pole), cut the ends into a point, and plant them upright in the snow. Coated with tar, they're set ablaze—torches to light and warm the cozy yet frigid occasion. In the distance, children ride old-time wooden sleds, going up and down, up and down.

For the Swiss, a communal pot of fondue is purely a winter

specialty. Invitations to a cozy Swiss party include the word *FIGUGEGL* (fee-GOO-geck-ul), which stands for *Fondue isch guet und git e gueti Lune*—"Fondue is good and gives a good mood." According to tradition, if you drop your bread into the pot, you must kiss the person to your left.

Each Christmas season, usually on St. Nicholas Day (December 6), Swiss children receive a visit from Samichlaus—that's Swiss German for St. Nicholas. With his black-clad, soot-faced henchman, Schmutzli, by his side, Samichlaus goes door to door, visiting the town's children. He knocks on the door, and when the frightened-but-excited kids answer, Samichlaus consults his big book of sins—co-authored by parents—and does some lighthearted mor-

alizing. Schmutzli stands by as a menacing enforcer, traditionally holding either a stick or switch for beating bad children, and a sack for carrying them away to be eaten (nowadays he only eats the really bad children). Then Samichlaus asks the kids to earn a little forgiveness by reciting a poem. After the poems and assurances of reform, Samichlaus allows them to reach deep into his bag for a smattering of tangerines, nuts, gingerbread, and other treats.

Cutting and decorating the Christmas tree—traditionally on December 24—is a family affair. Real candles, kept upright by dangling ornamental counterbalances, are attached, then lit by the children. (Locals are bold with their candles; to me, it feels as if their pine houses, with open beams, are ready to go up in flames.) Presents are opened while the candles burn. The tree stays up after Christmas; candles are lit again on New Year's Eve for good luck. Some traditional rural Swiss churches also light candles on their trees for Christmas Eve services.

OTHER FESTIVITIES

Second only to Christmas is *Fasnacht*, the Germanic equivalent of Mardi Gras or Carnival. Traditionally celebrated in the days before or after Ash Wednesday, *Fasnacht* features a parade of locals in traditional masks and garish, larger-than-life costumes. Quirky traditions vary from town to town (for example, in Basel—home to Switzerland's most outlandish *Fasnacht*—celebrations begin promptly at 4:00 in the morning, and feature roving fife-and-drum bands). This pre-Christian ceremony likely dates from a pagan tradition to frighten away evil winter spirits and welcome the renewal of springtime. The most famous *Fasnacht* celebrations in Switzerland occur in Basel (www.fasnacht.ch), Bern

(www.fasnacht.be), and Luzern (www.luzerner-fasnacht.ch). If you'll be in Switzerland at this time of year, it's worth the effort to catch one of these weird and wonderful celebrations.

SWITZERLAND: PAST & PRESENT

Switzerland has a unique and impressive story, forging unity from diversity and somehow remaining above the fray when Europe goes ballistic. Despite four languages, diverse geography, ill-defined borders, and many religious sects—and despite being surrounded by continental Europe's four big powers (France, Germany, Austria, and Italy)—the Swiss cantons banded together to form an independent federal system that still works today.

Even if you're not going to Switzerland for the history (who would?), you'll encounter it. You can play gladiator inside a fighting arena from Roman times or tour medieval castles and battlegrounds, left over from when the Swiss wrested their independence from foreign rulers. Stripped-down cathedrals attest to the religious violence of the Reformation, which almost tore the country apart. You'll ride the ingenious cogwheel trains and cliff-climbing funiculars of Switzerland's progressive 19th century, when the country was at the forefront of the emerging Industrial Age. The specters of Nazi Germany and the Soviet Union arise in underground fortresses and bomb shelters now open to the public. And finally, you'll see the Switzerland of today—gleaming cities, state-of-the-art transportation, and happy citizens. I love to go a-wandering along the history path, so strap on your rucksack, and let's go.

EARLY HISTORY: CELTS AND ROMANS
(c. 500 BC-AD 500)

The Alps—Switzerland's star attraction—were born 500 million years ago, when the ocean floor was rocked by earthquakes that folded the earth's crust upward and created this long range of peaks (see the sidebar on page 18). The rugged landscape shaped the history and character of the Swiss people. It kept early populations physically isolated, leading to still-present cultural divisions and fostering an ethos of independence. Switzerland's location at the heart of Western Europe forced it to be international in outlook, yet the impregnable mountains allowed it to remain apart and neutral.

The first Swiss to appear in written records (c. 500 BC) were a Celtic tribe called the Helvetii. Their name survives today in the country's official title, Confoederatio Helvetica. "Helvetia," the female symbol of Switzerland, appears dressed in robes and armed with a spear and shield on coins, stamps, and statues.

In 58 BC, the Helvetii were defeated by Julius Caesar, the Roman general and future ruler. The Romans established a capital at Avenches, near Murten (where evocative ruins remain); built the cities of Zürich, Geneva, Basel, and Lausanne; and assimilated the Helvetii into their Europe-wide empire. Roman culture thrived in Switzerland for almost 500 years.

As Rome fell (c. AD 400), the Alemanni and other Germanic tribes swarmed in from the north, snuffed out Roman culture, and established the German language. In the west, the Burgundians adopted Latin, which eventually evolved into French. But these tribes never penetrated the nooks and crannies of the most remote mountain areas, and in these regions, particularly in the southeast, people still converse in Romansh, a language that descends independently from the colloquial Latin spoken by Roman-era occupiers. South of the Alps, Latin gradually developed into modern-day Italian. These linguistic and cultural divides remain today.

THE MIDDLE AGES: THE HOLY ROMAN EMPIRE (c. 500-1291)

Like most of Europe during the dark medieval centuries, Switzerland was poor, feudal, and swept by barbarian invasions. The mostly pagan Swiss were slowly converted to Christianity by traveling Irish monks, including St. Gallus (seventh century), who gave his name to the canton of St. Gallen. Swiss lands became part of Charlemagne's empire (c. 800) and then of its successor to the east—the Holy Roman Empire.

Around the turn of the first millennium, Switzerland began to prosper. Cities such as Bern and Luzern were founded, welcoming skilled craftsmen and traders. High in the Alps, clever engineers built bridges and catwalks to open a vital north-south highway through the St. Gotthard Pass. Merchants bought luxury goods in Venice and shipped them over the high mountains to northern Europe. This trade route proved so lucrative that the Holy Roman Emperor ensured access to it by granting the Swiss a measure of independence. Switzerland got a taste of freedom, and when the emperor (a member of the powerful Habsburg family) later tried to bring the country under tighter control, the Swiss had had enough.

THE OLD CONFEDERACY (1291-1500)

On August 1, 1291 (celebrated today as the country's national day), representatives of Switzerland's three original cantons (Uri, Schwyz, and Unterwalden) gathered together and swore an oath. "We will be a single nation of brothers..." they asserted, and joined together to oppose Habsburg rule. According to a famous legend, a Swiss man named William Tell refused to bow to the Habsburg hat, a symbol of their power. As punishment, he was forced to shoot an apple off his own son's head. His son lived to see another haircut, and Tell led the rebellion. (Sadly, historians say that Tell probably never actually existed.)

The Swiss had to battle the powerful Habsburg family for two full centuries to completely drive them out. Meanwhile, in the west, the Swiss fought Burgundy, trouncing them at the pivotal Battle of Murten. One by one, other cantons and cities (Luzern, Zürich, Bern) joined the confederacy. By around 1500, Switzerland's territory had grown to become roughly similar to its current bounds.

During these centuries of warfare, the Swiss earned a reputation as Europe's fiercest warriors. Swiss mercenaries became a

valuable export, hired by foreign kings to fight their wars and defend their palaces (think of the Swiss Guards, who still protect the Vatican today). During the French Revolution in 1792, when crowds stormed the king's palace in Paris, it was Swiss mercenaries who went through with the hopeless defense. Six hundred of them were killed—an event memorialized in Luzern's famous Lion Monument to fallen Swiss Guards.

REFORMATION AND ENLIGHTENMENT
(c. 1500-1700)

The Protestant Reformation split Switzerland in two. Ulrich Zwingli preached Protestantism in Zürich (see sidebar on page 36), John Calvin brought his French flock to Geneva, and the Dutch humanist Desiderius Erasmus taught at Basel. While the cities went Protestant, the more rural cantons stayed true to the Catholic faith, plunging the country into religious warfare (1529-1531). Angry rioters stormed Catholic cathedrals, stripping them of their "graven images" and leaving the austere interiors travelers see today (including Zürich's Grossmünster, Bern's Münster, and Lausanne's cathedral). This destruction of religious symbology is known as "iconoclasm."

While Europe suffered through a century of religious wars, Switzerland's struggles were relatively short-lived. Swiss mercenaries fought other countries' wars more than their own. When peace came to Europe with the Treaty of Westphalia (1648), the agreement also officially recognized Switzerland as a fully independent nation.

1700s AND 1800s

Through the Age of Enlightenment, Switzerland bucked the European trend toward absolute monarchs. As the country steadily advanced economically and technologically, it moved in a firmly democratic direction. However, internal conflict about how to organize the country's government made for a rocky transition. Swiss Protestants generally favored a strong central government and were more open to new political and social ideas. The more remote, more Catholic cantons wanted to keep power in local areas and preserve traditional ways of life. This tension continues in Swiss politics to this day.

Riding the wave of the French Revolution, Napoleon Bonaparte occupied Switzerland (1798) and tried (unsuccessfully) to establish a unified central government—called the Helvetic Republic—which fell apart within five years. With Napoleon's defeat (and the 1815 Congress of Vienna), the European powers restored Switzerland's old status. They also set it on its future political course: neutrality in all conflicts.

In 1847, the Swiss fought a four-week, not-very-bloody civil war that ended in a victory for the advocates of centralization. In 1848, amid a Europe-wide wave of liberal reforms, Switzerland crafted a constitution that struck a balance between the two camps. The constitution created a strong central government but also allowed each canton much more autonomy than the regions in other European countries. (It was partly modeled on America's, as the Swiss struggles with centralism and federalism mirror American debates over states' rights.) The country's seat of government was established in the low-key town of Bern, at the boundary of the German- and French-speaking parts of Switzerland.

Around this time the country began to welcome hordes of tourists, beginning with French, English, and German aristocrats on the Grand Tour, who passed through Switzerland on their way to Italy. Next came the British mountaineers, whose reverence for the Alps was part of the Romantic outlook on nature: For the first time, Europeans looked at mountains as objects of beauty and inspiration, rather than as frustrating obstacles. Visitors marveled at

the mountain scenery and the "sublime" rush it gave them. The new technology of rail travel made trips more comfortable and affordable.

In this heyday of European travel, Switzerland virtually invented mass tourism as we know it—pioneering ways of marking its mountains, offering the first organized vacations, investing in a well-oiled infrastructure, and establishing a reputation for efficiency, cleanliness, quality, and ease (even inventing new names for places that had

local names that were considered too intimidating for foreign visitors). Switzerland's system of high-altitude trains, funiculars, and mountain lifts was built to carry 19th-century tourists to previously unheard-of heights. Today's visitors stay in the same resort towns (Interlaken, Zermatt, Luzern, St. Moritz), ride the same kind of lifts, and see echoes of themselves in the stylized travel advertisements from that Romantic Age.

As a neutral country, Switzerland fostered its reputation as

a leader in international relations. Like tourists, politicians loved to meet amidst its clear air and alpine vistas. The world's diplomats descended on Geneva in 1863 and 1864, producing two landmark institutions: the International Red Cross (still run from Geneva) and the Geneva Conventions war treaties. The United Nations and other international organizations still maintain a large presence in Geneva. And when the modern Olympic Games were founded by a French aristocrat in 1894, nearby Lausanne became the movement's world headquarters.

PAST & PRESENT

20TH CENTURY: WORLD WARS

Switzerland entered the 20th century on the cutting edge of progress. Its trains and communications systems were top-notch. The

artist Paul Klee (1879-1940), with his playful, eccentric style, contributed to the Modernist movement (see his works at the Rosengart Collection in Luzern and at the Paul Klee Center in Bern). Europe's rich flocked to visit Swiss doctors at alpine sanatoriums. Carl Jung (1875-1961) pioneered the blossoming field of psychoanalysis. And in the quiet city of Bern, an

anonymous patent clerk named Albert Einstein (1879-1955) was rewriting humankind's understanding of how the universe worked (see sidebar on page 116).

In World War I (1914-1918), Switzerland declared itself neutral and escaped the devastation that hit the rest of Europe. After the war, Geneva served as the seat of the League of Nations, a short-lived forerunner to the United Nations.

When World War II broke out (1939-1945), Swiss neutrality was not taken for granted. As Nazi Germany and fascist Italy flanked the country, 850,000 Swiss men grabbed their rifles and mobilized to protect the borders. They had an ambitious plan, in case of invasion, to assemble the country's leadership and military into the innermost, mountainous core of the country—sealing off a fortified Swiss National Redoubt (see page 94.) Switzerland avoided invasion through both "militarized neutrality," and by trading with (some would say "appeasing") the Nazis. Switzerland sheltered some refugees—and turned others away—and acted as a mediator between the Allies and the Axis.

Today, critics charge that, though neutral in the war, Switzerland actually helped the Nazi effort by continuing to do business with them. (It's no secret that a significant number of German-speaking Swiss weren't all that opposed to the Nazi regime.) They exchanged Swiss francs (the only currency accepted throughout Europe) for Nazi gold—knowing full well that the gold had been stolen from other nations and Holocaust victims. In the 1990s, lawsuits called Swiss banks to account for the ill-gotten bullion in their vaults. A 2002 commission formed by the Swiss government agreed that Switzerland could have done more to resist the Nazis and to help Jewish refugees...but restitution has been slow in coming.

After the war, Switzerland's policy of neutrality led the country to refuse membership in various international alliances and organizations, including the United Nations, NATO, and the European Union.

SWITZERLAND TODAY

Switzerland maintains a delicate balance between its traditional, neutral past and the high-tech, global future.

As it has been for 700 years, the government is a federalist democracy that gives considerable autonomy to each canton. On the national level, the executive branch is steered by a seven-member committee, and the presidency is just a figurehead position that rotates between the seven members. There's a strong bicameral parliament, in which no single political party has more than about a fourth of the seats. Since World War II, legislative power has been held by an ever-changing array of coalitions. No single point of view dominates, and collaboration is essential.

The federal government handles foreign affairs, national defense, currency, and the federal courts—and leaves most everything else to the 26 cantons. The person-on-the-street can always make their voice heard thanks to frequent referendums, held when citizens gather enough signatures to require a public vote on an issue. Unlike in most modern democracies, Swiss citizens have a direct say in many political matters and leave fewer decisions to elected representatives.

During the Great Recession, the euro zone's financial crisis posed a threat to Switzerland's financial stability by driving up demand for the Swiss franc—and making Swiss exports and tourism less competitive. Now, with Europe's economy on the rebound, Zürich continues to be a global center of banking and finance, and tourism remains a strong part of the economy. Stability is enhanced by strong social security and a collaborative approach to settling labor disputes between unions and employers.

In foreign affairs, Switzerland remains neutral...but ever-vigilant. Every able-bodied man serves in the army and stays in the reserves. Each house has a gun and a fully stocked bomb shelter. (Swiss vacuum-packed emergency army bread, which lasts two years, is also said to function as a weapon.) Altogether, the country bristles with 600,000 rifles in homes and 12,000 heavy guns in place. Airstrips are hidden inside mountains, accessed by camouflaged doors. With the push of a button, all road, rail, and bridge entries to Swiss territory can be destroyed, sealing off the country from the outside world. Sentiments are changing, though, and Switzerland has come close to voting away its entire military. Today, you can visit once-hidden military installations, now open to the public as museums (for example, Fortress Fürigen—covered in the Luzern & Central Switzerland chapter).

The question of how closely to integrate with Europe has dominated political discussion in Switzerland for the last few decades. In 2002, the Swiss made a big step away from total neutrality when voters approved a referendum to join the United Nations. In 2008, Switzerland joined the Schengen Agreement, opening its borders to its neighboring countries and most of the EU. Is EU membership next? Probably not. In referendum after referendum the Swiss have strongly rejected the idea of full economic and political integration with the EU, judging the costs to be more significant than the huge potential gains. Still, they've seen benefits in collaborating with Europe on practical matters such as scientific research. For example, Switzerland is home to Europe's high-tech particle accelerator laboratory, called CERN (the place where the World Wide Web was invented by a British scientist).

While it's nice to think of Swiss neutrality as born of pacifism, many realists argue that it's more about money: Switzerland's neutrality policy was key to one of its main sources of income. Traditionally, many Swiss banks allowed foreigners to deposit money with few questions asked. Critics charge that these secret bank accounts have harbored the dirty money of mobsters, terrorists, dictators, guidebook authors, tax evaders, and sleazy businessmen. Switzerland also has a reputation as a safe haven from prosecution, harboring a long list of foreigners (from Hollywood sex offender Roman Polanski to Ugandan dictator Idi Amin). But times are changing. Recently, Swiss politicians and bankers have responded to outside pressure and introduced legislation that will require banks to share information on clients with the tax authorities in other countries.

Another big issue in Switzerland is how to deal with the rising tide of immigrants. The country's high standard of living makes it an appealing place to live, and Switzerland has more noncitizen residents than most countries (about 24 percent, compared with 7 percent in the US). Many of those immigrants are wealthy Europeans enjoying the country's easy tax laws. Others are young Germans, Italians, or Portuguese who have taken jobs in the hospitality industry. Still others are the Swiss-born, Swiss-raised children of an earlier generation of immigrants (called "Secondos")—who still don't have Swiss citizenship due to the complicated application requirements. It's the "less-desirable" immigrants who have drawn fire—those who arrive with little wealth and then rely on generous social services—but it's not clear that there are really that many of them.

Opinions on this and many other issues are generally divided along geographic/linguistic lines. City dwellers, along with French and Italian speakers, tend to favor immigrants' rights, EU membership, and other progressive issues; rural German speakers are more likely to be conservative. In 2009, when Switzerland voted to ban the construction of new minarets—sparking controversy across Europe—only four cantons opposed the initiative, all of them in French-speaking areas.

Climate issues also loom large in Swiss politics. Swiss people are keenly aware of the widespread impact of climate change. In 2019 elections, the balance of parliamentary power was tipped not toward right-wing nativist parties (as in many other European nations), but toward environmental movements. Switzerland's various "green" parties took 20 percent of seats—one of the highest ratios in Europe.

With 2,500 years of history, Switzerland has seen many shifts—from Celts to Romans to Habsburgs, from wars to neutrality to technological prog- ress. But what's striking is how little Switzerland has changed. The Alps are still there, and they're still big and rugged (even if the glaciers are smaller than ever). The government, after 700 years in existence, remains a model of democracy and international cooperation. Switzerland is fully modern, but you'll also encounter quaint pockets of the past. Take time to see Swiss history alive today—from the cow parades of Appenzell to the Roman ruins in Avenches, and from the turrets of Château de Chillon to the farmers of Gimmelwald, who still make hay while the sun shines.

NOTABLE SWISS PEOPLE

William Tell (c. 1280-1354): On November 18, 1307, William (Wilhelm) Tell, a Swiss peasant, refused a bailiff's order to bow to a symbol of the Habsburg emperor. As punishment, Tell was forced to fire his crossbow at an apple resting on his son's head. He shot cleanly through the apple without injuring his son, and later ambushed and killed the bailiff—launching a revolt for Swiss independence. Though historians say the famous hero is fictional (a similar Danish legend predates the Swiss one), don't "tell" the Swiss—up to 60 percent still believe there was a real William Tell.

Huldrych Zwingli (1484-1531): The son of a farmer, Huldrych Zwingli started out as a Catholic true believer, but under the influence of Renaissance humanists, turned into a religious revolutionary. Known as the "third man of the Protestant Reformation" (the other two were Martin Luther and John Calvin), he used his position as the top pastor in Zürich to challenge Rome, insisting that Christians study the Bible to guide their beliefs. Many Protestant faiths, including the United Church of Christ and the Presbyterian Church, trace their theology back to Zwingli.

Jean-Jacques Rousseau (1712-1778): One of the most influential writers of the 18th century, Jean-Jacques Rousseau ran away from his humble Geneva home for France when he was 16, but he always considered himself Swiss, not French. His writings celebrated nature and human passion (over cold reason), unleashing forces that would result in the French Revolution, Romantic literature, and even a return to breastfeeding. Publishers couldn't print his books fast enough, so they rented them out by the day. Rousseau's descriptions of the Swiss countryside helped start the 19th-century craze for visiting the Alps.

Madame Tussaud (1761-1850): An entertainment empire began when Swiss-born Anna Maria Grosholtz moved to Paris and learned how to sculpt wax. It was an auspicious time and place—she was able to create figures of Voltaire, Jean-Jacques Rousseau, and Benjamin Franklin. Later, during the French Revolution, she made death masks from decapitated heads. After marrying François Tussaud (becoming "Madame Tussaud"), she moved to London and eventually opened a museum of wax figures, which still shows some of her original work.

Henri Dunant (1828-1910): In 1859, Geneva businessman Henri Dunant witnessed one of the bloodiest battles of the 19th century—the Battle of Solferino in northern Italy, where about 40,000 soldiers were killed or wounded. He wrote a book that not only described the carnage, but also proposed a neutral organization that would care for those wounded in wartime. His leadership led to the founding of the International Red Cross and the Geneva Conventions, which put humanitarian limits on the waging of war. He won the first Nobel Peace Prize in 1901.

Carl Jung (1875-1961): After Freud, Carl Jung had the greatest impact on modern psychology; there probably wouldn't be a New Age movement or the Myers-Briggs personality test without him. The Zürich psychologist popularized such terms as "introvert/extrovert," "personality complex," and "collective unconscious." He once said that the Swiss are a "primitive" people (their love of cows reminded him of African animism), and that under their legendary efficiency is a deeply buried "earth mysticism."

Hermann Hesse (1877-1962): German-born Hesse, who became a Swiss citizen in 1923, was into psychoanalysis, India, and Buddhism before they were cool. His writing was banned by the Nazis and later beloved by 1960s hippies for its themes of self-discovery and enlightenment. His best-known works—among them *Steppenwolf, Siddhartha,* and *Narcissus and Goldmund*—are still widely read today. He was particularly publicity-shy—upon winning the Nobel Prize for Literature in 1946, he wrote to a friend, "To hell with this damn business."

Paul Klee (1879-1940): Paul Klee's mastery of color and tone created highly individual art that critics have described as "musical" and "childlike." Born and raised in Bern, Klee became a teacher at the famous Bauhaus school in Weimar, Germany, but when Hitler came to power in 1933, he was fired. He returned to Switzerland as the Nazis stripped his paintings from museums and classified them as "degenerate." You can see his work at museums in Bern and Luzern—then decide for yourself.

Le Corbusier (1887-1965): "The house is a machine for living in." With this and other edicts, architect Charles-Edouard Jeanneret-Gris, better known as Le Corbusier, changed the shape of 20th-century cities. His plan for Paris' Marais district was emblematic—rows of identical towers set between freeways, replacing public squares and winding streets. The Parisians turned him down, but many office and housing projects in Europe and America followed his precepts. Le Corbusier was one of the most influential architects of his time, though today many regard his International Style as sterile and socially destructive.

Jean Piaget (1896-1980): According to *Time* magazine, Geneva psychologist Jean Piaget was "the first to take children's thinking seriously." Before the publication of his groundbreaking work, parents and teachers regarded children as empty vessels into which they poured knowledge. By studying his own three kids, Piaget deduced that children are constantly testing their own theories of how the world works, asserting that "children have real understanding only of that which they invent themselves."

Alberto Giacometti (1901-1966): The son of a Post-Impressionist painter, sculptor/painter Alberto Giacometti was born in a Swiss alpine valley near the Italian border. Best known for his stylized, elongated figures, he was an important Surrealist sculptor in the 1930s, while his later work explored existentialism, evoking the melancholy and alienation of a post-WWII world.

Elisabeth Kübler-Ross (1926-2004): She grew up in a strict, Protestant family, but Elisabeth Kübler-Ross defied tradition and got her MD in 1957. A year later, she left Zürich for the US, where she was appalled by the way doctors and hospitals treated the dying. The five stages of grief she first explained in *On Death and Dying*—denial, anger, bargaining, depression, and acceptance—

have become a modern touchstone, now commonly applied to any catastrophic personal loss.

Ursula Andress (born 1936): When the bikini-clad Andress walked out of the ocean in the first James Bond movie, *Dr. No,* the indelible image of the "Bond heroine" was born. Tough, smart, and outrageously beautiful, Andress was a great match for Sean Connery's 007, even though the producers dubbed her voice to mask her Swiss-German accent. Though many of her subsequent films were subpar, the list of her leading men is not: Laurence Olivier, Frank Sinatra, Marcello Mastroianni, Peter Sellers, and even Elvis Presley.

Roger Federer (born 1981): This Swiss ace was born and raised near Basel. By the age of 29, Federer had won a record 16 Grand Slam tennis titles, including all four majors. From 2003-2007, he reeled off five straight Wimbledon wins, and has since captured the title several more times. He also pulled off a five-peat at the US Open (2004-2008), making it clear why many regard him as one of the greatest tennis players of all time.

PRACTICALITIES

Tourist Information 409
Travel Tips. 410
Money 412
Sightseeing. 418
Sleeping 419
Eating. 429
Staying Connected 436
Transportation 441
Resources from Rick Steves 454

This chapter covers the practical skills of European travel: how to get tourist information, pay for things, sightsee efficiently, find good-value accommodations, eat affordably but well, use technology wisely, and get between destinations smoothly. For more information on these topics, see www.ricksteves.com/travel-tips.

Tourist Information

The Swiss national tourist office in the US is a wealth of information (tel. 800-794-7795, www.myswitzerland.com). Before your trip, download or request brochures (including regional and city maps, festival schedules, and hiking information).

In Switzerland, a good first stop in every town is generally the tourist information office (abbreviated TI in this book). While you can get plenty of information online, I still make a point to swing by to confirm sightseeing plans, pick up a city map, and get information on public transit, walking tours, special events, and nightlife. Anticipating a harried front-line staffer, prepare a list of questions and a proposed plan to double-check. Throughout Switzerland, you'll find TIs are usually well-organized and always have an English-speaking staff. Most TIs are run by the government, which means their information isn't colored by a drive for profit.

Some TIs have information on the entire country or at least the region, so try to pick up maps for destinations you'll be visiting later in your trip.

Travel Tips

Emergency and Medical Help: For any emergency service—ambulance, police, or fire—call **112** from a mobile phone or landline. Operators, who in most countries speak English, will deal with your request or route you to the right emergency service. If you get sick, do as the locals do and go to a pharmacist for advice. Or ask at your hotel for help—they'll know the nearest medical and emergency services.

ETIAS Registration: Beginning in 2021, US and Canadian citizens may be required to register online with the European Travel Information and Authorization System (ETIAS) before entering certain European countries (quick and easy process, $8 fee, valid 3 years). A useful private website with more details is www.schengenvisainfo.com/etias.

Theft or Loss: To replace a passport, you'll need to go in person to the US embassy (see next). If your credit and debit cards disappear, cancel and replace them (see "Damage Control for Lost Cards," on page 416). File a police report, either on the spot or within a day or two; you'll need it to submit an insurance claim for lost or stolen rail passes or travel gear, and it can help with replacing your passport or credit and debit cards. For more information, see www.ricksteves.com/help.

US Embassy in Bern: Tel. 031-357-7011, services by appointment only; Mon-Fri 9:00-11:30, closed Sat-Sun—after-hours tel. 031-357-7777; Sulgeneckstrasse 19, https://ch.usembassy.gov/embassy/bern.

Canadian Embassy in Bern: Tel. 031-357-3200; Mon-Fri 8:30-11:30, closed Sat-Sun; Kirchenfeldstrasse 88, http://switzerland.gc.ca.

Borders: Although Switzerland isn't in the European Union, it does belong to the Schengen Zone, which means border controls are a wave-through. Even so, remember that when you change countries, you also change currencies, country dialing codes, and *Unterhosen*.

Time Zones: Switzerland, like most of continental Europe, is generally six/nine hours ahead of the East/West Coasts of the US. The exceptions are the beginning and end of Daylight Saving

Time: Europe "springs forward" the last Sunday in March (two weeks after most of North America), and "falls back" the last Sunday in October (one week before North America). For a handy online time converter, see www.timeanddate.com/worldclock.

Business Hours: In large cities, shops are generally open Monday through Friday 9:00-18:30 (later on Thursday) and Saturday 8:00-17:00. Smaller shops, and all shops in villages, typically close for one or two hours at lunchtime—often from 12:00 to 14:00. Sundays have the same pros and cons as they do for travelers in the US: Sightseeing attractions are generally open, while shops and banks are closed, public transportation options are fewer, and there's no rush hour. Many sights are closed on Monday (head for the hills).

Watt's Up? Europe's electrical system is 220 volts, instead of North America's 110 volts. Most electronics (laptops, smartphones, cameras) and newer hair dryers convert automatically, so you won't need a converter, but you will need an adapter plug with two round prongs, sold inexpensively at travel stores in the US. Sockets in Switzerland only accept plugs with slimmer prongs: Don't buy an adapter with the thicker ("Schuko" style) prongs—it won't work. Avoid bringing older appliances that don't automatically convert voltage; instead, buy a cheap replacement in Europe.

Switzerland uses its very own style of electrical plugs, not shared with any other country in Europe: three slim round prongs arranged in a triangular shape. You'll often see wall sockets with a three-plug cloverleaf pattern. If you already have an adapter for European plugs, you may not need another adapter for Switzerland—European plugs will fit in Swiss sockets if the prongs are of the slimmer type and un-grounded, and if the body of the adapter is small enough to fit in a recessed outlet. If your adapter doesn't work in your hotel room's sockets, ask your hotelier if they have one you can borrow, or buy one locally.

Discounts: Discounts for sights are generally not listed in this book. However, seniors (age 60 and over), youths under 18, and students and teachers with proper identification cards (www.isic.org) can get discounts at many sights—always ask. Some discounts are available only to European citizens.

Online Translation Tips: Google's Chrome browser instantly translates websites; translate.google.com is also handy. The

Exchange Rate

Switzerland, which isn't a member of the European Union, has retained its traditional currency, the Swiss franc. The international abbreviation for the Swiss franc is "CHF."

1 Swiss franc (CHF) = about $1

Check www.oanda.com for the latest exchange rates. One Swiss franc is broken down into 100 rappen (or centimes in French Switzerland). There are coins for one, two, and five francs, plus several coins for very small denominations of rappen. The small coin with real value is the 50-rappen (marked with "½" rather than "50"). It looks like a tiny dime, but is equivalent to a half-dollar. In a handful of change, it's easy to identify as the only one with ridges.

Google Translate app converts spoken English into most European languages (and vice versa) and can also translate text it "reads" with your phone's camera.

Money

Here's my basic strategy for using money in Europe:

- Upon arrival, head for a cash machine (ATM) at the airport and withdraw some local currency, using a debit card with low international transaction fees.
- In general, pay for bigger expenses with a credit card and use cash for smaller purchases. Use a debit card only for cash withdrawals.
- Keep your cards and cash safe in a money belt.

PLASTIC VERSUS CASH

Although credit cards are widely accepted in Europe, cash is sometimes the only way to pay for cheap food, taxis, tips, and local guides. Some businesses (especially smaller ones, such as B&Bs and mom-and-pop cafés and shops) may charge you extra for using a credit card—or might not accept credit cards at all. Having cash on hand helps you out of a jam if your card randomly doesn't work.

I use my credit card to book and pay for hotel reservations, to buy advance tickets for events or sights, and to cover most other expenses. It can also be smart to use plastic near the end of your trip, to avoid another visit to the ATM.

WHAT TO BRING

I pack the following and keep it all safe in my money belt.

Debit Card: Use this at ATMs to withdraw local cash.

Credit Card: Handy for bigger transactions (at hotels, shops, restaurants, travel agencies, car-rental agencies, and so on), payment machines, and online purchases.

Backup Card: Some travelers carry a third card (debit or credit; ideally from a different bank), in case one gets lost, demagnetized, eaten by a temperamental machine, or simply doesn't work.

A Stash of Cash: I always carry $100-200 as a cash backup, which comes in handy in an emergency (such as when banks go on strike or if your ATM card gets eaten by the machine).

What NOT to Bring: Resist the urge to buy Swiss francs before your trip or you'll pay the price in bad stateside exchange rates. Wait until you arrive to withdraw money. I've yet to see a European airport that didn't have plenty of ATMs.

BEFORE YOU GO
Use this pre-trip checklist.

Know your cards. Debit cards from any major US bank will work in any standard European bank's ATM (ideally, use a debit card with a Visa or MasterCard logo). As for credit cards, Visa and MasterCard are universal, American Express is less common, and Discover is unknown in Europe.

Know your PIN. Make sure you know the numeric, four-digit PIN for all of your cards, both debit and credit. Request it if you don't have one, as it may be required for some purchases in Europe (see "Using Credit Cards," later), and allow time to receive the information by mail.

Report your travel dates. Let your bank know that you'll be using your debit and credit cards in Europe, and when and where you're headed.

Adjust your ATM withdrawal limit. Find out how much you can take out daily and ask for a higher daily withdrawal limit if you want to get more cash at once. Note that European ATMs will withdraw funds only from checking accounts; you're unlikely to have access to your savings account.

Ask about fees. For any purchase or withdrawal made with a card, you may be charged a currency conversion fee (1-3 percent) and/or a Visa or MasterCard international transaction fee (less than 1 percent). If you're getting a bad deal, consider getting a new debit or credit card. Reputable no-fee cards include those from Capital One, as well as Charles Schwab debit cards. Most credit unions and some airline loyalty cards have low or no international transaction fees.

IN EUROPE
Using Cash Machines
European cash machines have English-language instructions and work just like they do at home—except they spit out local currency

Why No Swiss Euros?

Though surrounded by countries enjoying the convenience of a shared currency, the Swiss have hung on to their old franc. They would have to be part of the European Union to join the euro zone—and compliance with European Union regulations would mean the end of Switzerland's fortress identity and subsidized agricultural system. Most Swiss are horrified by the idea of having to square their fiscal, military, and foreign policies with the cacophonous EU.

But it's not just fear of instability and loss of sovereignty that's kept the Swiss clinging to their francs. Having a separate currency helps bring business to Switzerland. A huge part of the Swiss economy is based on providing a safe and secret place for wealthy people from around the world to stash their money. When bank fees are figured in, people who "save" in Swiss banks actually earn negative interest—they pay the Swiss to keep their money. Switzerland's separate currency also means that residents enjoy lower mortgage interest rates than the rest of Europe.

Even though Switzerland hasn't adopted the euro, the majority of Swiss hotels, restaurants, and shops (especially in touristy areas) accept smaller euro bills. Most businesses will not take euro coins or larger bills, and you'll usually get bad rates (and your change in Swiss francs). But unless this is your last chance to use up leftover euros, spend francs in Switzerland instead—you'll save money, and they're prettier.

instead of dollars, calculated at the day's standard bank-to-bank rate.

In most places, ATMs are easy to locate—in Switzerland, ask for a *Bankomat* or *Geldautomat* in German, or a *distributeur* in French. When possible, withdraw cash from a bank-run ATM located just outside that bank. Ideally use it during the bank's opening hours so if the machine munches your card, you can go inside for help.

If your debit card doesn't work, try a lower amount—your request may have exceeded your withdrawal limit or the ATM's limit. If you still have a problem, try a different ATM or come back later—your bank's network may be temporarily down.

Avoid "independent" ATMs, such as Travelex, Euronet, Moneybox, Your Cash, Cardpoint, and Cashzone. These have high fees, can be less secure than a bank ATM, and may try to trick users with "dynamic currency conversion" (see below).

Exchanging Cash

Avoid exchanging money in Europe; it's a big rip-off. In a pinch you can always find exchange desks at major train stations or airports—convenient but with crummy rates. Anything over 5 percent for a transaction is piracy. Banks generally do not exchange money unless you have an account with them.

Using Credit Cards

Despite some differences between European and US cards, there's little to worry about: US credit cards generally work fine in Europe. I've been inconvenienced a few times by self-service payment machines that wouldn't accept my card, but it's never caused me serious trouble (I carry cash just in case).

European cards use chip-and-PIN technology; most chip cards issued in the US instead have a signature option. Some European card readers will accept your card as-is while others may generate a receipt for you to sign or prompt you to enter your PIN (so it's important to know the code for each of your cards). If a cashier is present, you should have no problems. At self-service payment machines (transit-ticket kiosks, parking, etc.), results are mixed, as US cards may not work in some unattended transactions. If your card won't work, look for a cashier who can process your card manually—or pay in cash.

Drivers Beware: Be aware of potential problems using a US credit card to fill up at an unattended gas station, enter a parking garage, or exit a toll road. Always carry cash as a backup and be prepared to move on to the next gas station if necessary. When approaching a toll plaza, use the "cash" lane.

Dynamic Currency Conversion

If merchants offer to convert your purchase price into dollars (called dynamic currency conversion, or DCC) refuse this "service." You'll pay extra for the expensive convenience of seeing your charge in dollars. If an ATM offers to "lock in" or "guarantee" your conversion rate, choose "proceed without conversion." Other prompts might state, "You can be charged in dollars: Press YES for dollars, NO for Swiss francs." Always choose the local currency.

Security Tips

Pickpockets target tourists, even in safe Switzerland. Keep your cash, credit cards, and passport secure in your money belt, and carry only a day's spending money in your front pocket or wallet.

Before inserting your card into an ATM, inspect the front. If anything looks crooked, loose, or damaged, it could be a sign of a card-skimming device. When entering your PIN, carefully block other people's view of the keypad.

Don't use a debit card for purchases. Because a debit card pulls funds directly from your bank account, potential charges incurred by a thief will stay on your account while you bank investigates the fraudulent use.

To access your accounts online while traveling, be sure to use a secure connection (see the "Tips on Internet Security" sidebar, later).

Damage Control for Lost Cards

If you lose your credit or debit card, report the loss immediately to the respective global customer-assistance centers. With a mobile phone, call these 24-hour US numbers: Visa (tel. +1 303/967-1096), MasterCard (tel. +1 636/722-7111), and American Express (tel. +1 336/393-1111). From a landline, you can call these US numbers collect by going through a local operator. European toll-free numbers can be found at the websites for Visa and MasterCard.

You'll need to provide the primary cardholder's identification-verification details (such as birth date, mother's maiden name, or Social Security number). You can generally receive a temporary card within two or three business days in Europe (see www.ricksteves.com/help for more).

If you report your loss within two days, you typically won't be responsible for unauthorized transactions on your account, although many banks charge a liability fee of $50.

TIPPING

Tipping in Switzerland isn't as automatic and generous as it is in the US. For special service, tips are appreciated, but not expected. As in the US, the proper amount depends on your resources, tipping philosophy, and the circumstances, but some general guidelines apply.

Restaurants: You don't need to tip if you order your food at a counter. At Swiss restaurants that have a wait staff, it's common to tip by rounding up (about 5-10 percent) after a good meal. For more details on tipping in restaurants, see the "Eating" section, later.

Taxis: For a typical ride, round up your fare a bit (for instance, if the fare is 13 CHF, pay 15 CHF). If the cabbie hauls your bags and zips you to the airport to help you catch your flight, you might want to toss in a little more. But if you feel like you're being driven in circles or otherwise ripped off, skip the tip.

Services: In general, if someone in the service industry does a super job for you, a small tip of a franc or two is appropriate...but not required. If you're not sure whether (or how much) to tip, ask a local for advice.

GETTING A VAT REFUND

Wrapped into the purchase price of your Swiss souvenirs is a Value-Added-Tax (VAT) of about 8 percent (one of the lowest in Europe).

You're entitled to get most of that tax back if you purchase more than 300 CHF (about $300) worth of goods at a store that participates in the VAT-refund scheme. Typically, you must ring up the minimum at a single retailer—you can't add up your purchases from various shops to reach the required amount. (If the store ships the goods to your US home, VAT is not assessed on your purchase.)

Getting your refund is straightforward...and worthwhile if you spend a significant amount on souvenirs.

Get the paperwork. Have the merchant completely fill out the necessary refund document. You'll have to present your passport. Get the paperwork done before you leave the store to ensure you'll have everything you need (including your original sales receipt).

Get your stamp at the border or airport. Process your VAT document at your last stop in Switzerland (such as the airport) with the customs agent who deals with VAT refunds. Arrive an additional hour before you need to check in to allow time to find the customs office—and wait. Some customs desks are positioned before airport security; confirm the location before going through security.

It's best to keep your purchases in your carry-on. If they're not allowed as carry-on (such as Swiss Army knives), pack them in your checked bags and alert the check-in agent. You'll be sent (with your tagged bag) to a customs desk outside security, where someone will examine your bag, stamp your paperwork, and put your bag on the belt. You're not supposed to use your purchased goods before you leave. If you show up at customs wearing your new Swiss watch, officials might look the other way—or deny you a refund.

Collect your refund. You can claim your VAT refund from refund companies such as Global Blue or Planet with offices at major airports, ports, or border crossings (either before or after security, probably strategically located near a duty-free shop). These services (which extract a 4 percent fee) can refund your money in cash immediately or credit your card. Otherwise, mail the stamped refund documents to the address given by the shop where you made your purchase.

CUSTOMS FOR AMERICAN SHOPPERS

You can take home $800 worth of items per person duty-free once every 31 days. Many processed and packaged foods are allowed, including vacuum-packed cheeses, dried herbs, jams, baked goods, candy, chocolate, oil, vinegar, mustard, and honey. Fresh fruits and vegetables and most meats are not allowed, with exceptions for some canned items. As for alcohol, you can bring in one liter duty-free (it can be packed securely in your checked luggage, along with any other liquid-containing items).

To bring alcohol (or liquid-packed foods) in your carry-on bag on your flight home, buy it at a duty-free shop at the airport. You'll increase your odds of getting it onto a connecting flight if it's packaged in a "STEB"—a secure, tamper-evident bag. But stay away from liquids in opaque, ceramic, or metallic containers, which usually cannot be successfully screened (STEB or no STEB).

For details on allowable goods, customs rules, and duty rates, visit https://help.cbp.gov.

Sightseeing

Sightseeing can be hard work. If you're spending time in urban Switzerland, use these tips to make your museum visits meaningful, fun, efficient, and painless.

MAPS AND NAVIGATION TOOLS

A good map is essential for efficient navigation while sightseeing. The maps in this book are concise and simple, designed to help you locate recommended destinations, sights, and local TIs, where you can pick up more in-depth maps.

You can also use a mapping app on your mobile device. Be aware that pulling up maps or looking up turn-by-turn walking directions on the fly requires a data connection: To use this feature, it's smart to get an international data plan. With Google Maps or City Maps 2Go, it's possible to download a map while online, then go offline and navigate without incurring data-roaming charges, though you can't search for an address or get real-time walking directions. A handful of other apps—including Apple Maps and Navmii—also allow you to use maps offline.

PLAN AHEAD

Set up an itinerary that allows you to fit in all your must-see sights. Most sights keep stable hours, but you can easily confirm the latest by checking with the TI or visiting museum websites.

Don't put off visiting a must-see sight—you never know when a place will close unexpectedly for a holiday, strike, or restoration. Many museums are closed or have reduced hours at least a few days a year, especially on holidays such as Christmas and New Year's. A list of holidays is in the appendix; check for possible closures during your trip. In summer, some sights may stay open late; in the off-season, hours may be shorter.

Going at the right time helps avoid crowds. This book offers tips on the best times to see specific sights. Try visiting popular sights very early or very late. Evening visits (when possible) are usually peaceful, with fewer crowds. Late morning is usually the worst time to visit a popular sight.

If you plan to hire a local guide, reserve ahead by email. Popular guides can get booked up.

Study up. To get the most out of the sight descriptions in this book, read them before your visit.

AT SIGHTS

Here's what you can typically expect:

Entering: You may not be allowed to enter if you arrive too close to closing time. And guards start ushering people out well before the actual closing time, so don't save the best for last.

Many sights have a security check. Allow extra time for these lines. Some sights require you to check daypacks and coats. (If you'd rather not check your daypack, try carrying it tucked under your arm like a purse as you enter.)

Photography: If the museum's photo policy isn't clearly posted, ask a guard. Generally, taking photos without a flash or tripod is allowed. Some sights ban selfie sticks; others ban photos altogether.

Audioguides and Apps: Many sights rent audioguides with recorded descriptions in English. If you bring your own earbuds, you can often enjoy better sound. If you don't mind being tethered to your travel partner, you'll save money by bringing a Y-jack and sharing one audioguide. Museums and sights often offer free apps that you can download to your mobile device (check their websites).

Temporary Exhibits: Museums may show special exhibits in addition to their permanent collection. Some exhibits are included in the entry price, while others come at an extra cost (which you may have to pay even if you don't want to see the exhibit).

Expect Changes: Artwork can be on tour, on loan, out sick, or shifted at the whim of the curator. Pick up a floor plan as you enter, and ask museum staff if you can't find a particular item.

Services: Important sights usually have a reasonably priced on-site café or cafeteria (handy places to rejuvenate during a long visit). The WCs at sights are free and generally clean.

Before Leaving: At the gift shop, scan the postcard rack or thumb through a guidebook to be sure you haven't overlooked something that you'd like to see. Every sight or museum offers more than what is covered in this book. Use the information I provide in this book as an introduction—not the final word.

Sleeping

Extensive and opinionated listings of good-value rooms are a major feature of this book's Sleeping sections. Rather than list accommodations scattered throughout a town, I choose hotels in my favorite neighborhoods that are convenient to your sightseeing.

PRACTICALITIES

My recommendations run the gamut, from dorm beds to fancy rooms with all the comforts. I like places that are clean, central, relatively quiet at night, reasonably priced, friendly, small enough to have a hands-on owner or manager, and run with a respect for Swiss traditions. I'm more impressed by a handy location and a fun-loving

philosophy than flat-screen TVs and a fancy gym. Most of my recommendations fall short of perfection. But if I can find a place with most of these features, it's a keeper.

Book your accommodations as soon as your itinerary is set, especially if you want to stay at one of my top listings or if you'll be traveling during busy times. See the appendix for a list of major holidays and festivals in Switzerland; for tips on reserving rooms, see the "Making Hotel Reservations" sidebar, later.

Some people make reservations as they travel, calling or emailing ahead a few days to a week before their arrival. If you're trying for a same-day reservation, it's best to call hotels at about 9:00 or 10:00, when the receptionist knows who'll be checking out and which rooms will be available. If you encounter a language barrier, ask the fluent receptionist at your current hotel to call for you. Some apps—such as HotelTonight—specialize in last-minute rooms, often at boutique or business-class hotels in big cities.

RATES AND DEALS

I've categorized my recommended accommodations based on price, indicated with a dollar-sign rating (see sidebar). The price ranges suggest an estimated cost for a one-night stay in high season in a standard double room with a private toilet and shower, including breakfast, and assume you're booking directly with the hotel (not through a booking site, which extracts a commission). Room prices can fluctuate significantly with demand and amenities (size, views, room class, and so on), but relative price categories remain constant. Part of the room price is a local tax (about $2-6 per person per night). In return, you get perks such as free local transport or museum discounts. In a few towns (and some types of accommodations) the tax is included in quoted room rates; in most others, it's broken out.

Room rates are especially volatile at hotels that use "dynamic pricing" to set rates. Prices can skyrocket during festivals and conventions, while business hotels can have deep discounts on weekends when demand plummets. Of the many hotels I recommend,

Sleep Code

Hotels in this book are categorized according to the average price of a standard double room with breakfast in high season.

$$$$	**Splurge:** Most rooms over 300 CHF
$$$	**Pricier:** 225-300 CHF
$$	**Moderate:** 175-225 CHF
$	**Budget:** 100-175 CHF
¢	**Backpacker:** Under 100 CHF
RS%	**Rick Steves discount**

Unless otherwise noted, credit cards are accepted, hotel staff speak basic English, and free Wi-Fi is available. Comparison-shop by checking prices at several hotels (on each hotel's own website, on a booking site, or by email). For the best deal, *book directly with the hotel.* Ask for a discount if paying in cash; if the listing includes **RS%,** request a Rick Steves discount.

it's difficult to say which will be the best value on a given day—until you do your homework.

Booking Direct: Once your dates are set, compare prices at several hotels. You can do this by checking Hotels.com, Booking.com, and hotel websites. After you've zeroed in on your choice, book directly with the hotel itself. Contact small family-run hotels directly by phone or email. When you go direct, the owner avoids the commission paid to booking sites, thereby leaving enough wiggle room to offer you a discount, a nicer room, or a free breakfast (if it's not already included). If you prefer to book online or are considering a hotel chain, it's to your advantage to use the hotel's website.

Booking directly also increases the chances that the hotelier will be able to accommodate any special needs or requests (such as shifting your reservation). Going through a middleman makes it more difficult for the hotel to adjust your booking.

Getting a Discount: Some hotels extend a discount to those who pay cash or stay longer than three nights. And some accommodations offer a special discount for Rick Steves readers, indicated in this guidebook by the abbreviation "RS%." Discounts vary: Ask for details when you reserve. Generally, to qualify for this discount, you must book direct (not through a booking site), mention this book when you reserve, show this book upon arrival, and sometimes pay cash or stay a certain number of nights. In some cases, you may need to enter a discount code (which I've provided in the listing) in the booking form on the hotel's website. Rick Steves discounts apply to readers with either print or digital books. Understandably, discounts do not apply to promotional rates.

Using Online Services to Your Advantage

From booking services to user reviews, online businesses are playing a greater role in travelers' planning than ever before. Take advantage of their pluses—and be wise to their downsides.

Booking Sites

Booking websites such as Booking.com and Hotels.com offer one-stop shopping for hotels. While convenient for travelers, they present a real problem for independent, family-run hotels. Without a presence on these sites, small hotels become almost invisible. But to be listed, a hotel must pay a sizeable commission... and promise that its own website won't undercut the price on the booking-service site.

Here's the work-around: Use the big sites to research what's out there, then book directly with the hotel by email or phone, in which case hotel owners are free to give you whatever price they like. Ask for a room without the commission mark-up (or ask for a free breakfast if not included, or a free upgrade). If you do book online, be sure to use the hotel's website. The price will likely be the same as via a booking site, but your money goes to the hotel, not agency commissions.

As a savvy consumer, remember: When you book with an online booking service, you're adding a middleman who takes roughly 20 percent. To support small, family-run hotels whose world is more difficult than ever, book direct.

Short-Term Rental Sites

Rental juggernaut Airbnb (along with other short-term rental sites) allows travelers to rent rooms and apartments directly from locals, often providing more value than a cookie-cutter hotel. Airbnb fans appreciate feeling part of a real neighborhood and getting into a daily routine as "temporary Europeans." Depending on the host, Airbnb can provide an opportunity to get to know a

TYPES OF ACCOMMODATIONS
Hotels

Plan on spending about $180-250 for a double room in a hotel or $120-175 for a double (with the bathroom down the hall) in a small guesthouse. Swiss hotels are, generally speaking, clean, comfortable, and efficiently run by English-speaking staff.

Some hotels can add an extra bed (for a small charge) to turn a double into a triple; some offer larger rooms for four or more people (I call these "family rooms" in the listings). If there's space for an extra cot, they'll cram it in for you. In general, a triple room is cheaper than the cost of a double and a single. Three or four people can economize by requesting one big room.

Arrival and Check-In: Hotels and B&Bs are sometimes lo-

local person, while keeping the money spent on your accommodations in the community.

Critics view Airbnb as a threat to "traditional Europe," saying it creates unfair, unqualified competition for established guesthouse owners. In some places, the lucrative Airbnb market has forced traditional guesthouses out of business and is driving property values out of range for locals. Some cities have cracked down, requiring owners to occupy rental properties part of the year (and staging disruptive "inspections" that inconvenience guests).

As a lover of Europe, I share the worry of those who see residents nudged aside by tourists. But as an advocate for travelers, I appreciate the value and cultural intimacy Airbnb provides.

User Reviews

User-generated review sites and apps such as Yelp and TripAdvisor can give you a consensus of opinions about everything from hotels and restaurants to sights and nightlife. If you scan reviews of a restaurant or hotel and see several complaints about noise or a rotten location, you've gained insight that can help in your decision-making.

But as a guidebook writer, my sense is that there is a big difference between the uncurated information on a review site and the vetted listings in a guidebook. A user-generated review is based on the limited experience of one person, who stayed at just one hotel in a given city and ate at a few restaurants there. A guidebook is the work of a trained researcher who forms a well-developed basis for comparison by visiting many restaurants and hotels year after year.

Both types of information have their place, and in many ways, they're complementary. If something is well reviewed in a guidebook and it gets good online reviews, it's likely a winner.

cated on the higher floors of a multipurpose building with a secured door. In that case, look for your hotel's name on the buttons by the main entrance. When you ring the bell, you'll be buzzed in.

Hotel elevators are becoming more common, though some older buildings still lack them. You may have to climb a flight of stairs to reach the elevator (if so, you can ask the front desk for help carrying your bags up). Elevators are typically very small—pack light, or you may need to send your bags up without you.

Switzerland requires that hotels collect your name, nationality, and ID number. When you check in, the receptionist will normally ask for your passport and may keep it for anywhere from a couple of minutes to a couple of hours. If not comfortable leaving your passport at the desk for a long time, ask when you can pick it up. Or, if you packed a color copy of your passport, you can generally leave that rather than the original.

Smoking is prohibited in many Swiss hotels, sometimes by law (depending on the region) and sometimes by choice. Nearly all the hotels I list are completely nonsmoking, and all of them offer nonsmoking rooms. If it's important to you to have a nonsmoking room, ask for one.

If you're arriving in the morning, your room probably won't be ready. Check your bag safely at the hotel and dive right into sightseeing.

In Your Room: Most hotel rooms have a TV, telephone, and free Wi-Fi (although in old buildings with thick walls, the Wi-Fi signal might be available only in the lobby). Simpler places rarely have a room phone, but often have free Wi-Fi.

More pillows and blankets are usually in the closet or available on request. Towels and linens aren't always replaced every day.

Breakfast and Meals: Swiss hotel breakfasts are usually excellent: fruit, eggs, muesli, cheese, fresh bread, and yogurt. Some places give you the option of skipping breakfast and paying less; you can buy breakfast items easily and cheaply at a bakery or supermarket—the savings add up, especially for families. Some places offer "half-board," which means that dinner is included in the room price. This is often a good deal and gets you a hassle-free, value-priced three-course meal, but limits your choices.

Checking Out: While it's customary to pay for your room upon departure, it can be a good idea to settle your bill the day before, when you're not in a hurry and while the manager's in.

Hotelier Help: Hoteliers can be a good source of advice. Most know their city well, and can assist you with everything from public transit and airport connections to finding a good restaurant, the nearest launderette, or a late-night pharmacy.

Hotel Hassles: Even at the best places, mechanical breakdowns occur: Sinks leak, hot water turns cold, toilets may gurgle or smell, the Wi-Fi goes out, or the air-conditioning dies when you need it most. Report your concerns clearly and calmly at the front desk.

If you think that night noise might be a problem (if, for instance, your room is over a nightclub or facing a busy street), ask for a quieter room in the back or on an upper floor. To guard against theft in your room, keep valuables out of sight. Some rooms come with a safe, and other hotels have safes at the front desk. I've never bothered using one and in a lifetime of travel, I've never had anything stolen from my room.

For more complicated problems, don't expect instant results. Above all, keep a positive attitude. Remember, you're on vacation.

If your hotel is a disappointment, spend more time out enjoying the place you came to see.

Pensions

Compared to hotels, pensions (small guesthouses) and rooms in private homes give you double the cultural intimacy for half the price. While you may lose some of the conveniences of a hotel—such as lounges, in-room phones, daily bed-sheet changes, and credit-card payments—I happily make the tradeoff for the lower rates and personal touches.

Small guesthouses go by several inexact German names: *Pension, Gasthaus, Gästezimmer,* even "B&B" (in French, it's also *pension*). In many parts of Switzerland, people rent out rooms *(Zimmer)* in their homes to travelers. Look for *Zimmer Frei, Zimmer mit Frühstück,* or *Privatzimmer* signs in German-speaking areas and *chambres d'hôte* in French Switzerland.

Don't confuse *Privatzimmer* with the *Ferienwohnung,* which is a self-catering apartment rented out by the week or fortnight.

Camping and Other Budget Beds

Campers can manage with listings at www.eurocampings.co.uk or with help from the local TI (ask for a regional camping listing). Your hometown travel bookstore should also have guidebooks on camping in Europe. You'll find campgrounds just about everywhere you need them. Look for *Campingplatz* signs. You'll meet lots of Europeans, as camping is a popular, middle-class-family way to go. Campgrounds are cheap ($10 per person), friendly, safe, more central and convenient than rustic, and rarely full.

A fluffy straw bed awaits you at a number of farms that have opened their haylofts to sleepy tourists. It's a fun hostel alternative and more comfortable than you'd think (see www.schlaf-im-stroh. ch for details).

Many hotels and campsites provide dormitory-style accommodations in bunk-bedded rooms. Also look for the word *Matratzenlager,* which usually indicates a loft lined with mattresses—common in mountain lodges. These slumber mills may be less charming than cozy hostels, but they're cheap and convenient.

For serious hikers and climbers, mountain huts and "refuges" are an essential alpine experience. Don't expect ski-lodge comfort: These practical, adventurous places are simple, offering a warm place to sleep and (usually) breakfast and dinner. Some mountain-hut guests are long-distance hikers, connecting one hut to another along an extended hiking trail. Others hike in from the parking lot one day and hike out the next, enjoying the fresh air and views for a night. You'll pay about $30 a night for your bunk and a little

Making Hotel Reservations

Reserve your rooms as soon as you've pinned down your travel dates. For busy national holidays, it's wise to reserve far in advance (see "Holidays and Festivals" in the appendix).

Requesting a Reservation: For family-run hotels, it's generally cheaper to book your room directly via email or a phone call. For business-class hotels, or if you'd rather book online, reserve directly through the hotel's official website (not a booking website). Almost all of my recommended hotels take reservations in English.

Here's what the hotelier wants to know:

- Type(s) of rooms you want and size of your party
- Number of nights you'll stay
- Your arrival and departure dates, written European-style as day/month/year (for example, 18/06/21 or 18 June 2021)
- Special requests (such as en suite bathroom vs. down the hall, cheapest room, twin beds vs. double bed, quiet room)
- Applicable discounts (such as a Rick Steves reader discount, cash discount, or promotional rate)

Confirming a Reservation: Most places will request a credit-card number to hold your room. If you're using an online reservation form, make sure it's secure by looking for the *https* or a lock icon at the top of your browser. If the hotel's website doesn't have a secure form where you can enter the number directly, it's best to share that confidential info via a phone call.

Canceling a Reservation: If you must cancel, it's courteous—and smart—to do so with as much notice as possible, especially for

more for grub (see www.sac-cas.ch for a map and database of Swiss mountain huts).

Short-Term Rentals

A short-term rental—whether an apartment, house, or room in a local's home—is an increasingly popular alternative, especially if you plan to settle in one location for several nights. For stays longer than a few days, you can usually find a rental that's comparable to—and cheaper than—a hotel room with similar amenities. Plus, you'll get a behind-the-scenes peek into how locals live.

Many places require a minimum stay and have strict cancellation policies. And you're generally on your own: There's no hotel reception desk, breakfast, or daily cleaning service.

Finding Accommodations: Websites such as Airbnb, FlipKey, Booking.com, and the HomeAway family of sites (HomeAway, VRBO, and VacationRentals) let you browse a wide range of properties. Alternatively, rental agencies such as InterhomeUSA.com and RentaVilla.com, which list more carefully selected accom-

From:	rick@ricksteves.com
Sent:	Today
To:	info@hotelcentral.com
Subject:	Reservation request for 19-22 July

Dear Hotel Central,

I would like to stay at your hotel. Please let me know if you have a room available and the price for:
• 2 people
• Double bed and en suite bathroom in a quiet room
• Arriving 19 July, departing 22 July (3 nights)

Thank you!
Rick Steves

smaller family-run places. Cancellation policies can be strict; read the fine print before you book. Many discount deals require pre-payment, with no refunds for cancellations.

Reconfirming a Reservation: Always call or email to reconfirm your room reservation a few days in advance. For B&Bs or very small hotels, I call again on my day of arrival to tell my host what time to expect me (especially important if arriving late—after 17:00).

Phoning: For tips on calling hotels overseas, see page 438.

modations that might cost more, can provide more personalized service.

Before you commit, be clear on the location. I like to virtually "explore" the neighborhood using the Street View feature on Google Maps. Also consider the proximity to public transportation, and how well-connected the property is with the rest of the city. Ask about amenities (elevator, air-conditioning, laundry, Wi-Fi, parking, etc.). Reviews from previous guests can help identify trouble spots.

Think about the kind of experience you want: Just a key and an affordable bed...or a chance to get to know a local? There are typically two kinds of hosts: those who want minimal interaction with their guests, and hosts who are friendly and may want to interact with you. Read the promotional text and online reviews to help shape your decision.

Confirming and Paying: Many places require you to pay the entire balance before your trip. It's easiest and safest to pay through the site where you found the listing. Be wary of owners who want

PRACTICALITIES

to take your transaction offline; this gives you no recourse if things go awry. Never agree to wire money (a key indicator of a fraudulent transaction).

Apartments or Houses: If you're staying in one place for four or more nights, it's worth considering an apartment or rental house, called *Ferienwohnung* in German (shorter stays aren't worth the hassle of arranging key pickup, buying groceries, etc.). Apartment or house rentals can be especially cost-effective for groups and families. European apartments, like hotel rooms, tend to be small by US standards. But they often come with laundry facilities and small, equipped kitchens, making it easier and cheaper to dine in.

Rooms in Private Homes: Renting a room in someone's home is a good option for those traveling alone, as you're more likely to find true single rooms—with just one single bed, and a price to match. These can range from air-mattress-in-living-room basic to plush-B&B-suite posh. Some places allow you to book for a single night; if staying for several nights, you can buy groceries just as you would in a rental house. While you can't expect your host to also be your tour guide—or even to provide you with much info—some may be interested in getting to know the travelers who come through their home.

Other Options: Swapping homes with a local works for people with an appealing place to offer (don't assume where you live is not interesting to Europeans). Good places to start are HomeExchange.com and LoveHomeSwap.com. To sleep for free, Couchsurfing.com is a vagabond's alternative to Airbnb. It lists millions of outgoing members, who host fellow "surfers" in their homes.

Hostels

Switzerland has a wonderful network of official hostels (*Jugendherberge* in German, *auberge de jeunesse* in French) that charge under $100 per night for beds (for a full list, see www.youthhostel.ch). Choose your hostel selectively: They can be cozy mountain chalets, serene lakeside villas—or antiseptic spaces overrun by noisy school groups. While official hostels are clean and predictable, they can also have an institutional feel.

Travelers of any age are welcome if they don't mind dorm-style accommodations and meeting other travelers. Most hostels offer kitchen facilities, guest computers, Wi-Fi, and a self-service laundry. Hostels almost always provide bedding, but the towel's up to you (though you can usually rent one for a small fee). Many hostels offer inexpensive evening meals (about 17-20 CHF), but there are also posh boutique hostels with in-house restaurants that are significantly more expensive. Expect youth groups in spring, crowds in the summer, snoring, and variability in quality from one hostel to the next. Family and private rooms are often available.

Independent hostels tend to be easygoing, colorful, and informal (no membership required; www.hostelworld.com or www.

swissbackpackers.ch). You may pay slightly less by booking directly with the hostel. **Official hostels** are part of Hostelling International (HI) and share an online booking site (www. hihostels.com). HI hostels typically require that you either have a membership card or else pay a bit more per night.

Eating

For listings in this guidebook, I look for restaurants that are convenient to your hotel and sightseeing. When restaurant-hunting, choose a spot filled with locals, not the place with the big neon signs boasting, "We Speak English and Accept Credit Cards." Venturing even a block or two off the main drag leads to higher-quality food for a better price.

The Swiss eat when we do and enjoy a straightforward, no-nonsense cuisine. Specialties include delicious fondue, rich chocolates, a melted cheese dish called raclette, *Rösti* (hash browns), fresh dairy products (try *Birchermüesli* for breakfast or an afternoon snack), 100 varieties of cheese, and Fendant—a good, crisp white wine.

The exorbitant prices at Swiss restaurants—up to double what you'd pay in neighboring Germany—mean that eating here demands some different strategies if you're on a budget. Think of restaurants with table service as a luxury for special occasions, and self-service cafeterias and supermarkets as your everyday options. Bakeries also sell sandwiches, quiches, and the like. If breakfast is included in your room price, don't miss it. But if your hotel gives you the option to skip an expensive breakfast and pay a lower rate, consider saying yes and eating more cheaply on your own.

Tipping: If you buy your food at a counter, don't tip. Service is included at Swiss restaurants with table service, but it's customary to round up the bill (5-10 percent; for a 19-CHF meal, pay 20 CHF. Some restaurants are getting clever about adding a tip line to their bills, hoping to take advantage of unsuspecting tourists who don't realize that service is included.) Give the tip directly to your

Restaurant Code

Eateries in this book are categorized according to the average cost of a typical main course. Drinks, desserts, and splurge items can raise the price considerably.

$$$$ **Splurge:** Most main courses over 45 CHF
$$$ **Pricier:** 30-45 CHF
$$ **Moderate:** 15-30 CHF
$ **Budget:** Under 15 CHF

In Switzerland, a kebab stand or other takeout spot is **$;** a self-service cafeteria or casual café is **$$;** a restaurant with table service is **$$$;** and a swanky splurge is **$$$$.**

server. Rather than leaving coins on the table, the Swiss usually pay with paper, saying how much they'd like the bill to be. For example, if paying for an 8.10-CHF meal with a 20-CHF bill, say "Nine francs" or *("Neun Franken").* The server will keep a .90-CHF tip and give you 11 CHF in change. Rounding up isn't required, though, and no one will come running after you if you don't.

RESTAURANT PRICING

I've categorized my recommended eateries based on the average price of a typical main course, indicated with a dollar-sign rating (see sidebar). Obviously, expensive specialties, fine wine, appetizers, and dessert can significantly increase your final bill.

The categories also indicate the personality of a place: **Budget** eateries include street food, takeaway, order-at-the-counter shops, and bakeries selling sandwiches. **Moderate** eateries are nice (but not fancy) sit-down restaurants, ideal for a straightforward, fill-the-tank meal.

Pricier eateries are a notch up, with more attention paid to the setting, presentation, and (often inventive) cuisine. **Splurge** eateries are dress-up-for-a-special-occasion swanky—typically with an elegant setting, polished service, intricate cuisine, and an expansive (and expensive) wine list.

BUDGET OPTIONS

Grocery Stores: The midrange Migros and Co-op grocery stores are the hungry hiker's best budget bet. Larger stores have a great selection of prepared foods and picnic fixings. These include a huge variety of salads (green, potato, pasta, or meat—all sold with a plastic fork), decorated hard-boiled eggs (called *Picknickeier*), sandwiches, delicious cheese, single portions of cake and ice cream, inexpensive chocolate bars, and sometimes, a hot-meal counter. You'll also see Manor ("mah-NOR"), a more elegant supermarket chain, and Aldi, a discount grocery store with a limited range. Manor is actually a department store (and many Migros and Co-ops are as well), with the supermarket typically hiding in the basement.

By law, most supermarkets are required to close on Sunday, with exceptions for stores in train stations and in some towns where grocery stores are allowed to open for a few hours on Sunday afternoons (a controversial issue in Switzerland). In larger cities, supermarket chains have skirted the law by building big stores in malls attached to train stations.

Self-Service Cafeterias and Buffets: Cafeterias have good food at much lower prices than restaurants with table service. You'll find them in most cities, usually at downtown branches of Manor, Co-op, and Migros supermarkets (in descending order of fanciness). Manor's cafeterias (called "Manora") feature lush salad bars, tasty entrées, and fresh-squeezed juices (I've listed several specific Manora locations in this book). A main course at a cafeteria is usually cooked to order in front of you and will cost 13-19 CHF; drinks and dessert run about 3 CHF each. Some self-service cafeterias have free tap water, often hidden in an inconspicuous place to encourage diners to pay for bottled drinks. Most have free Wi-Fi.

While cafeteria food may not be inventive, it is typical, fresh, and high-quality (these are supermarkets, after all); they're also popular with locals. Eating some of your meals at cafeterias can free up money for splurges on traditional dishes at fine restaurants with table service.

Another common type of self-service eatery is a gourmet buffet (often vegetarian) that is charged by weight. Look for Hiltl (in Zürich) and the Tibits chain (in Zürich, Bern, and Luzern).

Hostels: Swiss hostels that belong to the Hosteling International network usually offer a fine four-course dinner for 17-20 CHF, with free tap water—a great deal for guests. In a few cases this is open to nonguests, too, at a slightly higher price (call to reserve).

Global Food: Asian and Middle Eastern restaurants abound, but are generally not as much of a bargain as in neighboring countries (a *döner kebab* costs around 10 CHF and a main course at an Asian restaurant about 20 CHF). The same goes for pizzerias, which are often upscale places with table service and 20-CHF pies; takeout orders are often slightly cheaper than the sit-down price.

RESTAURANTS

The cheapest main courses at Swiss restaurants start at just under 20 CHF—typically starchy dishes topped with meat or cheese (pasta, pizza, and potato dishes) or sausages with kraut or potato salad. Meat courses (served with a starch and vegetable) will run you 25-45 CHF at an average restaurant. Many restaurants offer

PRACTICALITIES

a daily special—a main course for about 20 CHF (at least Mon-Fri at lunch, sometimes weekends and evenings, too). High-priced drinks can quickly run up the cost of a meal.

Different kinds of restaurants offer different experiences. Hotels often serve fine food. A *Gaststätte* is a simple, less expensive restaurant. A *Weinstübli* (wine bar) or *Bierstübli* (tavern) usually serves food. Mountain huts—called *Hütte*—generally have hot chocolate and hearty meat-and-potato meals. Smoking is no longer allowed inside Switzerland's eateries (though a few places skirt the laws with enclosed verandas for smokers). If you're not too hungry, order from the *kleine Hunger* (small hunger) section of the menu.

Most restaurants tack a menu onto their door for browsers and have an English menu inside. If you ask for the *Menü* (or *menu* in French), you won't get a list of dishes; you'll get a fixed-price meal of several courses. If you simply want a list of what's cooking, ask for *die Speisekarte* (dee SHPIE-zeh-kar-teh; *la carte* in French).

Only a rude waiter will rush you. Good service is relaxed (slow to an American). To wish others "Happy eating!" offer a cheery *"En Guete!"* When you want the bill, request *"Die Rechnung, bitte."* (See the survival phrases in the appendix for more tips.)

SWISS CUISINE

Here at this meeting point of European cultures, a region's food is heavily influenced by the cuisine of neighboring countries. You'll find heavy wurst-and-kraut fare in German-speaking areas; delicate, subtle French cuisine in the west; and pasta and polenta dishes *all'Italiana* in Ticino. In alpine regions, most meals are still built on the hardy ingredients that can be produced and stored in the mountains: cheese, potatoes, onions, cabbage, sausage, cured meat...and more cheese.

Traditional Dishes

Aside from clocks and banks, Switzerland is known for its cheese. Gruyère cheese is hard, with a strong flavor; Emmentaler is also hard, but milder (and looks like what we call "Swiss cheese"). Appenzeller is the incredibly pungent cheese from the northeast of Switzerland, with a smell that verges on nauseating...until you taste it.

Two of Switzerland's best-known specialties are cheese-based. (Swiss people typically eat these at home, so restaurants featuring them tend to cater to tourists.) **Käsefondue** is usually Emmentaler and Gruyère cheese melted with white wine, garlic, nutmeg, and other seasonings. You use a long fork to dip cubes of bread into it. The price for fondue is calculated per person (about 24-28 CHF), and many restaurants have a two-person minimum. While the Swiss consider fondue a winter-only meal, it's served year-round in touristed areas, and there's nothing silly about eating it "out of season." Note that "meat fondue," in which you cook raw meat in broth at your table, is not typically Swiss. Sometimes called *fondue chinoise* (Chinese fondue), this is an Asian-style hot pot.

Raclette is cheese slowly melted on a special dish; as it softens, scrape a mound off and eat it with potatoes, pickled onions, and gherkins. (In restaurants, raclette often comes as little slices of cheese already melted.)

Another must-try dish, most typical in the mountains of the German-speaking areas, is **Rösti**—sort of like hash browns. The potatoes are grated coarsely, then often molded into a loose, round patty, and topped with alpine cheese, a bit of bacon or ham, or with an egg cracked over it...yum.

Each region has its own specialties. In French-speaking Switzerland, white wine and heavy cream are used in many dishes, and you'll commonly see horsemeat (formerly imported from Eastern Europe, now imported from the US, New Zealand, and Australia). The cuisine in eastern Switzerland (Pontresina, St. Moritz) uses chestnuts in many forms, wild mushrooms, and air-dried beef. Southwestern Switzerland (Zermatt area) specializes in all kinds of cheese, and their favorite white wine is Fendant.

Despite all the cheese and potatoes, the Swiss tend to be health-conscious; after all, they invented **muesli.** While the dry muesli served at breakfast buffets is unremarkable, *Birchermüesli*—a yummy mixture of fresh yogurt, fresh fruit, and juice-soaked oats—is worth seeking out in supermarket delis and on café menus. Menus often feature a *Fitnessteller* ("fitness plate")—usually a large mixed salad that comes with steak, chicken, or fish. *Bio* means organically grown (a *Biolädeli* is a store that sells organic products).

Of course, on the other end of the health spectrum, there's the famous **Swiss chocolate.** The vast variety of chocolate flavors available in any Swiss supermarket—let alone a specialty chocolate shop—is staggering. Only chocolate actually produced in the country is granted the honor of being called Swiss. Stroll the chocolate aisle of a grocery store and take your pick.

Beverages

Wine: Swiss wine is good, but expensive because of high production costs and mostly small vineyards. The Swiss certainly have plenty of winemaking experience—they've been growing grapes

Swiss Chocolate:
The Souvenir that Disappears

Of Switzerland's well-known icons—watches, banks, gadgety knives, booze-bearing mountain dogs—only one makes would-be visitors salivate in anticipation: chocolate. But why does Swiss chocolate hold such cachet? The answer dates back to 1819, when François-Louis Cailler figured out how to mechanize chocolate production and set up a factory near Lake Geneva. The Swiss also invented milk chocolate (in 1875) and conching, the process that makes solid chocolate smooth (1879).

The 1890s Golden Age of Swiss tourism spurred a Golden Age of Swiss chocolate, when vacationers returned home with a chocolate habit and chocolatey gifts for friends and family. By the 1910s, about 75 percent of the chocolate produced here was being exported. Today, Swiss chocolate is still a popular souvenir, what had been a small collection of "manufactories" has become a billion-dollar industry, and the Swiss people are among the world's top chocolate consumers.

When looking for high-quality chocolate, notice the way the chocolate breaks (a clean break with no crumbles is best), how it melts (like butter?), how it feels in your mouth (the smoother the better), and whether it leaves any gritty, unchocolatey aftertaste.

Of course, the only way to know what you like best is to try lots of different kinds (in the name of science!). The big-name brands—such as Lindt, Toblerone, and Cailler—are everywhere;

since Roman times. Since Swiss wine is not well known outside of the country, and very little is exported, this is your chance to try the local *Wein/vin/vino*. About two-thirds of the production is white, and much of that is made from the Chasselas (a.k.a. Fendant) grape. Swiss specialties include the red Dole (a light-bodied blend of pinot noir and gamay grapes), Gutedel (or Chasselas; full, fruity, dry white); Fendant (a dry white that pairs well with cheese dishes), St. Saphorin (lovely, fruity white from Lake Geneva), and Merlot del Ticino (full-bodied red from Italian-speaking Switzerland).

Menus list drink size by the "deci"—a deciliter (dl, tenth of a liter). In German-speaking areas, order wine by the *Glas* (glass) or *Viertel* (quarter liter, or 8 ounces). Order it *süss* (sweet), *halb trocken* (medium), or *trocken* (dry); *weiss* (white), or *rot* (red). To order white wine, for instance, you can say, *"Ein Viertel Weisswein, bitte."* For fun, try ordering the same thing in colloquial Swiss German: *"Ä Viertel Wiisewyy, bitte"* (ih FEER-tehl VEE-seh-vee, BIT-teh).

In French Switzerland, wine comes either by *le verre* (a glass, 1-2 dl), *la carafe* (3 dl or 5 dl), or *la bouteille* (bottle). Order by requesting *"Un verre de vin blanc, s'il vous plaît"* (or *"vin rouge"* if you keep your eyes peeled for lesser-known brands like Läderach, a high-end favorite among many Swiss. In his book *Swiss Watching*, Diccon Bewes reports on a blind taste test in which Prix Garantie, the Co-op house brand, came in a close second to Cailler—despite costing only a fraction of Cailler's price.

If you prefer milk chocolate, look for bars marked *Vollmilch* or *Alpenmilch;* dark chocolate fans want the *edelbitter* or *dunkeler* stuff, and *weisse Schokolade* is white chocolate. Bars with percentages printed on them are boasting their high cocoa content (the higher the number, the more bitter the chocolate). Common additions include *Haselnuss* (hazelnuts), *Mandeln* (almonds), *Trauben* (grapes/raisins), and *Joghurt* (guess). Connoisseurs watch for seasonal flavors.

Switzerland offers surprisingly few worthwhile sights for the choco-curious. You can ride the Chocolate Train, which combines three Swiss greats—rail travel, beautiful vistas, and chocolate noshing—and stops for a visit at the Cailler factory in the hills above Lake Geneva (both sights described in the Lake Geneva & French Switzerland chapter). You can also visit the Alprose chocolate factory just outside Lugano (see the Lugano chapter). But my favorite Swiss chocolate experience is simply nibbling a bar on a high-mountain hike.

prefer red). In the Ticino region, *un boccalino* is a small, decorated 8-ounce ceramic jug filled with the local red wine.

Beer: Swiss beer is surprisingly good and inexpensive. Most of the beer is light, golden-colored lager, but you'll also find other types, such as *Hefeweizen* and *Dunkel* (dark) beers. Each pub has one brand of a local beer on tap, with others available in bottles. Feldschlössen is the largest brewery in the country, and you'll see its red-castle logo all over. But the Swiss are loyal to their local brews; for example, in the Appenzell region, Appenzeller is the beer of choice. The standard size, measured in centiliters (cl), is a *Stange* (33 cl); the smaller size is called a *Herrgöttli* (20 cl). Beer mixed with lemon-flavored soda or *Citro* (lemonade) is called a *Panaché*. In summer, this lightly sweet, sudsy drink is more refreshing than straight beer.

Water: Switzerland has a tradition of **free fountains,** with fresh, mountain-chilled water, in squares and other central points around cities and towns. I assume I can fill my bottle from any well-maintained public fountain unless I see a sign saying otherwise. At restaurants, tap water, which many waiters aren't eager to bring you, is *Leitungswasser* (*l'eau du robinet* in French). Ask for it by

PRACTICALITIES

name, or you'll receive—and be charged for—*Mineralwasser* (*mit/ ohne Gas,* with/without carbonation).

Other Nonalcoholic Drinks: Instead of Coke, try the local favorite, **Rivella,** a carbonated, vitamin-rich soft drink made with 35 percent whey (called "milk serum" on the label). Its unusual— but not unpleasant—taste isn't milky at all; it's more like chewable vitamins. It comes in four colors: Red is regular; blue is low-calorie; green is mixed with green tea; and yellow is soy-based. *Süssmost* is apple juice.

As an alternative to hot chocolate, try **Ovomaltine.** The Swiss have a fondness for this hot drink—a malt-derived vitamin supplement, flavored with chocolate so kids will drink it. (In the US, Ovaltine is an Asian variation on this drink—considered by the Swiss to be a cheap copy.) Chocolate bars mixed with crispy Ovomaltine wafers are also popular and worth trying.

Staying Connected

One of the most common questions I hear from travelers is, "How can I stay connected in Europe?" The short answer is: more easily and cheaply than you might think.

The simplest solution is to bring your own device—mobile phone, tablet, or laptop—and use it just as you would at home (following the money-saving tips below, such as getting an international plan or connecting to free Wi-Fi whenever possible). Another option is to buy a European SIM card for your US mobile phone. Or you can use European landlines and computers to connect. Each of these options is described next, and more details are at www.ricksteves.com/phoning. For a very practical one-hour talk covering tech issues for travelers, see www.ricksteves.com/mobile-travel-skills.

USING A MOBILE PHONE IN EUROPE

Here are some budget tips and options.

Sign up for an international plan. To stay connected at a lower cost, sign up for an international service plan through your carrier. Most providers offer a simple bundle that includes calling, messaging, and data. Your normal plan may already include international coverage (T-Mobile's does).

Before your trip, call your provider or check online to confirm that your phone will work in Europe, and research your provider's international rates. Activate the plan a day or two before you leave, then remember to cancel it when your trip's over.

Use free Wi-Fi whenever possible. Unless you have an unlimited-data plan, you're best off saving most of your online tasks

Hurdling the Language Barrier

Switzerland has four official languages: German, French, Italian, and Romansh (a Romance language spoken in far-flung corners of Graubünden). Most of the destinations in this book are in the German-speaking territory. No matter where you are, most young or well-educated people—especially those in larger towns and the tourist trade—speak at least some English. Still, you'll get more smiles by using the local pleasantries. See the German, French, and Italian survival phrases at the end of the appendix.

In German-speaking Switzerland, locals speak sing-songy *Schwyzertütsch* (Swiss German) around the house, but in schools and businesses, they speak and write in the same standard German used in Germany and Austria (called "High" German, *Hochdeutsch*—though many Swiss prefer to call it *Schriftdeutsch,* "Written German"). The standard greeting is a hearty *Grüezi* (GRIT-see). "Thank you" is derived from French, but pronounced a little differently: *Merci* (MUR-see). They also sometimes use the more German-like *Dankche* (DAHN-kheh with a very guttural "kh"). The exact pronunciation of Swiss German words varies substantially by region, and there's no standard spelling.

English—like Dutch, Danish, Swedish, and Norwegian—is a Germanic language, making German easier on most American ears than Romance languages (such as Italian and French). High German is spelled phonetically—its pronunciation rules are regular, and there are no silent letters.

These tips will help you pronounce German words: The letter *w* is always pronounced as "v" (e.g., the word for "wonderful" is *wunderbar,* pronounced VOON-dehr-bar). The vowel combinations *ie* and *ei* are pronounced like the name of the second letter—so *ie* sounds like the letter *e* (as in *hier* and *Bier,* the German words for "here" and "beer"), while *ei* sounds like the letter *i* (as in *nein* and *Stein,* the German words for "no" and "stone"). The vowel combination *au* is pronounced "ow" (as in Frau). The vowel combinations *eu* and *äu* are pronounced "oy" (as in *neu, Deutsch,* and *Bräu,* the words for "new," "German," and "brew"). To pronounce *ö* and *ü,* purse your lips when you say the vowel; the other vowel with an umlaut, *ä,* is pronounced the same as *e* in "men." (In written German, these can be depicted without an umlaut as the vowel followed by an *e: oe, ue,* and *ae,* respectively.) Written German always capitalizes all nouns.

Give it your best shot. The locals will appreciate your efforts.

For more tips on hurdling the language barrier, consider the *Rick Steves French, Italian & German Phrase Book* (available at www.ricksteves.com).

How to Dial

International Calls

Whether phoning from a US landline or mobile phone, or from a number in another European country, here's how to make an international call. I've used one of my recommended Gimmelwald hotels as an example (tel. 033-855-1658).

Initial Zero: Drop the initial zero from international phone numbers—except when calling Italy.

Mobile Tip: If using a mobile phone, the "+" sign can replace the international access code (for a "+" sign, press and hold "0").

US/Canada to Europe

Dial 011 (US/Canada international access code), country code (41 for Switzerland), and phone number.

▶ To call the Gimmelwald hotel from home, dial 011-41-33-855-1658.

Country to Country Within Europe

Dial 00 (Europe international access code), country code, and phone number.

▶ To call the Gimmelwald hotel from Germany, dial 00-41-33-855-1658.

Europe to the US/Canada

Dial 00, country code (1 for US/Canada), and phone number.

▶ To call from Europe to my office in Edmonds, Washington, dial 00-1-425-771-8303.

Domestic Calls

To call within Switzerland (from one Swiss landline or mobile phone to another), simply dial the phone number, including the initial 0.

▶ To call the Gimmelwald hotel from Geneva, dial 033-855-1658.

More Dialing Tips

Swiss Phone Numbers: Swiss numbers that begin with 075 through 079 are mobile phones, which cost more to call.

for Wi-Fi. You can access the internet, send texts, and even make voice calls over Wi-Fi.

Most accommodations in Europe offer free Wi-Fi, but some—especially expensive hotels—charge a fee. Many cafés (including Starbucks and McDonald's) have free hotspots for customers; look for signs offering it and ask for the Wi-Fi password when you buy something. You'll also often find Wi-Fi at TIs, city squares, major museums, public-transit hubs, airports, and aboard trains and buses.

Minimize the use of your cellular network. The best way to make sure you're not accidentally burning through data is to put your device in "airplane" mode (which also disables phone calls and texts), turn your Wi-Fi back on, and connect to networks as

Toll and Toll-Free Numbers: It's generally not possible to dial Swiss toll or toll-free numbers from a US mobile or landline (although you can sometimes get through using Skype). Look for a direct-dial number instead.

More Phoning Help: See HowToCallAbroad.com.

European Country Codes		Ireland & N. Ireland	353 / 44
Austria	43	Italy	39
Belgium	32	Latvia	371
Bosnia-Herzegovina	387	Montenegro	382
Croatia	385	Morocco	212
Czech Republic	420	Netherlands	31
Denmark	45	Norway	47
Estonia	372	Poland	48
Finland	358	Portugal	351
France	33	Russia	7
Germany	49	Slovakia	421
Gibraltar	350	Slovenia	386
Great Britain	44	Spain	34
Greece	30	Sweden	46
Hungary	36	Switzerland	41
Iceland	354	Turkey	90

needed. When you need to get online but can't find Wi-Fi, simply turn on your cellular network (or turn off airplane mode) just long enough for the task at hand.

Even with an international data plan, wait until you're on Wi-Fi to Skype, download apps, stream videos, or do other megabyte-greedy tasks. Using a navigation app such as Google Maps over a cellular network can take lots of data, so do this sparingly or use it offline.

Limit automatic updates. By default, your device constantly checks for a data connection and updates apps. It's smart to disable these features so your apps will only update when you're on Wi-Fi. Also change your device's email settings from "auto-retrieve" to "manual" (or from "push" to "fetch").

Tips on Internet Security

Make sure that your device is running the latest versions of its operating system, security software, and apps. Next, ensure that your device and key programs (like email) are password- or passcode-protected. On the road, use only secure, password-protected Wi-Fi hotspots. Ask the hotel or café staff for the specific name of their Wi-Fi network, and make sure you log on to that exact one.

If you must access your financial info online, use a banking app rather than accessing your account via a browser. A cellular connection is more secure than Wi-Fi. Avoid logging onto personal finance sites on a public computer.

Never share your credit-card number (or any other sensitive information) online unless you know that the site is secure. A secure site displays a little padlock icon, and the URL begins with *https* (instead of the usual *http*).

Use Wi-Fi calling and messaging apps. Skype, WhatsApp, FaceTime, and Google Hangouts are great for making free or low-cost calls or sending texts over Wi-Fi worldwide. Just log on to a Wi-Fi network, then connect with any of your friends or family members who use the same service. If you buy credit in advance, with some of these services you can call or send a text anywhere for just pennies per minute.

Some apps, such as Apple's iMessage, will use the cellular network for texts if Wi-Fi isn't available: To avoid this possibility, turn off the "Send as SMS" feature.

Buy a European SIM card. If you anticipate making a lot of local calls, need a local phone number, or your provider's international data rates are expensive, consider buying a SIM card in Europe to replace the one in your (unlocked) US phone or tablet. SIM cards are sold at department-store electronics counters, some newsstands, and vending machines. If you need help setting it up, buy one at a mobile-phone shop (you may need to show your passport).

There are no roaming charges when using a European SIM card in other EU countries, though to be sure you get this "roam-like-at-home" pricing, buy your SIM card at a mobile-phone shop and ask if this feature is included.

WITHOUT A MOBILE PHONE

It's possible to travel in Europe without a mobile device. You can make calls from your hotel and check email or get online using public computers.

Most **hotels** charge a fee for placing calls—ask for rates before you dial. You can use a prepaid international phone card (usually available at newsstands, tobacco shops, and train stations) to call out from your hotel. Dial the toll-free access number, enter the card's PIN code, then dial the number.

You'll see Swisscom **public pay phones** in a few post offices and train stations. The phones generally come with multilingual instructions; most don't take coins but instead require insertable phone cards (called a "taxcard"; sold at post offices, newsstands, etc.); these work only within Switzerland.

Some hotels have **public computers** in their lobbies for guests to use; otherwise you may find them at public libraries (ask your hotelier or the TI for the nearest location). On a European keyboard, use the "Alt Gr" key to the right of the space bar to insert the extra symbol that appears on some keys. If you can't locate a special character (such as @), simply copy and paste it from a web page.

MAIL

You can mail one package per day to yourself worth up to $200 duty-free from Europe to the US (mark it "personal purchases"). If you're sending a gift to someone, mark it "unsolicited gift." For details, visit www.cbp.gov, select "Travel", and search for "Know Before You Go." The Swiss postal service works fine, but for quick transatlantic delivery (in either direction), consider services such as DHL (www.dhl.com).

Transportation

Because Switzerland's train network is excellent, I recommend using public transportation here. Only a few areas—like the Appenzell region and the French Swiss countryside—are better by car. Cars are an expensive headache in the bigger cities. For more detailed information on transportation throughout Europe, including trains, flying, renting a car, and driving, see www.ricksteves.com/transportation.

TRAINS

Trains in Switzerland are generally slick, speedy, and punctual, with synchronized connections. They're also clean, roomy, and nonsmoking. Few places in Switzerland are out of reach of the train system—and nearly everywhere can be reached by

PRACTICALITIES

PostBus, which is also well-synchronized with Swiss Rail. However, due to frustrating schedules, some travelers might find a few out-of-the-way recommendations not worth the time or trouble.

Virtually all Swiss stations have luggage lockers. In smaller towns, lockers are sometimes too small to fit larger bags, but if asked nicely the ticket office will usually store bigger luggage for the same price.

Many Swiss trains and stations are marked "SBB CFF FFS." All those letters mean the same thing ("Swiss Federal Railways"), in three different languages: German, French, and Italian. Quite a few of Switzerland's trains are, however, run by small private companies—particularly in mountain areas. Though private, these companies all take part in the same website with schedule and pricing information.

Schedules

For timetables, visit the Swiss site (www.sbb.ch; www.rail.ch gets you straight to the English version; since the website is hard to navigate, use the search function for info on passes and scenic rail). Note: Prices shown on this website look deceptively low, as by default, it assumes you have a Swiss Half-Fare Card (as most Swiss do). To see the full price, select "No Discount." Germany's excellent all-Europe timetable, www.bahn.com, also covers Switzerland, but doesn't give fare information. Although Switzerland has a 24-hour train-info number you can dial from anywhere in the country, it's so expensive that using it is a last resort (toll tel. 0900-300-300).

Oddly for a country that prides itself on timeliness, the touchscreen ticket machines at train stations and bus stops don't provide schedule information. Some train stations have a kiosk or two near the ticket office that lets you use the Rail.ch website. Also look for printed schedule booklets (in racks) showing major intercity connections, and yellow posters in stations that show departures. At the cost of waiting in line, ticket-office staff will print out a step-by-step itinerary for you, free of charge. It can help to know that most routes follow a regular schedule, with the same pattern usually repeated every hour or half-hour.

Intercity trains (IC, ICN, and EC) are the fastest, interregional trains (IR) come next, "regional expresses" (RE) skip minor stops, and most other trains (including those beginning with S) stop at all stops. Knowing these codes can help you save time by zeroing in on the fastest train available, as the yellow schedule posters at stations don't list arrival times at destinations.

Tickets

If you're traveling without a rail pass, get train tickets online or at the station—either at the ticket windows, or at the easy-to-use machines. You're not normally allowed to buy your ticket on the train. The penalty for boarding a train without a ticket is 90 CHF—which Swiss conductors strictly enforce.

The Swiss rail system's website lets you purchase train tickets no earlier than one month in advance, and tickets purchased online are nonrefundable and nonchangeable (with very few exceptions). Purchasing tickets at a station counter, which you can do up to three months in advance, lets you change or cancel them much more easily.

Unlike in neighboring countries, Swiss trains don't offer much in the way of advance purchase discounts, so there's little incentive to book far in advance. Also, tickets on fast trains usually cost the same as those on slower trains. Most tickets are not tied to a specific departure time, but only to a given route. Occasionally, though, you'll see discounts on particular departures offered on the website.

At larger stations, ticket offices have separate windows for international travel, which close earlier than the regular domestic sales windows.

The Swiss rarely make seat reservations on trains. Reservations are important only on certain special or international trains (for example, they're required on the Glacier Express, the Gotthard Panorama Express, and on TGV trains to France). They can also provide peace of mind at busy travel times (the Rail.ch website helpfully indicates how crowded a train is expected to be). Buy seat reservations at any ticket counter or online.

If you're waiting on the platform for your train, and you have a reserved seat or are planning to sit in first class, look for blue diagrams that show the sector of the platform where the various cars in the train will stop (usually A through F). Stand in the appropriate sector to avoid a last-minute dash to your car or a long walk through the train to your seat.

Rail Passes

Because of high ticket prices, rail passes are a good deal in Switzerland, often even for just a three-day trip. For such a little country, Switzerland has a dizzying array of train passes and deals—but for most travelers, the Swiss Travel Pass is the way to go. For more detailed advice on figuring out the smartest rail pass options for your train trip, visit www.ricksteves.com/rail.

Swiss Travel Pass: The basic version covers all trains, boats, and buses, plus admission to most Swiss museums, and offers a half-price discount on most high-mountain trains and lifts. It comes in both consecutive-day and flexipass versions. Both versions cover the cost of most transportation options for a specified number of days (but do not cover seat reservations). Second class is 35 percent cheaper than first class.

PRACTICALITIES

Rail Pass or Point-to-Point Tickets?

Will you be better off buying a rail pass or point-to-point tickets? It pays to know your options and choose what's best for your itinerary.

Rail Passes

A Swiss Travel Pass lets you travel by train in Switzerland for three to fifteen days (consecutively or not) within a one-month period. This pass also covers boats, buses, many museum admissions, and gives discounts on mountain trains and lifts.

Switzerland is also covered (along with most of Europe) by the classic Eurail Global Pass. It's generally cheaper to buy one pass for your whole trip than separate, single-country passes. But since Eurail passes don't cover all the same extras that a Swiss Travel Pass does, different combinations are worth considering.

Switzerland's many travel options also include a one-month Half-Fare Card for discounts on individual point-to-point tickets and various local or regional passes.

While most rail passes are best purchased outside Europe (through travel agents or Rick Steves' Europe), the Swiss Travel Pass and related products are also sold at train stations in Switzerland and at www.rail.ch (search for "Swiss Travel Pass"). For more on rail passes, including current prices, visit RickSteves.com/rail.

Point-to-Point Tickets

Use this map to add up approximate pay-as-you-go train fares for your itinerary and compare that to the price of a rail pass. Keep in mind that a pass can help with expensive lift tickets and other bonuses in Switzerland, so remember to include these in your comparison.

Map shows approximate costs, in US dollars, for one-way, second-class tickets.

Comparing Swiss Pass Coverage

All passes that include Switzerland cover national network trains and many sightseeing and private rail and boat discounts.

Route or Bonus	Eurail Global Pass	Swiss Travel Pass
Swiss Museum admission	No	Covered
Postal buses	No	Covered
Urban buses and trams	No	Covered
Mt. Rigi above Vitznau, Arth-Goldau, or Weggis ($25–40 per leg)	50% off	Covered
Mt. Pilatus above Kriens or Alpnachstad ($70 for 2 legs)	50% off	50% off
Mt. Schilthorn lifts from Stechelberg ($105 roundtrip)	25% off	50% off above Mürren
Jungfrau Region Railways from Interlaken (e.g. $10 to Lauterbrunnen, $11 to Grindelwald, $15 to Wengen; $200 round-trip Jungfraujoch)	25% off above Interlaken	25% off above Grindelwald or Wengen
Glacier Express scenic train	Covered	Covered
Brig-Zermatt private train to see Matterhorn ($40 2nd class)	Covered	Covered
Le Châtelard, Switzerland, to Chamonix, France ($14)	Covered	Covered

All "covered" and discounted services start use of a travel day on a Swiss Travel Pass flexipass.
Eurail Global flexipasses allow discounts without using a counted travel day.

Swiss Half-Fare Card: This card gives you a 50 percent discount off all national and private trains, postal buses, boats, and many lifts ($125 for one month). This can save you money if your Swiss travel adds up to more than $250 in point-to-point tickets.

Swiss Family Card: This card allows children ages 6-15 to travel free with their parents who are using a Swiss Travel Pass or one-month Half-Fare Card for visitors (kids are free even on high-mountain routes where the parents may pay extra). If parents are not buying a pass, the similar Swiss Junior Travelcard costs 30 CHF/1 child or 60 CHF/2 or more children at Swiss stations, valid for one year. A Children's Co-Travelcard works for non-parents (30 CHF/each child). Children under 6 always travel free.

Eurail Global Pass: This pass covers most European railways for as few as three travel days within a month or as long as three months continuously in either first or second class. They can make sense if Switzerland is part of a multicountry trip. All Eurail passes allow up to two kids (ages 4-11) to travel free with each adult, and rates are discounted for youths under 28 or seniors age 60 or older.

Rail Pass Bonuses and Discounts: If you buy a rail pass, know what extras are included—for example, Swiss Travel Passes

Public Transportation

Rail

Boat

Bus

Note: Not all transportation routes shown.

50 Kilometers
50 Miles

can get you free entry to many museums and discounts on many mountain lifts. Always ask. The Eurail Global Pass also includes some deals in Switzerland beyond simple trains (such as discounts on lake boats and some mountain lifts), but the coverage and discounts aren't as extensive as the Switzerland-only passes. (For example, lifts in Zermatt are discounted and postal buses nationwide are free with a Swiss Travel Pass, but both are full price with a Global Pass.)

If your rail pass is a flexipass (covering a certain number of days spread over a longer span, rather than consecutive days), it pays to maximize the benefits you use on a single calendar day. With a flexi version of a Swiss Travel Pass, all coverage and discounts are offered only on the counted travel days. Even if you use the pass just for a short bus ride, a museum entrance, or a discounted ticket, you start the use of a flexi-day. If you don't have more travel planned on the same day, it can make sense to pay out of pocket rather than using a valuable day of your flexipass.

With a Eurail Global Pass, discounted (but not free) trips—most notably many mountain lifts—are still offered at the lower price anytime within the validity window (not just on a flexi-day).

Train Tips

Scenic Rail Journeys: In addition to being convenient for transportation, many of Switzerland's trains are also breathtakingly scenic. Several trips are particularly beautiful and billed as special "theme" routes for tourists. For many visitors, these are a Swiss highlight, and I've devoted an entire chapter to them (see the Scenic Rail Journeys chapter).

Using Rail Passes on Private Lines: Switzerland has some privately owned train lines. Most notably, the private Jungfrau Railway operates the trains from Interlaken up the Lauterbrunnen Valley and to the Jungfraujoch. In this region, Swiss Travel Pass coverage switches to just a discount above Wengen or Grindelwald, but Eurail Global Pass coverage switches to a discount once you board a Jungfrau Railway train at Interlaken. If your rail pass doesn't cover an entire journey, pay for the "uncovered" portion at the station before you board the train.

Check Your Bags: If you're town- or mountain-hopping through Switzerland by train, a great way to lighten your load is by sending your baggage ahead (drop it off at the station before 19:00, pay 12 CHF with ticket or rail pass, maximum 55 pounds). Your bag will show up at the designated station within 36 hours of your arrival (usually faster) and will be held for four days for free (after that, it's a few francs a day). Door-to-door delivery is available with an additional flat fee of 40 CHF per travel group and

Lift Lingo

The Swiss have come up with an impressive variety of ways to conquer peaks and reach the best viewpoints and trailheads with minimum sweat. Known generically as "lifts," each of these contraptions has its own name and definition. Use the right terms, and impress your new Swiss friends.

Cogwheel Train: A train that climbs a steep incline using a gear system, which engages "teeth" in the middle of the tracks to provide traction. Also known as "rack-and-pinion train" or "rack railway." In German, it's a *Zahnradbahn* (*train à cremaillère* in French and *ferrovia a cremagliera* in Italian).

Funicular: A car that is pulled by a cable along tracks up a particularly steep incline, often counterbalanced by a similar car going in the opposite direction (which you'll pass halfway through the ride). Funiculars, like cogwheel trains, are in contact with the ground at all times. In German, it's a *Standseilbahn* (*funiculaire* in French and *funicolare* in Italian).

Cable Car: A large passenger car, suspended in the air by a cable, which travels between stations without touching the ground. A cable car holds a large number of people (sometimes dozens at a time), who generally ride standing up. When a cable car reaches a station, it comes to a full stop to allow passengers to get on and off. In German, it's a *Seilbahn* (*téléphérique* in French and *funivia* in Italian).

Gondola: Also suspended in the air by a cable, but smaller than a cable car— generally holding fewer than 10 people, who are usually seated. Gondolas move continuously, meaning that passengers have to hop into and out of the moving cars at stations. Generally, gondolas have many smaller cars strung along the same cable. In German, it's a *Gondel* (*télécabine* in French and *telecabine* in Italian). Confusingly, the "car" compartment of a cable car is sometimes referred to as a "gondola."

offers a same-day express upgrade in some locations for another 30 CHF per group. See www.rail.ch for details.

Bike 'n' Rail: You can rent a bike at more than 80 Swiss rail stations, usually at the baggage counter, for 35 CHF per day (30 CHF with rail pass; 27 CHF/half-day, 22 CHF with rail pass, helmets included). You may be able to return the bike at another station (10 CHF extra). They also have electric bikes, tandem bikes, and kids' bikes. For more information, see www.sbbrail.ch/

mobilitaet and search "bike." Though not required, online reservations are encouraged. For general information on bike routes in Switzerland, visit www.veloland.ch.

TAXIS AND RIDE-BOOKING SERVICES

While most European taxis are reliable and cheap, Swiss taxis are expensive (Zürich's were recently ranked the priciest in the world). Public transit is extremely efficient; using it to get to outlying sights or an airport is still the best option. If you like ride-booking services like Uber, these apps work in Zürich, Lausanne, and Geneva just like they do in the US: You request a car on your mobile phone (connected to Wi-Fi or data), and the fare is automatically charged to your credit card.

RENTING A CAR

It's cheaper to arrange most car rentals from the US, so research and compare rates before you go. Most of the major US rental agencies (including Avis, Budget, Enterprise, Hertz, and Thrifty) have offices throughout Europe. Also consider the two major Europe-based agencies, Europcar and Sixt. Consolidators such as Auto Europe/Kemwel (www.autoeurope.com or the often cheaper www.autoeurope.eu) compare rates at several companies to get you the best deal.

Wherever you book, always read the fine print. Check for add-on charges—such as one-way drop-off fees, airport surcharges, or mandatory insurance policies—that aren't included in the "total price."

Rental Costs and Considerations

Figure on paying roughly $250 for a one-week rental for a basic compact car. Allow extra for supplemental insurance, fuel, tolls, and parking.

Manual vs. Automatic: Almost all rental cars in Europe are manual by default—and cars with a stick shift are generally cheaper. If you need an automatic, request one in advance. When selecting a car, don't be tempted by a larger model, as it won't be as maneuverable on narrow, winding roads or when squeezing into tight parking lots.

Age Restrictions: Some rental companies impose minimum and maximum age limits. Young drivers (25 and under) and seniors (69 and up) should check the rental policies and rules section of car rental websites.

Choosing Pick-Up/Drop-off Locations: Always check the hours of the locations you choose: Many rental offices close from midday Saturday until Monday morning and, in smaller towns, at lunchtime. When selecting an office, plug the addresses into a mapping website to confirm the location. A downtown site is generally cheaper—and might seem more convenient than the airport. But pedestrianized and one-way streets can make navigation tricky when returning a car at a big-city office or urban train station. Wherever you select, get precise details on the location and allow ample time to find it.

Have the Right License: If you're renting a car in Switzerland, bring your driver's license. If you're also planning to drive in Austria or Italy, you're technically required to have an International Driving Permit—a translation of your driver's license (sold at your local AAA office for $20 plus the cost of two passport-type photos; see www.aaa.com). While that's the letter of the law, I generally rent cars without having this permit. How this is enforced varies from country to country: Get advice from your car-rental company.

Picking Up Your Car: Before driving off in your rental car, check it thoroughly and make sure any damage is noted on your rental agreement. Rental agencies in Europe tend to charge for even minor damage, so be sure to mark everything. Find out how your car's gearshift, lights, turn signals, wipers, radio, and fuel cap function, and know what kind of fuel the car takes (diesel vs. unleaded). When you return the car, make sure the agent verifies its condition with you. Some drivers take pictures of the returned vehicle as proof of its condition.

Car Insurance Options

When you rent a car in Europe, the price typically includes liability insurance, which covers harm to other cars or motorists—but not the rental car itself. To limit your financial risk in case of damage to the rental, choose one of these options: Buy a Collision Damage Waiver (CDW) coverage with a low or zero deductible from the car-rental company (roughly 30-40 percent extra), get coverage through your credit card (free, but more complicated), or get collision insurance as part of a larger travel-insurance policy.

Basic **CDW** costs $15-30 a day and typically comes with a $1,000-$2,000 deductible, reducing but not eliminating your financial responsibility. When you reserve or pick up the car, you'll be offered the chance to "buy down" the deductible to zero (for an additional $10-30/day; this is sometimes called "super CDW" or "zero-deductible coverage").

If you opt for **credit-card coverage,** you must decline all coverage offered by the car-rental company—which means they can place a hold on your card for up to the full value of the car. In case of damage, it can be time-consuming to resolve the charges. Before relying on this option, quiz your card company about how it works.

If you're already purchasing a **travel-insurance policy** for your trip, adding collision coverage is an option. For example, Travel

Guard (www.travelguard.com) sells affordable renter's collision insurance as an add-on to its other policies; it's valid everywhere in Europe except the Republic of Ireland, and some Italian car-rental companies refuse to honor it, as it doesn't cover you in case of theft.

For more on car-rental insurance, see www.ricksteves.com/cdw.

Navigation Options

If you'll be navigating using your phone or a GPS unit from home, remember to bring a car charger and device mount.

Your Mobile Phone: The mapping app on your mobile phone works fine for navigating Europe's roads, but for real-time turn-by-turn directions and traffic updates, you'll need mobile data access. And driving all day can burn through a lot of very expensive data. The economical work-around is to use map apps that work offline. By downloading in advance from Google Maps, City Maps 2Go, Apple Maps, Here WeGo, or Navmii, you can still have turn-by-turn voice directions and maps that recalibrate even though they're offline.

You must download your maps before you go offline—and it's smart to select large regions. Then turn off your data connection so you're not charged for roaming. Call up the map, enter your destination, and you're on your way. Even if you don't have to pay extra

PRACTICALITIES

for data roaming, this option is great for navigating in areas with poor connectivity.

GPS Devices: If you want the convenience of a dedicated GPS unit, consider renting one with your car ($10-30/day). These units offer real-time turn-by-turn directions and traffic without the data requirements of an app. The unit may come loaded only with maps for its home country; if you need additional maps, ask. Also make sure your device's language is set to English before you drive off.

A less-expensive option is to bring a GPS device from home. Be sure to buy and install the European maps you'll need before your trip.

Paper Maps and Atlases: Even when navigating primarily with a mobile app or GPS, I always make it a point to have a paper map—ideally a big, detailed regional road map. It's invaluable for getting the big picture, understanding alternate routes, and filling in when my phone runs out of juice. The free maps you get from your car-rental company usually don't have enough detail. It's smart to buy a better map before you go, or pick one up at a local gas station, bookshop, newsstand, or tourist shop.

DRIVING

You can get anywhere quickly on Switzerland's fine road system, the world's most expensive per mile to build.

Road Rules: By law, you must use your headlights day and night in Switzerland (driving without them on will earn you a 40-CHF fine). Seat belts are required, and two beers under those belts are enough to land you in jail. Children under 12 (yes, 12) need to ride in a child-safety seat. Be aware of typical European road rules; for example, like many other European countries, Switzerland forbids handheld mobile-phone use. Ask your car-rental company about these rules, or check the "International Travel" section of the US State Department website (www.travel.state.gov, search for your country in the "Country Information" box, then click on "Travel & Transportation").

Tolls: Drivers pay an annual 40-CHF fee for a permit to use Swiss autobahns. Check to see if your rental car already has one of these windshield stickers, called a "vignette"—if you picked it up in Switzerland, it most likely does. If not, buy it at border crossings, gas stations, post offices, or car-rental agencies. Anyone caught driving on a Swiss autobahn (indicated by green signs with a white expressway symbol) without this tax sticker is likely to be stopped and slapped with a steep fine (200 CHF plus the 40-CHF fee).

Fuel: Gas and diesel are both expensive—often around $6 per gallon. US credit and debit cards may not work at pay-at-the-pump stations, but are generally accepted (with a PIN code) at staffed stations. Diesel rental cars are common; make sure you know what type of fuel your car takes before you fill up.

Signage: Know the universal road signs (shown in this chapter and explained in charts in most road atlases and at service stations). *Dreieck* (literally, "three corners") means a Y in the road; *Autobahnkreuz* is an intersection (*carrefour* in French). Exits are spaced about 20 miles apart and often have a gas station (*bleifrei/sans plomb* are German/French for "unleaded"), a restaurant, a minimart, and sometimes a tourist information desk. Exits and intersections refer to the next major city or the nearest small town. Look at your map and anticipate which town names to watch out for. Know what you're looking for—miss it, and you're long autobahn-gone. When navigating, you'll see *Nord, Süd, Ost,*

West, or *Mitte* (*nord, sud, est, ouest,* or *centre* in French).

To get to the center of a city, follow signs for *Zentrum* or *Stadtmitte* (or *centre-ville* in French). Ring roads go around a city.

Parking: Even in small towns, prime parking spots usually require payment. But it's easy to find free short-term parking in relatively central "blue zone" spaces, which require a blue cardboard "parking disc" clock (*Parkscheibe,* available free at TIs, gas stations, police stations, and *Tabak* shops). It's easy: Display your arrival time on the clock (you can scoot it up to the nearest full hour or half-hour) and put it on the dashboard, so parking attendants can see how long you've been there. Unless the sign indicates otherwise, you can park for free for an hour past the time set on your clock. If you arrive after 11:30, you can leave your car till 14:30, and if you arrive after 18:00, you're good until 9:00 the next day. Blue zones aren't patrolled overnight (19:00-8:00) or on Sundays, so you don't need to display a disc during those times.

FLIGHTS

To compare flight costs and times, begin with an online travel search engine: Kayak is the top site for flights to and within Europe, easy-to-use Google Flights has price alerts, and Skyscanner includes many inexpensive flights within Europe. To avoid unpleasant surprises, before you book be sure to read the small print about refunds, changes, and the cost for "extras" such as reserving a seat, checking a bag, or checking in and printing a boarding pass.

Flights to Europe: Start looking for international flights about four to six months before your trip, especially for peak-season travel. Depending on your itinerary, it can be efficient and no more expensive to fly into one city and out of another. If your flight requires a connection in Europe, see our hints on navigating Europe's top hub airports at www.ricksteves.com/hub-airports.

Flights Within Europe: Flying between European cities has become surprisingly affordable. Before buying a long-distance train or bus ticket, first check the cost of a flight on one of Europe's airlines, whether a major carrier or a no-frills outfit like EasyJet and Ryanair. Be aware that flying with a discount airline can have drawbacks, such as minimal customer service and time-consuming treks to secondary airports.

Flying to the US and Canada: Because security is extra tight for flights to the US, be sure to give yourself plenty of time at the airport. Charge your electronic devices before you board in case security checks require you to turn them on (see www.tsa.com for the latest rules).

Resources from Rick Steves

Begin Your Trip at RickSteves.com

My mobile-friendly **website** is *the* place to explore Europe in preparation for your trip. You'll find thousands of fun articles, videos, and radio interviews; a wealth of money-saving tips for planning your dream trip; travel news dispatches; a video library of my travel talks; my travel blog; my latest guidebook updates (www.ricksteves.com/update); and my free Rick Steves Audio Europe app. You can also follow me on Facebook, Instagram, and Twitter.

Our **Travel Forum** is a well-groomed collection of message boards where our travel-savvy community answers questions and shares their personal travel experiences—and our well-traveled staff chimes in when they can be helpful (www.ricksteves.com/forums).

Our **online Travel Store** offers bags and accessories that I've designed to help you travel smarter and lighter. These include my popular carry-on bags (which I live out of four months a year), money belts, totes, toiletries kits, adapters, guidebooks, and planning maps (www.ricksteves.com/shop).

Our website can also help you find the perfect **rail pass** for your itinerary and your budget, with easy, one-stop shopping for rail passes, seat reservations, and point-to-point tickets (www. ricksteves.com/rail).

Rick Steves Tours, Guidebooks, TV Shows, and More

Small Group Tours: Want to travel with greater efficiency and less stress? We offer more than 40 itineraries reaching the best destinations in this book...and beyond. Each year more than 30,000 travelers join us on about 1,000 Rick Steves bus tours. You'll enjoy great guides and a fun bunch of travel partners (with small groups of 24 to 28 travelers). You'll find European adventures to fit every vacation length. For all the details, and to get our tour catalog, visit www.ricksteves.com/tours or call us at 425/608-4217.

Books: *Rick Steves Switzerland* is just one of many books in my series on European travel, which includes country and city guidebooks, Snapshots (excerpted chapters from bigger guides), Pocket guidebooks (full-color little books on big cities), "Best Of" guidebooks (condensed, full-color country guides), and my budget-travel skills handbook, *Rick Steves Europe Through the Back Door.* A complete list of my titles—including phrase books, cruising guides, travelogues on European art, history, and culture, and more—appears near the end of this book.

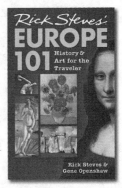

TV Shows and Travel Talks: My public television series, *Rick Steves' Europe,* covers Europe from top to bottom with over 100 half-hour episodes—and we're working on new shows every year (watch full episodes online for free). My free online video library, Rick Steves Classroom Europe, offers a searchable database of short video clips on European history, culture, and geography (http://classroom.ricksteves.com). And, to raise your travel I.Q., check out the video versions of our popular classes (covering most European countries as well as travel skills, packing smart, cruising, tech for travelers, European art, and travel as a political act—www. ricksteves.com/travel-talks).

Radio: My weekly public radio show, *Travel with Rick Steves,* features interviews with travel experts from around the world. It airs on 400 public radio stations across the US, or you can hear it as a podcast. A complete archive of programs is available at www.ricksteves.com/radio.

Audio Tours on My Free App: I've produced dozens of free, self-guided audio tours of the top sights in Europe. For those tours, and other audio content, get my free **Rick Steves Audio Europe app,** an extensive online library organized by destination. For more on my app. See page 11.

APPENDIX

Holidays & Festivals 457
Books & Films 459
Conversions & Climate 462
Packing Checklist 465
German Survival Phrases 467
French Survival Phrases 469
Italian Survival Phrases 471

Holidays and Festivals

This list includes selected festivals in major cities, plus national holidays observed throughout Switzerland. Many sights and banks close down on national holidays—keep this in mind when planning your itinerary. However, not every canton celebrates all holidays (particularly religious ones); if you find yourself in a town closed down for an unexpected holiday, consider going on to your next stop (call ahead), where everything may well be in full swing. Before planning a trip around a festival, verify the dates with the festival website, the Switzerland tourist office (www.myswitzerland.com), or my "Upcoming Holidays and Festivals in Switzerland" web page (www.ricksteves.com/europe/switzerland/festivals).

Jan 1	New Year's Day
Jan 2	Berchtoldstag (St. Berchtold's Day), Harder-Potschete (parade), Interlaken
Jan 6	Epiphany (closings)
Mid-Jan	Lauberhorn ski race, Wengen; Inferno ski race, Mürren (www.inferno-muerren.ch)

March	Fasnacht (Carnival), especially celebrated in Luzern, Zürich, Bern, and Basel
March 19	Josefstag (St. Joseph's Day)
March-May	International Jazz Festival (www.jazzfestivalbern.ch), Bern
Early April	Lucerne Festival at Easter (classical and sacred music, www.lucernefestival.ch), Luzern
Early to Mid-April	Sechseläuten (Spring Festival, www.sechselaeuten.ch), Zürich
April	Easter Sunday-Monday: April 4-5, 2021; April 17-18, 2022
Last Sun in April	Open-Air Parliament (public selection of delegates), Appenzell
May 1	Labor Day
May	Ascension (Christi Himmelfahrt): May 13, 2021; May 26, 2022
May or June	Pentecost and Pentecost Monday (Pfingsten and Pfingstmontag): May 23-24, 2021; June 5-6, 2022
June	Corpus Christi (Fronleichnam): June 3, 2021; June 16, 2022
June	Zürich Festival (www.zuercher-festspiele.ch)
Mid-June-Sept	William Tell Performance (open-air theater, www.tellspiele.ch), Interlaken
Late June-Early July	Montreux International Jazz Festival (www.montreuxjazz.com)
Early July	Estival Jazz (free open-air festival, www.estivaljazz.ch), Lugano
Early July	City Festival (www.festivalcite.ch), Lausanne
Mid-July	Gurten Open-Air Rock Festival (www.gurtenfestival.ch), Bern
Aug	Street Parade (citywide rave, www.streetparade.ch), Zürich
Aug 1	Swiss National Day (parades and fireworks)
Aug 15	Assumption of Mary (Maria Himmelfahrt)
Mid-Aug-Mid-Sept	Lucerne Festival in Summer (classical music, www.lucernefestival.ch), Luzern
Early Oct	Festa d'Autunno (food and wine festival), Lugano
Nov 1	All Saints' Day
Late Nov	Lucerne Festival at the Piano (www.lucernefestival.ch), Luzern

Late Nov	Zibelemärit (traditional onion market festival), Bern
Dec	Christmas fairs
Dec 6	St. Nicholas Day
Dec 8	Immaculate Conception
Dec 25	Christmas
Dec 26	St. Stephen's Day (Boxing Day)

Books and Films

To learn more about Switzerland past and present, check out a few of these books or films.

NONFICTION

Eiger Dreams (Jon Krakauer, 1990). In this collection of essays, Krakauer explores the trials and triumphs of mountaineering, including his attempt on the Eiger's north face.

La Place de la Concorde Suisse (John McPhee, 1983). Following a mountain unit of the Swiss Army, this book explores how mandatory military service (for men) keeps Switzerland from breaking apart.

Scrambles Amongst the Alps (Edward Whymper, 1871). This mountaineering classic recounts adventure and tragedy in the life of the first climber to summit the Matterhorn.

Swiss History in a Nutshell (Gregoire Nappey, 2010). Nappey delivers information that's concise and enjoyable, yet not dumbed down.

Swiss Watching (Diccon Bewes, 2010). This fun yet well-researched book covers all the basics in an easy-to-digest look at 21st-century Switzerland.

Target Switzerland: Swiss Armed Neutrality in World War II (Stephen P. Halbrook, 1998). Halbrook posits that Switzerland's robust preparation for armed resistance against the Nazis was a key to its success in maintaining neutrality.

A Tramp Abroad (Mark Twain, 1880). Twain humorously recounts his 1878 "walking tour" through the Alps.

The White Spider (Heinrich Harrer, 1959). This book chronicles the first successful ascent of the Eiger's north face in 1938.

Why Switzerland? (Jonathan Steinberg, 1976). Steinberg explains how a country with four official languages can still have a common culture.

FICTION

Einstein's Dreams (Alan Lightman, 1992). A young Albert Einstein wrests with his theory of relativity in turn-of-the-century Bern.

A Farewell to Arms (Ernest Hemingway, 1929). Two lovers struggle through the horrors of World War I, finding brief peace in Switzerland in the last act.

Frankenstein (Mary Shelley, 1818). Set partially in Geneva, this novel explores the nature of humanity when scientist Victor Frankenstein creates a monster and brings it to life.

Hotel du Lac (Anita Brookner, 1995). A writer of romance novels attempts to recover from her own misguided love affair by fleeing to Switzerland.

I'm Not Stiller (Max Frisch, 1954). In an attempt to reclaim his true identity, a prisoner in a small Swiss town recounts his adventurous life.

The Magic Mountain (Thomas Mann, 1924). An exclusive sanatorium high in the Alps is a microcosm for European society in the days before World War I.

The Night Manager (John le Carré, 1993). The fussy manager of a Swiss hotel is recruited by British intelligence to bring down a millionaire gunrunner.

The Watchers (Jon Steele, 2011). Three strangers in Lausanne must solve the mysteries haunting their town.

William Tell (Friedrich Schiller, 1804). William Tell, legendary Swiss marksman, fights for Swiss independence from the Habsburg Empire in the 14th century.

FILMS AND TV

The Bourne Identity (2002). This action movie, set mostly in Prague, pits an amnesiac spy against his pursuers in the heart of Zürich.

Clouds of Sils Maria (2014). Largely set (and filmed) in the Upper Engadine valley, this coming-of-middle-age drama stars Juliette Binoche as an aging actress and Kristen Stewart as the personal assistant who poses a subtle threat (as does the Engadine's unique weather patterns).

Dilwale Dulhania Le Jayenge (1995). In the longest-running film in Indian cinema (600 weeks in the movie theaters), two young people fall in love on a trip to Switzerland.

The Eiger Sanction (1975). A mountain climber (Clint Eastwood) joins an expedition on the Eiger's north face intending to expose a murderer among his climbing team. The film includes scenes from Kleine Scheidegg and on the Eiger itself.

Five Days One Summer (1982). Sean Connery stars in the tale of an incestuous love triangle, offset by breathtaking climbing sequences in the Swiss Alps.

Jonah Who Will Be 25 in the Year 2000 (1976). A group of student activists living in Geneva face disillusionment during the late 1960s.

Journey of Hope (1990). Three members of a Kurdish family search for a better life in Switzerland.

North Face (2008). Inspired by a true story, this adventure chronicles a 1936 attempt by two German soldiers to be the first to scale the Eiger's daunting north face.

On Her Majesty's Secret Service (1969). James Bond (George Lazenby) goes undercover in the Swiss Alps, with action sequences on the Schilthorn.

The Swissmakers (1978). The most popular Swiss movie ever made showcases a group of foreigners trying to get Swiss citizenship.

Three Colors: Red (1994). In the Oscar-nominated final film of the acclaimed *Three Colors Trilogy*, a young model living in Geneva forms an unlikely bond with a cynical old judge.

FOR KIDS

And Both Were Young (Madeleine L'Engle, 1983). In a tale for teens, Philippa struggles to find her place at a Swiss boarding school until she starts a secret romance and gains new friends.

Asterix in Switzerland (René Goscinny, 1970). Asterix and Obelix have adventures in Switzerland during Roman times in book number 16 of this beloved French cartoon series.

Banner in the Sky (James Ramsey Ullman, 1954). Young Rudi Matt tries to climb one of the world's most forbidding Alpine peaks in this Newbery Honor book.

A Bell for Ursli (Selina Chönz, 2007). High in the Alps, a boy named Ursli hikes alone into the snowy mountains to find a big bell with which to lead the spring procession.

Count Karlstein (Philip Pullman, 2000). Two girls escape the sinister plot of their uncle—an evil count—in this humorous middle-grade thriller set in a Swiss village in 1816.

Dear Alexandra: A Story of Switzerland (Helen Gudel, 1999). This charming picture book takes the form of letters from a grandmother who awaits her granddaughter's visit in a Swiss mountain village.

Heidi (Johanna Spyri, 1880). In the most famous novel about Switzerland, an orphan girl is sent to live with her grandfather in the Alps. A popular film version starring Shirley Temple was released in 1937.

Pitschi (Hans Fischer, 1947). In this Swiss children's classic, a kitten named Pitschi sets out to find her place among the animals on Old Lisette's farm.

A Tale of Two Brothers (Eveline Hasler, 2006). This Swiss-Italian folk tale of two brothers with vastly different worldviews delivers a moral about the power of positive thinking.

William Tell: One Against an Empire (Paul D. Storrie, 2008). This dynamic retelling of the legendary Swiss hunter's story is presented in graphic novel format.

Conversions and Climate

Numbers and Stumblers

- Europeans write a few of their numbers differently than we do. 1 = 1, 4 = 4, 7 = 7.
- In Europe, dates appear as day/month/year, so Christmas 2021 is 25/12/2021.
- Commas are decimal points and decimals are commas. A dollar and a half is $1,50, one thousand is 1.000, and there are 5.280 feet in a mile.
- When counting with fingers, start with your thumb. If you hold up your first finger to request one item, you'll probably get two.
- What Americans call the second floor of a building is the first floor in Europe.
- On escalators and moving sidewalks, Europeans keep the left "lane" open for passing. Keep to the right.

Metric Conversions

A **kilogram** equals 1,000 grams (about 2.2 pounds). One hundred **grams** (a common unit at markets) is about a quarter-pound. One **liter** is about a quart, or almost four to a gallon.

A **kilometer** is six-tenths of a mile. To convert kilometers to miles, cut the kilometers in half and add back 10 percent of the original (120 km: 60 + 12 = 72 miles). One **meter** is 39 inches—just over a yard.

1 foot = 0.3 meter	1 square yard = 0.8 square meter
1 yard = 0.9 meter	1 square mile = 2.6 square kilometers
1 mile = 1.6 kilometers	1 ounce = 28 grams
1 centimeter = 0.4 inch	1 quart = 0.95 liter
1 meter = 39.4 inches	1 kilogram = 2.2 pounds
1 kilometer = 0.62 mile	32°F = 0°C

CLOTHING SIZES

When shopping for clothing, use these US-to-European comparisons as general guidelines (but note that no conversion is perfect).

Women: For pants and dresses, add 30 in Switzerland (US 10 = Swiss 40). For blouses and sweaters, add 8 for most of Europe (US 32 = European 40). For shoes, add 30-31 (US 7 = European 37/38).

Men: For shirts, multiply by 2 and add about 8 (US 15 = European 38). For jackets and suits, add 10. For shoes, add 32-34.

Children: Clothing is sized by height—in centimeters (2.5 cm = 1 inch), so a US size 8 roughly equates to 132-140. For shoes up to size 13, add 16-18, and for sizes 1 and up, add 30-32.

Switzerland's Climate

First line, average daily high; second line, average daily low; third line, average days without rain. For more detailed weather statistics for destinations in this book (as well as the rest of the world), check www.wunderground.com.

J	F	M	A	M	J	J	A	S	O	N	D
Bern											
38°	42°	51°	59°	66°	73°	77°	76°	69°	58°	47°	40°
29°	30°	36°	42°	49°	55°	58°	58°	53°	44°	37°	31°
20	19	22	21	20	19	22	20	20	21	19	21

Fahrenheit and Celsius Conversion

Europe takes its temperature using the Celsius scale, while we opt for Fahrenheit. For a rough conversion from Celsius to Fahrenheit, double the number and add 30. For weather, remember that 28°C is 82°F—perfect. For health, 37°C is just right. At a launderette, 30°C is cold, 40°C is warm (usually the default setting), 60°C is hot, and 95°C is boiling. Your air-conditioner should be set at about 20°C.

Packing Checklist

Whether you're traveling for five days or five weeks, you won't need more than this. Pack light to enjoy the sweet freedom of true mobility.

Clothing

- [ ] 5 shirts: long- & short-sleeve
- [ ] 2 pairs pants (or skirts/capris)
- [ ] 1 pair shorts
- [ ] 5 pairs underwear & socks
- [ ] 1 pair walking shoes
- [ ] Sweater or warm layer
- [ ] Rainproof jacket with hood
- [ ] Tie, scarf, belt, and/or hat
- [ ] Swimsuit
- [ ] Sleepwear/loungewear

Money

- [ ] Debit card(s)
- [ ] Credit card(s)
- [ ] Hard cash (US $100-200)
- [ ] Money belt

Documents

- [ ] Passport
- [ ] Tickets & confirmations: flights, hotels, trains, rail pass, car rental, sight entries
- [ ] Driver's license
- [ ] Student ID, hostel card, etc.
- [ ] Photocopies of important documents
- [ ] Insurance details
- [ ] Guidebooks & maps

Toiletries Kit

- [ ] Basics: soap, shampoo, toothbrush, toothpaste, floss, deodorant, sunscreen, brush/comb, etc.
- [ ] Medicines & vitamins
- [ ] First-aid kit
- [ ] Glasses/contacts/sunglasses
- [ ] Sewing kit
- [ ] Packet of tissues (for WC)
- [ ] Earplugs

Electronics

- [ ] Mobile phone
- [ ] Camera & related gear
- [ ] Tablet/ebook reader/laptop
- [ ] Headphones/earbuds
- [ ] Chargers & batteries
- [ ] Phone car charger & mount (or GPS device)
- [ ] Plug adapters

Miscellaneous

- [ ] Daypack
- [ ] Sealable plastic baggies
- [ ] Laundry supplies: soap, laundry bag, clothesline, spot remover
- [ ] Small umbrella
- [ ] Travel alarm/watch
- [ ] Notepad & pen
- [ ] Journal

Optional Extras

- [ ] Second pair of shoes (flip-flops, sandals, tennis shoes, boots)
- [ ] Travel hairdryer
- [ ] Picnic supplies
- [ ] Water bottle
- [ ] Fold-up tote bag
- [ ] Small flashlight
- [ ] Mini binoculars
- [ ] Small towel or washcloth
- [ ] Inflatable pillow/neck rest
- [ ] Tiny lock
- [ ] Address list (to mail postcards)
- [ ] Extra passport photos

German Survival Phrases for Switzerland

In the phonetics, sounds like the long i in "light," and bolded syllables are stressed.

English	German	Pronunciation
Hello.	Grüetzi.	**grewt**-see
Do you speak English?	Sprechen Sie Englisch?	**shprehkh**-ehn zee **ehng**-lish
Yes. / No.	Ja. / Nein.	yah / nīn
I (don't) understand.	Ich verstehe (nicht).	ikh fehr-**shtay**-heh (nikht)
Please.	Bitte.	**bit**-teh
Thank you.	Merci.	**mur**-see
I'm sorry.	Es tut mir leid.	ehs toot meer līt
Excuse me.	Entschuldigung.	ehnt-**shool**-dig-oong
(No) problem.	(Kein) Problem.	(kīn) proh-**blaym**
(Very) good.	(Sehr) gut.	(zehr) goot
Goodbye.	Ciao.	chow
one / two	eins / zwei	īns / tsvī
three / four	drei / vier	drī / feer
five / six	fünf / sechs	fewnf / zehkhs
seven / eight	sieben / acht	**zee**-behn / ahkht
nine / ten	neun / zehn	noyn / tsayn
How much is it?	Wieviel kostet das?	**vee**-feel **kohs**-teht dahs
Write it?	Schreiben?	**shrī**-behn
Is it free?	Ist es umsonst?	ist ehs oom-**zohnst**
Included?	Inklusive?	in-kloo-**zee**-veh
Where can I buy / find...?	Wo kann ich kaufen / finden...?	voh kahn ikh **kow**-fehn / **fin**-dehn
I'd like / We'd like...	Ich hätte gern / Wir hätten gern...	ikh **heh**-teh gehrn / veer **heh**-tehn gehrn
...a room.	...ein Zimmer.	īn **tsim**-mer
...a ticket to ___.	...eine Fahrkarte nach ___.	ī-neh **far**-kar-teh nahkh ___
Is it possible?	Ist es möglich?	ist ehs **mur**-glikh
Where is...?	Wo ist...?	voh ist
...the train station	...der Bahnhof	dehr **bahn**-hohf
...the bus station	...der Busbahnhof	dehr **boos**-bahn-hohf
...tourist information office	...das Touristen-informations büro	dahs too-**ris**-tehn-in-for-maht-see-**ohns-bew**-roh
...toilet	...die Toilette	dee toy-**leh**-teh
men	Herren	**hehr**-ehn
women	Damen	**dah**-mehn
left / right	links / rechts	links / rehkhts
straight	geradeaus	geh-**rah**-deh-**ows**
When is this open / closed?	Um wieviel Uhr ist hier geöffnet / geschlossen?	oom **vee**-feel oor ist heer geh-**urf**-neht / geh-**shloh**-sehn
At what time?	Um wieviel Uhr?	oom **vee**-feel oor
Just a moment.	Moment.	moh-**mehnt**
now / soon / later	jetzt / bald / später	yehtst / bahld / **shpay**-ter
today / tomorrow	heute / morgen	**hoy**-teh / **mor**-gehn

In a German-Speaking Restaurant

English	German	Pronunciation
I'd like / We'd like...	Ich hätte gern / Wir hätten gern...	ikh **heh**-teh gehrn / veer **heh**-tehn gehrn
...a reservation for...	...eine Reservierung für...	**ī**-neh reh-zehr-**feer**-oong fewr
...a table for one / two.	...einen Tisch für eine Person / zwei Personen.	**ī**-nehn tish fewr **ī**-neh pehr- zohn / tsvī pehr-**zoh**-nehn
Is this seat free?	Ist hier frei?	ist heer frī
Menu (in English), please.	Speisekarte (auf Englisch), bitte.	**shpī**-zeh-kar-teh (owf **ehng**-lish) **bit**-teh
service (not) included	Trinkgeld (nicht) inklusive	**trink**-gehlt (nikht) in-kloo-**zee**-veh
cover charge	Eintritt	**īn**-trit
to go	zum Mitnehmen	tsoom **mit**-nay-mehn
with / without	mit / ohne	mit / **oh**-neh
and / or	und / oder	oont / **oh**-der
menu (of the day)	(Tages-) Karte	(**tah**-gehs-) **kar**-teh
set meal for tourists	Touristenmenü	too-**ris**-tehn-meh-**new**
specialty of the house	Spezialität des Hauses	**shpayt**-see-ah-lee-**tayt** dehs **how**-zehs
appetizers	Vorspeise	**for**-shpī-zeh
bread / cheese	Brot / Käse	broht / **kay**-zeh
sandwich	Sandwich	**zahnd**-vich
soup	Suppe	**zoo**-peh
salad	Salat	zah-**laht**
meat	Fleisch	flīsh
poultry	Geflügel	geh-**flew**-gehl
fish	Fisch	fish
seafood	Meeresfrüchte	**meh**-rehs-**frewkh**-teh
fruit	Obst	ohpst
vegetables	Gemüse	geh-**mew**-zeh
dessert	Nachspeise	**nahkh**-shpī-zeh
mineral water	Mineralwasser	min-eh-rahl-**vahs**-ehr
tap water	Leitungswasser	**lī**-toongs-**vahs**-ehr
milk	Milch	milkh
(orange) juice	(Orangen-) Saft	(oh-**rahn**-zhehn-) zahft
coffee / tea	Kaffee / Tee	kah-**fay** / tay
wine	Wein	vīn
red / white	rot / weiß	roht / vīs
glass / bottle	Glas / Flasche	glahs / **flah**-sheh
beer	Bier	beer
Cheers!	Prost!	prohst
More. / Another.	Mehr. / Noch eins.	mehr / nohkh īns
The same.	Das gleiche.	dahs **glīkh**-eh
Bill, please.	Rechnung, bitte.	**rehkh**-noong **bit**-teh
Do you accept credit cards?	Akzeptieren Sie Kreditkarten?	ahkt-sehp-**teer**-ehn zee kreh-**deet**-kar-tehn
tip	Trinkgeld	**trink**-gehlt
Delicious!	Lecker!	**lehk**-er

For more user-friendly German phrases, check out *Rick Steves German Phrase Book and Dictionary* or *Rick Steves French, Italian & German Phrase Book.*

French Survival Phrases

When using the phonetics, try to nasalize the n̲ sound.

English	French	Pronunciation
Good day.	*Bonjour.*	bohn̲-zhoor
Mrs. / Mr.	*Madame / Monsieur*	mah-dahm / muhs-yuh
Do you speak English?	*Parlez-vous anglais?*	par-lay-voo ahn̲-glay
Yes. / No.	*Oui. / Non.*	wee / nohn̲
I understand.	*Je comprends.*	zhuh kohn̲-prahn̲
I don't understand.	*Je ne comprends pas.*	zhuh nuh kohn̲-prahn̲ pah
Please.	*S'il vous plaît.*	see voo play
Thank you.	*Merci.*	mehr-see
I'm sorry.	*Désolé.*	day-zoh-lay
Excuse me.	*Pardon.*	par-dohn̲
(No) problem.	*(Pas de) problème.*	(pah duh) proh-blehm
It's good.	*C'est bon.*	say bohn̲
Goodbye.	*Au revoir.*	oh ruh-vwahr
one / two / three	*un / deux / trois*	uhn̲ / duh / trwah
four / five / six	*quatre / cinq / six*	kah-truh / sank̲ / sees
seven / eight	*sept / huit*	seht / weet
nine / ten	*neuf / dix*	nuhf / dees
How much is it?	*Combien?*	kohn̲-bee-an̲
Write it?	*Ecrivez?*	ay-kree-vay
Is it free?	*C'est gratuit?*	say grah-twee
Included?	*Inclus?*	an̲-klew
Where can I buy / find...?	*Où puis-je acheter / trouver...?*	oo pwee-zhuh ah-shuh-tay / troo-vay
I'd like / We'd like...	*Je voudrais / Nous voudrions...*	zhuh voo-dray / noo voo-dree-ohn̲
...a room.	*...une chambre.*	ewn shahn̲-bruh
...a ticket to ___.	*...un billet pour ___.*	uhn̲ bee-yay poor ___
Is it possible?	*C'est possible?*	say poh-see-bluh
Where is...?	*Où est...?*	oo ay
...the train station	*...la gare*	lah gar
...the bus station	*...la gare routière*	lah gar root-yehr
...tourist information	*...l'office du tourisme*	loh-fees dew too-reez-muh
Where are the toilets?	*Où sont les toilettes?*	oo sohn̲ lay twah-leht
men	*hommes*	ohm
women	*dames*	dahm
left / right	*à gauche / à droite*	ah gohsh / ah drwaht
straight	*tout droit*	too drwah
pull / push	*tirez / poussez*	tee-ray / poo-say
When does this open / close?	*Ça ouvre / ferme à quelle heure?*	sah oo-vruh / fehrm ah kehl ur
At what time?	*À quelle heure?*	ah kehl ur
Just a moment.	*Un moment.*	uhn̲ moh-mahn̲
now / soon / later	*maintenant / bientôt / plus tard*	man̲-tuh-nahn̲ / bee-an̲-toh / plew tar
today / tomorrow	*aujourd'hui / demain*	oh-zhoor-dwee / duh-man̲

In a French Restaurant

English	French	Pronunciation
I'd like / We'd like...	Je voudrais / Nous voudrions...	zhuh voo-dray / noo voo-dree-oh<u>n</u>
...to reserve...	...réserver...	ray-zehr-vay
...a table for one / two.	...une table pour un / deux.	ewn tah-bluh poor uh<u>n</u> / duh
Is this seat free?	C'est libre?	say lee-bruh
The menu (in English), please.	La carte (en anglais), s'il vous plaît.	lah kart (ah<u>n</u> ah<u>n</u>-glay) see voo play
service (not) included	service (non) compris	sehr-vees (noh<u>n</u>) koh<u>n</u>-pree
to go	à emporter	ah ah<u>n</u>-por-tay
with / without	avec / sans	ah-vehk / sah<u>n</u>
and / or	et / ou	ay / oo
special of the day	plat du jour	plah dew zhoor
specialty of the house	spécialité de la maison	spay-see-ah-lee-tay duh lah may-zoh<u>n</u>
appetizers	hors d'oeuvre	or duh-vruh
first course (soup, salad)	entrée	ah<u>n</u>-tray
main course (meat, fish)	plat principal	plah pra<u>n</u>-see-pahl
bread	pain	pa<u>n</u>
cheese	fromage	froh-mahzh
sandwich	sandwich	sahnd-weech
soup	soupe	soop
salad	salade	sah-lahd
meat	viande	vee-ahnd
chicken	poulet	poo-lay
fish	poisson	pwah-soh<u>n</u>
seafood	fruits de mer	frwee duh mehr
fruit	fruit	frwee
vegetables	légumes	lay-gewm
dessert	dessert	day-sehr
mineral water	eau minérale	oh mee-nay-rahl
tap water	l'eau du robinet	loh dew roh-bee-nay
milk	lait	lay
(orange) juice	jus (d'orange)	zhew (doh-rah<u>n</u>zh)
coffee / tea	café / thé	kah-fay / tay
wine	vin	va<u>n</u>
red / white	rouge / blanc	roozh / blah<u>n</u>
glass / bottle	verre / bouteille	vehr / boo-tay
beer	bière	bee-ehr
Cheers!	Santé!	sah<u>n</u>-tay
More. / Another.	Plus. / Un autre.	plew / uhn oh-truh
The same.	La même chose.	lah mehm shohz
The bill, please.	L'addition, s'il vous plaît.	lah-dee-see-oh<u>n</u> see voo play
Do you accept credit cards?	Vous prenez les cartes?	voo pruh-nay lay kart
tip	pourboire	poor-bwahr
Delicious!	Délicieux!	day-lees-yuh

For more user-friendly French phrases, check out *Rick Steves French Phrase Book and Dictionary* or *Rick Steves French, Italian & German Phrase Book*.

Italian Survival Phrases

English	Italian	Pronunciation
Good day.	Buongiorno.	bwohn-**jor**-noh
Do you speak English?	Parla inglese?	**par**-lah een-**gleh**-zay
Yes. / No.	Sì. / No.	see / noh
I (don't) understand.	(Non) capisco.	(nohn) kah-**pees**-koh
Please.	Per favore.	pehr fah-**voh**-ray
Thank you.	Grazie.	**graht**-see-ay
You're welcome.	Prego.	**preh**-go
I'm sorry.	Mi dispiace.	mee dee-spee-**ah**-chay
Excuse me.	Mi scusi.	mee **skoo**-zee
(No) problem.	(Non) c'è problema.	(nohn) cheh proh-**bleh**-mah
Good.	Va bene.	vah **beh**-nay
Goodbye.	Arrivederci.	ah-ree-veh-**dehr**-chee
one / two	uno / due	**oo**-noh / **doo**-ay
three / four	tre / quattro	tray / **kwah**-troh
five / six	cinque / sei	**cheeng**-kway / **seh**-ee
seven / eight	sette / otto	**seh**-tay / **oh**-toh
nine / ten	nove / dieci	**noh**-vay / dee-**ay**-chee
How much is it?	Quanto costa?	**kwahn**-toh **koh**-stah
Write it?	Me lo scrive?	may loh **skree**-vay
Is it free?	È gratis?	eh **grah**-tees
Is it included?	È incluso?	eh een-**kloo**-zoh
Where can I buy / find...?	Dove posso comprare / trovare...?	**doh**-vay **poh**-soh kohm-**prah**-ray / troh-**vah**-ray
I'd like / We'd like...	Vorrei / Vorremmo...	voh-**reh**-ee / voh-**reh**-moh
...a room.	...una camera.	**oo**-nah **kah**-meh-rah
...a ticket to ____.	...un biglietto per ____.	oon beel-**yeh**-toh pehr ____
Is it possible?	È possibile?	eh poh-**see**-bee-lay
Where is...?	Dov'è...?	doh-**veh**
...the train station	...la stazione	lah staht-see-**oh**-nay
...the bus station	...la stazione degli autobus	lah staht-see-**oh**-nay **dehl**-yee **ow**-toh-boos
...tourist information	...informazioni per turisti	een-for-maht-see-**oh**-nee pehr too-**ree**-stee
...the toilet	...la toilette	lah twah-**leh**-tay
men	uomini / signori	**woh**-mee-nee / seen-**yoh**-ree
women	donne / signore	**doh**-nay / seen-**yoh**-ray
left / right	sinistra / destra	see-**nee**-strah / **deh**-strah
straight	sempre dritto	**sehm**-pray **dree**-toh
What time does this open / close?	A che ora apre / chiude?	ah kay **oh**-rah **ah**-pray / kee-**oo**-day
At what time?	A che ora?	ah kay **oh**-rah
Just a moment.	Un momento.	oon moh-**mehn**-toh
now / soon / later	adesso / presto / tardi	ah-**deh**-soh / **preh**-stoh / **tar**-dee
today / tomorrow	oggi / domani	**oh**-jee / doh-**mah**-nee

In an Italian Restaurant

English	Italian	Pronunciation
I'd like...	Vorrei...	voh-**reh**-ee
We'd like...	Vorremmo...	vor-**reh**-moh
...to reserve...	...prenotare...	preh-noh-**tah**-ray
...a table for one / two.	...un tavolo per uno / due.	oon **tah**-voh-loh pehr **oo**-noh / **doo**-ay
Is this seat free?	È libero questo posto?	eh **lee**-beh-roh **kweh**-stoh poh-stoh
The menu (in English), please.	Il menù (in inglese), per favore.	eel meh-**noo** (een een-**gleh**-zay) pehr fah-**voh**-ray
service (not) included	servizio (non) incluso	sehr-**veet**-see-oh (nohn) een-**kloo**-zoh
cover charge	pane e coperto	**pah**-nay ay koh-**pehr**-toh
to go	da portar via	dah **por**-tar **vee**-ah
with / without	con / senza	kohn / **sehnt**-sah
and / or	e / o	ay / oh
menu (of the day)	menù (del giorno)	meh-**noo** (dehl **jor**-noh)
specialty of the house	specialità della casa	speh-chah-lee-**tah deh**-lah **kah**-zah
first course (pasta, soup)	primo piatto	**pree**-moh pee-**ah**-toh
main course (meat, fish)	secondo piatto	seh-**kohn**-doh pee-**ah**-toh
side dishes	contorni	kohn-**tor**-nee
bread	pane	**pah**-nay
cheese	formaggio	for-**mah**-joh
sandwich	panino	pah-**nee**-noh
soup	zuppa	**tsoo**-pah
salad	insalata	een-sah-**lah**-tah
meat	carne	**kar**-nay
chicken	pollo	**poh**-loh
fish	pesce	**peh**-shay
seafood	frutti di mare	**froo**-tee dee **mah**-ray
fruit / vegetables	frutta / legumi	**froo**-tah / lay-**goo**-mee
dessert	dolce	**dohl**-chay
tap water	acqua del rubinetto	**ah**-kwah dehl roo-bee-**neh**-toh
mineral water	acqua minerale	**ah**-kwah mee-neh-**rah**-lay
milk	latte	**lah**-tay
(orange) juice	succo (d'arancia)	**soo**-koh (dah-**rahn**-chah)
coffee / tea	caffè / tè	kah-**feh** / teh
wine	vino	**vee**-noh
red / white	rosso / bianco	**roh**-soh / bee-**ahn**-koh
glass / bottle	bicchiere / bottiglia	bee-kee-**eh**-ray / boh-**teel**-yah
beer	birra	**bee**-rah
Cheers!	Cin cin!	cheen cheen
More. / Another.	Di più. / Un altro.	dee pew / oon **ahl**-troh
The same.	Lo stesso.	loh **steh**-soh
The bill, please.	Il conto, per favore.	eel **kohn**-toh pehr fah-**voh**-ray
Do you accept credit cards?	Accettate carte di credito?	ah-cheh-**tah**-tay **kar**-tay dee **kreh**-dee-toh
tip	mancia	**mahn**-chah
Delicious!	Delizioso!	day-leet-see-**oh**-zoh

For more user-friendly Italian phrases, check out *Rick Steves Italian Phrase Book and Dictionary* or *Rick Steves French, Italian & German Phrase Book*.

INDEX

A

Aare River: 101, 102, 109–110, 160–161, 366; eating with views, 129–130; floating, 121–122
Accommodations: See Sleeping; and specific destinations
Aescher-Gasthaus am Berg: 267–268
Airbnb: 59, 422–423, 426–428
Airfares (air travel): 2, 454
Airports: Geneva, 278, 294; Milan, 333; Zürich, 55–56
Albula Tunnel: 382
Aletsch Glacier: 205
Allmendhubel: 151, 193, 211
Allmendhubelbahn: 192–193, 210
Almanac: 14–15
Alps: geology, 18–19. See also specific destinations
Alpenrose (Gimmelwald): 185
Alpine lifts: See Cable cars, funiculars and lifts
Alpine Museum (Pontresina): 342–343
Alpine Sensation (Jungfraujoch): 205
Alpin Palace Hotel (Mürren): 190–191
Alpin Raft (Interlaken): 165
Alpkäserei Chäserenholz: 98–99
Alp Languard: 343–344, 357
Alp Languard Viewpoint: 344
Alpnachstad: 85, 88, 366
Alprose Chocolate Factory (Caslano): 328–329
Altes Tramdepot (Bern): 121, 129
Altitude alert: 338
Ambulance: 410
Amrein's House (Luzern): 74–75
Ancient Romans: See Romans, ancient
Andermatt: 388
Andress, Ursula: 408
Appenzell (region): 5, 253–270; map, 254; planning tips, 254–255; sights/activities, 258–263; transportation, 255, 265
Appenzell Card: 256
Appenzell City Hall: 259
Appenzell Customs, Museum of (Urnäsch): 262

Appenzeller cheese: 20, 253, 260, 264
Appenzeller Dairy (Stein): 260
Appenzell Folklore Museum (Stein): 261–262
Appenzell Museum: 258
Appenzell Town: 255–265; eating, 264–265; helpful hints, 256–258; map, 257; sights/activities, 258–263; sleeping, 263–264; tourist information, 256; transportation, 256, 265
Apps: 8–9, 439; maps and navigation, 418, 451–452; messaging, 440; sightseeing, 419; sleeping, 420; user reviews, 423
Art Brut Collection (Lausanne): 285–286
Arth-Goldau: 97
ATMs: 412–415
Audio Europe, Rick Steves: 9, 11, 456
Avenches: 143–145

B

Bahnhofplatz (Bern): 105
Bahnhofplatz (Luzern): 62–64
Bahnhofplatz (Zermatt): 233
Bahnhofplatz (Zürich): 26–27
Bahnhofstrasse (Interlaken): 157
Bahnhofstrasse (Zermatt): 233–235
Bahnhofstrasse (Zürich): 22, 27–28, 39; eating, 53–54
Ballenberg: 151, 162–163
Ballooning: 165, 367–368
Banks (banking): alerting to travel, 8. See also Money
Barefoot Trail (Appenzell): 259–260
BärenPark (Bern): 120–121
Bärenplatz (Bern): 105–108, 130
Barfussweg (Appenzell): 259–260
BASE jumping: 174–175, 207
Basel: 396; population, 14
Bear Park (Bern): 102, 120–121
Beer: 264, 435; Luzern, 82; Zürich, 54
Bel Air Tower (Lausanne): 281
Bellagio: 377–378
Bellavita Pool and Spa (Pontresina): 345–346
Bellinzona: 323

Berggasthaus Ebenalp: 268
Berggasthaus Seealpsee: 267–268
Bergün: 382
Bern: 5, 101–132; eating, 128–131;
    helpful hints, 103; maps, 101,
    106–107, 126–127; planning tips,
    100; shopping, 111–112; sights/
    activities, 121–125; sleeping,
    125–128; tourist information,
    102; tours, 104; transportation,
    102–103, 104, 131–132; walking
    tour, 104–121
Bern Cathedral: 115–118
Berner Oberland: 5, 146–225; at a
    glance, 150–151; helpful hints, 153;
    hiking, 206–221; map, 148–149;
    planning tips, 146–147; sleeping
    and eating, 222–225; transporta-
    tion, 148–149, 152–153; winter
    sports, about, 392. See also specific
    destinations
Berner Oberland Regional Pass: 152
Bern Historical Museum: 124
Bernina Express: 373–383; Lugano,
    332; map, 374; orientation, 375–
    377; planning tips, 374–375; route
    overview, 373–374; self-guided
    tour, 377–383; tickets, 361–362;
    train types, 362–363
Bernina Pass: 344, 373, 380
Bern Museum of Fine Arts: 108, 122
Bern Natural History Museum: 124
Bern Symphony Orchestra: 110–111
Bern Train Station: 102–103,
    104–105
Berry Museum (St. Moritz): 356–357
Bever: 382
Beverages: 433–436. See also Wine
    and vineyards
Beyer Clock and Watch Museum
    (Zürich): 40
Biel: 139–140
Biking (bike rentals): Appenzell,
    257–258; Berner Oberland,
    221–222; Bike 'n' Rail, 448–449;
    Interlaken, 156, 165; Lausanne,
    278, 290; Lauterbrunnen, 172,
    221–222; Luzern, 60; Morges, 290;
    Mürren, 189; Murten, 140; Pon-
    tresina, 346; St. Moritz, 354–355;
    Zermatt, 232, 248
Birg Station: 151, 200, 220–221
Blatten: 234, 243
Blauherd: 231, 246–247

Blumental: 210
Boat travel: Château de Chillon,
    296; Gotthard Panorama Express,
    371–372; Interlaken, 163–164;
    Lake Brienz, 163–164; Lake
    Geneva, 273, 287, 301–302; Lake
    Lugano, 321, 326–328; Lake Lu-
    zern, 77–78, 93, 97; Lake Murten,
    139–140; Lake Thun, 163; map,
    446; Zürich, 45
Böcklin, Arnold: 44
Boltigen: 311
Bond World 007 (Schilthorn):
    201–202
Books, recommended: 459–460; for
    children, 461–462
Border crossings: 410
Bourbaki Panorama (Luzern): 73–74
Brienz, Lake: 154, 366; cruises,
    163–164
Brig: 388
Broc: 301, 310, 311
Brünig Pass: 366
Brusio: 378–379
Bryndli: 151, 220–221
Bubenberg, Adrian von: 133, 135, 136
Budgeting: 2–3
Budget tips: 8–9, 17, 411; Appenzell,
    256; eating, 430–431; Engadin
    Card, 340, 353; Luzern, 58–59;
    sleeping, 420–421; Swiss Travel
    Pass, 2, 6–7, 8–9; train travel, 443,
    445, 447; Zürich, 22, 23, 45
Bulle: 304, 309–310
Bundeshaus (Bern): 108–109
Bungee jumping, in Interlaken: 165
Bürkliplatz (Zürich): 45, 54
Busenalp: 218–219
Buses: Berner Oberland, 152–153;
    Bernina Express, 377–378;
    Lausanne, 278–279; Lugano, 318,
    332–333; map, 446; Montreux,
    301–302; St. Moritz, 354;
    Samedan, 349; Upper Engadine,
    336, 338, 359
Business hours: 411

C
Cabaret Voltaire (Zürich): 33
Cable cars, funiculars and lifts:
    Allmendhubelbahn, 192–193, 210;
    Berner Oberland, 148–149, 150,
    164, 198–206; map, 148–149; pass-
    es, 152; Diablerets, 313; Ebenalp,

266–267; Gimmelwald, 180–181; glossary of terms, 448; Gornergrat, 237, 244–245; Grütschalp, 178; Interlaken, 164; Jungfraubahn, 150, 202–203; Lugano, 317, 324–326; Matterhorn Glacier Paradise, 239–241, 243; Moléson, 308; Monte Brè, 325; Monte Generoso, 325–326; Mount Pilatus, 85–89; Mount Rigi, 96–97; Piz Nair, 357; Pontresina, 343–345; Rothorn, 231, 237, 245–246; San Salvatore, 324–325; Schilthornbahn, 150, 177–178, 198–199, 207; Zermatt, 230–231, 237–242, 246

Cabs: See Taxis

Cailler Chocolate Factory (Broc): 304, 310

Calvin, John (Calvinism): 37, 43, 135–136, 282, 400

Camping (campgrounds): 176, 425–426

Campione d'Italia (Lugano): 321–322

Cantine di Gandria (Lake Lugano): 327

Canyoning, in Interlaken: 165

Car insurance: 450–451

Car rentals: 2, 449–450

Car travel (driving): 452–453; Appenzell, 256; Bern, 103, 132; Berner Oberland, 152; best two-week trip, 7; distance and time, 451; Gruyères, 304–305; Interlaken, 171; Lausanne, 278, 295; Lauterbrunnen, 172; Les Alpes Suisses, 311–312; Luzern, 60; Murten, 133, 143; navigation options, 451–452; road signs, 453; St. Moritz, 354; Samedan, 349–350; Stansstad, 92–93; Zermatt, 230–231; Zürich, 23

Casino Kursaal (Interlaken): 160

Caslano: 328–329

Cassarate: 325

Castagnola: 318, 328

Castles and palaces: 166; Château de Chillon, 272, 295–300; Château d'Oex, 311, 367–368; Gruyères Castle, 305–306; Hünegg Castle, 166; Murten Castle, 138–139; Oberhofen Castle, 166; Thun Castle, 166

Cell phones: 8–9, 436–440. See also Apps

Central Switzerland: 5, 57–99; at a glance, 59; map, 86–87; planning tips, 85. See also specific destinations

Chagall, Marc: 44, 72; Fraumünster (Zürich), 36–39

Chantarella: 355, 357

Chapel Bridge (Luzern): 64–65

Chaplin, Charlie: 288, 301–302

Chaplin's World (Corsier): 301–302

Charmey: 311

Château de Chillon: 272, 295–300

Château d'Oex: 311, 367–368

Cheese: 17, 20, 111–112, 182–183, 184, 429, 432–433. See also Appenzeller cheese; Gruyère cheese

Chemin de St. Jacques (Lausanne): 284

Chesa Planta (Samedan): 352

Chexbres-Village: 289–290, 295

Chillon Château: 272, 295–300

Chocolate: 162, 301, 433, 434–435; Alprose Chocolate Factory (Caslano), 328–329; Cailler Chocolate Factory (Broc), 304, 310; Lugano, 322; Luzern, 76; Zürich, 27, 33

Chocolate Adventure (Luzern): 76

Chocolate Train (Montreux): 301, 304

Christmas celebrations: 394–395

Chur: 381, 383, 389–390

Churches and cathedrals: Bern Cathedral, 115–118; Fraumünster (Zürich), 35–39; French Church (Murten), 135–136; German Church (Murten), 136; Grossmünster (Zürich), 34; Holy Ghost Church (Bern), 105; Jesuitenkirche (Luzern), 66–67; Lausanne Cathedral, 282–283; St. Francis Church (Lausanne), 281; St. Ignazio Church (Poschiavo), 380; St. Mary Church (Pontresina), 342; St. Mary of the Angels Church (Lugano), 322; St. Peter Church (Samedan), 352; St. Peterskirche (Zürich), 31; Samedan Catholic Church, 351; Wasserkirche (Zürich), 35

Church Square (Zermatt): 235

Cinemas: See Movie theaters

Classroom Europe, Rick Steves: 11, 455

Climate: 4, 463

Clothing sizes: 462–463

Cogwheels: See Cable cars, funiculars and lifts

Col de la Croix: 312
Col du Pillon: 311, 312
Collection de l'Art Brut (Lausanne):
    285–286
Como, Lake: 333, 359, 377
Conditorei Schober (Zürich): 33
Corniche de Lavaux: 295
Corviglia: 338, 357
Costs of trip: 2–3
Cows: See Cheese; Dairy cows
Credit cards: 8, 412–416
Credit Suisse (Zürich): 40
Cruises: See Boat travel
Cuisine: 17, 20, 51, 429, 432–433;
    Graubünden, 337. See also Eating
Culture and Conference Center
    (Luzern): 64
Currency and exchange: 15, 412–413
Customs regulations: 417–418

D

Dairy cows (cow culture): 182–183,
    256–257, 305, 367. See also Cheese
Daub Peak: 218
Davos: 252
Debit cards: 8, 412–416
Diablerets Summit: 312–314
Diavolezza Peak: 345
Dining: See Eating; and specific
    destinations
Disentis: 387
Domaso: 378
Dongo: 377–378
Doyle, Arthur Conan: 366
Drinking water: 60, 435–436
Driving: See Car travel
Drug policy: 29
Dubuffet, Jean: 286
Dunant, Henri: 406
Duncan, David Douglas: 72
Dutch Tower (Bern): 106–107

E

Eating: 429–433; budgeting, 2–3;
    budget options, 430–431; French
    phrases, 470; German phrases, 468;
    Italian phrases, 472; restaurant
    pricing, 430; tipping, 416, 429–430.
    See also Cheese; Chocolate;
    Fondue; Markets; and specific
    destinations
Ebenalp: 266–268; hiking, 266–268;
    map, 266
Economy: 14–15

Eggishorn: 388
Eidgenössische Technische Hoch-
    schule (Zürich): 30–31
Eiger: 110, 202
Eigergletscher: 204
Einstein, Albert: 31, 102, 116–117,
    402; House (Bern), 114; Museum
    (Bern), 124
Eismeer: 204
Electric fences: 212–213
Electricity: 411
Embassies, in Bern: 410
Emergencies: 410
Engadin Card: 340, 353
Engadine architecture: overview, 351
Engadiner Museum (St. Moritz): 356
Engadine Valley: on Bernina Express,
    380–381. See also Upper Engadine
Entertainment: budgeting, 3. See also
    Music; Nightlife
Erlacherhof (Bern): 119
Escaliers du Marché (Lausanne): 284
Escher, Alfred: 26
Esel (Mount Pilatus): 91
Esplanade de la Cathédrale (Laus-
    anne): 283–284
ETH Zürich: 30–31
ETIAS (European Travel Informa-
    tion and Authorization System):
    4, 410
European Union (EU): 15, 16, 404
Events: See Festivals
Evian-les-Bains: 283
Exchange rate: 412

F

Faido: 373
Fasnacht: 60, 70, 395–396, 458
Faulhorn: 218
Federer, Roger: 408
Festivals: 395–396, 457–459;
    Gruyères, 305; Luzern, 60, 458;
    Murten, 133; Zermatt, 232
Festung Fürigen: 59, 92–95
Filisur: 382
Films, recommended: 460–461; for
    children, 461–462
Findeln: 247–248
Flag, Swiss: 15
Flüelen: 372
Fluhalp: 231, 246–247
Folklore Festival (Zermatt): 232
Folk museums: Appenzell Folk-
    lore Museum (Stein), 261–262;

INDEX

Engadiner Museum (St. Moritz), 356; Lauterbrunnen Valley Folk Museum, 175; Musée Gruérien (Bulle), 309–310; Museum of Appenzell Customs (Urnäsch), 262; Swiss Open-Air Museum (Ballenberg), 151, 162–163

Folk music: Appenzell, 259; Mürren, 195

Fondue: 20, 394–395, 432–433

Food: *See* Cheese; Chocolate; Cuisine; Eating; Fondue; Markets

Forest Fun Park Zermatt: 237

Fortress Fürigen: 59, 92–95

Fountain of Justice (Bern): 119

Fräkmüntegg (Mount Pilatus): 88–89, 91–92

Franc, Swiss: 15, 412

Frau Gerolds Garten (Zürich): 46

Fraumünster (Zürich): 35–39

Freitag (Zürich): 46

French Church (Murten): 135–136

French restaurant phrases: 470

French survival phrases: 469

French Switzerland: 5, 271–314, 367; at a glance, 272; map, 274–275; planning tips, 272. *See also specific destinations*

Fribourg: 136

Friedhof Fluntern (Zürich): 46

Fromagerie d'Alpage du Moléson: 307–308

Funiculars: *See* Cable cars, funiculars and lifts

Furi: 240, 243

Fürigen Fortress: 59, 92–95

Furka Base Tunnel: 388

Füssli, Johann Heinrich: 44

G

Gandria: 327–328

Geneva, Lake: 5, 271, 286–287, 295, 300; at a glance, 272; cruises, 273, 287, 301–302; map, 274–275; planning tips, 272; transportation, 272–273

Geneva Airport: 278, 294

German Church (Murten): 136

German restaurant phrases: 468

German survival phrases: 467

Giacometti, Alberto: 28, 44, 122, 407

Giacometti, Augusto: 34

Giardino Belvedere (Lugano): 322–323

Giger (H. R.) Museum (Gruyères): 306

Gimmeln: 211, 219

Gimmelwald: 150, 179–188; Christmas events, 394; eating, 187–188; hiking, 206–221; maps, 180, 208–209; nightlife, 187–188; sleeping, 186–187; tourist information, 179; tours, 179–180; walking tour, 180–186

Gimmelwald Fire Station: 185

Glaciers: about, 18–19; Aletsch, 205; Morteratsch, 344–345, 381

Glacier Express: 383–389; map, 384; orientation, 384–386; planning tips, 383–384; route overview, 383; self-guided tour, 386–389; tickets, 361–362; train connections, 252, 389; train types, 362–363; Zermatt, 236, 252

Glacier Garden (Luzern): 74–75

Glacier Palace (Zermatt): 242

Glacier Paradise, Matterhorn: 230, 239–242, 248–249

Glacier 3000 (Les Diablerets): 311, 312–313

Gletschergarten (Luzern): 74–75

Glockengasse (Zürich): 31

Goat Parade (Zermatt): 232

Golden Pass: 364–368; map, 365; orientation, 365–366; planning tips, 364–365; route overview, 364; self-guided tour, 366–368; tickets, 361–362; train types, 362–363

Goms: 388

Gondolas: *See* Cable cars, funiculars and lifts

Gontenbad: 259–260

Gorner Gorge: 237

Gornergrat: 237, 244–245

Gornergrat Top Station: 230, 237, 244–245

Gornerschlucht: 237

Gotthard Base Tunnel: 332, 369, 372–373

Gotthard Panorama Express: 369–373; Lugano, 315, 332; Luzern, 84; map, 370; orientation, 370–371; route overview, 369; self-guided tour, 371–373; tickets, 361–362; train types, 362–363

Gotthard Pass: 64, 323

Gourmetweg: 231, 247–248

Government: 14, 15–16, 403–405

Grand Café al Porto (Lugano): 320
Graubünden: language, 13, 337; overview, 337. *See also specific destinations*
Grauseeli Lake: 220
Gravedona: 378
Grossmünster (Zürich): 34
Gruèrien Museum (Bulle): 309–310
Grütschalp: 151, 211–213, 222
Grütschalp Cable Car: 178
Gruyère cheese: 20, 304–309
Gruyères: 272, 303–307, 311; eating, 307; sights, 305–307; sleeping, 307
Gruyères Castle: 305–306
Gryon: 312
Gstaad: 311, 312, 367
"Guardian Angel" (Zürich): 26
Guidebooks: Berner Oberland, 153; Rick Steves, 455; updates, 9, 454
Gurten (Bern): 110; Open-Air Rock Festival, 458

H

Hall of Mirrors (Luzern): 75
Hanftheke Bern: 114
Hanggliding: *See* Paragliding
Harderbahn (Interlaken): 151, 164
Harder Kulm (Interlaken): 151, 164
Hauptgasse (Appenzell): 256
Hauptgasse (Murten): 138
Heiliggeistkirche (Bern): 105
Helvetii tribe: 15, 26, 43, 135, 398
Herisau: 265
Hesse, Hermann: 406–407
Hiking: safety, 212–213, 238, 338; weather concerns, 213, 237–238; Appenzell, 259–260; Berner Oberland, 150–151, 206–221; Château de Chillon, 296; Ebenalp, 266–268; Gimmelwald, 206–221; Lausanne, 289–290; Lauterbrunnen Valley, 150–151, 206–221; Liechtenstein, 269; Mount Pilatus, 90–91; Mount Rigi, 97–99; Mürren, 194–195; Pontresina, 342, 343–344; St. Moritz, 357–358; Schilthorn, 200–201, 204; Weg der Schweiz, 372; Zermatt, 231, 237–248
Hilterfingen: 166
Hinterdorf (Zermatt): 230, 233
Hirschenplatz (Luzern): 69–70
Historisches Museum (Luzern): 72
History: 397–402; military readiness, 93

Hodler, Ferdinand: 44, 122
Hofmattstrasse (Zermatt): 233–234
Höhematte Park (Interlaken): 160
Holidays: 457–459
Holländerturm (Bern): 106–107
Holy Ghost Church (Bern): 105
Horner Pub (Lauterbrunnen): 175, 177
Hostels: overview, 428–429, 431. *See also specific destinations*
Hot-air ballooning: 165, 367–368
Hotels: overview, 422–425; rates and deals, 420–421; reservations, 8, 426–427. *See also specific destinations*
H.R. Giger Museum (Gruyères): 306
Hünegg Castle: 166
Husmättli (Gimmelwald): 183–184

I

Ice Palace (Jungfraujoch): 205
Interlaken: 150, 154–171, 311–312, 366; biking, 221–222; eating, 168–170; helpful hints, 153, 156; hiking, 217–218; map, 158–159; nightlife, 166–167; sights/activities, 162–166; sleeping, 167–168; tourist information, 154–155; transportation, 155–156, 170–171; walking tour, 157, 160–162
International Olympic Committee: 273, 287, 290
Internet security: 440
Iseltwald: 164
Italian restaurant phrases: 472
Italian survival phrases: 471
Italy: 321–322, 333; on the Bernina Express, 377–378

J

Jakobsbad: 259–260; luge, 262–263
Jaman Tunnel: 368
Jesuitenkirche (Luzern): 66–67
Joyce, James: 46
Jung, Carl: 402, 406
Jungfraubahn: 150, 202–203
Jungfraujoch: 202–206; ascending, 203–206; transportation, 178
Jungfrau Travel Pass: 149, 202–203
Junkerngasse (Bern): 119–120

K

Käfigturm (Bern): 105–106
Kapellbrücke (Luzern): 64–65
K44 (Interlaken): 165

Kilchbalm: 151, 208–209

Kirchenfeld Bridge (Bern): 110–111

Klee, Paul: 44, 72, 102, 122, 402, 407; Center (Bern), 121, 123

Kleine Scheidegg: 150, 215–217; sleeping and eating, 223–224

Klein Matterhorn: 239–241, 243

Klettersteig Mürren: 194–195

Kornhauskeller (Bern): 111, 129

Kornhausplatz (Bern): 111–112

Kramgasse (Bern): 113–114

Kreuzgang Fraumünster (Zürich): 39

Kriens: 88–89

Kronberg Luge Ride (Jakobsbad): 262–263

Kübler-Ross, Elisabeth: 407–408

Kühboden: 388

Kultur-und Kongresszentrum (Luzern): 64

Kulturzentrum Reithalle (Bern): 124–125

Kunsthalle Ziegelhütte (Appenzell): 259

Kunsthaus Zürich: 43–44

Kunstmuseum Appenzell: 259

Kunstmuseum Bern: 108, 122

Kunstmuseum Luzern: 64, 72

L

Lac Léman: *See* Geneva, Lake

Lake Lucerne Navigation Company: 77

Landsgemeindeplatz (Appenzell): 255, 256, 264

Landwasser Viaduct: 382

Language: 10, 13; French restaurant phrases, 470; French survival phrases, 469; German restaurant phrases, 468; German survival phrases, 467; Italian restaurant phrases, 472; Italian survival phrases, 471; online translation tips, 411–412

Language barrier: 437

Lausanne: 272, 273–295; eating, 292–294; helpful hints, 278; maps, 277, 280; nightlife, 290–291; sights/activities, 285–290; sleeping, 291–292; tourist information, 276; transportation, 276, 278–279, 294–295; walking tour, 279–284

Lausanne Cathedral: 282–283

Lausanne City History Museum: 284, 285

Lauterbrunnen: 150, 171–178; activities, 172, 174–175; biking, 221–222; eating, 176–177; helpful hints, 172; map, 173; sleeping, 175–176; tourist information, 172; transportation, 172, 177–178

Lauterbrunnen Valley: BASE jumping, 174–175; biking, 221–222; hiking, 150–151, 206–221; transportation, 177–178

Lauterbrunnen Valley Folk Museum: 175

Lavaux Express: 290

Lavaux-Oron: 289–290

Le Corbusier: 407

Le Moléson Mountain: 307

Le Musée et Parc Olympique (Lausanne): 287–289

Lenin, Vladimir: 33

Les Avants: 368

Les Diablerets: 311, 312–314

Le Sépey: 311

Leventina: 373

Licht Festival (Murten): 133

Liechtenstein: 269–270

Lifts: *See* Cable cars, funiculars and lifts

Limmat River: 22, 28, 30, 35; cruises, 45; eating along, in Zürich: 54

Lindenhof (Zürich): 19, 30–31

Lindt: 27, 120, 206

Lion Monument (Luzern): 73

Lothar: 368

Löwendenkmal (Luzern): 73

Löwenplatz (Luzern): 73–75

Lucerne: *See* Luzern

Lucerne Festival: 60, 458

Lucerne Museum Card: 58

Lucerne Navigation Company: 77–78

Lugano: 5, 315–333; eating, 330–332; helpful hints, 317; history of, 323; maps, 316, 318–319; planning tips, 315; shopping, 322; sights/activities, 324–329; sleeping, 329–330; tourist information, 316–317; transportation, 317, 318, 332–333; walking tour, 319–323

Lugano, Lake: 315, 316, 321; cruises, 321, 326–328; map, 316

Lugano Art and Cultural Center: 323

Lugano Art Museum of Italian Switzerland: 320

Lugano City Park: 321

Lugano Town Hall: 316–317

Luges: 90, 91, 262–263, 309, 313
Lungernsee: 366
Lutry: 289
Luzern: 5, 58–84; eating, 81–84; helpful hints, 60; maps, 62–63, 80–81; planning tips, 57; shopping, 70; sights/activities, 71–78; sleeping, 78–81; tourist information, 58–59; tours, 61; transportation, 59, 60–61, 84; walking tour, 61–71
Luzern, Lake: 59, 67–68, 70–71; cruises, 77–78, 92, 97; map, 86–87
Luzern Culture and Congress Centre: 64
Luzerner Fasnacht: 60, 396
Luzern Festival: 60, 458
Luzern History Museum: 72
Luzern Museum of Art: 64, 72
Luzern Visitor Card: 58–59

M
Mail: 441. See also specific destinations
Maison du Gruyère: 304, 306–307
Männlichen: 150, 215–217
Maps: navigation apps, 418, 451–452. See also Map Index
Marijuana: 29, 114
Markets: Bern, 103; Bulle, 309; Lausanne, 278; Lugano, 320; Luzern, 60; Zürich, 26, 32, 45
Mary of the Snow Chapel: 99
Marzilibad (Bern): 110, 121–122
MASILugano: 320
Matterhorn: 5, 226, 389
Matterhorn Glacier Paradise: 230, 239–242, 248–249
Matterhorn Glacier Paradise Summit: 230, 242
Matterhorn Gotthard Railway: 252
Matterhorn Museum (Zermatt): 230, 235–237
Matterhorn Trail: 231, 243
Matthorn (Mount Pilatus): 91
Medical help: 410; Luzern, 60; Zürich, 23
Meiringen: 366
Menaggio: 333, 359, 377
Mercury, Freddie: 301
Metric system: 462–463
Metropole Hotel (Interlaken): 157, 167, 168–169
Milan Airport: 333
Military readiness: 93
Mill Bridge (Luzern): 68–69

Mobile phones: 8–9, 436–440. See also Apps
Moléson Mountain: 307
Moléson-sur-Gruyères: 308–309
Mönchsjochhütte: 204–205
Money: 412–416; budgeting, 2–3
Money-saving tips: 8–9, 17, 411; Appenzell, 256; eating, 430–431; Engadin Card, 340, 353; Luzern, 58–59; sleeping, 420–421; Swiss Travel Pass, 2, 6–7, 8–9; train travel, 443, 445, 447; Zürich, 22, 23, 45
Montbovon: 368
Montebello: 381
Monte Brè: 325, 328
Monte Generoso: 325–326
Montreux: 272, 300–303, 368
Mont Vully: 132, 135, 140
Morges: 290
Morteratsch Glacier: 344–345, 381
Mountain biking: See Biking
Mountaineers' Cemetery (Zermatt): 235
Mountain lifts: See Cable cars, funiculars and lifts
Mountain View Trail: 211
Mount Bernina: 381
Mount Pilatus: 59, 85–92; ascending, 85–89; eating, 90; hiking, 90–91; sleeping, 89–90
Mount Rigi: 59, 95–99; ascending, 96–97; hiking, 97–99; sleeping and eating, 97
Mount Säntis: 253
Movies, recommended: 460–461; for children, 461–462
Movie theaters: 138, 232, 291
Muesli: 433
Mühlenplatz (Luzern): 69
Munch, Edvard: 44
Münstergasse (Zürich): 33
Münsterhof (Zürich): 39
Münsterplattform (Bern): 118
Muottas Muragl: 339, 343–344, 381
Mürren: 150, 188–198; activities, 193–195; eating, 197–198; helpful hints, 189; hiking, 151, 209–211, 212–214; map, 190–191; nightlife, 195; sleeping, 195–197; tourist information, 188–189; walking tour, 190–193
Mürrenbach: 213
Mürrenbach Falls: 207

Murten: 5, 132–143; activities, 139–140; eating, 141–142; helpful hints, 133; maps, 101, 134; nightlife, 140–141; planning tips, 100; sleeping, 141; tourist information, 132–133; transportation, 133, 143; walking tour, 133–139

Murten, Lake: 132, 135, 139; cruises, 139–140

Murten Castle and Town Museum: 138–139

Murten Classics Music Festival: 133

Murten Ramparts: 136–138

Murten Swimming Pool: 140

Murten Youth Festival: 133

Musée et Parc Olympique (Lausanne): 287–289

Musée Gruèrien (Bulle): 309–310

Musée Historique de Lausanne: 284, 285

Museo Casa Console (Poschiavo): 380

Museo Doganale (Lugano): 327

Museum Alpin (Pontresina): 342–343

Museum of Appenzell Customs (Urnäsch): 262

Museum of Fine Arts (Bern): 108, 122

Museum Rietberg (Zürichsee): 46

Music: Appenzell, 259; Luzern, 60; Murten, 133; Pontresina, 340–341; Zürich, 54

N

Naturweg: 231, 248

Niederdorf (Zürich): 22, 31, 32–33; eating, 51–52; sleeping, 48, 50

Nightlife: Gimmelwald, 187–188; Interlaken, 166–167; Lausanne, 290–291; Mürren, 195; Murten, 140–141; Zermatt, 251–252. See also Music

Nikolaital Valley: 228

North Face Trail: 151, 209–211

Nouvel, Jean: 64

Nydegg Bridge (Bern): 120

O

Oberalp Pass: 387–388

Obere Schwändihütte: 99

Oberhaupt (Mount Pilatus): 91

Oberhofen Castle: 166

Obersteinberg: 151, 219; sleeping, 225

Old Town (Lausanne): 276, 279–285; eating, 292–293; map, 280; sleeping, 291–292

Old Tram Depot (Bern): 121, 129

Olympic Museum and Park (Lausanne): 287–289

On Her Majesty's Secret Service (movie): 201, 202, 461

Oppenheim, Meret: 107–108

Ouchy (Lausanne): 276, 286–289; eating, 294

Ovomaltine: 436

P

Packing tips and checklist: 9, 465

Palm Express: 333, 359

Palü Gletscher: 380

Paradeplatz (Zürich): 39–40

Paradiso (Lugano): 323, 324

Paragliding: 165, 194, 248

Parco Civico Villa Ciani (Lugano): 321

Parliament (Bern): 108–109

Passerelle du Flon (Lausanne): 279, 281, 290–291

Passports: 4, 10, 269, 410, 415

Paul Klee Center (Bern): 121, 123

Pensions: overview, 425. See also *specific destinations*

Pestalozzi, Johann Heinrich: 27–28

Pestalozzi Park (Zürich): 27–28

Pfalzgasse (Zürich): 30

Phones: 8–9, 436–441

Piaget, Jean: 407

Pian di Spagna: 378

Piazza Comunale (Poschiavo): 379–380

Piazza della Riforma (Lugano): 320, 330–331

Piazza Indipendenza (Lugano): 320–321

Picasso, Pablo: 44, 71–72, 122

Pickpockets: 10, 410, 415–416

Pilatus: See Mount Pilatus

Piz Cambrena: 380

Piz Gloria: 198, 201

Piz Nair: 336, 357

Piz Palü: 380

Piz Varuna: 380

Place de la Palud (Lausanne): 284

Place de la Riponne (Lausanne): 284

Place St-François (Lausanne): 281

Planetarium, in Luzern: 75

Platzspitz Park (Zürichsee): 45

Police: 410
Police Department (Zürich): 28
Pont Bessières (Lausanne): 281–282
Pontresina: 339–348, 381; eating, 347–348; helpful hints, 340–341; map, 341; shopping, 341; sights/activities, 342–346; sleeping, 346–347; tourist information, 339; transportation, 340
Population: 14
Poschiavo: 379–380
Postgasse (Appenzell): 256
Post offices: 441. *See also specific destinations*
Praz: 139–140
Preda: 382
Prison Tower (Bern): 105–106
Pully (Lausanne): 289
Punt Muragl: 343

Q

Quai d'Ouchy (Lausanne): 286
Quartier du Flon (Lausanne): 279, 281, 290–291

R

Rafting: 165
Rail passes: 2, 443–447, 455
Rail travel: *See Scenic rail journeys; Tourist trains; Train travel*
Randa: 388
Rathausbrücke (Zürich): 32
Rathausgasse (Bern): 111–112
Reckingen: 388
Reichenau: 383, 387
Rental properties: 426–428
Resources from Rick Steves: 454–456
Restaurants: *See Eating; and specific destinations*
Reuss River: 58; walking tour, Luzern, 61–71
Reuss River Weir System: 67–68
Rhône River: 388
Richard Wagner Museum (Luzern): 77
Ried: 247–248
Rietberg Museum (Zürichsee): 46
Riffelberg Express: 239, 241, 245
Riffelseeweg: 231, 245
Rifle Museum (Bern): 124
Rigi Kaltbad: 98
Rigi Kulm: 97–98
Rindermarkt (Zürich): 32
Rivella: 436

Romans, ancient (Roman sites): 21, 30, 31, 43, 132, 135, 274, 323, 398; Avenches, 143–145; Vidy, 291
Rominger Möbel (Pontresina): 341
Röntgen, Wilhelm: 31
Room and board: *See Eating; Sleeping*
Rope courses, in Interlaken: 165
Roseg Valley: 345
Rosengart Collection (Luzern): 71–72
Rösti: about, 433
Rothorn: 237, 245–248
Rothorn Summit: 231, 246
Rousseau, Jean-Jacques: 42, 43, 297, 406
Rue de Bourg (Lausanne): 281
Rue du Grand-Pont (Lausanne): 281
Rütli: 372

S

Saanen: 311, 312
St. Beatus Caves: 163
St. Francis Church (Lausanne): 281
St. Ignazio Church (Poschiavo): 380
St. Mary Church (Pontresina): 342
St. Mary of the Angels Church (Lugano): 322
St. Moritz: 353–359, 381; eating, 358; helpful hints, 354–355; sights/activities, 355–358; tourist information, 354; transportation, 354, 358–359; winter sports, 392–393
St. Peter Church (Samedan): 352
St. Peter's Chapel (Luzern): 71
St. Peter's Church (Zürich): 31
St-Saphorin: 289–290
Salvatore Museum (Lugano): 325
Samedan: 349–352
Samedan Catholic Church: 351
Sammlung Rosengart (Luzern): 71–72
San Rocco Church (Lugano): 320
San Salvatore: 324–325
Santa Maria degli Angioli (Lugano): 322
Sarnen: 366
Sassal Masone: 380
Scenic rail journeys: 360–390, 447; Bernina Express, 373–383; Glacier Express, 383–389; Golden Pass, 364–368; Gotthard Panorama Express, 369–373; map, 361; tickets, 361–362; train types, 362–363
Scex Rouge: 313

Schaan: 269, 270

Schanf: 381

Schiltalp: 211

Schilthorn: 198–202; ascending, 199–201; eating, 201; hiking, 200–201, 202, 220–221

Schilthornbahn: 150, 177–178, 198–199, 207

Schipfe (Zürich): 30, 54

Schloss Hünegg: 166

Schloss Oberhofen: 166

Schloss Thun: 166

Schwarzenbach (Zürich): 33

Schwarzmönch: 179

Schwarzsee: 240, 243

Schwarzsee Ridge: 231, 243

Schweizer Heimatwerk (Zürich): 28

Schweizerisches Nationalmuseum (Zürich): 26, 40–43

Schynige Platte: 151, 217–218

Seasons: 4

Sedrun: 387

Seealpsee: 267–268

Sefinenfall Falls: 207

Sefinen Valley: 151, 185, 208–209

Segantini (Giovanni) Museum (St. Moritz): 355–356

Seilpark (Interlaken): 165

Shopping: budgeting, 3; clothing sizes, 462–463; hours, 411; VAT refunds, 416–417. *See also* Markets; *and specific destinations*

Sightseeing: at a glance, 5; best two-week trip, 6–7; budgeting, 3; general tips, 418–419; priorities, 3–4. *See also specific sights and destinations*

SIM cards: 436, 440

Simmental Valley: 311, 312, 367

Simonet Weapons (Murten): 138

Sitter River: 256

Skiing: 392–393; Berner Oberland, 153, 189; Corviglia, 338; Gstaad, 367; Mürren-Schilthorn, 189; Pontresina, 341; St. Moritz, 353, 354, 392–393; Zermatt, 232, 248–249

Skyline Walk (Schilthorn): 200

Sleep code: 421

Sleeping: 419–429; budgeting, 2–3; rates and deals, 420–421; reservations, 8, 426–427; types of accommodations, 422–429. *See also specific destinations*

Smartphones: 8–9, 436–440. *See also* Apps

Snowboarding: *See* Skiing

Snow Fun Park (Jungfraujoch): 205

Soaring: *See* Paragliding

Sonnenberg: 210

Sorico: 378

Special events: *See* Festivals

Sphinx Observation Deck (Jungfraujoch): 204–205

Spiez: 312

Sports: *See specific sports*

Sportzentrum (Mürren): 189

Spreuerbrücke (Luzern): 68–69

Sprüngli (Zürich): 39–40

Sprutz Waterfall: 151, 219–220

Spysi (Bern): 119

Staffel: 98–99

Stansstad: 92–94

Staubbach Falls: 174, 176, 207

Stauffacher (Bern): 103

Stechelberg: 198; hiking, 151, 207–208, 214; sleeping, 224–225; transportation, 177–178

Stein: 260, 261–262

Sternenplatz (Luzern): 70

Sunnegga: 231, 247

Sunnegga Viewpoint: 230, 247

Suppenalp: 210

Surselva: 387

Suspension Rope Park (Mount Pilatus): 91–92

Swimming: Bern, 110, 121–122; Murten, 140; Pontresina, 345–346

Swiss Army: 93, 185

Swiss Army knives: 16, 111, 138, 154

Swiss chocolate: *See* Chocolate

Swiss Chocolate Adventure (Luzern): 76

Swiss National Museum (Zürich): 26, 40–43

Swiss Open-Air Museum (Ballenberg): 151, 162–163

Swiss Parliament (Bern): 108–109

Swiss Rifle Museum (Bern): 124

Swiss Transport Museum (Luzern): 75–76

Swiss Travel Pass: 2, 6–7, 8–9, 23, 58, 443, 445

Swiss Wine Road: 295

Synagogengasse (Zürich): 32

T

Talmuseum Lauterbrunnen: 175

Tanzbödeli: 151, 219

Täsch: 388–389

Taxes: VAT refunds, 416–417
Taxis: 449; Appenzell, 260; Lausanne, 278, 279; tipping, 416; Zermatt, 232
Telephones: 8–9, 436–441
Tell, William: 32, 399, 405, 458, 460
Tell-Pass: 61
Tellskapelle: 372
Temperatures, average monthly: 463
Theft alerts: 10, 410, 415–416
Three Lakes cruise: 139–140
Thun, Lake: 154, 367; cruises, 163
Thun Castle: 166
Thusis: 382–383
Tibet Museum (Gruyères): 306
Ticino: 13, 315, 373. See also Lugano
"Times Square" (Gimmelwald): 181
Time zones: 410–411
Tipping: 416
Tirano: 378
Tomlishorn (Mount Pilatus): 91
Tour guides: tipping, 416. See also specific destinations
Tourist information: 409–410. See also specific destinations
Tourist trains: 363; Lausanne, 290; Luzern, 61
Tours: best two-week trip, 6–7; Rick Steves, 455. See also Walking tours, guided; and specific destinations
Train travel: 441–449; Appenzell, 255, 256, 265; Bern, 102–103, 131–132; Berner Oberland, 148–149, 152; best two-week trip, 6–7; Bike 'n' Rail, 448–449; budgeting, 2; Château de Chillon, 296; general tips, 447–449; Gruyères, 304; Interlaken, 155–156, 161, 170–171; Lake Geneva, 272–273; Lausanne, 276, 278, 294–295; Lauterbrunnen, 172, 178; Lugano, 317, 332–333; Luzern, 59, 84; map, 446; Montreux, 300, 301; Murten, 133, 143; Pontresina, 340; St. Moritz, 354; Samedan, 349; schedules, 442; tickets, 442–443; Upper Engadine, 336, 338, 358–359; Zermatt, 227, 230, 252; Zürich, 23, 55. See also Scenic rail journeys; Tourist trains
Transportation: 20, 441–454; budgeting, 2; map, 446; prebooking, 8. See also Boat travel; Buses; Car travel; Train travel
Transport Museum (Luzern): 75–76

Travel insurance: 8, 450–451
Travel smarts: 9–11
Travel tips: 4, 8–9, 410–412
Trip costs: 2–3
Trockener Steg: 240
Trümmelbach Falls: 151, 174, 207
Tschingelhorn: 219
Tussaud, Anne-Marie "Marie": 406
TV shows, recommended: 460–461
Twain, Mark: 66, 99, 459

U
Uber: 449
Uetliberg (Zürichsee): 46
University of Zürich: 30
Unterseen (Interlaken): 154, 157, 161, 166; eating, 170
Upper Engadine: 5, 334–359; helpful hints, 338; map, 335; planning tips, 336; transportation, 336, 338, 358–359. See also Pontresina; St. Moritz; Samedan
Uri: 371–372
Urnäsch: 262–263

V
Vaduz (Liechtenstein): 269–270
Valais: 392. See also Matterhorn; Zermatt
Valtellina Valley: 378
VAT refunds: 416–417
Verkehrshaus (Luzern): 75–76
Vevey: 273, 289, 291; sleeping, 301
Via Canova (Lugano): 320
Via Ferrata (Mürren): 192, 194–195
Via Nassa (Lugano): 322
Via Pessina (Lugano): 319
Vidy: 290
Vierwaldstättersee: 371–372
Villa Ciani (Lugano): 321
Visitor information: 409–410. See also specific destinations
Vispa River: 234, 388
Vitznau: 96–97
Vorderrhein Gorge: 387

W
Wagner (Richard) Museum (Luzern): 77
Walking tours, guided: Bern, 104; Interlaken, 156; Lausanne, 276; Luzern, 61; Zürich, 24
Walking tours, self-guided: Bern, 104–121; Gimmelwald, 180–186;

Interlaken, 157, 160–161; Lausanne, 279–284; Lugano, 319–323; Luzern, 61–71; Mürren, 190–193; Murten, 133–139; Samedan, 350–352; Zürich, 24–40
Wasenegg Ridge: 221
Wassen: 372
Wasserauen: 259, 266
Wasserkirche (Zürich): 35
Water, drinking: 60, 435–436
Water Tower (Luzern): 64–65
Weather: 4, 463
Weg der Schweiz: 372
Weggis: 96–97
Weggisgasse (Luzern): 70
Weinmarkt (Luzern): 69
Weinplatz (Zürich): 31
Wengen: 215, 457; hiking, 215–217; sleeping, 222–223; transportation, 178
White Lake: 380
Whymper, Edward: 235, 236, 459
Wilderswil: 217–218
Wildkirchli church: 267
William Tell Express: *See* Gotthard Panorama Express
Wine and vineyards: 289–290, 295, 433–435
Winkelmatten: 247–248
Winteregg: 212–213, 222
Winter in Switzerland: 391–396; Christmas celebrations, 394–395; top destinations, 392–393; winter sports tips, 393

Y
Yoga, in Mürren: 189
Youth Festival (Murten): 133

Z
Zähringen Fountain (Bern): 113

Zentrum Paul Klee (Bern): 121, 123
Zermatt: 5, 226–252, 388; at a glance, 230–231; eating, 250–252; helpful hints, 232; maps, 229, 240–241; nightlife, 251–252; planning tips, 227–228; sights/activities, 233–249; sleeping, 249–250; tourist information, 228; transportation, 227, 230–232, 252
Zermatt Church Square: 235
Zermatt City Hall: 235
Zermatt Folklore Festival: 232
Zermatt Forest Fun Park: 237
Zermatt Goat Parade: 232
Zermatt Matterhorn Museum: 230, 235–237
Zermatt Train Station Square: 233
Zürich: 5, 21–56; Christmas events, 394; eating, 51–54; helpful hints, 23; maps, 25, 49; planning tips, 22; shopping, 23, 28, 30, 33, 46; sights/activities, 40–46; sleeping, 47–51; tourist information, 22; tours, 24; transportation, 23, 55–56; walking tour, 24–40
Zürich, Lake (Zürichsee): 22, 40; cruises, 45
Zürich Airport: 55–56
Zürich Card: 22, 23, 45
Zürich City Archive: 33
Zürich Town Hall: 32
Zürich Train Station: 23, 24, 26, 55; sleeping near, 47–48; supermarkets near, 54
Zürich University: 30
Zürich West: 22, 45–46
Zürich Zoo: 46
Zweisimmen: 311, 364, 367
Zwingli, Huldrych: 33, 34, 36–37, 400, 405–406
Zytglogge-Turm (Bern): 112–113

AP INDEX

r Maps
zerland: V
zerland Overview: IX

oduction
Destinations in Switzerland: 3
Two-Week Trip by Train: 7

ch
ch: 25
ch Hotels & Restaurants: 49

rn & Central Switzerland
rn: 62
rn Hotels & Restaurants: 80
Luzern Area: 86

& Murten
& Murten: 101
: 106
Hotels & Restaurants: 126
en: 134

er Oberland
er Oberland: 148
er Oberland Transport Time/
ost: 149
laken: 158
erbrunnen: 173
melwald: 180
en: 190
melwald Area Hikes: 208

natt & the Matterhorn
natt: 229
natt Area: 240

Appenzell
Appenzell Region: 254
Appenzell Town: 257
Epenalp: 266

Lake Geneva &
French Switzerland
French Switzerland: 274
Lausanne: 277
Lausanne City Center: 280

Lugano
Lugano: 316
Lugano Center: 318

Upper Engadine
Upper Engadine: 335
Pontresina: 341

Scenic Rail Journeys
Scenic Swiss Rail Routes: 361
Golden Pass: 365
Gotthard Panorama Express: 370
Bernina Express: 374
Glacier Express: 384
Glacier Express Elevations: 386

Practicalities
Public Transportation: 446
Driving in Switzerland: 451
Road Signs: 453

Explore Europe

At ricksteves.com you can browse through thousands of articles, videos, photos and radio interviews, plus find a wealth of money-saving travel tips for planning your dream trip. And with our mobile-friendly website, you can easily access all this great travel information anywhere you go.

TV Shows

Preview the places you'll visit by watching entire half-hour episodes of *Rick Steves' Europe* (choose from all 100 shows) on-demand, for free.

your travel dreams into affordable reality

Radio Interviews

Enjoy ready access to Rick's vast library of radio interviews covering travel tips and cultural insights that relate specifically to your Europe travel plans.

Travel Forums

Learn, ask, share! Our online community of savvy travelers is a great resource for first-time travelers to Europe, as well as seasoned pros.

Travel News

Subscribe to our free Travel News e-newsletter, and get monthly updates from Rick on what's happening in Europe.

Classroom Europe

Check out our free resource for educators with 400+ short video clips from the *Rick Steves' Europe* TV show.

Audio Europe™

Pack Light and Right

Gear up for your next adventure at ricksteves.com

Light Luggage

Pack light and right with Rick Steves' affordable, custom-designed rolling carry-on bags, backpacks, day packs and shoulder bags.

Accessories

From packing cubes to moneybelts and beyond, Rick has personally selected the travel goodies that will help your trip go smoother.

Shop at ricksteves.com

Save time and energy

This guidebook is your independent-travel toolkit. But for all it delivers, it's still up to you to devote the time and energy it takes to manage the preparation and logistics that are essential for a happy trip. If that's a hassle, there's a solution.

Rick Steves Tours

A Rick Steves tour takes you to Europe's most interesting places with great

with minimum stress

guides and small groups of 28 or less. We follow Rick's favorite itineraries, ride in comfy buses, stay in family-run hotels, and bring you intimately close to the Europe you've traveled so far to see. Most importantly, we take away the logistical headaches so you can focus on the fun.

Join the fun

This year we'll take 33,000 free-spirited travelers— nearly half of them repeat customers—along with us on 50 different itineraries, from Athens to Istanbul. Is a Rick Steves tour the right fit for your travel dreams?

Find out at ricksteves.com, where you can also request Rick's latest tour catalog. Europe is best experienced with happy travel partners. We hope you can join us.

See our itineraries at ricksteves.com

BEST OF GUIDES

Full-color guides in an easy-to-scan format. Focused on top sights and experiences in the most popular European destinations

Best of England
Best of Europe
Best of France
Best of Germany
Best of Ireland
Best of Italy
Best of Scotland
Best of Spain

COMPREHENSIVE GUIDES

City, country, and regional guid printed on Bible-thin paper. Pa with detailed coverage for a m week trip exploring iconic sigh and venturing off the beaten p

Amsterdam & the Netherlands
Barcelona
Belgium: Bruges, Brussels,
 Antwerp & Ghent
Berlin
Budapest
Croatia & Slovenia
Eastern Europe
England
Florence & Tuscany
France
Germany
Great Britain
Greece: Athens & the Peloponn
Iceland
Ireland
Istanbul
Italy
London
Paris
Portugal
Prague & the Czech Republic
Provence & the French Riviera
Rome
Scandinavia
Scotland
Sicily
Spain
Switzerland
Venice
Vienna, Salzburg & Tirol

E BEST OF ROME

Italy's capital, is studded with remnants and floodlit-fountain From the Vatican to the Colos-th crazy traffic in between, Rome ful, huge, and exhausting. The he heat, and the weighty history

of the Eternal City where Caesars walked can make tourists wilt. Recharge by tak-ing siestas, gelato breaks, and after-dark walks, strolling from one atmospheric square to another in the refreshing eve-ning air.

antheon—which
me until the
000 years old
er 1,500).

hens in the Vat-
he humanistic

ators fought
er, entertaining

me ristorante,

:KET GUIDES

pact color guides for shorter trips

terdam	Paris
·ns	Prague
elona	Rome
·nce	Venice
s Cinque Terre	Vienna
don	
·ch & Salzburg	

PSHOT GUIDES

used single-destination coverage

·que Country: Spain & France
·enhagen & the Best of Denmark
·lin
·rovnik
·burgh
Towns of Central Italy
·ow, Warsaw & Gdansk
·on
·e Valley
·rid & Toledo
·n & the Italian Lakes District
·les & the Amalfi Coast
·· & the French Riviera
·mandy
·thern Ireland
·way
·kjavík
·enburg & the Rhine
·ttish Highlands
·lla, Granada & Southern Spain
·etersburg, Helsinki & Tallinn
·ckholm

CRUISE PORTS GUIDES

Reference for cruise ports of call

Mediterranean Cruise Ports
Scandinavian & Northern European
Cruise Ports

Complete your library with...

TRAVEL SKILLS & CULTURE

*Study up on travel skills and gain
insight on history and culture*

Europe 101
Europe Through the Back Door
Europe's Top 100 Masterpieces
European Christmas
European Easter
European Festivals
For the Love of Europe
Travel as a Political Act

PHRASE BOOKS & DICTIONARIES

French
French, Italian & German
German
Italian
Portuguese
Spanish

PLANNING MAPS

Britain, Ireland & London
Europe
France & Paris
Germany, Austria & Switzerland
Iceland
Ireland
Italy
Spain & Portugal

Credits

RESEARCHERS
For help with this edition, Rick relied on...

Cameron Hewitt

Born in Denver and raised in central Ohio, Cameron settled in Seattle in 2000. Ever since, he has spent three months each year in Europe, contributing to guidebooks, tours, radio and television shows, and other media for Rick Steves' Europe, where he serves as content manager. Cameron married his high school sweetheart (and favorite travel partner), Shawna, and enjoys taking pictures, trying new restaurants, and planning his next trip.

Cary Walker

Cary discovered international travel during college and has been feeding her wanderlust ever since. A former teacher, she believes that Europe is the best classroom for those who travel with an open mind. When not researching guidebooks or leading Rick Steves' Europe tours, she resides in Dallas where she helps busy families plan trips around the world.

CONTRIBUTOR
Gene Openshaw

Gene has co-authored more than a dozen Rick Steves books, specializing in writing walks and tours of Europe's cities, museums, and cultural sights. He also contributes to Rick's public television series, produces audio tours on Europe, and is a regular guest on Rick's public radio show. Outside of the travel world, Gene has co-authored *The Seattle Joke Book.* As a composer, he has written a full-length opera called *Matter,* a violin sonata, and dozens of songs. He lives near Seattle with his daughter, enjoys giving presentations on art and history, and roots for the Mariners in good times and bad.

ACKNOWLEDGMENTS
Thanks to Susana Minich for writing the original version of the Zürich, Central Switzerland, Lugano, Upper Engadine, and Scenic Rail Journeys chapters; and to Cameron Hewitt for writing the original versions of the Luzern and Zermatt chapters.

Avalon Travel
Hachette Book Group
1700 Fourth Street
Berkeley, CA 94710

Text © 2020 by Rick Steves' Europe, Inc. All rights reserved.
Maps © 2020 by Rick Steves' Europe, Inc. All rights reserved.

Printed in Canada by Friesens.
10th Edition. First printing May 2020.

ISBN 978-1-64171-229-3

For the latest on Rick's talks, guidebooks, tours, public television series, and public radio
show, contact Rick Steves' Europe, 130 Fourth Avenue North, Edmonds, WA 98020, tel.
425/771-8303, www.ricksteves.com, rick@ricksteves.com.

Rick Steves' Europe
Managing Editor: Jennifer Madison Davis
Assistant Managing Editor: Cathy Lu
Special Publications Manager: Risa Laib
Editors: Glenn Eriksen, Julie Fanselow, Tom Griffin, Suzanne Kotz, Rosie Leutzinger,
    Alison Lockhart, Jessica Shaw, Carrie Shepherd
Editorial & Production Assistant: Megan Simms
Editorial Intern: Bridgette Robertson
Researchers: Cameron Hewitt, Cary Walker
Contributor: Gene Openshaw
Graphic Content Director: Sandra Hundacker
Maps & Graphics: David C. Hoerlein, Lauren Mills, Mary Rostad
Digital Asset Coordinator: Orin Dubrow

Avalon Travel
Senior Editor and Series Manager: Madhu Prasher
Associate Managing Editors: Jamie Andrade, Sierra Machado
Copy Editor: Maggie Ryan
Proofreader: Patrick Collins
Indexer: Stephen Callahan
Cover Design: Kimberly Glyder Design
Production and Typesetting: Lisi Baldwin, Jane Musser
Maps & Graphics: Kat Bennett

Photo Credits
Front Cover: The historic Gornergrat train and the Matterhorn © Roberto Moiola /
Sysaworld / Getty Images
Title Page: Cheesemakers at Schiltalp © Rick Steves
Public Domain via Wikimedia Commons: 116, 406
Additional Photography: Dominic Arizona Bonuccelli, Rich Earl, Glenn Eriksen, Trish
    Feaster, Simon Griffith, Cameron Hewitt, David C. Hoerlein, Sandra Hundacker, Rosie
    Leutzinger, Gene Openshaw, Steve Smith, Rick Steves, Gretchen Strauch, Ian Watson.
    Photos are used by permission and are the property of the original copyright owners.